ATHLETICS AND LITERATURE IN
THE ROMAN EMPIRE

From the first to the third century AD Greek athletics flourished as never before. This book offers exciting new readings of those developments. Drawing on a wide range of evidence, it sheds new light on practices of athletic competition and athletic education in the Roman Empire. In addition it examines the ways in which athletic activity was represented within different texts and contexts, and the controversies it attracted. Above all, the book shows how discussion and representation of athletics could become entangled with other areas of cultural debate and used as a vehicle for many different varieties of authorial self-presentation and cultural self-scrutiny. It also argues for complex connections between different areas of athletic representation, particularly between literary and epigraphical texts. It offers re-interpretations of a number of major authors, especially Lucian, Dio Chrysostom, Pausanias, Silius Italicus, Galen and Philostratus.

JASON KÖNIG is Lecturer in Greek and Classical Studies at the University of St Andrews. He has written a wide range of articles on the Greek literature and culture of the Imperial period.

GREEK CULTURE IN THE ROMAN WORLD

Editors
SUSAN E. ALCOCK, University of Michigan
JAŚ ELSNER, Corpus Christi College, Oxford
SIMON GOLDHILL, University of Cambridge

The Greek culture of the Roman Empire offers a rich field of study. Extraordinary insights can be gained into processes of multicultural contact and exchange, political and ideological conflict, and the creativity of a changing, polyglot Empire. During this period many fundamental elements of Western society were being set in place: from the rise of Christianity, to an influential system of education, to long-lived artistic canons. This series is the first to focus on the response of Greek culture to its Roman imperial setting as a significant phenomenon in its own right. To this end, it will publish original and innovative research in the art, archaeology, epigraphy, history, philosophy, religion and literature of the Empire, with an emphasis on Greek material.

Forthcoming titles

Describing Greece: Landscape and Literature in the Periegesis of Pausanias
William Hutton

Philostratus
Edited by Ewen Bowie and Jaś Elsner

Reading the Self in the Ancient Greek Novel
Tim Whitmarsh

Image, Place and Power in the Roman Empire: Visual Replication and Urban Elites
Jennifer Trimble

ATHLETICS AND LITERATURE IN THE ROMAN EMPIRE

JASON KÖNIG

CAMBRIDGE UNIVERSITY PRESS
Cambridge, New York, Melbourne, Madrid, Cape Town, Singapore, São Paulo

Cambridge University Press
The Edinburgh Building, Cambridge CB2 2RU, UK

Published in the United States of America by Cambridge University Press, New York

www.cambridge.org
Information on this title: www.cambridge.org/9780521838450

© Cambridge University Press 2005

This book is in copyright. Subject to statutory exception
and to the provisions of relevant collective licensing agreements,
no reproduction of any part may take place without
the written permission of Cambridge University Press.

First published 2005

Printed in the United Kingdom at the University Press, Cambridge

A catalogue record for this book is available from the British Library

ISBN-13 978-0-521-83845-0 hardback
ISBN-10 0-521-83845-2 hardback

Cambridge University Press has no responsibility for the persistence or accuracy of URLs for external or third-party internet websites referred to in this book, and does not guarantee that any content on such websites is, or will remain, accurate or appropriate.

For Alice

Contents

List of illustrations	page xi
Note on texts and translations	xiii
Preface	xv
List of abbreviations	xvi

1 Introduction — 1
   Competing voices — 2
   Reading athletic texts — 7
   Athletic history — 22
   Ancient athletics in the modern world — 35

2 Lucian and Anacharsis: *gymnasion* education in the Greek city — 45
   Introduction — 45
   Education in the *gymnasion* — 47
   Gymnasion and festival — 63
   Lucian's Thanatousia — 72
   Lucian and Anacharsis — 80

3 Models for virtue: Dio's 'Melankomas' orations and the athletic body — 97
   Viewing the athletic body — 97
   Athletic statues and their inscriptions — 102
   Athletics and philosophical virtue — 132
   The virtues of Melankomas — 139

4 Pausanias and Olympic Panhellenism — 158
   Pausanias and the compilatory texts of the Roman Empire — 158
   Copying the Olympics — 163
   Dating the Olympics — 171
   Visiting the Olympics — 180
   Ordering the Olympics: Pausanias — 186

5 Silius Italicus and the athletics of Rome	205
Greek athletics and Roman stereotypes	205
Athletic institutions in Rome	212
Greek contests and Roman emperors	225
Silius Italicus and the athletics of Roman epic	235
6 Athletes and doctors: Galen's agonistic medicine	254
Doctors in competition	254
Training in moderation	274
Galen's *Protrepticus*	291
7 Philostratus' *Gymnasticus* and the rhetoric of the athletic body	301
Rhetoric and the body	301
Athletic trainers in action	305
Medicine and training in the *Gymnasticus*	315
Interpreting the body and analysing the past	325
Philostratean athletics and the uses of Hellenism	337
Conclusion	345
Bibliography	353
General index	379
Index locorum	390
Index of inscriptions and papyri	397

Illustrations

1. Asterix' Greek rivals training in the *gymnasion* at Olympia: Goscinny, R. and Uderzo, G. (1972) *Asterix at the Olympic Games* (translated by Bell, A. and Hockridge, D.), London: 31 (top frame). *page* 41
2. Athlete mosaics from the Baths of Caracalla: watercolour (artist unknown) of their appearance at the time of discovery. Photo: DAI Rome 2142a. 108
3. Detail of athlete mosaics from the Baths of Caracalla (pictured here in the form in which they were displayed in the Lateran Museum; now rehoused in the Museo Gregoriano Profano, Musei dei Vaticani, in a format closer to their original appearance). Photo: DAI Rome 41.888. 109
4. 'Doryphoros' of Polykleitos (Roman copy; original *c.* 440 BC); discovered in Pompeii (Naples, Museo Nazionale). Photo: DAI Rome 66.1831. 111
5. 'Diadoumenos' of Polykleitos (Roman copy; original *c.* 430 BC). All rights reserved, The Metropolitan Museum of Art. 112
6. Prima Porta statue of Augustus, early first century AD, marble, after a bronze of *c.* 20 BC; Musei Vaticani, Rome. Photo: DAI Rome 91.72. 114
7. Head of the boxer Satyros, Olympia, fourth century BC (by Silanion?). Athens, NM Br. 6439. Photo: DAI Athens 1972/333. 116
8. Bronze statue of a seated boxer ('Terme Boxer'), second or early first century BC, Museo Nazionale Romano inv. no. 1055. 117
9. Boxer statue A, theatre of Aphrodisias (=Inan-Rosenbaum no. 190). Inv. 70-508-511 (*et al.*). Aphrodisias Archive, New York (forthcoming new study by Julie Van Voorhis). Reproduced by permission of the Ashmolean Museum, Oxford. 118

10 Boxer statue B, theatre of Aphrodisias (=Inan-Rosenbaum no. 191). Inv. 60–287 (*et al.*). Aphrodisias Archive, New York (forthcoming new study by Julie Van Voorhis). Reproduced by permission of the Ashmolean Museum, Oxford. 120
11 View of the stage (looking east), theatre of Aphrodisias. Reproduced by permission of the Aphrodisias Excavations, New York University. 121
12 Copy of Polykleitos' 'Diskophoros', theatre of Aphrodisias. Inv. no. 70-502/3. Reproduced by permission of the Aphrodisias Excavations, New York University. 122

Note on texts and translations

Greek and Latin texts are cited from the most recent Oxford Classical Text (or, where none exists, from the most recent Teubner edition), with the following exceptions:
- Dio Chrysostom is cited from von Arnim, J. (ed.) (1893–6) *Dionis Prusaensis quem vocant Chrysostomum quae extant* (two volumes), Berlin.
- Galen's *Protrepticus* is cited from the edition of Barigazzi in *CMG* 5.1.1. All works of Galen are numbered by volume and page number from Kühn, K. G. (ed.) (1821–33) *Opera omnia Claudii Galeni* (twenty-two volumes), Leipzig [= K].
- Philostratus' *Gymnasticus* is cited from Jüthner, J. (ed.) (1909) *Philostratos über Gymnastik*, Leipzig. I have used Jüthner's numbering of the text, but for clarity have at times combined that with page and line number from volume 2 of Kayser's Teubner edition of Philostratus (1870–71). The *Heroicus* is referred to by page and line number from volume 2 of Kayser's Teubner edition.

Many of the texts I discuss are included in translation in the source-book of Miller (ed.) (1991). Where that is the case (with the exception of his extracts from the authors I discuss at most length: Lucian, Dio, Pausanias, Silius Italicus, Galen and Philostratus), I have given the extract number from Miller. All translations are my own.

In transcribing Greek words into English I have generally preferred the original Greek form, but I have used Latinate versions where these seemed to me to be so widely accepted that the Greek version would look out of place. However, I have deliberately not followed a rigid system in doing so, and I have chosen to maintain Greek spelling in the case of some widely used Latinate words (e.g. *gymnasion* instead of *gymnasium*, and for some Latin names in Greek inscriptions) in order to signal the fact that they were presented in their Greek form in the texts I am discussing.

Preface

Many people have helped with the writing of this book. I wish first of all to thank Simon Goldhill, who has read more drafts than he would like to remember, and whose challenging and supportive advice spurred me on during the PhD which was the starting-point for this book and afterwards. I am also very grateful to Jaś Elsner and Richard Hunter, who examined my PhD and discussed several years' worth of later drafts; to the series editors and the anonymous readers for Cambridge University Press, who rightly prompted me to re-evaluate this project's aims; and to Michael Sharp, Muriel Hall and Sinead Moloney at the Press. I would like to thank the Master and Fellows of St John's College, Cambridge, who elected me to the Research Fellowship during which most of this book was written. I have been fortunate to have many conversations with others working on the athletic history of the Roman Empire and of earlier periods: I wish to thank especially Helen Lovatt, Zahra Newby and Onno van Nijf, who have been very generous in showing me drafts of their work and in commenting on my own. I want to thank my parents for their constant support. And I am grateful, finally, to the many others who have given advice or read drafts of some or all of the book at various stages, in particular Elton Barker, Ewen Bowie, James Davidson, Lucy Grig, Heidi Houlihan, Polly Low, Stephen Mitchell, Robin Osborne, Nigel Spivey, Tim Whitmarsh, Greg Woolf; and (especially) Alice Weeks, for reading this so many times, and for her love and encouragement.

It has not been possible to take account of material published after October 2003. A number of books on ancient athletics were published to coincide with the Athens Olympics in 2004 (including, amongst many others: Llewellyn Smith, M. (2004) *Olympics in Athens 1896. The Invention of the Modern Olympic Games*, London; Miller, S. (2004) *Ancient Greek Athletics*, New Haven; Spivey, N. (2004) *The Ancient Olympics. War Minus the Shooting*, Oxford).

Abbreviations

ABSA	*Annual of the British School at Athens*
AC	*L'Antiquité classique*
AEph.	Ἀρχαιολογικὴ Ἐφημερίς
AHB	*The Ancient History Bulletin*
AJA	*American Journal of Archaeology*
AJP	*American Journal of Philology*
AncSoc	*Ancient Society*
AncW	*The Ancient World*
ANRW	*Aufstieg und Niedergang der Römischen Welt*
APF	*Archiv für Papyrusforschung und verwandte Gebiete*
AS	*Anatolian Studies*
BASO	*Bulletin of the American Schools of Oriental Research in Jerusalem and Baghdad*
BCAR	*Bollettino della Commissione Archeologica Comunale di Roma*
BCH	*Bulletin de correspondance hellénique*
BE	'Bulletin épigraphique', in *Revue des études grecques*
Belleten	*Türk Karih Kurumu Belleten*
BHM	*Bulletin of the History of Medicine*
BICS	*Bulletin of the Institute of Classical Studies*
CAJ	*Cambridge Archaeological Journal*
CID	*Corpus des Inscriptions de Delphes*
CIG	*Corpus Inscriptionum Graecarum*
CJ	*Classical Journal*
ClAnt.	*Classical Antiquity*
CMG	*Corpus Medicorum Graecorum*
CPh	*Classical Philology*
CPHerm.	*Corpus Papyrorum Hermopolitanorum*
CQ	*Classical Quarterly*

CRAI	Comptes rendus de l'Académie des Inscriptions et Belles-Lettres
CW	The Classical World
Dig.	Digesta
EAH	Τὸ Ἔργον τῆς Ἀρχαιολογικῆς Ἑταιρείας
F.Delphes	Fouilles de Delphes
FGH	F. Jacoby, Die Fragmente der griechischen Historiker
GIBM	The Collection of Ancient Greek Inscriptions in the British Museum
GRBS	Greek, Roman and Byzantine Studies
HSCP	Harvard Studies in Classical Philology
ICS	Illinois Classical Studies
I.Délos	Inscriptions de Délos
I.Didyma	Didyma. Die Inschriften
IE	M. L. West, Iambi et Elegi Graeci
I.Eph.	Die Inschriften von Ephesos
I.Erythrai	Die Inschriften von Erythrai und Klazomenai
IG	Inscriptiones Graecae
IGR	Inscriptiones Graecae ad res Romanas pertinentes
IGUR	Inscriptiones Graecae Urbis Romae
I.Magnesia	Die Inschriften von Magnesia am Maeander
I.Milet	Inschriften von Milet
Inan-Rosenbaum	J. Inan and E. Alföldi-Rosenbaum (1975) Römische und frühbyzantische Porträtplastik aus der Turkei. Neue Funde, Mainz
IOSPE	Inscriptiones antiquae orae septentrionalis Pontis Euxini Graecae et Latinae
I.Pergamon	Die Inschriften von Pergamon
I.Priene	Inschriften von Priene
I.Smyrna	Die Inschriften von Smyrna
IvO	Inschriften von Olympia
JEA	Journal of Egyptian Archaeology
JHM	Journal of the History of Medicine and Allied Sciences
JHS	Journal of Hellenic Studies
JÖAI	Jahreshefte des Österreichischen Archäologischen Institut
JRA	Journal of Roman Archaeology
JRS	Journal of Roman Studies
K	Kühn, K. G. (ed.) (1821–33) Opera omnia Claudii Galeni (twenty-two volumes), Leipzig

LBW	P. Le Bas and W. H. Waddington, *Voyage archéologique en Grèce et en Asie Mineure fait pendant les années 1834 et 1844*
LSJ	H. G. Liddell, R. Scott, and H. Stuart Jones, *Greek-English Lexicon* (ninth edition)
MAL	*Memoria della Classe di Scienze morali e storiche dell' Accademia dei Lincei*
MDAI(A)	*Mitteilungen des Deutschen Archäologischen Instituts (Athenische Abteilung)*
Miller	Miller, S. G. (ed.) (1991) *Arete. Greek Sports from Ancient Sources*, Berkeley (revised edition; first published in 1979)
MNIR	*Mededelingen van het Nederlands Historisch Instituut te Rome*
OMS	Robert, L. (1969–90) *Opera Minora Selecta*, Amsterdam (seven volumes)
P&P	*Past and Present*
PBSR	*Papers of the British School at Rome*
PCPS	*Proceedings of the Cambridge Philological Society*
PGR	A. Giannini, *Paradoxographorum Graecorum Reliquiae*
Platon	Πλατων. Δελτίον τῆς Ἑταιρείας Ἑλλήνων Φιλολόγων
P.Lond.	*Greek Papyri in the British Museum*
P.Oxy.	*Papyri Oxyrhynchi*
PP	*La Parola del passato: rivista di studi antichi*
P.Zenon	C. C. Edgar, *Catalogue général des antiquités égyptiennes du musée du Caire, numbers 59001–59139; Zenon Papyri* 1
RA	*Revue archéologique*
REA	*Revue des études anciennes*
REG	*Revue des études grecques*
REL	*Revue des études latines*
RhM	*Rheinisches Museum*
RIL	*Rendiconti dell' Istituto Lombardo*
RPh	*Revue de philologie*
RSA	*Rivista storica dell' Antichità*
SEG	*Supplementum Epigraphicum Graecum*
SIG³	*Sylloge Inscriptionum Graecarum* (third edition)
SO	*Symbolae Osloenses*

TAM	*Tituli Asiae Minoris*
TAPA	*Transactions of the American Philological Association*
TGF	A. Nauck, *Tragicorum Graecorum Fragmenta*
WS	*Wiener Studien*
YCS	*Yale Classical Studies*
ZPE	*Zeitschrift für Papyrologie und Epigraphik*

CHAPTER I

Introduction

... I am Markos Aurelios Asklepiades, also called Hermodoros, senior temple warden of the great god Sarapis, chief priest of the Universal Athletic Guild, Guild president for life, Director of the Imperial Baths; I am a citizen of Alexandria, Hermopolis, and Puteoli; a member of the City Council of Naples, Elis and Athens; and also a citizen and member of the Council of many other cities. I was a *periodos*-victor in the *pankration*. I was undefeated, I was never thrown from the wrestling ring, I never made an appeal. I won all of the contests I ever entered ... In all I competed for six years, but withdrew from competition at the age of twenty-five, because of the dangers and jealousies I encountered. After I had been in retirement for some time I was forced to compete in the Olympic festival of my home city of Alexandria in the sixth Alexandrian Olympiad and I won the *pankration* there.

(*IG* xiv, 1102 (=*IGUR* 240), lines 4–12 and 35–41; *c.* AD 200)[1]

Come on, boys, all of you who have listened to my words and are preparing to commit yourselves to an art, make sure that no swindlers and conjurers can deceive you by teaching arts that are useless or bad. You must realize that any activity whose aim is not useful for life is not really an art. As far as most activities are concerned, I am confident that you are under no illusion – things like acrobatics

---

[1] ... Μάρκος Αὐρήλιος | Ἀσκληπιάδης ὁ καὶ Ἑρμόδωρος, ὁ πρεσβύτατος τῶν νεω⁻ | κόρων τοῦ μεγάλου Σαράπιδος, ὁ ἀρχιερεὺς τοῦ σύνπαντος | ξυστοῦ, διὰ βίου ξυστάρχης καὶ ἐπὶ βαλανείων τοῦ Σεβαστοῦ, | Ἀλεξανδρεύς, Ἑρμοπολείτης, Ποτιολανός, Νεαπολείτης καὶ | Ἡλεῖος καὶ Ἀθηναῖος βουλευτὴς καὶ ἄλλων πόλεων πολλῶν | πολείτης καὶ βουλευτής, πανκρατιαστὴς περιοδονείκης ἄλειπτος, | ἀσυνέξωστος, ἀνέκκλητος, ὅσους ποτὲ ἀγῶνας ἀπεγραψάμην | πάντας νεικήσας ... ἀθλήσας τὰ πάντα ἔτη | ἕξ, παυσάμενος τῆς ἀθλήσεως ἐτῶν ὢν κε΄ | διὰ τοὺς συνβάντας μοι κινδύνους καὶ φθό⁻ | νους, καὶ μετὰ τὸ παύσασθαι μετὰ πλείονα χρόνον | ἀνανκασθεὶς ἐν τῇ πατρίδι Ἀλεξανδρείᾳ καὶ | νεικήσας Ὀλύμπια πανκράτιον | Ὀλυμπιάδι ἕκτῃ. Miller 153 translates the whole forty-one-line text; translation of some of the technical terms in the inscription is much disputed: for commentary, see esp. Moretti (1953) no. 79 (pp. 228–35) and his notes on *IGUR* 240; cf. Poliakoff (1981); Robert (1969a) 183, 191–2, 263, who compares the conventions on which this inscription draws with the satirical epigrams of Lucillius.

and tightrope-walking and spinning round in a circle without feeling dizzy, or the kind of stunts Myrmekides the Athenian or Kallikrates the Lakedaimonian are famous for. You realize, I am sure, that none of these is an art. The only thing I am afraid of is the activity of the athletes, in case it deceives any one of our young men into preferring it to a genuine art, through offering, as it does, bodily strength and popular fame and daily public payments from the elders of our cities, and honours equal to those given to outstanding citizens.

(Galen, *Exhortation to Study the Arts (Protrepticus)* 9 [K1.20–21]; c. AD 180)[2]

COMPETING VOICES

Two very different views of athletic life in the Roman Empire. Galen, a doctor from the second century AD, whose voluminous work influenced medical practice and theory for many hundreds of years after his death, writes with professional rivalries in mind, to advertise his vision of medicine as a profoundly philosophical activity. He launches a vigorous attack, in this work and others, against athletic trainers who claim that their own harmful training methods are based on medical expertise, and who use the promise of glory to entice young men into following them. He draws on long-standing literary and philosophical traditions to represent athletics as an absurd activity (although there are very few authors, in the second century or before, who can match his vehemence). It is, he suggests, as pointless as the frivolous twirlings of acrobats, and yet dangerous – the most dangerous temptation of all – through pretending to be very much more than that.

The athletic inscriptions of the Roman Empire tell a different story. My first quotation here is one of many thousands of inscriptions surviving from this period which celebrate the virtues and the achievements of athletic victors, and of the benefactors who spent an enormous amount of money on festivals of all sizes throughout the Mediterranean world. We

---

[2] Ἄγετ᾽ οὖν, ὦ παῖδες, ὁπόσοι τῶν ἐμῶν ἀκηκοότες λόγων ἐπὶ τέχνης μάθησιν ὡρμήσθε, μή τις ὑμᾶς ἀπατεὼν καὶ γόης ἀνὴρ παρακρουσάμενός ποτε ματαιοτεχνίαν ἢ κακοτεχνίαν ἐ<κ>διδάξηται γιγνώσκοντας, ὡς, ὁπόσοις τῶν ἐπιτηδευμάτων οὐκ ἔστι τὸ τέλος βιωφελές, ταῦτ᾽ οὐκ εἰσὶ τέχναι. καὶ περὶ μὲν τῶν ἄλλων ὑμᾶς καὶ πάνυ πέποιθα γιγνώσκειν, ὅτι μηδὲν τούτων ἐστὶ τέχνη, οἷον τό τε πετευρίζειν καὶ βαδίζειν ἐπὶ σχοινίων λεπτῶν ἐν κύκλῳ τε περιδινεῖσθαι μὴ σκοτούμενον <ἢ> οἷα τὰ Μυρμηκίδου τοῦ Ἀθηναίου καὶ Καλλικράτους τοῦ Λακεδαιμονίου. τὸ δὲ τῶν ἀθλητῶν ἐπιτήδευμα μόνον ὑποπτεύω, μή ποτ᾽ ἄρα τοῦτο, καὶ ῥώμην σώματος ἐπαγγελόμενον καὶ τὴν παρὰ τοῖς πολλοῖς δόξαν ἐπαγόμενον, δημοσίᾳ παρὰ τοῖς πατράσι ἡμερεσίαις ἀργυρίου δόσεσιν καὶ ὅλως ἴσα τοῖς ἀριστεῦσι τετι[μη]μένον, ἐξαπατήσῃ τινὰ τῶν νέων ὡς προκριθῆναί τινος τέχνης.

would know very little of Markos Aurelios Asklepiades if it were not for the discovery of the several stones on which his achievements are listed[3] – the longest of which is the inscription partially quoted here – and yet in his day his fame must have surpassed that of Galen. He won victories in the *pankration* (one of the Greek combat sports, a combination of the techniques of wrestling and of boxing) at the Olympic, Isthmian, Nemean and Pythian festivals, the four most ancient and most prestigious athletic contests of the Greek world (the first of which was extensively imitated, as Asklepiades' mention of the 'local Olympics in Alexandria' shows), and also in a large number of other festivals. He held high office within the Empire's powerful Universal Athletic Guild, a huge organization which promoted the interests of athletes from all over the Mediterranean. The breadth of his fame is attested by the geographical range of the cities which have honoured him with citizenship, and sometimes also with membership of their City Councils: Alexandria, the great city of Egypt and his birthplace, along with nearby Hermopolis; Naples and Puteoli in southern Italy; and Athens and Elis, traditional centres of mainland Greece (to name only those he has chosen to mention). All of these were famous festival centres.[4] All of them have adopted Asklepiades, as if in the desire to participate in his glory. Asklepiades was a very unusual athlete, and this text is far from typical of the athletic epigraphy of the Roman Empire. It goes far beyond any standard format in its length and in its boastfulness.[5] Nevertheless, it gives a revealing illustration of the wide popularity of athletics, which other honorific athletic inscriptions attest to in less strident but equally confident terms.

Two other famous pankratiasts, the athletes Aurelios Helix and Aurelios Alexander, grace the front cover of this book. Like Asklepiades they offer a striking illustration of the widespread fame of the most successful athletic victors. They are depicted here on an early third-century AD mosaic from Ostia, just west of Rome, which adorns the floor of what seems to have been an inn, much as pictures of sporting personalities adorn the walls of

---

[3] The text quoted here is an inscription put up by Asklepiades in honour of his father, who was also a famous athlete and Guild official, although Asklepiades devotes most of the inscription to his own achievements. The other inscriptions are: *IG* XIV 1103 (=*IGUR* 241), in honour of Asklepiades, put up by the Athletic Guild; *IG* XIV 1104 (=*IGUR* 239), another inscription put up by Asklepiades in honour of his father; and *IGUR* 250 (originally published and discussed in more detail by Moretti (1953–5) no. 1 (pp. 73–8)), a fragmentary inscription half in Latin, whose precise significance is not clear; Asklepiades is also mentioned in *CPHerm.* 5.7.

[4] E.g., see Criscuolo (1995) on Alexandria.

[5] However, many features of the text are widely paralleled: e.g., see Robert (1930) for examples of agonistic stars with multiple citizenship; Pleket (1998) 158–60 gives parallels for athletes who return to compete in their home towns in the course of glorious international careers.

modern bars. In addition, however, Helix shows his face in more elevated surroundings through being mentioned twice in the writing of the third-century Greek author Philostratus whose work is the subject of my final chapter.[6] In that sense Helix is a wonderful example of an athlete who bridges east and west, and who makes his mark on both the popular and literary imaginations.

The two texts quoted above thus hint between them at differences of opinion within Greek and Roman society about the degree to which athletes were worthy of admiration. The criticisms Galen makes may be untypical in their intensity, but they are widely paralleled. Athletics was never short of opponents. And yet it was at the same time enormously popular. Greek cities like those mentioned by Asklepiades used their own festivals, and the victories of their citizens, amongst other things as advertisements for their own pre-eminence. On a more day-to-day level, athletic training, carried out in the *gymnasion*, played a central role in the education of the young elite in the eastern half of the Empire through the first to third centuries AD, the period which is the main focus of this book.

However, despite the differences of perspective between them, the details of athletic activity which these two texts present to us confirm rather than contradict one another. Galen's knowledge of the practices referred to in the Asklepiades inscription is intricate (both in this extract and elsewhere in his writing). The positive spin on athletics which Asklepiades offers does nothing to prove Galen wrong; it is, in fact, a perfect example of what Galen is afraid of. Galen's warnings against the temptations of strength, wealth and glory all find close echoes in the boasts of Asklepiades – boasts of invincible and precocious physical prowess, and of popular fame, so great that it provokes envy from lesser men and provides a passport into the very highest levels of society (although many athletes came from the highest, most wealthy levels of society in the first place). Moreover this athlete's involvement with the Imperial Baths is reminiscent of Galen's worries – frequently repeated in the *Protrepticus* and other works, as we shall see in chapter six – about men without philosophical or medical training having influence over public health. Even Galen's comparison between athletes and acrobats has some grounding in 'real-life' festival activity. Acrobats played a central role in providing informal entertainment at festivals – along with conjurers, jugglers, contortionists (all of whom share with the athletic

---

[6] See Jones (1998) on the identification of Helix and Alexander in this mosaic; the mentions by Philostratus are in *Heroicus* p. 147, line 15 and *Gymnasticus* 46; Helix is also mentioned by Cassius Dio (80.10.12 [=Miller 69]); Newby (2002) 192–3 discusses this image in the context of other athletic mosaics from Ostia.

trainer, so Galen implies in this passage, the capacity to deceive or beguile) – and there is epigraphical evidence for such people being honoured by cities for their performances, and recording their own prowess and even their own victories in competition, in the language of athletic victory inscriptions.[7] Galen's account is thus more firmly grounded in detailed reference to the festival traditions mentioned in Asklepiades' boasts than might at first sight appear to be case.

In some ways Galen and Asklepiades even use similar strategies in presenting their own accomplishments, and in promoting their own viewpoints and achievements ahead of those of their competitors. Both athletes and doctors were constantly engaged in rivalry, not only with men of the same profession, but also with representatives of other types of entertainment and education. Both Galen and Asklepiades, in other words, were involved in processes of professional competition where success required, amongst other things, fierce, assertive self-promotion. Both denigrate their rivals dismissively, while at same time acknowledging the dangers those rivals have posed, as if to emphasize more firmly their own ability to rise above forces which have the potential to threaten their dominance. Galen mocks the athletic trainers as absurd, but also acknowledges their power. Asklepiades draws attention to some of the threats he has managed to overcome, in his mention of the 'dangers and jealousies' (presumably at the hands of rival competitors) which forced him into retirement, but which have not been able to prevent his further accumulation of administrative glory; and in the mention of his continued physical prowess even after his days of regular competition are over, which gives him victory on his comeback in Alexandria after several years of retirement. There are also geographical parallels between them. Asklepiades – like Galen throughout most of his work – takes on the persona of one who is not narrowly tied to his place of birth, but whose ability has instead made him a universally applicable icon for the whole of the Empire (although he is far from typical in that, since many athletes emphasize instead their contributions to the life of a single city). Galen moved to Rome from the east of the Empire, and was closely associated with the imperial family. Asklepiades, too, was based in Rome, the home of the Universal Athletic Guild – at least after he had retired from competition – and the inscription quoted above was set up there (although no doubt he would have been honoured similarly in the many other cities which were linked with him). Moreover, Galen regularly borrows from the

---

[7] See van Nijf (2001) 330; Perpillou-Thomas (1995) 228; Spawforth (1989) 197; Robert (1938) 76–108; Robert (1929a) 433–8; Robert (1928b) 422–5; cf. Lada-Richards (2003), esp. 34–40 on pantomime dancing in festival contexts.

language and imagery of athletics in his writing, in broadcasting his own effortless superiority over his rivals, and in representing his own skills as more elevated equivalents of the debased and vulgarly self-advertising skills of the athletic trainers, as I shall argue further in chapter six. Asklepiades, conversely, shares with Galen the desire to claim philosophical accomplishment (of a sort). One of the other inscriptions commemorating Asklepiades' career mentions the fact that he held some kind of sacred office within the association of philosophers in the Mouseion of Alexandria.[8] That is perhaps not a surprising honour given the similar appointments made to other non-philosophers for their military or political achievements, but it is an extraordinary detail in the light of Galen's criticism of athletic trainers as the most ignorant and unphilosophical of all pretended experts. Clearly there *were* ways in which one could claim close links between athletics and philosophy, despite Galen's arguments to the contrary. The badge of philosophical accomplishment is far from unique to Galen. Even Asklepiades uses it, albeit in a diluted form, as so many people did in advertising their claims to elite status.

Such similarities of self-advertisement may be partly due to the fact that both of these texts were intended to be similarly impressive to elite readers, despite their startling differences. The fact that such a large proportion of ancient athletes came from the elite, as Galen implicitly acknowledges, points in the same direction. The audiences envisaged by these two texts, in other words, may be closer than initially seems to be the case, despite the fact that the texts approach their subjects from such different viewpoints (although I certainly do not mean to suggest that they are appealing to *exactly* the same audience, or that they would have been perceived as generically similar to each other). Both texts are jostling for position, clamouring for attention against each other, and against many other voices, against many other claimants for public attention.

These passages, then, illustrate between them some of the alluring challenges and difficulties which stand in the way of any attempt to analyse the athletics of the ancient world. For one thing, they hint at the diversity of athletic material available to us. The variety of evidence becomes even richer and more bewildering if one moves away from concentration on the evidence of a short time-period (these two texts were composed within about twenty years of each other) in search of a more diachronic understanding of Greek athletics across its whole history. No single picture of ancient athletics will ever give us the whole story. We find debated archaeological evidence for the very earliest days of the great athletic sites, where the Olympics

---

[8] *IG* xiv 1103 (=*IGUR* 241); see Moretti (1953–5) 76.

and other Panhellenic festivals were held; scenes of competition on fifth-century BC pottery painted in idealizing or sometimes parodic style for an elite market; polished Platonic descriptions of Socrates philosophizing in the *gymnasia* of Classical Athens; complex Hellenistic decrees for the foundation of festivals, with the detailed arrangements for sending and receiving ambassadors which accompanied that process; idealized statues of impossibly well-formed athletic competitors; Roman denunciations of effeminate Greeks, trained in the *gymnasion*, mostly recorded at second or third hand in later historical writing; mutilated victory inscriptions celebrating athletic and musical prowess from the cities – both Greek and non-Greek cities – of the Roman Empire; appropriations of traditional athletic imagery in formulations of Christian virtue, which often seem strangely inconsistent with Christian resistance to pagan spectacle – all of these things spanning between them over a thousand years. This book focuses mainly on the first to third centuries AD, the period of Greek history when athletic activity flourished perhaps more vigorously than at any other. Much of my central evidence is taken from the second century, at the end of which both of the texts I have quoted were produced. But even within that time-span, as we have seen, the evidence we have is varied and often at first sight contradictory.

Even more importantly, I believe, these two snapshots give a powerful illustration of the controversial nature of athletic activity, even if they can offer only a selective view of the issues around which such controversy clustered. Athletics stirred passion and rivalry and obsession, as we shall see repeatedly in later chapters. It played a central role, over a long period, within civic life and festival culture, within education, within art and literature, and within the forms of self-perception and self-presentation which were characteristically associated with these things throughout the Mediterranean world. But it was a role whose significance was far from uniformly envisaged. In everything which follows I will be aiming to expose the controversies and contradictions which lie beneath the surface of so many of the representations of athletics which survive from the Imperial period. As we shall see, even the most confident and imposing ancient valuations of athletics tend to show traces of the alternative viewpoints they are in competition with.

READING ATHLETIC TEXTS

How, then, are we to read the inscriptions and literary works which serve as our main window on to the athletic culture of the ancient world? This book is intended to be of interest to those who seek a basic understanding of the ways in which ancient athletics was practised, in the sense that it brings together — at least in outline form — a vast body of Imperial-period evidence which has never before been presented with any coherence. But it is more than anything a book about the *texts* of athletics, and about the particular challenges and pleasures and manipulations of cultural ideals which they offer. Within that broad framework the book has two main aims. First, to show how textual portrayals of athletics within the Imperial period were so often entangled with much broader debates about contemporary culture, and used as vehicles for powerful strategies of elite self-representation. Recognition of that fact has generally been submerged beneath the desire for empirical reconstructions of the realities of ancient athletic practice, as we shall see further in a moment. And second, to show how very different types of text often have striking overlaps in their performance of those functions. Over and over again we shall see how the extended 'literary' treatments of athletics which I discuss at the end of each chapter draw on and contribute to patterns of representation which were central to the athletic inscriptions of the Roman Empire. Literary and epigraphical representations need to be studied together if we are to gain a complete picture of either.

Both of these projects require one to pay close attention to the complexities of individual athletic texts. Cursory, face-value presentations of textual evidence for ancient attitudes to athletics — in other words the kinds of discussion which seek to collect and extract the 'opinions' of individual authors from a wide range of texts without paying any attention to the rhetorical contexts in which those statements of 'opinion' are embedded, and which fail to acknowledge that these texts have any purpose other than the faithful portrayal of athletic techniques and procedures — have been all too common within writing on ancient athletics in the past. Analysis of that kind risks over-simplifying the opinions and values it purports to illuminate, by ignoring the fact that even the most confident of ancient claims about the significance of athletic activity are necessarily controversial, made in response to a wide variety of different possible assessments, and the fact that the vast majority of these texts carry deeply ingrained tensions and ambiguities beneath their compelling surfaces. If we are to avoid unnuanced reading of that sort it is vitally important to set these texts in their wider contexts of cultural polemic, and to be sensitive to their internal ambiguities, which are so heavily influenced by the kinds of controversy and variation in opinion which I illustrated briefly above.

I turn now — as a test case for those principles — to the relation between athletics and identity in the Roman world. One of the reasons why athletics was such a controversial activity and such a highly charged subject of discussion within the first three centuries AD was the fact that it was seen to have conspicuous implications for the identities of those who involved themselves with it. For that reason, as we shall see in several of the chapters which follow (especially chapters two and seven, on Lucian and Philostratus respectively), it was often seen as a promising topic by writers who were interested in theorizing the cultural boundaries and identities of their contemporary society. However, my emphasis on questions of identity in the rest of this section is not meant to suggest that athletics was significant in the Roman Empire *only* because of its role within performances and explorations of identity. Clearly there were many other aspects of Greek and Roman culture for which athletic activity and athletic representation were thought to have significance – although one might argue that *all* of the pronouncements which I will analyse in this book were necessarily tied up with their authors' (and readers') strategies of self-presentation and experiences of self-identification. Instead, I emphasize the issue of athletic identity in the rest of this section because it illustrates so vividly – more vividly than any other single aspect of athletic history – the points I have been making up to now. Most importantly, it sheds a fascinating light on the way in which even the most confident and apparently straightforward of statements about the significance of Imperial-period athletics is likely to show traces of a more complicated story lying behind it.

My starting-point is the observation that all expressions and experiences of identity necessarily involve some tension between self-confidence, fixity and typicality on the one hand, and uncertainty, instability and innovativeness on the other. It should not be controversial to state that cultural identities are constantly open to reconfiguration, and necessarily reshaped in each new expression of them. Recent scholarship has rightly moved away from the idea that specific 'cultures' have fixed qualities and fixed patterns of self-perception associated with them. Instead it has increasingly recognized the fact that self-perception and self-presentation are much more variable, much more malleable and unstable than was previously understood. The 'culture' (however that difficult word is defined)[9] of any community or geographical area or period of history may often be imagined and represented as something monolithic, but it is always in reality shifting and many-sided. 'Culture', in other words, is never something that has objective reality. It is rather an ideal which is imagined and presented

---

[9] See Goldhill (2001a) 15–18.

in different ways by different individuals for a great variety of different purposes. Individuals respond to what they envisage as cultural norms in selecting and evaluating their own activities and identities, and for their own understandings of social hierarchies and group boundaries. However, they also necessarily refashion those perceived norms in highly creative though often unintentional ways. Any cultural history which seeks to summarize and condense, which irons out the specificities and ambiguities of this kind of individual response to cultural resources and individual experiences of identity, is necessarily at risk of oversimplifying the object of its analysis.[10]

However, while acknowledging that fact, I also follow recent trends in anthropological and sociological thinking in resisting the idea of identity as something which is purely rhetorical, purely a matter of playful and infinitely flexible self-fashioning.[11] It is worth making that point clearly partly because the accusation of privileging playfulness and multivalence too highly is one of the criticisms most often made against theoretically informed approaches to cultural history and, especially, literary analysis.[12] As I aim to show throughout the chapters which follow, acknowledging the inevitability of multivalence and inventiveness within any act of cultural self-positioning, textual or otherwise, is very far from being incompatible with recognition of the existence of firmly held opinions. The fact that 'Greek' identity – for example – was a highly contested commodity, repeatedly and controversially refashioned in every new statement of it, is in no way irreconcilable with acknowledgement of the fact that such statements were often expressions of firmly and passionately held beliefs.

To put that point in rather different terms, analysis of contested values, which are constantly and necessarily open to subjective variation, needs to be *combined* with recognition of the enormous investment individuals

---

[10] On the drive towards recognizing the importance of individual agency within recent anthropological and sociological scholarship, see, e.g., Daniel and Peck (1996) esp. 18–20; Dirks, Eley and Ortner (1994) 11–17; see also Brannigan (1998), who gives a clear account of some of the pay-offs of New Historicist analysis – with its strategy of bringing together roughly contemporary texts of very different types and examining their common implication in the power relations of the culture from which they arise – but also points out, especially in his concluding pages (218–21) the danger that this approach can neglect close reading of the capacity of individual texts to manipulate cultural pressures in surprising and independent ways.

[11] See, e.g., Cohen (2000), esp. 4–6 for a concise account of some of these trends. He emphasizes the importance of the move away from Goffmanesque interest in the 'gamelike character of social interaction' (5) (with particular reference to Goffman (1969)); cf. Davies (2000).

[12] E.g., see Swain (1996) 12–13 for an example of that kind of criticism within recent writing on the Greek literature of Roman Empire.

make in identities which are often envisaged and represented as firmly bounded categories.[13] The vision of identity as an ongoing process, subject to manipulation and rhetorical posturing, by no means implies an entirely self-conscious, controlling subject. Acknowledging the fact that identity is never a fixed and essential attribute does not require one to imagine that all people are always able to be whoever they want to be, to take the masks of identity on and off at will. Rather, identity, or perhaps better 'identification', is the never-ending and always partly subconscious activity of negotiation between perceived communal norms on the one hand, which themselves help to shape subjectivity around distinctive contours, and individual experiences and impulses of self-formation and resistance to those norms (sometimes self-consciously acknowledged resistance, but most often not) on the other. As Stuart Hall suggests, analysis of these processes of identification requires

a theory of what the mechanisms are by which individuals as subjects identify (or do not identify) with the 'positions' to which they are summoned; as well as how they fashion, stylize, produce and 'perform' these positions, and why they never do so completely, for once and all time, and some never do, or are in a constant, agonistic process of struggling with, resisting, negotiating and accommodating the normative or regulative rules with which they confront and regulate themselves.[14]

Identification – the making and experience of one's own identity – always involves tensions, whether consciously perceived or not, between ostensibly fixed standards and the various instabilities and contradictions and insufficiencies which lie behind them. Often individuals seek to reject or refashion the values which they encounter, or the social and cultural status and identity with which society presents them. In some cases, however, they fall short of the values they aspire to embody or find their own self-imaginings in conflict with the ways in which they are viewed by others; and in some cases they find their own self-presentations in conflict with very different versions of cultural accomplishment. Often, too, individuals seek to conform to perceived social norms, but find themselves unable to do so fully. Looking at identity, in other words, requires one to look not only at the confident statements of affiliation and confident evaluations of culture which are so easy to find, but also at the uncertainties

---

[13] Cf. Morris (2000) 9–17 for an ideal of cultural history which recognizes 'both individual agency and the limits of self-fashioning' (17).
[14] Hall (1996) 13–14.

and anxieties which give rise to and are contained within those statements and evaluations.[15]

That point, I believe, is an important one for cultural history in all its forms, but it has particular relevance for the subject of this book. The painstaking processes of self-fashioning which pervaded so many areas of elite Greek and Roman culture (in athletic training as in many other spheres of activity, not least rhetorical education) attracted and required extraordinary commitment and self-belief, and brought with them tangible marks of prestige. And yet there were always ways in which individual experiences and manipulations of elite self-fashioning were in conflict with alternative perceptions of the norms of elite culture. Moreover, the combination of firm commitment and self-belief with inconsistency and anxiety would have been particularly marked in the example of athletic training and display through being tied to the struggles of individuals for control over their own bodies. Recent sociological analysis has emphasized the way in which the human body is on one level a discursive formulation, shaped by wider social forces and ideals. It has also emphasized, however, the way in which individuals shape their own bodies as part of a process of independent response to such forces, and the way in which bodily self-fashioning in itself always risks failure.[16] The human body always eludes control, always thwarts the practical achievement of one's ideals, whether they involve conformity with or resistance to societal norms. In that sense physical training provides a vehicle and an appropriate image for a wide range of (only partially achievable) cultural aspirations. Moreover, psychoanalysis points to similar tensions between desire and the frustration of desire in our experiences of our own bodies and our perceptions of the bodies of others. Psychoanalytic analyses of modern literature have pointed to links between physical and textual desire, between the desire for knowledge and the yearning for perfect possession of and identification with the objects of corporeal longing as they are presented in textual form, neither of which is ever fully attainable.[17] The ancient world's textual representations of athletic bodies (as I will argue in chapter three in particular), fit in with that pattern, repeatedly using the human form as a vehicle for exploring the meaning of contemporary society, but also for articulating the unattainability of any fixed version of traditional virtue or secure identity.

---

[15] Cf. Kurke (1999), esp. 23–32 for the argument that even texts which offer statements intended to be definitive will nevertheless often give us access to the debates and anxieties within elite culture which lie behind them (with reference to Archaic Greek texts).

[16] E.g., see Turner (1996) and Shilling (1993), discussed further in chapter three (pp. 99–101).

[17] E.g., see Brooks (1993).

The sense that athletics marked identity clearly was bolstered by the public portrayal of its importance for city life and local prestige, and for the elites who invested so much in those communities. Athletic competition and the festivals which framed it played a crucial role – not only during the events themselves, but also within the inscriptional records which commemorated them – in defining and advertising local achievements and local allegiances. Proclamation of athletic victory included mention of the victor's home city, and victors were often honoured extravagantly on their return home, although we also see examples of athletes being poached by cities other than their own, and some of the greatest of them, like Markos Aurelios Asklepiades, accumulated multiple citizenships. The participation of young men within festival processions which dramatized local history was crucial to their education as citizens.[18] At the same time, athletics was often associated with Hellenic culture and identity more broadly, not least through the idea that the Olympic festival and the other major contests of the festival calendar were Panhellenic gatherings, in other words occasions for the whole of the Greek world to gather together, as we shall see further in the next section. Athletic activity also impacted on the self-presentation of individuals through its central place in educational institutions like the *gymnasion* (discussed in chapter two), which was one of the most important centres of Greek education (and very different from the modern gymnasium), and for that reason was one of the places where young men were prepared to play their part as citizens in their own cities.[19]

However, the association of athletics with elite identity was also precisely the thing which exposed it to denigration as well as praise. The status of athletics as an elite activity was always open to debate. My main focus in this book will be on the significance of athletics as a male, Greek, high-status activity, simply because most of the athletic exponents and commentators I will discuss fit into that category: those whose wealth and social status gave them access to a *gymnasion* education; those politically consequential men who were most likely to be involved in the erection of the agonistic inscriptions on which so much of our understanding of ancient athletics relies; and those who mainly wrote and read the kinds of sophisticated literary texts which I will be discussing in the second half of all of the chapters which follow. Beyond that broad statement, however, I make no attempt to define the contours of 'elite' identity in this period. My reason for not doing so is the fact that the boundaries

---

[18] E.g., see Rogers (1991a). [19] E.g., see van Nijf (2003).

between different levels of social status, and the relative valuation of different types of educational and honorific accomplishment, are some of the things which are most consistently debated precisely *through* the representations of athletic activity which I will analyse. High social status was not a fixed and self-evident phenomenon, but rather something which people laid claim to in a variety of different ways,[20] even if that is not always immediately obvious, since individuals tend to represent their own versions of high status as self-evident and unchallenged. The pre-eminence of athletic activity as an elite activity was therefore very far from being self-evident and undisputed.

More specifically, declarations of the value (or otherwise) of athletics tended to be informed by wider debates: about how to care for the body in practice, and how bodily deportment should contribute to elite self-presentation; about what elite education should involve, and how young men should best be prepared for lives of civic responsibility within the cities of the Greek east.[21] For one thing, athletics was in competition with private forms of self-care, not just with those which were enshrined within educational institutions. Michel Foucault has influentially charted an intensification of elite interest in bodily and spiritual self-attention within the Imperial period.[22] It may not be right to suggest that athletics was part of the move he identifies. Certainly he resists that idea himself.[23] Nevertheless, athletic training would have interacted significantly with many of these trends, whether as a practice which was influentially in conflict with and obstructive of philosophical self-attention; or else as a practice which could be harmonized and made compatible with that kind of self-attention, if performed in the right way. One of the things I aim to do here is therefore to contribute towards a picture of some of the nuances and contestations which underlie the trends Foucault outlines, nuances which he often chooses not to emphasize.[24]

There are also signs of contest over the relative value of athletics and rhetorical or literary accomplishment. Many of our literary sources suggest that rhetorical skill and literary or philosophical erudition were the most significant focuses for elite education. However, as I have suggested already, the inscriptions of the Greek east give a different impression, and it seems

---

[20] Cf. Edwards (1993) 12–17 on Roman elite identity.
[21] Cf. Lada-Richards (2003) on pantomime dancing as a site of cultural contest, which was 'fitted into the complex set of broader discourses on education, gender, performance and civic memory, imitation, spectatorship, and acting' (70).
[22] Foucault (1986).   [23] Foucault (1986) 56–7.
[24] Cf. the criticisms of Miller (1998); Davidson (1997) xxiv; Goldhill (1995), esp. xi–xii.

that many wealthy Greeks actually gave their main attention to athletic activity, if we are to judge by the huge expenditure of time and money to which the epigraphic record attests.[25] Proclamations of rhetorical skill and of the importance of rhetorical education should therefore be seen against the background of an elite culture where rhetoric had constantly to compete with other forms of education and spectacle.

The status of athletics as a threat to the dominance of rhetoric is one of the reasons why I have avoided throughout the phrase 'Second Sophistic' which seems to me to be an unhelpful term for description of this period, not least because of its implicit undervaluation of non-rhetorical forms of cultural accomplishment.[26] Among ancient writers, the phrase itself is used only by Philostratus in his *Lives of the Sophists* (*VS*).[27] Much of the impetus for study of this period has come from the claims he makes in that work about the importance of rhetoric, especially display rhetoric, within elite culture. Even within the *VS*, however, there are signs of rivalry between sophistry and other forms of education and display; in fact Philostratus at times seems to be drawing attention to the significance of rival disciplines even as his sophists belittle them. For example, they are often scathing in their encounters with other types of performer, parading their own superiority over these men, but also at the same time drawing parallels between sophistry and these other professions. We see that effect most famously in the sophist Polemo's encounter with a gladiator, where he suggests that the gladiator's fear before fighting makes him look as if he is about to face the terrors of speaking in public: 'Seeing a gladiator dripping with sweat out of terror at the coming battle (ἀγῶνα) for his life, he said, "You are as anxious (οὕτως ἀγωνιᾷς) as if you were about to declaim"' (*VS* 541).[28] Polemo's comment hints, through the repetition of agonistic vocabulary (ἀγῶνα, ἀγωνιᾷς), at similarities between the competitive arts of the gladiator and

---

[25] E.g., see van Nijf (2003), who challenges not only the exclusive modern emphasis on rhetorical accomplishment, but also (p. 278) the suggestion made by Dickie (1993) that the Imperial-period elite increasingly left athletics to professionals, turning their attention instead to callisthenics; see also van Nijf (2001); Robert (1934b) 54–8.

[26] For recent debate about this term and about the significance of the sophistic activities it describes, see (amongst many others) Whitmarsh (2001) 42–5, who seeks to challenge the crude conceptual split between Greek culture and Roman power, and the denigration of Imperial Greek literature which the term 'Second Sophistic' has been used to underpin; Goldhill (2001a) 14–15; Korenjak (1999), esp. 12–14; Schmitz (1997) 11–18, who makes a strong case for the centrality of sophistic rhetoric to all parts of Greek society and politics; Swain (1996), esp. 1–7; Brunt (1994) who goes too far in denying the distinctive importance of sophistic rhetoric for this period; Anderson (1993), esp. 13–21, (1990) and (1989); Bowie (1982) and (1974); Bowersock (1969) 8–9.

[27] *VS* 481 and 507.

[28] ἰδὼν δὲ μονόμαχον ἱδρῶτι ῥεόμενον καὶ δεδιότα τὸν ὑπὲρ τῆς ψυχῆς ἀγῶνα, οὕτως, εἶπεν, ἀγωνιᾷς, ὡς μελετᾶν μέλλων.

the sophist — in much the same way Philostratus often draws comparisons between the shared skills of sophists and athletes[29] — but it also draws attention to Polemo's superiority. Not only does it remind us that the skills of sophistic display grant a far superior social status, but it also reminds us that Polemo himself has complete mastery over these skills. The implication, perhaps, is that the gladiator would be frightened if *he* had to declaim, as any normal mortal would, whereas Polemo's erudition and rhetorical brilliance allow him to approach the sophistic stage without a hint of self-doubt.[30] However, we should not necessarily take gestures of effortless sophistic pre-eminence like these as face-value evidence for the unchallenged importance of sophistry in second-century society, not least because they resemble closely the way in which Philostratus' sophists assert superiority over their own sophistic rivals through a strategy of belittlement elsewhere in the text.[31] Bearing in mind that thematic preoccupation in the *VS*, dismissal of athletic and other rivals might just as well mark an acknowledgement of the way in which other agonistic disciplines represented serious challenges to the popularity of sophistic performance. Even Philostratus, in other words, hints at the background of disciplinary rivalry which sophistry arises from, equating that rivalry with the forms of hostility which his sophists use between themselves.

In interrogating the relationships between rhetoric and athletics, I aim to extend the conclusions of Maud Gleason[32] and Thomas Schmitz,[33] both of whom have analysed the significance of upper-class rhetorical activity within the Roman Empire, but have, I believe, underestimated the significance of physical training and athletic competition within elite life and elite identity. Gleason uses the famed rivalry between the sophists Favorinus and Polemo to demonstrate the way in which the masculine identity of highly public figures like these relied on deeply ingrained habits of bodily deportment. The process of constructing and advertising an identity was one which had to be always repeated and renewed through performance, and Favorinus and Polemo had constantly to struggle against

---

[29] See Whitmarsh (2001) 188–90; cf. Korenjak (1999) 195–9 for general discussion on the use of agonistic metaphors for sophistry.
[30] Cf. Polemo's disqualification of an actor from the Olympic Games in Smyrna in *VS* 541–2, which humorously implies similarities between Polemo's sophistic skills and those he is judging but also suggests again his own effortless superiority.
[31] E.g., see *VS* 514 on the detractors of Scopelian who attempt to belittle him by refusing to allow him the label of 'sophist'; *VS* 542 on Polemo's combative (ἐναγώνιος) style of speech; *VS* 490–91, where Philostratus describes the famous quarrel between Polemo and Favorinus, quoting Hesiod's maxim that the spirit of rivalry is always directed against men of the same craft (τοὺς ἀντιτέχνους); by that principle Polemo is closer to the gladiator he belittles than he would admit.
[32] Gleason (1995); cf. Gleason (1999a).   [33] Schmitz (1997).

negative representations, fighting to justify the different models of manliness they had chosen to follow. That compelling insight needs to be extended further, it seems to me, by comparison with areas which lay outside the recriminatory arena of sophistry, and one of the most obvious places to look must surely be the fiercely competitive field of the agonistic festival, with the painstaking habits of gymnastic training which lay behind it. Gleason seems wrong, for example, to write (in her conclusion):

> Perhaps physical strength once had been the definitive criterion of masculine excellence on the semi-legendary playing fields of Ilion and Latium, but by Hellenistic and Roman times the sedentary elite of the ancient city had turned away from warfare and gymnastics as definitive agonistic activities, firmly redrawing the lines of competitive space so as to exclude those without wealth, education, or leisure.[34]

The 'sedentary' elite may have turned away from these things, but there was clearly a very large segment of the elite which was far from sedentary, and devoted itself to the life of the *gymnasion* with more eagerness than ever before. Others enjoyed their 'sedentariness' by packing the seats of the stadia of the east to watch athletic competition. By putting the Roman Empire's *gymnasia* and competitive festivals back into the picture I aim to broaden Gleason's analysis of the roles played by bodily deportment and agonistic excellence within elite self-representation, and of the variety of ways in which elite identity and authority were physically displayed and embodied. I also aim to demonstrate something of the way in which masculine identity could be inculcated and advertised and in the process (controversially) defined through the repeated actions of physical training, and through idealizing display of the athletic male body.

Athletics was important as a defining factor of Roman-Empire Greek identity partly because of its antiquity, the way in which it dramatized links between the Greek past and the present. In that sense it had much in common with the archaizing literary and rhetorical culture of the period. Schmitz draws on insights from sociology to shed light on the roles played by rhetorical display in the maintenance of social hierarchies, as an instrument of elite self-distinction.[35] He argues that mastery of the heritage of the past, which required long years of learning, ensured high social status, which was inaccessible to men who had no contact with the (sometimes

---

[34] Gleason (1995) 159; van Nijf (2003) 265 and (1999) 193 quotes and criticizes the same passage; however, see Gleason (1995) 87 for a more balanced view.
[35] In that sense he reacts against Bowie's (1974) argument that Imperial-period obsession with the Classical past was linked with political disempowerment.

abstruse) processes of elite education. Like Gleason, however, he seems to me to overestimate the dominance of rhetoric, and to underestimate the great variety of ways in which 'elite' virtue could be constructed, and the potential for debate about how exactly elite manhood might best be achieved. He analyses the competitive ethos of elite culture, for example in schools and festivals, but emphasizes musical events at the expense of athletic ones.[36] He discusses the way in which individual sophists acted as surrogate representatives of elite superiority for other members of their class who could not come close to matching their improvisational brilliance, and in doing so rightly acknowledges the fact that there was a great deal of variation in the degree of erudition attained by different members of the elite.[37] Surely, however, it was not only the sophists who performed this kind of role, but also the many athletes who are honoured so conspicuously as role models in the victory inscriptions of the east, often with mention of their distinguished family backgrounds and their post-retirement political appointments.

I shall also be engaging not only with questions about the constitution of elite identity and education, of the kind examined by Gleason and Schmitz, but also with recent debates about the construction of cultural boundaries in this period.[38] Much recent scholarship, for example the work of Simon Swain,[39] has rightly emphasized the importance of a carefully guarded sense of Greekness as a key element in elite self-perception in the east of the Empire. Like Gleason and Schmitz, he tends to focus on the evidence of 'literary' and rhetorical self-expression. However, his insight, into the way in which advertisement and definition of Hellenic virtue and identity – often in contrast with Roman identity – was a central concern for many second- and third-century authors, is equally relevant to the traditionally Hellenic characteristics of athletic activity. It is also relevant to many of the representations of athletic activity within 'literary' texts which I will analyse here, since some of the authors I will discuss (especially Lucian and Philostratus) are interested in presenting and exploring Hellenism and its boundaries and proper use through their discussions of athletic tradition.

'Greek' identity was prestigious and widely advertised, then. However, it was certainly not something fixed or self-evident. Commitment to an

---

[36] Schmitz (1997) 97–135, esp. 108–12.   [37] Schmitz (1997) 63–6.
[38] For recent studies on Roman Empire cultural identities not discussed elsewhere in this introduction, see esp. Ostenfeld (2002); Salomies (2001); Spawforth (2001) and Saïd (2001); Woolf (1998) and (1994); Laurence and Berry (1998); and many of the essays in Saïd (1991).
[39] Swain (1996).

emphasis on the strength of Hellenic feeling in this period could lead one into excessively monolithic views of Greek culture, and monolithic interpretations of the 'opinions' of those authors through whose work our views of Roman-Empire Hellenism are formed.[40] In reaction to that tendency there have been a number of recent attempts, most sustainedly in the work of Tim Whitmarsh, to emphasize the dialogic, processual character of 'Second-Sophistic' literary constructions of Hellenic identity.[41] In line with that approach, I will be paying close attention, as I have already explained, to the way in which the definition of elite, Hellenic virtue was constantly open to contestation, and the way in which the dazzling and provocative literary and rhetorical texts of this period do not simply offer a neutral reflection of that identity, but allow and provoke the formation of Hellenic self-perception precisely through the process of reading, or listening, and responding. Personal response is often represented as crucial to learning, and many writers are interested in exploring the instabilities of Hellenic culture. I aim, in other words, to give full weight to the flexibility of Hellenic identity as it is presented in the writing of the Roman Empire. That said, I also believe that it is crucial to hold on to the balance which I discussed above between the rhetorical features of identity construction on the one hand, and the widespread experience and perception of identity as self-evident and natural on the other. The identities of the Roman Empire may have been flexible and unstable, but that certainly does not mean that they would have been widely perceived as such, or that Hellenic identity was nothing more than a rhetorical game. Of course many of the Greek writers of this period are self-consciously and provocatively playful. But for the majority of texts the important point seems to me to lie rather in the way in which even confident expressions of identity tend to be in tension with – and always potentially undermined by – the force of inherent contradictions and alternative evaluations.

Finally, in addition to examining representations of Hellenic identity, we shall also be seeing regular glimpses of the importance of local identities within the Roman Empire, which were so closely entangled with the activities of the *gymnasion* and with local festival calendars (although the primary aim of this book is to analyse patterns of representation which are not restricted to specific locations; detailed study of the athletics of

---

[40] On the second of those two problems, see the criticism of Swain (1996) by Whitmarsh (2001) 3.
[41] See Whitmarsh (2002), (2001), (1999) and (1998); cf. Goldhill (2001c), especially the introduction by Goldhill (2001a); also König (2001) for application of some of those principles to one text, the *Corinthian Oration* of Favorinus, which has often been read too cursorily, as I argue there, in order to support monolithic visions of second-century AD cultural boundaries.

particular areas[42] (or indeed detailed study of the chronological development of the athletics of the Imperial period) will have to wait for other studies). 'Hellenic' culture and identity was very far from being the only significant focus of allegiance for the inhabitants of the east of the Empire. Images of a coherent, universally applicable, chronologically uninterrupted Hellenic culture, based on literary *paideia*, are often in tension with the reality of the Roman Empire present, with its great variety of local allegiances and practices.[43] Rhetorical education, like athletic education, at least in some forms, allowed one to claim membership of an Empire-wide Hellenic community, which stretched back over hundreds of years (although of course that often led people to be more closely associated with their own cities, in positions of political authority, rather than less). But that kind of vision was always in tension with other sources of allegiance and other arenas for self-presentation.

How, then, can this cursory sketch of athletic identities illuminate the challenge of reading athletic texts which is the main subject of this section? For one thing, many of the texts I will examine in later chapters are written with the performance and exploration of identity in mind. Inscriptions from festivals and from *gymnasia* make assertions about the social class and communal affiliations of the men (or boys) they celebrate, and about the identities of the cities in which they are displayed. 'Literary' representations of athletics, as I have already suggested, sometimes use athletic subject matter in order to explore contemporary cultural boundaries and cultural norms. In deciphering these texts we need to be alert to the range of competing ways in which athletics could be mobilized as a vehicle for self-presentation in the ancient world. More importantly, however, examination of the uncertainties and controversies underlying athletic identities can, I believe, provide a valuable model for reading athletic texts even where issues of identity are not prominent, not least because it reveals so clearly the principle that even apparently firm and typical statements of opinion tend to carry signs of their own internal contradictions, and traces of the range of options from which they have been formed. That point is valid – in fact crucial – for all of the interventions in broader cultural debate which I will discuss in what follows, whether or not they are explicitly concerned with questions of communal identity and social self-positioning.

That is not to suggest that we can read the complexities of athletic ideology in exactly the same ways in different contexts and different types

---

[42] Extended study of the numismatic evidence for athletic festivals, which has not been possible in this book, would make a major contribution to that project.
[43] Cf. Schmitz (1997) 181–93 on the importance of local identity.

of evidence. Clearly there are differences between the operations of different kinds of text. Some of the authors I examine actively prompt us towards playful interpretations, whereas others attempt to shut out alternative readings of the topics they discuss, with varying degrees of success. I will distinguish as far as possible between different degrees of playfulness and ambivalence in what follows. Genre is one important factor. Satirical texts, for example, invite very different kinds of reading from agonistic victor lists, or from technical works of medical instruction. At the same time, however, generic boundaries of this kind are often not quite so firm as they initially seem. There is always a potential for cross-contamination between different genres at least for readers who are familiar — as many in the first to third centuries AD must have been — with the wide range of contexts in which athletic imagery and athletic subject matter were regularly used. We shall see that point illustrated perhaps most vividly of all in my discussion of Dio Chrysostom's funeral orations in honour of the boxer Melankomas, in chapter three, where traditions of philosophical consolation jostle for position with athletic satire, without either ever gaining the upper hand.

I return, then, to summary of the two main aims of this book, in the hope that they will have been nuanced a little through the intervening discussion of athletic identities. First, to show how textual portrayals of athletics within the Imperial period were so often caught up with broader debates about contemporary culture, and used as a vehicle for powerful strategies of elite self-representation. And second, to show how very different types of text — epigraphical and 'literary' texts in particular — often have striking overlaps in their performance of those functions despite the enormous differences between them. In both cases I will be giving close attention to the controversies and contradictions and variations in opinion which lie in the background to all athletic representations.

In pursuing the second of those aims — in other words in examining the interaction between 'literary' and epigraphical representations — I have been helped by the work of Louis Robert, who published a huge number of articles on athletics between the mid-1920s and the mid-1980s.[44] The volume of his writing and his breathtaking command of the ancient Greek inscriptional record are awe-inspiring, along with his method of conjuring up sweeping synoptic visions of ancient agonistic life, by setting tiny

[44] Robert's work is widely dispersed; in addition to the many articles listed in my bibliography he was responsible (jointly with his wife, J. Robert) for yearly production of the 'Bulletin épigraphique' (BE) in the *Revue des études grecques* between 1938 and 1984, which is packed with detailed comment on agonistic inscriptions as well as many other subjects. Also important are the works of Christopher Jones (1986), (1978) and (1971), which situate the work of Imperial-period Greek authors in their social and political backgrounds, as those backgrounds are revealed through epigraphical texts.

fragments of individual inscriptions within the context of long series of parallels. He regularly extends that method to 'literary' evidence, pointing to the ways in which literary texts draw on the same language and the same situations as the decrees and boasts which we find inscribed on stone.[45] I have drawn heavily on this insight, as well as on his detailed accounts of specific institutions and of common patterns of epigraphical language, although my approach is for the most part different in aiming for sustained accounts of literary works, rather than exposition of individual inscriptions, as its primary focus.

The organization of my chapters, finally, reflects that desire to cover a broad range of interlinking and conflicting representations, and to integrate literary portrayals of Imperial-period athletics with attention to texts of other kinds. Each chapter of this book is structured as a move from examination of athletic institutions and broad patterns of textual representation, with examination especially of inscriptional evidence, towards a detailed final reading of one single text or set of texts – works by Lucian, Dio Chrysostom, Pausanias, Silius Italicus, Galen and Philostratus, in that order. I begin in the opening chapter with examination of the processes of *gymnasion* education within the Greek city, and the complex traditions and debates which lay behind them. I then move beyond the boundaries of civic activity to view the scene of celebrated athletes on display in festival contexts and elsewhere, parading athletic beauty and athletic virtue which was both alluring and morally suspect at the same time. From there I move to the great Panhellenic festivals which formed the pinnacle of Greek festival activity, and offered one of the most powerful but also tantalizingly unstable emblems of continuity between the past and the present; and then further west to look at the athletics of Rome and its contested place in formations of Roman identity there. Finally in the last two chapters I change focus again to look in detail at some of the more private uses and techniques of care of the body, examining conflicts between doctors and trainers which give a vivid illustration, from these two opposing perspectives, of the range of conflicting opinions which clustered around athletic activity.

ATHLETIC HISTORY

Before I launch any further into those chapters, however, I want to step back from the Imperial period for a moment to outline some of the most distinctive features of ancient athletics as it developed throughout its long

---

[45] E.g., see Robert (1969a).

history, and some of the ways in which modern sports historians have approached the challenges that history poses. My aim in doing so is to explain some of the much-imitated institutions and ideals of the Classical and Hellenistic periods, whose Imperial-period manifestations I will be discussing in later chapters. In the process I will be drawing attention to ways in which the athletics of the Roman Empire was both similar to and different from what had come before; and I will be emphasizing especially the tendency for momentous changes within ancient athletic practice and significance to be concealed or downplayed beneath a mask of continuity.

I also want to make clear some of the most significant similarities and differences between ancient and modern practice. The functions of ancient athletics within society were in many ways very different from the functions of modern sport. Athletics was linked, as we shall see, with religious ritual, in ways which are largely alien to modern practice; it was a political tool even more conspicuously than it is now, through its institutionalized connections with public ceremony and public benefaction; and its role within ancient educational ideals and practices was far removed from what we expect of sport within educational contexts in the present. Paying attention to those differences, as well as to similarities between ancient and modern sport, makes it easier to form a picture of ancient practice which is not too badly skewed by the importation of modern assumptions. In the section following this one I will extend my account of those differences and similarities by looking at some of the ways in which ancient athletic practice and ideology have been appropriated and adapted within the modern world.

The origins of Greek athletics – whose earliest dateable institutional presence within the Greek world is the first Olympic festival, held in 776 BC – are far from clear, but it does seem even in its early days to have been marked as a mainly elite activity,[46] although athletic victory and training were never the exclusive prerogative of the highest social classes.[47] Certainly, the Classical *gymnasion* was an elite institution, as it continued to be in the Hellenistic and Roman periods. Ancient and modern authors alike have plausibly seen the demands of elite military training as an important context for the growing prestige of athletics. More specifically, it has been suggested that the new demands of hoplite warfare in the early sixth century BC were a factor in the intensification of interest in athletic training

---

[46] See Young (1985), discussed by Golden (1998) 142–4.
[47] See Golden (1998) 141–75; Pleket (1975) and (1974).

at that time, and those new demands have been linked especially with the more or less simultaneous rise of the *gymnasion*. As Mark Golden points out, however, that relationship can only have been an oblique one, since the skills required for hoplite fighting were in many of their features unconnected with the exercises of the *gymnasion*. If anything, the popularity of the *gymnasion* may have been an elite reaction against the dominant forms of warfare, looking back to the traditions of heroic one-to-one combat.[48] These traditions were enshrined most famously in the funeral games for Patroclus in *Iliad* 23.[49] The relevance of athletics to warfare, and also to democratic life, was constantly questioned, and there is a whole collection of fifth-century texts (many of which were influential for Roman-Empire literature, as we shall see) which mock athletes for the uselessness of their activity. According to that widespread stereotype, the skills the *gymnasion* offered were irrelevant to the requirements of any ordinary citizen-soldier.

That said, ancient athletics was not always associated with out-of-touch aristocrats. Athletic contest – especially in Athens, although also elsewhere – was just one of many areas of public activity which were centred around performance and competition, processes which were often represented as crucial to democratic life. It may therefore be right to see a conceptual split between popular enthusiasm for festival competition and spectatorship on the one hand, and elite interest in the *gymnasion* and the *palaistra* on the other.[50] This broad split between elite and non-elite uses of athletics illustrates well the way in which the social significance of 'agonistic' (i.e. competitive) excellence was open to a variety of formulations. It also illustrates the fact that the conventional characterization of Greek culture as an 'agonistic' or 'performance' culture, while often revealing, requires qualification,[51] not least because it ignores the distinctions between different reactions to agonistic ideology at different levels of society. I will argue further for the need to qualify that 'agonistic'

---

[48] See Golden (1998) 25–8.
[49] =Miller 1; discussed further in chapter five, below, in relation to athletic games in Latin epic poetry.
[50] See, e.g., Osborne (1993) on the prominence of public competition in the festivals of democratic Athens, but also on attempts to downplay the association between athletic victory and elite political glory by reorganizing existing contests on a tribal basis; cf. Henderson (1990) 275–9 on the Old Oligarch's criticisms of the way in which the *demos* has adapted pre-democratic traditions, athletic competition included.
[51] For an influential nineteenth-century view of Greek society as 'agonistic' see the recently republished work of Burckhardt (1998) 160–213. For attempts to nuance that view, see Goldhill (1999), on 'performance' in Classical Athens, esp. 24–5 on the *gymnasion*; Golden (1998) 28–33; Lloyd (1996), esp. 1–19, on ancient Greek scientific culture. In terms of athletic ideology specifically, see Crowther (1992), whose collection of ancient sources attesting to commemoration of second-place finishes in competition challenges the notion that ancient athletes were interested in winning and nothing else.

label, especially with reference to the Imperial period, in the chapters which follow.[52]

The link between athletics and Panhellenism – the ideals of collective Greek identity and political and military co-operation – like the *gymnasion*, went back long before the Classical period. The Olympic festival was the first competitive festival to have 'Panhellenic' status, through its role as gathering point for the whole of the Greek-speaking world from the moment of its foundation in the early eighth century BC. Another important moment seems to have been the granting of similar Panhellenic status to three other great festivals – the Pythian, Isthmian and Nemean games – in the space of just ten years in the early sixth century BC, roughly at the time when the flourishing of the *gymnasion* seems to have begun.[53] It is tempting to feel that this is more than coincidence, that both of these institutional innovations were consequences and at the same time causes of an increasing sense that athletic training and competition was one of the things which marked out a distinctively Hellenic lifestyle. Between them the Olympic festival and these three others formed the Panhellenic 'circuit' (*periodos* in Greek). Winning victory at all four periodic festivals, as Markos Aurelios Asklepiades boasts of having done, was one of the greatest achievements any athlete could aspire to. In addition, the Olympic festival was accompanied by a 'truce', which was used to justify claims about Panhellenism as a force for harmony throughout the Greek world, although the truce in itself may not have led to a significant reduction in fighting, since it was confined to wars waged by or against the host city, and to hostilities against those travelling to or from the festival.[54]

The practice of exercising nude was another feature which marked out the distinctiveness of Greek athletics. The origins of that custom are much debated within modern scholarship, and do not seem to have been obvious even to ancient writers.[55] What is clear, however, is that athletic nudity came to be associated with the concept of a distinctively Hellenic type of youthful, male beauty, representative of the virtues which athletic training could bring, although there are also signs of anxiety about the potential for such beauty to be a marker and cause of immorality, in line with traditions that the *gymnasion* was a place for seduction of young boys by older men. In the Imperial period, as we shall see in chapter five,[56] the nudity of Greek

---

[52] Esp. pp. 254–74.
[53] See Morgan (1993) and (1990), esp. 212–23 on the development of the Panhellenic festival circuit; cf. Golden (1998) 10–23, 25.
[54] See Golden (1998) 16–17. [55] See Scanlon (2002) 205–10; Golden (1998) 65–9.
[56] Pp. 208–9, 217.

athletics was one of the things which seems to have marked it out for a long time as a foreign import when it was brought into Rome. That is another sign that Hellenism and athletics – at least in certain distinctive forms – went hand-in-hand, for Greeks and non-Greeks alike.

Athletic competition thus came to be represented as a distinctively Hellenic activity. Nevertheless there were enormous local variations. The gruelling Spartan educational system, for example, which was widely famous and often held up as an example, was in many ways different from the Athenian model, in particular through having a more direct claim to military relevance. Local agonistic festivals – generally much smaller than the festivals of the *periodos* – proliferated, with highly varied programmes. Athletic, musical and horse-racing events were staple ingredients and many contests boasted all three, but athletic events did not always play a part. Moreover, the 'Greek-speaking world' was in itself very far from being a clearly bounded entity, and many people adapted the ideology of Panhellenism opportunistically. Claims about the Panhellenic significance of agonistic festivals are not always as straightforward as they appear. Thus Herodotus describes the Athenians appealing to shared festivals as a proof of common identity in their request for Spartan help in the war against Persia in the early fifth century BC. However, the claims the Athenians make would have been far from self-evident at the time, even for Herodotus' first readers half a century after the events he describes, and their attempt to draw a straightforward association between festival participation and Greek allegiance is repeatedly complicated by the surrounding narrative. Herodotus' work is in itself a record of, and on some level a contribution to, the first steps in the formation of a Panhellenic identity, and certainly not a reflection of something which was already securely in existence.[57] In the early fourth century BC, similarly, we see Isocrates in his *Panegyricus* appealing opportunistically to sentiments of Greek unity through festival culture, and

---

[57] For the Athenians' appeal, see Herodotus 8.144; for the point that the claims made here may have been far from self-evident to all of Herodotus' readers, see Whitmarsh (2001) 22–3; Cartledge (1997) 26–30; J. Hall (1995) 92–3; cf. Hall (2002) for the argument that a broad sense of Greek identity emerged much later than has often been assumed. Herodotus acknowledges the fact that the concept of Panhellenic unity through shared festival culture is a fragile one in his account of the permission given to the Macedonian king Alexander to compete in the Olympics, in 5.22. Only Greeks were allowed to enter, and Alexander satisfies the *hellanodikai*, the Olympic judges, of his Greek ancestry. Later, however, we see that this permission is no guarantee that he will act with the interests of his fellow Greeks at heart, as he negotiates repeatedly with the Persians; the Athenian speech discussed above is in fact a response to overtures from Persia conveyed by Alexander; on Alexander in Herodotus, see Badian (1994); Scaife (1989).

representing Athens as the archetypal festival city, as part of a controversial argument for Athenian leadership of the Greek world.[58]

The tradition of the *gymnasion* as a place for physical education and for informal intellectual discussion, which we see in Platonic dialogues like the *Lysis*, was transformed and increasingly formalized in the Hellenistic period, as a defining feature of Greek city life. In the fourth century BC Athens developed a system of *gymnasion*-based military training for young men – ephebes – which quickly spread to become one of the central features of education within the Greek *polis* until well into the fourth century AD. The military character of the institution gradually declined – although it seems never to have been lost entirely – and was increasingly supplemented with literate and rhetorical education. The *gymnasion* itself became one of the central markers of Greek identity for cities well beyond the traditional centres of the Greek world, and so contributed to the maintenance and inculcation of civic loyalty and social hierarchies. Membership of the *gymnasion* in Egypt, for example, required proof of Greek ancestry, and brought with it exemptions from tax.[59]

The Hellenistic period also saw a huge expansion in the number of festivals held, partly no doubt as a result of the growth in regular contact between different cities of the Hellenic world, which made festivals increasingly attractive vehicles for displaying communal identity to the world outside. We see the development of a distinction between local festivals, rewarded with money prizes, and more prestigious 'crown' festivals, where victory was rewarded with garlands, occasionally supplemented by money prizes but usually not (although such victory was lucrative in other ways, not least because victors were usually rewarded financially by their home cities). The foundation of a crown festival, or the upgrading of a local festival to a crown festival, was always accompanied by the sending out of envoys to cities all over the Greek world to seek agreement, in a way which reinforced the impression that these were celebrations of communal Greek identity as well as celebrations of the local glory of the host city.[60] Hellenistic kings were often honoured through the foundation of festivals by their subject communities, and were frequently involved in founding new festivals on their own initiative. This period also saw the expansion of the institution of euergetism, that is civic benefaction. The offices of

---

[58] On Isocrates' Athenian Panhellenism see Cartledge (1997) 33; Usher (1994), and the response by Cartledge (1994); Perlman (1976), esp. 25–9; cf. Shapiro (1996) on the Panathenaia and Athenian imperialism under Perikles.
[59] See Bowman (1986) 125–6; cf. Giovannini (1993) 272–3.
[60] See Robert (1984) 36–8 for an overview of these developments in the Hellenistic period.

gymnasiarch and agonothete – head of the *gymnasion* and festival president, responsible for providing year-round facilities and festival funding respectively – were among the most prestigious public duties to which wealthy men and women could aspire.

Many of these things did not change in the Imperial period, but there were some significant shifts. There seems to have been a slight reduction in the scale and volume of agonistic festivals after the subjugation of Greece in the mid second century BC, and it is not until a century and a half later, with growing prosperity and growing imperial encouragement, that we begin to see signs of a revival whose momentum carried well into the third century, and which surpassed anything the Mediterranean world had known before.[61] Extravagant *gymnasia* were built in many of the great cities of the east, and the *gymnasion* was regularly represented as one of the basic requirements of civilized urban life.[62] The rich cities of Asia Minor overtook mainland Greece as the centre of the athletic world, at least in the sense that this area now held more contests and produced more athletes than any other, although the old mainland festivals of the *periodos* continued to be the most prestigious of all.

Some of the most striking changes in Greek athletics in this period were due to the influence of Rome. Augustus was an enthusiastic watcher of athletics, and himself founded a number of festivals, one of which – the Aktia at Nikopolis, founded to commemorate his victory over Mark Antony at Actium – was made part of the *periodos*. These new foundations attracted large numbers of competitors from all over the Empire. Augustus' athletic sponsorship was carried forward, with different styles and degrees of obsessiveness, by Nero, who had the timetable of the great games of Greece changed, so that he could compete (and win) in their musical contests; by Domitian, who in AD 96 founded the first agonistic festival in Rome, the Capitolia, which was also made part of the *periodos*; and later by Hadrian, who bolstered the festival calendar in Athens as part of his promotion of an Athens-based Panhellenism. However, despite evidence of Roman enthusiasm for Greek athletics there were also strong traditions of Roman hostility towards the (perceived) degeneracy of the Greek *gymnasia*. This does not – for the most part – seem to have been matched by eastern resistance to Roman styles of entertainment; certainly

---

[61] For overviews of Imperial-period festival organization, see, amongst others, van Nijf (2001), esp. 307–12; the articles in volume 24.1 of the journal *Stadion*, especially the contribution by Pleket (1998), who focuses on the cities of Asia Minor; Roueché (1993), esp. 1–11; Mitchell (1993) 217–25 and (1990) 189–91; Spawforth (1989) on festivals in Achaia; Robert (1984) 38–45.
[62] See Forbes (1945) 32–3.

gladiatorial entertainments became enormously popular in the Greek cities of the Empire.[63] Many agonistic festivals of the east were closely connected with celebration of imperial cult, which was routinely integrated with the festivals of local deities,[64] although there are also signs that festivals could be the focus for struggles over the balance of power between local and imperial control, not least because imperial consent was now required for the foundation of a festival with 'sacred', Panhellenic status, with the result that we sometimes see signs of negotiation about the precise form a festival should take.[65] The rise of the athletic guilds (originally two organizations, unified at some point before the mid second century AD), whose importance we have seen already in the boasts of Markos Aurelios Asklepiades, must have contributed to the sense of a unifying, Empire-wide athletic culture.[66]

Of course, the changes within Imperial-period athletics were not associated only with public, institutional developments. The work of Michel Foucault[67] and others, which I mentioned in the previous section, raises the possibility that attitudes towards private exercise may also have undergone adjustment. The techniques of *gymnasion* training may not have been the most obvious vehicle for the intense, philosophically informed self-attention which those studies have focused on, but it seems likely that athletic training would at least have been influenced by those trends in some of its manifestations. It may be the case, for example, that these developments at least partly explain the proliferation of treatises which harmonize gymnastic exercise with the demands of a moderate physical regimen (discussed in chapter six),[68] in ways which are far removed from the more vigorous training methods of athletic competitors.

The early-Imperial athletic revival was far from being a passing craze. This book will limit itself to analysing Imperial-period athletics up to the first half of the third century AD, since that is when the 'literary' and epigraphical production related to athletic training and athletic contest begins to thin. However, we hear of large-scale foundations well into the third century,[69] and there is plenty of evidence for athletic training and athletic competition continuing long after Theodosius' proclamation banning the Olympics in

---

[63] See Robert (1940). [64] See Price (1984), esp. 101–32 and 143–4.
[65] On negotiations over the foundation of the Demostheneia at Oinoanda, discussed further in chapter two (p. 71), see Wörrle (1988) with the comments of Rogers (1991b); but also the disagreements of Mitchell (1993) 210, n. 73.
[66] See Roueché (1993) 49–60; Pleket (1973); Forbes (1955); discussed further in chapter five (pp. 221–5).
[67] Foucault (1986). [68] Pp. 274–91. [69] See Mitchell (1990) 191; Robert (1970).

AD 393 as part of a crackdown on pagan festivals.⁷⁰ We should probably not take the decline in athletic inscriptions from the late third century onwards as automatic evidence for a dramatic decline in the importance of athletic institutions. The fact that the epigraphic habit waned in all areas of public life, and not just in relation to athletics, should make us cautious of that conclusion. It does, however, seem likely that the two were connected, as consequences of a gradual decline in the importance of benefaction within the city, which may have been related to financial pressures, and to the increasing importance of imperial rather than civic administration as a focus for elite ambition.⁷¹

Until recently, the most ambitious surveys of ancient 'sport' have been those by E. N. Gardiner⁷² and H. A. Harris.⁷³ Their works are surveys of ancient athletic institutions and athletic technique. Both make impressively broad reference to a great range of ancient literary evidence. However, they also have a number of features which consistently hamper their conclusions. For one thing, both authors are interested as a first priority in the details of sporting practice. That preoccupation with *realia* often leads them to be credulous in their treatment of the complex literary and epigraphic texts which they use as 'sources'. They also often fail to illustrate – Harris especially – the way in which athletics functioned in relation to other areas of ancient culture. And they tend to retroject anachronistic modern assumptions on to ancient practice. In particular, Gardiner's view of the decline of ancient athletics from the aristocratic amateur ideal, due to the corrupting influences of professionalism, is an extraordinary, and by now notorious, distortion of the facts, though very much in step with other accounts contemporary with his own.⁷⁴ The idea that amateurism was an ancient concept has been widely discredited.⁷⁵

The study of ancient athletics has moved on from these foundations,⁷⁶ although in some areas it is still, to my mind, further in thrall to an obsession

---

[70] For continued festival activity, see Cameron (1993) 74–6; Roueché (1993) 6–7; Chuvin (1990) 80; Robinson (1955) 205–8; more specifically, on the continuation of the Olympic games of Antioch, see Millon and Schouler (1988); also Price (1999), who refers to Downey (1961) 493–4, 455–6, 482–3, 504–7 and 518.

[71] See Roueché (1993) 7–11, 137.   [72] Gardiner (1930).   [73] Harris (1972) and (1964).

[74] See Kyle (1990) on Gardiner's devotion to the early twentieth-century amateur movement.

[75] See esp. Young (1985).

[76] Important works on ancient athletics include the epigraphical studies of Louis Robert, Harry Pleket and Onno van Nijf; the collections of inscriptions by Moretti (1953) and (1957); the sourcebook of translated athletic texts assembled by Miller (1991); Scanlon (2002), esp. 3–24, on the social and ritual significance of ancient athletics in a wide range of contexts; Newby (forthcoming) on Imperial-period athletic statues; Lovatt (forthcoming) on the funeral games in Statius, *Thebaid* Book 6. There are also surveys of athletic literature by Visa-Ondarçuhu (1999) and Müller (1995), the former confined

Introduction

with *realia* than is profitable. My aim here is not to reject the study of athletic *realia*, but rather to situate them within a broader cultural context. In that I partly follow the lead of Mark Golden, who has emphasized the influence of ancient sport on ancient constructions of identity, by analysing it as a practice through which individuals were able to situate themselves and others within the complex map of social hierarchies, age boundaries, and gender distinctions.[77] I wish to go beyond his project in two main ways, however: first of all by analysing the Imperial period as a distinctive context for ancient athletics, resisting the tendency, which is apparent within much recent athletic scholarship, to mix together Imperial-period sources and earlier evidence without clear differentiation; and secondly, by paying more attention to sustained reading of the individual pieces of textual evidence on which our knowledge of ancient athletics for the most part relies, in the conviction that it is only through detailed excavation of the agendas and rhetorical strategies which underlie these complex productions that we can properly assess their significance.

There is also a large scholarly industry of modern sports studies. Sport, so this literature often tells us, has not been treated as seriously as it should be.[78] In reaction to that neglect, the last thirty years or so have seen many diachronic accounts of sporting activity from the sixteenth century onwards, and many fascinating analyses of the roles played by modern sport within constructions of gender and social hierarchies, and within processes of national and local self-definition.[79] Many of these studies have a claim to political importance through their capacity to influence contemporary practice. However, there is still a great deal of work to be done in relating sporting activity – conceptually and institutionally – to other areas of society. The very concept that 'Sports Studies' should exist as an independent field of study, separate from historical research more broadly, is in danger of perpetuating the idea that sport is a subject unworthy of serious historical attention. Conversely, some writing in this field has concentrated on large-scale and often speculative analysis of the meaning and development of modern sport, as if in an attempt to emphasize its 'seriousness', and so

---

to the fifth century BC; for athletic bibliography, see Scanlon (1984a) and Crowther (1984–5) and (1985–6); other survey accounts of ancient sport include Decker (1995) and Vanoyeke (1992); and the journals *Nikephoros* (a journal of ancient sports history, founded in 1988) and *Stadion* (a journal of general sports history, founded in 1975) contain many articles on detailed points of ancient athletic activity.

[77] Golden (1998), esp. 33–45.
[78] See, e.g., Polley (1998), esp. 1–11; MacClancy (1996a), esp. 1–2 and 17–18.
[79] See, e.g., Polley (1998); MacClancy (ed.) (1996b).

has failed to provide nuanced analyses of the range of representations and valuations which sporting activities tend to provoke in specific texts and contexts.[80]

Ancient athletics especially has had a bad deal within studies of modern sport, even though many of these studies have rightly given it a starring role within their accounts of the extraordinary processes by which modern sporting practices were formed. In particular the tendency to focus on general questions about what makes modern sport distinctive, and where it comes from, has led to superficial treatment of the distinctive characteristics of ancient practice. Comparative approaches might ideally be expected to encourage and assist contextualization,[81] but in this case they have often done the opposite, being too often focused on just one half (the modern half) of the comparison. Allen Guttmann's book, *From Ritual to Record*, is a good example. He isolates seven characteristics which he feels distinguish modern sport (or at any rate modern American sport), and compares them systematically with more 'primitive' traditions, to see how well his characterization holds up.[82] His seven principles (secularism, equality of opportunity, rationalization, quantification, the quest for records, bureaucratic organization, specialization) – formulated in defiance of Neo-Marxist critiques of modern sporting organization – are themselves in danger of sounding highly idealized. When they are tested out against the ancient world they produce a very skewed picture of Greek athletic practice, diverting attention from more important questions about its role within Greek culture. Most of these principles turn out on closer inspection to be applicable to the ancient world in some form anyway. In confining himself to stark comparison of this sort, Guttmann pays little attention to how people have imitated and adapted ancient models in developing and theorizing modern practice.

All of this, of course, raises questions about what exactly the subject of a book on ancient 'athletics' should be. Are there ancient categories which correspond to our own notions of sport and exercise and competition, as far as those are consistently employed in themselves within modern usage? How can we get behind our modern conceptions to see how 'sporting' activities were conceived within the Roman Empire?

---

[80] See Rader's (1979) (still relevant) criticisms of Guttmann (1978) and others; for surveys of recent trends in sports theory, see Golden (1998) 6–8; Rojek (1992).
[81] E.g., see Bassnett (1993), esp. 138–61, on the recent drive towards contextualization in comparative literature, and its related links with cultural studies; also Lloyd (1996) 1–19 on the methodological difficulties and advantages of comparative history.
[82] Guttmann (1978), esp. 15–55; restated with no account of intervening criticisms in Guttman (1994) 2–4.

We can gain some impression of the connotations of athletic contest by looking at the other activities with which it was institutionally linked. Competitive festivals contained many activities which we would not immediately associate with 'athletics' or 'sport', or even with public competition of any sort. For example, agonistic festivals often included horse-racing in a variety of forms.[83] The combination of athletics and horse-racing survives in the modern Olympics but is not otherwise found at modern athletics meetings. Even more frequently, athletic contests tended to be juxtaposed with events which are referred to within ancient sources as 'musical': music, dancing, acting, declamation and poetic composition.[84] In the majority of festivals, athletes shared the limelight with musical and dramatic performers of many different types, whose fame was often of a similar magnitude, although there were also some conceptual boundaries between these activities, to judge by the fact that some festivals were purely 'athletic', and some purely 'musical'.[85] Musicians advertised their victories in much the same way as athletes. And they were similarly represented by large guild organizations, which seem to have predated the athletic guilds by a considerable period. Physical and spiritual or intellectual training, according to some accounts, following Plato, represented the two essential halves of civilized education. The shared prominence of athletics and 'music' in festival contexts may therefore be due, amongst other things, to the fact that agonistic festivals were valued for displaying in a highly specialized form skills which were seen as central to civilized education (although it would be wrong to suggest that festival competition was always viewed as an unproblematic extension of educational activity, as I will argue further in the next chapter).

Within the category of events which would be classed as 'athletic' or 'sporting' in the modern world, it is hard to work out why some activities gained institutional acceptance within agonistic programmes and some did not. However, one distinctive feature of ancient athletic competition was the high valuation attached to individual achievement. For example, racing in armour made it into many 'athletic' festival programmes, while

---

[83] Crowther (1995) 119–23 argues that horse-racing played a bigger part in the Greek festival culture of the early Empire than is sometimes thought; however, see Farrington (1997) 32–3 on the almost total absence of evidence for hippic contests in the many festivals which purported to follow the Olympic programme; see also Golden (1998), esp. 169–75 on equestrian competition in the Classical period; Decker (1995) 105–15.

[84] On musical contests, see Herz (1990); Larmour (1999) argues that the conceptual boundaries between athletic and musical/dramatic activity were less firm than we usually assume.

[85] See Potter (1999) 256–325 for an overview of the broad range of entertainers and agonistic stars within the Roman Empire, esp. 258–83 on the parallel development of athletic and dramatic activity.

ball games did not, although there is a great deal of evidence for ball-playing rooms attached to *gymnasia*. Probably the reasons for these traditional patterns, which had been formed many hundreds of years before, were not clear to the Greeks of the Imperial period (or even before that) themselves. But one of the most distinctive requirements for inclusion seems to have been a focus on individual prowess, as a distant descendant of the heroic ideology I mentioned above.[86] That may be one reason why team sports (in which category ball games would sometimes have been placed) were generally not taken as agonistic events. Where team sports – including ball sports played in teams – did sometimes feature was in competition between ephebes, the young men who underwent official training in the *gymnasion*.[87] That may be a consequence of the tendency for the practices of the *gymnasion* to be more firmly linked to the skills required for participation in everyday civic and political life than were the events of the competitive festivals. I will argue for that point in more depth in chapter two.[88]

These details go some way towards illuminating the qualities most likely to have been seen as essential features of athletic activity in its different forms, and towards illustrating differences between ancient and modern definitions, but they also give rise to a set of further questions which are difficult to answer. What exactly was the conceptual relationship between *gymnasion* activity and the competitions of the *stadion*? Did private exercise for health outside the *gymnasion* count as 'athletics' in any sense? Is athletics still athletics when it is transposed to the context of the Roman arena, for display rather than prestigious competition? Is it even possible to draw firm lines around these different practices, given the variety of associations which are attached to them within ancient sources? My solution to that problem is a partial one, as perhaps any solution must be. My main focus will be on the physical training and competition which were associated with the *gymnasion* and with the athletic sections of Greek agonistic festivals. I will also, however, be interested precisely in the range of ways in which the links between these two institutions were conceived, and in the range of ways in which people stated and questioned their relationships with activities which were not, or not unanimously, associated with them. Often the question of what should or should not 'count' as legitimate athletic activity is precisely the thing which ancient athletic texts are most interested in debating.

---

[86] Cf. Potter (1999) 324.   [87] E.g., see Golden (1998) 9.   [88] Pp. 63–80.

The contours of these different possibilities for conceiving relations between athletic and other activities can to some extent be mapped out in the uses of 'athletic' vocabulary. The varied employment of words for athletic training and competition both reflects and contributes to the fact that the activities they describe were themselves open to a range of valuations, and associated with a range of contexts.[89] For example, *athleuô* (ἀθλεύω) and related words often carry connotations of 'competition' or 'struggle' for a prize not only in sporting contexts, but also in battle, which tends to reinforce the links which are sometimes drawn between athletics and warfare. It can also refer, however, to training, and the term *athletês* (ἀθλητής) can be used simply to mean one who is skilled or trained in a particular field, or sometimes even a 'star performer'. It is also used in a metaphorical sense, especially of moral struggles, and this semantic connection reflects, and contributes to, the fact that athletes are set up as moral role models, for example in inscriptions. The term *gymnazô* (γυμνάζω) and related words are more clearly confined to training, but can similarly be used for skill or training outside sport (including, again, warfare) although less often with a moral sense. In particular they are often used to refer to rhetorical training.[90] Similarly, the word *agôn* (ἀγών) is used in rhetorical (especially legal) contexts, and can also refer to moral or military struggle.[91] The validity of links between sporting accomplishment and literary and military skill was, as we shall see further in what follows, a common area of disagreement. The idea that such things might be connected with each other is deeply ingrained within the Greek words used to describe them. The language used for athletic activity can thus shed light on the complex network of associations which I have outlined here – a network which had been built up over a long time-period through a range of institutional links.

ANCIENT ATHLETICS IN THE MODERN WORLD

We have seen, then, something of the way in which ancient athletics developed over its thousand-year history, and something of the way in which the ancient world tended to categorize athletics in relation to other spheres of activity. In the rest of this chapter I want to look in more detail at some of the ways in which ancient athletics continues to exert influence over the modern

---

[89] Cf. Scanlon (1983) on the words *agôn* and *aethlos* and related forms.
[90] Cf. ἀσκέω and ἄσκησις, which can refer to training in non-athletic fields, and also to physical and moral discipline in a Christian context.
[91] Cf. Korenjak (1999) 195–6; Goldhill (1999) 2–3; E. Hall (1995), esp. 39–40; Pfitzner (1967) on the word *agôn* in the letters of Paul.

world. I do so partly in order to expand the points I have made about distinctions between modern and ancient practice, distinctions which can easily be obscured by the belief that we have inherited important features of ancient athletic ideology. If we assume that ancient athletics had the same social and cultural functions as modern sport we are likely to come away with a distorted picture of it. However, I will also be pointing to a number of similarities between them, which can alert us to distinctive and important features of ancient practice. Most importantly, as a bridge into the next chapter, I will emphasize the way in which the opportunistic adaptation of Classical customs and ideals within the nineteenth and twentieth centuries – for example, within the early history of the Olympic movement – is paralleled within ancient culture, especially within the athletics of the Imperial period, which accommodated enormous social and political changes, and the substantial changes of athletic ritual and education which accompanied them, beneath a mask of continuity. The multi-layered traditions of modern sporting practice have the capacity to intrigue and fascinate modern viewers, as soon as we stop to delve beneath the surface of activities which often seem natural to us. There is, I believe, a parallel in the fascination which many ancient authors and readers seem to have experienced in encountering the strangeness and complexity of ancient athletic traditions, as soon as they stopped to question the appearance of continuity which those things presented.

The ideals of the Olympic movement have often been presented as an inheritance of the values of the ancient world. However, that is not to suggest an unqualified naivety in those who were responsible for the institutional developments which have given us the modern Olympics as they now function, since that process of 'inheritance' was often accompanied by carefully orchestrated adaptation.[92] There are signs of a degree of credulousness in interpretation of ancient evidence, and we might expect such credulousness to have been even more marked in the case of spectators who received these ideas without any access to specialized knowledge of the ancient world. But that kind of credulousness is often combined with a self-conscious and pragmatic approach to recreation of ancient practice, which accepted the importance of updating this practice for contemporary needs. The writings of Pierre de Coubertin, who was largely responsible for

---

[92] For surveys of the nineteenth- and early twentieth-century Olympic movement, and its exploitation of ancient precedents within debates about national and international regeneration and educational innovation, see Biddiss (1999); Hill (1992) 5–30; cf. Hobsbawm (1983) 298–303 on invention of sporting traditions in late nineteenth-century Europe.

the Athens Olympics of 1896[93] – which is generally taken as the starting-point for the modern Olympic movement – illustrate that mixture well, oscillating between pragmatism and gullibility.[94] In a speech made just before the decision to refound the games, for example, we hear him verging on an acknowledgement of the freedom with which he and others have treated their ancient models: 'The Greek heritage is so vast, Gentlemen, that all those who in the modern world have conceived physical exercise within one of its multiple aspects have been able legitimately to refer to Greece, which contained them all'.[95] Elsewhere, however, de Coubertin frequently expresses his conviction that there was a powerful and uncorrupted Olympic ideal within ancient Greece, which could be recovered even if its precise forms could not be recaptured.[96]

One of the most notorious distortions of ancient athletic ideals has been the notion that Greek athletics attained its glory because of the amateur status of its aristocratic competitors. While it would be wrong to deny that ancient athletics was imbued with idealism, and while it would be wrong to deny the fact that many successful ancient athletes came from elite backgrounds, and might therefore have been able to finance their own training without any reliance on cash prizes, it has nevertheless long been clear that the retrojection on to ancient athletics of nineteenth- and early twentieth-century ideals of amateurism, which were so closely bound up with the class structures of European and American society at the time, was highly anachronistic.[97] The idea of a link between ancient and modern amateurism had a great influence on the early Olympic movement; in fact it continues to have some influence on modern sporting organization. It also influenced much of the scholarship of ancient athletics in the first half of the twentieth century, as I suggested in the previous section.[98]

There are many other less blatant examples of modern distortion and adaptation of ancient practice and ideology, some of them no doubt more self-consciously planned than others. For example, the interest in promoting physical fitness at all levels of society in the late nineteenth and early twentieth centuries was largely a response to the perceived need for military preparedness within the uneasy political atmosphere of that period: de Coubertin's own views seem to have been shaped partly by his concerns

---

[93] For biography on de Coubertin, see MacAloon (1981).
[94] E.g., see Biddiss (1999) 132–3; Guttmann (1994) 122–3; Hill (1992) 8–9; MacAloon (1981) 142–3.
[95] MacAloon (1981) 173.   [96] See Müller (1997).
[97] See Young (1985).   [98] See Kyle (1990), esp. 23–6.

about France's humiliation in the Franco-Prussian War of 1870–71.[99] That interest owed something to ancient ideas about the importance of athletics as training for warfare, of which we will see more in later chapters, but the forms in which those ideas were expressed and implemented were, not surprisingly, distinctively tailored to modern needs. The programming of the early Olympics, partly in reaction to these needs, shows signs of an odd mixture of pedantic imitation of ancient practice and pragmatic adaptation of it, combining painstaking recreation of ancient athletic events with the inclusion of modern disciplines like shooting and fencing.[100]

At the same time, the early Olympic movement also reacted against contemporary militarism by its expressed aim of uniting the different nations of the world harmoniously. It did so partly by appropriating ancient ideals of Panhellenism, perhaps encouraged by the ancient practice of declaring a truce for the host city during the period of a Panhellenic festival. The concept of international harmony does have something in common with ancient ideals. However, the adaptation of these ideals for the modern world has resulted in a number of features very much alien to ancient practice. For example, the idea of world-wide harmony was one of the main motivating factors for de Coubertin's insistence that the Olympics should be moved, rather than remaining in one place as it did in the ancient world, although there were many Greek voices which argued that Athens should be a permanent home for the games, encouraged by the fact that Athens had held a number of smaller 'Olympic' festivals of its own earlier in the nineteenth century.[101] Host nations have used many (if not all) of the subsequent Olympics as opportunities for national self-advertisement, twisting the ideals of internationalism to suit their own purposes. The Berlin Olympics of 1936 – especially as they are portrayed within Leni Riefenstahl's extraordinary documentary *Olympia* – mapped a picture of international collusion with Nazi self-glorification on to the ancient vision of Panhellenic co-operation.[102] More recently, the Atlanta Olympics of 1996 gave a platform, amongst many other things, for a vision of the global corporate dominance of Coca-Cola, a vision which is of course far removed from ancient Panhellenic ideals, but which one can hardly avoid reading as a distant and distorted descendant of them. Many of these ideals of international harmony continue to influence current Olympic ideology, despite the fact that the commercialized foundations of that ideology are largely at odds with ancient

---

[99] See MacAloon (1981) 83–112.   [100] See Guttmann (1994) 122–3.
[101] See Hill (1992) 24–6.   [102] See Guttmann (1994) 123.

practice (though perhaps not entirely so, given that the financial boost of a huge influx of spectators must have been one of the benefits an ancient city could gain from hosting a large festival) and indeed with the original intentions of de Coubertin and others. Even as the Olympics strives to throw off its Eurocentric and Americocentric image, for example, it is plain that the desire to reach out to all corners of the globe is partly driven by commercial motives, which in themselves contribute to the domination of western culture and western business, although that situation may not be incompatible with more idealistic aims in the minds of those who implement and react to those changes.

Some of the flexibility of the ancient Olympic ideal can be illustrated, finally, by the variety of ways in which it was used even well before the modern Olympics 'started' in 1896. Those 'first' Olympics arose out of a whole series of other events which had previously claimed to be the inheritors of the Classical Olympic model, and had used the Olympic name:[103] the Cotswold Olympicks of seventeeth-century England, which featured shin-kicking and stick-fighting contests along with more authentically ancient athletic events; Greek Olympic games organized in Athens on the initiative of the wealthy patriot Evangelios Zappas from 1859 onwards; and a whole raft of festivals in nineteenth-century England, most famously the Shropshire Olympian games (which is still celebrated annually, and was formed originally for the improvement of local labourers), but also the lesser-known Olympic games of Liverpool, Leicester and Morpeth (to name only a few examples). De Coubertin was in contact with the organizers of many of these events. There was already a long established tradition, in other words, of manipulating the Olympic name in a variety of ways throughout Europe.

I have emphasized, then, the way in which modern appropriation of ancient athletics has tended (not surprisingly) to involve distortion and adaptation, both deliberate and otherwise, as well as admiring imitation. This is one explanation for the huge differences between ancient athletic customs and the modern sporting practices which have so often claimed affinity with them. I also wish to show, however, that the tendency to adapt and recreate ancient practice while claiming affinity with it is (again perhaps not surprisingly) one of the things which ancient and modern athletics have most obviously in common. Some of the appropriations I have discussed have vivid parallels with what we know of ancient festival history. For example, the appropriation of Panhellenic ideology for the purposes of local

---

[103] See Young (1996), esp. 13–67; Hill (1992) 9–17; MacAloon (1981) 146–53.

self-advertisement has many parallels within the civic festivals, small and large, of the Roman east. We see signs within the ancient world of a similar readiness to refound festivals, self-consciously repackaging local traditions in response to new political or social situations. We also hear of regular imitation of the programming of great festivals like the Olympics. The accommodation of imperial cult within traditional festival structures is a good example of the way in which distinctive contemporary concerns and needs were often fitted within an avowedly traditional framework. The ideals of Panhellenism were also themselves sometimes adapted for the Imperial present by writers who associate the concept of harmony throughout the Greek world with the pacific benefactions of Roman imperial government.[104] We see similar examples of the manipulation of Panhellenic ideology in a much earlier period in the fourth-century BC *Panegyricus* of Isocrates, who uses the traditions of harmonious Greek festival culture opportunistically within his arguments for Athenian leadership of the Panhellenic community. Often these adaptations passed unnoticed, as they tend to do in the modern world. Sometimes, however, we see signs within ancient texts – as within modern writing on modern sports history – of a fascination with the way contemporary custom represents itself as a natural development continuous with ancient tradition, but turns out on closer inspection to be complex and multi-layered. Analysis of athletic tradition makes the past present, but it has the capacity to make it seem alien and distant at the same time. I will return to that theme in a number of later chapters, especially in discussing works by Lucian, Pausanias and Philostratus, all of which exhibit a fascination with delving into the conflicting strands inherent within the traditions on which the athletic institutions and ideals of the Roman Empire were founded.

Here I want to turn finally to a single comic image of the athletics of the Roman Empire (Figure 1), which sums up many of the themes I have been discussing within this section, offering a picture of ancient athletes whose bewilderment and fascination with Classical athletics is similar to our own. One of the most striking features of the Asterix comic series from which my example comes is its insistence on advertising its own liberation from the authority of classical scholarship.[105] That liberation is mirrored in the refusal of its Gallic heroes, Asterix and Obelix, to conform to Roman control, or to

---

[104] E.g., see Aelius Aristides 26.97–9, in his speech *On Rome*.
[105] Cf. Beard and Henderson (1995) 106–8; on the resistance of these works to modern, bureaucratic realities, see Nye (1980) 192–3; on their reaction to the abstruseness of more elevated literature and on the way in which Asterix and Obelix embody stereotypical, plain-speaking French virtues, see Duhamel (1985); Pinet (1977).

Figure 1 Asterix' Greek rivals training in the *gymnasion* at Olympia.

conform to modern stereotypes of ancient appearance (athletic appearance included). At the same time, however, the authors, Goscinny and Uderzo, frequently insert pedantically researched historical details into that anarchic frame, producing an intriguing mixture of familiarity and distance, accuracy and invention, without ever quite allowing us to be sure where to draw the line between these different qualities.

Asterix at the Olympics offers a vision of the ancient games which follows that pattern closely, combining pedantic recreation of the ancient world with deliberately careless anachronism. In doing so it parodies Olympic and scholarly and popular attempts to recreate ancient athletics, attempts which have often failed to escape from anachronism despite, or perhaps because of, the passion with which they have been made. There is a strange mixture, in other words, of pedantry and absurd inaccuracy in the pictures of ancient athletics which the work offers us. That mixture may be a result of, or even a comment on, modern failures of interpretation or modern carelessness of interpretation. One of its other consequences, however, is that the text shows us 'ancient' characters who are themselves confused about how to treat 'their own' athletic traditions. In doing so it reproduces in uncannily – and perhaps unintentionally – perceptive ways the creativeness of ancient responses to athletic tradition which I have just been discussing. It seems unlikely that René Goscinny and Albert Uderzo would have discussed their work in those terms, or that they deliberately set out to make the point that the inhabitants of the Roman Empire sometimes distorted their own heritage. Goscinny on a number of occasions stated his dislike of attempts to find deep meaning in their work.[106] But their inclusion of this picture of ancient Greeks misusing their own past is thematically consistent with their tendency throughout their work to drop in tantalizingly accurate points of detail within their portrayals of the ancient world.

Here I want to focus on just one frame, which shows us Greeks training in the Olympic *gymnasion* before the games. The scene has details which suggest accurate research, but those details are often presented with a carelessness and distortion which may not be deliberate or knowing in these individual manifestations, but which clearly is deliberate as a broader strategy for the work as a whole, which repeatedly uses scholarly insights but also flaunts its freedom to depart from them. For example, the high jumper carries jumping weights, of the kind which were widely used for the long jump, but never, from the evidence we have, for high jumping, an event

[106] See Nye (1980) 188–90.

which as far as we know did not exist in the ancient world. That detail is a good example of deliberately careless use of accurate detail – accurate portrayal of the jumping weights combined with inaccurate and anachronistic portrayal of their function. It parodies, whether knowingly or not, the pedantic attempts of modern scholars to recreate the technique of the ancient long jump, pedantry which has often led to explanations just as absurd as the idea which is presented here of using jumping weights for the high jump.[107] And in the process it projects this sense of distorting pedantry on to the ancient characters themselves, who seem uncertain about how to use their own athletic equipment.

Even more tellingly – on the far right-hand side – we see a trainer teaching his athlete how to throw the discus by making him copy the painting on a pot. Some modern attempts to recreate ancient technique have gone about it in exactly this kind of way, by drawing on visual or textual representations without taking account of the contexts or agendas lying behind those representations, sometimes with ludicrous results which take no account of the original contexts of the artefacts they are drawing on. Moreover, one of the famous images which has been influential in forming modern perceptions of ancient athletics is the *Diskobolos* statue of Myron, depicting an athlete in exactly the pose we see on the trainer's pot. This frame thus parodies the frustrations and distortions which are inevitable in any modern attempt to recreate the athletic past. At the same time, the picture conjures up an image of Imperial-period athletes who are themselves faced with exactly the same problems. What is the expression on the athlete's face? Is it one of rigorous but dull-witted concentration, born of the determination to imitate faultlessly? Or is it rather an expression of disinterest, even puzzlement, in reaction to a model whose relevance is far from obvious? Either way, it comically foregrounds his simultaneous dependence on and dislocation from any living version of his Classical heritage. And it offers a teasing image of the possibility that this combination of dependence and dislocation is one of the things which the ancient world may share with us in its view of the Classical athletic past.

Goscinny and Uderzo's entertainingly confused picture of Imperial-period Greeks training at Olympia thus reproduces with a deliberate carelessness the distortions of modern interpretation. It also leaves behind it a lingering suspicion that the vision of ancient athletes both mechanically reproducing and at the same time distorting their own heritage may in itself be one of the many strangely accurate details which these authors

[107] See Golden (1998) 60–2.

repeatedly insert into the anarchic refashionings of ancient history which their work presents. In other words it hints at the possibility that the tendency to distort Classical athletic ideals in imitating them is one of the things which the modern world shares with the inhabitants of the Roman Empire.

In that sense, their text is reminiscent of some of the patterns we find within ancient satirical writing. The resemblance is perhaps most obvious of all in the work of the second-century AD satirist, Lucian, whose humorous portrait of the confusing variety of opinions and practices which underlie ancient athletic convention will form the focus of the second half of my next chapter. The self-consciousness with which Lucian dissects and parodies the contradictions and absurdities of traditional culture as it manifests itself in his contemporary world makes his work an appropriate bridge into everything which follows, through its unusually vivid capacity to illuminate not only the practice of ancient athletics and the outline contours of ancient attitudes to athletics, but also some of the complex debates and layers of tradition which underlay those things, and which have left their provocative traces on so many ancient textual representations of athletics in all its forms.

CHAPTER 2

Lucian and Anacharsis: gymnasion *education in the Greek city*

Why are your young men doing these things, Solon? Some of them embrace each other and then trip each other, some of them throttle and twist each other, and wallow around with each other, rolling around in the mud like pigs. First of all they took their clothes off – I saw it with my own eyes! – and anointed one another richly and smoothed each other down peacefully. But then straight afterwards some kind of madness takes over them, and they lean together and start shoving each other, and clash their heads together like rams.

(Lucian, *Anacharsis*, or *Concerning Gymnasia* 1)[1]

INTRODUCTION

These are the uncomprehending words of the barbarian Anacharsis viewing the *gymnasion* exercises of the Greeks. They form the opening words of Lucian's dialogue of the same name, an imagined conversation between the iconic wise men Anacharsis and Solon in a *gymnasion* of ancient Athens. It is a text which brilliantly confronts us – and its second-century AD audience – with the multivalence of Greek tradition and the pitfalls of cultural translation. The sense of mockery in Anacharsis' increasingly incredulous questions is so strong that Solon's defence of Greek athletics, which emphasizes especially the way in which *gymnasion* training brings civic and military excellence, can only ever be partly convincing. Why do the Greeks humiliate their young men in public, in laughable exercises which have no practical usefulness? And why, we might ask, do they continue to do so even at the time Lucian himself is writing, 700 years after the dialogue's sixth-century BC setting?

[1] Ταῦτα δὲ ὑμῖν ὦ Σόλων, τίνος ἕνεκα οἱ νέοι ποιοῦσιν; οἱ μὲν αὑτῶν περιπλεκόμενοι ἀλλήλους ὑποσκελίζουσιν, οἱ δὲ ἄγχουσι καὶ λυγίζουσι καὶ ἐν τῷ πηλῷ συναναφύρονται κυλινδούμενοι ὥσπερ σύες. καίτοι κατ' ἀρχὰς εὐθὺς ἀποδυσάμενοι – ἑώρων γάρ – λίπα τε ἠλείψαντο καὶ κατέψησε μάλα εἰρηνικῶς ἅτερος τὸν ἕτερον ἐν τῷ μέρει. μετὰ δὲ οὐκ οἶδ' ὅ τι παθόντες ὠθοῦσί τε ἀλλήλους συννενευκότες καὶ τὰ μέτωπα συναράττουσιν ὥσπερ οἱ κριοί.

One of my aims in this chapter is to set out some answers to Anacharsis' enquiries. What were the exercises of the *gymnasion* really for? Why did they attract so much devotion? And what other areas of civic life were they linked with? I will outline some of the most important features of ancient *gymnasion* culture, as far as we can reconstruct it, and some of the ways in which it was linked with other areas of education and civic life. And in the process I aim to illustrate the social and political distinction which athletic benefaction and athletic training could bring. In addition, however, I will be looking – unlike many previous accounts of the athletics of the Roman Empire – at some of the ways in which the educational and civic usefulness of the *gymnasion* was denied and debated, both within Roman Empire society and within the literary heritage which was so important to that society, and some of the ways in which debating the value of the archaizing customs of *gymnasion* education could have implications for one's evaluation of Hellenic tradition and contemporary Hellenic culture more broadly. In order to illustrate these points, I will discuss, in the section following this one, the athletic functions of the *gymnasion*, examining especially its role within the education of young men as 'ephebes'. In the third section, I will move beyond the walls of the *gymnasion* in order to analyse its relationship with festival competition and benefaction. And then in the final two sections I will discuss the way in which Lucian's work illustrates and questions the significance of these institutions and of the valuations which are standardly attached to them. Like all of the authors I will be engaging with, Lucian draws on common literary and epigraphical patterns of representing athletic education and reshapes them for his own characteristic – in this case satirical – purposes.

Throughout this chapter (as in all of the chapters following) I will rely as far as possible on Imperial-period sources (roughly defined as the period from the beginning of the reign of the emperor Augustus in 31 BC). I will nevertheless also discuss a great deal of Hellenistic evidence, partly because there were many elements of continuity between Imperial and Hellenistic gymnastic practices. Hellenistic inscriptions in some cases give us the most vivid and detailed portraits of institutional features which still existed in the Imperial period. Many Hellenistic inscriptions would still have been visible in their original positions, contributing by their juxtaposition with more recent inscriptional material to an impression of broad continuity with the Classical past. It is also clear, however, that there were major changes in the function of the *gymnasion* between the Imperial and Hellenistic periods, and my other reason for using Hellenistic sources is to give some impression of what those changes consisted of (although a detailed chronological account of the development of *gymnasion* activity is not the main purpose of this chapter). The most conspicuous shift was the change in the *gymnasion*'s military significance. Throughout the first three centuries AD, the cities of the Greek east were no longer responsible for organizing their own defence or military training on a large scale, although there are occasional exceptions to that generalization, as we shall see. Nevertheless, the content of ephebic training was remarkably little changed from the Hellenistic period. This continuity seems to have been related to the much broader archaizing tendency within Imperial-period Greek culture. The value of anachronistic military training must often have been accepted unquestioningly by those who trained in the *gymnasion*, but we can also see that the anachronism of that military programme was sometimes acknowledged. The Greek literary tradition had even in the seventh and sixth centuries BC criticized athletics for the absurdity of its pretensions to military usefulness. But those criticisms take on a special force, I suggest, when they are reused within the Greek literature of the Roman Empire.

In examining these issues one of the themes I shall come back to repeatedly is the range of ways in which the disjunctions between the *gymnasion* and the world outside it could be represented. The insulation and archaism of the *gymnasion* could be taken as a marker of distinction, a sign of its maintenance of prestigious Classical tradition, and a sign of its capacity to impose rigid discipline on the students for whom it was responsible, far removed from less rigorous lifestyles outside its walls. However, that insulation could also be taken as a cause of its absurdity and anachronistic uselessness of the kind Anacharsis insists on in his scathing commentary. The sense of the *gymnasion* as a place set apart from normal life was one of the areas, in other words, around which contest over its significance tended to focus. Mockery – of the kind we will be seeing in the work of authors like Galen and Lucian – of the *gymnasion*'s isolation from the realities of contemporary day-to-day necessity, military necessity included, is not just mockery of qualities which were generally unnoticed or merely tolerated. Rather it is mockery of an ideal which was often advertised as a source of the *gymnasion*'s importance.

EDUCATION IN THE *GYMNASION*

The *gymnasion* was the most important educational institution of the Greek east within the Roman Empire. Wealthy young men were trained in the *gymnasion* in a number of different age groups, most prestigiously during their *ephebeia* (a training period which lasted usually for one or two years, at around the age of eighteen),[2] and then afterwards, less intensively, as members of the official category of *neoi* ('young men').[3] There was some local variation within that custom between different Greek cities, and indeed between different periods, but also a remarkable degree of uniformity. The *gymnasion* was an official building, maintained at city expense, but the day-to-day running and funding of the institution was left in the hands of the gymnasiarch or his or her deputies. Gymnasiarchy was usually a yearly office, filled by wealthy members of the community, and viewed as one of the most important benefactions individuals could perform for their cities, as we shall see further in the next section. The buildings themselves usually had a number of different rooms – including changing rooms and rooms for ball games (*sphairisteria*)[4] – in addition to their central, uncovered exercise areas.[5] In addition to publicly administered *gymnasia*, many cities also had *palaistrai*, smaller athletic buildings which were usually not large enough to accommodate running or other more extensive activities[6] (although the word *palaistra* could also be used to describe a specific training area within a *gymnasion*). These *palaistrai* could be either public or private, and were similarly staffed by athletic trainers (*paidotribai*). *Paides* (children under sixteen) generally received their physical education in *palaistrai* rather than *gymnasia*, although there are many attested exceptions (including the Beroia decree which I will examine in a moment).[7]

Athletic and military training nearly always dominated the activity of the *gymnasion* throughout its history, but that dominance did not go entirely unchallenged. Ephebes, and to a lesser extent the members of other age groups, were generally put through a rigorous programme of training in athletic events of the kind which featured in festival competition, as well as military drill and weapons training, for which a range of different instructors

---

[2] For overviews of the *ephebeia* see Kleijwegt (1991) 91–101; Marrou (1965) 161–80; on the Hellenistic *gymnasion* as venue for ephebes and *neoi*, see Gauthier (1995) 3–7; on the Athenian *ephebeia* in the Imperial period, see Graindor (1934) 98–102 and (1931) 85–97.
[3] See Forbes (1933).
[4] See Roux (1980), arguing against Delorme (1960) 281–6, who takes *sphairisteria* to be rooms for boxing training.
[5] On *gymnasion* architecture and its functions, see Delorme (1960); cf. Tréheux (1988) for debate about the layout of the *gymnasion* in Delos, as revealed in a second-century BC inventory of the offerings in the *gymnasion*, with separate lists for each room (*I.Délos* 1417 A 1, 118–54) (=Miller 122).
[6] On distinctions between *gymnasia* and *palaistrai*, and on the difficulties of distinguishing between them, see Glass (1988); Marrou (1965) 197–201; Delorme (1960) 253–71.
[7] See Delorme (1960) 262–6; cf. Gauthier (1995) 4–7 on the Hellenistic tendency to exclude *paides* from the *gymnasion*.

was often employed in numbers which depended on the size of the institution and the city in question. These functions were, however, always to some extent balanced by use of the *gymnasion* for other purposes. For instance, the widespread evidence for ball-play areas in *gymnasion* buildings even long before the Imperial era implies that *gymnasion* exercise was not solely about training for the athletic events which formed part of agonistic festival programmes, given that ball-play is usually represented in literary and medical sources as an activity for private pleasure and maintenance of health.[8] In the Imperial period, moreover, *gymnasia* were increasingly combined with bath buildings in both the east of the Empire and the west,[9] a development which suggests an increasing tendency to juxtapose prestigious ephebic training with facilities designed for enjoyment and relaxation and public health.

We also know that literary and musical education was sometimes conducted within the space of the *gymnasion*.[10] Admittedly there is not enough firm evidence for us to conclude that such education took place routinely and systematically in *gymnasion* and *palaistra* buildings,[11] and most of the indications we have give the impression that physical education – whether explicitly military or not – was nearly always predominant, putting aside special cases like the *gymnasion* of the Lykeion where Aristotle's school was founded (and which is also the setting of Lucian's *Anacharsis*, a detail whose significance I will return to in the final section of this chapter).[12] But we do have a great deal of evidence for less formalized educational activities in the libraries and auditoria which sometimes formed part of *gymnasion* building complexes. Many of these activities would have involved ephebes and their near contemporaries.[13] For example, there are many surviving inscriptions, both Hellenistic and Imperial, which decree honours for outsiders who have lectured in *gymnasia*, or for gymnasiarchs who have entertained foreign lecturers, some of whom would have stayed only briefly, while others took up semi-permanent teaching duties.[14] Some *gymnasion* talks may have been open not only to those undergoing formal education, but also to the wider public, at least that seems to be the implication of decrees for doctors who are honoured for improving public health by their lectures.[15] *Gymnasia* also

---

[8] See Harris (1972) 75–111; and further discussion in chapter six (pp. 280–91).
[9] See Farrington (1999); Farrington (1995) 133–6; Yegül (1992) 250–313.
[10] See esp. Delorme (1960) 316–36 and Forbes (1945) 33–7, both of whom draw on the discussions by Robert (1938) and (1937) which I cite below.
[11] See Cribiore (2001) 34–6; T. Morgan (1998) 29, esp. n. 95.   [12] Pp. 85–6.
[13] See Manganaro (1974); Delorme (1960) 324–36; Robert (1937) 79–81.
[14] See Robert (1963) 58–9 and (1938) 13–17, 42–3; BE 1959 no. 330 (pp. 233–4).
[15] See, e.g., Wilhelm (1915) no. 33.1, lines 1–21 (pp. 54–6).

had permanent teaching staff attached to them, not only athletic trainers but also in some cases musical or literary instructors.[16] Many wealthy and powerful men boast of literary and athletic accomplishments together – a combination of interests which the mixed education of the *gymnasion* would have encouraged – and we even have evidence for one teacher of literature involved in athletic benefaction in the third century AD.[17]

I offer here just one example of the *gymnasion* as lecture theatre. At some time in the late first century BC, probably in the reign of Augustus, an astronomer of Roman origin, whose name has not survived, gave a series of classes in the *gymnasion* at Delphi. He was honoured by the city for his efforts with a short public inscription: 'A . . . of Rome, an astronomer (ἀστρόλογος), a man of excellence, visited our city and gave many classes (σχολάς) in the *gymnasion*, in which he distinguished himself greatly'.[18] This text shows us a typical example of erudite education in a *gymnasion* context. It also has some unusual and very revealing features. First of all, it reveals something of the great range of subjects which could be fitted into the *gymnasion* schedule and thought relevant for the educational life of the city (the audience of these classes is not clear, and they may have been open to non-ephebes). Astronomy was popular in Rome in this period, but was a marginal subject in standard programmes of education. Nevertheless it finds a place, anyway in Delphi, beside more conventional lectures by orators and grammarians. Secondly, it shows that *gymnasia* could offer the chance to see famous men of many professions (musical and scholarly as well as athletic) in action, a privilege which was not confined to periods of festival activity. Delphi was famous especially for the musical elements of its Pythian festival, and it may be that its reputation as a centre of learning and literary culture extended well beyond the weeks which were devoted to the Pythian festival every four years. If so, the *gymnasion* could have been an important focus for this distinctive identity, hence perhaps the unusually large number of inscriptions of this type which survive from Delphi. Thirdly, it is interesting to see a Roman in this period performing in a Greek agonistic and educational centre,[19]

---

[16] See Delorme (1960) 318–20; for a good example from third-century BC Teos, which records regulations for the appointment of *gymnasion* staff, discussed further in chapter seven (p. 311, n. 32), see *SIG*³ 578 (=Miller 125).

[17] E.g., see Hall and Milner (1994) 8–30 on the athletic festival founded in Oinoanda by Iulius Euarestos, a 'grammaticus'; cf. van Nijf (2001) 315–16.

[18] Ἀ – λου Ῥωμαῖος, ἀστρολόγος, ἀνὴρ ἀγαθός, ἐνδα[μήσας ἐν τὰν ἀμετέραν πόλιν ἐποιήσ]ατο σχολὰς καὶ πλείονας ἐν τῶι γυ[μνασίωι ἐν αἷς καὶ εὐδοκίμησε] μεγαλείως; see Robert (1938) 15, following Wilhelm's corrections of *SIG*³ 771.

[19] Cf. Robert (1938) 13–17 for a Roman orator similarly honoured at Delphi, also in the first century BC.

at a time when Augustus himself was about to make the first of his large-scale contributions to the agonistic calendar of the Empire through his foundation of the Aktian games at Nikopolis. That example shows how the *gymnasion* could sometimes replicate on a smaller scale the processes of cultural exchange which were among the most distinctive features of the ancient world's agonistic festivals. *Gymnasia* in the Hellenistic and Roman world, in other words, potentially had a great deal in common with festivals as venues for musical and literary learning and display, although no doubt most *gymnasion* instructors could only dream of lecture-lists like Delphi's.

The *gymnasion*, then, was regularly associated with the inculcation of the rhetorical, literary and musical skills which were seen as central to civilized elite identity. However, these associations were never widespread enough or formalized enough to be viewed as the main function of *gymnasion* education, or as the main reason for its prestige. Instead, the central place in nearly all ephebic *gymnasion* activity was occupied by a combination of athletic and military exercises. That might, in turn, lead one to suspect that the *gymnasion* was primarily valued as a venue for military training. And yet on closer inspection, as I have already suggested, that suspicion turns out to be hard to justify, anyway for the Imperial period.

In discussing the significance of military training in the *gymnasion* I want to begin by looking at one Hellenistic piece of evidence, that is the famous gymnasiarchal law of Beroia in Macedonia, which was set up within that city, at public expense, at some time in first third of the second century BC.[20] I start with this inscription partly because it gives us a vivid view of day-to-day *gymnasion* activity, including a number of features which seem to have continued as standard elements of *gymnasion* life well into the Imperial period. For one thing, the inscription gives us an extraordinary picture of education in the *ephebeia* as something meticulously regulated and harshly enforced, and in that sense it illustrates well some of the general points I have made about the way in which the *gymnasion* could be valued for its separateness from the normal conditions of city life. But I also use it in order to give some impression of how the *gymnasia* of the Imperial period departed from Hellenistic precedent

---

[20] *SEG* 27.261; translated by Austin (1981) no. 118 (pp. 203–7) and by Miller 126; for commentary and for the text followed here, see Gauthier and Hatzopoulos (1993); cf. *EAH* 1984, 22–4 and BE 1987 no. 704 (pp. 434–5) for summary of another similarly detailed and important *gymnasion* law from second-century BC Macedonia, which deals, amongst other things, with recruitment and disciplining of teachers, age and conduct and attendance requirements for ephebes, and plans for contests and processions.

through being largely divorced from the realities of military activity in the wider world.

The inscription opens as follows:

> During the generalship of Hippokrates, son of Nikokrates, on the 19th day of the month of Apellaios, during a meeting of the Assembly, the gymnasiarch Zopyros son of Amyntas, along with Asklepiades son of Heras and Kallipos son of Hippostratos made the following proposal: since all the other public offices of the city are conducted in accordance with the law, and since, in cities in which there are *gymnasia* and oiling is practised, the gymnasiarchic laws are deposited in the public archives, it would be best for the same thing to be done also in our city, and for the law which we gave to the auditors to be inscribed on a *stelê* in the *gymnasion* and also placed in the public office; for once this has been done, the young men will feel more shame and will be obedient to their leader, and their revenues will not be wasted, since the chosen gymnasiarchs will always hold office according to the law and will be answerable for their actions. (Side A, lines 1–16)[21]

This opening is striking partly because of the insistence with which the practices described, and their codification, are presented as a natural concern of the city as a whole. The inscription emphasizes the importance of uniformity between the gymnasiarchy and other magistracies. It also suggests that its own provisions are closely in line with those of other cities, painting the *gymnasion* as an institution which guarantees this community's association with the civilized values which unite the whole of the Greek world. Most interestingly of all, perhaps, the decree stresses the beneficial effects it will itself have for the orderly running of the *gymnasion*, for inculcating morally admirable behaviour in the young men of the city, and for preventing wrong-doing on the part of the gymnasiarch, as if these are crucial members of the citizen body whose behaviour cannot be left to chance. There is a curious mixture here of publicization and restriction. The decree will open up the *gymnasion* to public view, standardizing it with other areas of civic practice. In doing so, however, it will enforce a special status on the *gymnasion*, imposing on it unusually rigid disciplines. These disciplines are to be imposed on the gymnasiarch too, not only on the young men in his care. In that sense the inscription throws a

---

[21] Ἐπὶ στρατηγοῦντος Ἱπποκράτου τοῦ | Νικοκράτου, *vac* Ἀπελλαίου ΙΘ. *vac* | Συναχθείσης ἐκκλησίας Ζώπυρος Ἀμύντου, | ὁ γυμνασίαρχος, Ἀσκληπιάδης Ἡρᾶ, Κάλλιπος | Ἱπποστράτου εἶπαν· ἐπεὶ καὶ αἱ ἄλλαι ἀρχαὶ πᾶσαι | κατὰ νόμον ἄρχουσιν καὶ ἐν αἷς πόλεσιν γυμνάσιά | ἐστιν καὶ ἄλειμμα συνέστηκεν οἱ γυμνασιαρχι⁻ | κοὶ νόμοι κεῖνται ἐν τοῖς δημοσίοις, καλῶς ἔχει καὶ πα⁻ | ῤ ἡμῖν τὸ αὐτὸ συντελεσθῆναι καὶ τεθῆναι ὃν δεδώ⁻ | καμεν τοῖς ἐξεταστοῖς ἐν τῶι γυμνασίωι ἀναγραφέν⁻ | τα εἰς στήλην, ὁμοίως δὲ καὶ εἰς τὸ δημόσιον· τού⁻ | του γὰρ γενομένου οἵ τε νεώτεροι μᾶλλον αἰσχυνθή⁻ | σονται καὶ πειθαρχήσουσι τῶι ἡγουμένωι αἵ τε πρόσο⁻ | δοι αὐτῶν οὐ καταφθαρήσονται, τῶν αἱρουμένων ἀεὶ | γυμνασιάρχων κατὰ τὸν νόμον ἀρχόντων καὶ ὑπευθύ⁻ | νων ὄντων.

fascinating light on the conventions of praising gymnasiarchs which are so widespread in honorific inscriptions throughout the Greek east, not least because it suggests that gymnasiarchy was often far from being a sinecure. It often required close personal involvement rather than just faceless generosity.

Many of those patterns continue in the text which follows. The *gymnasion* is represented as an institution of great public importance, mimicking the structures of civic life, but also in many ways as a self-enclosed institution, with its own distinctive rules and rituals, preparing young men for the military disciplines of the outside world, but also providing them with an independent arena in which to exercise those disciplines. For example, the decree lays down rules for the election of gymnasiarchs, with built-in guarantees of accountability, and for the holding of a yearly set of competitions within the *gymnasion* in honour of Hermes, including instructions for the selection of judges and for the organization of the torch-race which formed its centrepiece. It sets out heavy fines (and sometimes flogging, in the case of *paides* or *gymnasion* officials who are slaves) as punishment for misbehaviour and strict procedures for their enforcement. The timing of exercise is strictly controlled, and social hierarchies and age categories are to be carefully maintained. The trainers, for example, are to be present twice every day at fixed times. The ephebes, and those who are in the two years following their *ephebeia*, are to train for their javelin throwing and archery while the *paides* are occupied with athletic exercise, in order to maintain the separation of the two groups. In other cities the *paides* and the *neaniskoi* (ephebes and *neoi*, for this purpose categorized together) were more usually educated in different institutions from each other, but Beroia's single *gymnasion* was used for both, and apparently for little else. There is an age limit of thirty on the use of the *gymnasion*, while young men under thirty can use *palaistrai* elsewhere in the city only by special permission. Even speech is to be carefully regulated. The *neaniskoi* are not permitted to distract the *paides* with talk; nor is anyone allowed to answer back to the gymnasiarch in the *gymnasion*.

The ephebic training itself is (unusually) compulsory, but undesirable elements are carefully excluded, at the risk of fines very much greater than those imposed for other offences:

Those who may not enter the *gymnasion*. None of the following may enter the *gymnasion* and strip for exercise: a slave, a freedman or one of their sons, a man who is incapable of physical training (ἀπάλαιστρος), a man who has prostituted himself (ἡταιρευκώς), a man who works in commerce (τῶν ἀγοραίαι τέχνῃ κεχρημένων), a man who is drunk, a madman. If the gymnasiarch knowingly allows one of these men to oil himself, or continues to allow it after someone has reported this and pointed it out to him, he shall pay a fine of 1000 drachmas ...' (Side B, lines 26–32).[22]

This huge fine – double the annual salary specified for a *paidotribês*, and much higher than any of the other (large) fines the decree threatens – is to be exacted by the city auditors, with the implication that any transgression threatens the social order of the city and the integrity of its educational institutions. It is not at all clear what all of these categories refer to, or what, if anything, they have in common. The clause may have as much to do with military practicalities as with social hierarchies, for example because those who must work every day will not be able to fulfil the demands of daily training.[23] But the explicitness of this exclusiveness, whatever its precise purpose, is remarkable. The decree deliberately and publicly cultivates a sense of regulated detachment from the everyday city life, as a positive advantage in the struggle to instil discipline in an orderly way, offering a positive spin on the kind of detachment from the 'real world' which Anacharsis and others mock.

The Beroia inscription can give us many useful and vivid insights into the most characteristic features of *gymnasion* organization throughout that institution's long history. Its opening insistence on the typicality of its own *gymnasion* regulations, in line with regulations in other cities, is a good example of the way in which standardized *gymnasion* practice was often represented as a sign of a city's participation in universalized Hellenic culture. However, there are also signs that the *gymnasion* it describes was far from typical. We cannot be sure, for one thing, how effectively the idealized vision of the decree was enforced. We should also bear in mind the possibility that this decree might have chronological and geographical peculiarities, especially in the intensity of its stress on military priorities. Different regions sometimes had very different models for commemorating and organizing *gymnasion* activity.[24] One of the main concerns of the

---

[22] Οἷς οὐ δεῖ μετεῖ⁻ | ναι τοῦ γυμνασίου· μὴ ἐγδυέσθω δὲ εἰς τὸ γυμνάσιον δ[ο]ῦ[λ]ος μηδὲ ἀπε⁻ | [λ]εύθερος μηδὲ οἱ τούτων υἱοὶ μηδὲ ἀπάλαιστρος μηδὲ ἡταιρευκὼς μη⁻ | [δ]ὲ τῶν ἀγοραίαι τέχνηι κεχρημένων μηδὲ μεθύων μηδὲ μαινόμενος· ἐὰν | [δ]έ τινα ὁ γυμνασίαρχος ἐάσηι ἀλείφεσθαι τῶν διασαφουμένων εἰδώς, | [ἢ] ἐνφανίζοντος τινὸς αὐτῶι καὶ παραδείξαντος, ἀποτινέτω δραχμὰς | χιλίας ... (B26–32).

[23] See Gauthier and Hatzopoulos (1993) 78–92 for one attempt at explaining these categories; they suggest that the main criteria for inclusion are decency, liberty, physical capacity (hence the exclusion of the *apalaistroi*, men of good families whose physical condition makes them unsuitable for military training), and way of life (which excludes men of merchant occupation, who will be unable to fulfil the requirements of regular attendance).

[24] E.g., see Robert (1960a) 369–77 for examples of ephebic inscriptions distinctive to Odessos and Dionysopolis in Thrace.

Education in the gymnasion 55

commentary of P. Gauthier and M. B. Hatzopoulos is to probe the tensions between typicality and specificity in this Beroia decree, and in the *gymnasia* of Macedonia more generally. They argue convincingly that the *gymnasia* of Macedonia were unusual in being so closely geared to military training, and they suggest that one of the most striking things about the decree is precisely the way in which it does not conform to modern ideas of the ancient *gymnasion* as a place for rounded elite education. They even suggest that it is not by chance that the only surviving gymnasiarchal laws come from this area, and that the intensity of civic involvement in *gymnasion* life in Beroia is due partly to the *gymnasion*'s unusual status in Macedonia as a centre not only for military training but also for military administration.[25] Even the *gymnasia* of Macedonia would probably have modified their military focus shortly after this decree was inscribed, in response to defeat by Rome.[26] We should be very careful, in other words, about taking the preoccupations of this decree as standard ones for the Hellenistic, let alone Imperial period.

How much had changed by the second century AD, when Lucian was writing? Certainly the heyday of the military *ephebeia* had come long before, in early Hellenistic Athens, which itself looked back in idealizing ways to a glorious military past.[27] Nevertheless, the military features of the Athenian system continued to be important, and to be widely imitated, for a long time.[28] The Athenian system began to lose its military focus from the second century BC onwards, but even then the change was not a sudden or a complete one. And even in the second century AD there are some signs of links between military and gymnastic activity. The Greek inhabitants of the Roman Empire were not entirely sheltered from the need for military skills. The *Pax Romana* was in many respects a convenient fiction, undermined in practice by regular incidents of banditry, rebellion and instability on the edges of the Empire, throughout the

---

[25] See esp. Gauthier and Hatzopoulos (1993) 173–6; however, Pleket (1999a), in his review of their commentary, suggests that they overemphasize the extent to which the aims of the Beroia regulations are *exclusively* military.
[26] See Gauthier and Hatzopoulos (1993) 37.
[27] On military activity in the Hellenistic Athenian *ephebeia* see Reinmuth (1974) and (1961), esp. 15; Robert (1938) 296–307.
[28] I will discuss the Athenian *ephebeia* further in chapter seven (p. 309); see also Newby (forthcoming) chapter six; Pélékidis (1962); Graindor (1934) and (1931). For military activity in the *ephebeia* in other cities in the Hellenistic period, see Pleket (1999b) 514–15, who rejects the arguments of Decker (1995) 170 that the growing importance of mercenary armies in the Hellenistic period led to demilitarization of the *gymnasion*; Gauthier and Hatzopoulos (1993), esp. 68–72; Kleijwegt (1991) 92–6 on the military activities of ephebes, with some Roman Empire examples to parallel his Hellenistic evidence; by contrast Delorme (1960) 469–74 is more sceptical about the military significance of the *gymnasion* even at an early period, and rejects the idea that the *gymnasion* was ever used for exclusively military purposes.

first three centuries AD.²⁹ There is evidence for armed opposition to Roman control amongst Greeks.³⁰ From the middle of the second century AD onwards the Empire was seriously threatened by enemies outside its borders³¹ and emergency militias from Greek cities – made up at least partly of young men trained in a *gymnasion* education – took on some of the burden of dealing with these threats.³² Pausanias writes about an Olympic victor leading a force against the invading Costobocci in 170 AD.³³ We hear of youth organizations patrolling the countryside around Greek cities, both in the Roman period and before: for example, one late second- or early third-century inscription records young men (*neaniskoi*) from the city of Apollonia in Caria, serving as mountain guards, under a chief of police (παραφύλαξ).³⁴ There also seem to have been plenty of Greeks from Asia Minor serving in the Roman army.³⁵ Sometimes Greek service in the Roman army had archaizing links with *gymnasion* culture, for example in the participation of members of the Spartan *ephebeia* in Marcus Aurelius' Parthian campaigns, and the eastern campaigns of Caracalla.³⁶ Athletic spectacle may also have had links with Roman militarism, not least because many festivals established in the Greek east were in places through which the Roman army regularly passed.³⁷ There is even evidence, in a fourth-century AD inscription from Panamara in Asia Minor, for a pair of gymnasiarchs extending their benefactions not only to citizens of their communities and foreign visitors but also to soldiers in the area.³⁸

Nevertheless this evidence for links between *gymnasion* activity and military activity is significant most of all for its sparseness. These examples are the exception, rather than the rule. The *gymnasia* of the Imperial period do seem to have followed closely the Hellenistic precedents for military training in the *ephebeia*. But the frequency with which that training was used in

---

²⁹ See Woolf (1993).   ³⁰ E.g. see *Historia Augusta, Antoninus Pius* 5; cf. Bowersock (1965) 101–11.
³¹ See de Blois (1984) 363–4.   ³² See de Blois (1984) 376–7; Millar (1969) 28–9.
³³ Pausanias 10.34.5.
³⁴ See Reinach (1909) and (1908), with the comments of Robert and Robert (1954) 281–3; Robert (1937) 106–8.
³⁵ Speidel (1980) argues that legionary recruitment from Asia Minor was common and prestigious, although military service must have been attractive most of all to poorer citizens (see Goldsworthy (1996) 30), in other words those least likely to have had a *gymnasion* education; see also Holder (1980) 109–39, esp. tables 8.9–8.12 (pp. 134–6); and Forni (1953) 99, who makes the point that Asia tended to supply adjacent provinces, since it did not have its own permanently stationed legion.
³⁶ See Herodian 4.8.3; Cartledge and Spawforth (1989) 105–19, esp. 115, 118; Caracalla himself took an archaizing approach to the expedition by dressing up as Alexander the Great.
³⁷ See Robert (1970) 23–4; cf. Mitchell (1990) 193 (with reference to Cassius Dio 77.9–10 and 77.16.7) on athletic contests between Roman soldiers serving under Caracalla, although he stresses that these were separate occasions from the agonistic festivals of the Greek cities.
³⁸ See *SIG*³ 900, lines 21–3.

Education in the gymnasion 57

situations of armed conflict must have been drastically reduced. In line with that change, a number of Imperial-period authors express scepticism about the military elements of this archaizing educational programme. The kinds of criticisms we hear from Anacharsis – who mocks the military uselessness of the exercises he is watching, boasting that he could defeat all of the naked, prancing Athenians single-handedly, with his tiny Scythian dagger – are widely paralleled. Their frequency suggests widespread, if certainly not unanimous, doubt about the relevance of archaizing military activity.

Many of these criticisms rely on older precedents, and Classical and Archaic attacks on athletics are widely quoted in Roman Empire literature. Passages by Xenophanes[39] and Euripides[40] are the most extravagant examples. Euripides' speaker (in a fragment of his *Autolykos* play) strings together a line of incredulous questions: 'What wrestler, what swift-footed man, or discus-thrower, or chin-puncher, has ever benefited his city by winning a garland? . . . Nobody tries these absurd manoeuvres when they get near hard iron in the battle-line. It's wise and good men who ought to get the garlands' (fr. 282, 16–19, 21–24).[41] The phrase 'wise and good' (σοφούς τε κἀγαθούς), instead of 'beautiful and good' (καλούς τε κἀγαθούς), which was one of the fifth-century watchwords of elite virtue, implies criticism of the way in which athletic prowess and athletic beauty contribute to political influence and upper-class status. The speaker suggests that intellectuals should be the ones taking all the glory. This is a claim which is widely paralleled and imitated, both in the centuries immediately following,[42] and in the later period on which this book focuses. Galen, for example, quotes this Euripides speech twice in his denunciation of athletic trainers in the *Protrepticus*. This picture of widespread doubt about the military usefulness of athletics is reinforced, but also complicated, by the fact that some of these Classical ideas coincide with stereotypically Roman opinions about athletics as an effeminate activity unsuitable for anyone committed to the

---

[39] *IE* 2.186–7 (=Miller 167); discussed by Visa-Ondarçuhu (1999) 229–46; Müller (1995) 88–99; Lesher (1992) 55–61 and 73–7; Kyle (1987) 127–8; Markovich (1978) 16–26; Bowra (1938); cf. also Tyrtaios fragment 12 (*IE* 2.177–9), whose criticisms are similar but less uncompromising.
[40] Euripides *Autolykos* fragment 282 (*TGF* pp. 441–2) (=Miller 168); discussed by Visa-Ondarçuhu (1999) 239–46; Müller (1995) 99–108; Kyle (1987) 128–31.
[41] τίς γὰρ παλαίσας εὖ, τίς ὠκύπους ἀνὴρ | ἢ δίσκον ἄρας ἢ γνάθον παίσας καλῶς | πόλει πατρῴᾳ | στέφανον ἤρκεσεν λαβών; . . . οὐδεὶς σιδήρου ταῦτα μωραίνει πέλας | στάς. ἄνδρας χρὴ σοφοὺς τε κἀγαθοὺς | φύλλοις στέφεσθαι . . . (lines 16–19 and 21–24).
[42] E.g. in Isocrates *Panegyricus* 1–2, who ingeniously combines denigration of athletes (whose lack of usefulness is contrasted with his own publicly beneficial intellectual skills) with exaltation of Athenian festival culture, which contributes to Athenian political hegemony (as discussed in chapter one, pp. 26–7), and which he represents as an appropriate forum for his own rhetorical skill.

military ideals of Roman citizenship, although those ideas were of course in tension with widespread elite Roman enthusiasm for Greek culture (as we shall see further in chapter five). Lucian, I will suggest, deliberately plays on this coincidence in order to raise the possibility that Anacharsis' bewilderment is in *some* ways similar to the reactions of Romans confronted with Greek tradition, as well as being in line with attitudes deeply ingrained within Greek literary tradition.

There were Classical precedents, then, for denigration of athletes, which were applied eagerly to Imperial-period activity. That said, the prevalence of sceptical portrayals of athletes is to some extent balanced by imitation of more positive Classical assessments of the military value of athletics. Of course, the ranting of Euripides' speaker here cannot be taken in itself as representative of common fifth-century BC opinion, not least because it seems to be from a satyr play, in which mockery of athletes may have been a common ingredient.[43] Elsewhere in Classical literature we find opinions that are much more athlete-friendly. The victory odes of Pindar often value athletics precisely for its military uses.[44] Plato not only sets several of his works in *gymnasia* or *palaistrai*, thus exploring the possibility that there are potential connections between physical training and education in virtue and philosophy, but also finds a central place for physical training in the educational schemes of the *Republic* and the *Laws*,[45] although he stresses that it should always be linked with military preparation, and criticizes contemporary practice for its excesses. He admits the potential benefits of physical training, but is also scathing about the suitability of specialist athletes for public office.[46] His views, especially his ideals of balanced education, which takes account of the mind and the body equally, were highly influential, although they were also appropriated and distorted in a great range of different ways, as we shall see in looking at Galen and Philostratus in the final two chapters of this book.

Why, then, was so much energy invested in the training of the *gymnasion*? I have argued that the full answer cannot lie with either the military or the

---

[43] See Kyle (1987) 129–30 and Sutton (1980) 59–61; Visa-Ondarçuhu (1999) 375 makes the point that the fragment runs contrary to more positive representations of athletes elsewhere in Euripides' work.
[44] See, e.g., Perysinakis (1990); on athletics in Pindar more generally, see Visa-Ondarçuhu (1999) 108–52; Lefkowitz (1991) 161–8; Lee (1983).
[45] E.g., see *Laws* 794d–796d (=Miller 129).
[46] E.g. *Republic* 3.403c–412b; *Laws* 8.794c–796e and 829e–834d; for discussion see Goldhill and von Reden (1999), esp. 284–8 on the way in which the social and physical context of the *gymnasion* in the *Lysis* frames the philosophical arguments; Müller (1995) 141–61; Kyle (1987) 137–40; Jeu (1986); Meinburg (1975).

musical/literary elements of ephebic training. Military training seems to have kept a strong foothold within the *gymnasion* activity of the Roman Empire, but its anachronism was far from going uncriticized. Similarly, literary and musical training in the *gymnasion* was often too cursory to be impressive, outweighed by the obsession with physical education. One answer to the question, I suggest, must be that agonistic accomplishment, and the badge of *gymnasion* education, were markers of high social status within the eastern, Greek half of the Roman Empire, and sometimes even necessary passports to participation in local politics,[47] precisely because of the institution's traditional, archaizing connotations. For many members of the Greek elite, in other words, the archaism and 'uselessness' of the *gymnasion* must have been precisely the thing which marked it out as a distinguished accomplishment, only available to those who had the time and money to devote themselves to skills which were not essential to the business of everyday living.

The elite character of the *gymnasion* is revealed glaringly by much of the evidence which survives. In many cities membership of each year's *ephebeia* was publicly and prestigiously recorded.[48] One Hellenistic inscription even makes a point of mentioning those who would normally have been excluded from competition by disability, presumably to make sure that all those who had participated in any form would benefit from the prestige which was attached to membership.[49] A second-century AD inscription from Paros shows the son of the gymnasiarch elected as *protephebos*, the senior ephebe[50] – a well-deserved honour, for all we can tell, but nevertheless in line with the tendency for elite families to monopolize agonistic glory. That elite dominance often also extended to local festivals. For example, there is evidence for elite monopoly over victories in the local festival of the Meleagria at Balboura.[51]

One of the reasons for the prestige attached to membership of the *ephebeia* was the assumption that it prepared young men to play a leading role within their local communities, and also within the wider Greek

---

[47] On the elite status of many Imperial-period athletes, see van Nijf (2003) and (2001); cf. Robert (1934b) 54–8 for examples of elite athletes named on coins.
[48] E.g., see Themelis (2001) 121–2 on ephebe lists in Roman Messene.
[49] See Tod (1951), discussed in BE 1952 no. 180 (pp. 190–91); cf. *P.Oxy.* 9.1202 for a plea on behalf of an ephebe missed off an ephebic list in third-century AD Egypt.
[50] *EAH* 1963 pp. 139–41.
[51] See Milner (1991) esp. 27; cf. van Nijf (2001) 326–7, who gives several examples of drawn contests where the joint victors are apparently of unequal status, and suggests that these contests may have been fixed to prevent the higher-status competitors from losing.

world. The *ephebeia* encouraged allegiance to individual cities through the participation of ephebes in public processions which threaded their way through iconic local sites, as we shall see further in the next section.[52] At the same time, it allowed communities and individuals to advertise their Hellenic identity, both communities where that status would not have been in doubt, and communities which were on the margins of the Hellenic world, and could not match the depth of tradition which older Greek cities could lay claim to.[53] There is also evidence that young men sometimes enrolled as ephebes in cities to which they were not native. For example, we hear of non-Athenians participating in the Athenian *ephebeia* and gaining citizenship as a result, from the late first century BC until well into the second century AD.[54] It is interesting, too, that the law of Beroia does not mention non-citizens among its list of excluded categories.[55] According to that evidence, athletic education – at least in some cases – could give one access to communities other than the city of one's birth (although of course Athenian ephebic training and citizenship might have been unusually sought after), just as athletic victory at the highest level could open doors to membership of cities other than one's own native community, as we saw in the Introduction in the case of Markos Aurelios Asklepiades. *Gymnasion* training was an important stepping stone to membership of one's local citizen elite, in other words, but the benefits of status it conferred also seem to have been transferable in some circumstances beyond the city of one's birth.

Many (though not all) of the literary accounts we have tend to confirm the view that athletics was a high-status activity. On closer inspection, however, some of these statements turn out to be far from unequivocal. Athletics was generally seen as an elite activity, in other words, but that elite character was often an object of debate. To illustrate this point I want to conclude this section by looking at just one example, from Ps.-Plutarch's *Education of Children*, in order to show how one author sheds light, but also throws doubt, on some of the uses of *gymnasion* education which I have been outlining. This work provides a useful reference point for many of the texts which follow later in the book, not least because the ideas it uses (taken from Plato and Xenophon in particular) are widely paralleled, and because it tends to represent its views (in contrast with Lucian, who dramatizes a clash between two different, confidently held opinions) as uncomplicated

---

[52] Pp. 67–8.
[53] E.g., see van Nijf (2001) 315–16 on Lycia; cf. Mehl (1992), who gives evidence, amongst other things, for non-Greeks gaining access to Hellenic education and affiliation through *gymnasion* membership.
[54] See Follet (1988); Reinmuth (1948) 222–30. [55] See Gauthier (1995) 8–9.

and conservative, even though many people would no doubt have disagreed with them.[56]

The work opens with discussion of the importance of choosing the right mother and the right teachers and slaves for one's children. Next we hear about the need for inculcation of orderly habits by constant good example and devotion to philosophy instead of public fame and pleasure-seeking. Halfway through the work, the author steps aside from his discussions of philosophy in order to proclaim the importance of athletic education: 'Nor is it right to overlook the struggles (ἀγωνίαν) of the body. But you should send your children to a trainer (ἐς παιδοτρίβου), to work at these things as is appropriate, both for the sake of their bodily gracefulness, and also to build their strength' (*Education of Children* 11.8b–c).[57] At the end of this paragraph, after discussing Plato's views on the *gymnasion*, he admits that the kind of education he is advocating will not come cheap: 'What should my response be, if somebody says to me, "Having promised to give us information on the education of free men, you are now neglecting the upbringing of poor men and ordinary people (τῶν πενήτων καὶ δημοτικῶν), giving your instructions only to the rich"? It is not hard to refute this accusation' (11.8d–e).[58] He would like the best education to be available to everyone equally, he says. But those who cannot afford it should blame their bad fortune, rather than him.[59]

At first sight this looks like a straightforward and unashamed expression of the elite status of *gymnasion* education. The author has earlier criticized fathers who stint on getting in the best teachers they can afford (7). His mention of the *paidotribês* suggests participation in a formal educational programme, and the word 'struggles' (ἀγωνία), from the same root as the word *agôn*, even hints at a link with the agonistic festival culture with which these things were so closely linked. If we look more closely, however,

---

[56] The sense that this work may be unusual despite its normative pretensions is backed up by Berry's (1958) suggestion that it is exceptional for the Imperial period because of its philosophical preoccupations, in contrast with other educational texts which tend to be more interested in rhetorical training.

[57] Οὐ τοίνυν ἄξιον οὐδὲ τὴν τῶν σωμάτων ἀγωνίαν παρορᾶν, ἀλλὰ πέμποντας ἐς παιδοτρίβου τοὺς παῖδας ἱκανῶς ταῦτα διαπονεῖν, ἅμα μὲν τῆς τῶν σωμάτων εὐρυθμίας ἕνεκεν, ἅμα δὲ καὶ πρὸς ῥώμην.

[58] τί οὖν, ἄν τις εἴπῃ· "σὺ δὲ δὴ περὶ τῆς τῶν ἐλευθέρων ἀγωγῆς ὑποσχόμενος παραγγέλματα δώσειν ἔπειτα φαίνῃ τῆς μὲν τῶν πενήτων καὶ δημοτικῶν παραμελῶν ἀγωγῆς, μόνοις δὲ τοῖς πλουσίοις ὁμονοεῖς τὰς ὑποθήκας διδόναι;" πρὸς οὓς οὐ χαλεπὸν ἀπαντῆσαι.

[59] See Pleket (1999a) 235 on the financial sources available to the gymnasiarch at Beroia and on the possibility that financial contributions were sometimes required for membership of the Hellenistic *ephebeia*, with reference to Pélékidis (1962) 177.

we see that the picture is not quite so straightforward. The term ἀγωνία, for one thing, also links this section of the work with preceding advice about the painstaking individual devotion required for progress in education (and in this sense the work has much in common with pieces whose Plutarchan authorship is not doubted). Excellence requires personal effort. Fathers must be involved in the education of their sons, providing a constant example for them. To farm them out to experts is not enough. The work repeatedly conjures up an image of personal devotion to philosophy, unencumbered by striving for recognition, as the true sign of class. It actually gives strikingly little attention to formal educational systems. Bodily training, with only this one paragraph from nearly thirty Teubner pages, gets a particularly bad deal.

The author's constant reference to Platonic doctrine also complicates any straightforward acceptance of athletic lifestyle. He follows Plato in insisting on moderation in physical exercise, and in advocating military exercise as the primary goal of gymnastic education.[60] Ps.-Plutarch tells us that the slim soldier (ἰσχνὸς . . . στρατιώτης), trained for battle, will easily worm his way through the ranks of over-sized athletes (11.8d). In doing so he aims a Platonic jibe at excessively fleshy *gymnasion* fanatics, who neglect the need for restraint in their treatment of their own bodies. Such pleas for moderation are repeated elsewhere in relation to other areas of educational activity, and often articulated through the imagery of bodily condition. Two chapters before, for example, he discusses the best habits of speech (λέξις). Speech which is bulky or immoderate (ὑπέρογκος) is unfit for public affairs (ἀπολίτευτος); speech which is dry, withered, slim (ἰσχνή) is similarly ineffective, through being unable to make any impression (ἀνέκπληκτος) (9.7a). Avoidance of the extremes of physical condition – whether athletic fleshiness or ungymnastic feebleness – thus stands for and parallels devotion to moderation in other areas of life. The author advocates sampling athletic exercise in moderation, then, as part of general exposure to standard education, which is marked out explicitly as something expensive. At the same time he places it, along with the public education of the city, on a much lower level than the philosophical devotion he is advocating, and which he represents as the mark of real quality in a man. Money and good birth, he tells us (8.5d–e) – in a passage which is closely reminiscent of Galen's anti-athletic recommendations in the *Protrepticus*, which I touched on in the previous chapter and will examine further in chapter six – are not on their own enough for a proper education.

---

[60] Cf. Plato *Laws* 832d–834d.

I have argued here, to summarize, that the athletic education of the *gymnasion* was routinely taken, in line with strong historical precedent, as central to the formation of wealthy, elite citizens. That was the case in part because the athletic training which the *gymnasion* provided was regularly supplemented by musical and military training. However, claims about the value of the *gymnasion* were often under threat, partly because neither the musical nor the military uses of the *gymnasion* were secure enough or sufficiently relevant to other areas of public life to meet with universal approval; and also because athletics was always in competition with other disciplines – other forms of spectacle or of education or of self-care (philosophical education and self-care, in the case of the *Education of Children*) – which sought to impose different disciplinary hierarchies.

I have also suggested that the exclusive and narrow nature of *gymnasion* training must have been one of its prime attractions for those intent on reinforcing their own social position, much as the exclusiveness and archaizing quality of sophistic skill made it a prestigious accomplishment, as Thomas Schmitz has argued.[61] In some cases, as in the *gymnasion* law from Beroia, the exclusiveness of the *gymnasion* is even represented as precisely the thing which makes disciplined and useful training possible, through the exclusion of those who are unable to offer full commitment. From less approving perspectives, however, the detachment of the *gymnasion* from everyday life could be exploited as an argument for its irrelevance to other more 'useful' forms of skill. Anacharsis uses that argument in Lucian's dialogue, in mocking the idea that the Athenians' exercises could be relevant to the realities of warfare, or indeed to any other useful sphere of human activity.

GYMNASION AND FESTIVAL

We have seen that the relevance of the *gymnasion* to 'real life' was sometimes in doubt. However, one way in which the *gymnasion* was routinely and plausibly linked with the world outside it was by its links with civic festival culture. In this section I want to illustrate that point by examining some of the prominent connections which existed between *gymnasion* and festival practice, although I will also at the same time draw attention to a number of disjunctions between them, which might in some cases have suggested that the *gymnasion* was a *more* valuable contributor to civic cohesion and traditional values than any agonistic festival ever could be.

---

[61] Schmitz (1997), discussed above in chapter one (pp. 17–18).

Most of the cities of the Greek world held at least one agonistic festival regularly, often many more than one. The activities of the *gymnasion* generally had more than a passing resemblance to the agonistic activities which those festivals contained. Contests were held at least once a year in most *gymnasia* (and in some cases more often), usually in honour of Hermes, one of the *gymnasion*'s patron gods (the other was Herakles).[62] Many ephebic inscriptions record the names of victors in these internal contests. Clearly one of their functions was to prepare young men for participation in larger festivals, and to encourage them to imitate the athletes who were so often held up as role models to the young.[63] All festival events were things for which a *gymnasion* education could have prepared one,[64] and many end-of-year Hermaia contests mimicked festival programmes closely in some of their events. Moreover, ephebes and even *paides* often competed in public *agones* in their own age categories.[65] Many inscriptions survive commemorating child victors, some of whom acknowledge their *gymnasion* education by praising their trainers. That said, the Hermaia do not always seem to have lived up to the prestige of their public equivalents. For example, the inscriptions of Oinoanda show a surprising lack of overlap between the names on ephebic records and those in victory inscriptions for local festivals. This may have been because the most prominent and wealthy members of the elite had a monopoly on victory inscriptions and on the honorific statues which usually accompanied them.[66] If so, that may be a sign that the very highest echelons of the elite were interested above all in agonistic victories as an indicator of outstanding physical prowess, beyond the lot of 'ordinary' people, and that membership of the *ephebeia* tended to be viewed as a less remarkable achievement.

Gymnasion activities thus imitated festival competition. However, there were also ways in which the internal *agones* of the *gymnasion* were

---

[62] For discussion of these contests, see van Nijf (2001) on *TAM* III.1, 199–213; Mitchell (1993) 218, esp. n. 136; Follet (1976) 318–28 on second- and third-century AD ephebic contests in Athens; Robert (1944) 24–7 and (1939c) 122–8 on two closely connected third-century AD inscriptions (*IG* VII 2450 and Peek (1934) no. 28 (pp. 77–80)) which record ephebes from Tanagra competing in a wide range of locations within the territory of their city, with the names of those who have funded each of these competitions; see also BE 1962 no. 248 (pp. 193–4) on a Hellenistic inscription (*IOSPE* IV 432) recording large numbers of victors in regular contests at Gorgippia on the Black Sea coast; Tod (1951) (mentioned above), with discussion in BE 1952 no. 180 (pp. 190–6) for an inscription from third-century AD Egypt which records victors in ephebic contests in the *gymnasion*, and afterwards the names of all other ephebes.
[63] See Roueché (1993) 191–2; Pleket (1975) 74–89.
[64] For this point see Roueché (1993) 135–6; Delorme (1960) 273–4.
[65] On the age categories of Greek *agones*, see Golden (1998) 104–12; Frisch (1988).
[66] See van Nijf (2001) 325–6.

distinguished from public festival contests, not least because they often contained events which were not part of standard festival programmes. The regulations for the Hermaia in the Beroia decree exemplify that point well. They specify a *hoplitodromos* (race in armour), an event which was widely paralleled in festival competition, and also a *lampadedromia* (torch race), which was a much less regular feature of agonistic programmes. In between come three other contests – contests in *euexia* (good condition), *eutaxia* (discipline) and *philoponia* (hard work).[67] There are no athletic events specified. We cannot know exactly what the criteria for victory in these three competitions were, but the prizes sound as though they are awarded for behaviour throughout the year, rather than for performance on a single occasion, and they seem to have been open to all men between 18 and 30. The virtues rewarded are often represented elsewhere, in non-athletic contexts, as desirable characteristics for men in public life. *Eutaxia* (good discipline), for example, is a quality regularly valued in other types of honorific inscription in the second century AD, particularly associated with political achievement.[68] Similar competitions are regularly attested in other *gymnasion* inscriptions well into the Roman Empire period.[69] Equivalent inscriptions sometimes also record contests in disciplines like reading (*anagnosis*) and writing (*kalligraphia*), which similarly have more practical, educational overtones than the standard programmes of the agonistic festivals, and so remind us of the *gymnasion*'s capacity to combine physical education with many other forms of training.[70] None of these contests has any agonistic equivalent outside the *gymnasion* (although they do have something in common with the way in which athletes are praised within victory inscriptions for their devotion and hard work, as a model for the young, as we shall see further in the next chapter). All of that evidence points to a fundamental difference between the *gymnasion* and the public *agôn*. Far from being a poor shadow of the 'real world' of athletic competition, the *gymnasion* in this case seems to be claiming much greater relevance for its own activities. It has taken on the forms of the public *agôn* in order to reward good behaviour and devotion in themselves, rather than simply honouring athletic victory as something which stands for these things indirectly.

There seem to have been conceptual differences, then, between public festival contests and the *gymnasion* celebrations of the Hermaia, with their

---

[67] Side B, lines 46–58.   [68] See Salmeri (2000) 81.
[69] See Gauthier and Hatzopoulos (eds.) (1993) 99–108; cf. Crowther (1991a); Knoepfler (1979) 173–5.
[70] E.g., see BE 1996 no. 408 (p. 634); *SIG*³ 959; cf. *CIG* 3088 and *I.Erythrai* 81, lines 3–7 for contests in learning (πολυμαθία).

greater claim to civic relevance and moral usefulness. There were many other features, however, which the *ephebeia* and the *agôn* had in common. Both, for example, tended to exclude women.[71] There is little evidence for systematic female athletic education, in the *gymnasion* or elsewhere, to parallel the male instruction of the *ephebeia* and the years of education surrounding it.[72] There is slightly more evidence for women competing in festivals, and this may be a sign that festival competition was felt to be less exclusively linked with the training of (male) citizens who could play an active role in city life than was gymnastic education, but that distinction is far from conclusive. We have a mid first-century AD inscription from Delphi, for example, which was set up by Hermesianax from Caesarea of Tralles to honour his three daughters, who have been victorious in a variety of events at both Corinth and Delphi, including the *stadion* and a race in armour.[73] Similarly, an inscription from Corinth seems to indicate that L. Castricius Regulus set up a contest for young women (*virgi[num certamen]*) as part of the complex of Isthmian games, although it seems likely that this women's competition did not stay on the Isthmian programme for long.[74] All of this material is shadowy, however, and very sparse in volume by comparison with the colossal amount of material attesting to male athletic victory. Even if female contests did take place more regularly than was once thought, the most significant point must surely be that they are mentioned so rarely in the epigraphic record. Athletic prowess and athletic education, at least as something to be publicly advertised, was nearly always strongly associated with masculine virtue. We cannot automatically conclude that women rarely did athletics, but it does seem to be the case that people were rarely interested in advertising the fact, or debating the way in which it should be done.

There were, of course, other ways of taking part in festivals besides competing. Spectatorship, for example, often required active participation, and offered opportunities for displaying social status and civic allegiance,[75] and

---

[71] For discussion of women's sport, see Golden (1998) 123–32; also Scanlon (2002), esp. 98–120 (revised from Scanlon (1984b)), 121–38 (revised from Scanlon (1988b)) and 175–98; Dillon (2000), esp. 460–9 on female competition; Mantas (1995); Lee (1988); Arrigoni (1985).

[72] However, see Mantas (1995) 130–1 for examples of distribution of oil to women in Asia Minor; cf. SIG^3 578, line 10 (=Miller 125) for a third-century BC inscription which records the teaching of grammar to girls, as well as *paides*, by grammarians affiliated to the *gymnasion* of Teos.

[73] SIG^3 802 (=Miller 106) (=Moretti (1953) no. 63 (pp. 165–9)).

[74] See Kent (1966), no. 153; discussed along with SIG^3 802 by Robert (1966a) 743–4. For a women's competition in the second century AD at the Sebasta in Naples, see Büchner (1952) (=*SEG* 14.602); on races for women in Domitian's first Capitolia festival in Rome, see Suetonius, *Domitian* 4.9.

[75] See van Nijf (1997) on the way in which festivals provided opportunities for reinforcing group identities and displaying social hierarchies, especially for civic associations.

Gymnasion *and festival*

the young men of the *gymnasion* were often closely involved in their local *agones* by that means.⁷⁶ For example, an inscribed Hellenistic *gymnasion* law from Macedonia prescribes attendance of ephebes at dramatic and musical and athletic contests, requiring that they should 'not clap or whistle, but should watch in silence and in an orderly way (κόσμωι)'.⁷⁷ The requirement for orderly behaviour recalls the virtues of good conduct (εὐκοσμία) which the same decree demands in its first half. The implication is that these young men ought to be advertising their virtue precisely through their lack of self-advertisement. The demands of proper spectatorship, in other words, are represented as equivalent to the toils of the competitors (an idea we shall see more of in chapter three).

Paides and ephebes and *gymnasion* officials also often played central roles within agonistic ritual, and their integration into the fabric of festival timetables was often carefully regulated, through instructions set out in detail at the time of foundation in inscribed decrees. Guy Rogers has analysed the first-century AD foundation of Vibius Salutaris at Ephesus (*I.Eph.*27), emphasizing especially the way in which the young men of the city were involved in the festival's processions, which educated them in their civic responsibilities and allowed them to explore the question of what their identity as citizens might mean.⁷⁸ Much of the recent scholarship on festive foundations in the Roman Empire has started from the long decree which records the foundation of the Demostheneia at Oinoanda during the reign of Hadrian,⁷⁹ which like the Vibius Salutaris inscription in Ephesus includes detailed instructions for the processions which are to accompany the festival. Ephebes do not play so prominent a role in the Demostheneia as they do in the Vibius Salutaris inscription, but we do see officers of the *gymnasion* taking their place with other city officials in the list of those who are to join the procession, each being required to contribute one bull for sacrifice. Similarly, the office of *amphithalês* in the Imperial period, with responsibility for cutting and ceremonially transporting the foliage used in victory crowns, was given to young boys, who were routinely represented as involved in the life of the *gymnasion*, whether as the sons of magistrates or as members of the *gymnasion*.⁸⁰ In addition ephebes were

---

⁷⁶ See Roueché (1993) 83–156 on spectatorship in Aphrodisias, esp. 94–5 and 123–4 on reserved seating for ephebes and *neoi*.
⁷⁷ μήτε κροτεῖν, μήτε συρίζειν, ἀλλὰ σιωπῆι καὶ κόσμωι θεωρεῖν; summarized in *EAH* 1984, 22–4; see also BE 1987 no. 704 (pp. 434–5); Gauthier and Hatzopoulos (1993) 161–3.
⁷⁸ Rogers (1991a), esp. 58–60, 67–9, 114–15.
⁷⁹ Published by Wörrle (1988) with detailed commentary; English translation with review by Mitchell (1990); other reviews by Rogers (1991b) and Jones (1990).
⁸⁰ See Robert (1973).

often on show, representing the city, on occasions which were not part of the regular calendar. One inscription from Ephesus, for example, records the performance of hymns by ephebes in the theatre in honour of a visit by the emperor Hadrian.[81] Presumably these were young men who had regularly participated in the processions of Vibius Salutaris during the year.

Gymnasion and festival were also often linked with each other by their common reliance on benefaction, from the Hellenistic period onward.[82] Many people boast of having performed both gymnasiarchy and agonotheteship (funding and organization of agonistic festivals), or of having combined these posts with other public offices. The office of agonothete was a prestigious and expensive one, which often involved holding regular banquets for large numbers throughout the festival period (many of which were held in the *gymnasion*)[83] and financing prizes and victory statues, as well as close personal involvement in the details of administration.[84] Gymnasiarchy, too, was expensive and often onerous, as we began to see in looking at the Beroia inscription in the last section. The most important task of the gymnasiarch was to provide the oil with which all *gymnasion* participants would anoint themselves before exercise, and which was seen as essential to bodily health.[85] There are signs that good *gymnasion* facilities were seen as crucial for any city's reputation. For example, P. Vedius Antoninus is honoured by the Ephesians for holding the gymnasiarchy with great generosity during the visit of the emperor Lucius Verus, with the implication that this was an occasion when putting on a good face to the outside world was particularly important.[86] The *gymnasion* building itself could add to the glory of the city. Thus a later Ephesian inscription, from the late third century AD, praises a man who has restored the 'Imperial *gymnasion*' (one of several in the city) 'with much effort and great generosity'.[87] There

---

[81] *I.Eph.* 1145.
[82] See Veyne (1990) for an overview of Hellenistic- and Imperial-period euergetism, with frequent mention (e.g. 147) of gymnasiarchy and festival funding; cf. van Minnen (2000) on euergetism in Hellenistic and Imperial Egypt, for which the *gymnasion* was one of the most important focuses; Gauthier (1985) on Hellenistic euergetism.
[83] See Schmitt-Pantel (1992) 323–4, 367–71.
[84] For a vivid example of the expenses and duties of agonotheteship, see *I.Priene* 112–14, three first-century BC inscriptions in honour of a single benefactor; see also Wörrle (1988), esp. 151–64; Pleket (1976) 1–4 on the most common sources of funding for festivals, which often relied on revenues from taxation or trust funds, as well as the one-off benefactions of individuals; BE 1961 no. 336 (pp. 169–71) on the Sarapeia at Tanagra (with reference to a first-century BC inscription, published with commentary by Christou (1959), which is part of *IG* VII 540) and many other examples, some from the Imperial period; Robert (1948b) 72–9 and 127–30.
[85] See Robert (1935) 450–2 on distinctions between oil of different qualities signalled in inscriptions; and 448, on *I.Magnesia* 116, an honorific decree for a gymnasiarch which praises oil for its health-giving properties.
[86] *I.Eph.* 728.   [87] *I.Eph.* 621.

was considerable pressure on wealthy men to provide oil for their fellow citizens, and the fact that gymnasiarchy is so often mentioned in the same breath as provision of food suggests that it was regarded as similarly essential for civilized city life.[88] Some inscriptions show signs of concern about difficulties involved in finding someone willing or able to fulfil the duties of gymnasiarchy, and we hear of a number of makeshift solutions, which sometimes involved the city as a body taking on the financial burden.[89] Nevertheless the prestige athletic benefaction offered attracted many. We see vivid examples of this prestige in inscriptions which record posthumous honours, like burial in the *gymnasion*, for those who have given money to it, or the right of having one's coffin carried by the ephebes.[90] One inscription from Xanthos, dating from the early second century BC, records the institution of cult worship of a gymnasiarch, as an expression of the gratitude of the city's *neoi*.[91] The *gymnasion*, like the athletic festival foundation, was thus able to ensure the preservation of benefactors' reputations. Benefaction was also frequently a family affair. For example, the relatives of Demosthenes of Oinanda seem to have had a continued involvement with athletic benefaction, and with the Demostheneia in particular, long after his death.[92] These practices of commemoration marked the institutions of athletic benefaction as vehicles for the perpetuation of hereditary elite prestige.

Both gymnasiarchy and agonotheteship were thus often represented as beneficial for the city as a whole. That said, we should be cautious about concluding that such an assumption would have been unanimously and enthusiastically shared, or that *gymnasion* benefaction and *agôn* benefaction would have been equally popular. As I have suggested, many wealthy men would have been reluctant to take on large financial commitments.[93] Moreover, euergetism often benefited members of the elite, rather than the city as a whole, especially in the case of gymnasiarchy, which would therefore probably not have been popular with the mass of any one city's population to the same degree as festival benefactions.[94] Any proclamation of civic consensus and public approval for benefaction was always a function of the processes of personal and dynastic

---

[88] As van Nijf (2001) 312–13 suggests.
[89] See, e.g., van Minnen (2000), esp. 454–60; Knoepfler (1979) 172; BE 1954 no. 158 (p. 145); Robert (1935).
[90] See, e.g., Robert (1968) 414–16; (1966c) 422–3 (esp. n. 7); (1937) 312–14; (1929c) 155–8; cf. BE 1984 no. 351 (pp. 479–80).
[91] See Gauthier (1996) no. 1 (pp. 1–27). [92] See Milner and Mitchell (1995).
[93] See esp. van Minnen (2000) 454–60. [94] See van Minnen (2000) 463–4.

self-promotion, as much as a universally shared ideal.[95] *Polis*-religion was certainly not the only focus for religious devotion and ritual activity.[96] It may even be that the frantic festival expenditure of the second century AD was a sign of the way in which civic cohesion was threatened, and was an attempt to shore up the position of those whose political pre-eminence depended on it, as much as an expression of undisputed common feeling.[97]

Nor did athletic benefaction always involve the same degree of personal effort and involvement as is attested within the inscription from Beroia. Gymnasiarchy in particular was a very flexible office. Many wealthy men took on gymnasiarchies which were for life, or even permanent, to continue after death, in line with common practice for presidency of *agones*.[98] We also hear of very young boys from wealthy families taking on festival or *gymnasion* benefactions (and presumably undergoing *gymnasion* education at the same time),[99] although the lower age-limit for gymnasiarchy was usually thirty, the age at which men ceased to be officially associated with the *gymnasion* as *neoi*.[100] Sometimes gods or emperors were gymnasiarchs. In all of these cases, as also with posthumous benefactions, deputies called *epimeletai* took over the detailed running of the *gymnasia*.[101] This was presumably also the case with female gymnasiarchs, of whom there were many, at least within Asia Minor.[102] In other words the low incidence of female involvement in *gymnasion* education does not seem to have extended to financial arrangements. This trend may be a symptom of the weakening of traditional associations between military achievements and political office, which made it easier for women to play politically prominent roles.[103] Thus, even as women funded training which claimed some conformity with the traditions of citizen-soldier education, their very involvement enacted the distance between past and present in this respect.

---

[95] E.g., see Bendlin's (1997) arguments for a variety of local versions of religious practice driven by individual elite interests, rather than any single homogeneous model of civic religion.
[96] See Woolf (1997) on alternatives to *polis*-religion.
[97] See Woolf (1997), esp. 80; Mitchell (1990) 191 discusses this possibility, but sees a continuation in 'the vitality of civic patriotism and pride' as the reason for continued enthusiasm for festival foundation.
[98] See, e.g., Robert (1966b) 83–5; Robert (1960b) 294–6.
[99] For Imperial-period boy gymnasiarchs, see, e.g., Hatzopoulos and Loukopoulou (1992) K9 (pp. 87–90); Robert (1948b) 73–4.
[100] See Gauthier and Hatzopoulos (1993) 50–2.
[101] See Knoepfler (1979) 171–2; Robert (1967) 43, n. 6; (1960b) 295, n. 5; (1935) 449–50.
[102] See van Bremen (1996), esp. 66–76, for women gymnasiarchs (and also women agonothetes); Casarico (1982) lists 41 examples of female gymnasiarchs; cf. Frei-Stolba (1998) on women founding festivals.
[103] See Levick (2000) 629.

Both *gymnasion* and festival were also subject to imperial influence. That influence was partly due to the Roman administration's desire to control overspending and other misuse of funds.[104] However, the more widely visible manifestation of the emperor's involvement was the association of civic festival life with imperial cult, which was sometimes accompanied by imperial benefactions.[105] The foundation of 'crown' festivals – more prestigious than local festivals, which had cash prizes – required imperial permission, and a striking number of these festivals are named as Sebasteia or Sebasta ('Sebastos' being the Greek version of 'Augustus'), or by the names of individual emperors. Imperial cult was often combined, no doubt often on local initiative, with local traditions already in place.[106] Nevertheless the process was not one of unqualified acceptance, and we do see some signs of resistance to excessive central control. The Demostheneia inscription reveals some of the complex negotiations between imperial and local authorities, and some of the conflicts between Greek, Roman and local identity, which the process of setting up a new festival often prompted.[107] There is also evidence that at least one of the other festivals at Oinoanda was used to assert the primacy of local geographical conceptions over Roman divisions of territory: the festival founded by Markos Aurelios Artemon and his wife makes provision for the participation of two cities outside the boundaries of the Roman province.[108] *Gymnasia* were similarly linked with worship of the emperors. They had been focuses for royal cult in the Hellenistic period,[109] and this continued for imperial worship. The *gymnasia* of the Roman Empire seem sometimes to have had special rooms for imperial worship, and may have played an important role within many festival processions for that reason.[110] Common involvement in imperial cult, in other words, was one of the things which tied *gymnasia* and festivals together.

---

[104] On Roman interest in the expense of payments to athletic victors, see Spawforth (1989) 193–4; on Roman interest in preventing the diversion of funds endowed for festivals, see Rigsby (1979), who cites Oliver (1953) 953–80.

[105] The grant of sacred status was probably not standardly accompanied by financial assistance: see Robert (1984) 38–9; cf. Boatwright (2000) 94, disagreeing with Mitchell (1990) 191.

[106] See, e.g., Price (1984) 102–7.

[107] See Rogers (1991b), esp. 93; however, Mitchell (1993) 210, n. 73 disagrees with the suggestion that the founder's original intentions were significantly altered as they were put into practice; cf. Price (1984), esp. 65–77 on the way in which imperial cult offered space for the exploration of relationships between Greek cities and Rome.

[108] See Hall and Milner (1994a) 33.   [109] E.g., see Robert (1960a) 124–5 and (1925) 425–6.

[110] See Price (1984) 110, 143–4; however, Newby (forthcoming), chapter eight, expresses reservations about the evidence for these rooms.

The *gymnasion* and the city's festivals, to summarize, were closely but not inextricably linked. The *gymnasion* often sought to link ephebic training with the wider world through its imitation of festival culture. Such connections, however, could not guarantee the value of a *gymnasion* education, partly because festival contests themselves were not self-evidently 'useful' events. Athletes were taken as role models and often commanded huge pensions and great political influence, but they also tended to be problematic figures, whose prowess was a useful metaphor for virtues of many different types, as we shall see in the next chapter, but who were useful so long as one imitated them only selectively. Solon, in Lucian's *Anacharsis*, attempts to defend the activity of the *gymnasion* precisely by the way in which it prepares men for winning garlands at Olympia, as if this will silence his critic, but his claim in itself induces even more vigorous mockery from Anacharsis. The prospect of fighting for garlands in front of crowds from the whole of Greece seems even more absurd to him than what they are doing in the enclosed *gymnasion*. Sometimes, in fact, perhaps in reaction to those kinds of criticism, the *gymnasion* was represented as *more* directly relevant to the day-to-day realities of civic life than was the glorious spectacle of great athletes competing in public, for example through the prevalence of ephebic competitions in virtues like *eutaxia* and *philoponia*.

LUCIAN'S THANATOUSIA

I want now to examine some of the ways in which Lucian engages with this background of traditional representation and practice, and with the controversies it gave rise to, within the provocative and slippery prose of the *Anacharsis*. Many of the details Lucian presents us with in this work recall the details of athletic life I have outlined so far. Solon is not simply an absurdly old-fashioned fifth-century Athenian being paraded as an object of curiosity for Lucian's second-century AD audience. The ideals and practices he defends were still important (albeit often treated with scepticism, in this period as before): for example, the education of young men in the *ephebeia* within an avowedly military framework; the claim that insulation of the *gymnasion* from the conditions of everyday life made it more suitable as a place for inculcating civic virtue rather than less; and the claim that training in the *gymnasion* was inextricably linked with participation in athletic festivals, as if these two types of institution were related elements of a coherent, agonistic way of life. By juxtaposing these commonly expressed ideals with the old-fashioned but also in some ways contemporary figure of Solon,

I will argue, Lucian comically challenges his readers to reconsider the value of the archaizing features of their own society.

One way of approaching many of the issues I want to address here is to ask what relation the *Anacharsis* has with Lucian's own society. One of the most prominent strands within twentieth-century Lucian scholarship was debate about the extent to which Lucian had his eyes open to the world around him. Some have emphasized Lucian's sophisticated engagement with literary models,[111] whereas others have stressed the way in which Lucian's work reflects its political and intellectual surroundings, as we know them from other sources.[112] More recently, Bracht Branham has reconfigured this debate by rejecting the choice between these two positions as a false dichotomy,[113] representing Lucian as a writer who is interested above all in dramatizing and questioning the precarious links between past and present with which contemporary sophistic culture was imbued. He analyses Lucian's exploitation of sophistic role-playing techniques, and his technique of parodic reflection on 'the staider forms of contemporary traditionalism'. These techniques, he suggests, allow Lucian to explore the 'logic of contemporary Hellenism and the intricate and obsessive ties of Greek society to its own cultural origins'. Branham exposes brilliantly the way in which '. . . the images the Greeks had projected of themselves over the centuries become in Lucian's hands the medium for reflecting on their cultural identity in its problematic relation to the historical present'.[114]

The *Anacharsis*, with its irreverent presentation of a traditional institution which was in many ways in its heyday in the second century, is a promising focus for precisely this kind of analysis, and indeed Branham does give it a great deal of attention.[115] Many scholars have used this dialogue, especially the pronouncements of Solon, as evidence for the athletic ideals of earlier periods.[116] It would be wrong, however, to ignore the way in which it invites comment on the educational and festive practices which were specific to the Greek city life of second-century AD. Branham, by contrast, grounds the work more firmly in its Roman Empire context. He discusses the way in which Lucian repeatedly in his writing presents us with scenes of confrontation between 'interlocutors whose lack of a shared language inhibits mutual comprehension', '. . . in order to evoke a

---

[111] E.g., Bompaire (1958).   [112] E.g., Jones (1986); Baldwin (1973).
[113] E.g., see Branham (1989) 1–8; cf. Jones (1986) 1–5 on the recent history of Lucian scholarship.
[114] Branham (1989) 5–6.   [115] Branham (1989) 82–104.
[116] E.g., see Scanlon (2002) 15–17, although he does acknowledge briefly the significance of the work's Imperial date.

recognition of the incongruous multiplicity of literary styles, stances, and genres that Greek culture had accumulated . . .'[117] He rightly demonstrates the frequency of athletic subject matter within the Greek literature of this period, and argues that '[t]hrough the estranging device of Anacharsis' uninformed glance Lucian makes the sight of Greeks exercising a matter of renewed curiosity and puzzlement for a second-century audience'.[118] And he analyses the debate about athletics which the *Anacharsis* stages as part of a wider process of questioning the value of traditional institutions and cultural forms.[119]

Despite Branham's sensitivity to the present-day implications of this imagined and ancient conversation even he, however, seems to me to underestimate the intricacy of Lucian's interest in present-day institutions and of his engagement with contemporary patterns of athletic representation. To take just one striking example, Branham, like most other commentators, fails to mention the fact that Anacharsis' recommendation of training with weapons, and Solon's horrified rejection of his suggestion, are surely meant to remind us of contemporary reactions to gladiatorial activity.[120] This in itself may not be a crucial omission (I will draw out some of the implications of this effect in more detail below), but it is symptomatic of a tendency to be vague about the ways in which this dialogue achieves its contemporary resonances, and the means by which Lucian conjures up his absurd but also sometimes uncannily familiar vision of traditional culture.

In what follows, therefore, I aim to build on Branham's analysis by looking in more detail than he does at two of the dialogue's most striking effects: first, the way in which Lucian engages with the variety of possibilities available for valuing athletic activity not only within Classical tradition but also within his own second-century society; and second, the way in which the text prompts its readers to consider their own cultural self-positioning, and the cultural positioning of Lucian himself, in relation to the stances taken up by its two speakers. Both Solon and Anacharsis at times sound as though they could be Lucian's contemporaries, as well as mouthpieces for long-standing stereotypes of traditional opinion.

One of the most tantalizing of those contemporary resonances lies in the frequent hints that we should take Anacharsis as a figure for Lucian himself. That effect is typical of Lucian's work. Many of his other texts show a similar fascination with figures who come from the margins of dominant culture.

---

[117] Branham (1989) 81.   [118] Branham (1989) 88.   [119] See esp. Branham (1989) 102.
[120] As far as I am aware this has been acknowledged only by Kokolakis (1958) 331–3 and Robert (1940) 249.

In presenting these marginal figures, Lucian often hints at parallels between their experiences and his own encounters with the conventions and practices of traditional Hellenism and of the cultural centres of the Empire, as a Syrian who has encountered and learned Greek culture from the outside.[121] That is not to claim that Lucian necessarily was so far removed from Greek culture, by origin, as he claims to be, although the region in which he was brought up did have a strong strand of indigenous local culture and local language underlying its Hellenic veneer.[122] My point is rather that he consistently takes up the pose of ambivalence towards Hellenic convention. In doing so he implies that detachment from unthinking acceptance of dominant cultural forms may in fact make one more representative of Hellenic culture than those who try to disguise the hybridity and constructedness of their own identities by claiming close links with the heritage of the past. In the *Anacharsis*, in line with that pattern, Lucian hints that one way of reading Anacharsis' encounter with Greek custom is to see it as the response of a contemporary observer who takes a sceptical attitude to received practices, and who is therefore more able to see the oddities and realities underlying long-standing traditions than those who invest in those traditions in more unthinking ways.

Before I look at the *Anacharsis* more closely, however, I wish to turn briefly to one related scene of athletic activity elsewhere in Lucian's work. Book 2 of Lucian's *True History* (*Vera Historia*, referred to in what follows as *VH*), includes a narrative of a visit to the Isle of the Blessed, within which is a short account of the *agôn* of the dead, the 'Thanatousia', which is said to be held there regularly (2.22). Louis Robert has analysed this short description in the light of contemporary epigraphical language to make his own contribution to the debate outlined above on Lucian's relation with the 'real world'.[123] He shows that Lucian draws on and distorts conventional language and institutions to produce a very funny and at times disconcerting picture of a world which combines the familiar with the unfamiliar, mixing contemporary reality with fantastical reconfigurations of much imitated but internally contradictory Classical traditions. One effect of that strategy

---

[121] E.g., see Goldhill (2002) 60–107, who also discusses the way in which Lucian's 'real' identity is hidden behind a range of fictional masks; Whitmarsh (2001) 122–8, with reference to the *Anacharsis* amongst other texts; Elsner (2001a) on the *De dea Syria* (although the authorship of that text is disputed); Gera (1995) on the ambiguity of Lucian's picture of the goddess *Paideia* in the *Somnium*, which implies less than whole-hearted approval of the path of Hellenic education he has chosen; Dubel (1994); Saïd (1994a) and (1993), who argues that Lucian's provocative use of first-person masks is part of a deliberate rejection of autobiography, which constantly challenges the reader to find a firm identity for the author; Bompaire (1993) 202–4; Branham (1989) 28–37.
[122] See Swain (1996) 298–308.   [123] See Robert (1980) 427–32.

is to draw attention to the extraordinary and potentially ludicrous range of strands which underlie contemporary agonistic culture.

The work as a whole is an account of a fantastical voyage, parodying the *Odyssey*, the traveller's tales of Herodotus, and a dizzying range of other literary models.[124] Lucian, in contrast with those mendacious fathers of literary deception, as he represents them, famously warns his reader in the opening paragraphs not to believe a word of what follows (*VH* 1.1–4), and proceeds to use that warning as licence for recounting an increasingly bizarre series of adventures which prefigure the inventions of Swift in *Gulliver's Travels*. At the end of the first book, the narrator undergoes a long imprisonment in the stomach of a colossal whale, along with hundreds of other people, who live there growing crops and fighting wars with each other. At the beginning of the second book he escapes, with his crew, and sails on, stopping at a number of islands with outlandish inhabitants. They then make a longer stop on the Isle of the Blessed, where the narrator spends some months enjoying fantastical banquets in the company of Homer and other famous heroes and poets. The juxtaposition of all of these different cultural superstars, and the attempt to accommodate them, with all their heroic idiosyncrasies, within the context of something approximating to contemporary city life, leads to some distinctly odd results.[125]

Lucian's account of the athletic events of the Thanatousia ('Festival of the Dead') is a good example of this ludicrous and uneasy mixture.[126] The account is a brief one, imitating in some ways the economical language of athletic victory inscriptions. The contest's agonothetes, we hear, are Achilles (holding that honour for the fifth time) and Theseus (for the seventh time). The choice of Achilles gives the event Homeric overtones, looking back to the presiding role Achilles plays within the funeral games of Patroclus in *Iliad* 23. We are pitched straight into a scene of heroic competition from the earliest days of Greek athletics. That identification is immediately complicated, however, by the addition of modern details. The office of agonothete, for one thing, is a post-Classical one, as Robert points out.[127] Achilles is never described as agonothete in the *Iliad*. At the same time, that modern addition is in turn distorted by the heroic context into which it is inserted. The appointment of two agonothetes instead of one was not common practice for the festivals of the Roman Empire. Robert suggests that Lucian chooses to record two agonothetes here in order to give prominent status to the Athenian Theseus – whose

---

[124] See Saïd (1994a); Morgan (1985), esp. 476–80.   [125] See Rütten (1997) 67–70.
[126] For commentary on this passage see Georgiadou and Larmour (1998) 204–6.
[127] Robert (1980) 427.

experience as benefactor surpasses even that of the archetypal heroic festival-organizer Achilles – consistently with the renewed prestige of Athens, and especially Athenian festivals, in the reign of Hadrian. There may also, however, be heroic overtones to their shared presidency, as if neither of them, like Achilles and Agamemnon, is willing to yield to the other. This departure from second-century norms is consistent with the strategy we see elsewhere of deliberately introducing slight inaccuracies within otherwise plausible versions of contemporary custom. If these heroes have brought themselves up to date, they have done so in a slightly eccentric way.

Many of the competitions Lucian describes suggest the possibility of harmony between heroic and contemporary custom. Of the various competitors, for example, we hear first of all that the wrestling was won by Kapros the Heraklid (ὁ ἀφ' Ἡρακλέους). This is a technical term used to describe athletes who, like Herakles in the first Olympics, have won in both wrestling and *pankration* contests on the same day. The insertion of this detail imbues the Thanatousia's heroic setting with the jargonized language of institutionalized post-heroic festival culture.[128] Lucian also pits modern athletes against Homeric heroes, matching Epeios, the winner of the boxing match in *Iliad* 23, with the modern Egyptian athlete Areios.[129] Their match is drawn, in line with the Homeric precedent of the wrestling contest between Odysseus and Aias in *Iliad* 23.735–7 (although that result is not one which would necessarily have been out of place in a modern festival context, given the records of drawn contests which survive in a number of Imperial-period victory inscriptions).[130] Lucian even transposes the traditions of poetic competition between Homer and Hesiod (in the *Certamen Homeri et Hesiodi*)[131] into a festival context, portraying them as modern festival poets. Lucian's use of contemporary detail thus suggests surprisingly close links between ancient and modern practice, while the equality between modern athlete and feared Homeric boxer suggests that modern competitors may be quite justified in taking on heroic styles of self-representation.

Once again, however, there are all sorts of inconsistencies which destabilize that assumption of compatibility between contemporary practice and the customs of the heroes in entertaining ways, since the Thanatousia always refuses to fit in perfectly with what might be expected from a second-century celebration. We hear, for example, that this is not a full programme: 'contests in the *pankration* do not take place among them

---

[128] See Robert (1980) 427–9.   [129] See Robert (1980) 428–31.   [130] See van Nijf (2001) 326–7.
[131] This text seems to date from the same period as Lucian's work, although it draws on much earlier sources: see West (1967), esp. 433 on its Antonine date.

(παρ' αὐτοῖς)' (*VH* 2.22).¹³² The *pankration* was one of the most prestigious events of Roman-Empire athletics, and while there are examples of the *pankration* being omitted from programmes which contained wrestling and boxing, the claim that the heroes do not practise the *pankration* at all (which mirrors the absence of that event from the games of *Iliad* 23) suggests their distance from the contemporary world. Furthermore, their prizes for the Thanatousia are not the woven leaves of various kinds which were sanctioned by Greek tradition, but rather garlands of peacock feathers. Both of these observations are made in ethnographical tones which recall Herodotus, and also the *Odyssey*, and more recent traditions of fictional journeys to strange lands. The phrase 'among them' (παρ' αὐτοῖς) in particular casts the heroes as alien to both readers and narrator of the text.

One effect of this mixture of alienness and familiarity is to hint (as in the *Anacharsis*) at absurdities in contemporary Greek custom by showing how it might look from the outside. Perhaps, Lucian seems to be hinting, contemporary athletic customs would look equally strange to an outsider. Herodotus is a particularly important model for that effect, given his consistent interest in the relativity of custom, and in the way in which encounters with the alienness of outside cultures can help one to understand the peculiarities of one's own.¹³³ At the same time this outsider's view is reminiscent of expressions of disapproval and wonderment which we find within Greek responses to Greek athletic tradition. For example the peacock feathers, whose relevance to athletic victory is far from obvious, recall comments elsewhere about the absurdity of garlands made from plants.¹³⁴ The detail of the peacock feathers also invites the kind of aetiologizing treatment which is often given to the various types of garland which were used at different festivals – celery at Olympia, for example, or pine at Isthmia, to name only two of the most famous.¹³⁵ That reminiscence suggests a parallel between fascination with the strangeness of the Thanatousia, and fascination with the obscurities of the ancient agonistic past, of the kind we see in so much Greek writing of the Roman Empire.¹³⁶

In the process, these details also once again provoke comical questions about the 'authenticity' of contemporary agonistic convention. If

---

¹³² παγκρατίου δὲ οὐ τίθεται ἆθλα παρ' αὐτοῖς.
¹³³ On Herodotus see, amongst many others, Cartledge (1997) 27–30; see also Saïd (1994a) on Lucian's manipulation of Herodotean ethnographic strategies, both in the *VH* and in other works.
¹³⁴ E.g., see Dio Chrysostom 66.2, 66.5.
¹³⁵ See Robert (1980) 431–2 on the variety of types of garland used at different festivals in this period; Broneer (1962) on the history of Isthmian garlands.
¹³⁶ Cf. my discussions of Pausanias and Philostratus, in chapters four and seven respectively.

the archetypally Greek Homeric heroes miss out the *pankration*, and use crowns from the exotic peacock,[137] and need to be described in ethnographical language, what implications should we draw for the authenticity of present-day customs which claim direct links with the Greek past? Does it mean that the archaizing pretensions of second-century Greeks are in fact misguided, dependent as they are on departures from ancient, heroic precedent, as if Lucian's contemporaries ought to be using peacock feathers if they want to do things properly? Or does it mean that they are following a model which is not quite so dignified as is usually thought, as if they have over-estimated the extent to which the ancient heroes – whose true character Lucian exposes in his own account – are admirable role models?

These provocative and comical effects have a certain amount in common with Lucian's challenge to the naturalness of the Hellenic credentials of some of the island's most distinguished inhabitants, most conspicuously Homer. Homer's origins were hotly debated within the Roman Empire, in part because a suspiciously large number of cities claimed him as their own most glorious son.[138] Here he reveals to the narrator that he is in fact not a Greek at all, but a hostage taken from Babylon (*VH* 2.20). Lucian humorously hints, through that detail, at similarities between Homer's position, as hellenized outsider to Greek culture, and the kind of outsider's pose which he so often takes on for himself and for the characters he creates, and which he has adopted within this narrative towards the society of the Isles of the Blessed and the other strange communities he visits. The detail of Homer's foreignness suggests that Hellenism may always have relied on absorption of outside influences. Perhaps Homer's famed wisdom and perceptiveness are precisely a result of his outsider's perspective?

One of the things Homer and Lucian have in common, however, is the falsity of the narratives they create. Homer's Odysseus is criticized in the opening section of Book 1 (*VH* 1.3) for his deceptiveness, along with many other historians and lying storytellers. Lucian admits to similar falsification, but suggests that he should be pardoned because of his openness about what he is doing. It may even be that Homer's lying – expressed through the mouth of his character Odysseus – is a consequence of his outsider's status, just as the extravagance of Herodotus' description, at least on Lucian's account, may be a consequence of the need for inventive interpretation

---

[137] Peacocks are associated with foreign luxury and finery elsewhere in Lucian: e.g. *Navigium* 23; *Nigrinus* 13; cf. Morales (1995) 45 on the common association of peacocks with exhibitionism; Dio Chrysostom *Or.* 12.2–5 for peacocks associated with sophists.

[138] See Heath (1998); Jones (1986) 54–5, esp. n. 45.

in deciphering alien conventions which would seem natural to those who practise them. Lucian suggests, in other words, that outsider status can make cultural observation unusually perceptive. But he also draws attention to the possibility that that kind of perceptiveness is always based on a degree of creative and fantastical distortion of reality. In much the same way, I will suggest, he makes Anacharsis in many ways a more authoritative and perceptive commentator than Solon. At the same time, however, he also leaves open the possibility that Anacharsis' own certainties are themselves based on a kind of distorting misapprehension.

This brief athletic interlude in the *VH*, then, illustrates well some of the entertaining and destabilizing effects which recur throughout Lucian's writing. The mixture of realistic contemporary athletic detail with archaizing fiction – sometimes in an incongruous combination, and sometimes in a disconcertingly smooth fit – is typical of the way in which Lucian revels in exposing the ambiguities and complexities of backward-looking Hellenic tradition.[139] He suggests that that kind of exposure, and the authoritativeness it brings with it – like the authoritativeness of Anacharsis – may require or imply a degree of detachment from whole-hearted Hellenic affiliation. At the same time, however, he slyly flaunts the fact that any such authoritativeness is in itself likely to be based on a degree of inventive distortion and misrepresentation.

LUCIAN AND ANACHARSIS

What are we to make, then, of Solon and Anacharsis? Neither side of the argument comes out clearly on top, as has often been noted, and the work exposes many of the ambiguities of Greek athletic activity.[140] That does not mean that the text is inviting an entirely open reading, giving us a free choice between two evenly presented viewpoints. It is hard to deny that the overall effect is likely to be one of absurdity, given the work's emphasis on destabilizing strongly stated certainties, Solon's certainties in particular. It is important, however, to acknowledge that even Anacharsis' certainties are not given unequivocal approval, as I shall argue further

---

[139] Some of Lucian's other works achieve similar effects in relation to athletic tradition by echoing Anacharsis' mockery (for example, in Charon's outsider's incredulity (as an inhabitant of the underworld touring the land of the living) at the vanity of athletic victory in *Contemplantes* 8 and 17); cf. Biliński (1960) 120–1 for Lucian's varied portrayal of athletics elsewhere.

[140] See Branham (1989) 101–2 for rejection of traditional approaches to this dialogue, which try to identify one side of the argument as validated above the other: e.g., Müller (1995) 304–6 surely overstates Lucian's agreement with Anacharsis' side of the argument, as does Anderson (1976) 114–16.

in what follows. In the rest of this chapter I want to examine the way in which the text comically dramatizes and responds to the great variety of conflicting ideals which I outlined in the first half of this chapter.[141] I will also argue that Lucian challenges us through this dramatization to think through the implications for cultural affiliation of a variety of different attitudes towards Hellenic tradition. Is Solon a true representative of Greek tradition? Or is the Scythian Anacharsis paradoxically more Hellenic and more admirable precisely through his sceptical, interrogatory attitude to received custom?

The very first words of the work (quoted at the beginning of this chapter) sum up Anacharsis' bewilderment bluntly, but also in a strikingly unemotional way, in comparison with the extravagant mockery and impassioned defence which follow: 'Why, Solon, do your young men (οἱ νέοι) do these things?'[142] The whole of the rest of the dialogue hovers around that question. Ostensibly it is uttered from a position of barbarian ignorance. It is also, however, the kind of question which was asked extensively from within Greek culture, as we have seen, and it turns out to be a harder question to answer than Solon at first imagines. Anacharsis' use of the word νέοι (young men) presents us with an interesting dilemma. How does he know the technical language of the *gymnasion* age categories (language used most of all in the Hellenistic and Roman periods) if he has no experience of the *gymnasion*? Is it that he has stumbled on this jargonized language by chance, not realizing that his own simple vocabulary has been (or will be, in post-Classical Greek) contaminated with so many complex associations in Athenian speech? Or does he know more than we would expect from a barbarian? Anacharsis was famous for having come to Athens and learnt about Greek culture, and it is difficult for us to know at the very beginning of this work what stage in the process of hellenization he has reached. Lucian seems to be alerting us immediately to the possibility that this sixth-century conversation will have implications for athletic institutions which developed much later. He also seems to be signalling to us, through the initial difficulty of deciphering the degree of Anacharsis' knowledge, that the question which structures the whole dialogue can be asked from a range of vantage points, from a position of complete ignorance of Greek culture as from a position of partial familiarity.

This immediate problem of working out exactly what position Anacharsis is speaking from is intensified by his use of ornate and allusive language

---

[141] Cf. Lada-Richards (2003) on Lucian's strategy of juxtaposing conflicting assessments of a similarly controversial icon of Hellenic culture – pantomime dancing – in his *De saltatione*.
[142] Ταῦτα δὲ ὑμῖν ὦ Σόλων, τίνος ἕνεκα οἱ νέοι ποιοῦσιν;

only a few sentences later, when he describes the way in which the young men 'anointed each other richly' (λίπα τε ἠλείψαντο). This phrase, and variants of it, are used a number of times in Homer,[143] although always to describe the use of oil after washing. Does Anacharsis' use of the language of heroic epic reveal to us that he is better acquainted with Greek culture than he claims? Or are we to assume that he is himself closer to the primitive ideal of heroic life than the Athenians, who have distorted the original, heroic uses of oil for their strange new *gymnasion* acrobatics? The text hints at both possibilities, without making either of them clear. These effects are further complicated by the fact that the phrase also echoes Thucydides (1.6.5), who talks about the way in which the Spartans were the first to strip for exercise and oil themselves afterwards.[144] In the same passage he states that the Athenians, in the mean time, were the first to give up the wearing of weapons (a renouncement Solon boasts of and Anacharsis mocks in paragraphs 33–5 of Lucian's dialogue), and to adopt a more luxurious lifestyle. The echo of Thucydides casts the *Anacharsis* as a scene of confrontation between primitive and new-fangled lifestyles. Anacharsis, in mocking the habit of oiling, seems to belong to the era which preceded this Spartan habit. This passage also plays on the ambiguity of Thucydides' own statement, which does not make it clear how negatively we should interpret this 'new' Athenian luxury, and what its implications might be for the account of Athenian belligerence and defeat which follows. It is hard to know, in other words, whether we should take Solon's renunciation of weapons as a sign of admirable sophistication, or as a sign of Athenian degeneracy in contrast with Anacharsis' heroic virtues. The intertext prompts us to ask ourselves whether Anacharsis is an admirable traditionalist or just a primitive, by these Thucydidean standards. It also prompts us to ask how significant is the difference between Thucydides' Spartans, oiling *after* exercise, and Solon's (more sophisticated? more new-fangled?) fellow citizens in the *Anacharsis*, who oil *before*. This single phrase, like the dialogue as a whole, challenges us – humorously and infuriatingly – to identify and interpret the differences between Anacharsis and those he is watching, and to work out which of them we are closer to.

The main concern of both speakers is to explain what athletic training might be *useful* for. Solon is confident that he will succeed. He seeks to do that in a number of different and overlapping ways, with reference especially to the military and civic and philosophical advantages of *gymnasion* training. He attempts – not always successfully – to give to athletic

---

[143] *Iliad* 3.350, 10.577, 14.171; *Odyssey* 3.466, 6.96, 10.364, 10.450, 19.505.   [144] =Miller 4.

training the civic and political and educational significance which I argued for in the opening half of this chapter, and which Anacharsis' mockery has undermined. And in doing so he anticipates Anacharsis' conversion to Hellenism, although the text makes it very difficult for us to imagine how that conversion from incredulous mockery to acceptance might take place. Anacharsis' opening speech (1–5) expands on his initial string of mocking questions, describing familiar athletic activities through unfamiliar language. He ends defiantly, assuring Solon that it will not be an easy job to persuade him of the Athenians' sanity. Solon, however, seems to think that it will only be a matter of time. He excuses his companion on the grounds that everything is unfamiliar to him, but promises that Anacharsis too will soon be rolling around in the dust, if he sticks around in Athens for a while (6). It is tempting to think that Solon underestimates the difficulty of what he is up against here, and that his own easy acceptance of Athenian custom is a sign of a comical failure to think with any originality about his own culture. However, that impression is humorously undercut by the knowledge we have with hindsight. Anacharsis was renowned more than anything for the way in which he took on Hellenic culture, and he is said to have been killed on his return to Scythia because of his devotion to foreign rituals, as we hear from Herodotus, amongst others, who makes Anacharsis emblematic of admiration for Hellenism and openness to cultural exchange.[145] Solon's promise (or is it a threat?) hangs over the whole dialogue. When they part at the end of the day and of this dialogue, agreeing to continue their discussion on the next day, we are left to wonder how the famous rapprochement between them could possibly have come about. It seems hard to avoid the conclusion that Anacharsis is about to abandon his principles.

That said, there are signs that Solon might be about to learn from Anacharsis in turn. In paragraph 6, for example, he at least envisages the possibility of learning from the Scythians, in pointing out that an Athenian would similarly struggle to comprehend Scythian education and customs (μαθήματα καὶ ἐπιτηδεύματα), though perhaps he overestimates even here the convergence between the two cultures in his assumption that the Scythians *have* an education system (unless we are to assume that he has some familiarity himself with Herodotean ethnographic literature). Later he is more explicit, stating that Athens has a tradition of learning from foreigners, although admittedly he gives little sign elsewhere of having learnt

---

[145] See Herodotus 4.76–7 for this story; cf. Kindstrand (1981) 9–11 for other versions; many of his examples come from Roman Empire texts.

from Anacharsis, nor does it seem to occur to him that their debate might be concluded in a state of productive uncertainty:

> We cannot fail to accomplish one of two things. Either you will be firmly persuaded, having exhausted all the objections which you think are necessary, or I will be taught that my own opinions about these things are wrong. And in the latter case the whole city of the Athenians would not be slow to express their gratitude; for if you teach me or persuade me of anything, the city will be the greatest beneficiary. For I will not hide anything from her . . . (17)[146]

Solon uses the language of athletic benefaction to describe Anacharsis' advice, suggesting that he will be rewarded as a benefactor (εὐεργέτης) with a statue and a public inscription. Anacharsis' benefaction is hard to identify, however, not least because we cannot know whether the 'advice' comprises the mocking comments he has already made, or whether we should imagine that he will have other things to say at a later stage. Lucian seems to be hinting that Anacharsis is himself responsible for the strong strand of scepticism about athletics within Greek literature.[147] The tradition of Solon's own views on athletics is rather confused, and he is sometimes said by Imperial-period writers to have held a negative view of athletics.[148] Lucian may be inviting us to consider the possibility that this confusion in the tradition is due to a change of heart in Solon, inspired by the influence of Anacharsis. Who is learning from whom? And which of the two is more representative of what we 'now' call Hellenism, in the second century? These questions are set up conspicuously in the dialogue's opening exchanges. They become increasingly difficult to answer as the dialogue goes on.

That effect is complicated by the fact that Anacharsis' homeland of Scythia – or at least the Scythian–Greek settlements on the north coast of the Black Sea – is represented in some Imperial writing, most famously in

---

[146] δυοῖν γὰρ θατέρου πάντως οὐκ ἂν ἁμάρτοιμεν, ἢ σὲ βεβαίως πεισθῆναι ἐκχέαντα ὁπόσα οἴει ἀντιλεκτέα εἶναι ἢ ἐμὲ ἀντιδιδαχθῆναι ὡς οὐκ ὀρθῶς γιγνώσκω περὶ αὐτῶν. καὶ ἐν τούτῳ πᾶσα ἄν σοι ἡ πόλις ἡ Ἀθηναίων οὐκ ἂν φθάνοι χάριν ὁμολογοῦσα· ὅσα γὰρ ἂν ἐμὲ παιδεύσῃς καὶ μεταπείσῃς πρὸς τὸ βέλτιον, ἐκείνην τὰ μέγιστα ἔσῃ ὠφεληκώς. οὐδὲν γὰρ ἂν ἀποκρυψαίμην αὐτήν . . .

[147] See Müller (1995) 304 on the likelihood that Lucian has Euripides' *Autolykos* in mind; perhaps we are meant to think that Anacharsis' words here prefigure and give rise to that text, rather than echoing it.

[148] Solon's views on athletics are discussed by Diodorus Siculus 9.2.5; Plutarch *Solon* 23.3; Diogenes Laertius 1.55–6; all of these sources point to a desire to control athletics and to prevent an excessive interest in it at the expense of devotion to the city (in line with Kyle's (1984) assessment of what Solon's athletic legislation really involved). Diodorus Siculus in particular ascribes a very negative view of athletics to Solon, which sounds very similar to those expressed by Xenophanes or Euripides, or even Lucian's Anacharsis.

Dio Chrysostom's *Borystheniticus* (*Oratio* 36), as a relic of a bygone age of Greek culture, even more conspicuously archaizing than the rest of the Hellenic world. The version of Greek life Dio describes in Borysthenes sounds like an oddly imperfect imitation of Classical culture, a strange combination of ignorance with rigid and pious adherence to tradition. That version of the area's cultural heritage is in part confirmed by the material record for the Bosporus area in the Imperial period.[149] For a reader aware of those stereotypes, Lucian's text prompts a number of further considerations. One possible implication is that the patchy archaism of that area is a result of Anacharsis' eventual conversion to Solon's viewpoint – marred, however, by his inability to decipher Solon's imperfect explanations properly.

Solon makes his arguments confidently, but there are signs that he is out of step with the some of the most prominent features of post-Platonic valuation of athletic activity – not surprisingly given that he died well over a century before Plato was born – in particular because he fails to rise to the challenge of integrating athletic training with a more balanced, philosophically informed approach to education. He begins by teaching Anacharsis some names, presumably as a first step on the road to unthinking familiarity. He also explains immediately that they are standing in the *gymnasion* of the Lykeion, with its statue of Apollo Lykeios. Lucian's setting of this athletic scene in Athens has contemporary resonances, recalling the continued prominence of the Athenian *ephebeia* which I touched on earlier, and the privileged position given under Hadrian and afterwards to Athenian athletic festivals.[150] Lucian's picture may even be consistent with the uses of the Lykeion in Imperial Athens. Certainly, there is evidence for ephebic training in the Lykeion as late as the first century BC.[151] Nevertheless it is striking that there is no mention in this text of the Lykeion's association with post-Solonian Peripatetic philosophy. As we shall see shortly, Solon often tries to justify *gymnasion* training in philosophical terms, but finds it very difficult to do so. At times he draws closely on Platonic arguments,[152] but at others his own philosophical understanding seems very underdeveloped by comparison with the glories of Athenian philosophy in later centuries, as we shall see. His ignorance of the

---

[149] See Mitchell (2002).
[150] On gymnastic and agonistic activity in Athens in the second and third centuries AD, see Follet (1976), esp. 201–46 and 317–50; cf. Oliver (1970) 107–9 on imperial letters which set out to prevent athletes from avoiding the Athenian festival of the Panhellenia; one of these may be from Marcus Aurelius, and so roughly contemporary with Lucian; and see Follet (1994) on the wealth of contemporary detail in Lucian's portrayals of Athens.
[151] See Delz (1950) 66–7.   [152] See Müller (1995) 301.

Aristotelian afterlife of the Lykeion is perhaps meant to contribute to that impression.

Solon first of all attempts to justify the Athenians' athletic obsessions by reference to the glory of festival victory, but in doing so he once again fails to make enough allowances for his interlocutor. He seems to be unable to see beyond the appearance of naturalness in his own narrow conceptions. He imagines that the motives for fighting in front of the huge crowds of people at Olympia for the glory of being awarded a traditional victory crown will be self-evident (12), but Anacharsis replies by mocking the whole concept of leaves for prizes, and suggests that the presence of so many spectators, and the consequent risk of even greater humiliation, make competition very much more unattractive, rather than less so (13). In the first half of this chapter I discussed some of the ways in which the gaps between festival culture and *gymnasion* life are both emphasized and downplayed within the processes of individual and institutional self-representation. Lucian shows Solon arguing for close links between them, but struggling to demonstrate clearly how the two institutions reinforce rather than undermine each other. In doing so Lucian offers us a comic challenge to the logic of traditional culture, undermining the idea that these different elements of Hellenic tradition can function together coherently and usefully.

At this stage (14), Solon finally realizes that Anacharsis' incomprehension is more deeply rooted than he had expected, and that he must do something more to justify his assumptions.[153] He launches into a longer explanation of the place of *gymnasion* training within the wider Athenian military and political system, but it is an explanation which often falls short of what he promises. Solon first suggests that Anacharsis can never have given any thought to what is the best type of state (πολιτείας ὀρθῆς περί (14)), and Anacharsis assures him that that has been his main reason for coming to Athens and for seeking out Solon in the first place. Solon then sets out to explain his vision of the way in which a city should treat its young men. He hints at a much higher prize, which the strange garlands of vegetation stand for and lead to, the prize of freedom, switching to much more idealistic language than in his previous, matter-of-fact explanation: 'There is another contest open in common to all decent citizens, and another type of crown, which is not made of pine or olive leaves or celery leaves, but which contains within itself all human happiness, I mean the freedom

---

[153] See Branham (1989) 92–4.

of each man individually, and of the state collectively . . .' (15).[154] This sounds obscure without further explanation, even mysterious. Anacharsis is for the moment willing to accept the possibility of some higher purpose (16) (although he later resumes his mockery, even more savagely in fact, when he sees that the concrete details of Solon's explanation do not, as far as he is concerned, live up to the promise of this impressive but abstract preamble). Solon then explains the Athenian concept of the *polis* (20), as a body whose whole significance lies in its citizens, who must be educated in both body and soul in order to be useful in peace, and keep the city free and safe in war. He discusses the education of citizens (20–1), and then, at Anacharsis' request, gives a more detailed account than he had at first intended of how men are trained for public affairs, mentioning especially the moral education of the theatre (22). Much of Solon's language, both in this passage and elsewhere, is consistent with the representations of athletic prowess as a civic asset in Hellenistic and Roman inscriptions. For example, his earlier praise of athletic glory in paragraph 12 lists the range of virtues on show in agonistic competition in terms which recall the boasts of victory inscriptions. And his mention there of good condition (*euexia*) recalls the categories of ephebic *gymnasion* contests. In 22 he mentions specifically the importance of inscriptions in teaching young men the laws of the city.

His account thus represents an attempt at broader explanation, which takes account of civic and philosophical issues, the latter not least through the way in which it shares the educational concerns of Plato's *Republic* and *Laws*. Nevertheless it is clear that Solon is still jumping to conclusions, and avoiding detailed philosophizing (although that may, of course, be from consideration of the inexperience of his interlocutor). Anacharsis, who seems to have a natural thirst for elevated discussion, several times has to press him for information. In paragraph 21, he criticizes Solon, 'Because you are omitting the things which are best, and which I most want to hear about, the things of the soul (τὰ περὶ τῆς ψυχῆς), and you intend to talk about what is less necessary, *gymnasia* and the toils of the body.' (21)[155] A few pages later, Solon still does not seem to have got the point, when he says to Anacharsis: 'As far as their bodies are concerned – the thing you were most eager to hear about – we train them as follows.' (24)[156] Earlier, just before

---

[154] κοινὸς γάρ τις ἀγὼν ἄλλος ἅπασι τοῖς ἀγαθοῖς πολίταις πρόκειται καὶ στέφανος οὐ πίτυος οὐδὲ κοτίνου ἢ σελίνων, ἀλλ' ὃς ἐν αὑτῷ συλλαβὼν ἔχει τὴν ἀνθρώπου εὐδαιμονίαν, οἷον ἐλευθερίαν λέγω αὐτοῦ τε ἑκάστου ἰδίᾳ καὶ κοινῇ τῆς πατρίδος . . .

[155] Ὅτι τὰ κάλλιστα καὶ ἐμοὶ ἀκοῦσαι ἥδιστα παρείς, τὰ περὶ τῆς ψυχῆς, τὰ ἧττον ἀναγκαῖα λέγειν διανοῇ, γυμνάσια καὶ διαπονήσεις τῶν σωμάτων.

[156] Τὰ δὲ δὴ σώματα, ὅπερ μάλιστα ἐπόθεις ἀκοῦσαι, ὧδε καταγυμνάζομεν.

Solon has started his attempt at a more politically pointed explanation, Anacharsis has asked if they can sit down out of the sun (16), and away from the noise of the wrestlers. This passage slyly replays the scene of philosophizing in the shade in Plato's *Phaedrus*.[157] It is the barbarian who gravitates most naturally towards this archetypal place for philosophy, whereas the Athenian's endurance, learned in the *gymnasion*, means that he has no inclination to approach it. The dialogue as a whole uses Platonic forms, as Branham has pointed out, as many of Lucian's works do.[158] Branham I think overemphasizes the idea that Plato's dialogues themselves endorse single solutions, in contrast with Lucian's open-endedness, but it is clear that the lack of any Socratic authority figure in the *Anacharsis* intensifies the dilemma we face in our responses. Which of them is the real philosopher? Which of the two is wiser?

Later the first hints of rapprochement between them are lost, as they slip back into a disjointed exchange of mockery and self-defence. One of the questions we have to grapple with is whether Anacharsis is right to lose patience. Has he just misunderstood Solon's metaphorical style of explanation, or is Solon's story really as absurd and unexamined as Anacharsis suggests? Once again we see in Solon's account little sign of the tradition of the *gymnasion* as a place of philosophy which was prominent from the fifth century BC onwards. Nor is there much sign of literary and musical training here. It does get a passing mention in 21, but even there the main advantage of poetic education comes from its function of encouraging young men to emulate ancient heroes. Is that a reminder that Solon has not had the benefit of reading Plato's pleas for balanced education? Or is it rather a reflection of the biases of Lucian's own society, which often gave its main attention, in its public proclamations, to athletic skills, rather than to literary or scholarly accomplishment, at least if we are to believe common complaints like those of Galen? It is also striking that Solon gives little attention to the importance of philosophical self-care which forms such a high priority in Ps.-Plutarch's *Education of Children*, as in so many other texts of this period. In this sense, again, Anacharsis' preoccupations are closer than Solon's to those of Roman Empire philosophical writers.

Solon returns more specifically to the subject of physical education between 24 and 30, and it is here that we find his most detailed concentration of 'military' arguments. Even these, however, sometimes seem curiously unconvincing. We hear, for example, that the *gymnasion* exercises

---

[157] See Goldhill (2001a) 2–3.   [158] Branham (1989) esp. 81–2, 103–4; cf. Müller (1995) 301.

of the young Athenians will often turn out to be useful when they find themselves in battle: 'For it is clear that a man like this, grappling even with the enemy, will trip and throw him more quickly, and that when he has fallen he will be able to get back on his feet very easily' (24).[159] At 25 Solon praises their appearance, especially their tanned skin: 'You can imagine, I am sure . . . how they must look with weapons, men who would put fear in their enemies' hearts even when naked',[160] and then at 27 we hear that the *gymnasion* makes them good at throwing the javelin, and jumping ditches and carrying heavy weights. He also explains that the discus resembles a small shield, as if that fact alone is enough to demonstrate the military usefulness of training with it. The most ingenious argument of all comes in 28, where Solon tells us that wrestling against men covered in oil is useful practice for grabbing things which are difficult to hold on to in warfare: 'in case it is necessary to take a wounded friend out of battle with ease, or grab hold of an enemy and come away carrying him in the air'.[161] Solon's assertions do reflect a strong current of positive representations in the second century, as we have seen,[162] but in many ways the details of his account are less than convincing, at least if one takes them at face value, even before Anacharsis lays into them. They are exaggeratedly ludicrous versions of the traditional arguments in favour of training with weapons which are given by the Athenian general in Plato's *Laches* 181e–182d, which first Laches, and then Socrates, less conventionally, take issue with.

It is possible, however, that the absurdities of Solon's explanation – of which the point about wrestling with oil as preparation for carrying bodies out of battle is only the most blatant – are in fact examples of Hellenic ingenuity, as if Solon is joking but making a serious point at the same time. Perhaps Solon's insistence on the value of *gymnasion* training really is a result of blind devotion to Greek tradition, but the dialogue raises the possibility that his attitude is in fact much more knowing and less naïve. If that latter is true, it may be the case that Anacharsis is not yet able to understand Solon's reasoning, although he is apparently beginning to catch on in 18, where he responds to Solon's point that Athenians are willing to learn from foreigners like him as if Solon is joking: 'This is exactly what I heard about

---

[159] δῆλον γὰρ ὅτι καὶ πολεμίῳ ἀνδρὶ ὁ τοιοῦτος συμπλακεὶς καταρρίψει τε θᾶττον ὑποσκελίσας καὶ καταπεσὼν εἴσεται ὡς ῥᾷστα ἐξανίστασθαι.
[160] Ἐννοεῖς γάρ, οἶμαι . . . οἵους εἰκὸς σὺν ὅπλοις ἔσεσθαι τοὺς καὶ γυμνοὺς ἂν φόβον τοῖς δυσμενέσιν ἐμποιήσοντας . . .
[161] εἰ δέοι φίλον τρωθέντα ῥᾳδίως ἀράμενον ὑπεξενεγκεῖν ἢ καὶ πολέμιον συναρπάσαντα ἥκειν μετέωρον κομίζοντα.
[162] See Angeli Bernadini (1995) xxxii–iii on the way in which Lucian draws on contemporary debate about how to train soldiers.

you Athenians, that you are ironical in your conversations (εἴρωνες ἐν τοῖς λόγοις)' (18).¹⁶³ It is hard to know quite how to read this response: is it a misinterpretation of Solon's sincere expression of an important principle; or is it rather an attempt in itself at ironic mock-humility, as if Anacharsis is playing at being Athenian? We are left to puzzle over those questions for ourselves.

There is a problem, then, about how far we should see Solon's speech of justification as ironic, and deliberately ingenious. Perhaps this is just a typically Athenian style of metaphorical speech, which cannot find any common ground with Anacharsis' blunter approach to reasoning. It may be that he is articulating serious principles light-heartedly and obliquely, in other words, when he describes the connections of warfare with gymnastic training. Or perhaps Solon really is unaware of the absurdities he is falling into. Maybe Anacharsis is more hellenized – more ironic – than the archetypal Solon, precisely because of his barbarian perspective. The same problem is raised in the closing moments of the dialogue, where Anacharsis admits that his own forthcoming account of Scythian custom will not live up to Solon's picture of harrowing physical training: 'for we are cowards (δειλοὶ γάρ ἐσμεν)' (40). Does Anacharsis mean this seriously (a sign that he is beginning to be won round?) or ironically, in line with his tone in the rest of the dialogue?

Anacharsis' mocking response to Solon's military arguments draws out some of the absurdities which are implicit, but not necessary, in Solon's account, again making Greek life seem strange by his literal-minded and very funny outsider's perspective. At 31, for example, he asks whether they would fight their enemies using the combat techniques of the *gymnasion*, if the city were attacked. He wonders, mockingly echoing Euripides' *Autolykos*, if their statuesque and tanned (like bronze?) bodies would ward off their enemies' arrows, or if the ridiculous costumes they wear on stage would frighten their enemies (32). He also laughs at them for not carrying arms, saying that he could capture the whole *gymnasion* with just his own tiny sword (ξιφίδιον) (33), and urges them to train with weapons (32).¹⁶⁴

Some of his arguments seem strikingly appropriate to an Imperial-period context, and in many instances they reinforce the impression that

---

¹⁶³ Τοῦτ' ἐκεῖνο ἦν ἄρα, ὃ ἐγὼ περὶ ὑμῶν ἤκουον τῶν Ἀθηναίων, ὡς εἴητε εἴρωνες ἐν τοῖς λόγοις.
¹⁶⁴ Greeks did race in full armour in the hoplite race, but this was a late addition to the Olympic and Pythian programmes (see Golden (1998) 26–7), well after the dramatic date of this dialogue. It may even be that Lucian is inviting us to see this as another development provoked by Anacharsis' criticisms.

Anacharsis' views have something in common with stereotypical representations of Roman reactions to the oddities of Greek culture.[165] For example, as we have seen, the idea that athletics and warfare were connected was often undermined, in the eyes of Roman writers, by the perception of Greek military weakness and effeminacy brought about by long subjection to Roman rule. Anacharsis' scathing remark at the end of 33 seems to be an expression of precisely this kind of view: 'Long peace has so greatly affected you, that you cannot easily bear to see even one plume of an enemy's helmet.'[166] He suggests that the Athenians are just as cowardly as the Trojan child Astyanax, who famously cries when he sees the plume of his father Hector in *Iliad* 6.466–73. One implication, in the context of Roman rule, seems to be that the old Classical Greek way of life is outmoded. Solon sounds like a second-century Hellene making absurd and incoherent justifications for an institution many hundreds of years out of date, while Anacharsis' observation echoes the Latin topos of Empire-wide peace as a debilitating influence on Rome's subjects.[167] Anacharsis' point about training with arms also sounds very much like a claim that Roman gladiatorial combat is a more suitable vehicle for inculcating military virtues, as I suggested earlier. Solon's response, which criticizes the cruelty and bestiality of such training, recalls the attacks made by Imperial writers like Dio Chrysostom on gladiatorial entertainment:[168] 'But as for testing them in weapons and watching them get wounded, don't even suggest it. For it is bestial and uncivilized (σκαιόν), and moreover entirely pointless to slaughter the best men and the ones one would most want to make use of against the enemy' (37).[169] The word σκαιόν implies lack of sophistication or refinement, and perhaps even 'westernness'.[170]

Solon thus attempts to set boundaries between civilized, traditional activities, and excessively fierce modern innovations. These boundaries are challenged, however, by the fact that the very thing which Anacharsis mocks

---

[165] See Dubuisson (1984–6) on Lucian's interest elsewhere in the boundaries and overlaps between Greek and Roman identity, esp. 197–9 on the way in which Lucian's works (e.g., *De saltatione*) often 'contain' stereotypical Roman prejudices.

[166] οὕτως ὑμᾶς ἡ εἰρήνη διατέθεικε βαθεῖα οὖσα, ὡς μὴ ἂν ῥαδίως ἀνασχέσθαι λόφον ἕνα κράνους πολεμίου ἰδόντας.

[167] E.g., see Tacitus, *Agricola* 11.4, with many parallels from both Greek and Latin texts listed by Ogilvie and Richmond (1967) 178.

[168] For discussion of Greek responses – mainly enthusiastic, but occasionally critical – to Roman gladiatorial 'imports', see chapter five (pp. 214–16), where I argue that Greek criticisms of gladiatorial spectacle do sometimes imply disapproval of its Roman origins.

[169] Τὸ δὲ δὴ ἐν ὅπλοις πειρᾶσθαι αὐτῶν καὶ ὁρᾶν τιτρωσκομένους – ἄπαγε· θηριῶδες γὰρ καὶ δεινῶς σκαιὸν καὶ προσέτι γε ἀλυσιτελὲς ἀποσφάττειν τοὺς ἀρίστους καὶ οἷς ἄν τις ἄμεινον χρήσαιτο κατὰ τῶν δυσμενῶν.

[170] See LSJ for σκαιός meaning 'western'.

most strongly is the violent, agonistic nature of what he sees around him.[171] He seems to be suggesting that Greeks should not complain, hypocritically, about the uncivilized violence of gladiatorial contest, since their own *agones* are equally vicious and senseless. This violence reaches its most absurd peak in the Spartan rituals which Solon defends immediately after this attack on the cruelty of training with weapons, at the end of their conversation (38–40). In many ways this climax sums up the clash of perspectives the rest of the dialogue has dramatized. Solon argues for open-minded acceptance of a custom which is even odder than the Athenian practices he has been defending. Anacharsis, rather than accepting those arguments, only intensifies his mockery. Solon refers, amongst other rituals, to the public trials of endurance where young men were whipped at the sanctuary of Artemis Orthia in Sparta. This ceremony was often mentioned in Roman Empire texts as a showpiece of Spartan civic identity, and as an event which embodied close links with the city's ancient traditions of military training, even though in reality the system was largely an archaizing invention.[172] It is often mentioned as one of the more bizarre sights available to the Roman Empire traveller, and it clearly attracted many visitors. Solon here instructs Anacharsis not to mock the Spartans if he should see these things, and suggests that Lykourgos would be able to give a convincing justification of them, although he does not attempt to give one himself. Anacharsis is again unconvinced. He asks whether Lykourgos himself was ever flogged, and also why the Athenians have not adopted the custom themselves, and finally declares his intention to laugh at the Spartans just as he has done at the Athenians (39). Solon, meanwhile, explains that the Athenians have no need for the Spartan habits, because they are very happy with their own: 'These things work for us very well, being home-grown (οἰκεῖα); we prefer not to pursue foreign customs (τὰ ξενικά)' (39).[173] He then reminds Anacharsis, however, that he should wait to hear the Spartan side of the story before he makes up his mind. Solon's plea for understanding of the Spartans repeats his point that Anacharsis must spend some time in Greece before making up his mind about it. And it acts as an argument for tolerant acceptance of invented tradition in all its forms, whatever its superficial oddity, by providing a defence of the most extreme examples of such tradition.

---

[171] See Branham (1989) 99–103.
[172] See Kennell (1995), esp. 70–83 on the endurance contest and 25–6 on this passage of Lucian's *Anacharsis*; Cartledge and Spawforth (1989) 184–9.
[173] Ὅτι ἡμῖν ἱκανά, ὦ Ἀνάχαρσι, ταῦτα τὰ γυμνάσια οἰκεῖα ὄντα· ζηλοῦν δὲ τὰ ξενικὰ οὐ πάνυ ἀξιοῦμεν.

However, Solon's plea for open-mindedness about the oddities of Spartan custom – which looks suspiciously like a last-ditch attempt to salvage the argument – in itself throws doubt on the success of his praise of the *gymnasion*, as if he has finally given up pretending that Anacharsis can be persuaded to agree with anything fully. Persuasion, it seems, will not work, so Solon must resort to pleading for tolerance. Solon is also tricked into proclaiming a lack of interest in foreign customs, undermining his statement of openness to Anacharsis' advice earlier in the dialogue. Moreover, Solon's statement here exposes the difficulties an outsider like Anacharsis faces in distinguishing between the different faces of Hellenism. If even Solon cannot explain Spartan custom, and sees Sparta as 'foreign', what hope is there for someone coming to Greece for the first time, especially someone who has come, like Anacharsis, to 'learn about the laws of the Greeks'? Ironically Anacharsis finds that question easier to answer than we might expect. From his mocking perspective, Athens and Sparta are in fact very close to each other, united in absurdity, in the similarities of their agonistic excesses.

I have argued, then, that debate about the value of athletics within this text has implications for how we see the interlocutors themselves. One of the jokes the text plays on us, in other words, lies in its constantly shifting combination of the familiar and the unfamiliar, the contemporary and the archaic. It is hard for us to know how exactly each of these two men relates to contemporary cultural categories and how their visions and valuations of athletic activity relate to contemporary 'reality'. Does detachment from Hellenic affiliation bring authority? Or is scepticism towards received tradition always based on wilful or literal-minded misunderstanding of the values of archaism? Which of these men is closer to the opinions any 'real' second-century Greek ought to hold? Lucian flirts with a variety of possibilities for answering those questions, but repeatedly trips us up as soon as we think we have reached firm ground.

The scene of confrontation with an intimidating but mockable culture is one which has resonances for other cultural exchanges too, not just in the idea of eastern 'barbarians' negotiating their relationship with the central ideals of Hellenism. I have already suggested that Anacharsis stands on some level for the stereotypical image of the Roman confronted with unwarlike, archaizing Greeks. There are other examples of similar comparisons elsewhere in Roman Empire literature. Fronto, in a letter from approximately the same period as Lucian's work (*Ad M. Caesarem* 2.3)[174] compares himself

---

[174] Teubner edition (van den Hout) pp. 21–4.

self-deprecatingly with Anacharsis, as a Roman whose command of Hellenic culture and language is very shaky. Anacharsis may even have been an attractive subject for writers of this period precisely because of the way in which his story could be made to stand for processes of cultural encounter which were central to the experience of many members of the Roman Empire elite in this period. There are even similarities between Lucian's representation of Anacharsis in Athens, and his descriptions of Greeks facing up to the horrors and absurdities of Rome, for example in his account in the *Nigrinus* of that philosopher's denunciation of life in Rome, the 'Big City', after returning there from Greece.[175] If we bear those links in mind, Anacharsis seems to represent anyone who confronts alien cultural forms, of any sort. The problems and jokes which that kind of experience produces also apply potentially to Greeks, struggling to deal with the incongruities of traditions which constitute their own heritage, but which are in many ways alien to them.

Those themes may also have implications, finally, for the persona of the author himself, if we read the text with an awareness of the way in which Lucian hints at similarities between himself and outsider figures like Anacharsis elsewhere. How hellenized is he in writing this text? Does his authority, in producing this clear-sighted but fantastical exposure of the complexities of athletic convention, arise from his detachment from Hellenic affiliation; or is it dependent equally on traditions of self-interrogation which are enshrined within Greek tradition? Lucian uses Anacharsis as one of his masks elsewhere, most explicitly in the *Scytha*. He describes there the help given by the hellenized Scythian Toxaris to Anacharsis, on his arrival in Athens, and equates that with the help he has received himself from the unidentified addressees of the work on arriving in one of the cities of Macedonia.[176] Toxaris is described as already dressed in a properly Greek way, and speaking fluently (*Scytha* 3), providing a model for his fellow Scythian's later hellenization. Is Anacharsis' own assimilation with Greek culture a similar kind of weakening of resistance? Or does it still have the capacity to maintain its independence from hellenized conformity?[177] None of those questions about the cultural affiliations either of Lucian or of Anacharsis is ever clearly answered.

---

[175] *Nigrinus* 17.
[176] See Branham (1985), esp. 241, on Lucian's technique in his prologues of introducing in an apparently casual way figures who turn out to be in some way analogous to himself; cf. Nesselrath (1990).
[177] Anacharsis is also one of the few barbarians present on the Isles of the Blessed (in *VH* 2.17), another sign of the way in which his wisdom, like the Babylonian Homer's, could be assimilated to become an essential part of the Hellenic heritage in itself.

I have illustrated in this chapter something of the way in which *gymnasia* and festivals were organized and advertised within the Greek cities of the Roman Empire. I have also attempted to shed light on some of the many ways in which such activities were characteristically valued within Roman Empire writing, and some of the ways in which such valuations could involve their authors in commenting on the wider significance of contemporary culture, and especially on the value of the archaizing tendencies which were so conspicuous in the elite Greek culture of this period. Athletics was a promising subject partly because it was closely linked with so many other important and controversial areas of contemporary life and elite identity: education, civic ceremony, the individual care of the body as an embodiment of masculine virtue (more on this last point in chapters three and seven especially), to name only a few. Both positive and negative representations of athletics – focused especially on the physical space of the *gymnasion*, a place of fantasy but also of everyday reality – were deeply ingrained within Hellenic rhetorical and philosophical tradition, and at the same time had immediate relevance for practical questions of how life should be lived in the Roman Empire present. Debating or proclaiming the value of athletics necessarily involved one in positioning oneself within this network of opinions.

That is clear perhaps more than anywhere in the fantastical but also strangely familiar vision Lucian conjures up for his second-century readers in the *Anacharsis*. I have chosen to start with that work partly because it shows just how odd the athletics of the Roman Empire could sometimes seem. Our own uncertainties about the precise function of highly traditional institutions are paralleled even in second-century opinion. I have chosen it also because it plays so entertainingly with the varied valuations of athletic culture which I introduced in the first half of this chapter, and with the idea that choosing between those valuations is always an act of cultural self-positioning. Lucian dramatizes the question of whether unthinking reception of archaizing tradition within the contemporary world, of the kind Solon for the most part seems to represent, or tenacious interrogation of it, is the more properly Hellenic response. In the process he ingeniously undermines the certainties of both of his interlocutors, and humorously challenges his readers to re-examine the significance of their own pre-conceptions.

Not all representations of athletics are so knowing. In what follows, however, I hope to show that representing athletes and physical education in the Roman Empire always involves one on some level in navigating through a network of competing claims and conceptions, and always involves one in taking up positions within much wider cultural controversies. Even texts which are less self-conscious and playful about excavating the contradictions and varieties within athletic tradition show signs of the variety of valuations against which their (often idealized, sometimes dismissive) pictures of athletic life are drawn.

CHAPTER 3

Models for virtue: Dio's 'Melankomas' orations and the athletic body

He was a very tall and beautiful young man. The exercises he was taking, as you would expect, made his body seem taller and more beautiful still. He was exercising brilliantly, and with great spirit, so that you would have thought he was competing rather than practising. When he stopped exercising and the crowd was drawing away we began to study him (κατενοοῦμεν αὐτόν) more closely. He was like a carefully wrought statue. His complexion was like blended bronze.
(Dio Chrysostom, *Oratio* 28.2–3)[1]

VIEWING THE ATHLETIC BODY

The athletic body was an object of spectacle, a conspicuous and familiar image within a society where spectatorship and display of many different kinds played central roles.[2] It was viewed, however, in a great range of different ways. For many people, athletes, and the idealizing statues which represented them, stood as exemplars, repeatedly imitated in the day-to-day physical education of the *gymnasion* (although the most highly muscled and famous of competitors must often have been seen as objects of wonderment, examples of a semi-divine physical and spiritual perfection which was unattainable for all but a few). For others, however, athletes were comical embodiments of excess, warnings of the dangers of mistreating the body and neglecting the mind. They could be symbols of luxury and stupidity and gluttony, qualities which left their mark on the overfed and showy athletic body. Often those contradictory associations

---
[1] ἦν οὖν νεανίσκος πάνυ μέγας καὶ καλός, ἔτι δέ, ὡς εἰκός, μεῖζον αὐτοῦ καὶ κάλλιον ὑπὸ τῆς γυμνασίας τὸ σῶμα ἐφαίνετο. πάνυ δὲ λαμπρῶς ἐγυμνάζετο καὶ μετὰ φρονήματος, ὥστε ἀγωνιζομένῳ μᾶλλον ἐῴκει. ἐπεὶ δὲ ἐπαύσατο γυμναζόμενος καὶ τὸ πλῆθος ἀνεχώρει, κατενοοῦμεν αὐτὸν ἐπιμελέστερον. ἦν δὲ ὅμοιος τοῖς ἀνδριᾶσι τοῖς ἀκριβῶς εἰργασμένοις· εἶχε δὲ καὶ τὸ χρῶμα ὅμοιον χαλκῷ κεκραμένῳ.
[2] See Bergmann and Kondoleon (eds.) (1999) for some of the many faces of ancient spectacle culture.

clustered around the eroticization of athletic beauty, which is regularly represented as having the capacity to display and stimulate desire for virtue, but which also had the capacity to arouse less admirable kinds of passion.[3] The ancient athletic body, in other words, often found it hard to throw off its negative associations. Many of those who praised athletes avoided negative overtones like these by attaching a kind of metaphorical value to athletes in their ideal form, while also dissociating themselves from the realities of athletic activity. Others, as we shall see, took the risk of endorsing athletic activity and athletic physique in a more concrete form, while simultaneously struggling against – or sometimes humorously drawing attention to – the negative connotations which clustered around these things.[4]

Interpretation of the ambiguities of athletic physique is often represented in ancient texts as having implications for the identity of the interpreter. Viewing in the Roman Empire, and the theorization of viewing, erotic viewing in particular, is frequently tied up with projects of political and social self-positioning.[5] How you look can say a great deal about who you are. That was true perhaps most strikingly of all for viewing of the athletic body, not least because athletic spectatorship was often in itself represented as an act of social display and communal self-definition, part of the experience of Greek citizen life, as we saw in looking at the presence of ephebes as spectators at agonistic festivals in the previous chapter. Moreover, athletic beauty was unusually revealing as an object of viewing because of its capacity to provoke a great range of reactions. If there are a number of different possibilities for reacting to athletic visions of beauty, if the athletic body carries a bewildering range of marks and connotations on its surface, as I have suggested, that must be partly because of the variety of viewers who have access to it. Many of the texts I will examine in this chapter are interested precisely in the question of how to look at athletes and their bodies: how the educated, philosophical man looks at athletes, for example, how the chaste man should look at athletes, how the citizen should look. They legislate for looking, they explore the implications for the looker's identity of different ways of looking. They also often draw attention to the difficulties of looking in a consistent way, without being dragged away from a clear-cut interpretation. The eyes are very hard to control. Athletic

---

[3] See Scanlon (2002), esp. 199–273, on links between athletics and Eros; cf. Steiner (1998) on athletic statues as erotic objects, which advertise their capacity to affect the viewer.
[4] Cf. Lada-Richards (2003) on the controversies and debates which clustered round the body of the pantomime dancer in the same period.
[5] E.g., see Goldhill (2001b).

beauty prompts one, with an almost physical insistence, to reactions which one might choose to exclude.

Consideration of the connotations of athletic physique also raises questions about the ways in which people understood their own bodies. No doubt the inhabitants of the Roman Empire often felt that their own bodily selves had fixed and self-evident significance, perhaps more so than in our own society, which modern sociologists have characterized as unusually fixated on the body as a focus for the project of moulding and altering personal identity in flexible ways, because of weakened bonds between the physical self and the fixed realities of the communal, political and economic structures which previously framed it and gave it meaning.[6] Even in the ancient world, however, there are signs of interest in the degree to which the body could be self-consciously fashioned, and deep-rooted anxiety about the extent to which the male body could bear the weight of semiotic expectations which were put on it.[7]

That anxiety about physical self-presentation may have been particularly prominent among members of the male elite in this period, when attention to *self*-control as a fundamental factor within masculine virtue seems to have been increasingly highly valued,[8] although signs of an interest in elite self-control are of course also conspicuous within the Classical texts which had such a strong influence over the values of this period.[9] It has recently been suggested that this intensification of interest in self-attention may have led to widespread doubts about the value of traditional paradigms of male elite virtue and physique, which were based on the ability to dominate others rather than to control oneself,[10] although it would be wrong to imagine that conventional ideals of masculine aggression and competitiveness were superseded entirely.[11] Athletic activity – and the athletic body – may, I suggest, have gained its allure partly from its ability to *combine* agonistic and self-disciplinary requirements. Athletics (at least according to some perceptions of it) combined a traditional ability to overcome external forces in competitive contexts with rigorous techniques of self-care, requiring a balance between the two, both of which could be signalled in the powerful

---

[6] See Turner (1996), esp. 1–6; Shilling (1993).
[7] E.g., see Gleason (2001), (1999a), (1999b) and (1995).
[8] See esp. Foucault (1986).   [9] See Davidson (1997), esp. 167–82, 253–5 and 313–14.
[10] E.g., see Alston (1998) on increasing uncertainty about the image of the soldier as a suitable model for elite manliness.
[11] Harries (1998) seems to me to overestimate the significance of the move away from agonistic virtues within political life in the Greek east under Roman rule; the popularity of athletic activity surely points in the other direction.

symmetries of the ideal athletic physique, although of course even this balance between competing paradigms of masculine virtue was very far from being universally approved.

Recent sociological work has emphasized the way in which the human body acts as a bearer of symbols which are closely linked with the structuring categories of society. The body is, amongst other things, a metaphor which societies often use for understanding and regulating their own distinctive customs and self-perceptions.[12] Sociologists have also characterized the human body as a surface over which political struggles are played out, a 'system of signs which stand for and express relations of power'.[13] That insight is tied in with increasing awareness of the way in which bodily identity – like gender identity – is to a large degree socially constructed.[14] The body, in other words, is conceptualized, and to some extent moulded, through the influence of wider forces, in different ways at different periods of history.

At the same time, many scholars have been wary of carrying social constructionism too far, and have called for continued recognition of the phenomenological aspects of bodily experience, that is the way in which we experience our bodies as inescapable and always in some respects unalterable facts of everyday life, and the way in which we use them in inventive ways for our interventions within society. The human body is not only shaped by the social and economic and gender hierarchies of society at large, but also provides a site for resistance to and transformation of those hierarchies. The body is formed from its participation in culture-wide practices, subject to and shaped by repeated regimes. Its identity is shaped through habits and patterns which are learnt from society. But the body is also always out of step with those patterns, independently and creatively moulded by each individual.[15] Individuals, in other words, often shape their own bodies in ways which self-consciously depart from communal norms as well as imitating them. At the same time, that gap between perceived norms and lived reality often exists even when we try to minimize it. As I suggested in

---

[12] See Turner (1996) 26–7.   [13] Turner (1996) 27.
[14] See Turner (1996) 27–31 for discussion of this trend, which has been influenced especially by Butler (1993); Messner and Sabo (eds.) (1990) have questioned the links between masculinity, power and sporting success which have underpinned male authority in western societies; from that perspective the naturalness of the male athletic physique (in both the ancient and the modern world) seems less self-evident than it is often assumed to be.
[15] On the body as a set of social practices, see Turner (1996) 24–6, drawing on the work of Bourdieu, but also criticizing Bourdieu's notion of *habitus* (cf. Shilling (1993) 146) for its failure to account adequately for individual agency and experience; cf. Hall (1996) 11–12 on the inadequacy of Foucault's constructivist view of the body.

my introduction,[16] our own self-fashionings rebel against and fall short of perceived communal norms. And our bodies constantly rebel against what we have in mind for them.[17]

Many recent studies of gender and the human body in ancient society – some of them directed specifically at ancient masculinities – have drawn on sociological insights such as these in order to explore the cracks and inconsistencies within ancient constructions of gender identity, in ways which are highly relevant to my discussion of athletic physicality.[18] Maria Wyke, for example, in the introduction to her edited volume *Parchments of Gender* has summarized many of these developments well, in discussing the way in which ancient taxonomies of gender 'requir[ed] constant iteration through the technologies of performance, spectatorship, self-examination, display, or concealment in order to sustain their claims to authority'.[19] She identifies '[t]ension, contradiction, change, and failure'[20] as themes which are central to that volume's readings of ancient bodies. Elsewhere she draws attention to 'recent trends in scholarship which examine ancient constructions of masculinity as complex and vulnerable, manifestly subject to slippages and contradictions, and fraught with considerable anxiety for the male elites who wrote the vast majority of ancient texts available for analysis'.[21] The athletic body, I will suggest, is subject to many of the same cracks and anxieties, even though they often hide behind a mask of confident self-presentation.

My aim in this chapter, then, is to discuss some of the connotations and ambiguities of idealized athletic physique, examining the way in which such ambiguities are both suppressed and highlighted within a number of media. In doing so I will be carrying forward my discussion of the contested nature of Imperial-period athletics, moving away from the controversial civic institutions of Greek athletics which I examined in the previous chapter, to analysis of the bodies which peopled them, as they were both experienced and imagined. I will look first of all at the inscriptional encomia of athletes which survive in such great numbers; and at the athletic statues which so often accompanied them; and then at a wide body of (for the most part) moralizing texts, culminating in the writing of Dio Chrysostom, the controversial orator-philosopher of the late first and early second centuries AD, who draws on and reshapes many of the

[16] Pp. 9–12.
[17] Cf. Turner (1996) 32–4 on the tensions between subjective and objective experience of the body.
[18] E.g., Porter (1999); Wyke (1998a); Wyke (1998b); Foxhall and Salmon (eds.) (1998a); Foxhall and Salmon (eds.) (1998b); Montserrat (ed.) (1998).
[19] Wyke (1998b) 4.   [20] Wyke (1998b) 5.   [21] Wyke (1998a) 2.

patterns of representation which are familiar from these other texts. Dio's representations of athletes, and more particularly the bodies of athletes, are connected, I will argue, with ambiguities in his own self-representation, whereby he explored, throughout his career, the difficulties and possibilities of harmonizing philosophical detachment from the world with active political engagement in the traditional life of the city and of the Empire.

The passage quoted at the beginning of this chapter comes from one of Dio Chrysostom's texts in praise of a recently deceased boxer, Melankomas (to which I will return at the end of the chapter). It gestures towards the inherent virtue of the athletic body by the way in which the statuesque subject engages the mental and philosophical sensibilities of his spectators – at least those who bother to stay on with the narrator – as well as their physical appreciation. We hear that they 'watched' him (κατενοοῦμεν: 'considered', 'apprehended'), as if they were contemplating some image and principle of virtue as much as a physical body. The boxer described in statuesque terms in the passage quoted is not Melankomas but his great rival Iatrokles. Even he, we are told, could not match Melankomas' physical and moral perfection, which the reader, like the onlooker, is left to imagine for him- or herself, as if it is too elevated to be adequately represented by any physical copy or textual description. However, as the description of Melankomas proceeds it also becomes clear that Dio is humorously exploiting the risk that Melankomas' beauty may carry negative connotations as much as positive ones, and is thus in the process drawing attention to the difficulties involved in trying to equal his virtue in practice or indeed in trying to achieve unflawed philosophical virtue of any kind. Thus Dio's representation of Melankomas illustrates well, I will argue, the way in which idealized portrayals of athletes often show some awareness of the negative representations they must exclude. In that sense it illuminates vividly the contested, controversial nature of athletic ideology which is the main subject of this book, and the deeply ingrained tensions which lie at the heart of so many individual examples of athletic representation.

ATHLETIC STATUES AND THEIR INSCRIPTIONS

Of course, this chapter is not only about the bodies of athletes, as they were looked at and lived in, but also about the uses to which the marble and bronze bodies of athletic statues were put.[22] That focus raises problems

---

[22] See Newby (forthcoming) on Imperial-period athletic statues and other athletic images; Rausa (1994) on Classical and Hellenistic agonistic statues, with only brief discussion of the Imperial period (161–6), no doubt largely because of lack of evidence.

of its own. What were these images really for? How do they relate to the real athletic bodies of the *gymnasion* and the *stadion*? And what range of reactions were they expected to conjure up in their viewers?

Some scholars have emphasized the way in which athletic statues – which nearly always represented entirely naked bodies, in line with the practice of exercising unclothed – were vehicles for idealized images of manly excellence. Athletic nudity in fact seems to have been directly linked with perceptions of distinctively Greek athletic virtues.[23] The canonization of ideal proportions for the athletic body in sculpture – carried out most famously by Polykleitos in the fifth century BC – was linked, at least in the minds of some writers who came afterwards, with philosophical interest in the relation of the different parts of the body. By this logic, the statue portrayed the virtues of the spirit through the order of the body, and signalled the workings of organizing forces which lay behind the arrangement of nature.[24] This may have involved a kind of elevation of the ideal athlete above the mortal sphere.[25] One might expect the naked athletic body to have democratic connotations, unadorned by the distinguishing marks of social class and wealth. Many scholars, however, have stressed the opposite, the status of athletic nudity as a kind of costume which marked the athlete as exceptional, distinctively Greek and distinctively upper-class.[26] The athletic physique is a heroic image, whose implausibly regimented stomach muscles recall the heroic cuirass.[27] On this interpretation the athlete in statue form is separated from the realities of everyday dress – at least for those who were not regulars in the *gymnasion* – and stands as a marker of elite superiority.

Others, by contrast, have stressed the realism of classical sculptural traditions – by comparison with earlier, less naturalistic trends – arguing that sculptors sought to portray the human body in plausible though exemplary form, selecting and combining typical physical traits, although in the process freeing them from the imperfections of their real-life manifestations in the bodies of individuals.[28] Athletic statues were also eroticized objects. That quality may not have been incompatible with a degree of idealism, but it does suggest that we should be careful about emphasizing too strongly the idea that the figures they represented would have seemed

---

[23] E.g., see Scanlon (2002) 205–10.   [24] See, e.g, Spivey (1996) 36–42; Beardsley (1966) 70.
[25] This is one of the main arguments of Rausa (1994).
[26] On nudity as costume, perhaps connected with the status of athletics as religious ritual, see Bonfante (1989); cf. Stewart (1990) 105–6.
[27] See, e.g., Spivey (1996) 111–13; Himmelmann (1990); by contrast, Stewart (1997) 95 connects muscular order with the order of the hoplite phalanx.
[28] E.g. see Stewart (1990) 78–81.

remote from everyday experience.[29] Similarly – as we shall see for Melankomas and others – the nudity of athletes always had the potential to arouse less philosophically admirable versions of desire, in line with comic Classical traditions of the *gymnasion* as a place of seduction. Classical sculptors also seem to have drawn on contemporary theories on the workings of the human body, accommodating themselves to medical opinion,[30] which warned constantly against the dangers of exercising the body unevenly and excessively, although they were also criticized by philosophically minded physicians for their ultimate failure to get beneath the surfaces of the body or to reveal the human soul adequately.[31]

Modern scholarship, then, has followed ancient patterns of representation in imposing a great range of interpretations on the Greek athletic body.[32] There are times when this depth of modern interpretation is in danger of seeming anachronistic. Ancient commemorative statues must often have been viewed as sacred objects, whose primary function was to stand as gifts to the gods, and to articulate the continued presence of the commemorated man within his community. Honorific statues – athletic statues included – were put up in huge numbers in prominent public places in the ancient world, in a density which is easy to underestimate from a modern perspective. One of the functions of this marble and bronze population within the central spaces of Greek cities – which I discuss further in the next chapter – must have been to remind the living of the continued (though in some ways inaccessible) presence of the heritage of the past, and of the long-lasting glory which those who distinguished themselves in the present could expect. In that capacity, it seems likely that the majority of athletic statues – unlike many modern objects of art – would not have been created with the possibility of critical analysis in mind. Nevertheless, as we shall see, there are also signs that athletic statues could sometimes become open to a more critical gaze, could sometimes invite interrogation of their moral or social significance.

Often the different possibilities for viewing which I have outlined seem to have coexisted with one another. Between them they point to a constantly unresolved tension between the accessibility, the typicality of the athletic body on the one hand, and its unattainability and unimaginable perfection on the other. This tension, I suggest, was one of the distinctive features, perhaps even one of the defining attractions, of ancient athletic statuary.

---

[29] E.g. see Steiner (2001) 222–34 and (1998); Osborne (1998a); Stewart (1997).
[30] E.g. Métraux (1995); Leftwich (1995). [31] See Métraux (1995) 96–7.
[32] Spivey's (1997) review of Stewart (1997) emphasizes the ambiguities of the statuesque athletic body; cf. Golden (1998) 65–9 for a review of (highly diverse) recent explanations of athletic nudity.

Greek athletic sculpture hovers between the human and the divine, the attainable and the unattainable.³³ Its ambiguous status is consistent with the inescapable tensions between idealized, conceptualized bodies and real ones in all human experience, as they are illuminated by modern sociological thinking, in other words tensions between the body's capacity to act as a vehicle for ambitious and romanticized values and self-perceptions and its simultaneous tendency to frustrate the attainment of those things. For example, viewing of an idealized, eroticized image may prompt onlookers to identify with the perspective from which it was created, ensnaring them into complicity with the social hierarchies which informed its creation.³⁴ Such viewing might also create the urge to identify with the physical perfection on display and to possess it. However, that process is always likely to be one which ends in frustration or uncertainty. Sculpture fixes the eroticized object of viewing, 'captures' it; it also sets it in stone, however, fixing the remoteness and alienness of that object from its viewers.³⁵ Onlookers may desire the sculpted bodies they see on display, and desire to be like them, while also knowing that they are never attainable.³⁶ Only the rich and powerful can have bodies like this, only those who can afford the training, or those who can afford the bronze and the sculptor's fees. They may be mystified, too, or indifferent, overcome by an inability to interpret, to see the point. That is a skill – if we are to believe the many elite writers who theorize visuality as something whose interpretation depends on proper education – which only the cultured man, the *pepaideumenos*, can lay claim to.

Reactions like these are ones which the texts I examine here often invite and illustrate. Lacanian psychoanalytic theory points to a close correspondence between our encounters with bodies and with texts. In particular it is interested in the way in which fulfilment of desire and frustration of desire tend to be intextricably related to each other. That insight applies to our strivings for identification with and possession of the objects of corporeal longing, strivings which always carry with them the signs of their own insufficiency even as they come closest to fulfilment. It also applies to our experiences of language and of knowledge, which are so much dependent on our perceptions and experiences of our own bodies and the bodies of

---

[33] Cf. Spivey (1996) 122; Stewart (1990) 78–81.
[34] Cf. Stewart (1997) 18–19; see also Osborne (1998c) on the way in which athletic statuary in the classical period helped to articulate a new vision of masculinity, in competition with traditional versions.
[35] Cf. Stewart (1997) 43.
[36] E.g., see Spivey (1996) 39–40 on the physically impossible features of many statuesque torsos.

others within earliest childhood and beyond, and which so often slip from our grasp as we come close to gaining control over them. Studies of modern literature have emphasized the way in which representation of the human body is often used in fictional texts to articulate this complex interplay of desire and frustration in the unlocking of meaning which all narrative demands – from fictional characters and readers alike. Peter Brooks, for example, has argued that:

> In modern narrative literature, a protagonist often desires a body (most often another's, but sometimes his or her own) and that body comes to represent for the protagonist an ultimate apparent good, since it appears to hold within itself – as itself – the key to satisfaction, power, and meaning. On the plane of reading, desire for knowledge of that body and its secrets becomes the desire to master the text's symbolic system, its key to knowledge, pleasure, and the very creation of significance.[37]

The combination of allure and inscrutability in the human body, in other words, is often a driving force of narrative. The desire to know the characters we encounter, to see beneath the surfaces of the body and of the text, spurs on readers and characters alike, although in both cases desire is always necessarily veined with dissatisfaction, as we are confronted with the impossibility of ever completely knowing or possessing another's body, or ever fathoming fully the physical surfaces of the texts we look at or listen to. Many of the Imperial texts I will examine below exploit similar effects, enacting – within their own textual opacities and ambiguities – the difficulty of extracting any clear meaning from athletic images and ideals; and in turn using the multivalence of athletic statuary as a model for the attractions and inaccessibilities of human virtue.

In the rest of this chapter, drawing on those principles, I want to discuss some of the characteristic features of Imperial-period agonistic statues and agonistic inscriptions. I will then turn to representations of athletic prowess within a selection of 'literary' texts, in the conviction that they share with honorific portrayals of athletes some of the basic conceptions and tensions I have been outlining, even though they tend to manipulate those conceptions in very different, and often more extravagant ways. Those overlaps exemplify once again the close interconnections between very different types of athletic text, and the way in which recurring tensions and thematic preoccupations tend to be spread across the whole spectrum of athletic discourse, as we have seen already with reference to Lucian's

---

[37] E.g., see Brooks (1993) 8.

Anacharsis, and as we shall be seeing further in all of the chapters which follow.

The aim of analysing images of victorious athletes together with the inscriptions which accompanied them is made more difficult by the fact that few, if any, clearly identifiable victory statues survive from this period. Many of the athletic figures which have been preserved are copies of famous Classical statues displayed in Roman collections in the west of the Empire. Most of these would probably never have been used for commemoration of real-life athletes, although a small number of them do seem to have been statues removed by Roman collectors from Greek cities or Panhellenic sanctuaries, where they would originally have had honorific functions. It is therefore almost always impossible for us to see how the interplay between victory inscriptions and their statues would have worked in any specific case. There are signs, however, that the 'copies' of Greek statue types which were so popular in the west were sometimes placed in contexts which had at least some agonistic connotations, for example in bath buildings, sometimes juxtaposed with realistic mosaic images of contemporary athletes as we shall see in a moment.[38] There is also some evidence for Classical-style athletic statues in the east placed in *gymnasia*.[39] This association between traditional statue types and venues loosely associated with athletic competition makes it more likely that Classical styles of athletic statuary would also have continued to be used for honouring specific athletes in the east throughout the Roman period, although that argument is of course far from conclusive.

The bath-buildings of Rome – the third-century AD Baths of Caracalla especially – give good examples.[40] The exercise rooms of these baths contained a number of Classical-style athletic statues,[41] juxtaposed with mosaics depicting a large number of more realistic athletes (figures two and three).[42] Many of these mosaic figures are combat athletes depicted in mid-fight, surrounded by details – for example, symbols of victory or items of athletic equipment – which recall the contemporary world of festival competition. Most of them share the exaggerated musculature of the athletic statues which would have stood near them, but combine that statuesque bodily form with ostentatiously brutal and disfigured facial features. The decoration of these rooms must have prompted reflection from the members of the

---

[38] E.g., see Rausa (1994) 161–6 for a brief survey of athletic statues from the Imperial period.
[39] E.g., see Themelis (2001) 123 on a copy of Polykleitos' Doryphoros in the *gymnasion* at Messene.
[40] See Newby (forthcoming) chapter three.
[41] See DeLaine (1997) 78–80; Rausa (1994) 162; Marvin (1983) 365–6 and 374.
[42] E.g., see Dunbabin (1999) 68; cf. Newby (2002) on athletic scenes on mosaics in Ostia, many of which similarly represent scenes of contemporary competition.

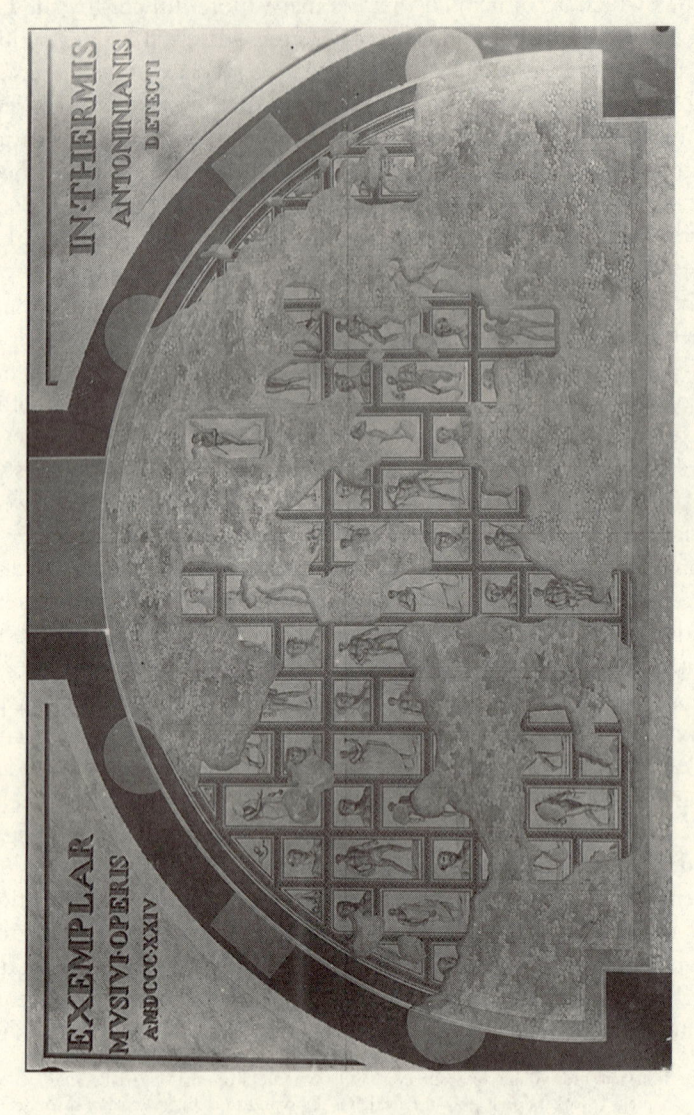

Figure 2 Athlete mosaics from the Baths of Caracalla.

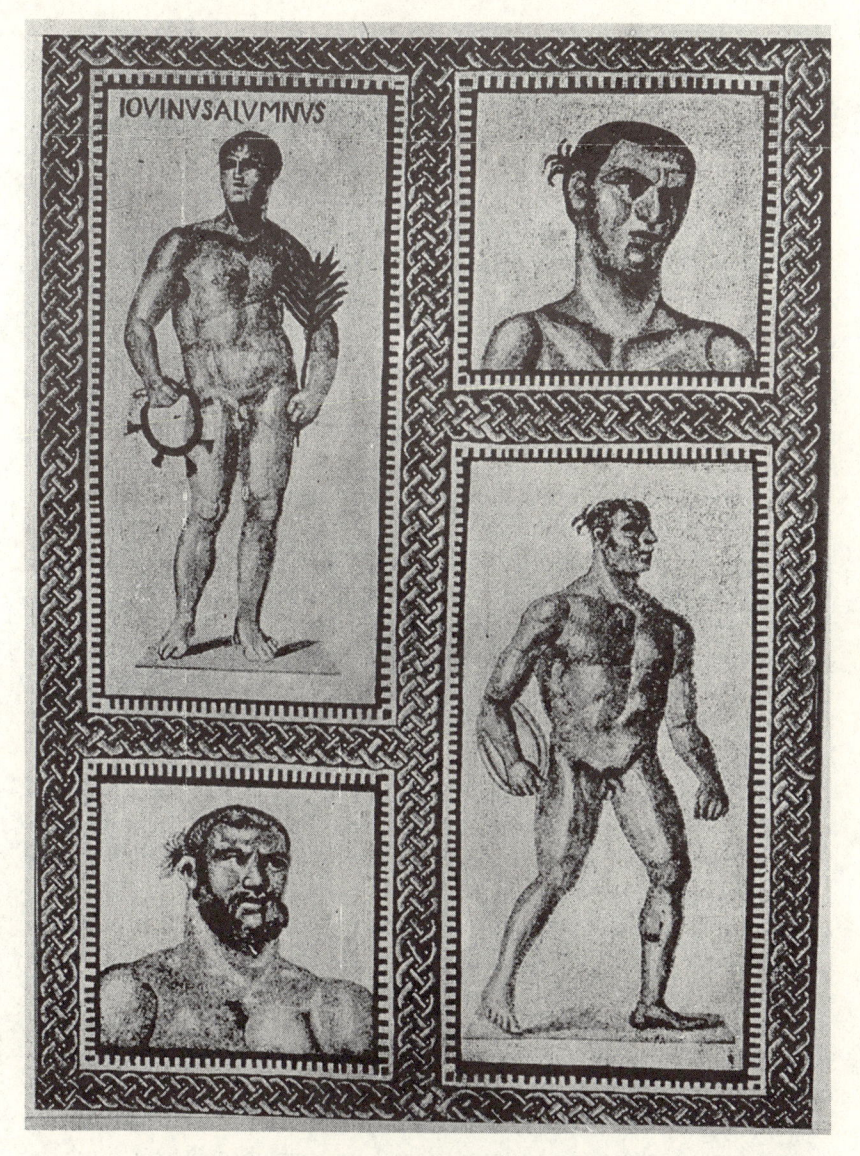

Figure 3 Detail of athlete mosaics from the Baths of Caracalla.

public who used them on the status of their own exercises, offering a variety of paradigms for understanding the activities they were engaged in, and prompting exercisers to ask a number of questions about their own activity. Was athletic exercise the route to physical and spiritual equilibrium, the route to private embodiment of ancient tradition? Or was it more akin to the violent and brutal (although in some ways equally idealized and inimitable) self-display of the career athletes who fought in public competition, and who had the headquarters of their powerful Athletic Guild in the nearby Baths of Trajan?

It seems likely, then, that analysis of Classical sculpture *is* relevant to our understanding of the now lost, or at least unidentifiable, victory statues of the Imperial period. Clearly ancient sculptural representations of athletic beauty continued to be familiar images throughout the Empire, and continued to be associated in some contexts with contemporary athletic competition. I turn now to some examples of that 'idealizing' Classical tradition. First, one of the most famous and influential (and much analysed) of all athletic statues, the 'Doryphoros' ('Spear-bearer') of Polykleitos (figure four), which embodies strikingly the combination of realism and fantasy which I have been discussing.[43] It was sculpted in the mid fifth century BC, but the original does not survive. It is here represented in one of its many Imperial-period 'copies'. It is often taken to represent the physical manifestation of the famous Polykleitan 'canon' discussed briefly above. Central to its effects is a sense of harmony and balance between opposing forces. It offers an extraordinary vision of symmetry arising from the juxtaposition of unsymmetrical body parts. Its balanced but uneven posture points to a mixture of stillness and alertness. The paradoxical combination of unbearded youthfulness and highly-developed musculature suggests a figure who mixes inimitability and universality in equal measure.[44] It thus seems to offer support for idealizing visions of athletic prowess which focus on spiritual and physical harmony. At the same time, however, it has paradoxical images of unattainability written into it. It is hard to avoid the feeling that the magical moment of balance it embodies may not be an easy one to maintain or even ever recapture. We see similar effects in the many Imperial-period copies of the 'Diadoumenos' ('Athlete binding his head') (figure five) by the same sculptor, Polykleitos, which depicts a similarly muscled and similarly positioned youth tying a ribbon around his hair, presumably celebrating victory in competition, frozen, I suggest, in the

---

[43] For detailed analysis, see, e.g. Moon (1995); von Steuben (1990).
[44] Cf. Osborne (1998b) 163.

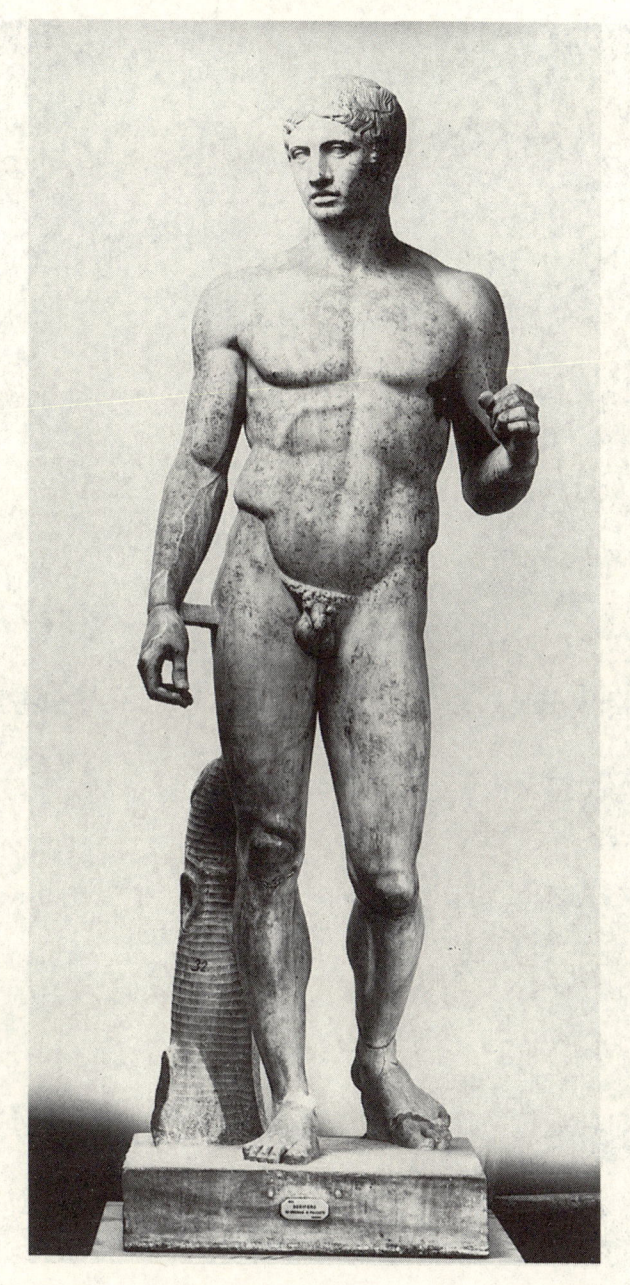

Figure 4 'Doryphoros' of Polykleitos (Roman copy; original *c.* 440 BC).

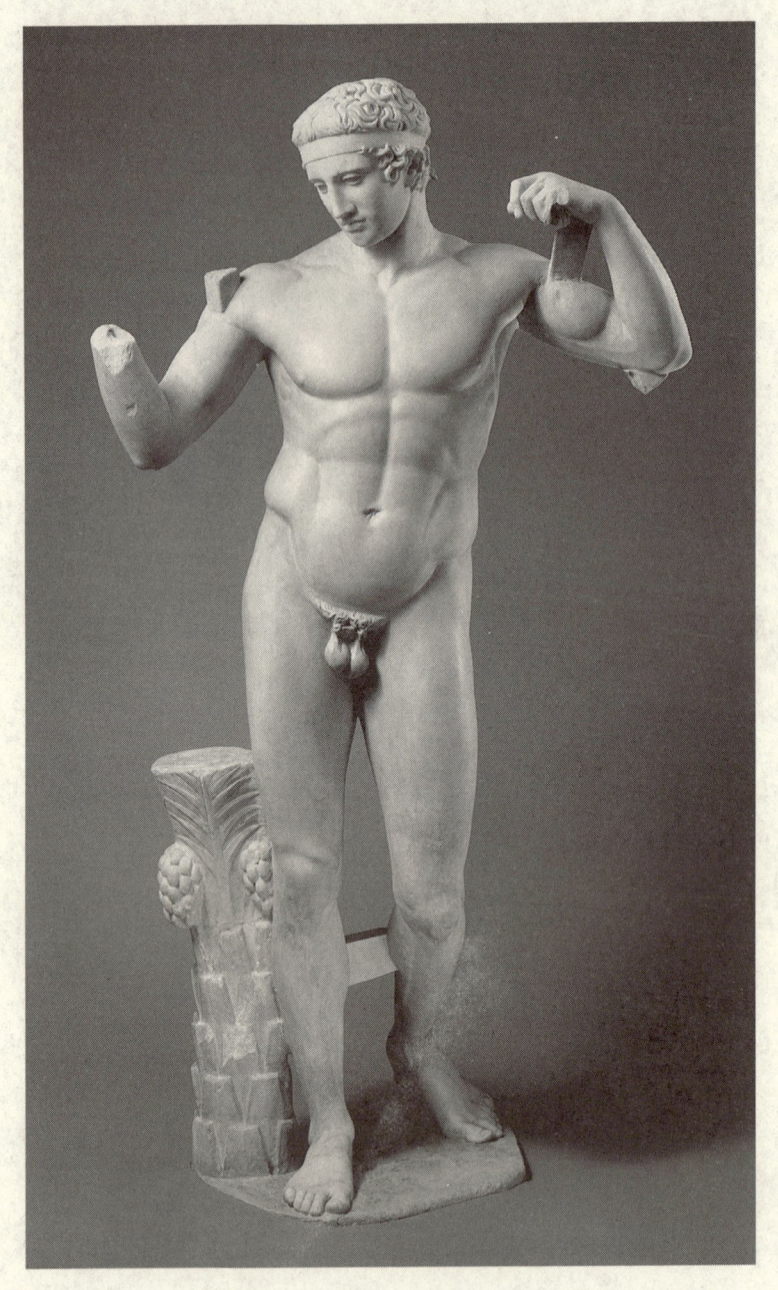

Figure 5 'Diadoumenos' of Polykleitos (Roman copy; original c. 430 BC).

fleeting moment of transition between victory and the glory which follows from it.[45]

These two statues, along with a number of other athletic figures ascribed to Polykleitos, were amongst the most widely copied of all Classical Greek statues in the Imperial period.[46] The recurrent use of these two images in decorative contexts in the west suggests a degree of uniformity in Imperial-period athletic sculpture. If the eastern agonistic statues of this period tended to follow the same repetitive pattern, as seems likely, that may be one sign that they would not often have been analysed for their semiotic complexities, or prized primarily for their originality. The victory statue was an offering to the gods as well as a reward, and dedication of a statue was thus always an act of impersonal ritual, as much as an opportunity for creative sculpting and self-advertisement. There is some evidence, for example, that victors could only in exceptional circumstances commission statues in their own likeness.[47]

However, there are also reasons to assume that sculptors and viewers alike could take an interest in the semiotic complexities of these figures. It would be wrong to envisage this kind of 'copying' as a process of mechanical and unthinking reproduction. As has often been noted, that assumption involves the transposition of anachronistic notions of creative genius and originality, of the kind which has similarly led the Greek literature of the Roman Empire to be undervalued until recently. Copying was often a highly creative exercise, which had the capacity to endow familiar images with new and striking significance, partly by variations in form, and partly also by their insertion within new contexts.[48] For example, Greek athletic body types were widely used within imperial portraiture, most famously in the Prima Porta statue of Augustus (figure six), which seems to imitate the stance and hairstyle of the Doryphoros, although the emperor is depicted wearing a breastplate rather than naked.[49] This statue attaches Roman overtones to Greek heroic virtues.[50] It borrows from the imagery of athletic exceptionality and exemplarity, making the emperor present through display of his corporeality, but at the same time advertising his almost unimaginable power, based on military victory of a kind very different from any agonistic

---

[45] See Bol (1990) for discussion of this statue.
[46] See Marvin (1997), esp. 23; Maderna-Lauter (1990); Leibundgut (1990).
[47] See Golden (1998) 85–6.   [48] See Marvin (1997) and (1993).
[49] See Elsner (1995) 161–72; Pollini (1995), who emphasizes this statue's Roman transformations of Polykleitan heroic ideals; Ramage and Ramage (1991) 86–9; Lahusen (1990); Zanker (1988) 188–92; however, see also Smith (1996) 41–5 for scepticism about the claim that this statue is modelled closely on the Doryphoros.
[50] As Pollini (1995) has emphasized.

Figure 6   Prima Porta statue of Augustus, early first century AD, marble, after a bronze of c. 20 BC.

triumph. The breastplate makes the emperor more accessible, endowing him with the familiar uniform of Roman soldiery in contrast with alien Greek nudity. But it also restricts access, locking away the emperor's body behind its elaborate and monumental covering, covering which may even be divinely crafted, as we might suspect if we are familiar with epic traditions of decorated heroic armour made by the gods for their favourites. It shuts away his vulnerability behind the imagery of semi-divine heroism, which is signalled also by the bareness of his feet, reserved for heroes and gods in Roman sculptural idiom. Polykleitan sculptural models were also adapted, sometimes with considerable alteration, for small devotional bronzes of Mercury, the Roman god of trade. In that case the athletic virtues of hard work and vigour seem to have been taken as appropriate for the non-athletic ideals of commerce.[51] This combination of idealized divinity with the capacity to exemplify very practical virtues draws on and transforms the similar combination of imitability and inaccessibility which I have argued for as a crucial feature of the Polykleitan tradition.

The sense of idealized, but almost graspable, Polykleitan beauty is thus regularly reinterpreted for new Imperial-period contexts. Some statues, however, both from the Imperial period and before, depart from Polykleitan models, insisting more firmly on the sense of realism and naturalness to which the Doryphoros and its near relatives never commit themselves. That is obvious especially in the many works which depict athletes, boxers especially, not with the smooth-skinned, unblemished beauty of the Doryphoros, but rather as experienced and often bearded fighters with heavily scarred faces. Most frequently we see statues with mangled or swollen ears. Many of these also have distorted noses and facial cuts. Two famous images, the head of the bronze statue of Satyros, a fourth-century BC Olympic victor (figure seven),[52] and the scarred body of the Terme Boxer (figure eight),[53] illustrate the furthest reaches of that tendency.

However, even these vicious scars come to have their own idealized overtones. Mangled ears occur so frequently in statues that they seem to have been taken as a standard means of identifying an athlete as a wrestler or boxer.[54] There is an implied association in these features between deformity and experience, so that scarring in itself becomes a badge of athletic prowess, and a sign of the almost inconceivable toils and pains which have been required to achieve that. We should surely be wary of assuming automatically that even the most extravagant examples of this tendency, like

---

[51] See Marvin (1997) 24. [52] See Stewart (1990) 180. [53] See Rausa (1994) 156–8.
[54] On mangled ears, see Rausa (1994) 30–2; Hyde (1921) 167–71.

Figure 7 Head of the boxer Satyros, Olympia, fourth century BC (by Silanion?).

Figure 8 Bronze statue of a seated boxer ('Terme Boxer'), second or early first century BC.

Figure 9 Boxer statue A, theatre of Aphrodisias.

the Terme boxer, are intended as caricature figures, in contrast with more glorious, unbearded figures.

I have argued, then, that tension between idealization and realism continued to be a crucial feature of post-Classical athletic sculpture in a great range of forms. Here I want to look at just one more example of that phenomenon, through a brief examination of athletic statues from the theatre of Aphrodisias in Asia Minor. The two images of boxers (figures nine and ten) which stood on either edge of the theatre's stage,[55] along with many other honorific and devotional pieces, give us perhaps the most reliably identifiable examples we have of agonistic victory statues from the Imperial period.

Aphrodisias had a thriving agonistic culture. Excavations there have yielded large numbers of agonistic inscriptions,[56] one of which I will examine in more detail shortly. Many of them date from the early third century, roughly the period when the boxer statues were sculpted. The theatre itself was an important context both for public competition and for honorific commemoration.[57] These agonistic connotations were celebrated by the many statues of the winged goddess of Victory (*Nikê*) which adorned the stage building (pictured in figure eleven).[58] Dotted between them are a number of other statues of gods, and a number of clothed portrait statues, presumably honorific in function. There is also an early-Imperial statue copy of the 'Diskophoros' ('*Diskos*-bearer') of Polykleitos (figure twelve), another of the famous Classical athletic statues which was widely imitated and adapted within many Imperial-period contexts.[59] Whether this is meant to represent the god Hermes or a victorious athlete is not clear. But regardless of which interpretation is correct – and presumably that would not have been clear to many viewers from the seats of the theatre – it introduces into this competitive space a conventional reminder of the enshrinement of athletic virtue in physical excellence.

How do the two boxer statues function within that context? It seems likely that they were intended to honour local victors, in line with the several non-athletic honorific statues which surround them. They seem to be meant as a pair, balancing each other at the opposite ends of the stage, as if to advertise the fact that they are equally deserving of honour from their city.[60] We cannot identify the men depicted for certain, but it seems likely

---

[55] Smith and Erim (1991) numbers 19 and 20 (pp. 84–6). I am grateful to Zahra Newby for pointing out these statues to me, and for sharing her own conclusions on them.
[56] See Roueché (1993), esp. numbers 66–87 (pp. 191–221).   [57] See Roueché (1993) 67.
[58] Smith and Erim (1991) numbers 7–11 (pp. 74–9).   [59] Smith and Erim (1991) no. 5 (pp. 72–4).
[60] See Smith and Erim (1991) 84.

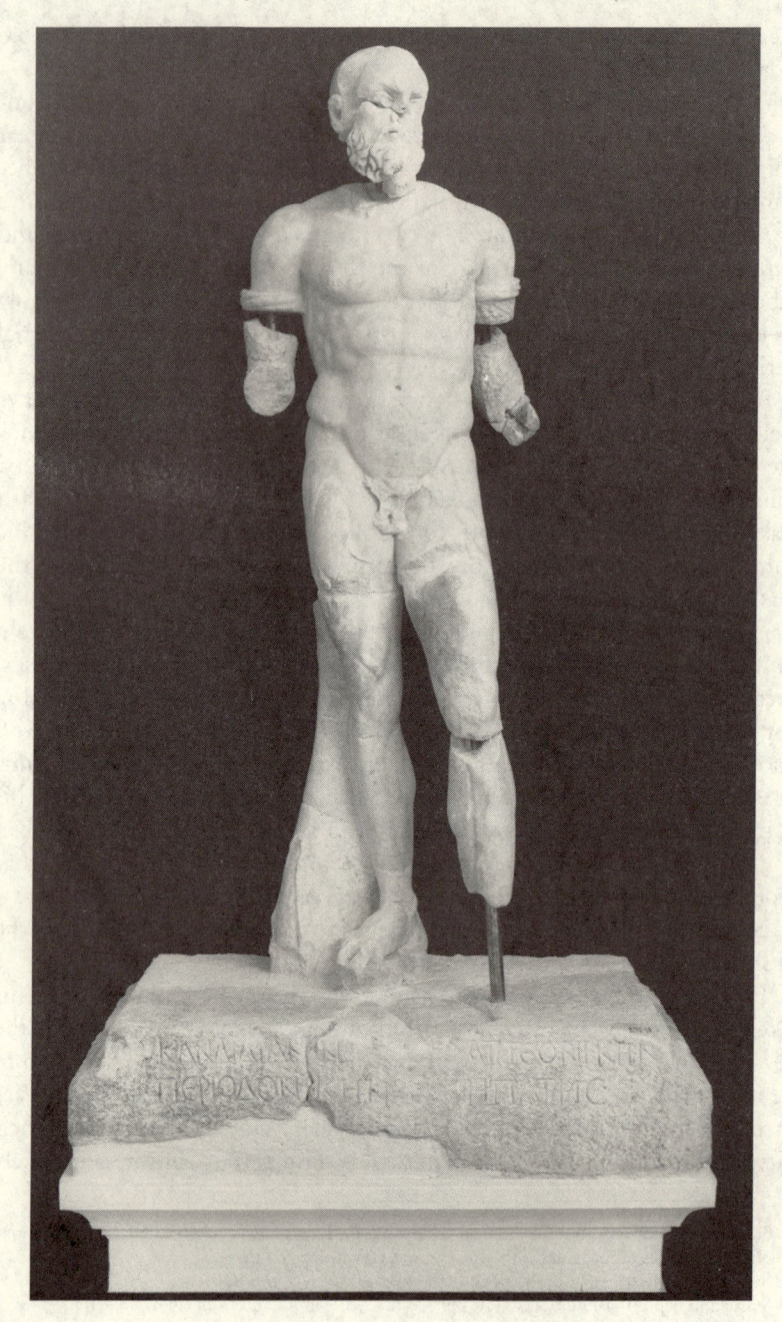

Figure 10   Boxer statue B, theatre of Aphrodisias.

Figure 11 View of the stage (looking east), theatre of Aphrodisias.

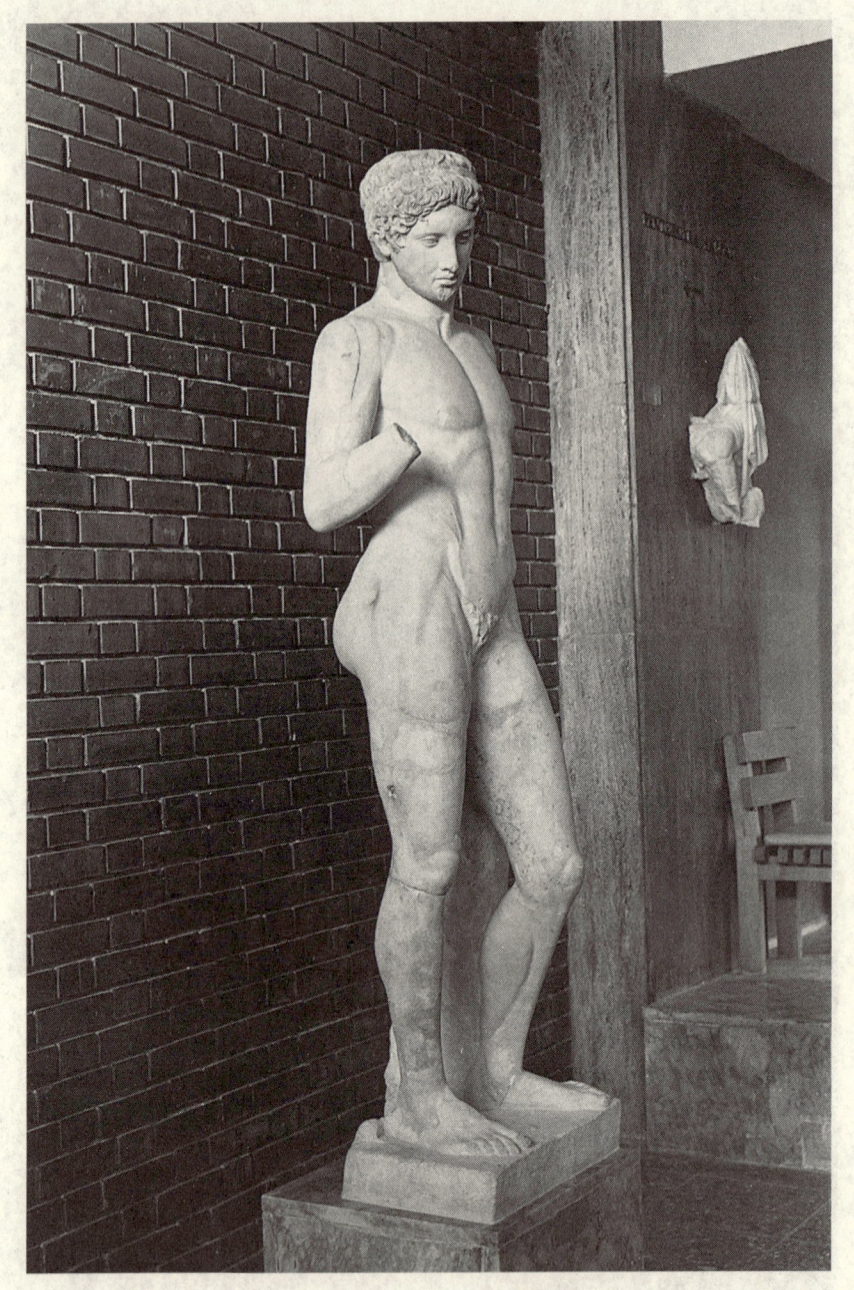

Figure 12 Copy of Polykleitos' 'Diskophoros', theatre of Aphrodisias.

that the statues should be linked with two brief honorific inscriptions for *periodos*-victors which were found close to them on the stage.[61] The first of those inscriptions records that: 'The fatherland honours Kandidianos, victor in the Aktian games, *periodos*-victor'.[62] The second is similar: 'The fatherland honours Piseas, son of Piseas, *periodos*-victor'.[63] There is no sign within these inscriptions of any attempt to proclaim these men's virtues. That is in line with the tendency towards unelaborated listing of victories which we find in the majority of victory inscriptions (though certainly not all), as we shall see further in a moment, although it seems likely that they would have been honoured in much longer inscriptions elsewhere.

Do the statues follow that strategy of avoiding any specific reference to these men's virtues? Or are there signs of any more specific claim to moral or physical excellence? And if so, how does that interact with the common tensions between realism and idealism which I have outlined? At first sight they seem to opt for an ostentatiously realistic and down-to-earth presentation, in place of any extravagant idealization. They fit the pattern of 'realistic' boxers which I discussed above. Their bearded faces are heavily scarred. One of them (figure ten) frowns, as if weighed down by cares, in contrast with the unconcerned abstraction of the Doryphoros. These are clearly figures of flesh and blood. And yet there are also indications that their realistic nature, their deformities and their anxieties are precisely the things which make them embodiments of inaccessible virtues, and thus paradoxically in line with the more godlike 'Diskophoros' which stood close to them. Their grizzled features are signs of the long experience and effort which has brought them their almost inconceivable prowess. That prowess is signalled too by their highly developed musculature, of the kind which is characteristic of all athletic statues, realistic, bearded statues and otherwise. Both of them are sculpted with their arms wrapped in boxing 'gloves' (which in ancient boxing were made from leather straps, sometimes with metal attachments). These are the tools of their trade, brutally physical objects of combat which anchor these men in the real and familiar world of *stadion* competition. At the same time, however, they act as markers of their distinctiveness. On figure nine in particular the 'gloves' are carefully ornamented, covered with intricate patterning which suggests idealized presentation, removed from the sweat and untidiness of real-life combat. They also fit the boxer's arms closely, almost as though they are an inextricable part of his flesh (although that effect is no doubt exaggerated

---

[61] See Roueché (1993) numbers 74–5 (pp. 207–8).
[62] Κανδιδιανὸν Ἀκτιονίκην | περιοδονίκην ἡ πατρίς.
[63] Πίσεαν Πισέου | περιοδονίκην | ἡ πατρίς.

by the loss of the original paint). It is almost as though the thongs and the flesh have blended together as a result of their long attachment, and as a result of this boxer's glory, which has made it possible for his body to be hardened and immortalized in its only half-human marble form. These two boxer statues thus offer a more realistic, accessible version of athletic beauty and athletic prowess than some of their idealizing counterparts. And yet even they have a sense of inaccessibility and unreality deeply ingrained within them.

I have illustrated, then, the way in which 'idealizing' athletic statue types were familiar and widely circulated within the Roman Empire, and adapted for a wide range of uses. We also find, less frequently, more 'realistic' statues of boxers and wrestlers, distinguished by their scars and their experience. Both types seem, from the small amount of evidence we have, to have been regularly placed within locations associated with agonistic performance and training, although we cannot identify many of them with specific agonistic victors. As one of the defining features of their attraction all of these statues share with their Classical models a fundamental tension, differently expressed in different cases, between opposing forces – between realism and abstraction, between exemplarity and inaccessibility.

In what follows I will argue that we can see signs of similar tensions within many of the athletic inscriptions of this period. Agonistic dedications were put up for a great range of different reasons, by a range of different groups or individuals, as we shall see in more detail shortly. One thing most agonistic inscriptions have in common, however, is a tendency to commemorate athletic glory as something which is accumulated, acquired through a repeated series of victorious achievements. Inscriptions sponsored by agonothetes, who were often responsible for commemoration of victors, regularly present unelaborated lists of each event with the name of its victor, as if the fact of victory is the important thing, and not the means by which it was attained. Inscriptions honouring individual athletes, whether erected by themselves or by others (for example by their cities or guilds, to commemorate outstanding achievement), often rely for their breathtaking effects on exhaustive catalogues of agonistic success from festivals all over the Empire, usually listed in descending order of prestige. The inscription with which this book opened, the bloated CV of Markos Aurelios Asklepiades, is a good example, worth quoting in part again here. It begins, as we saw, with brief honorific mention of his father, followed by a long list of his own recent administrative triumphs, as if to emphasize the continuity of his accumulatory endeavour beyond retirement. It then moves on to his earlier, agonistic achievements:

I was a *periodos*-victor in the pankration. I was undefeated, I was never thrown from the wrestling ring, I never made an appeal. I won all of the contests I ever entered; I never had to challenge a decision, nor did anyone ever dare to challenge one of my victories; I never drew a contest or deserted a contest or refused a fight, nor did I ever miss any competition or win by imperial favour, nor were any of my victories in contests which had to be re-run; instead I was crowned in all of the contests I ever entered in the wrestling ring itself, having come through all of the preliminary tests of eligibility beforehand. I competed among three peoples, in Italy and in Greece and in Asia, winning all of the contests listed here: I won the *pankration* of the Olympics in Pisa in the 240th Olympiad [AD 181], the Pythia at Delphi, the Isthmia twice, the Nemean games twice (on the second occasion all my rivals pulled out), the 'Shield games' of Hera in Argos, the Capitolia in Rome twice (on the second occasion all my rivals pulled out after the first lot-drawing), the Eusebia at Puteoli twice (on the second occasion all my rivals pulled out after the second lot-drawing), the Sebasta at Naples twice (on the second occasion all my rivals pulled out after the second lot-drawing), the Aktia in Nikopolis twice (on the second occasion all my rivals pulled out) . . .' (*IG* XIV, 1102 (= *IGUR* 240), lines 10–25)[64]

And so it goes on, for another sixteen lines, the relentlessness of the inscription matching the implacability of Asklepiades' ambitions and perhaps also his physical bulk. He seems determined to leave no stone unturned, not pedantically, but in a spirit of rhetorical showmanship, separating himself repeatedly and exuberantly from those who use the conventions of epigraphical language to twist the truth. These cowardly opponents have dropped away without fighting, at the first lot-drawing ceremony, at the very first sight of his naked body, as if this carries the marks of his invincibility on its surface.[65] Not many athletes could match Asklepiades'

---

[64] . . . πανκρατιαστὴς, περιοδονείκης ἄλειπτος, | ἀσυνέξωστος ἀνέκκλητος, ὅσους πότε ἀγῶνας ἀπεγράψαμην | πάντας νεικήσας· μήτε ἐκκαλεσάμενος μήτε ἑτέρου κατ' ἐμοῦ τολμή¯ | σαντος ἐκκαλέσασθαι μήτε συστεφανωθεὶς μήτε ἐπεξελθὼν μήτε παραι¯ | τησάμενος μήτε ἀγῶνα παραλιπὼν μήτε κατὰ χάριν βασιλικὴν ἀγῶνα | ἔχων μηδὲ καινὸν ἀγῶνα νεικήσας, ἀλλὰ πάντας οὕς ποτε ἀπεγρα¯ | ψάμην ἐν αὐτοῖς τοῖς σκάμμασιν στεφανωθεὶς καὶ ταῖς προπείραις | τούτων πάσαις δοκιμασθείς· ἀγωνισάμενος ἐν ἔθνεσιν τρισίν, Ἰταλίᾳ, | Ἑλλάδι, Ἀσίᾳ, νεικήσας ἀγῶνας τοὺς ὑπογεγραμμένους πάντας πανκρα¯ | τίου· Ὀλύμπια τὰ ἐν Πείσῃ σμ' ὀλυμπιάδι, Πυθια ἐν Δελφοῖς, Ἴσθμια δίς, | Νέμεα δίς, τὸ δεύτερον στήσας τοὺς ἀνταγωνιστάς, καὶ τὴν ἀσπίδα Ἥρας ἐ[ν Ἄρ¯ | γε]ι, Καπετώλια ἐν Ῥώμῃ δίς, τὸ δεύτερον μετὰ πρῶτον κλῆρον στήσας | τοὺς ἀνταγωνιστάς, Εὐσέβεια ἐν Ποτιόλοις δίς, τὸ δεύτερον μετὰ δεύτερον | κλῆρον στήσας τοὺς ἀνταγωνιστάς, Σεβαστὰ ἐν Νεαπόλι [δίς], τὸ δεύτερον μετὰ | δεύτερον κλῆρον στήσας τοὺς ἀνταγωνιστάς, Ἄκτια ἐν Νεικοπόλι δίς, τὸ δεύ¯ | τερον στήσας τοὺς ἀνταγωνιστάς . . . (= Miller 153, although his translation is misleading in places); some of the athletic terms translated here are far from certain in meaning: for discussion, see Moretti (1953) no. 79 (pp. 228–35) and his later notes on *IGUR* 240 (esp. pp. 210–11), with intervening discussions by Bean (1956) 198–9 and Harris (1962) 19–20.

[65] See Robert (1949) 105–13 on that claim, both in this inscription and others, and on the procedures to which it refers; cf. Crowther (2001b).

comprehensiveness, but his boasts do have in common with other victory inscriptions a striving to go beyond the claims of others, and also a tendency to let the accumulation of athletic glory speak for itself, without moral elaboration. It enacts Asklepiades' social distinction precisely through its lack of explanation, its lack of any specified usefulness. In much the same way, I have suggested, athletic victory statues would often have been viewed as morally neutral objects, memorials of victory but not of any further claim to moral excellence. This characteristic lack of any moral claim within Asklepiades' boasts seems at first sight to reinforce the impression of a clear distinction between athletes, who value being 'undefeated' for its own sake, and the recipients of other types of honorific decree, whose actions tend to be praised for the ways in which they have benefited their communities. This inscription also suggests that there may have been a distinction between the amoral boasts of athletes and the claims of moralists, philosophers and orators, who turn statements about athletic invincibility into metaphors, valuing the ability to be undefeated not in wrestling or in running, but in virtue and in self-control.

Sometimes, however, athletes do move beyond the language of accumulated victory to make claims for their own moral exemplarity, setting themselves up as role models in ways which match the ever-present potential for athletic statuary to take on overtones of moral virtue. One means of achieving that effect was by drawing attention to the links between festival victory and the virtues of the *gymnasion* (links which were of course never far from view for festival spectators given the large number of boys and young men trained in the *gymnasion* who competed in pre-adult age categories). For example, Pseudo-Dionysius' rhetorical treatises contain instructions for the praise of athletes, which should always end, the author suggests, with mention of great athletes of the past, who are to be praised 'because they have achieved their success through temperance (*sophrosynê*), self-control and training'.[66] Such references are in line with the more consistently moralizing and educational concerns of inscriptions in the *gymnasion*, where *Aretê* (Virtue) and *Sophrosynê* (Wisdom and Self-Control) were patron deities.[67] Qualities like *philoponia* (hard work) and *sophrosynê* are the ones most often mentioned in agonistic inscriptions. The first of these would have recalled ephebic prizes given for *philoponia* in the *gymnasion* inscriptions which I discussed in the previous chapter. Similarly, statuesque depictions of the beauty of athletic victors may have had the potential to recall ephebic prizes

---

[66] ὅτι ἀπὸ σωφροσύνης, ἀπὸ ἐγκρατείας, ἀπὸ τῆς ἀσκήσεως τοιοῦτοι ἐγένοντο (Ps.-Dionysius, *Ars rhetorica* 7.292 (for translation see Russell and Wilson (1981) 381)).
[67] See Robert (1967) 65–6.

in 'good condition' (*euexia*), and in 'good manliness' (*euandria*),[68] which were probably awarded not only for physical attractiveness but also in recognition of the qualities of excellence and devotion to training which made such attractiveness possible.[69] Admiration for unsullied youthful beauty and virtue often signalled the value of ephebic identity for the well-being of the city, emphasizing the importance of the body of potential held by the city's youth, to be brought to fruition at some future stage. The recalling of ephebic virtues is most common in inscriptions honouring athletes who have died young, where mastery of those virtues, which would in happier circumstances have facilitated glorious service to the city, is a particularly poignant and flattering boast (both for the subject of the decree and for his family).

It may also be significant that many agonistic inscriptions are enthusiastic about signalling participation in matches which were drawn,[70] and that we sometimes even see athletes boasting of second prizes or lower.[71] This contradicts the stereotype of Greek athletes concerned with winning at all costs, unwilling to tolerate anything less than outright victory (although of course the alternative stereotype – where participating is the only thing that counts – is equally crude). That zero-sum, winning-is-everything mentality was sometimes modified, in other words, by approval of individual endeavour, dependent upon the ability to remain undefeated, rather than the ability to master one's opponents, although these occasional signs of a less victory-centred ideology are far from universal. Markos Aurelios Asklepiades, for one, crushes his rivals with his rhetoric, as he had done with his punches, claiming never to have drawn a match,[72] with the implication that boasting of a draw is suitable only for those inferior specimens who have no other claim to glory.

Louis Robert has commented in a number of places on athletes who are praised for body and soul together.[73] I wish to look here at just two of his examples in detail. The first of those is a statue base from Aphrodisias in honour of one of its citizens, the athlete Aurelios Achilles, probably from the early third century AD, roughly the same period as the boxer statues

---

[68] On these contests, see Crowther (1991a), (1987) and (1985).
[69] E.g., see Wilson (2000) 38 on the meanings of the word *euandria* in Classical Athens, arguing that it denotes the kinds of qualities which make a community proud of its youth (however that might have been decided in practice), rather than qualities of manly beauty specifically.
[70] See van Nijf (2001) 326–7; Robert (1938) 278–9; Robert (1930) 27–9, 32 and 43–4; cf. Robert (1939a) 735–8 on *SEG* 7.825, for a second-century AD agonothete entertaining winners and losers alike.
[71] See Crowther (1992).
[72] Cf. *I.Magnesia* 180, line 15 for another example of that claim, discussed by Robert (1930) 28.
[73] E.g., see Robert (1965) 140–1; (1960a) 342–9; (1939b) 235–6; cf. Merkelbach (1974a) and (1970); and, especially, Robert and Robert (1989) 11–62.

discussed above.⁷⁴ On one side of the stone is part of a decree from the nearby city of Ephesus, congratulating Aphrodisias and Aurelios Achilles on the occasion of his victory at the Ephesian Olympic festival, one of that city's largest *agones*. On the side of the stone to the left of the decree is an epigram, some of which is missing, purporting to be a boast, in the first person, by the same athlete. The decree begins by proclaiming the admiration of the Ephesian people for distinguished men from other cities, and by assuring its readers of the special place Aphrodisias holds in their hearts. We then hear about the virtues of Aurelios Achilles,

who has undertaken the training of the body, and who is most distinguished of men (γενναιότατον) in athletics, and the most impressive of men (σεμνότατον) for his life and for his character, so that in him all types of virtue are mixed, both those of the soul and of the body. The city has honoured him many times in contests in the past, which he has adorned by fighting magnificently, and with all possible manliness, and especially in the contest of the Olympics . . . (lines 16–26)⁷⁵

The decree then describes the way in which the city persuaded him to compete in the *pankration* in the men's category, and tells us that the glorious manner of his victory has caused this to be numbered among the most renowned of all victories. The Ephesians have thought it right that knowledge of his glory should not be confined to those who were present, but should be spread more widely, in his homeland.

This inscription has certain features in common with the statuesque traditions which I pointed to in the Doryphoros, especially in its paradoxical combination of intimidating and inaccessible virtues with elements of realism and moderation. The application of the morally charged word γενναιότατον ('most excellent', 'noblest', 'most well-born') conjures up a vision of athletics as something which in its most elevated form exemplifies the virtuous behaviour which belongs to the very highest level of society (although the word is so common that it may not have attracted more than passing attention from the original readers of the inscription). The word σεμνότατον ('most impressive', perhaps even 'most revered') implies awe-inspiring qualities above the common run of mortal accomplishment. At the same time, the decree is shot through with a sense of moderation and

---

⁷⁴ Published by Robert (1939b) 230–44, with discussion; see also Rouéche (1993) no. 72 (pp. 202–6), for text, translation and short discussion; BE 1984, numbers 410 and 411 (pp. 493–4); Merkelbach (1982); Jones (1981) (whose text I follow here); Ebert (1981).

⁷⁵ . . . σώματος μὲν ἄσκη⁻ | σιν ἐπανελόμενον, ἀθλήσεως δὲ | τὸν γενναιότατον, βίου δὲ καὶ προ⁻ | αιρέσεως τὸν σεμνότατον, ὡς ἐν αὐ⁻ | τῷ πᾶσαν κεκρᾶσθαι τὴν ἀρετὴν ὅσην | ψυχῆς ἐστιν καὶ σώματος, ἀποδε⁻ | ξαμένης μὲν πολλάκις, καὶ ἐν τοῖς | φθάνουσιν ἀγῶσιν οἷς ἐκόσμησεν | διαπρεπῶς καὶ μετὰ πάσης ἀγω⁻ | νισάμενος ἀνδρείας, μάλιστα δὲ | ἐν τῷ τῶν Ὀλυμπίων ἀγῶνι . . .

modesty, both in the balanced virtues it praises and in the carefully balanced sentences used to describe them. Asklepiades, too, had been persuaded to compete in a local contest, after his retirement. He had used that fact as proof of his own envy-provoking fame. For Achilles, by contrast, the fact that he has succumbed to persuasion signals a tendency to avoid aggressive self-advertisement, and a willingness to co-operate with, even submit to (ὑπακούσας, 'obeying' (line 30)) the wishes of his friends the Ephesians. The boastful epigram on the left-hand face to some extent counters that impression, although even there it is interesting to see a degree of defensiveness, since the epigram opens with criticism of people who honour Achilles' rivals more than him. That criticism signals at least an awareness of the fragility and fickleness of athletic adulation. The decree also suggests a combination of youthfulness and experience in Achilles. We know that Achilles is a young man by the fact that he has been persuaded to compete in the men's category, presumably after a victory in the boys' *pankration*. We know of other victors who similarly won amongst both boys and men on the same day of a contest.[76] Despite Achilles' youth, however, the Ephesians stress their familiarity with him: they have honoured him 'many times in contests in the past'. They also put a special stress on his manliness (ἀνδρεία), using that word twice, as if to endorse his move to the men's competition.[77] Finally the decree gives a strong impression of Achilles' victory as a rare moment, a moment which is hard to recapture, but which is nevertheless to be replayed over and over again, reported and enshrined in bronze so that those who were not there can experience at least the distant echoes of it: 'For that reason it has been decided that testimony of these things should not be confined to those who were present and who happened to be in the *stadion* at the time . . .' (lines 37–42).[78] The inscription thus combines humility with boasting, youth with experience, moral exemplarity with unattainability.

The contrast between this inscription and the more strident boasting of Markos Aurelios Asklepiades is immediately apparent. However, concern with moral virtue is not the only thing which marks it out as unusual. One of its most striking features is the fact that the Ephesians explicitly reject the rivalries between different cities which so many other athletic inscriptions reveal to us. That rejection of inter-city rivalry has a certain amount in common with Achilles' avoidance of competitiveness. Cities invested huge

---

[76] See Jones (1981) 118–19; cf. Robert (1949) 112–13.   [77] See van Nijf (2003) 275.
[78] διὰ ταῦτα ἔ˔ | δοξεν μὴ μέχρις μόνης τῆς γνώ˔ | σεως τῶν παρόντων μηδὲ τῶν ἀ˔ | παντη-σάντων κατὰ καιρὸν τῷ στα˔ | δίῳ στῆναι τὴν περὶ τούτων μαρτυρί˔ | αν . . .

resources in the advertisement of athletic success,[79] and athletes regularly accumulated citizenships from different communities eager to share in their glory, and dedicated their victories to cities other than their own, as we have seen already from Asklepiades' claims.[80] There was also competition from other sources of allegiance. Inscriptions and statues were often financed by the relatives of athletes, or by the athletic guilds, as we shall see in a moment, rather than by the city or the agonothete for the games, although sometimes the costs seem to have been shared, and dedications from both families and guilds often emphasized civic pride as well as their own claims on the victor. Agonistic inscriptions paid for by the relatives of victors tend to conjure up pictures of athletic dynasties, proclaiming devoted service to the city over many generations.[81] Some inscriptions also supplement the victor's primary loyalty with claims about his value as a role model for the whole of Greece.[82] All of these groups and allegiances jostled for position, competing for the right to claim the victor's glory for themselves, but also with co-operative overtones when these were consistent with self-serving interests, in line with the high valuation given to ideals of harmony in inter-city relations in the Roman east. In the decree for Achilles the Ephesians choose to emphasize co-operation ahead of competition to an unusual degree. The juxtaposition of that attitude with Achilles' own distinctively moderate approach to agonistic self-advertisement is striking, and it seems hard to avoid the conclusion that we are meant to see a deliberate parallel between the two. Achilles' ability to see beyond the narrow bounds of competitiveness for its own sake is matched by the city's insistence on doing the same. Athletic prowess is thus a metaphor here for the goodwill of the city towards its neighbours. Achilles and his Ephesian admirers show their true community, united in an elevated version of the agonistic virtues which were central to the civic life of the Roman Empire in so many ways, distinguished by its harmoniousness, a quality which was valued in inter-state politics (not least in the speeches of Dio Chrysostom),[83] just as much as in the self-fashionings of individuals.

Finally a brief look at an extraordinary commemorative inscription from Asia Minor, set up by members of the Athletic Guild of Sacred Victors and their trainers in honour of a young athlete, Markos Alfidios, one of their number, who died in Naples in the first century AD during the Sebastan

---

[79] E.g., see Robert (1967) 14–32; Robert (1934b) 54–6.
[80] See Robert (1978a) 286–8; Robert (1949) 105–6.
[81] On athletes from wealthy families, see van Nijf (2001); Robert (1934b) 56–8.
[82] E.g., see Robert (1967) 23–4.   [83] See Salmeri (2000) 77–81; Swain (1996) 219–20.

games.⁸⁴ As we shall see, the situation described is uncannily similar to what is presented in Dio's Melankomas orations, which are also set in Naples, at roughly the same date. Much of the text is taken up with the grief of this young man's fellow athletes, and the example his virtue, and his undefeated record, will set for them. As with Aurelios Achilles, the inscription mixes physical and moral or philosophical virtue in equal measure, as if the two are to be inextricably connected with each other. We hear, for example, that he represented the 'strongest possible (κράτιστον) example, both of temperance (σωφροσύνην) and of athletic prowess' (lines 21–2).⁸⁵ The word 'strongest' implies links between competitive and moral dominance. This athlete is a powerful, and empowering, role model. And yet at the same time there is a sense of disappointed expectation here, an awareness of the fragility of the virtues Markos Alfidios embodied; but also, combined with that, an urge to fight against that fragility, to perpetuate those virtues and advertise them, which finds its outlet in art. The decree conjures up the funeral cortege, the way in which the athletes of the guild were united in their grief, surging forward spontaneously to share the burden of the coffin, as if this is the task all their muscles were made for. They are inspired by their grief to set up statues and pictures of many kinds ('honouring him with crowns and with engraved pictures on gold armour and with statues' (lines 43–5)).⁸⁶ It is almost as though they acknowledge the impossibility of holding on to Markos Alfidios' uniqueness, but nevertheless embrace a strategy of proliferation, allowing his virtue to multiply in a variety of visual commemorations, much as the Ephesians try to spread the glory of Aurelios Achilles beyond its original confines. The decree is vague about the form of these commemorative pieces, almost as though their precise relationship with Markos Alfidios' actual physical appearance is not the important thing. The tension between loss and gain, unattainability and universality of the athletic ideal, is thus focused on the honorific image which (presumably) we have in front of us as we read the decree, which represents the athlete, but which cannot claim to capture his spirit in a pure or unmodified form. This inscription, in other words, explicitly and vividly associates athletic images with a paradoxical combination of imitability and inaccessible idealization, of the kind I have been discussing.

---

⁸⁴ Published by Bean (1965) no. 2 (pp. 588–93); see also discussion by Robert (1968) 406–17; cf. Rouché (1993) numbers 89–92 (pp. 228–36) for similar examples, from second-century AD Aphrodisias, of athletes honoured by the athletic guilds for their achievements.
⁸⁵ ... τὸ κράτιστον ὑπόδειγμα καὶ κα⁻ | τὰ σωφροσύνην καὶ κατὰ πρᾶξιν; cf. lines 6–8 and 51–4.
⁸⁶ ... χρυσοῖς στεφά⁻ | νοις καὶ εἰκόσι γραπταῖς ἐν ὅπλοις ἐπιχρύ⁻ | [σ]οις καὶ ἀνδριᾶσιν ...

In this section I have offered some suggestions about the range of connotations which agonistic inscriptions and their statues could carry. I have illustrated the habit of accumulating claims to glory in intimidating bulk, and suggested that the dedication of traditional athletic statues – with little variation of design over hundreds of years – must often have fitted in with that pattern. The precise significance or originality of a statue may not have been the important thing; what mattered was the fact that it was there at all. I have also indicated, however, that some inscriptions do show an interest in making their subjects moral exemplars, especially when they are set up in honour of young athletes, and that this aim may have resonated with the moralizing potential of Classical sculptural traditions, and with the resources athletic sculptors had for signalling individuality even within the fairly rigid limits of tradition. In such cases the desire for an accessible model of virtuous behaviour within inscriptions is often mixed with a sense of athletic glory as something fragile and inimitable, difficult to live up to. Representations of this sort within the agonistic inscriptions of the Roman Empire must often have been reinforced by the tensions between realism and idealism in the traditional images which accompanied them. We shall see similar tensions – though often treated more conspicuously and irreverently – within the 'literary' representations of athletic bodies which I will discuss in what follows.

ATHLETICS AND PHILOSOPHICAL VIRTUE

The Aurelios Achilles decree, if it does invite us to see parallels between athlete and city as I have suggested, is a good example of the way in which athletic prowess could be used as a metaphor for actions and virtues of many different sorts within both the literary and the epigraphical language of the Greek east. The benefactions of athletic officials, for example, are repeatedly described through athletic language. We sometimes hear that benefactors have 'defeated' their rivals in generosity,[87] an image which is particularly appropriate in cases where successful athletes go on to have distinguished and generous public careers.[88] Nor is athletic metaphor confined to those who have had some relation with athletic activity. It is used, in fact, to describe a very diverse range of skills and achievements, in both inscriptions

---

[87] E.g., see Robert (1934a) 267–8 for two examples.
[88] For a good example, see Robert and Robert (1989) 11–62; cf. Robert (1960a) 340–1 and Robert (1937) 121–2 on the phrase 'undefeated envoy' (ἄλειπτος πρεσβευτής), used of a man who has also had a career as a pankratiast, in *IGR* IV, 1252.

and literary texts, from soldiery to medicine (more of that in chapter six) to gladiatorial prowess.[89]

My particular focus in this section is the way in which athletics is used as a metaphor for philosophical *aretê* (virtue). This is a trope which surfaces repeatedly in the literature of the Roman Empire, both in Greek and in Latin. We saw in the last section how athletes could themselves be portrayed as directly imitable models of moral virtue. Most of the writers I wish to examine here tend to take a different line, either mocking the whole concept of connections between athletic skill and moral virtue, or else using athletes as metaphorical aids for understanding how virtue should be gained but at the same time rejecting the value of athletic training itself. Others, however, like Dio Chrysostom in his Melankomas orations, deliberately – and often ingeniously – take up the challenge of imagining varieties of real athletic activity which *can* boost philosophical development and which are not hopelessly marred by negative connotations.

Athletic metaphor is not only common but also widely dispersed throughout the whole bulk of Roman Empire literature and its Classical models,[90] and no single study can hope to do justice to it. In what follows I wish simply to exemplify these tendencies by looking at a number of specific examples, focusing especially on two 'serious' philosophical authors, Epictetus and the younger Seneca, both of them interpreters of Stoic philosophy, which exercised an important influence on the thinking of Dio Chrysostom – whose work I will turn to in the final section of the chapter – and which was closely related to the Cynicism which attracted Dio's primary allegiance.

The list of promising sources could be extended almost endlessly, of course, from the many Greek writers (for example, Philo and Artemidorus and Diodorus Siculus) whose use of athletic metaphor has been dissected by Louis Robert,[91] through to the even more numerous Christian texts which follow Paul's epistles in applying athletic metaphors to Christian virtue.[92] Horrifying and sensational Christian martyr texts, for example, transform Christian martyrs into athletes of virtue, who offer a far greater spectacle, for those who can see it, than anything which the arena culture

---

[89] E.g., see chapter six (pp. 259–61) on the decree in honour of the medical writer Herakleitos of Rhodiapolis (*TAM* II.910); Robert (1940), esp. 16–23, for athletic terminology used to describe gladiators, although there the usage is as much due to similarities of technique and spectacle involvement as it is to metaphorical connections.

[90] See Müller (1995) 189–206 for a useful survey; cf. Grodde (1997) on athletic metaphor in the work of Quintilian; Harris (1976) on athletic imagery in Jewish writing, esp. 51–95 on Philo.

[91] E.g. see Robert (1960a) 330–49.

[92] See Kuefler (2001) 176–7 and 210–13; Lendon (1997) 92–3; Merkelbach (1975) 108–36; Pfitzner (1967).

to which they fall victim can provide.[93] Tertullian's *De spectaculis* illustrates that point well through its drive to recuperate and transform the non-Christian festival customs which it criticizes so viciously, conjuring up a dazzling picture, in its final lines, of the glorious spectacle of Christian triumph.[94]

Some writers take on the links between athletic appearance and virtue and exploit them for more light-hearted purposes. Images of idealized beauty recur frequently in the Greek novels. Beauty, in both male and female characters, is associated in these texts with bodily self-control and bravery and moral virtue.[95] At the same time, however, the novels joke about the possibility that their protagonists may fall short of those admirable qualities, and about the possibility that their beauty affects those who view it in less admirable ways than it should. For example, they often represent the beauty of their protagonists as capable of inspiring almost religious awe, while at the same time hinting that those who are looking at them are more interested in seduction than they claim.[96] The beauty of the novels is not often specifically athletic beauty. Scenes of athletic activity are not so common in the Greek novels as one might expect. That is partly because so much of the action takes place away from the safe haven of the protagonists' cities, in places where the certainties of Hellenic civic life are harder to guarantee, and where the absence of athletic culture is one symptom of the protagonists' distance from the centres of the Hellenic world.[97] It is perhaps also because of a tendency to concentrate on heterosexual relations, at the expense of the homosexual interests for which the *gymnasion* would provide a natural setting,[98] although the novels do of course dramatize the way in which homosexual forces threaten to disturb the exclusiveness of that narrative focus and of the idealized vision it articulates. Nevertheless there are moments where athletic beauty is treated simultaneously as an object of awe and of humour. For example, the hero Theagenes gives a breathtaking

---

[93] E.g. see Robert (1982) on athletic imagery in the martyr story of Perpetua.
[94] See Goldhill (2001b) 181–4. [95] E.g., on beauty in Heliodorus, see Keul-Deutscher (1996).
[96] E.g., see Heliodorus, *Aithiopika* 1.4, 1.7 and 1.19–21; Chariton, *Chaireas and Kallirhoe* 2.3; see Hunter (1994) on the juxtaposition of a historiographical style with epic and comic markers in Chariton's novel, and the way in which Chariton makes it difficult for his readers to know which generic codes to use in interpreting what he describes; esp. 1073–7 on the beauty of Kallirhoe.
[97] Several of the novels open with festivals, which represent the sheltered life of the Greek city, from which the protagonists are soon removed: e.g. Xenophon of Ephesus, *Ephesiaka*, 1.2–3; Chariton, *Chaireas and Kallirhoe*, 1.1.4–6; cf. mention of Chaireas' membership of the gymnasium at 1.1.5, 1.1.10 and 1.2.6. In Heliodorus' *Aithiopika*, there is an implicit link between the Pythian scenes of athletic contest at the beginning of the story (esp. 2.35–3.6 and 4.1–4) and Theagenes' wrestling bout in the Ethiopian festival at the end of it (esp. 10.28–32), which helps to articulate the similarities and differences between these two locations: see J. Morgan (1998) 72–7.
[98] See Saïd (1994b) 221.

display in the Ethiopian games at the end of Heliodorus' novel (Book 10), as he had in Delphi earlier in the narrative, where his dazzling beauty strikes all of his spectators speechless, but these shows of Greek youthful perfection are also comically at odds with the indecisiveness and lack of control which he exhibits in the rest of his travels.

The satirical epigram-writer Lucillius, as Louis Robert has shown, takes these novelistic hints of parody further by making athletes into archetypes not of manly virtue, but of sluggishness and deformity and stupidity.[99] One of them is so battered that his face looks like a sieve or a moth-eaten book (*Greek Anthology* 11.78). Another (11.85) is such a slow runner that he still has not finished his race by the end of the day (this parodies the common boast to have drawn a fight by drawing it out till nightfall) and the attendants lock him in the *stadion*, mistaking him for a statue. And another epigram (11.80) reverses the common claim never to have been defeated, or even wounded, by describing an athlete who has never managed to hurt his opponents: 'The fellow-fighters of the boxer Apis have buried his body here; / For he never wounded anyone'.[100] Lucillius ingeniously rises to the challenge of removing *all* moral and inspirational usefulness from athletic stereotypes, turning his victims into models of unqualified hopelessness. In that sense his work humorously follows a strategy which is diametrically opposed to many of the more complimentary portraits of athletics which survive from this period, which seek to extract all conceivable negative overtones from their portrayals.

This kind of mockery is common also in philosophical texts, which foreground the absurdity of brainless athletic activity, as we shall see in a moment in the writings of the younger Seneca. However, such texts are usually much keener to salvage some positive, *metaphorical* value from what they mock. That tendency is particularly prominent in Stoic and Cynic philosophy. Indifference towards the body was a distinctive feature of Stoic thought, closely related to the belief that moral virtue was the only good. Stoics drew a distinction between events and objects which were internal, and so subject to human control, and externals, which were outside human control and therefore matters of indifference. The body was situated in the latter category, as something to be ignored. By that scheme, the glory-seeking of conventional, large-scale athletics was very far beyond the boundaries of acceptable Stoic behaviour. At the same time, however, the attraction of athletics as a metaphor for the development

---

[99] See Robert (1969a).
[100] Οἱ συναγωνισταὶ τὸν πυγμάχον ἐνθάδ ἔθηκαν | Ἆπιν· οὐδένα γὰρ πώποτ' ἐτραυμάτισεν.

of Stoic virtue is easy to see, not least because Stoicism emphasized the importance of constantly training oneself to control one's reactions, and to interrogate rigorously the external impressions which the outside world presents.[101]

Epictetus, who was roughly contemporary with Dio (and with Seneca), takes disdain for the body further than many other Stoic thinkers, although that does not lead him to advocate complete neglect of it.[102] He uses athletic imagery repeatedly in his *Discourses* to illustrate the importance of devoted attention to philosophy, setting himself up as an equivalent of the athletic trainer.[103] He tells us, for example, that we should treat books not as ends in themselves, but as material which can train us for the struggles of life, just as the externals of the *gymnasion* are only training for the athlete's moment of contest (4.4.11–12). Elsewhere, a young follower of philosophy is likened to an athlete in training (2.17.29–31), as are those who struggle against the temptation to succumb to external impressions (2.18.22–7, 3.20.9–10). In *Discourse* 1.24, Epictetus suggests that God has matched us with our bodies, and with our physical circumstances, in order that we may achieve virtue, just as an athletic trainer matches his athletes with challenging opponents to train them to greater heights. The athletic image is picked up again implicitly in the second half of that short text, when Epictetus praises the nakedness of the philosopher who rejects worldly preoccupations, with reference to the Cynic Diogenes, who was also an important model for Dio, as we shall see. Nakedness of this sort results from indifference towards physical objects and conventions (1.24.7, 1.24.12). The naked philosopher's obsession with disregarding the body, he suggests, is more valuable than the naked athlete's obsession with training it. Stoic virtue, in other words, requires disregard of the physical world. However, that disregard is represented as something which can be achieved only through a constant and difficult process of almost physical struggle with external impressions.

Many of the same images are exploited similarly in the work of Seneca. He repeatedly uses the imagery of publicly experienced pain in organized spectacle as a framework for understanding bodily suffering and endurance.[104] Like Epictetus, he stresses the importance of self-control and repeated training of one's reactions and impulses, although he often seems to be even more interested than Epictetus in the way in which the challenges of very specific situations should be met, and his philosophical advice often arises out

---

[101] See Hadot (1998) 82–100, with special reference to Epictetus, esp. 86–8 for summary of the three areas of training which Epictetus and others demanded.
[102] See Long (2002) 157–62.   [103] See Long (2002) 107–25; 169; 195–6.
[104] See Edwards (1999).

of apparently mundane personal experiences, which are integral elements of the epistolary genre which much of his writing uses. At times, in fact, the careful regulation of the body which his Stoic disregard of the physical world requires comes to seem bizarrely similar to the athletic projects of self-mastery which he rejects,[105] in the sense that the training and self-control he recommends themselves require and arise from a very direct engagement with the realities of the physical world.

In order to illustrate that tendency to combine mockery of athletic activity with close imitation of its more admirable features, I want to look briefly at two of Seneca's letters. In Letter 15 Seneca advises his addressee to devote himself to the life of the mind. Without philosophy, he claims, the mind is ill, and even the strong body is only strong with the strength of lunatics: 'For the habit of building up one's arms and thickening one's neck and strengthening one's lungs is absurd, my dear Lucilius, for any cultivated man' (15.2).[106] Popular obsession with athletic physique, by that judgement, is laughable, most conspicuously so for the danger that it can lead men away from philosophical devotion. The affectionate, personal style of second-person address seems designed to strike a chord with all readers, not only with this specific recipient, Seneca's friend Lucilius, who is named only sporadically in the text. It also reminds us, perhaps, of the paradox that Stoic detachment from external objects did not demand complete withdrawal from the world, since encouraging the moral education of others was consistent with an attempt to 'place [oneself] in the service of the human community, and bring about the reign of justice', and thus constituted an attempt to ensure the dominance of that moral virtue which is Stoicism's highest goal.[107] We are given a list of reasons for thinking that athletics is damaging: it wastes energy which could be better used for study; it contributes to sluggishness from eating too much; and it requires one to take orders from slaves – presumably Seneca is thinking of athletic trainers – who do nothing but oil themselves and drink. It is better, he suggests, to stick with less strenuous exercises – running, jumping, reading aloud, or being carried around in a divan. Here he finds varieties of physical exercise

---

[105] Habinek (1998) 150 analyses some of the contradictions within Seneca's self-presentation, as it relates to traditionally Roman patterns of elite identity, suggesting that 'throughout Seneca's writing, an aristocracy of virtue supplements, even as it purports to supplant, the age-old aristocracy of birth'. Similarly, I suggest, in claiming to replace obsessive bodily training and self-display with mental self-control he often seems instead to be *supplementing* bodily training with mental self-control, mixing the two in a way which is in fact highly traditional even within the most public, glory-seeking manifestations of the athletic activity he criticises.

[106] *Stulta est enim, mi Lucili, et minime conveniens litterato viro occupatio exercendi lacertos et dilatandi cervicem ac latera firmandi.*

[107] Hadot (1998) 87.

which are not only not incompatible with philosophy, but may actually present opportunities to reinforce it (depending on what book you choose to read in your divan). The rejection of bodily training becomes instead a recuperation and redefinition of it.

Letter 80 is set (like the decree for Markos Alfidios discussed above), in Naples, the same city as the Dionian encomia for Melankomas which this chapter has been working towards. As in Letter 15, Seneca rejects athletic activity, while at the same time recommending forms of spiritual discipline which are metaphorically related to it. Seneca takes pleasure in the fact that everyone in the city has gone to watch a boxing match (*sphaeromachia*), leaving his mind, he hopes, undisturbed to follow its own independent path. Here he seems to be exploiting stereotypical distinctions between Greek and Roman attitudes to athletics (to be discussed further in chapter five)[108] in order to make claims about his own Stoicism as a distinctively Roman discipline. *Sphaeromachia* is a rare word in Latin, transliterated from Greek. As such it breaks the flow of the opening Latin sentence, intruding on its Roman tranquillity, as if standing for the kind of intrusion Seneca hopes to avoid in his own case ('no-one will interrupt, no-one will hold up my thoughts' (*nemo inrumpet, nemo cogitationem meam impediet* (*Ep.* 80.1)). It stands in contrast with the morally solid Romanness of the 'good arts' (*artes bonas*) (80.2), words which do not have any simple equivalent in Greek, and whose neglect Seneca criticizes. At the beginning of the second paragraph, he breaks off his original train of thought. He has spoken too soon, it seems, for he suddenly hears a cheer from the *stadion* in the distance – is this adulation for the fellow-athletes of Markos Alfidios, perhaps, or even for Melankomas? – and this time he changes tack, taking these audible manifestations of the fighting as a starting-point for reflection: 'I think to myself how many people train their bodies, but how few train their minds; what a great crowd flocks to spectacles which are frivolous and not trustworthy; but what great solitude there is surrounding the good arts; and how weak are those men whose arms and shoulders we admire' (80.2).[109] If the body can be trained to endure such horrifying extremes of treatment, he asks, how much easier should it be to train the mind in the same way, given that the mind is self-sufficient, and has no need of external stimuli. There is a contrast here between the external nature of physical training and the internal development of the mind, although this glosses over the

---

[108] Pp. 205–12.
[109] *Cogito mecum, quam multi corpora exerceant, ingenia quam pauci; quantus ad spectaculum non fidele et lusorium fiat concursus, quanta sit circa artes bonas solitudo; quam inbecilli animo sint, quorum lacertos umerosque miramur.*

fact that Seneca's own virtue, and that of his reader(s), is being brought to higher levels by external stimuli precisely within the text we have in front of us (by the cheering, for example, or – in the reader's case – by the letter itself). Seneca's final advice is to strip away all the pretensions which cover up a man's true self – money, property, honours – and to look inside the soul. Here, as for Epictetus, we have an implicit continuation of the athletic image, which contrasts spiritual nakedness with the nudity of the *gymnasion*. There are nevertheless many features in common between these two types of training – spiritual and athletic – as Seneca represents them, not least the requirement for careful attention to proper treatment of the human body, and the need for constant awareness and interrogation of the temptations of the physical world.

I have aimed in this section to give some impression of the variety of ways in which athletics was linked with philosophical virtue in texts of many different sorts, especially through the use of athletic training as a metaphor for spiritual discipline. That process often involved rejection of the possibility that athletes could in real life embody philosophical virtue, even though it provided a valuable metaphor for that virtue. At the same time, however, rejection of the physical world and of the athletic mentality may not *always* be as firm as it purports to be, and some writers flirt with the possibility that real-life athletic training may not, after all, be so far removed from the techniques which philosophical self-fashioning requires. That is a paradox particularly evident in, and appropriate to, Stoic thinkers, whose doctrine of indifference to external factors is modified in so many ways, in order to sanction engagement with the world in its concrete form. In what follows I aim to show in more detail how another writer, Dio Chrysostom, who was himself influenced by Stoic thought in many areas,[110] wrestled with some of the same themes and the same paradoxes.

THE VIRTUES OF MELANKOMAS

For Dio, I believe, these paradoxes – focused around an uneasy tension between mockery and praise of agonistic practices – are if anything more evident. That is partly because of his distinctive combination of philosophical allegiance (which did not harmonize naturally with practical involvement in agonistic life) with devotion to the political and social life of the Greek city in which athletics played such an important role. That combination was probably not untypical in the most highly educated layers of the

---

[110] On Dio's Stoicism, see Swain (1996) 197–206; Jones (1978) 11–14; Brunt (1973).

Greek elite, but few men carried their devotion in either of these spheres to anything like the same level as Dio. He is notoriously a difficult author to pin down.[111] His career, at least as he presents it in his work, seems to have gone through a number of metamorphoses, not least because he was banished by Domitian and spent a number of years in exile before returning to his native city of Prusa to resume a distinguished but acrimonious career in local politics. Traditionally he was thought to have abandoned a devotion to rhetoric at the time of his banishment, and turned instead to Cynic philosophy. That idea is now discredited,[112] although a number of scholars have continued to demonstrate the benefits of investigating chronological developments in Dio's interests.[113] However, that kind of approach has also been supplemented with other explanations for the variations of Dio's self-presentation. Often such variations are determined by context, by the different demands of philosophical dialogue and political oratory. Dio also tends to present himself through a series of different masks, associating himself with famous heroic or philosophical figures like Diogenes, Odysseus and Socrates.[114] Role-playing of this sort gives him the opportunity to explore a number of different moralizing perspectives, hinting, in the process, at his own philosophical and political importance, but also neutralizing the capacity of his listeners to take offence, by presenting advice without committing himself to it unequivocally. Many of his works use a narrative frame to interrogate the models for virtuous action which they present, thus avoiding the impression that the opinions they contain necessarily reflect the opinions of Dio himself. All of this means that it is much harder than was once thought to make any firm distinction between Dio's pre- and post-exile preoccupations,[115] or to separate Dio in his exiled Cynic phase from the more pragmatic figure we see in his Bithynian speeches.[116] The political and the philosophical are both present throughout his career (sometimes, though not always, within the same works), and the Melankomas texts, I will argue, offer a good illustration of that. Through this emotionally charged and rhetorically ingenious pair of works (apparently composed at an early stage in his career) Dio explores the problem of how philosophy can be fitted into long-standing traditions of civic action, which he elsewhere repeatedly tries to regulate and correct.

---

[111] See Swain (2000) for a collection of essays which are between them consistently interested in the problem of how to explain Dio's variety and ambiguity. Other important works on Dio include Whitmarsh (1998); Moles (1995) and (1978); Jones (1978); Desideri (1978).
[112] See especially Moles (1978).   [113] See Desideri (2000) for a recent example.
[114] See especially Moles (1990), (1983) and (1978).   [115] Cf. Moles (1978), esp. 81–93.
[116] Cf. Whitmarsh (2001) 156–67.

His work provides a vivid illustration of the range of valuations which were attached to athletic beauty. It also illustrates well the difficulties of achieving the combination of beauty and moral standing which athletics was sometimes portrayed as offering. Athletic prowess could be made compatible with virtues of many different sorts, but any such representation required suppression of alternative interpretations. The value of athletic and other types of beauty was also unstable because it depended in part on the reactions of those who viewed it. Beauty, Dio repeatedly suggests, is a kind of mirror, which in part reflects back the assumptions and character of the person who is looking into it. Beauty may prompt not just moral admiration, but also acknowledgement of its own unattainability, or else the urge to debunk or corrupt the absurdly idealized perfection which is on display. The athletic body stands for perfect manliness, perfect harmony between divergent impulses, and perfect embodiment of the traditions in which so much identificatory energy was invested in this period. However, these athletic beauties are also always hard to grasp hold of, just as the narratives which present them to us tend to frustrate as well as rouse our attempts to envisage them and identify with them.

Dio's fictionalized accounts of the career of the Cynic philosopher Diogenes, especially *Orationes* 8 and 9, offer some of the most vehement anti-athletic opinion anywhere in his work. They seem at first sight incompatible with the very different encomia for Melankomas, which have often been taken as insincere rhetorical exercises, in contrast with 'more serious' later work,[117] signs of the way in which Dio moved from the insincerities of sophistry to a more mature espousal of uncompromising Cynicism. That interpretation is misleading, not least because the athletic Melankomas and the anti-athletic Diogenes in fact have a surprising amount in common. The Cynic virtues of resistance to pleasure and toleration of hardship which Diogenes embodies are virtues which Melankomas too has mastered, representing as he does a kind of philosopher's fantasy, an idealistic attempt to make philosophy compatible with a field of activity which it more often condemns.

Orationes 8 and 9 both recount Diogenes' visit to the Isthmian festival.[118] In both texts, Diogenes – like Seneca – uses athletics as a metaphor for his own philosophical disciplines, while mercilessly mocking the athletes of the festival. On being exiled from his home city, Dio tells us, Diogenes travels to Athens, where he meets many of the famous philosophers of the day. There the philosopher Antisthenes trains him in Cynicism, as a

[117] E.g. by Jones (1978) 15–17; Desideri (1978) 139.   [118] Miller 93 gives extracts from both texts.

horse-trainer trains a spirited and uncontrollable horse (8.3), as if in preparation for the very public struggles he will face in his chosen philosophical path. After the death of Antisthenes, Diogenes travels to Corinth, and then on to Isthmia, where he denounces the absurdities of athletic competition and the folly of the spectators who travel for miles to see it, setting himself up as an alternative object of spectacle. He crowns himself with a pine garland, the standard reward for Isthmian victors, and when the Isthmian officials complain he refers to his own victory over effort (*ponoi*) and pleasure (*hedonê*), setting himself on an incomparably higher pedestal than the agonistic competitors around him (9.10–13). At one point he interrupts a victory parade, and harangues the triumphant *stadion*-winner, proclaiming, in stock Cynic mode, the absurdity of celebrating his speed when so many animals can do better: even cowardly hares, he says, can run faster (9.14–20).[119] His criticisms have mixed success. *Oratio* 9 tells us that Diogenes was, for some, the main reason for coming to Isthmia (9.5–7); and that some spectators leave without waiting to see the athletes, prompted by Diogenes' mockery (9.22). *Oratio* 8, by contrast, ends with Diogenes' spectators getting tired of his crudity and drifting away (8.36), back to the chattering of the sophists who have already been described scathingly, along with other attention-seeking intellectuals, in 8.9. That scene recalls Dio's complaints, in *Oratio* 27, about the way in which philosophers are ignored, while all the other con men and frauds who gather at festivals are inundated with attention. Diogenes' scrawniness, based on rigorous self-discipline, is the true sign of merit, for those who have eyes to see it; the musclemen he mocks (like the babbling sophists) have nothing beneath the surface. Here, then, Dio (like Seneca and Epictetus) attempts to confine the virtues of athletic training to metaphorical ones and nothing more. The Melankomas orations, as we shall see, take up the opposite challenge, going as far as possible towards presenting the athlete as a concrete model for virtue who does not rely on metaphorical justifications for admiration, although they also at the same time explore the difficulties of attaining that goal.

On one level, of course, Diogenes is Dio, the Cynic wanderer who devotes himself, on returning to Prusa, to enticing his fellow-citizens away from folly, although there are also differences between them. Like Diogenes, Dio carries the marks of his philosophical devotion on his body, which separates him by its oddity from his fellow-citizens. He often represents his own appearance as a distinctive marker of his philosophical profession,

---

[119] On the Cynic elements of these dialogues, see Jouan (1993); Brancacci (1980) and (1977).

especially his dress and hairstyle, which many people criticize him for.[120] The mask is not a perfect fit, however.[121] Dio, as civic adviser, is a more constructive, less nihilistic character than his Cynic prototype, more firmly bound by ties and responsibilities of community. His overriding concern lies in correcting the abuses of Hellenic tradition. In doing so he repeatedly criticizes the frivolities of agonistic institutions, as Diogenes does, but he also leaves space for athletic education to play a positive role in the formation of the ruling classes of the Greek elite.

He is particularly worried about the danger of improper spectatorship, which drags people away from philosophy and distorts the nobility of the Hellenic heritage. Such worries sometimes spill over into criticism of the officials who are responsible for degrading that heritage. In *Oratio* 32, for example, he complains about the Alexandrians' obsession with horse racing and theatres, criticizing their over-excitement as undignified and unworthy of their status as citizens of a leading Greek city.[122] At 34.31, he expresses doubt about the suitability of gymnasiarchs to give advice to the city of Tarsos, offering his own, more reliable, services by contrast. In *Oratio* 66 he criticizes those who aim for glory and fame, mentioning the vanity of athletics at 66.5.

The picture is not a purely negative one, however. In *Oratio* 31, for example, he appeals to a vision of properly regulated festival organization, in criticizing the Rhodian practice of honouring people by putting new names on old statues. It is clear that he is thinking partly of athletic victory statues, since he suggests in 31.21 that present-day athletes will not come to Rhodes if they think that they are going to be treated dishonourably. He compares the people of Rhodes with the Eleans, who still conduct the Olympic festival fairly and honourably despite the influence of Rome (31.110–11). The Athenians, on the other hand, have debased their festivals, and the glory of their ancestors, by granting honours to men who do not deserve them (31.116), and also by holding gladiatorial shows inside the city, and so defiling the great centres of Hellenic civilization (31.121). The Greek, athletic heritage of Rhodes is something to be valued, but also protected, since it is readily open to abuse. In several works, moreover, athletic festivals are represented as important places of philosophical exposition. Dio's own *Olympic Oration* (*Or*. 12) seems to have been delivered at the Olympic games of AD 97, probably in sight of Pheidias' statue of Zeus which is its

---

[120] E.g., see Dio 47.25; 49.11–12. [121] Cf. Moles (1978) 97–100.
[122] Cf. 31.163, where he praises the dignified conduct of the Rhodian spectators, and 80.2, where he praises the man who can remain free from popular obsession with athletic and other sorts of spectacle.

subject. There he makes no specific mention of the athletic content of the festival, but dwells rather on the role of philosophy in giving advice, as well as emphasizing the role of Olympian religion in encouraging Hellenic and universal harmony, something he is often keen to foster in his speeches to rival cities in Bithynia.

There is thus a sustained tension between approval and disapproval of athletic activity running through Dio's work. How do these preoccupations fit in with Dio's more explicit representations of statuesque beauty? Do we find similar tensions there between positive and negative representation? In order to answer those questions I wish to look first, briefly, at his *Oratio* 21, *On Beauty*, which presents a short dialogue between two men, one of them apparently Dio himself, admiring the statue of a young man. Their remarks are focused on the idea that distinctive types of beauty reflect distinctive types of discipline and cultural affiliation. They are dazzled by the statue, and take it as an example of an ancient kind of beauty, something which is seen more and more rarely in the present-day: 'How tall and youthful (or 'graceful' (ὡραῖος)) this young man is. His form (εἶδος) is an ancient one, of the sort which I have never seen in today's statues (or men?: τῶν νῦν), apart from those very ancient ones dedicated at Olympia' (21.1).[123] There is an ambiguity in these opening words between statues and the men they represent, which immediately raises questions about the extent to which sculpture can really capture and convey reality.[124] That theme continues in the lines which follow, where they speculate about whether the rarity of this ancient form is due to the declining skill of sculptors, or the decline in human beauty in the young men thZy take as their models. That point reminds us again that sculptural reproductions of beauty may often be insufficient and flawed. The speakers go on to distinguish between a number of different types of beauty. The beauty which is under threat, and which this statue exemplifies, is a specifically male and Hellenic type of beauty, formed by exercise of young men together in the *gymnasion*, a practice which also inculcates the ability to *appreciate* male beauty. Feminine beauty in men, by contrast, is on the increase, here exemplified by the Persians, whose young men spend too much time with their mothers and nurses; and by Nero, who barbarically had his lover castrated, as the Persians also do for their most beautiful specimens. The speakers claim, in other words,

---

[123] ὡς ὑψηλὸς ὁ νεανίσκος καὶ ὡραῖος· ἔτι δὲ ἀρχαῖον αὐτοῦ τὸ εἶδος, οἷον ἐγὼ οὐχ ἑώρακα τῶν νῦν, ἀλλ' ἢ τῶν Ὀλυμπίασιν ἀνακειμένων τῶν πάνυ παλαιῶν.

[124] Newby (forthcoming) chapter four takes that point about ambiguity further, in arguing that Dio deliberately makes it impossible for us to be sure about whether the object of discussion is a statue or a real person.

that it is possible to see the marks of identity and training in the nuances of physical form, and that there is a variety of beauty directly linked with traditional Hellenic virtues.

They are also aware, however, that beauty is not something which can ever be taken at face value. For one thing it means very different things to different viewers; in fact the way you view beauty, the assumptions you bring to it, inevitably transform it. Dio (if it is Dio who is speaking) suggests that there are very few people now who can appreciate male beauty properly. Those who do notice it treat it badly, so that it very quickly fades and disappears through being corrupted. It is as if the onlooker's gaze, and the reactions which accompany that gaze, can have a concrete effect on the character of the man who is looked at, and through that on his physical appearance. Similarly if no-one appreciates and honours beauty it will fade away. It is a kind of mirror, which reflects back at us the very qualities we bring to it: 'For it is not only virtue which is increased by praise, but beauty, too, is increased by those who honour and respect it. And if it is neglected, or looked at only by those who are corrupt, it will be extinguished, as a mirror is' (21.2).[125] The speakers are also made aware by their own reactions that beauty is able to affect the viewer in turn, in its capacity to make one turn one's head in shame, to make even immodest people (ἀναιδεῖς) seem modest, although for them the effect is only a temporary one (21.13–14). That assumption is of course deeply ingrained within the Classical philosophical texts which Dio often follows, as we shall see further for the Melankomas orations.[126] Beauty offers an improving influence, and offers us the pleasure of seeing traditional virtue embodied. Those pleasures and benefits are not available to all, however, but only to those who can bring their own Hellenic integrity to bear on the objects of their viewing, in the knowledge that they will necessarily modify what they are looking at, just as they cannot help contributing to the time-honoured Hellenic tradition which beautiful statues and beautiful men stand for through their contemplation of it. These insights into the active nature of viewing, the way in which viewing – especially viewing of athletic beauty – is always a two-way process, are ones which the Melankomas texts share, with a similar awareness of the dangers in store – for both viewed and viewer – when people get it wrong.

---

[125] οὐ γὰρ μόνον ἡ ἀρετὴ ἐπαίνῳ αὔξεται, ἀλλὰ καὶ τὸ κάλλος ὑπὸ τῶν τιμώντων αὐτὸ καὶ σεβομένων· ἀμελούμενον δὲ καὶ οὐδενὸς εἰς αὐτὸ βλέποντος ἢ πονηρῶν βλεπόντων σβέννυται, ὥσπερ τὰ κάτοπτρα.

[126] Xenophon, *Symposium* 9–10, which describes the improving effects of the youthful beauty of Autolykos, especially on his lover Kallias, is a good example.

Dio's two Melankomas orations (*Orationes* 28 and 29) are celebrations of the life of a young boxer, Melankomas, who has died in Naples, like Marcus Alfidios, in the lead-up to the Sebastan games.[127] Much of the attention this work has received has been directed at the problem of whether or not Melankomas was a real person.[128] Certainty about that is impossible with the evidence we have, however, and the effects I analyse here are not dependent on the reality or otherwise of these works' subject. In fact, debate about this problem has often ignored the fact that a tension between reality and unreality in Melankomas' character is central to the effects Dio sets out to achieve. It is quite appropriate, in that case, that the reader should be uncertain about whether or not Melankomas really existed, just as we are bound to be uncertain about whether he could possibly have existed in precisely the form in which he is described. Where we can anchor these works more firmly in 'reality' is by illustrating the way in which they draw on the traditions of epigraphical praise which I illustrated earlier in this chapter, and on the rhetorical traditions for praising athletes and festivals which are preserved for us in the treatises of Pseudo-Dionysius.[129] Both Louis Robert and Christopher Jones have illustrated some of those correspondences, although neither of them has attempted a sustained reading of these two texts of Dio – which are of course very much more than a weaving together of epigraphical conventions – on their own terms.[130]

Oratio 29, which I will discuss first, is a speech by an athletic official, who is also a friend of Melankomas, and who presents a passionate and extravagant speech of commemoration. *Oratio* 28, apparently set several days later, is a short dialogue between Dio and an athletic trainer, who repeats many of the passionate pronouncements of that speech in abbreviated form.[131] Both texts contain highly emotional expressions of grief, which mix nostalgic longing for Melankomas' uniqueness, and for the glories of

---

[127] See Jüthner (1904) for criticism of doubts about the Neapolitan setting.

[128] Interest in that question is partly due to the tradition that Melankomas was a lover of the Emperor Titus. The evidence for that – based on a passage of Themistius (139a–b) – is very insecure. It is not difficult to see how Titus' reputation for an interest in athletics (see Geer (1935) 215 and Leiwo (1994) 46 for evidence that he held office at the Sebasta in Naples) and for an obsession with homosexual love affairs (see Julian, *Caesares* 7 (311a) and Suetonius, *Titus* 7) could have given rise to unsubstantiated assumptions about his involvement with Melankomas. Many scholars have assumed that the information is correct, in the light of evidence for Dio's connections with the Flavians elsewhere (and some have used it in turn as evidence of exactly this): see, e.g., Jones (1978) 15–17 and (1973) 307; Moles (1978) 84; Desideri (1978) 139. By contrast, Sidebottom (1996), esp. 449–50, is sceptical about both Dio's Flavian connections and the links between Melankomas and Titus. For the (necessarily inconclusive) argument that Dio invented Melankomas, see Poliakoff (1987a); Lemarchand (1926) 25–32.

[129] See esp. Ps.-Dionysius, *Ars Rhetorica* speech 7 (translated by Russell and Wilson (1981) 377–81).

[130] See Jones (1978) 17; Robert (1969a) 235–6; (1968) 409–11; (1960a) 330–49.

[131] Jüthner (1904) gives a convincing reconstruction of the precise order of the events described.

the past which he embodied, with stirring exhortations to resist the temptations of unrestrained grief, and to live up to the example he has left behind. At the same time, however, they are shot through with humorous glimpses of the difficulty Melankomas will have in escaping from negative connotations.

Melankomas is praised in *Oratio* 29 for a wide range of different virtues. For one thing, the speaker emphasizes (as do the inscriptions I looked at earlier) the athlete's mixture of youth and experience, telling us that he fought in an unprecedented number of matches despite his youth (29.11). This image is one which the speaker appropriates for himself in his opening words, in combining the authority of his office with reminders about his own unsuitability to speak, due to the difficulty he will have in battling against his grief, as one who is so inexperienced in the world (29.1–2). That self-deprecating claim intensifies our impression of the enormity of what Melankomas has achieved despite his young age, by inviting us to contrast the speaker with his much more impressive subject. At the same time, the speaker's determination to continue with his task despite his grief and inexperience – as Melankomas continued with his training despite its difficulty – hints at the inspirational potential of Melankomas' example, potential which the speaker later draws attention to explicitly, as we shall see. Melankomas is also an embodiment of the virtues of the distant heroic past. The speaker claims that he could have held his own with any of the Homeric heroes. None of them, in fact, could have matched up to his perfection, since all, unlike him, had flaws accompanying their beauty (29.17–20). Moreover, Melankomas embodies a kind of continuity with the past through his membership of an athletic family, a boast which finds many parallels in epigraphic encomia (exemplified well in the inscriptions of Markos Aurelios Asklepiades in honour of his father). In Melankomas' case, the speaker is keen to emphasize, this was an aristocracy of *aretê*, not an aristocracy of wealth or birth, since his father similarly combined victory with virtue (29.2–3).

By far the biggest focus of the speech, however, is on Melankomas' indescribable and unparalleled beauty, which is represented as a transparent marker of his virtues, as if these shone through into the dazzling physical surface of his body. Melankomas, we hear, was the most beautiful of men, the most beautiful of all time, not in the temporary sense in which most young men are called beautiful, before their youthful bloom begins to fade, but in a much fuller and truer sense, which would never have disappeared in old age (29.3–5). He stood out not amongst ordinary people, but amongst athletes, who are themselves the most beautiful of men, and he was admired and talked about throughout the world (29.6). Beauty is the most wonderful of all the blessings a man can have, since it is never envied, and since it can never be hidden from view (29.7). But the most marvellous thing of all was that Melankomas combined his bodily beauties with beauties of the soul: 'For he seems to me to have competed (φιλονικῆσαι), with his soul, against his body, striving, with the help of his soul, to become more renowned' (29.9).[132] The word 'competed' (φιλονικῆσαι) suggests a metaphorical link between the external *agones* which his body underwent, and the far more important *agôn* within him. He chose athletics because it was the most effort-filled and the most manly of all careers, more so than warfare, which requires only bravery (εὐψυχία), in contrast with the manly courage (ἀνδρεία) and self-control (σωφροσύνη) of boxing (29.9–10). Here the conventional contrast between frivolous, morally worthless athletics and socially useful military prowess is ingeniously reversed.

The links which the speaker draws between Melankomas' *aretê* and his physical form are very concrete ones. His beauty is a direct consequence of his athletic skill. At 29.11, we hear that his record was the most glorious there has been, for he was never beaten in a fight, despite meeting so many glorious opponents. As it happens, the claim to be undefeated (ἄλειπτος) is a common one in agonistic inscriptions, as Louis Robert has illustrated extensively.[133] It is also a claim which could be elaborated in a variety of ways, as part of the process of trumping conventional epigraphical claims. We saw a good example of this in the inscription for Markos Aurelios Asklepiades, who is keen for his readers to know not just that he has been undefeated, but that he has never even drawn a match – his victories have always been outright. In the case of Melankomas the elaboration takes a different path, with the extraordinary claim that he won all of his victories not only without being wounded (this idea, too, is paralleled in athletic record-keeping, at least in one example, from Iulius Africanus' Olympic victory lists, for the 135th Olympiad in 240 BC),[134] but bizarrely, and surely comically, without even hitting any of his opponents (29.11–12):

> For many times he fought through the whole day in the hottest season of the year, and even though it was possible for him to win more quickly he chose not to, thinking that occasionally a worthless boxer can overcome even the best of fighters by a lucky punch. The truest victory, he thought, lay in forcing his opponents to give up unwounded; for that meant they were being defeated not by wounds but by themselves. (29.12)[135]

---

[132] δοκεῖ γάρ ἔμοιγε τῇ ψυχῇ φιλονικῆσαι πρὸς τὸ σῶμα καὶ σπουδάσαι ὅπως ἂν διὰ ταύτην ἐνδοξότερος γένηται.
[133] See esp. Robert (1960a) 330–42.   [134] See Robert (1969a) 235–6.
[135] πολλάκις γὰρ δι' ὅλης τῆς ἡμέρας ἠγωνίσατο ἐν τῇ σφοδροτάτῃ ὥρᾳ τοῦ ἔτους, καὶ δυνάμενος θᾶττον ἂν περιγενέσθαι παίων οὐκ ἐβούλετο, νομίζων τὸ μὲν πληγῇ νικῆσαι καὶ τοῦ

The virtues of Melankomas

That claim is more plausible than we might at first imagine, but even so it strains the bounds of credibility, in ways which make us doubt the possibility of imitating Melankomas' virtues as they are described to us. Ancient boxing seems to have been a more defensive sport than the modern version of it, although the differences have sometimes been overstated.[136] Blows to the head – and so also the ability to defend one's head with outstretched arms – were valued highly, and we hear in 28.7 that Melankomas had trained himself to hold his arms stretched out in front of him for two days on end. Exaggeration, moreover, was often thought quite compatible with the aims of 'sincere' encomium.[137] Even by those standards, however, it is hard to avoid the impression of absurd humour. Surely this is a joke? Surely this is a sign of the speaker's overenthusiasm? Are we really meant to *believe* this, even bearing in mind encomiastic licence? It enhances Melankomas' philosophical credentials, ingeniously linking his physical beauty with the endurance he has cultivated. His unscarred beauty, his ability to stop other people from hitting him – so unusual in boxing, whose adherents were often represented even in victory statues with cauliflower ears – is a *direct result* of the philosophical virtue he has shown through his devotion to training in the *gymnasion*. At the same time, the extraordinary boldness of the claims his encomiasts make for him challenges us to wonder to what degree Melankomas is an unrealistic, even comical figure, a figure whose virtues can act as metaphors for philosophical discipline, but never as directly imitable contributions to it.

There are a number of passages which connect Melankomas' virtues specifically with philosophical principles.[138] The praise of combined mental and physical prowess is a commonplace of encomiastic literature,[139] but it also looks back to Platonic ideas about the value of balanced education (which I discussed in chapter two),[140] and balanced constitution of the body and soul. In *Republic* Book 3, 402d, for example, Socrates defines

---

φαυλοτάτου ἔσθ' ὅτε εἶναι τὸν βέλτιστον, εἰ τύχοι· τὴν δὲ ἀληθεστάτην νίκην, ὅταν ἄτρωτον ἀναγκάσῃ τὸν ἀντίπαλον ἀπειπεῖν· οὐ γὰρ τοῦ τραύματος ἀλλ' ἑαυτοῦ ἡττῆσθαι.

[136] Poliakoff (1987a) rejects the common picture of slow and brutal heavyweight fights (favoured, e.g., by Gardiner (1930), esp. 201–8); he is too quick, however, to assume that this automatically means that we should read the claims about Melankomas on a metaphorical level only; the practice of covering the hands with leather straps, instead of padded gloves, and the lack of any deadline for ending fights clearly did make it a more defensive sport than modern boxing (see Poliakoff (1987b) 68–88); there is also evidence for fights lasting until nightfall, and we have at least one example (*SIG*³ 1073, lines 35–6) of an athlete boasting of having drawn a match in this way: see Robert (1969a) 255 and (1960a) 336–7.

[137] See Pernot (1993) 403–10, 675–80; Russell and Wilson (1981) xxi–ii.

[138] For discussions of the relative importance of Stoic and Platonic philosophical ideas and models for Dio, see Trapp (2000) and Brancacci (2000).

[139] See Pernot (1993) 134–78, esp. 159–61.   [140] P. 58.

beauty in the light of the educational theories he is expounding: 'Imagine a situation where someone combines good character in the soul and in the appearance, so that the two are harmonious with each other and share the same form, would this be the most beautiful of sights for anyone who is capable of seeing?'[141] That final stress on the viewer is important. As for Dio in *Oratio* 21, not all people can appreciate a good thing when they see it. There are also echoes of Plato's *Symposium* and *Phaedrus*, both of which are interested in the idea that the sight of physical beauty can lead one to perception of higher, ideal forms of beauty. For example, the claims made at 29.7, that beauty does not lead to envy, and that beauty is the thing 'most clearly seen', recall *Phaedrus* 250b–e;[142] and the picture of perfect beauty as a thing which is beautiful in all its aspects, and does not wane (29.5), recalls *Symposium* 211a.[143] Melankomas is also made into an icon of Cynic virtue, in terms which recall Diogenes' struggles against pleasure and against hardships, most strikingly in 28.12, as we shall see further shortly.

The speaker of *Oratio* 29, then, offers his friend a bold and sophisticated and highly emotional encomium. There are, however, problems with Melankomas' paradigmatic status, which the speaker sometimes acknowledges. At times the work even threatens to tip over into absurdity and humour, in line with the way in which athletic beauty always risks criticism and mockery, and can never guarantee its moral exemplarity. For one thing, the constant stress on Melankomas' uniqueness suggests the practical difficulties of living up to his example, although this does not stop the speaker from urging his listeners to take up that challenge in his final paragraph. They should honour their departed friend, he tells them, not with tears, but through their memory and their training (29.21–2), recreating his image in their own bodily forms. There are also more specific problems, however, which cluster in particular around his beauty. Very few people, we are told, are able to combine beauty with other virtues. That reminds us again of the problems anyone will have in matching the high ideals which are presented here. Even more worryingly, and at times entertainingly, we are reminded that beauty is not only rarely found in combination with virtue, but that it actually tends to threaten virtue and corrupt it, as Dio had similarly suggested in *Oratio* 21:

---

[141] ... ὅτου ἂν ξυμπίπτῃ ἔν τε τῇ ψυχῇ καλὰ ἤθη ἐνόντα καὶ ἐν τῷ εἴδει ὁμολογοῦντα ἐκείνοις καὶ ξυμφωνοῦντα, τοῦ αὐτοῦ μετέχοντα τύπου, τοῦτ' ἂν εἴη κάλλιστον θέαμα τῷ δυναμένῳ θεᾶσασθαι;

[142] Pointed out by Cohoon (ed.) (1939) 381.   [143] Cf. *Phaedo* 78d–e.

If any man has beauty of the body combined with manliness and courage, and also self-control and the ability to remain undefeated, who could be called more fortunate? And yet for this same man, manliness and self-control are very difficult to achieve; for beauty more than anything makes men vain and persuades them to turn to luxuriousness, as if they do not need any other claim to glory, when they are already famed for their appearance, and as if a life of ease were more pleasant. (29.16–17)[144]

This, it seems, is the reason why so few of the beautiful ancient heroes were virtuous as well. The warning is in line with Dio's rejection elsewhere of any male homosexual relation which is not subject to the controls of philosophy.[145] By this description beauty sounds like a rather dangerous thing to aim for.

Melankomas' importance comes, of course, from his ability to sidestep these corrupting effects, to have beauty and virtue at the same time.[146] There are moments, however, when even he seems in danger of being liable to the negative representations which his encomiast has tried so hard to suppress, not least because the value of beauty is dependent partly on the reactions of those who are viewing it. That in particular makes Melankomas' reputation hard to protect, even if his virtue is secure. The speaker repeatedly goes out of his way to counter the possibility of criticism, but Dio also seems keen to show us the difficulty he has in closing off all the loopholes. Some of the moments of praise early in the speech, for example, come to seem less flattering when we read them in the light of the statement of beauty's corrupting effects quoted above. The speaker tells us in 29.6 that Melankomas was the most beautiful of athletes, themselves the most beautiful of men. If athletes are the most beautiful of men, however, they are also likely (by the principles which are outlined in 29.16–17, discussed above) to be the most luxurious, with the result that defeating them in combat comes to seem very much less impressive. In 29.7, similarly, we hear that beauty is one of the most fortunate of gifts, since it does not provoke envy, but rather makes people 'friendly' (φίλους). Read with the later reminder of erotic corruption in mind, that friendliness comes to seem rather more sinister, as does the admiration of the many cities Melankomas

---

[144] ὅτῳ ἄρα ὑπῆρξε μὲν κάλλος σώματος, ὑπῆρξε δὲ ἀνδρεία καὶ εὐψυχία, ἔτι δὲ σωφροσύνη καὶ τὸ ἀήττητον γενέσθαι, τίνα ἂν τοῦδε τοῦ ἀνδρὸς εὐδαιμονέστερόν τις φήσειεν; καίτοι αὐτῷ τούτῳ παραγενέσθαι χαλεπωτάτω ἐστὸν ἀνδρεία καὶ σωφροσύνη· κάλλος γὰρ ἀνθρώπους μάλιστα δὴ χαυνοῖ καὶ ἀναπείθει τρυφᾶν, ὡς ἂν δόξης μὲν ἑτέρας οὐ δεομένους, ὅταν τις περιβόητος ᾖ τὸ εἶδος. ἡδίονος δ' οὔσης τῆς ῥαθυμίας.

[145] See Hawley (2000) 134–8, who summarizes recent debate about Dio's attitudes to homosexual love.

[146] Cf. Pernot (1993) 708–9 on the way in which encomium often aims to demonstrate the combined presence of two apparently incompatible qualities.

has visited (29.6). If nothing else, Melankomas may often have been looked at in the wrong way. We might even conclude that the reason why beauty is not envied is the fact that it so often leads men into ruin. In 29.8 the speaker anticipates, rather tortuously, the potential criticism that beauty should be viewed simply as an external quality, out of the beautiful man's control, and so not something he can be praised for:

> But if anyone says that I am giving an encomium of beauty, and not of the man himself, his criticism is wrong. That is made clear by the fact that an account of someone's manliness would automatically be called praise of the man himself. When the existence of the quality is in doubt, then we must prove it; but when it is acknowledged, then we need only praise the nature of the man's quality. For praise of that quality will also automatically be praise of the man himself.[147]

There may be an implication here that beauty is something which is under the control of its possessor. Beauty, in this representation of it, is more than just a random quality one is born with. Rather, it is praiseworthy because it springs from deliberately chosen actions and deliberately cultivated discipline. If that is the case, however, it becomes harder to sustain the claim – which is made in the other Melankomas text at 28.6 – that Melankomas has paid no attention to his appearance, although of course both speakers get round that by suggesting that his beauty was an unintended consequence of other actions. If the argument here is tortuous and obscure, as some have claimed for the speech as a whole,[148] that may, I suggest, be an orchestrated attempt to articulate the difficulty of the task the speaker has set himself.

Oratio 28 shows us a different attempt to interpret Melankomas. It contains many of the same arguments in strikingly similar form, but it also simplifies and recontextualizes them. The athletic trainer who talks to Dio (if that is who the first-person persona of the dialogue represents) is shown – with comical effect – struggling to restate the sentiments presented by the speaker of *Oratio* 29, and struggling to live up to his exhortations. The version of Melankomas' virtues he offers is briefer and less sophisticated. He is given interpretative help by Dio, who puts a more philosophical spin on his account, and who does his best to prevent the trainer from abandoning himself to tears. Athletic models, it seems, have the capacity to provoke personal response in a range of more or less philosophical ways, and that is where their value, but also their danger, lies.

---

[147] εἰ δέ τίς φησι κάλλους με ποιεῖσθαι ἐγκώμια, ἀλλ' οὐχὶ τοῦ ἀνδρός, οὐκ ἂν ὀρθῶς αἰτιῷτο. αὐτίκα γὰρ ἔπαινος ἀνδρὸς ἂν λέγοιτο, ἐπειδὰν τὴν ἀνδρείαν αὐτοῦ ἐπεξίωμεν. ὅπου μὲν γὰρ ἀμφίλογον τὸ εἶναί τινα τοιοῦτον, τότε ἀποδεικνύναι χρή· ὅπου δὲ γιγνώσκεται, τὴν φύσιν ἐπαινεῖν τοῦ προσόντος ἀγαθοῦ τινι. ὁ γὰρ τοῦδε ἔπαινος ἅμα ἂν εἴη καὶ τοῦ ἔχοντος αὐτό.
[148] E.g. see Pernot (1993) 383.

The virtues of Melankomas

The dialogue opens with description of Dio's arrival in the city, apparently with friends, in order to watch the games (κατὰ θέαν τοῦ ἀγῶνος (28.1)). These opening scenes introduce the figure of Melankomas' rival, Iatrokles, whose role in the dialogue, as I will argue here, is partly to emphasize the unrecapturability of Melankomas' unparalleled virtues. Dio and his companions go up from the harbour to the *gymnasion*, where they see a number of athletes training, and lots of onlookers, clustered especially around Iatrokles, whose statuesque physique is described in the passage quoted at the opening of this chapter. There are Platonic overtones in this opening. Dio himself is cast as a Socratic figure, following the pattern in several of Plato's dialogues – for example *Lysis*,[149] *Charmides* and *Laches* – whereby Socrates takes physical training as a starting point for discussion, or sets philosophical discussion in a *gymnasion* context. In the first two of those dialogues Socrates described himself in the very opening words entering the city, much as Dio does here.[150] At the same time Iatrokles himself is also portrayed, paradoxically, with Socratic overtones, in 28.2, where Dio describes their struggle to see over the heads of the crowd: 'To begin with we tried to see him by peeping over the top . . .' (τὸ μὲν οὖν πρῶτον ἐπειρώμεθα ὁρᾶν ὑπερκύπτοντες . . .). This echoes Crito's account of his attempt to see through the crowd surrounding Socrates, in a conspicuous position at the beginning of the *Euthydemus* (271a), which similarly uses the word ὑπερκύψας ('peeping over'). Iatrokles is thus offered to us as someone who may be a source of philosophical benefits, although it is tempting to feel that he may also share some of Socrates' notoriously frustrating characteristics.

Iatrokles has his arms outstretched, the trademark exercise of Melankomas himself, and we may even wonder, if we have heard or read *Oratio* 29, whether we are seeing that most famous boxer in the flesh, at some time before his death. If so, that illusion is broken by the words of the trainer who explains everything. Iatrokles, he tells us, was the only one who could hold Melankomas at bay, but even he was not on the same level. Even Iatrokles' body, it seems, is an insufficient substitute for Melankomas' perfections, just as the statues to which Iatrokles is compared will presumably be insufficient to represent Melankomas' departed virtue. That sense of unattainability mirrors the reader's frustrations, and the impossibility of ever seeing through the opacities of the text to recapture a clear image of physical and spiritual perfection, especially when that is lost in the past,

---

[149] Extracts reproduced by Miller 123.
[150] Cf. the opening sentence of Plato's *Republic* (327a), where Socrates goes down to the Peiraeus in order to see a newly instituted festival.

as it is here. It may be even the case that this frustration is one which all viewers of beauty share. Perhaps there is no unmediated beauty without personal response, and without all the unclarity which that necessarily risks. Dio, however, in conspicuous contrast with the trainer, seems to set the best example of how to deal with those frustrations, seeing with immediate simplicity to the heart of Melankomas' philosophical value, and in the process setting aside anxiety about the impossibility of capturing and holding on to his specific image.

The trainer praises Melankomas in passionate and extravagant terms, emphasizing as in *Oratio* 29 the apparently indisputable fact of his unparalleled beauty (28.5). He was as healthy (ὑγιής (28.7)) as a runner, we hear, an image which conjures up Melankomas' lack of scarring, and also suggests that he was not subject to the unhealthy condition – the consequence of overeating and overexercising – for which heavy athletes in particular (boxers, wrestlers, pankratiasts) were criticized by medical writers. He was not interested in his beauty, but his exercises increased it, paradoxically given the physical risks of injury inherent in his profession (28.6). He could hold up his hands for two days on end, and he would make his opponents concede without even hitting them (28.7–8). Dio agrees at this point (28.8), echoing in condensed form an argument from 29.13 that abandoning a defensive pose is a sure sign of weakness and desperation and lack of self-control for men in battle. The trainer then continues, claiming that Melankomas was 'the first man we know of to be undefeated' (πρῶτος . . . ὧν ἴσμεν ἄλειπτος διεγένετο) (28.9). As I mentioned earlier, the claim to be undefeated is actually a common one in agonistic inscriptions. Perhaps the trainer is simply exaggerating (as such inscriptions themselves frequently do), but he may also be displaying his own lack of reliable experience of the traditions on which he is passing judgement. Finally, he laments Melankomas' misfortune, and tells us that even on his deathbed he demonstrated his competitiveness by asking his childhood friend, the pankratiast Athenodoros, how many days of the games were left (28.10).

Here, then, we have another passionate eulogy. Once again, however, there are signs that the speaker has difficulties in guaranteeing his own representation of Melankomas. He is aware, for one thing, of the problems beauty brings with it: 'Beauty usually leads to luxuriousness, even for those who only have a moderate amount of it; but his self-control was even greater than his beauty, despite the fact that he looked as he did' (28.6).[151] He

---

[151] εἰωθότος δὲ τοῦ κάλλους εἰς τρυφὴν ἄγειν καὶ τοὺς μετρίως αὐτοῦ μετειληφότας, τοιοῦτος ὢν τὸ εἶδος ἔτι σωφρονέστερος ἦν.

seems to be unaware, however, that the general admiration for Melankomas' beauty, perhaps even his own admiration and judgement of it, is not easy to separate from precisely the kind of lustful looking he deprecates. That point also comes across humorously – and apparently without the speaker's intention – in the previous sentence, where he proclaims Melankomas' lack of vanity: 'And yet he did not adorn himself with clothes nor did he seek to be noticed, rather than ignored, in any other way. But when he had stripped nobody looked at anyone else, even if there were many men and boys exercising' (28.6).[152] Conventional praise for those who choose not to beautify themselves with fine clothes is particularly appropriate when applied to athletes, who don't wear *any* clothes. However, it also eroticizes Melankomas' unadorned body. In trying to prove Melankomas' modesty, in other words, the trainer falls into the trap of making him an object of lust, as if neither he nor Melankomas can ever escape from the erotic potential of the exchange between viewer and viewed which he describes.

The trainer also falls short of the ideals of *Oratio* 29 when he breaks down in tears, as he tells of Melankomas' dying words. In doing so he contradicts the instructions in 29.21–2, where we are told to commemorate Melankomas by imitating his training, and not by mourning. Dio, however, persuades him to control his emotions, and the trainer's brief (too brief?) closing words show that his optimism and determination have been restored, and that Dio's words of wisdom have been absorbed (at least in their superficial implications): 'Now it is time to go and train the boy, so I must leave' (28.13).[153] Dio brings about this transformation in the trainer's attitude through his words of philosophical consolation. Melankomas should be regarded as blessed, not wretched, he suggests:

for he had a distinguished ancestry, and beauty, and also courage and strength and self-control; and the most amazing thing of all in a man is to have been undefeated not only by opponents, but also by hardship and tiredness and greed and sex. For anyone who intends to be undefeated by his opponents must first of all be undefeated by these. (28.12)[154]

---

[152] καίτοι οὔτε ἐσθῆτι ἐκόσμει ἑαυτὸν οὔτε ἄλλῳ τῳ γιγνώσκεσθαι μᾶλλον ἐπετήδευεν ἢ λανθάνειν· ἀποδυσαμένου δ' οὐκ ἔστιν ὅστις ἄλλον ἐθεᾶτο, πολλῶν μὲν παίδων, πολλῶν δὲ ἀνδρῶν γυμναζομένων.

[153] ἀλλὰ γὰρ ὥρα γυμνάζειν τὸν παῖδα, καὶ ἀπέρχομαι.

[154] ᾧ καὶ γένους ὑπῆρξε λαμπροῦ τυχεῖν καὶ κάλλους, ἔτι δὲ ἀνδρείας καὶ ἰσχύος καὶ σωφροσύνης, ἃ δὴ μέγιστα τῶν ἀγαθῶν ἐστι· τό γε μὴν θαυμαστότατον ἐν ἀνθρώπῳ, ἀήττητον γενέσθαι οὐ μόνον τῶν ἀνταγωνιστῶν, ἀλλὰ καὶ πόνου καὶ καύματος καὶ γαστρὸς καὶ ἀφροδισίων· δεῖ γὰρ πρῶτον τούτοις ἀήττητον εἶναι τὸν μέλλοντα ὑπὸ μηδενὸς τῶν ἀνταγωνιστῶν λειφθήσεσθαι.

Dio lists here precisely the threats – hardship and pleasure – which Diogenes boasts of conquering in *Oratio* 8. Dio expands the trainer's praise, turning Melankomas into an icon of Cynic virtue. His words also echo again those of the speaker in *Oratio* 29, as if to add Dio's own guarantee of philosophical respectability to the sentiments expressed there.

The Melankomas speeches, then, between them offer a poignant portrait of unrecapturable but inspiring virtues, embodied in the alluring beauty of the athletic physique. Both of them are also aware, however, of the problems which are inevitably involved in analysis and viewing of such beauty. They navigate through those problems with an ingenuity which constantly verges on absurd humour but which nevertheless need not detract from these texts' commemoratory power. The humour of the texts may even enhance that power, as a reminder of the difficulties which are always present in the attempt to live up to remembered and dimly grasped perfections, and the constant difficulty of sidestepping the risks of absurdity and luxuriousness which athletic beauty can so easily bring with it.

Looking, I have suggested, in particular looking at the iconic manliness of the athletic physique, often says something about who you are, and about how you position yourself within the social and educational structures of your society. Athletic beauty always requires a response; it reflects back at the viewer the qualities he or she brings to it. It also has a life of its own. It can prompt reactions which are unexpected and undesirable. If you look at images in the wrong way, if beauty brings the wrong things out of you (as for the tearful trainer of Dio's *Oratio* 28) that may be partly your own fault. It is also, however, a function of the ever-present potential for disruption which athletic beauty carries with it. Looking, like the social distinction it signals, is always hard to control.

Bodies, especially athletic bodies, can be idealized. They can act as models for manliness and for the philosophical and civic virtues which the elite claimed for their own *gymnasion* traditions; and they can act as embodiments of the glorious Hellenic past. There are always gaps, however, between idealized bodies and real ones, between idealized models and what we can possibly hope to gain from them. Such gaps are disguised or exploited in different contexts for a wide range of ends. Agonistic inscriptions, and the statues which accompanied them, use the tension between universality and unattainability of the athletic ideal in order to proclaim both the exemplarity and the incomparability of the victors they celebrate, and of the communities and families from which they arise. Satirical writing, by contrast, turns the gap between athletic ideals and athletic realities not into a source of glorification for the commemorated athlete but rather into a source of mockery, by portraying beautiful athletes as creatures deprived of brains and unsuited to the practical requirements of everyday life, and so demonstrating that beautiful athletes can never *in reality* have any spiritual virtues at all, whatever their idealized statuesque forms might suggest.

Moralizing, philosophical texts tend to play down direct, causal links between bodily and spiritual virtues – sometimes with satirical language – replacing them with metaphorical connections, so that the discipline of the *gymnasion* becomes an image for the disciplines and struggles of the spirit, rather than a direct vehicle for philosophical self-improvement. At the same time, however, many of these texts prefer to avoid a complete separation of the two, and so flirt with the possibility that real-life and metaphorical athletics may have *some* elements in common after all, as if athletics in some forms can actually be made compatible with philosophy, even if that compatibility is difficult – often humorously difficult – to guarantee. In doing so, they feel their way towards answers to much wider problems, about the extent to which body and spirit ever can be detached from one another; and the extent to which the civic traditions which athletic competition contributes to can be harmonized with equally long-standing Hellenic traditions of philosophical life, a harmonization which – for Dio, at least, in his Melankomas works and elsewhere – requires constant and careful attention. For Dio – as for Lucian in his *Anacharsis* and as for all of the other authors whose work we shall be examining in later chapters – navigating through the contested terrain of Imperial-period athletics is a powerful means of exploring the values and challenges of contemporary society.

CHAPTER 4

Pausanias and Olympic Panhellenism

There are many other things one can see or hear about among the Greeks which are worthy of amazement. But the things done in Eleusis, and the *agôn* in Olympia, these have the greatest share of divine attention.

(Pausanias 5.10.1)[1]

PAUSANIAS AND THE COMPILATORY TEXTS OF THE ROMAN EMPIRE

With the words quoted above Pausanias introduces his account of the precinct at Olympia, the Altis, in the central books of his guide to the sacred landscape of mainland Greece. Included in his discussion of the altars and temples and treasuries is a breathtakingly detailed enumeration of some two hundred commemorative victor statues, which had been erected there over the course of many hundreds of years. Pausanias takes these statues as starting-points not for the kind of ethical reflection we saw in the previous chapter, but rather as gateways for historical and mythological story-telling. He flaunts his ability to see beyond their ancient surfaces to a virtual world of unified Hellenic tradition, in which each statue is linked by an intricate web of connections with the whole sweep of Greek history and Mediterranean geography.

On this model, the athlete stands not only as an icon of personal virtue, but also as a reminder of all the political and historical forces which have jointly contributed to, and coincided with, the moment of his victory and his commemoration, even though accessing those memories may be fraught with all sorts of almost insuperable challenges. Commemoration of athletic glory was a way of preserving the present for the future, and a way of linking

---

[1] Πολλὰ μὲν δὴ καὶ ἄλλα ἴδοι τις ἂν ἐν Ἕλλησι, τὰ δὲ καὶ ἀκοῦσαι θαύματος ἄξια· μάλιστα δὲ Ἐλευσῖνι δρωμένοις καὶ ἀγῶνι τῶι ἐν Ὀλυμπίαι μέτεστιν ἐκ θεοῦ φροντίδος.

the present with a long line of similar commemorations in the past. Victory statues held the promise of access – for both athlete and spectator (not to mention benefactor and sculptor) – to a shared community of Panhellenic achievement. That function of athletic record-keeping will be one of the main focuses of this chapter. Pausanias is both the most vivid illustrator of this assumption, and also the most untypical, obsessive pursuer of it, and yet the link between Pausanias' text and the practices of athletic and other forms of commemoration has never been adequately explored.

This chapter begins with some discussion of the ways in which the festivals of the Greek world – large and small – tended to be represented in relation to the age-old traditions of the Panhellenic *periodos*. I start by discussing the continued importance of the original *periodos* festivals (Olympic, Pythian, Isthmian and Nemean)[2] in the Roman period, but also the ways in which their dominance was challenged by the growth in prestige of more recent imperial foundations. I will also examine the way in which much smaller local foundations imitated the programmes of the big Panhellenic festivals, as if claiming for themselves a part of the Panhellenic aura of Olympic identity, while nevertheless also maintaining distinctive local traditions, holding Panhellenism and local identity, not to mention Roman influence, in a delicate balance.[3] In the next section I will deal with the practice of using Olympic victor lists as a basis for dating, for pinning down the Greek past. Knowledge of a victor's name, I will argue, gives access to an almost infinite vista of chronologically simultaneous historical memories. The name of the victor is the link which binds all these different moments of history together. In the third section I will look at Olympia itself – why did people visit Olympia? And what did they find when they got there? – focusing especially on the combination of old and new which would have confronted Pausanias, like others, on his arrival.

Finally I will turn to Pausanias, in an attempt to illustrate his sense of the numinous powers of the commemorated athlete as a carrier of traces of the distant past (numinousness which my opening quotation proclaims boldly for the Olympic site as a whole), but also his awareness of the impossibility of ever recapturing the past as an authentic and complete whole. All of Pausanias' writing is concerned with accessing an imagined totality of Hellenic culture and topography through specific monuments, in the sense that any single artefact can prompt him, in his analysis of it, to mention almost any part of the Mediterranean world. That unlimited

---

[2] The pre-Imperial *periodos* may also have included the Heraia at Argos: see Spawforth (1989) 193.
[3] See Boatwright (2000) 95–8 for a good summary of that balancing act.

geographical potential is Panhellenism in a distinctively Pausanian sense, which borrows from contemporary patterns of Panhellenic imagery in a whole range of genres, but also manipulates them in extraordinary ways. It is a Panhellenism which is at home most of all in the Altis of Olympia, which lies at the very centre of Pausanias' work and occupies more space in the text than any other region. Olympia, more than anywhere, condenses all corners of the Greek world into one space. At the same time it confronts us with the difficulty of reading that severe condensation, of deciphering the extraordinary historical depths which lie beneath the surfaces of the inscribed stones and statuesque bodies Pausanias comes up against.

In examining Pausanias' ordering of his material, I will be interested above all in the political and cultural implications of the way in which he manipulates traditions of large-scale compilation of geographical and historical information. Pausanias' ambitious text was very far from untypical of its time. The elite, literate culture of the ancient world, the Imperial world in particular, was preoccupied with works which attempted to aggregate knowledge, collecting and setting in order huge amounts of disparate material from a great range of different sources. We catch glimpses of this huge industry – unless industry is too restrictive a word for a habit of thought and textual production which was so deeply ingrained, and which manifests itself in so many different forms – in a great range of different texts and practices, which are themselves very difficult to separate into firm categories. To name only a few: the 'encyclopedic' works of writers like Pliny; which shades into the genre of paradoxography and miscellany (for example, Aelian, Phlegon, Favorinus, Aulus Gellius, Athenaeus), and into the (ostensibly) didactic projects represented by more 'technical' compilations of knowledge, for example in the work of Galen or Frontinus or Vitruvius; projects of lexicography and anthologization and epitomization, all of them partly shaped by contemporary reading habits and principles of library organization; large-scale projects of philosophical enquiry, which may be partly based on a systematizing Aristotelian agenda (for example within the *Moralia* of Plutarch); works of universalizing history (Diodorus Siculus, Dionysius of Halicarnassus, Appian), which draw on and imitate the practices of historical (e.g. annalistic) record-keeping; the genre of geographical writing, which often had a strong historical focus, represented for example by Strabo and Pomponius Mela;[4] and finally (and most importantly for this chapter) the practices of chronological record-keeping and chronography (i.e. the recording of historical events in chronological

---

[4] On ancient geography, see Dueck (2000), on Strabo; Clarke (1999); Nicolet (1991); Jacob (1991).

Pausanias and the compilatory texts of the Roman Empire 161

order).⁵ Pausanias relies on and adapts all of these modes of composition – the last one in particular – in ways which have not been adequately appreciated in recent scholarship.

'Encyclopedic', systematizing texts of this sort have generally been given little attention within modern scholarship. For the Roman Empire period this lack of respect has been part of a persistent underrating of 'Second Sophistic' literature for its derivative, secondary nature.⁶ That lack of attention is now beginning to seem increasingly misguided. For one thing, systematizing habits have the capacity to reveal a great deal about the cultures in which they arise, as work on the sociology of knowledge in a range of other disciplines has emphasized.⁷ The way in which societies organize and control knowledge in textual form – both within sophisticated writing and in utilitarian texts, as far as the two can be separated – both reflects and contributes to the underlying practices and patterns of thought which structure their social and political relations. That said, a systematizing habit does not imply or require cultural conformity, if anything quite the opposite. Systematization of knowledge is often profoundly political because of its capacity to conceal highly charged choices about what to exclude and include behind the mask of objectivity. Each systematizing text has its own prioritizing logic, imprinting its own vision of how the world is ordered on to the material it contains. Texts which categorize and collect large amounts of material offer their authors distinctive opportunities for self-dramatization. Often they advertise authorial control, even while the author is at his most self-effacing. Often, too, they foreground the particular problems which their own projects of controlling knowledge may face, the difficulties of wrestling with material, of getting it into shape. Such texts also have the capacity to draw their readers into the same processes. They hold out the promise of universal knowledge, but often at the same time frustrate our expectations, prompting us to explore further and order the material for ourselves. That challenge is particularly acute in Pausanias' case because he tends to avoid explicit statements about the taxonomic criteria he is using, making us work much

---

⁵ See Bickerman (1980) 62–79; Mosshammer (1979), esp. 84–112.
⁶ See, e.g., Whitmarsh (2001), esp. 41–89.
⁷ The bibliography on knowledge and society from other disciplines is huge, but there has been very little application of these ideas to the compilatory and didactic texts of the ancient world; the most obvious exception for the Imperial period is Barton (1994a); see also my forthcoming volume on 'Ordering Knowledge in the Roman Empire' (edited jointly with Tim Whitmarsh), for one attempt to deal with this topic. Much of the modern writing on this subject is prompted by the work of Michel Foucault (see McNay (1994), esp. 48–84); see also Burke (2000) 1–17 for a clear introduction to recent work on social histories of knowledge.

harder than some of his knowledge-ordering contemporaries do to decipher those criteria. Moreover, within elite Imperial writing the prevalence of categorizing of this sort often seems to have reflected a desire to imitate or even surpass the systematization of expertise on which the Empire was founded, and the textual extent of their compilations of knowledge often implicitly rivals the Empire's geographical spread. These styles of writing also reflected and influenced the particular ways in which the contemporary world was reliant on and in dialogue with the past. The texts of the Roman Empire often proceed through rearrangement and reassessment of the many texts which lie behind them, as if the textual tradition they depend upon is a world in its own right, the stuff from which their own new creations are to be moulded. From that perspective, the past comes to seem impressively and intimidatingly complex, but also at the same time flexible and manipulable.

How do those principles impact on the textual categorizations of Olympia and Olympic chronology which I will examine here? The system of dating by Olympic chronology was a way of bringing all time – Roman time included – beneath a Greek aegis. At the same time, as we shall see for Phlegon's *Olympiads* especially, universalizing visions of this sort often acknowledge the fragility of the visions of independent but all-embracing Greek structuration which they conjure up. Similarly, the erection of athletic (and other) victory statues within civic or sacred space proclaims a kind of community between past and present. The victors of the past are still visible, standing in dialogue with each other in almost human form, and lining the routes of processions so that they seem to participate in the city's viewing of its rituals. The practice of commemorating victories also reflects a distinctively Greek geographical conception of the world, an awareness of the way in which the whole of the Greek world, represented by a range of victory-locations, can be unified within a single figure or a single space, mentioned together within a single inscription, just as the returning Panhellenic victor brings home with him the spoils of a kind of territorial conquest along with his victory wreath. At the same time, the idealized community these statues stand for is a very difficult one to access. How do we join the community of stone figures the city displays to us? How do we recapture and imitate the precise moments which gave rise to the bare inscriptions which commemorate them? That tension has a great deal in common with the ambiguity between presentness and unattainability which is so deeply ingrained in ancient attitudes towards the ideal athletic body as a model of moral perfection, as I argued in the previous chapter. The past, as it is articulated through the annotated bodies of athletic statues, and through the universalizing claims of the Olympic victory chronicles, is made present to us, yet in a way which is tantalizingly difficult to grasp and to control. And that, surely, must be one of the reasons for its attraction. My argument here will be that Pausanias, in the very central section of his *Periegesis*, exploits fundamental similarities between his own systematizing, Panhellenic project, and the systematizing presentations of athletic history which we find in so many inscriptional and chronographical texts. He both illustrates and exploits the tensions between presence and absence, familiarity and distance, which were central to so much athletic commemoration. And in doing so he also provides another powerful illustration of the close overlaps between literary and inscriptional representation of athletics in the Roman period.

COPYING THE OLYMPICS

The ideals of Panhellenism played a central role in the prestige of festival activity.[8] By Panhellenism I mean not only the idea of shared Greek religious and educational traditions, but also – more specifically – the sense of geographical (and also historical) comprehensiveness which was enshrined in Olympic tradition. The Panhellenic sanctuaries were renowned as gathering places for the whole of the Greek-speaking world, and also for their combination of artefacts and memories from an extraordinary range of historical and geographical sources, as Pausanias' account shows. But Panhellenism was not confined to these very unusual spaces. Other festivals – even very small festivals – drew on the imagery of Panhellenism in their struggles for self-promotion. Hadrian's Panhellenion project, for example, which relied amongst other things on an extraordinary expansion in the Athenian festival progamme, was clearly meant (though perhaps with limited success) to complement or even rival the older Olympic-centred version of Hellenic identity.[9] Inscriptions in honour of victorious athletes often claim a kind of Panhellenic status for their subjects, mentioning victories at the great games of Greece in a prominent position in order to proclaim their membership of a very exclusive club of *hieronikai* (victors at 'sacred' *agones* with

---

[8] See chapter one (pp. 25–7) for brief discussion of the development of Panhellenic ideals in the Classical period, and for (often self-serving) appropriations of them.

[9] The Panhellenion seems to have been significant more as a religious than as an administrative entity, and much of the impetus for its founding seems to have come from the Greeks themselves, rather than from Hadrian; nevertheless it seems likely that Hadrian at least recognized and encouraged the institution's political and symbolic significance, as Spawforth (1999) argues; see also Jones (1999) and (1996); Spawforth and Walker (1985), esp. 90–2 on Hadrian's Athenian focus, and (1986); on the festivals of Athens, see Spawforth (1989) 194; Geagan (1979) 397–9.

Panhellenic status), while also enumerating lesser victories over a great range of locations.

How exactly did the imagery of Panhellenism come to be attached to festivals whose claims to Panhellenic significance seem at first sight highly tenuous? The answer lies partly in the system by which ancient agonistic festivals were categorized, since the more prestigious categories of festival were implicitly linked with Panhellenic qualities. As we saw briefly in chapter one, there was a distinction in prestige between sacred, crown festivals, where victors were rewarded with a garland (although sometimes money prizes were available as well,[10] and victors in these contests could expect huge financial benefits from their home cities, in recognition of the glory they had brought to their fellow citizens);[11] and local prize festivals (*themides*), where the rewards were purely financial ones.[12] In the Hellenistic period, sacred festivals had been established by a process of sending out envoys across the Greek world to seek permission for the new foundation, and they were therefore associated with a degree of Panhellenic consensus. Greek cities would then send representatives to subsequent celebrations of the festival,[13] which would be accompanied in some cases by a sacred truce, applicable at least to the organizing city and to everyone travelling to it.[14]

In the Imperial period, the prominence of Roman influence on Greek festivals must sometimes have left the impression that Panhellenism was dependent upon Roman harmonization of the Empire. Permission for foundation of a sacred festival, or for the upgrading of a local festival to sacred status, came under the control of the emperor (and sometimes also the senate), partly because these decisions had serious financial implications for the cities in question.[15] Imperial cult was in fact one of the most significant driving forces behind the expansion of the Greek festival programme,[16]

---

[10] For cash prizes at crown games, see, e.g. Spawforth (1989) 194; cf. Pleket (1975) 57–8 on prizes at crown games in the Classical period and before.

[11] On rewards for Olympic victory especially, see Dillon (1997) 116–18; Drees (1968) 106–7.

[12] For that distinction see, amongst others, Robert (1984) 36. However, Mitchell (1990) 189 stresses that there was no clear dividing line between them in terms of the competitors they attracted and the prestige they offered.

[13] See Robert (1984) 36–8 and (1970) 6, with mention of the long set of third-century BC inscriptions from Magnesia on the Maiandros (*I.Magnesia* 17–87) which give some of the most vivid and detailed evidence for these processes.

[14] E.g., see Dillon (1997) 1–8; cf. Golden (1998) 16–17 on the Olympic truce.

[15] See Mitchell (1990) 191; Robert (1984) 38–9, (1977) 33 and (1970) 6–7; there is also evidence for *themides* receiving imperial approval (the Demostheneia at Oinoanda is a good example: see Wörrle (1988) 172–82).

[16] For the combination of imperial cult worship with local festival traditions, see Price (1984) esp. 102–7; this phenomenon is discussed also in chapter two (p. 71) and chapter five (p. 214).

and the number of sacred *agones* increased rapidly as the second and third centuries went on, although much more rapidly under some emperors (e.g. Hadrian and the Severans) than others.[17] Some of these sacred festivals were founded on the initiative of the emperor, while others received imperial permission in response to specific requests. Sacred games were also themselves further subdivided. Some received the title *eiselastikos*,[18] entitling victors to triumphal entry to their home cities on returning home; and a few of the most prestigious *agones* were even added to the *periodos* by imperial decree, as we shall see further below.

The status of a city's festivals could have implications for its prestige, not least because the right to hold a sacred, Panhellenic *agôn* was a sign of imperial favour. A festival's name and status would presumably also have affected its potential to attract famous competitors. There is evidence for festival status being used as a weapon within rivalries between neighbouring cities, for example in squabbling between Nikaia and Nikomedia in Bithynia in the late second century AD.[19] According to Louis Robert's reconstruction, the emperor Commodus at some stage granted Nikomedia the right to celebrate a sacred festival, along with the title of *neokoros*, which signalled the presence in the city of the provincial centre of the imperial cult.[20] Later, however, he seems to have removed those rights and simultaneously to have given permission for a sacred festival – the Commodeia – to the Nikaians. Septimius Severus then reversed the situation once again, removing the right to a sacred festival from Nikaia, along with the title of 'first city' of the province which the two cities had for some time shared, in punishment for Nikaia's support for his rival Pescennius Niger; and at the same time returning the neocorate to Nikomedia, together with the right of a sacred festival, named the Severeia. Both cities advertised these privileges. Nikaia in particular seems to have broadcast its celebration of the Commodeia frenetically, not least in its coin issues,[21] drawing attention to its exaltation at the expense of the Nikomedians.

Cities often advertised Panhellenic status, then, through their holding of crown festivals. The pursuit of Panhellenic legitimacy was sometimes

---

[17] For discussion of chronological variations in the patterns of agonistic foundation in the Imperial period, see Mitchell (1993) 219–24 and (1990) 189–91; Robert (1984) 39–40; see also Boatwright (2000) 94–104 on evidence for Hadrian's involvement with festivals in 21 different cities.

[18] See Spawforth (1989) 193–4; others (e.g. Robert (1984) 43 and Mitchell (1990) 189) give the impression that all crown contests were *eiselastikoi*, which was not the case.

[19] See Boatwright (1977).

[20] See Boatwright (2000) 96–7 on the neocorate.

[21] See Robert (1977) 34–5; on coin issues celebrating festivals elsewhere, see Ziegler (1985); Robert (1960a) 360–8.

carried to further extremes, as I have already suggested, through a strategy of imitating the ancient *periodos* festivals. There were large numbers of festivals classified as 'isolympian' (i.e. 'equal to Olympia') or 'isopythian', and often also named as Olympia or Pythia in their own right.[22] In most cases, however, their imitation was far from exact. The title 'isolympian' seems to have referred most often to the use of Olympic age categories and prize regulations, rather than imitation of the Olympic programme.[23] Some festivals imitated the administrative structures of Panhellenic foundations, for example by appointing *hellanodikai* or *alytarchai*, offices which originated at the Olympic festival.[24] Outside Olympia, however, their services would usually have been supplemented by appointment of an agonothete, whereas this seems to have been only sporadically the case in the Elean games themselves, which probably did not rely on benefactions by agonothetes as a regular institution.[25] Moreover, this kind of imitation was far from incompatible with other advertised focuses for allegiance. Many festivals accumulated lengthy names, combining both Panhellenic and imperial titles,[26] and even in festivals which conformed to Empire-wide patterns of programming and nomenclature there would always have been plenty of room for distinctive local rituals.

The traces of Panhellenic styles of self-advertisement are, I believe, often visible in victory inscriptions, which were designed to promote victors and benefactors and cities, often all at the same time. For example, inscriptions which are set up by agonothetes to record the results of the festivals they have funded often record the way in which athletes from all over the Mediterranean world have converged on the host city, transforming it into a microcosm of the Panhellenic gatherings of the *periodos*. We see a good

---

[22] Louis Robert has discussed this topic in a number of places: e.g., see Robert (1974a) 180–1 for a summary of the most prominent imitations of both Olympic and Pythian traditions; Robert (1967) 40–4 for inscriptions from the Olympia at Ephesus (in which we saw Aurelios Achilles competing in chapter three (pp. 127–30)); Robert (1938) 60–1; see also Farrington (1997) 32–4 (with appendix 35–43), who catalogues known occurrences of local Olympic festivals while also noting many divergences from the original Olympic programme; Nollé (1987) 254 and Weiss (1981) on Side in Pamphylia, which seems to have held its own Pythian *and* Olympic festivals; Spawforth (1986) on the Olympia Commodeia at Sparta.

[23] See Frisch (1988), esp. 181 (although see also Crowther (1989) 101 for some qualifications).

[24] See Robert (1948a) 59–63 on the *hellanodikai* of the Olympia at Ephesus; cf. Robert (1974a) for the argument that the title *theoros* at Ephesus was an imitation of the title of the priestess of Demeter at Olympia.

[25] See Pleket (1976), esp. 6 and 12–13.

[26] E.g., see Boatwright (2000) 94 for the Olympia Pythia Hadriana of Tralles; cf. Price (1984) 103–4 on local and imperial titles combined.

example of that in one late-Hellenistic victory catalogue from the Romaia at Xanthos in Lycia,[27] which lists the *agôn*'s victors as follows:

In the *agonothesia* of Andromachos son of Andromachos son of Andromachos from Xanthos, these men have won in the *agon* of the Romaia, established by the confederacy of the Lycians:
  Among the *aulos* players: Theogenes son of Apollogenos, from Sardis;
  Among the *kithara* players: Pythion son of Pythion from Patara;
  The prize for singing to the *kithara* I dedicated at the altar of Rome because the competitors were disqualified;
  The boys' *dolichos*: Glaukos son of Artapatos from Patara;
  The boys' *stadion*: Menephron son of Theophanos from Ephesus;
  The boys' *diaulos*: Poseidonios son of Ktesippos from Magnesia on the Maiandros;
  The youths' *stadion*: Nikandros son of Nikandros from Argos;
  The youths' wrestling: Miltiades son of Xenon from Alexandria;
  The youths' boxing: Pateres son of Diodoros from Philadelphia;
  The men's *dolichos*: Aristokritos son of Charixenos from Argos;
  The men's *diaulos*: Aristokritos son of Charixenos from Argos;
  The men's *stadion*: Antiochos son of Menestratos from Myra . . .
(lines 1–27)[28]

And so on. The text records a geographically diverse set of victors, including men from cities as remote and famous as Argos and Alexandria, but also a good proportion of local winners (for example from Patara and Myra), recording the fact that Lycia can more than hold its own against the finest men of Greece (although the high percentage of local winners presumably has just as much to do with the small proportion of non-local entrants). The inscription's second half (not translated here) also offers an early example of the way in which Rome was often involved in and written into this world of Panhellenic commemoration (a technique which is carried to much more conspicuous extremes within the second-century AD *Olympiads* of Phlegon, which I will examine in the next section): the festival is not only

---

[27] Published with discussion by Robert (1978a).
[28] Ἀγωνοθετοῦντος | Ἀνδρομάχου τοῦ Ἀνδρομά⁻ | χου τοῦ Ἀνδρομάχου | Ξανθίου, οἵδε ἐνίκων ἐν τῶι ἀγῶνι τῶν | Ῥωμαίων τῶι τεθέντι ὑπὸ τοῦ κοινοῦ | τῶν Λυκίων. Αὐλητάς· | Θεογένης Ἀπολλογένους Σαρδιανός. | Κιθαριστάς· | Πυθίων Πυθίωνος Παταρεύς. Τὸν δὲ τῶν | κιθαρῳδῶν στέφανον ἀνένεκα ἐπὶ τὸν τῆς | Ῥώμης βωμὸν διὰ τὸ ἐκπεσεῖν τοὺς ἀγωνι⁻ | ζομένους· | Παῖδας δόλιχον· Γλαῦκος Ἀρταπάτου | Παταρεύς· | Παῖδας στάδιον· Μενέφρων Θεοφάνου Ἐφέσιος. | Παῖδας δίαυλον· Ποσειδώνιος Κτησίππου | Μάγνης ἀπὸ Μαιάνδρου. | Ἀγενείους στάδιον· Νίκανδρος Νικάνδρου | Ἀργεῖος· Ἀγενείους πάλην· | Μιλτιάδης Ξένωνος Ἀλεξανδρεύς. | Ἀγ(ε)νείους πυγμήν· Πατερῆς Διοδώρου | Φιλαδελφεύς.| Ἄνδρες δολιχόν· | Ἀριστόκριτος Χαριξένου Ἀργεῖος. Ἄνδρας | δίαυλον· Ἀριστόκριτος Χαριξένου Ἀργεῖος. | Ἄνδρας στάδιον· Ἀντίοχος Μενεστράτου | Μυρεύς . . .

in honour of Rome, but also includes a Roman winner, who has had himself declared a citizen of Telmessos for the purposes of participation (lines 40–2). The technique of unelaborated categorization draws on the traditional style of agonistic enumeration. The victors are slotted into their place within Panhellenic tradition as if that is something they can lay claim to without any need to justify their position there or to narrate the means by which they have achieved it. This unelaborated style of exposition is in some ways very far removed from the never-endingly hypertextual catalogue Pausanias gives us, with its tendency to use the victors under discussion as starting-points for telling stories about other subjects. Nevertheless, it shares with Pausanias' text an aspiration towards comprehensiveness, in its systematic recording of the different age-classes and events. In the process it also bears witness to the broad topographical scope of the many competitors who have contributed to the festival. Even within this economical cataloguing, moreover, there are moments where the text hints (as Pausanias repeatedly does) at the possibility of further stories lying behind its bare surface, not least in the double victory of Aristokritos, in *dolichos* and *diaulos*.

Inscriptions in honour of individual athletes often advertise their subjects' home citizenship but in the same breath boast about the geographical range of their victories, as if to demonstrate the way in which the community involved has exported home-grown talent far beyond its own bounds, spreading its victorious influence over the whole of the Hellenic world. In doing so they often give a prominent position to the old and most prestigious festivals of the Greek agonistic calendar. That technique paints the athlete as a Panhellenic figure, a man whose victory extends far beyond the edges of the *stadion* to encompass territorial domination. Markos Aurelios Asklepiades, whose career record formed the opening quotation of this book, and whom we have encountered several times already, once again offers us an exceptional example. He boasts of a perfect periodic pedigree, which nevertheless also embraces a whole raft of smaller, local festivals, in what is no doubt a unique combination, so many that he does not see the need to name them all, and a whole collection of different citizenships:

. . . I competed among three peoples, in Italy and in Greece and in Asia, winning all of the contests listed here: I won the *pankration* of the Olympics in Pisa in the 240th Olympiad [AD 181], the Pythia at Delphi, the Isthmia twice, the Nemean games twice (on the second occasion all my rivals pulled out), the 'Shield games' of Hera in Argos, the Capitolia in Rome twice (on the second occasion all my rivals pulled out after the first lot-drawing), the Eusebia at Puteoli twice (on the second occasion all my rivals pulled out after the second lot-drawing), the Sebasta at Naples twice (on the second occasion all my rivals pulled out after the second lot-drawing), the Aktia in Nikopolis twice (on the second occasion all my rivals pulled out) . . . (*IG* XIV, 1102 (=*IGUR* 240), lines 17–25)[29]

The hierarchy Asklepiades sets up between these different games is typical. The *periodos* games, and the Olympics especially, continued to cling to first position in lists like these,[30] although not without competition, since there were a number of other imperial foundations of almost equal prestige, and occasionally these foundations even took precedence over the older festivals within victory lists.[31] The Aktia, founded by Augustus at Nikopolis, was the first new festival to be added to the *periodos*, and several others followed. The ability to claim victory in the whole *periodos* (to be a *periodonikês*) continued to be valued, but a number of different festival combinations seem to have been acceptable, not only the traditional quartet of Olympic, Pythian, Isthmian and Nemean.[32]

Often even less muscular festivals attempted to push their way to the top of the list, and so to draw on the Panhellenic prestige of the *periodos* festivals. Local *agones* are sometimes given unusually prominent positions within victory inscriptions of this sort. An early third-century AD inscription from Ankyra honours a triple-victor at the festival of the Asklepieia Sotereia Pythia in that city.[33] The home festival is, not unusually, listed

---

[29] . . . ἀγωνισάμενος ἐν ἔθνεσιν τρισίν, Ἰταλίᾳ, | Ἑλλάδι, Ἀσίᾳ, νεικήσας ἀγῶνας τοὺς ὑπογεγραμμένους πάντας πανκρα⁻ | τίου· Ὀλύμπια τὰ ἐν Πείσῃ σμ' Ὀλυμπιάδι, Πύθια ἐν Δελφοῖς, Ἴσθμια δίς, | Νέμεα δίς, τὸ δεύτερον στήσας τοὺς ἀνταγωνιστάς, καὶ τὴν ἀσπίδα "Ηρας ἐ[ν Ἄρ⁻ | γε]ι, Καπετώλια ἐν Ῥώμῃ δίς, τὸ δεύτερον μετὰ πρῶτον κλῆρον στήσας | τοὺς ἀνταγωνιστάς, Εὐσέβεια ἐν Ποτιόλοις δίς, τὸ δεύτερον μετὰ δεύτερον | κλῆρον στήσας τοὺς ἀνταγωνιστάς, Σεβαστὰ ἐν Νεαπόλει [δίς], τὸ δεύτερον μετὰ | δεύτερον κλῆρον στήσας τοὺς ἀνταγωνιστάς, Ἄκτια ἐν Νεικοπόλι δίς, τὸ δεύ⁻ | τερον στήσας τοὺς ἀνταγωνιστάς . . .
[30] Farrington (1997) discusses the revived prestige of Olympic victory and commemoration of it in this period, especially within Asia Minor, Syria and Egypt; see esp. 30 on the increasing desire to commemorate Olympic victory locally rather than in the Olympic sanctuary itself. Sacred victors (*hieronikai*) seem to have been entitled to certain legal privileges; Spawforth (1989) 193 notes that Diocletian restricted such privileges to those who had won victories in the festivals of old Greece, keeping in check the proliferation of accepted routes to athletic glory.
[31] E.g., see Reinach (1916) no. 9 (pp. 354–8) (=Moretti (1953) no. 69 (pp. 191–6)) for a victory inscription which lists the Capitolia in Rome, the Sebasta in Naples and the Aktia in Nikopolis ahead of the Isthmian, Pythian and Olympic games (in that order), although Moretti (1953) 192 suggests that these may be the Olympic games of Athens; cf. LBW 1620b (pp. 380–1) (=Moretti (1953) no. 72 (pp. 206–11)), for an inscription which lists the Sebasta at Naples ahead of the Nemean and Isthmian games.
[32] See BE 1954 no. 57, pp. 113–15 (commenting on Moretti (1954)); Kennell (1988) discusses this phenomenon in the course of his argument that Nero was not interested in visiting Athens and Sparta because neither of these cities had festivals which were of any use to him in his quest to gain the status of *periodonikês*.
[33] Mitchell (1977) no. 8 (pp. 75–7).

first. It is followed by mention of a number of other victories, apparently presented in a rough order of prestige. These do not include an Olympic victory, almost as though the Asklepieia at Ankyra can compensate for that lack by taking over the characteristic position of the Olympics at the top of the list. The Pythian festival at Delphi is also (surprisingly) demoted below the Isthmian which it usually precedes. Presumably the reason for that is desire to avoid a confusing clash with the Asklepieia Sotereia Pythia,[34] although that pragmatic adjustment might in the process have the effect of suggesting that the local festival has displaced the Delphic original. We even see signs that athletes may have tried to pass off victories in imitation Pythian and Olympic festivals as the real thing, hence the much-paralleled phrase Asklepiades uses at the beginning of his list, reminding his readers (in case there is anyone bold enough to doubt it) that he has won at the real Olympics, 'the Olympics in Pisa' (line 19).[35] An athlete honoured in a late second-century AD inscription from Smyrna, for example, gives an ambitious list of victories and citizenships, and yet cannot disguise the fact that he has no Olympic victory from Pisa to show for his pains. The text does, however, mention two other Olympic triumphs, in Smyrna and in Athens, both at the very beginning of the list, and it is tempting to feel that they are meant to stand in for the most glaring gap in his resumé.[36]

I have argued, then, that some of the most distinctive features of agonistic commemoration can be explained by a desire to draw on the tropes of Panhellenic self-representation. The accumulation of Panhellenic overtones, in other words, is one of the ways in which the athletics of the Roman Empire celebrates its prestige. That is not to suggest that Panhellenic connotations were always applied in formulaic and unthinking ways. We see all sorts of ways of combining Panhellenic imagery with an emphasis on the individuality of the athlete or the community being honoured, with the sense that nothing else is quite like what we have in front of us. In many ways the Olympic sanctuary conforms to the same pattern, as we shall see, sucking the whole of the Greek world into its orbit, and yet proclaiming a kind of uniqueness and inimitability at the same time.

---

[34] See BE 1978 no. 489 (p. 485) for restoration of the word Pythia and for that explanation of its position.
[35] See Robert (1948a) 63, n. 1 for a number of other examples; cf. van Nijf (2001) 324, n.74 on *I.Milet* II, 500.
[36] See Robert (1949) 105–13, esp. 106; cf. Robert (1948a) 62–3 on an Ephesian inscription (*I.Eph.* 1127) in praise of an Ephesian athlete and benefactor whose claims to have been *olympioneikês* and *hellenodikês* may be deliberately vague about the fact that both his victory and his office-holding must have been at the Olympia at Ephesus, rather than at Pisa.

DATING THE OLYMPICS

The Olympic programme was not the only vehicle by which Olympic Panhellenism was exported. The practice of dating Greek history by Olympiads was also widespread, both within texts which provided comprehensive lists of past Olympic victors and in works of history where Olympic dating was used to give a chronological anchor to records of political or military activity (amongst other things). By this system any four-year period could be identified either by the position its Olympic festival held within the overall series (thus 776–772 BC formed the first Olympiad, 772–768 BC the second, and so on); or by the name of the man who won the *stadion* race in that Olympiad.

Olympic chronography was useful partly because it allowed historians to synchronize different dating systems. We have evidence for a great variety of chronographical practices within the ancient world, many of them specific to individual communities.[37] Most often they were based on the names of yearly office-holders. Many of these systems would have been perfectly adequate for local administrative or commemorative uses, but they must always have had the potential to cause confusion when it was necessary to compare events in different regions. However, some local systems, like the Athenian archonship, did come to have wide currency outside their original contexts. Olympic dating was one of the most important of these synchronizing systems.[38] Its widespread use no doubt both relied on and reinforced the concept of Olympic Panhellenism as a force capable of bringing together many different regions and cultures.

Dating by local festival was also common. That practice may have been influenced by the prominence of Olympiad dating, as part of the process of Olympic imitation described in the previous section. Inscriptions from Smyrna, Alexandria, Kyzikos and Tralles (Phlegon's home town) all dated local events by their own Olympic festivals, and there is similar evidence in relation to a number of non-Olympic festivals elsewhere.[39] The inscription for Asklepiades exemplifies this tendency well in recording his victory in the Olympian festival of his native Alexandria, dated to the 'sixth (Alexandrian) Olympiad' (Ὀλυμπιάδι ἕκτῃ) (*IG* XIV, 1102, line 41).

However, Olympic chronicles were not simply utilitarian texts for administrators and antiquarians. The project of Olympic listing also attracted

---

[37] See Bickerman (1980) 62–79; cf. Follet (1976) on the many different dating systems (including Roman consular dating) in use in the inscriptions of second- and third-century AD Athens.
[38] See Bickerman (1980) 75–6. [39] See Robert (1930) 39, esp. n. 2 for several examples.

distinguished scholars, and chronographical texts offered promising vehicles for the exploration of cultural hierarchies. The first list of Olympic victors is said to have been compiled by the sophist Hippias in the fifth century BC.[40] Many others followed his example, including Aristotle,[41] the Hellenistic writer Eratosthenes,[42] and the second-century author Phlegon of Tralles, whose *Olympiads* (which survive only in fragments)[43] will be the main focus of this section. Philostratus, in his *Gymnasticus*, the athletic training 'manual' which will be the subject of chapter seven, devotes many pages to early Olympic history, with precise attention, so he claims, to the dating recorded within the official records of Elis. As we shall see, he uses those records to explore the way in which athletic material – both this body of historical evidence and the body of the athlete – is to be shaped in creative ways for the contemporary world, in response to the interpretative challenges they pose.

We also have surviving work from two Christian authors who attempted to synchronize Greek and Hebrew history: Sextus Iulius Africanus[44] and Eusebius (who was also a biblical scholar, and bishop of Caesarea in the first half of the fourth century).[45] Both of them rely heavily on Olympiad dating. In neither case does the use of Olympiads imply unqualifiedly admiring acknowledgement of the antiquity of non-Christian Greek tradition. Rather, it implies, amongst other things, the lack of power in non-Christian dating systems by comparison with Christian chronography. Eusebius, for example, represents Olympiad dating as a comparatively young system. His text sets out parallel tables of dates and important events from a number of different cultures, starting from the birth of Abraham, dated to 2016 BC, and working forward. It is more than 1200 years before the Olympics puts in its first appearance, nearly halfway through the chronicle. Eusebius' aim, it seems, was 'partly to make clear the greater antiquity of Hebrew history relative to most others'.[46] The continued use of the Olympiad system into the Byzantine period, widespread despite the fact that the Olympics themselves had been abolished at the end of the fourth century AD, may paradoxically have carried with it similar implications, drawing attention in some cases to the fleeting nature of pagan tradition. The *Chronicon Paschale*, for example, written in the early seventh century, chronicles world events, dated by

---

[40] See Jüthner (1909) 67–9.   [41] See Jüthner (1909) 65–7.   [42] See Jüthner (1909) 64–5.
[43] *FGH* 257, F1 and F12; translated by Hansen (1996) 58–62, with commentary; discussed by Jüthner (1909) 62–3.
[44] See Mosshammer (1979) 146–57; Jüthner (1909) 61–2.
[45] See Mosshammer (1979) who discusses Eusebius' work against the background of Greek precedents for Olympic chronology (esp. 22–168).
[46] Mosshammer (1979) 34.

their Olympic years, down to AD 628, which is catalogued as the 352nd Olympiad.[47] On one level this is a tribute to the power of the Olympic name. At the same time, however, it may have been meant as a gesture to the greater power of Christianity, which has survived well beyond the greatest of the old festivals of Greece.

Like Eusebius' work, many pre-Christian Olympic chronographical texts achieve effects which are more sophisticated and challenging than they are sometimes given credit for, not least through their capacity to interrogate cultural hierarchies by their endlessly intriguing juxtapositions. Phlegon's Olympic chronicle, as we shall see in a moment, is no exception. Of course not all Olympic lists were so intricately integrated with non-Olympic events as those I have referred to so far.[48] For example, we have one surviving papyrus fragment from Egypt (*P.Oxy.* 2, 222),[49] dating from the mid third century AD, which contains unembellished lists of winners (with name and city of origin) in a number of events from the 75th to the 78th Olympiad, in the fifth century BC. The existence of this list on papyrus, in a relatively small centre like Oxyrhynchos, points to the easy availability and widespread dispersal of such information, in what appears to be a very uncomplicated form.[50] This text should not, however, be taken as an unsophisticated document, or categorized on an entirely different level from the other works we have looked at, even if it does at first sight fall short of the complexities of presentation we find in Phlegon or Eusebius. For one thing, the order in which the information is presented to us on the papyrus is very close to the order Phlegon uses in his fragmentary record of the 177th Olympiad which I will discuss below,[51] and the most significant difference between them is simply that the papyrus fragment omits all the non-Olympic happenings which Phlegon includes after his Olympic lists. It may even be the case that the Egyptian list is based on Phlegon's work, or at least shares a common source with it. More importantly, even this unelaborated Egyptian fragment participates in a style of presentation – often denigrated by modern scholars as encyclopedic and derivative – which had great prestige and popularity in the Imperial period, as I have suggested already. Systematization not only is useful, but also has the capacity to offer its readers distinctive pleasures and challenges. Systematizing texts impose a vision of order on

---

[47] Translated with notes by Whitby and Whitby (1989).
[48] See Ebert (1982), commenting on *IG* II/III², 2326, for the possibility that Olympic and other victor lists may sometimes have been made publicly available in order to provide a context for the details recorded in other victory inscriptions.
[49] =Miller 86; discussed by Jüthner (1909) 63–4.
[50] E.g. see Habicht (1985) 22; Grenfell and Hunt (1899) 87.   [51] Cf. Grenfell and Hunt (1899) 86.

the world, albeit often a deliberately fragile, illusory order, including and excluding information according to their own priorities, and often hinting at tantalizing connections and disjunctions between items of information they choose to hold on to (although of course some kinds of listing are more challenging and complex than others). This Egyptian list presents to us a microcosm of Olympic diversity transformed to harmony, through the juxtaposition of victors from a great range of different communities. It also preserves that harmony, fixing and universalizing in its own text each fleeting moment of victory, in a vision of precisely preserved and self-contained Greek tradition. And it casts its readers as spectators with a vision far more elevated than those who watched the original contests, able to look back over the whole sweep of Olympic contest in a single glance, so that the agglomeration of detail becomes an object of wonder in itself. That, of course, is an effect which many other Olympic texts share. Pausanias, I will suggest, carries the project of Olympic enumeration as thaumatography furthest of all.

How far does Phlegon's work fit in with these patterns? He, too, treats the summation of athletic history as a source of wonder in his *Olympiads*, a text which has been almost entirely ignored by recent scholarship as an object of critical analysis. For Phlegon, it seems, as for Pausanias, the wonder of Olympic chronography comes partly from the way in which his listing of Olympic victories allows him to jump to all sorts of superficially unconnected facts and events. If the pattern of the surviving fragments is typical, it seems that each Olympiad's victory list was followed by an account of noteworthy events which coincided with it, drawn from a wide range of geographical locations. It may be significant that Phlegon's *oeuvre* also included a famous work of paradoxography, the *Book of Marvels*,[52] a collection of bizarre stories gathered from all over the Mediterranean world. That work parallels the wonder-inspiring topographical range of the *Olympiads* by the geographical diversity of its stories, although it dates those stories, if at all, by Athenian archons and Roman consuls, perhaps because it is less interested in the project of drawing together its many disparate details into a coherent whole.

The *Olympiads* shares the project of interrogating inter-cultural relations which I have identified as crucial to other chronographical texts like that of Eusebius. Most importantly, I believe, the surviving fragments suggest a preoccupation with the way in which Greek autonomy is circumscribed and defined by Roman control. It may be no accident that Phlegon's status as a freedman of the emperor Hadrian is advertised so conspicuously in the

---

[52] *PGR* 169–219 (=*FGH* 257, F36); translated by Hansen (1996) 25–49 (with commentary at 65–176).

opening sentence of the text as we have it, as it is in several other ancient testimonies.[53] Phlegon's halfway status – as one who has been freed from his original servitude, but nevertheless defines himself with reference to it, and hints in a number of places at his unquestioning service of the emperor – serves as a powerful introduction to the theme of oscillation between Greek independence from and subjection to Rome which dominates the passages of the work which survive.

The first fragment we have (*FGH* 257, F1) deals with the foundation of the Olympic festival, and introduces themes which surface again in later parts of the surviving text. Phlegon tells us that it was initially established by Peisos and Pelops and Herakles, but then fell into neglect for a period of 27 Olympiads. It was then refounded in an attempt to restore peace to the Peloponnese, in the year afterwards dated as the starting-point of the first Olympiad. Here, immediately, the text reflects on its own chronographical method. The fact that this period of neglect is dated by Olympiads even when the festival was not being maintained, in fact even before that system was invented, looks like a gesture of Phlegon's control over his material, advertising his ability to extend the genre of Olympic time-keeping beyond its usual limits and to apply it to a period whose dates were even more hotly disputed than those of the early Olympiads.[54] He then lists the second set of founders – Lykourgos and Iphitos and Kleosthenes – tracing Lykourgos' ancestry back to Herakles over nine generations. This unwieldy description of Lykourgos' pedigree is perhaps meant to remind us of the precision of Olympic dating, by contrast with the system of generational calculation on which many ancient accounts of early historical and mythological events rely. Most of the rest of the fragment is then taken up with an account of the reluctance of the Peloponnesians to support the Elean festival, and of the oracles which were necessary to coerce them into acceptance. That theme of coercion of small communities into a wider entity, accompanied by the promise of universal peace, resonates with similar themes in Phlegon's record of Roman expansion in the other surviving fragment, to which I will now turn, although the distance between these two passages within his text of course makes it dangerous to draw any tight correspondences.

Phlegon's account of the 177th Olympiad (72–69 BC) opens with a list of victors in the Olympic games.[55] This list shares the unelaborated style which we have seen already in *P.Oxy.* 2. 222, and in many of the inscriptions

---

[53] E.g., see *FGH* 257, F1, lines 1–2, and T1–3.
[54] Photius mentions that dispute over early Olympic dating in *FGH* 257, T3.
[55] This fragment (*FGH* 257, F12) is preserved by Photius: he tells us that he read Phlegon's work up to the end of the fifth book, as far as the account of the 177th Olympiad, which he then quotes; he does not explain why he stopped when he did.

discussed in the second section of this chapter, recording the Olympic events followed by the name and origin of each victor. Even within this list, however, there are moments when Phlegon hints at some further story lying behind his bare record-keeping (as does the inscription from the Romaia at Xanthos which I discussed above), gesturing towards hypertextual possibilities of the kind Pausanias' work relies on so heavily, but without cashing them in. For example, we hear at the start of the list that 'Hekatomnos the Milesian won in three contests: *stadion, diaulos* and hoplite race'.[56] The *stadion* and the *diaulos*, the two Olympic sprint races, are traditionally mentioned first in lists of this type, without any other events between them. Here, this single sentence covers both events together. The hoplite race, however, is usually held back until after the other athletic events, and Phlegon insists on sticking to that convention by repeating the record of Hekatomnos' triple victory there. This repetition advertises Phlegon's determination to maintain a precise devotion to traditional patterns of commemoration in this part of his account, while also in the process re-enacting the multiple celebration of Hekatomnos' glory and so allowing us to share to some degree the perspective of the original audience. Similarly, the home city of Elis seems to have done conspicuously well, winning the boys' boxing and the boys' *pankration*, as well as all of the six horse-racing events, two of them with horses owned by the same man, another example of how Phlegon's catalogue gestures towards narrative possibilities – stories he could expand on if he chose to – without carrying them through.[57]

This was a period when Roman control over Greece was firmly established, and when the cities of mainland Greece could not match the wealth and influence they had held in the Classical period. Nevertheless, this victor list is able to conjure up an image (of sorts) of the continuing strength of autonomous Greek tradition and Panhellenic harmony, at least within the temporary suspension of everyday diplomatic relations which the Olympics brought with them. It papers over other worries or upheavals, and maintains a Panhellenic face despite the lack of large-scale participation in some events from beyond the western Peloponnese. And yet even here we see one specific sign of forces intruding on Panhellenism from the outside, in the intriguing mention of a Roman victor, Gaius, who is said to have won the *dolichos*, the long-distance running race. Oddly, his name is listed after that of Hypsikles of Sikyon, who is also recorded as winner of the *dolichos*. The precise explanation for that – apparently self-contradictory – repetition is

---

[56] ἐνίκα Ἑκατόμνως Μιλήσιος στάδιον καὶ δίαυλον καὶ ὁπλίτην, τρίς.
[57] See Scanlon (2002) 43 on the lack of non-Elean interest in Olympic equestrian events in this period.

far from clear, but it may have the effect (whether it was a deliberate choice[58] on Phlegon's part or just a mistake) of throwing doubt on the legitimacy of this Roman's victory, leaving the impression that he has been admitted to Phlegon's Panhellenic catalogue only grudgingly, an impression which I believe the lines following it, to which I will now turn, strongly reinforce.

In the second half of the fragment we move away from Olympia abruptly, and the Roman world breaks in upon this image of ordered Greek ritual much more bluntly as Phlegon launches into his account of significant events which occurred elsewhere during the Olympiad. These incidents have a geographical diversity to match the variety of communities named within the victory list, but that diversity is here a result of Phlegon's focus on the actions of the Roman army, as he follows a number of generals on their campaigns, juxtaposing Roman geographical dominance to the imagery of Olympic Panhellenism. The Greek word 'to win' (νικᾶν), which is used for agonistic victory, is repeatedly applied to Roman victories in battle:

[Lucullus] ordered Hadrianus to fight against Mithridates. Having done so, he defeated him (καὶ πολεμήσας ἐνίκησε)... In the fourth year Tigranes and Mithridates gathered 40,000 foot soldiers and 30,000 cavalry, and having drawn them up in the Italian manner, they fought against Lucullus. Lucullus defeated them (καὶ νικᾶι Λεύκολλος)... And Metellus, having set out for the Cretan war with three divisions, arrived at the island. Having defeated Lasthenes in battle (μάχηι νικήσας τὸν Λασθένη), he was declared imperator.[59]

The second of those examples in particular – the phrase 'Lucullus defeated them' – mirrors the unelaborated tone of the preceding victory listings, as if the Roman army is indulging in its own rival form of competition and display. We hear, too, about non-military events: for example an earthquake in Rome, the appointment of the philosopher Patron as head of the Epicurean chair in Athens, and the birth of the poet Virgil. Phlegon also tells us that 910,000 Roman citizens were enrolled in a census in the third year of the Olympiad, a reminder, perhaps, that the combined demographic bulk of Rome can more than parallel the assembled Panhellenic community at Olympia, which must in itself have been one of the wonders of that festival. The fragment ends with enumeration of the military

---

[58] Even if that choice involved simply transcribing self-contradictory information which was already present in the records Phlegon used.

[59] καὶ Ἀδριανὸν ἐπέταξε πολεμῆσαι Μιθριδάτηι· καὶ πολεμήσας ἐνίκησε... τῶι δὲ τετάρτωι ἔτει Τιγράνης καὶ Μιθριδάτης ἀθροίσαντες πεζοὺς μὲν τέσσαρας μυριάδας ἱππέας δὲ τρεῖς καὶ τὸν Ἰταλικὸν αὐτοὺς τάξαντες τρόπον ἐπολέμησαν Λευκόλλωι· καὶ νικᾶι Λεύκολλος... καὶ Μέτελλος ἐπὶ τὴν Κρητικὸν πόλεμον ὁρμήσας, τρία τάγματα ἔχων, ἦλθεν εἰς τὴν νῆσον, καὶ μάχηι νικήσας τὸν Λασθένη αὐτοκράτωρ ἀνηγορεύθη.

events of the fourth year, partly quoted above. Particularly striking here is a sense of ambiguity about whether these Roman generals are to be taken as protectors of the Greek world, or as its oppressors. It is worth quoting the exploits of Metellus again to bring out that effect:

> And Metellus, having set out for the Cretan war with three divisions, arrived at the island. Having defeated Lasthenes in battle, he was declared imperator. And he put the Cretans under siege (τειχήρεις κατέστησε). And the pirate Athenodoros enslaved Delian citizens, and defiled the statues of their . . . gods.[60] But Gaius Triarius restored what was damaged in the city, and fortified Delos (ἐτείχισε τὴν Δῆλον).[61]

Here we see Roman generals crushing Greek resistance in Crete, but also protecting Greek populations from marauding, in Delos. The final verb 'fortified' (ἐτείχισε) embodies that ambiguity, marking an act which is simultaneously a gesture of protection and of occupation. In line with the second of those two gestures, it is disturbingly close to the phrase 'under siege' (τειχήρεις) in the previous sentence, replaying the idea of enclosing a Greek population behind fortifications. Delos had in fact been subject to Roman impositions for some time, having been handed over to Athenian control by Rome in 166 BC. Moreover, the massacre in Delos in 69 BC – described here – was remembered as one of the most cataclysmic events of the Mithridatic wars, and Delos never fully recovered from the trauma. It is hard, in other words, to see the Roman restoration of Delos as an act of unequivocally successful and beneficent restoration, or of unequivocal harmonization between the Greek and Roman worlds, since mention of it carries a reminder of Greek decline in the context of Roman 'protection'.

Phlegon's Olympic victory listings (like those of Pausanias) are thus represented as valuable partly for the stories and events which they give access to, events which are linked, in Phlegon's case, by their chronological contiguity. They are also used, I believe, as vehicles for meditation on the place Greek tradition holds within the Mediterranean world, both in Phlegon's contemporary second-century milieu and in the centuries of inter-cultural encounter which had preceded it. In that sense they offer a vivid example of the way in which the compilatory literature of this period so often had the capacity to confront its readers with provocative questions

---

[60] The text transmitted by the Christian Photius refers to their 'so-called' gods (τῶν λεγομένων θεῶν), but presumably the word λεγομένων ('so-called') is his interjection.
[61] καὶ Μέτελλος ἐπὶ τὴν Κρητικὸν πόλεμον ὁρμήσας, τρία τάγματα ἔχων, ἦλθεν εἰς τὴν νῆσον, καὶ μάχηι νικήσας τὸν Λασθένη αὐτοκράτωρ ἀνηγορεύθη· καὶ τειχήρεις κατέστησε τοὺς Κρῆτας. καὶ Ἀθηνόδωρος πειρατὴς ἐξανδραποδισάμενος Δηλίους τὰ τῶν . . . θεῶν ξόανα διελυμήνατο· Γάιος δὲ Τριάριος τὰ λελωβημένα τῆς πόλεως ἐπισκευάσας ἐτείχισε τὴν Δῆλον.

about the cultural and political relations of their contemporary world. That is an insight which has all too rarely been articulated both for Phlegon's much neglected *Olympiads*, and for the systematizing habits of composition to which it is so closely indebted. It would be wrong, of course, to suggest that Phlegon's text has any clear message about Roman domination or Greek autonomy, not least because there is not nearly enough of it surviving to support such a claim. However, Phlegon does at least acknowledge the potential status of the Olympic festival as a site for autonomy from Roman control, while at the same time foregrounding the precariousness of that autonomy and the potential of Roman imperial ambition to swallow up Greek tradition in its path. At the same time, of course, like Pausanias,[62] Phlegon hints at the idea that it is Rome's empire which enables the new Panhellenism which his own journalistic versatility represents. It is the movements of Roman military might which have made it possible for him to range so widely over the centuries and spaces of Mediterranean history. Similarly, it is partly his own status in the service of the emperor which makes it possible for him to collect his information, as he hints several times in the *Book of Marvels*, where he records curiosities which have been brought to Rome to satisfy the curiosity of the emperor, or which he has come across in the course of travelling with the emperor.[63]

Whether Phlegon's work can throw light on the significance of contemporary festival activity, and on the continued use of Olympic dating for contemporary events, is harder to say. Nevertheless, the continuation of his work right up to very recent Olympiads must surely have hinted at the continuing capacity of second-century *agones* to link the present with the past via centuries-old traditions and rituals, while also provoking exploration of the relation between that cultural continuity and the changing political realities around it. Louis Robert argues for connections between Phlegon's work and living performance culture in analysing an inscription recording honours given to Titus Aelius Alkibiades of Nysa by the Artists of Dionysus, partly in gratitude for a gift of 'marvellous books' (θαυμαστὰ βιβλία) donated to their organization.[64] Robert identifies the recipient of these honours as a relative of the Publius Aelius Alkibiades who was a fellow-freedman of Phlegon in the service of Hadrian, and who was the dedicatee of the *Olympiads*.[65] He speculates that the books Titus Aelius

---

[62] See Elsner (1994) 248 and (1992) 19.
[63] See esp. *Book of Marvels* 35; cf. *Long-Lived Persons* (*FGH* 257, F37) 97.
[64] Robert (1938) 45–53; the decree was originally published by Clerc (1885) Face A (pp. 124–7) (but see also the corrections of Robert and others, signalled by Robert (1938) 45, n. 2).
[65] See *FGH* 257, T3.

Alkibiades has donated were the works of Phlegon, which are said to have included a book on the festivals of Rome as well as the *Olympiads*.[66] If that is right, this inscription provides the most concrete evidence we have that Phlegon was in touch with the interests of those who competed in public in the Roman Empire.

I have argued, then, that each Olympic festival, and each Olympic victory, stood as an epochal event, a marker around which other incidents could be categorized, although that conception was of course in competition with a great many other systems of chronological marking. Olympic victory listing thus offered a starting-point for the challenges of setting the past in order, of accessing a shared historical heritage. Texts like those of Phlegon and Eusebius parade their universal coverage, while also advertising the awe-inspiring complexity of the tasks they have undertaken, and acknowledging their reliance on the communal efforts of many generations of scholars. Victory listing was also a way of integrating local identity with wider community, conjuring up a picture of diversity within Panhellenism. Often we see Rome being written into that traditional pattern, represented as one community of many within the Hellenic world; or else as an enabling force, a force which makes possible forms of Panhellenism broader than any which have come before.[67] However, such representations are also often aware of the difficulties of constraining Rome within any Panhellenic system. In Phlegon's work, I believe, we see Rome not only participating in Panhellenic tradition (for example through the victory of Gaius in the *dolichos*) and perhaps even safeguarding it (if we take Roman protection of Delian religion as a model for Rome's relationship with the Olympic sanctuary), but also at the same time threatening to burst out of that frame, threatening to overshadow it, or to refashion it under its own control.

VISITING THE OLYMPICS

In what ways, then, was the act of visiting Olympia represented and understood as a Panhellenic experience? And how was the imagery of Panhellenism projected within the Olympic sanctuary itself?

I do not intend to provide here a summary of the Olympic site and the Olympic programme (as far as they can be reconstructed), partly because

---

[66] See *FGH* 257, T1.
[67] Cf. Aelius Aristides, *On Rome* 26.97–9, for harmonization of the ideals of festival Panhellenism with the imagery of Roman global benefaction.

there are a number of such accounts already available,[68] and partly because some of these things will emerge from my discussion of Pausanias, whose text has formed one of the main bases for modern descriptions of the Olympic site. Nevertheless, some basic points are worth making. Athletic and religious space were closely integrated within the Olympic sanctuary.[69] In the centre of the sacred grove (the Altis) stood the huge Temple of Zeus, with its famous statue of Zeus by Pheidias. Around that were a number of smaller temples and 'treasuries', buildings housing dedications from Greek cities. Dotted between the temples and lining the site's processional routes were hundreds of dedicatory statues, most, though certainly not all, put up to honour the victors in athletic and horse-racing competitions.[70] The dedication of non-agonistic statues reflects amongst other things a tradition of speech-making at the Olympics, unconnected with the festival's competitions, by philosophers and orators and historians keen to advertise their own work or to reach an audience symbolic of the Greek people as a whole.[71] To the east stretched the *stadion* and the hippodrome, while to the south and west stood a *palaistra* and a *gymnasion* for the training of athletes, as well as a number of buildings used for administration and accommodation (although all but the most distinguished of the spectators would probably have slept in the open around the site). The festival lasted for five days.[72] It began with a swearing-in ceremony for judges and competitors, followed by the boys' contests on the same morning, and then the men's athletic and horse-racing competitions on days two to four (Olympia was the only one of the four main *periodos* festivals to have no musical events). The third day also included a sacrifice of one hundred oxen at the altar of Zeus, and no doubt the festival as a whole saw other sacrifices and processions on a smaller scale.[73] The administrative complexity of the event, in the hands of the city of Elis twenty-five miles away, must

---

[68] E.g., see Sinn (2000); Swaddling (1980); Finley and Pleket (1976); Drees (1968); Gardiner (1925); on the archaeology of the site, see Raschke (1988); Herrmann (1972), esp. 183–95 on the Imperial period; cf. the reports by Ulrich Sinn and others on the Olympic excavation project 'Olympia während der römischen Kaiserzeit', published in *Nikephoros* 5 (1992) and a number of subsequent issues.

[69] Swaddling (1980) 13–37 gives clear maps, with brief commentary.

[70] On athletic statues in Olympia, see Rausa (1994) 39–51; Herrmann (1988) (who lists all statues mentioned by Pausanias, and then all of the known statues not mentioned by Pausanias); Hyde (1921).

[71] For an Imperial-period example, see Dio Chrysostom *Oratio* 12; cf. Lucian's *Peregrinus*, which satirizes the philosopher Peregrinus' perversion of those traditions in his sensationalistic suicide at the Olympics.

[72] On the order of the programme see Lee (2001); Drees (1968) 66–86.

[73] See the evidence collected by Miller (1991) numbers 60–83 (pp. 63–78), much of it drawn from Pausanias; Finley and Pleket (1976) 59–67 discuss Olympic rules and the duties of Olympic officials in general terms, apparently relying on much of the same evidence.

have been awe-inspiring, as it would also have been for other Panhellenic festivals.[74] And yet the number of competitors for each event may often have been very small.[75] Universal Panhellenic virtue was thus condensed, focused on a very small number of individuals, just as the geographical variety of the Panhellenic world was condensed within the physical space of the Altis.

Clearly Pausanias' textual tour of Olympia was a very unusual one. There are good reasons, however, for thinking that even less learned visitors would have viewed their own experiences there as something much more than passive tourism or spectatorship 'for its own sake'. Festival attendance, along with the viewing of contests and sacred objects which accompanied that, was often represented as an experience which required active response from the viewer, not least because it constituted a participatory performance of Hellenic identity (although the version of Hellenic identity which was on show at Olympia was of course an unusual one in some ways). Visiting Olympia involved being part of a gathering of people from all over the Hellenic world, and confronting the great range of traditions on show there, in all their chronological and geographical variety. It was also an act of religious significance, as Ian Rutherford has recently argued in challenging the idea of a clear boundary between tourism and pilgrimage within the ancient world.[76] The simple fact that sporting venues and the (to modern eyes) museum-like sites which accompanied them were also religious sanctuaries immediately makes the separation between spectatorship and religious observance seem suspect. Cities from all over the Greek world would send out envoys to sacrifice in Panhellenic sanctuaries and to attend their games, in a process known as *theoria* (literally 'spectatorship'). Similarly envoys (*theoroi*, a word also used in other contexts to mean 'spectators') from those sanctuaries would travel widely issuing invitations before the festivals began (and sometimes engaging in diplomatic activity on the way), following itineraries which survive in temple records. This was necessary partly because the distinctions between different local dating systems made certainty about the exact timing of these festivals difficult. The act of broadcasting Panhellenic timekeeping was thus embedded within ritual and diplomatic custom, as well as in historiographical practice. The attendance of athletes similarly had ritual dimensions: competitors were required, having satisfied the judges

---

[74] Some of our best inscriptional evidence for the organization of Panhellenic festivals comes from elsewhere, for example from third-century BC records of accounts from the Pythian games at Delphi: e.g., see *CID* 2.139 (=Miller 60).
[75] See Crowther (1993).
[76] See Rutherford (2001); cf. Rutherford (2000); Dillon (1997), esp. 1–26 and 99–123.

of their Hellenic ancestry, to train in Elis under supervision for at least one month before the Games started.[77] Private contemplation of sacred images was also often represented in ancient texts as an act of religious observance.[78] Pausanias' preoccupation with religious sites in his viewing of Greece seems to have been anticipated by earlier *periegesis* writing.[79] Philosophical texts used the experience of visiting the Panhellenic festivals, the Olympics especially, as a metaphor for the journey of self-discovery which was central to the *theoretikos bios*, the contemplative life.[80] Between them, these concepts and patterns of representation must have influenced the spectators who flocked to Olympia every four years. For some, at least, Olympic attendance was not simply an act of tourism, nor was it simply an opportunity to marvel at the athletes and buildings and to join in with the Panhellenic crowd. It was also a challenging, active, religiously charged experience, which had implications for their perceptions of personal and communal identity.

The old and the new seem to have been combined with each other within the Olympic site in very distinctive ways. For example, there seems to have been a strong concentration of Classical statues in the Altis, partly because victors in some later periods were commemorated more often in their home cities than in Olympia itself.[81] Pausanias' neglect of post-Classical statues is thus partly a reflection of what he saw in front of him, although he very much intensifies that bias. Ancient statues were interspersed with other dedications from the distant past, many of which had been brought to Olympia hundreds of years before to celebrate victories in battle. Modern excavations have unearthed a large amount of weaponry and armour from Classical and Archaic campaigns between Greek states, and even from the wars against Persia.[82] Here the Panhellenic past was at its most acccessible, and yet also at its most alien and exotic. Where else (apart from Athens and Delphi, perhaps, the cities Pausanias places at the beginning and end of his text) could one have set eyes on so many concrete links with the past, on the very arms used by the old heroes of Greece, and even on the helmets of their legendary Persian enemies, taken as booty in battle?

---

[77] See Dillon (1997) 221–7; Crowther (1991b), who emphasizes the fact that this must have made participation at the Olympics difficult for all but the wealthiest of athletes.
[78] See Rutherford (2001) 43.   [79] See Rutherford (2001) 45–6.   [80] See Rutherford (2001) 47–8.
[81] See Farrington (1997) 29–30; also 44–5 (figures 2 and 3), for tables comparing the number of inscriptions found in each fifty-year period of Olympic history with the number mentioned by Pausanias.
[82] E.g. see Kunze (1961) 129–37 on a Persian helmet taken as booty; Kunze (1956) 69–74 on a helmet with an inscription identifying it as a dedication from the Athenian general Miltiades; on other pieces of ancient armour found at Olympia, see Kunze (1961) 56–128, (1958) 74–151 and (1956) 35–68.

Combined with these ancient artefacts, by the time Pausanias visited the site in the second half of the second century AD, there were conspicuous signs of recent building activity and Roman imperial influence,[83] although Pausanias notoriously fails to mention many of the site's modern buildings, as we shall see shortly. Olympia seems to have flourished in the Imperial period more than any of the other Panhellenic festivals because of the exceptional imperial interest it attracted, and the sanctuary's position in western Greece, more easily accessible from Italy, may even have contributed to that.[84] For example, the Metroön, temple to the Mother of the Gods, contained a three-times-life-size statue of Augustus, with a thunderbolt in hand in imitation of the great statue of Zeus, surrounded by other Roman emperors and other members of the imperial family.[85] Similarly, Herodes Atticus in the mid second century built a Nymphaion, an elaborate fountain building backed by statues of the imperial family and his own relatives, providing the festival with a more reliable water supply than it had ever had before, in a combined act of self-glorification and benefaction.[86] Some prominent Romans had interfered with the Olympic site and the Olympic programme in even more obtrusive ways. Sulla seems to have brought most of the Olympic athletes to Rome in 80 BC, with the result that only the boys' *stadion* race was held in Olympia;[87] and Nero postponed the Olympic *agôn* to fit in with his visit to Greece, and arranged for the festival to contain (unprecedented) musical contests, which he then won himself, just as he is said to have 'won' the Olympic chariot race despite having fallen out of his chariot halfway.[88] These intrusions left only temporary marks. For example, there are signs of attempts to destroy records of Nero's Olympic visit.[89] However, other signs of forcibly imposed Roman control survived, for instance in dedications connected with the Roman general Mummius, who brought Greece under Roman control in the mid second century BC, and removed famous votive offerings from Corinth and other Greek cities in the process. Pausanias describes offerings, including

---

[83] See esp. Scanlon (2002) 40–63, a revised version of Scanlon (1988a); cf. Alcock (1993) 189–91; Price (1984) 160–1; Gardiner (1925) 158–74.
[84] See Alcock (1993) 180 for that suggestion.   [85] See Hitzl (1991).
[86] See Walker (1987) 60–2; Bol (1984).
[87] See Scanlon (2002) 42 and 354, n. 5, with further references.
[88] See Cassius Dio, *Roman History* 62.14; Suetonius, *Nero* 23–4.
[89] Pausanias (10.36.9) tells us that this false Olympiad was not included in official Elean records; Cassius Dio 62.14 reports Galba's recovery of the huge bribe given by Nero to the Olympic *hellanodikai* for giving oracles in his favour; one Olympic inscription (*IvO* 287) has Nero's name carefully erased; however, commonly made claims about destruction of a triumphal arch of Nero after his death (e.g., see Alcock (1993) 190; Drees (1968) 127; Gardiner (1925) 164) seem to me to have no clear evidence, as Arafat (1996) 149, n. 27 also notes.

statues of Zeus, said to have been made by Mummius in commemoration of his victory;[90] and excavations have uncovered statue bases (ignored by Pausanias) which supported statues of Mummius, one of them (*IvO* 319) set up by the city of Elis in honour of Mummius' benefactions.[91] It is possible that these statues would have been taken as uncompromising reminders of Greek debasement. But it also seems likely that even Mummius' dedications (three centuries old by the time Pausanias was writing) could have been rationalized as equivalents to the many artefacts which commemorated ancient wars between Greek neighbours who now lived in harmony.

Olympia was thus the most modern of festivals — as well as being the most widely plagiarized, as I argued in this chapter's first section — but it also maintained its own inimitable air of archaism and even (with some exceptions) of autonomy. We have seen already that the Roman authorities took a close interest in the foundation of sacred festivals, and that the mixture of local festival foundations with imperial cult was the rule rather than the exception by the middle of the second century AD. Few festivals could match the degree of Roman imperial interest which Olympia attracted, and yet Olympia was also unusual in maintaining its own traditional name, without the addition of any imperial title like Kaisareia or Sebasta, or the addition of any imperial festival in combination with the original.[92] Similarly, as noted above,[93] its own funding arrangements, which did not rely on *agonothesia* as a permanent institution, remained unique, despite the fact that its programme and administrative systems were so widely imitated.[94] There are signs that the culture of Olympic imitation was itself acknowledged within the Olympic sanctuary, for example in an inscription which records the programme of the isolympic festival of the Sebasta in Naples.[95] The inscription is usually treated as an advertisement for the great new *agôn* of Magna Graecia, but it is presumably also meant to comment on the Olympic festival itself, given its location. The inscription implies a shared Roman and Panhellenic festival culture, in which Olympia participates on an equal footing even with the newest of foundations. However, it is also

---

[90] See Pausanias 5.10.5, 5.24.4 and 5.24.8.
[91] See Arafat (1996) 95–7; Tzifopoulos (1993); Philipp and Koenigs (1979).
[92] See Robert (1969b) 49–58 for the name Kaisareia added to the Pythia (admittedly in one inscription only, from the first century AD, and (much more frequently) to the Isthmia, along with many examples from other sacred festivals; Scanlon (2002) 40–63 emphasizes the deliberately unobtrusive nature of imperial interventions in Olympia, as well as their frequency.
[93] P. 166.   [94] See Pleket (1976), esp. 6.
[95] *IvO* 56 (with the modifications of Crowther (1989) and Merkelbach (1974b)) (translated in part by Miller 140); discussed also by Frisch (1988); Arnold (1960) 246–7; Geer (1935).

striking that the programme of the Sebasta as it is presented diverges from Olympic precedent widely, not least by the addition of musical competition, and it may even be that this inscription is a record of Augustan additions to an original festival known as the Italika Isolympia.[96] If that is the case, the very mention of the Sebasta's isolympian programme, with its conspicuous departure from its model, would, I suggest, have had the capacity to remind its readers not only of the homage the Olympics customarily received, but also of the Olympic festival's own ultimate resistance to imitation, and to modifications like the ones the Neapolitan festival had just undergone.

Olympia, in summary, blended old and new in a way which was typical of the world around it, indeed paradigmatic, fitting Roman influence into a long tradition of syncretism between past and present, east and west. At the same time it radiated an aura of uniqueness, despite its typicality. The visible traces of this distinctive blend, I believe, must always have had the potential to draw its spectators into the experience of participation and interpretation. Pausanias, I will argue, draws on all of these images and traditions, but also transforms them. Not only does he cast himself – and his readers – as Panhellenic travellers in a conventional sense, sharing the experiences which any spectator would have access to, but he also holds out the promise of an expanded and elevated version of those experiences for those who are able to follow the threads and challenges which his own mapping of Olympia presents to us. He distinguishes Olympia from Isthmia and the other Panhellenic sanctuaries, even Delphi, for example by the number of pages he devotes to it, and by the fact that he gives almost no attention to victory statues outside Olympia. At the same time, however, he is interested in the things Olympia shares with the Greek world around it, in particular the way in which anyone who visits the site inevitably struggles to recapture, to set in stone, the essence of Hellenism which this sanctuary, more than any other, purports to embody.

ORDERING THE OLYMPICS: PAUSANIAS

Pausanias' description of Elis opens with an intriguing description of the origins of the different races inhabiting the Peloponnese:

Those Greeks who say that the Peloponnese has five parts and no more must agree that both the Eleans and the Arkadians live in the first part, the territory of the Arkadians; that the second part is inhabited by the Achaians; and that the three

---

[96] See Geer (1935) 218–21.

remaining parts are inhabited by the Dorians. The autochthonous races of the Peloponnese are the Arkadians and the Achaians . . . The rest of the Peloponnese belongs to immigrants (ἐπηλύδων ἐστιν ἀνθρώπων). The modern Corinthians are the latest inhabitants, and from my time to the time when they received their land from the Roman emperor is 217 years. (5.1.1–2)[97]

The Arkadians and the Achaians are the only races who have always lived in the Peloponnese, and even the Achaians, as we hear immediately after this passage, do not inhabit the territory they originally did. The inhabitants of Elis, the guardians of Olympic tradition, are newcomers, like so many others, categorized in the same breath as the Corinthians, whose Hellenic status appears to be so precarious when Pausanias describes them at an earlier stage in his text, as we shall see in a moment. Even as Pausanias prepares to celebrate Olympia's continuity with its own past, he pointedly reminds us that very few communities can tie themselves to their own soil without qualification.

This programmatic passage, with its awareness of the difficulty of establishing unbroken links with the land of the Peloponnese itself, provides vivid support for recent developments within Pausanian scholarship, which has increasingly shown an interest in the tensions which underlie Pausanias' at-first-sight straightforward and celebratory cataloguing of the monuments of mainland Greece. His text, as Jaś Elsner[98] and James Porter,[99] amongst others, have recently stressed, conjures up an imagined vision of everything which is most marvellous and memorable within the Hellenic heritage. Pausanias uses specific monuments and art-works as gateways to a world of virtual Panhellenism, drawing on an image of internally consistent Hellenic tradition to make dazzling links between the different artefacts and stories he presents us with. As an essential part of that process, however, the absence of the things Pausanias describes paradoxically becomes the very feature which makes them so powerful.[100] Porter in fact makes Pausanias a paradigmatic figure for 'Second-Sophistic' culture, which he characterizes as obsessed with exploration of the uncertainties

---

[97] Ὅσοι δὲ Ἑλλήνων Πελοποννήσου πέντε εἶναι μοίρας καὶ οὐ πλείονάς φασιν, ἀνάγκη σφᾶς ὁμολογεῖν ὡς ἐν τῆι Ἀρκάδων οἰκοῦσιν Ἠλεῖοι καὶ Ἀρκάδες, δευτέρα δὲ Ἀχαιῶν, τρεῖς δὲ ἐπὶ ταύταις αἱ Δωριέων. γένη δὲ οἰκεῖ Πελοπόννησον Ἀρκάδες μὲν αὐτόχθονες καὶ Ἀχαιοί · . . . τὰ δὲ λοιπὰ ἐπηλύδων ἐστὶν ἀνθρώπων. Κορίνθιοι μὲν γὰρ οἱ νῦν νεώτατοι Πελοποννησίων εἰσί, καὶ σφισιν, ἀφ' οὗ τὴν γῆν παρὰ βασιλέως ἔχουσιν, εἴκοσιν ἔτη καὶ διακόσια τριῶν δέοντα ἦν ἐς ἐμέ· . . .
[98] Elsner (2001b).   [99] Porter (2001).
[100] E.g., see Porter (2001) 67–76; Elsner (2001b) 17–18; cf. Elsner (1994), esp. 244–52, on the way in which Pausanias uses monuments of the Greek past (both ruined and intact) to construct an identity for the present.

which underlie its own constructed, manipulated identities.[101] The fact that the past can be accessed only through the tantalizing traces it leaves in the present, and the fact that firm explanations for the wonders Pausanias puts on view so often slip away from the grasp of even this most learned of guides, is the very thing which guarantees their fascination, drawing us – like Pausanias himself – into the endless task of putting the Panhellenic world into order.

That is a paradox, I believe, which Olympia is ideally suited to express, given the combinations of ancient and modern, continuity and disjunction which I have argued for as deeply ingrained features of Olympic representation, in the Imperial period as before. Pausanias (who seems to have come from Lydia in Asia Minor)[102] is both an insider to mainland Greece, describing sites and monuments which play a central role in his own self-definition,[103] and an outsider, articulating his encounter with the awe-inspiring alienness of the Greek landscape and the Greek past through the language of Herodotean ethnography.[104] Both of these perspectives have been well studied (although usually without acknowledgement of the way in which Pausanias constantly oscillates between them).[105] I will argue in what follows that the tension between order and disorder, between accessibility and absence, within Pausanias' portrayal of the Olympian Altis – which is thematized within the opening sentences of Book 5 quoted above – is central to the way in which he draws us, as spectators, into the process of grappling with Panhellenism for ourselves. That kind of tension was also central to the conventions of athletic commemoration, Olympic record-keeping especially, as I have argued above. The sense of a glorious but only half-visible world is thus especially appropriate and prominent within Pausanias' portrayal of athletic victor statues in Book 6, which offers, I will suggest, an intensified version of effects which are central to the whole of his *Periegesis*.

The works of Elsner and Porter are part of a wider move towards growing appreciation of Pausanias' *Periegesis* as a text which not only hides a sophisticated structure beneath its matter-of-fact surface, but also engages with the contemporary Greek and Roman culture of the mid second century

---

[101] See Porter (2001), esp. 90–2.
[102] On Pausanias' Lydian identity, see Swain (1996) 331; Arafat (1996) 8; Habicht (1985) 13–16.
[103] See Elsner (1995) 125–55, esp. 131 and 135.
[104] On Pausanias as ethnographer, see Alcock (1996); on Herodotus as Pausanias' most important stylistic model, see Bowie (2001) 25–6.
[105] For a good statement of that paradox, see Elsner (2001b) 5; cf. Elsner (1995) 127, on the way in which the multiplicity of Pausanias' viewings hints at the different strands of his identity.

AD in provocative and complex ways.[106] This is very much more than an ancient guide book. One of the stumbling blocks to moving beyond that conception has been the difficulty, from a modern perspective, of seeing how systematizing works of this kind can provide their own entertainment and their own challenges, as they clearly did in the ancient world, and in the Roman Empire in particular, as I suggested at the beginning of this chapter.[107] That stumbling block has proved oddly difficult to shift, despite the fact that modern scholarly writing owes so much to the Pausanian aesthetic, through having relied so heavily on the exercise of Pausanian-style commentary.[108] Given that resemblance it should be easier than many have thought – at least for classical scholars – to appreciate the seductiveness of the vision of Greek history and Greek geography Pausanias offers us. That said, appreciating Pausanias' seductive qualities should not blind us to the fact that he makes it difficult for his reader to take any pleasure or any enlightenment from his text. We have to work hard for the vision he promises to us, reading his opaque and difficult work painstakingly, just as he reads painstakingly the traces of the Greek past in the landscape through which he passes. I share the aim of taking Pausanias' writing seriously '*as writing*',[109] attempting to take up the challenge of reading consecutively. That challenge, I suggest, requires not only appreciation of the text's sweeping and coherent pleasures, but also acknowledgement of the bewilderment and frustration his work provokes.

In what follows, I want to focus on the way in which the virtual world of Pausanian Panhellenism reveals itself behind the facade of Olympic statue bases[110] (many of which still survive for us). First, however, a brief look at Corinth and the famous Isthmian festival which was under that city's control, and which acts as one of several foils to Olympia within Pausanias'

---

[106] See esp. Alcock, Cherry and Elsner (2001) (of which the essays of Elsner and Porter form a part); Knoepfler and Piérart (2001), esp. the article in this collection by Lafond (2001); also Bingen (ed.) (1996); Elsner (1995) 125–55, (1994) and (1992); and less recently Habicht (1985).

[107] Konstan (2001) argues that the attraction of Pausanias' text comes partly from its status as a catalogue, offering a comparison with the work of Athenaeus. He must certainly be right to stress the importance of linking Pausanias with the systematizing work of his contemporaries, although to my mind he underestimates the extent to which systematization can in itself be a politically charged project.

[108] E.g., see Beard (2001) 235–6 on similarities between Pausanias' text and the writings of James Frazer, his most famous commentator.

[109] Elsner (2001b) 3–4.

[110] See Whittaker (1991) on the unusually detailed attention Pausanias gives to inscriptions in his work, especially within Books 5 and 6. On Pausanias' interest in the large number of cities which have left their mark on Olympic history, see Newby (forthcoming) chapter seven, who discusses the way in which Pausanias' mentions of Olympic victors in the other cities he visits help to structure his account, revealing the connections these cities have with Hellenic history more broadly.

narrative.¹¹¹ A 'brief look' is in fact all that Pausanias offers to us, since his treatment of Corinth is strikingly short, in contrast with his extended two-book treatment of Olympia. At first sight – at least if we follow Pausanias' version – the two sites could hardly be more different. Corinth had been destroyed by the Roman army of Mummius in 146 BC, along with most of its ancient buildings and art works, and then refounded over 100 years later as a Roman colony. There are strong signs of identification with Rome amongst the city's elite population well into the third century AD, but also increasing signs of Greek influences on the city's public life and on its population as a whole. For the most part these different strands must have coexisted with each other quite harmoniously, as Corinth came to enjoy ever-increasing prominence as a landmark city of the new Roman Greece.¹¹² Nevertheless there are signs that in some contexts the disjunctions between Greek and Roman identity within Corinth came closer to the surface, and even apparently confident statements of the city's affiliations often conceal doubts about the image of a unified Greco-Roman culture. Favorinus, for example, in his mid second-century *Corinthian Oration*, announces that the city has become entirely hellenized despite its Roman origins, just as he has been hellenized himself, as a westerner devoted to Greek culture.¹¹³ Those claims have too often been taken by modern scholars at face value.¹¹⁴ When we look more closely, it becomes clear that Favorinus' 'praise' of Corinth is heavily ironic, even sarcastic, not least because the whole speech is aimed at criticism of the Corinthians for their failure to live up to the Hellenic facade they project; and that his comparison between the city's identity and his own contributes to playful acknowledgement of the insecurities of his own constructed, marginal identity.¹¹⁵ Corinth's claims to 'Hellenic identity', it seems, always had the potential to prompt doubts and to demand qualification.

The Isthmian festival may have been one context where the paradoxes of Corinthian Hellenism were most conspicuously on show. Semi-Roman Corinth was in some ways an odd setting for the third-oldest Panhellenic festival. The festival had been removed from the sanctuary at Isthmia, close

---

¹¹¹ For an extended version of the arguments presented here, see König (2001), esp. 156–60.
¹¹² Engels (1990) 66–91 gives most of the important evidence for the cultural affiliations of post-refoundation Corinth, but he underestimates drastically the complexities of the relationship between Greek and Roman culture within the city: see König (2001) 146–7.
¹¹³ Favorinus, *Corinthian Oration* 26.
¹¹⁴ E.g. by Piérart (1998) 86–7; Arafat (1996) 95; Bowie (1996) 220; Alcock (1993) 169; Engels (1990) 71.
¹¹⁵ See König (2001) 160–7; cf. Whitmarsh (2001) 119–21; Gleason (1995) 8–20 discusses Favorinus' teasing of the Corinthians, but pays little attention to the text's Corinthian context.

to Corinth, at the time of the city's destruction, and had been administered instead by the city of Sikyon. It was returned to Corinthian control when the city was refounded, or soon afterwards.[116] Despite being slow to regain momentum, it rebuilt itself into an increasingly grand and prestigious celebration from the second half of the first century AD onwards, as far as we can tell from archaeological evidence for building activity on the site, and from the evidence of victory inscriptions, perhaps prompted in part by Nero's visit there on his agonistic tour of Greece.[117] The juxtaposition of ancient Isthmian tradition with Corinth's conspicuous modernity must often have been interpreted in positive terms, as an example of the way in which Roman influence could be integrated into Panhellenic tradition, in line with the prominence of imperial foundations like the Aktia at Nikopolis and the Capitolia in Rome.[118] In other cases, however, this combination of ancient and modern seems to have left the impression of profound disjunction and inconsistency, of the kind Favorinus hints at in his teasing criticisms of the Corinthians.[119]

Pausanias does not seem keen to give Corinth detailed attention within his own vision of Panhellenism, as we have seen. However, that lack of detail should not necessarily be taken as a sign of unqualified disapproval.[120] Like Favorinus, Pausanias seems to have been aware of the variety of possibilities available for conceptualizing Corinthian identity, and his account shows signs of a deeply rooted ambivalence about Corinth's (and Isthmia's) status which is in many ways programmatic for his work as a whole.[121] On the surface, he takes exactly the opposite tack from Favorinus' 'praise' of Corinthian Hellenism, foregrounding the distance of the present-day Corinthians from their past and insistently referring to them as 'colonists',[122] although he stops

---

[116] See Kajava (2002); Gebhard (1993) 79–89.
[117] See, e.g., Gebhard, Hemans and Hayes (1998), esp. 417; Gebhard (1973), esp. 63–87 and 141–3.
[118] E.g., see Aelius Aristides, *Oratio* 46, esp. paragraphs 20–4.
[119] E.g., see Spawforth (1994) on Pseudo-Julian *Letter* 198, which seems to have been written in support of an Argive embassy, sent to Corinth in the late first or early second century AD to complain about the requirement that Argos should contribute financially to Corinthian spectacles. The text argues that Argos should be immune from these contributions because of its control over the Nemean games; and in 408a–409d the author criticizes Corinth's expenditure on wild beast shows, which are, he suggests, incompatible with the dignity of the Isthmian games, as a Roman import.
[120] Arafat (1996) 110–14 appears to suggest that it should.
[121] For the idea that Corinth is important for Pausanias despite the brevity of his description of it, cf. Lafond (1996), esp. 196–7; she emphasizes the prominence of Corinth, not only geographically and textually (at the entrance to the Peloponnese, which takes up most of his attention, from Book 2 onwards), but also historically (since the sack of Corinth signals the end of Greek freedom, although it was also the place where Greek 'freedom' was proclaimed by Flamininus and later by Nero); cf. Arafat (1996) 109.
[122] 2.1.2, 2.3.7.

short of denying their Greekness altogether. He seems to find very few monuments or statues worth reporting, in line with his tendency to be interested mainly in Classical and Hellenistic artefacts.[123] That lack of interest applies also to the Isthmian sanctuary, which is given only two Teubner pages of commentary. Nevertheless, even here, I believe, his text offers us the chance to interpret the site rather differently, not as a sign of discontinuity, but rather as an example of the way in which sparks of ancient Hellenism do survive even within the most desolate ruins of ancient Greece.[124] In 2.1.5, to take just one example, Pausanias describes Nero's attempt to cut a canal through the Isthmus: 'The man who tried to make the Peloponnese into an island gave up digging through the Isthmus before he got to the end . . . and it remains part of the mainland as it was created . . . so difficult is it to do violence to the things of the gods (τὰ θεῖα βιάσασθαι)'.[125] The word θεῖα ostensibly refers to the Greek land itself, but it also seems designed to remind us of the survival of the festival, which was so closely associated with Poseidon, and which Pausanias has just mentioned. The spark of ancient Isthmian tradition cannot be extinguished entirely, it seems, even when it is buried beneath the unremarkable creations of present-day Roman Greece.

Corinth is thus both the nadir of ancient Hellenism within contemporary Greece and its archetype, and Pausanias navigates between those two versions of its identity, in fact draws attention to the way in which they are intertwined with each other. In many ways, paradoxically, Olympia shares Corinth's ambiguous characteristics. Olympia was the archetypal symbol of continuity between past and present, marked as such by stories like the one Pausanias tells about the Messenians (6.2.10–11), who did not win any Olympic victories so long as they were in exile from their own land, and only began to do so again when they returned home. His neglect of some of the modern monuments of the Altis, for example the Nymphaion of Herodes Atticus,[126] may be meant to contribute to that effect, as if there is so much ancient material that his attention is consumed by it entirely, in contrast with Isthmia where a dedication by Herodes Atticus in the Temple of Poseidon is presented as one of the few things

---

[123] Arafat (1996), esp. 43–79, takes Pausanias' neglect of modern artefacts as a sign of his dissatisfaction with Greek subjection to Rome; cf. Swain (1996) 330–56 for a similar view.

[124] Cf. Bowie (1996) 219–20; Elsner (1992) 15. Arafat (1996) 95, n. 34 and 113 (esp. n. 17) is surely wrong to disagree with the latter, being to my mind too keen to isolate a unified attitude to Rome in Pausanias' work.

[125] ὃς δὲ ἐπεχείρησε Πελοπόννησον ἐργάσασθαι νῆσον, προαπέλιπε διορύσσων Ἰσθμόν . . . μένει δὲ ὡς πεφύκει καὶ νῦν ἤπειρος ὤν . . . οὕτω χαλεπὸν ἀνθρώπωι τὰ θεῖα βιάσασθαι (2.1.5).

[126] See Arafat (1996) 37–8; Habicht (1985) 134–5.

worth mentioning (2.1.7–8). Nevertheless in some areas Olympia too is imbued with a sense of secondariness, and a sense that the past is almost impossibly difficult to access, available to its visitors only through traces and remains, although of course those traces are present on an entirely different scale from those Pausanias encounters in Corinth. The opening of Book 5, quoted at the beginning of this section, suggests, through its combined categorization of Corinthians and Eleans as newcomers, ultimately detached from their land's ancient past, that the difference between them is a difference only of degree.

In the paragraphs of Book 5 which follow that opening passage, Pausanias picks his way through the labyrinth of evidence surrounding the foundation of the early games and the conflicts which preceded it (5.1.1–5.5.1). He goes into great detail, advertising his own control over ancient knowledge prominently, very much more prominently than Phlegon does in the confident but much briefer account of Olympic prehistory at the opening of his *Olympiads*. In doing so, however, Pausanias confronts us with the complexity of that project, and with some of the differences between the Olympic past and the Olympic present. He jumps from one community and one leader to the next, while cross-referencing between them compulsively, recording the many points of contact which link them together. In doing so he produces an impression of an ordered system, but makes us work hard to produce for ourselves the interlinking genealogical and historical map he seems to have in mind. He also refers repeatedly to uncertainties in his material, for example gaps communities have in knowledge of their own pasts, or contradictions between the answers different communities or individuals give for the same question.[127] Similarly, in Book 6, he sometimes corrects common mistakes about the origins of the victor statues he records,[128] or uses the inscriptions on statues to draw inferences which are not explicitly attested;[129] but he also sometimes admits defeat, for example in listing statues whose identities or iconographic connotations cannot be reconstructed.[130] His account of pre-foundation Olympia is a Panhellenic one in the sense that it mentions a great range of different cities and peoples, and in the sense that all four of the cities responsible for the

---

[127] E.g. see 5.1.4; 5.1.5; 5.1.6; 5.2; 5.5.5–6; 5.6.2; cf. Snodgrass (2001), esp. 137, on the possibility that Pausanias was interested in giving such a long description of the Chest of Kypselos (in the temple of Hera at Olympia) (5.17.5–5.19.10) precisely because of the difficulties of interpretation it posed for him.

[128] E.g., see 6.9.4–5; 6.13.2.

[129] E.g., see 6.4.7; at 6.25.1 he leaves a detail of iconography unexplained, inviting us to guess at the matter for ourselves.

[130] 6.3.1; 6.9.1; 6.10.5.

Panhellenic *periodos* festivals – Delphi, Corinth, Argos, as well as Elis – have a crucial role to play within the narrative. But this is not Panhellenism in any second century AD sense, not least because Pausanias stresses the way in which hostility between these communities both preceded and followed the founding of the first festival, for example through struggles over the right to control it.[131]

After a description of the land around Olympia (5.5.2–5.7.5), the history of the foundation itself is then taken up again in more detail (5.7.6–5.9.6), along with post-foundation developments in the Olympic programme. Pausanias first describes the way in which the games developed from a number of different precursors. He then deals with alterations made since foundation, representing repeated changes in the Olympic programme as part of a gradual process of recapturing the memory of ancient tradition: 'When Iphitos . . . renewed the games, men still had no memory of the ancient things; but they progressed gradually to remembrance of them, and whenever they remembered something they would make an addition to the *agôn*' (5.8.5).[132] By that account, the Olympic records themselves are testimony to a centuries-long striving towards the past. That claim seems to hold out the promise of an increasing approximation to authenticity, the promise of an ever-closer progression towards knowledge of how things used to be. At the same time, however, it removes Pausanias' own account even further from its ultimate object, representing it as an attempt to commemorate and decipher isolated moments which are themselves part of a long process of reinventing some dimly remembered past. It is also at odds with the picture which has emerged from the preceding paragraphs of a huge diversity of ancient practice. The Olympic past is thus represented throughout these opening sections of Book 5 as something only vaguely recalled and controversially recorded, and fundamentally different from the established institution of the present-day, riven by inter-state hostilities and competing traditions. Nevertheless, Pausanias also holds out at least the promise of something more, the promise of imagined access to an originary moment of completeness in the past, available to us still through its tantalizing and opaque traces.

From there Pausanias launches into his descriptions of the Altis. Jaś Elsner has analysed the way in which Pausanias flirts with a number of different modes of categorization here, dealing with different types of

---

[131] See 5.4.7; cf. 6.22.2–3.
[132] Ἰφίτου δὲ τὸν ἀγῶνα ἀνανεωσαμένου . . . τοῖς ἀνθρώποις ἔτι ὑπῆρχε τῶν ἀρχαίων λήθη· καὶ κατ' ὀλίγον ἐς ὑπόμνησιν ἤρχοντο αὐτῶν, καὶ ὁπότε τι ἀναμνησθεῖεν, ἐποιοῦντο τῶι ἀγῶνι προσθήκην.

artefact in turn – altars, statues of Zeus, votive offerings, victory statues – and following a different route around the Altis for each.[133] Pausanias here acts as an idiosyncratic stand-in for the Olympic guides who seem to have held official positions within the sanctuary, and who are mentioned in his text in a number of places.[134] His account of the altars follows the route taken by the Eleans when they sacrifice. The other three categories of monument are structured with a more rigid adherence to their topographic arrangement, combined (differently for each group) with gestures towards other organizing criteria (for example groups of monuments which share the same artist, or the same dedicator). The impression of geographical variety – artefacts from communities all over the Hellenic world – is prominent throughout. One of the effects of this patterning is to conjure up a picture of Pausanias' imagined Panhellenic past as an entity which can boast internal unity in a number of different dimensions, although those dimensions may not be easy to disentangle from one another. In that sense there is almost too much of the past in Olympia,[135] so much material that it takes a superhuman organizational effort to put it into place.

Pausanias' account of the athletic victory statues, which occupies most of Book 6, is the fourth (and longest) of these groups. One of the most immediately striking features of this section, by comparison with chronographical texts like Phlegon's *Olympiads*, is the lack of chronological differentiation between the different statues. We see athletes from many different periods rubbing shoulders with each other (as of course they would have done within the statuesque community of the Altis at the time Pausanias is writing). That is not to say that control over chronological knowledge is unimportant for Pausanias, in fact it is crucial to his ability to identify them and to classify them in different ways, but his narrative nevertheless resists the model of the Olympic chronographers, making it clear to us that other ordering criteria are to take priority (though without making it clear what those criteria are). Unlike the chronographers he mixes athletes from different eras, not only from different regions. Also striking, I think, is the way in which the physical appearance of the statues Pausanias deals with is hardly mentioned. Their bodily, athletic appearance is written out of the account, in line with the way in which Pausanias' travel narrative finds no space for the living people he must have encountered on the way, and even sometimes seems to lose sight of the very monuments which are ostensibly its primary subject, as Pausanias gets carried further and

---

[133] See Elsner (2001b) 8–18.   [134] See Jones (2001), esp. 37.
[135] Cf. Porter (2001) 69 for a similar point in relation to Pausanias' work as a whole.

further away from them by the material they prompt him to present. It is not the physical traces the past has left which claim his attention, but the secrets and stories which hide behind them, not the athletic bodies which stared out at him in the shade of the Altis, but the lifeless surfaces of their inscribed bases. The voices of the past are overwhelming in their volume, clamouring so insistently for his attention that he must shut everything else away. And yet that volume does not make it any easier for Pausanias to impose order on his material. As in the rest of the Altis description, he hints at many different ways of ordering the statues – by event, by origin, by artist – but none of these systems is on its own powerful enough to dominate the account. Up to a point he keeps topography in view, joining the statues together in a long chain by links of contiguity, which are shown to coincide in a variety of ways with other forms of organization, but he also makes it difficult for us to imagine breaking in on that chain at any point. All he tells us is that a certain statue is next to certain others, at least until he stops at 6.17.1 to pause for breath and reorientate himself at the Leonidaion, one of the sanctuary's landmark monuments. If we have not started from the beginning and followed him carefully all the way it will be hard to avoid the sense of being lost in a virtual sea of historical references, with no meaningful way of orientating ourselves in relation to the actual space of the sanctuary. Navigating through the traces of the past, it seems, is far from easy.

In the programmatic passage that opens Book 6, where he introduces his discussion of the victory statues, Pausanias rejects conventional genres of categorization, although without being explicit about what alternative patterns of organization he may be prompted to replace them with. He tells us that not all Olympic victors have had statues erected in their honour: 'My work has ordered (ἐκέλευσεν) me to leave out these people, because it is not a register (κατάλογος) of athletes who have gained Olympic victories, but rather an account (συγγραφή) of statues and other offerings' (6.1.2).[136] In this passage, in other words, he separates his own work from Olympic chronographies, resisting the model of textual organization which that genre offers.[137] He speaks as if he is under the control of his text, as if its organizational imperatives have a mind of their own, and as if he

---

[136] τούτους ἐκέλευσεν ἀφεῖναί με ὁ λόγος, ὅτι οὐ κατάλογός ἐστιν ἀθλητῶν ὁπόσοις γεγόνασιν Ὀλυμπικαὶ νῖκαι, ἀναθημάτων δὲ ἄλλων τε καὶ εἰκόνων συγγραφή.

[137] He implicitly acknowledges the usefulness of Panhellenic record-keeping at 6.13.8, and sometimes uses Olympiad dates himself, e.g. at 6.5.3; however he also advertises the greater flexibility his own method provides, for example at 6.2.3, where he includes details which the unelaborated Olympic lists do not seem to contain.

must follow them wherever they lead. He then announces that not all of the statues in the sanctuary will be listed, since some athletes have won without deserving victory, through having had a lucky draw. He will list instead all those who have won some glory, as well as those whose statues are better made than others. He seems here to be raising himself above the authority of the Olympic umpires, suggesting that the contest he will judge himself is fairer and more elevated. The overall effect is to mark his own representation of Olympic history and Olympic activity as an elevated and original version of alternative paradigms of record-keeping and judging.

In what follows he is consistently interested in showing how these Olympic artefacts allow themselves to be sorted according to a great range of different criteria. The magic of this Panhellenic material, I suggest, lies in the way in which it gestures towards unexpected links in so many dimensions, prompting us to spot surprising connections however we look at it, although without ever quite yielding up its secrets of structuration. The opening statue group offers a good example of what is to come:

On the right of the Temple of Hera is the statue of a men's wrestling victor, whose origin was from Elis, Symmachos son of Aischylos; next to him is Neolaidas son of Proxenos, from Pheneos in Arcadia, who won a victory in the boys' boxing-match; and next along is Archedamos son of Xenios, a victorious wrestler, like Symmachos, but in the boys' category, and another Elean. The statues of these men I have mentioned were made by Alypos the Sikyonian, pupil of Naukydes from Argos. (6.1.3)[138]

David Konstan quotes this passage, without detailed comment, to illustrate the way in which Pausanias' text offers a kind of numbing pleasure by the bare, unreflecting qualities of its enumeration.[139] It must be right that the rhythms of Pausanias' text are beguiling precisely because they lull us away from the realities of the contemporary world, in a way which is potentially disorientating. I wonder, however, if there is more to say, even about this simple opening. Not only does it appeal to us through its hypnotic accumulation of detail; it also provokes us to respond, inviting us to decipher the principles on which its own categorization of these different victors is based, and hinting at surprising depths beneath its matter-of-fact

---

[138] Ἔστιν ἐν δεξιᾶι τοῦ ναοῦ τῆς Ἥρας ἀνδρὸς εἰκὼν παλαιστοῦ, γένος δὲ ἦν Ἠλεῖος, Σύμμαχος Αἰσχύλου· παρὰ δὲ αὐτὸν ἐκ Φενεοῦ τῆς Ἀρκάδων Νεολαΐδας Προξένου, πυγμῆς ἐν παισὶν ἀνῃρημένος νίκην· ἐφεξῆς δὲ Ἀρχέδαμος Ξενίου, καταβαλὼν καὶ οὗτος παλαιστὰς παῖδας, γένος καὶ αὐτὸς Ἠλεῖος. τούτων τῶν κατειλεγμένων εἰργάσατο Ἄλυπος τὰς εἰκόνας Σικυώνιος, Ναυκύδους τοῦ Ἀργείου μαθητής.
[139] Konstan (2001) 58–9.

surface. For one thing it contains geographical variety within its condensed space, with four cities mentioned in the course of two sentences (although Pausanias' writing here is less digressive than the more anecdotal style which often carries us away from the physical space of the Altis in what follows).[140] There is also a fascinating profusion of categorizing criteria on show. The athletes are classified not only by topographical co-ordinates, which tie them to their communities and to their precise locations within the sanctuary (at least relative to the other statues surrounding them), but also by their age-categories, by their specialist events, and by their paternity. The artistic master-pupil relation of the final sentence then adds yet another way of categorizing, paralleling the father-son relations which precede it. All three of these men are thus linked with each other, and with the multitude of victors which follows, in a variety of ways. Chronological contiguity is also implied, by the fact that they share the same sculptor (although we should perhaps be careful about jumping to that conclusion given that some statues within the sanctuary seem to have been produced hundreds of years after the victories they celebrate). There is a constant impression, in other words, that these individual athletic victories are all part of a much larger network of interconnected Panhellenic activities and achievements.

Pausanias continues with similar effects, although his second paragraph emphasizes more firmly the fact that there are limits to the freedom with which we can draw links between different victors:

> The epigram on the statue of Kleogenes the son of Silenos says that he was one of the people of that country (τῶν ἐπιχωρίων) (i.e. an Elean), and that he won victory with a racehorse from his own herd. Near to Kleogenes lies Deinolochos son of Pyrrhos, and Troilos son of Alkinoos. Their origin too is from Elis, but their victories were not in the same things. Troilos happened to carry off victories in the chariot-race for full-grown horses and the chariot-race for foals when he was *hellanodikês*; he won in the hundred-and-second Olympiad, and from then the law came into being for the Eleans that none of those serving as *hellanodikês* should enter horses in the future; his statue was made by Lysippos. The mother of Deinolochos saw herself in a dream clasping her garlanded son to her breast, and for that reason Deinolochos was trained for the contest, and he outraced the other boys in running. The artist is Kleon of Sikyon. (6.1.4–5)[141]

---

[140] Sometimes Pausanias makes it hard to be sure whether the athlete under discussion is actually situated next his predecessor in the narrative, or whether he has digressed to talk about an athlete commemorated elsewhere in the sanctuary, for example at 6.6.3 (Paraballon) and 6.14.2–3 (Artemidoros); that effect may go some way towards explaining the divergence between different modern attempts to count the number of statues Pausanias refers to (Habicht (1985) 65 lists several different results).

[141] Κλεογένην δὲ Σιληνοῦ τὸ ἐπίγραμμα τὸ ἐπ' αὐτῶι φησιν εἶναι τῶν ἐπιχωρίων, ἐκ δὲ ἀγέλης αὑτὸν οἰκείας ἵππωι κρατῆσαι κέλητι. πλησίον δὲ τοῦ Κλεογένους Δεινόλοχός τε κεῖται

Once again we see a cluster of men from Elis, reminiscent of the cluster of Elean victors in Phlegon's fragment for the 177th Olympiad, and matched by many Elean groups later in Pausanias' text. The mention of Kleogenes' locally bred horse intensifies the sense of geographical concentration here. And the mention of another artist from Sikyon, so soon after the final sentence of 6.1.3, suggests another tie with the group of figures which has come before. However, the narrative also attempts to close down certain categorizational possibilities at this point. Pausanias cautions us against jumping to conclusions, in noting that Deinolochos and Troilos did not win in the same events, despite the fact that they were from the same city. There are limits, it seems, to the number of connections between adjacent statues. The narrative here reminds us that Panhellenic interconnectedness is based on something more subtle and inscrutable than the principle that everything is directly linked with everything else. We even see the Eleans themselves restricting those who are tempted to belong to too many categories at once, imposing boundaries between officialdom and competition. The later narrative, similarly, several times refers to punishments meted out to athletes who have attempted to change citizenship,[142] as if stressing the dangers of being overwhelmed by Panhellenism, the dangers of a situation where everything is so easily interconnected with everything else that it becomes almost impossible to guarantee individuality. The mention of Deinolochos' mother's dream, finally, opens a theme of divine inspiration, which is picked up in frequent later references to the numinous powers of deceased athletes and their statues.[143] These athletes have links with divine powers which take them beyond the normal level of mortal achievement, giving them an air of inaccessibility and unreality, even while mention of their Elean origins familiarizes them, reminding us that their statues are not so far from from the ground they trod while they were still alive.

The opening of Book 6 thus offers us the first threads of a web of mutual correspondences which will become more and more intricate

Πύρρου καὶ Τρωίλος Ἀλκίνου. τούτοις γένος μὲν καὶ αὐτοῖς ἐστιν ἐξ Ἤλιδος, γεγόνασι δέ σφισιν οὐ κατὰ ταὐτὰ αἱ νῖκαι· ἀλλὰ τῶι μὲν ἑλλανοδικεῖν τε ὁμοῦ καὶ ἵππων ὑπῆρξεν ἀνελέσθαι νίκας τῶι Τρωίλωι τελείαι τε συνωρίδι καὶ πώλων ἅρματι· ὀλυμπιάδι δὲ ἐκράτει δευτέραι πρὸς ταῖς ἑκατόν, ἀπὸ τούτου δὲ καὶ νόμος ἐγένετο Ἠλείοις μηδὲ ἵππους τοῦ λοιποῦ τῶν ἑλλανοδικούντων καθιέναι μηδένα· τούτου μὲν δὴ τὸν ἀνδριάντα ἐποίησε Λύσιππος· ἡ δὲ τοῦ Δεινολόχου μήτηρ εἶδεν ὄψιν ὀνείρατος ὡς ἔχοιτο τοῦ παιδὸς ἐν τοῖς κόλποις ἐστεφανωμένου, καὶ τοῦδε ἕνεκα ἐς τὸν ἀγῶνα ὁ Δεινόλοχος ἠσκήθη καὶ τοὺς παῖδας παρέθει τρέχων. Σικυωνίου δὲ Κλέωνός ἐστιν <ἡ> εἰκών.

[142] E.g., see 6.2.2–3; 6.13.1; 6.18.6; cf. 6.2.6 where an athlete dedicates his victory for his own city, resisting bribery.
[143] E.g. see 6.6.4–11; 6.8.2; 6.9.3; 6.9.6–8; 6.11.2–9.

as the book proceeds. However, Pausanias also foregrounds the way in which those correspondences obey certain laws and restrictions. We cannot automatically recapture the real figures lying behind the statues, nor can we force our own view of indiscriminate Panhellenic interconnectedness on to this material. Rather we must wait and see what emerges from it.

There is space here only to indicate some of the most notable moments within Pausanias' continuation of those effects in the long narrative which follows. At times we find him hinting at much more unusual links, rather than restricting himself to the conventional co-ordinates – paternity, age category, and so on – which he has introduced in his opening sentences. In 6.4.1–2, for example, we are shown the statue of a Sikyonian pankratiast, Sostratos, who was nicknamed 'Akrochersites' ('Finger-breaker'), because he used to fight by breaking his opponents' fingers until they submitted. Next to him (6.4.3–4) is a wrestler, Leontiskos from Messene in Sicily. He, too, used a finger-breaking style of fighting; in fact Pausanias tells us that he did not even know how to throw his opponents to the ground, so heavily did he depend upon that unconventional method. As usual, Pausanias does not make it clear whether this bizarre juxtaposition is coincidental, or whether it is due to deliberate thematic arrangement of the statues within the Altis. But it is hard to avoid the impression from his text that links of this sort would emerge however the statues were arranged, simply because of the mysterious richness of the Panhellenic system in which they all participate.

The Panhellenic space of the Altis also brings together figures who would not normally be joined. There is surely some humour in the matter-of-fact way in which Pausanias (in 6.4.8) juxtaposes a man named Molpion, said by his inscription to have been crowned by the Eleans – that is all the information we are given – and a statue said to be of the philosopher Aristotle, introduced as 'Aristotle, the one from Stageira in Thrace' ('Ἀριστοτέλης . . . ὁ ἐκ τῶν Θραικίων Σταγείρων), as if we might mistake him for some athlete or other without that further explanation. Here, athletes and philosophers alike are part of a continuum of Hellenic excellence.[144] There is another interesting intrusion into the stream of athletic and horse-racing victors at 6.18.2–6, where Pausanias introduces the statue of the historian Anaximenes: 'who compiled in one place all the ancient things of Greece (τὰ ἐν Ἕλλησιν ἀρχαῖα . . . συνέγραψεν ὁμοίως ἅπαντα), and the deeds of Philip son of Amyntas, and after him

---

[144] Gorgias is similarly listed in harness with a boys' wrestling victor (6.17.7–9).

of Alexander' (6.18.2).¹⁴⁵ Much of that description applies equally well to Pausanias' own text, recalling his aim of bringing together 'all Greek things' (πάντα ... τὰ Ἑλληνικά) at 1.26.4.¹⁴⁶ He seems to be making an oblique claim here for the Panhellenic status of his own work, not only as a text which can contain within itself all of the victors he lists, along with a diverse range of other individuals, but also as an achievement which deserves to be honoured in the same way, and which will allow him to participate in their Panhellenic glory.

The final statues of Pausanias' catalogue, just a few lines after the end of his account of Anaximenes, turn out to be the very first athletic statues ever put up in the Altis. Through his description of them Pausanias reminds us again of both the presence and absence of the athletic past:

> The first statues of athletes dedicated at Olympia were of Praxidamas the Aiginetan, who won at boxing in the fifty-ninth Olympiad, and the Opuntian Rhexibios who defeated the other pankratiasts at the 61st Olympiad. These statues stand not far from the pillar of Oinomaos, and they are made from wood, that of Rhexibios from fig-wood, and that of the Aiginetan from cypress, and his statue is less decayed than the other one. (6.18.7)¹⁴⁷

The reference to the pillar of Oinomaos gives us an independent landmark within the space of the Altis, allowing us to reorientate ourselves in relation to the physical world (the only other opportunity being at the Leonidaion at 6.17.1, as noted above) as we emerge once again from the self-contained trail of victor statues, with their disorientating proliferation of hypertextual possibilities. Pausanias here advertises again his resistance to the model of Olympic chronography, inverting conventional chronographical order by ending at the beginning. In doing so he portrays his own text as a journey back towards the past (even though most of his preceding narrative has never conformed to any chronological pattern explicitly), just as the development of the festival itself is represented as a gradual movement back towards authenticity, in the passage quoted above from 5.8.5. At the same time, however, it is striking that his backward progress must come to a halt at the 59th Olympiad, more than 200 years after foundation, frustrating any efforts to go further. The final reference to the statues' decay gives a startling

---

¹⁴⁵ ὃς τὰ ἐν Ἕλλησιν ἀρχαῖα, καὶ ὅσα Φίλιππος ὁ Ἀμύντου καὶ ὕστερον Ἀλέξανδρος εἰργάσατο, συνέγραψεν ὁμοίως ἅπαντα.
¹⁴⁶ Discussed by Porter (2001) 68–9.
¹⁴⁷ Πρῶται δὲ ἀθλητῶν ἀνετέθησαν ἐς Ὀλυμπίαν εἰκόνες Πραξιδάμαντός τε Αἰγινήτου νικήσαντος πυγμῆι τὴν ἐνάτην ὀλυμπιάδα ἐπὶ ταῖς πεντήκοντα καὶ Ὀπουντίου Ῥηξιβίου παγκρατιαστὰς καταγωνισαμένου μιᾶι πρὸς ταῖς ἑξήκοντα ὀλυμπιάδι· αὗται κεῖνται μὲν αἱ εἰκόνες οὐ πρόσω τῆς Οἰνομάου κίονος, ξύλου δέ εἰσιν εἰργασμέναι, Ῥηξιβίου μὲν συκῆς, ἡ δὲ τοῦ Αἰγινήτου κυπαρίσσου καὶ ἧσσον τῆς ἑτέρας πεπονηκυῖά ἐστιν.

vision of the traces of the past imperceptibly but relentlessly crumbling away from view.

The rest of the book is taken up with an account of several areas not yet mentioned, including the treasuries next to the Temple of Hera, and the *stadion* and hippodrome; followed by an account of the city of Elis and the territory around it. In 6.26.6, finally, Pausanias leaves Elis, and mentions briefly the fact that the territory surrounding the city is well-suited to the cultivation of flax. This was one of the first points he had made about the land in Book 5 (5.5.2), and that ring-composition takes him back to the edges of his narrative, mirroring his movement back towards the edges of Elean territory. However, it also gives him the opportunity of moving into an intriguing and not obviously relevant ethnographical digression, as he contrasts the flax and hemp grown in lands like this one with the fine thread which is produced from insects by the people of Seria, whose obscure and exotic origins he then debates. Even as he is about to come up against territorial boundaries, he here proclaims his own ability to go beyond them in the most ambitious and geographically unbounded way imaginable. The ending of the book then follows abruptly:

That is how these things are said to be. When a man goes into Achaia (ἀνδρὶ ... ἐς Ἀχαίαν ἰόντι) from Elis there are one hundred and fifty-seven *stadioi* (στάδιοι) to the River Larisos, and the River Larisos is the boundary between the Eleans and the Achaians in our day; although the even older boundary used to be Cape Araxos on the coast. (6.26.10)[148]

There are familiar themes even in these short sentences, for example in the mention of changes in Elean boundary marking, with its implied awareness of discrepancies between the established facts of the present and the still traceable alienness of the past, lying behind what is taken for granted in the contemporary world. It is hard, too, to avoid the impression that we might have the athletic material of the rest of the book still ringing in our ears as we leave Olympia behind us. The word 'man' (ἀνδρί), and the reference to *stadioi* as units of measurement, respectively recall the age categorizations and the athletic events (especially the *stadion* race) which we have heard about so often in the preceding narrative, casting Pausanias himself, and perhaps his reader as well, as athletes returning from the festival. Pausanias' geographical activity is thus portrayed as an elevated version of the struggles of the Olympic running races. We are reminded,

---

[148] Ταῦτα μὲν δὴ οὕτω λέγεται· ἀνδρὶ δὲ ἐς Ἀχαῖαν ἰόντι ἐξ Ἤλιδος ἑπτὰ καὶ πεντήκοντα στάδιοι καὶ ἑκατὸν ἐπὶ ποταμόν εἰσι Λάρισον, καὶ Ἠλείοις ὅροι πρὸς Ἀχαιοὺς τῆς χώρας ὁ ποταμός ἐστιν ἐφ' ἡμῶν ὁ Λάρισος· τὰ δὲ ἔτι ἀρχαιότερα ἄκρα σφίσι πρὸς θαλάσσῃ ὅρος ἦν ὁ Ἄραξος.

too, of how the language and convention of Olympic competition are deeply ingrained in the way we measure out our own movements through the world of present-day Greece, movements which may at first sight seem too mundane to deserve any Olympic comparison, but which themselves have the potential to participate in an imagined community of centuries-old Panhellenic tradition, if only we can learn to see the world the way Pausanias does.

Athletic commemoration was not only about setting moral examples and proclaiming civic loyalties. It was also, I believe, a way of advertising membership of an imagined Panhellenic community which stretched back over many centuries. That effect was common to the practice of inscribing records of athletic victory and the practice of structuring historical compilations with reference to catalogues of Olympic victors. Crucially, however, the imagery of Panhellenism was often veined with an awareness of its own inaccessibility and instability. Athletic festivals advertised their own mimicry of the Olympic *agôn*, drawing on Panhellenic tropes in boasting of the geographical range of competitors they had attracted, while also implicitly acknowledging the ultimate inimitability of the Olympic paradigm. The Panhellenic dating system attempted to accommodate the modern world, for example through writing the Roman Empire into an already existing vision of worldwide community, but chronographic texts like Phlegon's often also recognize the fragility of that project. The rows of victory statues which filled so many Greek cities had the function of perpetuating and broadcasting the achievement of individuals, and proclaiming their relevance beyond the bounds of the city, but also served to elevate them, shutting them off within their own glorious but barely accessible community. Through the athletic statue, I have suggested, the Greek past was made present, but also remained tantalizingly absent at the same time. Even Olympia itself sometimes showed signs of strain in its projected unity between ancient tradition and contemporary practice.

Those tendencies, I suggest, fit closely with some of the most characteristic features of Pausanias' own attempt at Panhellenic systematization. Central to that attempt is a vision of the contradictions between mysterious presence and frustrating inaccessibility which saturate the traces of the Greek past as it survives within the second century AD world. In Books 5 and 6 of his *Periegesis*, at the very centre of his work, he draws on and extends the conventions of athletic Panhellenism – in ways which have never been fully appreciated within modern accounts of Pausanias' work – in order to articulate this distinctive vision through his portrayal of the brilliant but half-vanished glory of Olympia's dazzlingly interrelated community of victory statues. Despite his neglect of the physical characteristics of the statuesque bodies which confront him, Pausanias' description of the Olympic Altis is a profoundly and paradigmatically athletic account, not only in its insistence on the highly charged attractions and glories of the fleeting moment of athletic victory, and of the traces it leaves behind it; but also in its insistence on the exhilarating difficulties any observer will have in seeing beneath the inscrutable surface of those traces, and in recapturing or fixing the momentary impressions of perfect Panhellenic community which they seem to promise.

CHAPTER 5

Silius Italicus and the athletics of Rome

> Marcellus shouted, thrusting the hesitant squadrons forward with the boss of his shield: 'Press forward, mow down this unwarlike herd, cut them down with your swords. Through their slothful study of wrestling (*pigro luctandi studio*), these men are erudite (*docta*) in the endurance of soft contests (*certamen . . . molle*) in the shade. They are only happy when they are shining with oil. Look at them, the cowardly youth of Syracuse. What a meagre prize for victors in battle! The only chance of glory you have is that the enemy might admit defeat just through looking at you.'
>
> (Silius Italicus, *Punica* 14.134–9)[1]

GREEK ATHLETICS AND ROMAN STEREOTYPES

My aim in this chapter is to examine some of the ways in which Greek athletic activity spread to the west of the Empire, and some of the many ways in which the inhabitants of the west reacted to it. In dealing with that subject I will not be suggesting that we can chart any clear progression in the degree of cultural overlap and interchange between east and west. For one thing, the model of gradually but steadily intensifying rapprochement between Greek and Roman culture throughout the first to third centuries AD is, I believe, an oversimplification of complex and varied patterns of shifting self-perception. Moreover, it would clearly be wrong to argue that the spread of 'Greek culture' is something which can be measured simply by charting the spread of typically Greek institutions. Recent cultural and archaeological scholarship has moved away from a straightforward association between 'style' and ethnicity, and it is now generally accepted that using the geographical distribution of culturally marked institutions, or of distinctive features of material culture, to chart the expansion of the

---

[1] '*ite, gregem metite imbellem ac succidite ferro!* | *clamat cunctantes urgens umbone catervas.* | *'pigro luctandi studio certamen in umbra* | *molle pati docta et gaudens splendescere olivo* | *stat, mediocre decus vincentum, ignava iuventus.* | *haec laus sola datur, si viso vincitis hoste.*'

'cultures' with which they are associated will lead to over-simplistic conclusions.[2] The very idea of cultural interchange as something quantifiable depends on a dubious model of 'cultures' as clearly defined units which can be mixed together with each other in reliably identifiable proportions. It ignores the fact that 'Greek culture' and 'Roman culture', like all 'cultures', were the product of a great range of different definitions and imaginings, made for a great range of different purposes, rather than entities with any objective reality (although that insight should not of course disguise the fact that they would often have been perceived as meaningful and consistent categories; in fact we shall see in everything which follows that Greekness and Romanness continued to be important as ideals, albeit ideals which were variably perceived, and as powerful conceptual markers by which individuals understood their own cultural and political inheritances).

Instead of seeing cultural interaction as a clearly quantifiable process it is, I believe, important to acknowledge the way in which the highly varied *responses* which accompanied cultural 'importations' in the Roman world played a crucial role in determining the contours of changing self-perceptions. I will argue here that the increasing visibility of stereotypically Greek practices and values in the west of the Empire was often significant above all for the fact that it prompted westerners to reflect on their *own* traditions and self-perceptions. The increasing popularity of athletics in the west, in other words, was not in any sense a straightforward reflection of increasing 'hellenization' of the western population; instead Greek athletic habits were incorporated and adapted and reconceived in a great range of different ways by different individuals and communities, and taken as a spur to confirmation or reassessment of existing self-perceptions, rather than as a vehicle for quantifiable and steadily increasing absorption of Greek culture.

For the purpose of this chapter my main focus will be on the city and literature of Rome itself, since there is not space here to deal in detail with the many different but equally complex spectacle cultures of any of the other urban centres of the western provinces, although I will give some hints about the way in which Rome's treatment of athletic activity related to the situation in southern Italy and Gaul. The extensive evidence we have for reactions to Greek culture within Rome backs up my point that Hellenic imports tended to be treated above all as starting-points for the display and exploration of Roman tradition. In the Republican and

---

[2] E.g., see Morris (2000) esp. 9–17; Woolf (1998) esp. 1–23; Jones (1997); Hall (1997) 17–33.

early-Imperial periods, for example, the ability to adopt Greek culture selectively was itself seen as a crucial skill for any educated Roman.[3] That ability required not only a high level of the right kind of education, but also a tactful sense of when Hellenic behaviour might or might not be appropriate, qualities which were represented as being specific to Roman elite culture. On that model, selective adoption of Hellenic habits may also have served to strengthen the significance of traditional icons of Roman identity by contrast, so reinforcing a sense of the individuality of Roman culture rather than diluting it.

These points about the workings of 'cultural interaction' have implications for the way we analyse stereotypes. Just as culturally marked practices and conventions become the focus for a great variety of reactions, so the forms those reactions most commonly take sometimes themselves act as provocative starting-points for discussion. Stereotypes, in other words, are used not only for reflecting and reinforcing established assumptions, but also for debating and re-evaluating them. The use of stereotypes within modern literature has recently been the focus of reassessment. Astrid Franke, for example, has analysed their use in American novels from the first half of the twentieth century in order to challenge the notion that stereotypes necessarily and straightforwardly reinforce the assumptions they proclaim.[4] She pays close attention to the interplay of stereotypes with other features of the texts they inhabit, in order to show how they can be refashioned creatively and inscribed with new significance, and thus in turn have the capacity to influence the cultural milieu from which they have arisen. And she demonstrates that stereotypes can be used – sometimes very self-consciously (for example within blatantly parodic representation) and sometimes more instinctively (by their recontextualization within unfamiliar narrative situations) – as starting-points for challenging cultural and social hierarchies as much as for restating them. I am not suggesting that stereotypes were always used and conceptualized in the ancient world in exactly the same way as they are now. I do believe, however, that they often had a similar capacity to play creative and provocative roles within ancient texts.

I am interested here especially in the stereotypically Roman criticisms of Greek athletic activity which resonate through Latin literature. These criticisms have been much documented,[5] and some modern scholars, in less guarded moments, have even taken them as straightforward reflections of widespread Roman opinion. Roman writers often suggest that the Greek

---

[3] See Wallace-Hadrill (1998).   [4] Franke (1999).
[5] E.g., see Müller (1995) 216–23; Mähl (1974), esp. 40–54; Harris (1972) 49–74; for more nuanced accounts of stereotyping in Roman encounters with Greece, see Gruen (1993) 260–71; Rawson (1992).

habit of unwarlike exercise in the *gymnasion* leads inevitably to luxury, which in turn has brought about the subjection of Greece to Roman rule. That anxiety is frequently linked with the Greek tradition of exercising nude,[6] and with the charge of effeminization, related to traditions of the Greek *gymnasion* as a venue for pederastic encounters.[7]

Clearly stereotypes do help to form common opinion, and it is no doubt the case that many Romans subscribed to the view that Greek gymnastic activity was a dangerous influence, at least when pursued to excess. It is striking, however, that many of the most clearly stated examples of Roman opposition to Greek athleticism occur in the context of highly tendentious accounts of Roman identity, as we shall see. Often, for example, conventional perceptions of Roman identity are challenged through the doubts which readers are prompted to feel about hackneyed expressions of long-standing prejudices. Such prejudices, in other words, tend to be used as objects of parody and debate more often than as 'sincere' expressions of opinion.

In some cases we see Greek writers using these stereotypes of Roman anti-athleticism in similarly complex ways. For example, Plutarch in his life of the archetypal Roman moralizer Cato the Elder reports Cato's vehement opposition to the Greek custom of exercising naked. Afterwards, however, he adds a short parenthesis which makes the picture much more complicated: 'having learned from the Greeks the practice of exercising naked, the Romans themselves in turn infected the Greeks with the habit of doing the same thing in the presence of women' (*Cato Maior* 20.8).[8] One effect of that addition is to challenge the assumption of Roman moral superiority which lies behind Cato's opinion. It also emphasizes the fact that Cato's reaction is far from typical, through the suggestion that Roman culture is in fact much more susceptible to moral corruption than its Greek equivalent.[9] Plutarch, in other words, gives us a stereotypical example of Roman objection to Greek athletics, but at the same time undermines the

---

[6] See Crowther (1980/1) for a survey of disapproving references to Greek nudity within Latin literature.
[7] See Williams (1999) 63–72.
[8] εἶτα μέντοι παρ' Ἑλλήνων τὸ γυμνοῦσθαι μαθόντες, αὐτοὶ πάλιν τοῦ καὶ μετὰ γυναικῶν τοῦτο πράσσειν ἀναπεπλήκασι τοὺς Ἕλληνας.
[9] This passage is discussed briefly by Gruen (1993) 75, who seems to me wrong to read this scathing comment as Cato's own, aimed 'primarily at his lapsed fellow countrymen'; the comment can equally well be read in Plutarch's own voice, as a characteristic reminder of the way in which morally admirable Greek custom is perverted in the west through being misunderstood; cf. Goldhill (2002) 261–3 on this passage; also 263–71 (cf. Goldhill (2001a) 1–2) on similar effects in Plutarch, *Roman Questions* 40 (=Miller 5). On Plutarch's sustained project of comparison between Greek and Roman culture in the *Parallel Lives*, see Duff (1999); Humbert (1991); Swain (1990); Pelling (1989); on similar effects in the *Greek* and *Roman Questions* see Preston (2001); Boulogne (1992) and (1987).

validity of that stereotype in the text which surrounds it – as so many of his Latin contemporaries also do – in a way which throws a spotlight on Roman culture, making it seem rather more complicated than it at first sight appears.

In the rest of this section I want to look in detail at just one (similarly challenging) Latin example of athletic stereotyping, in order to illustrate the way in which these tropes are often used by Roman writers to analyse the problems and developments of Roman identity. Tacitus, in *Annals* 14.20–1, describes Nero's foundation of the Neronian festival in AD 60, and some of the negative reactions which, according to his account, followed it. The Neronia, which was abolished after Nero's death, having been held only twice, was the first clearly attested Greek-style *agôn* established in Rome, as we shall see further in the next section.[10] It thus represented a crucial moment in the institutionalization of Greek athletics within Rome itself, a point which Tacitus acknowledges in discussing the festival's novelty for its Roman audience, and which is similarly stressed by Suetonius in his account of Nero's reign. I have chosen to look at this account here partly because it is one of the passages most often quoted in surveys of Roman attitudes to Greek athletic culture. In 14.20 we hear that many Romans criticized the festival as a sign of capitulation to foreign luxuries. They complain about the way in which the youth of Rome is exposed to corrupting influence – '*gymnasia* and idleness and disgraceful love affairs' (*gymnasia et otia et turpis amores*): 'What remained, they asked, but for the Roman leaders to strip their bodies and take up boxing gloves, and spend their time on boxing fights instead of military service and weapons?' (14.20).[11]

Perhaps the first thing to notice – a fairly straightforward point – is that this speech forms just one half of a debate, counterbalanced by the opinions of the festival's supporters in 14.21. These second speakers conceal their licentiousness behind a mask of propriety – 'they simulated honourable pretexts' (*honesta nomina praetendebant*) – and argue that a few days of frivolity cannot do the city any harm. At first sight, we might feel that Nero's later obsession with agonistic glory, and the moral decline which Tacitus, like others, associates with that, is enough to prove the first speakers right. Their scandalized question quoted above ('What remained...?' (*quid superesse...?*)) sounds like an ironic foreshadowing of Nero's later excesses, which in the end surpass their wildest suspicions. The things which 'remain'

---

[10] See Caldelli (1993) 37–43 for evidence on the Neronia; also Beacham (1999) 214–19.
[11] *quid superesse nisi ut corpora quoque nudent et caestus adsumant easque pugnas pro militia et armis meditentur?*

in store for Nero's Rome are worse than they could imagine. And yet in the short term the second speakers are right. They raise the possibility of a controlled and selective use of Greek spectacle culture within Rome, and their confidence seems to be justified by events, since the festival passes off without great disturbance. Tacitus even tells us that: 'the Greek dress, which many people had adopted during the days of the festival, afterwards died out' (14.21)',[12] an image which seems strikingly consistent with the idea that Greek behaviour was something which members of the Roman elite – at least according to their own idealized self-representations – could put on and off at will.

This juxtaposition of these two rival attitudes to Greek influence, at such a conspicuous moment in the city's – and the emperor's – institutional acceptance of Hellenic influence, thus raises questions which will be crucial for all of the narrative which follows, and which are central to Tacitus' broader project of exploring Neronian identities.[13] Is Nero's obsession with Greek competition a cause of his degeneration? Or is it his natural tendency to excess which causes him to misuse so monstrously something which is essentially harmless? Does the problem perhaps lie in his lack of restraint, in contrast with the second speakers, who at least know how to disguise their immorality beneath a veneer of Roman virtue?[14] And what is the long-term effect of all of these innovations on the city's moral health? Will Rome itself be able to throw off the cloak of Greek luxury with which Nero has smothered it, after his death, as easily as it removed the Greek clothing temporarily in fashion during the first Neronia? The last question especially surely has implications for Tacitus' contemporary readers, as they struggle to adjust themselves to Hadrian's Hellenic enthusiasms, which in some ways matched the intensity of Nero's own even though Hadrian also distanced himself from Nero's treatment of Hellenic tradition in many areas.[15]

That is not to suggest, however, that Tacitus' work dwells on the problems of philhellenism as a dominant theme. Rather he uses this stereotypical claim opportunistically within a narrative which is always ultimately about Rome, about imperial excess and the sycophancy which makes it possible.

---

[12] *Graeci amictus quis per eos dies plerique incesserant tum exoleverunt.*

[13] For discussion of this passage as part of a cumulative series of scenes exploring the influence of luxury and theatricality on Nero and on the people of Rome, see Mellor (1993) 52–3 and Aubrian (1990); however, both of them overestimate the extent to which disapproval of Nero's philhellenism is presented here as a straightforward expression of Tacitus' opinion.

[14] Ginsburg (1993) 87 uses this passage to illustrate the way in which the past is manipulated flexibly in the *Annals* to justify actions in the present.

[15] See Syme (1958) 515–19.

In doing so he seems to be interested as much in the hypocrisy of the second set of speakers, whose habit of self-serving accommodation to Nero's whims is one of the things which makes his later madness possible, as he is in the precise focus of their argument. Roman criticism of Hellenic *gymnasion*-culture becomes a peg on which to hang inward-looking Roman self-examination.

I have argued, then, that Greek athletics, and the stereotypes of Roman resistance to Greek athletics, were often highly charged starting-points both for defining *and* (in some cases) questioning the proper composition of elite Roman culture. In the two sections following this one I want to look mainly at ways in which those processes of Roman self-scrutiny were related to the agonistic innovations of individual emperors. And then in the final section I will draw together some of these ideas in discussing the way in which Roman epic poets, Silius Italicus especially, replay the scene of Greek-style funeral games, in imitation of the games for Patroclus in *Iliad* 23. The epic poems of the Flavian era are texts which on the surface seem to be less closely connected with real-life events and problems than the historical accounts of Suetonius and others which I will examine. And yet the fact that both Statius and Silius had close contact with Domitian, and the fact that both of their poems were published soon after Domitian's foundation of the Capitolia – the first long-lasting Greek *agôn* within Rome, founded in AD 86 – might make us doubtful about that conclusion. My argument here will be that these writers engage closely with that background by replaying scenes of Greek athletic activity in ways which comment on traditional Roman virtues and their relation with contemporary realities; and that variations between their agonistic narratives articulate wider differences between the cultural projects their poems represent.

The marks of Roman stereotypes are visible even within these poems, as this chapter's opening quotation from Silius Italicus shows. Here, too, the stereotype turns out to be a vehicle of debate, rather than a simple reflection of Silius' or even the speaker's opinion. The passage quoted is a short speech by the Roman general, Marcellus, encouraging his troops as they face battle with the Syracusan allies of Hannibal. He mocks the enemy for the unwarlike effeminacy which they have learned in the *gymnasion*, ironically applying the imagery of Greek erudition (*pigro luctandi studio* ('slothful study of wrestling'); *docta* ('erudite')) to their luxurious skills, and commenting scathingly on conventional comparisons between warfare and athletics, through the repetition of the word *certamen* ('contest'), to expose their contemptible (and stereotypically Greek) inadequacy for the contests of war. The final image, in line 139, intensifies that point, twisting the boasts commonly made by victorious athletes (Markos Aurelios Asklepiades among them, as we have seen) that their opponents have withdrawn from combat through fear at the ceremony of lot-drawing, before any fighting has taken place. In the same way, Marcellus suggests, these Greek athletes from Syracuse will be defeated by the very sight of the advancing Roman army. And yet Silius complicates Marcellus' distinction between effeminate, athletic Greeks and manly Romans elsewhere in his poem, as we shall see later, not least by describing Scipio's orchestration of a Greek-style *agôn* (of sorts) for the Roman army two books afterwards. These two scenes, as I will argue, between them form small parts of a much larger, sustained exploration of the relation between the Roman Republican identity of Scipio and his compatriots, and the contemporary and mythical alternatives against which that identity is implicitly set.

This chapter is thus structured in the same way as the other chapters of the book, in setting detailed exploration of a single text – Silius Italicus' *Punica* – against the background of a wide range of other representations. It differs from the others, however, in the fact that Silius' work – even the short section of it from Book 16 which is my main focus – is not 'about' athletics in the sense that the Greek texts of the rest of the book are. Silius' funeral games are only a very minor part of a poem which ranges over a broad canvas of military and political and social interaction in many different settings. I would go so far as to suggest, in fact, that none of the Latin writers of the Roman Empire who address the athletic ideals and anxieties of Greek tradition chooses to take those ideals and anxieties as their main subject, in contrast with many of the Greek writers of the same period. Instead, athletics within Roman literature tends to be more cursory, more incidental, a topic to take up and set down at will, much as the Romans of *Annals* 14 take up Greek dress for the Neronia and then set it down immediately afterwards. Athletics in Latin literature is always a peg for discussing Roman problems and values, an imported starting-point for inward-looking response, rather than a subject for extended discussion in its own right.

ATHLETIC INSTITUTIONS IN ROME

The first thing I want to do here is to outline some of the major developments in the growing institutionalization of Greek athletics within Rome. As we shall see, the earliest Roman appropriations of Greek athletics tended to advertise their Roman characteristics conspicuously. As time went on, there was a gradual move towards a more 'faithful' borrowing of Greek customs, but even then – even when Greek conventions came to be imitated more closely – Roman appropriations of Greek athletics still tended to be presented as expressions of Roman identity and Roman control, veined with subtle reminders of how they had been adapted for their new western context. One of my aims here is to challenge commonly expressed modern assumptions about a close rapprochement between Greek and Roman elite culture in the second century AD and afterwards. If the Roman uses of athletic culture are anything to go by, 'Greekness' and 'Romanness' continued to be envisaged as distinctive and separate categories in many circumstances. In some cases Romans used Greek athletic custom paradoxically to advertise the continuing independence of Roman culture from outside influence. In other cases, by contrast, questions about the degree of Hellenic influence implied by the practices in question seem to have aroused only minimal interest, displaced by the tendency to use debates about athletics as a convenient vehicle for commenting on issues which were specific to Roman society.

First, though, a quick glance at the situation in the east of the Empire, which I hope will help to clarify the situation in the west by comparison. Does imperial influence extend to the athletics of the east? And are there signs of a desire to adapt western influence which parallel Roman adaptations of Greek agonistic culture? For the first question the answer is certainly yes. The second is less clear-cut. Signs of imperial cult and even direct imperial intervention are hard to miss within the institutional history of eastern athletics, but the desire to mitigate the effects of outside influence on traditions of entertainment seems to have been less conspicuous than it was in the west. Nevertheless there are, I suggest, some signs of attempts to reassert local tradition and local initiative in reaction to that influence.

Roman involvement in the festivals of the Greek cities began to make itself felt on a large scale many years before the foundations of Augustus. There is extensive evidence for Roman influence on the major Panhellenic sites, Olympia especially, as I showed in the previous chapter.[16] Small numbers of Roman competitors also seem to have been allowed to compete in Greek *agones* from an early date (although the exact circumstances of such participation are hard to reconstruct, since many of these athletes are known to us only from unelaborated victory inscriptions).[17] From 189 BC onwards

---

[16] See esp. Scanlon (2002) 40–63.

[17] That point is made briefly by Caldelli (1993) 19; for one prominent example of such authorization, see Polybius 2.12.8 (=Miller 134) on the Corinthian decision to allow Roman competitors at the Isthmian games from the late third century BC; I discussed one Roman victor briefly in chapter four (p. 168), from the festival of the Romaia at Xanthos.

a huge number of festivals were founded in honour of the city of Rome, which was the object of cult worship throughout the east. These *agones* were usually named as 'Romaia', and grafted on to existing local festivals, by local initiative.[18] We also hear of a number of Republican Roman generals holding *agones* in the east to celebrate their own victories, in a small-scale anticipation of the later rush of imperial initiatives, although these triumphal festivals were always one-off events.[19] During the Imperial period, Roman approval became increasingly important for all festival foundations, not least because permission for 'sacred' status lay in the power of the emperor.[20] Roman officials took an interest in such things in part because of the financial implications of festival funding.[21] Moreover, imperial cult was regularly accommodated within local festival structures.[22] On the whole, Roman influence of this sort seems to have been tolerated, at least without the kind of resistance which would make its mark in the archaeological or epigraphical record, although we do see occasional signs of conflict between local and imperial officials, for example in debate over the form to be taken by new festivals.[23]

Long-standing Roman practices of spectacular display and physical recreation also found their way east, and were absorbed eagerly, apparently in ways which were not widely perceived as posing a threat to the integrity of Greek identity, at least if we are to judge by the evidence of literary and epigraphical material (although admittedly that evidence can give access to only a tiny fraction of the spectrum of reactions these things would have provoked). Roman-style bath-buildings were built and heavily used in most Greek cities, often grafted on to *gymnasion* buildings.[24] Gladiatorial

---

[18] See Mellor (1975), esp. 165–80 for a survey of the inscriptional evidence for 'Romaia' festivals; Price (1984) 40–7, who sets the cult of Rome in the context of other forms of cult worship of the Roman authorities; cf. Gruen (1984) 177–9; and for vivid discussion of the possible circumstances of foundation of one such festival, Robert (1978a) 288–9 (with reference to BE 1950 no. 183 (pp. 188–9)) on the inscription from the Romaia at Xanthos which I analysed briefly in chapter four (pp. 166–8).

[19] E.g., see Edmondson (1999) and Ferrary (1988) 547–72 on the *agôn* held by the Roman general L. Aemilius Paullus at Amphipolis in 167 BC (attested by Livy 45.32.8–11); Ferrary characterizes these as the first authentically Greek-style games held by a Roman general (although he also notes (561–2) the nominal *agonothesia* of Flamininus at the Nemean games of 195 BC). He contrasts them with a number of other less obviously 'Hellenic' spectacles organized by Roman generals before then, including the (at least partly gladiatorial) games held by Scipio in 206 BC in Sicily; those games of Scipio are described by Silius Italicus in *Punica* Book 16, in the passage which will form the main focus of this chapter's final section.

[20] As discussed in chapter four (pp. 164–5), with reference to Robert's (1977) analysis of Commodus' festival grants in Bithynia.

[21] See Mitchell (1990) 190.   [22] See Price (1984), esp. 101–32.

[23] E.g. see Rogers (1991a), esp. 140–3 and (1991b), discussed in chapter two (p. 71).

[24] See Farrington (1995) and (1987), esp. 117–44; Yegül (1992) 250–313.

games and wild beast shows were held throughout the Greek east to widespread acclaim in the Imperial period,[25] and were often listed together with Greek agonistic events in inscriptions honouring wealthy men with lists of their benefactions.[26] These events were regularly held in theatres and *stadia*, many of which, especially in Asia Minor, were rebuilt in architectural styles of western origin.[27] Many of the Greek terms used to describe gladiatorial activity were borrowed from athletic vocabulary.[28] There are some criticisms of gladiatorial games by Greek authors,[29] but surprisingly few of those express explicit disapproval of their Roman connotations.[30] Greg Woolf has discussed that phenomenon in demonstrating that material culture played a less important role in Greek than in Roman self-definition, one result being that western leisure and entertainment practices – which were often accompanied by the distinctive architectural forms so prominent in the material record – were widely accepted in the east.[31]

However, that formulation should not disguise the fact that tensions between gladiatorial imports and ancient Panhellenic traditions always had the potential to resurface, and that gladiatorial combat never seems to have lost its potential to be viewed as a distinctively Roman custom, even if that potential was submerged in the majority of the contexts we have access to. Greek writers do sometimes hint disapprovingly at the modernness and the western origins of these events, as I argued in chapter two with reference to Lucian's *Anacharsis*; and close juxtaposition of Roman-style games with ancient Greek agonistic customs seems to have been one of the things most likely to stir up adverse comment on their innovatory status amongst Greek philosophers and moralists. Dio Chrysostom's criticism (in *Oratio* 31.121) of the way in which his Athenian contemporaries hold gladiatorial games within the theatre of Dionysus, one of the great agonistic centres of Greek tradition, is a good example. Many of the authors whose criticisms of gladiators survive compare the things they are criticizing with the gladiatorial enthusiasms of the city of Corinth,[32] whose status as a hybrid Greek-Roman city, famous for its mixed spectacle culture, was well known,

---

[25] See Robert (1940).
[26] There are many examples of this (too many to list here) in the catalogue of gladiatorial inscriptions made by Robert (1940) 75–237; notable examples include no. 15 (pp. 81–2) and no. 86 (pp. 135–7).
[27] See Welch (1999) and (1998).   [28] See Robert (1940), esp. 16–23.
[29] E.g., see Robert (1940) 248–53, who warns against the danger of taking them, as many people have done, as signs of widespread Greek feeling about Roman forms of entertainment.
[30] See Swain (1996) 417–21.   [31] Woolf (1994), esp. 126–30.
[32] E.g., Dio Chrysostom 31.121; Lucian, *Demonax* 57; Philostratus, *VA* 4.22; Corinth is criticized in Ps.-Julian *Ep.* 198 for its juxtaposition of Roman-style *venationes* with the ancient Panhellenic traditions of the Isthmian festival (discussed briefly in chapter four, p. 191, n. 119; see also Spawforth (1994)).

as I have argued in chapter four. That repeated link with Corinth, I believe, is a sign that moralizing resistance to gladiatorial games and suspicion of Roman novelties were sometimes implicitly connected with each other.[33] These passages, in other words, illustrate vividly the way in which generally smooth acceptance – at least within the epigraphical and literary record – of Roman influence over eastern spectacle culture was veined with occasional anxiety, very much like the tensions which clustered around the importation of Greek athletics into Rome, albeit on a strikingly smaller scale.

In Rome we see much clearer signs of the impulse towards ostentatious adjustment of foreign influence which I have argued leaves only quiet traces in the spectacle record of the eastern half of the Empire. In the Republican period, for example, Greek athletes were occasionally brought into the city to perform in public spectacles.[34] That often involved significant distortion of traditional Greek practice, for instance by presentation of Greek athletic contests in combination with gladiatorial combat. For example, M. Fulvius Nobilior held *ludi* at Rome in 186 BC after his campaign in Aitolia.[35] These included performances by actors and athletes from Greece, as well as *venationes* (wild animal shows). Others followed his example sporadically. Sulla held games in Rome in 80 BC to celebrate his victory over Mithridates, attracting (or perhaps coercing) so many Greek athletes that the Olympic games were nearly put out of action for the year.[36] That gesture must have been at least as much about advertising Roman subjection of Greece, in line with Sulla's plundering of Panhellenic sites, Delphi especially,[37] as it was a reflection of growing Hellenic influence over Roman culture and of the 'philhellenic' interests of Sulla himself.[38] We also have evidence for athletic performances organized by M. Aemilius Scaurus in 58, Pompey in 55, C. Scribonius Curio in 53, and Julius Caesar in 46 BC. These triumphal games of Caesar, as described by Suetonius, mixed athletic contests with gladiatorial combat, plays, chariot races, and even a mock naval battle,[39] in

---

[33] See König (2001) 148–53 for a longer discussion of these issues.
[34] Caldelli (1993) 15–18 catalogues the recorded instances of this; as does Crowther (1983); Müller (1995) 207–23 discusses these developments in the context of Rome's broader cultural and political relationship with Greece; Thuillier (1982) distinguishes between the appearances of professional Greek boxers cited here, and the frequent earlier appearance of non-Greek boxers within the Roman *ludi*; the latter were perhaps connected with Etruscan sporting practices which Thuillier elsewhere ((1996a) and (1993) 15–36) sees as an important influence on Roman spectacle.
[35] See Livy 39.22.1–2 (=Miller 135).   [36] See Scanlon (2002) 42.
[37] E.g., see Plutarch, *Sulla* 12.1–6 and 19.6 (=Miller 136).
[38] Cf. Derow (1990) 200 for doubts about the claim made by Ferrary (1988) that 'philhellenism' was the most important motive for the games of Aemilius Paullus which I discussed above.
[39] See Suetonius, *Divus Iulius* 39 (=Miller 142).

a combination which would have been almost unthinkable for any Greek civic festival in this period.

The connection of displays of this sort with triumphal celebrations of Roman victory in the east suggests that they functioned partly as advertisements for the all-controlling superiority of Roman military might, and for the territorial acquisitions of the individual Roman generals who orchestrated them.[40] By that model, the athletes who appeared within Republican spectacles were put in the position of exotic foreign curiosities. The Greek practice of exercising nude (whether within day-to-day physical training or within public athletic combat) does not seem to have been followed within Roman tradition, although it is not at all clear how long Roman resistance to that Greek custom lasted.[41] If these early athletes did appear naked in the *ludi* (games) of Republican Rome that would presumably have enhanced the aura of alienness attached to them. Paradoxically, in other words, the display of Greek conventions in their 'authentic' form led to distortion of that 'authenticity', since it marked out the exotic outsider status of Greek athletes within Rome, a status which was inconsistent with the civic focus of agonistic festivals in the cities of the east, where competitors were nearly always citizens of Greek cities, often of the city holding the festival itself.

There were also signs of interest in Greek *gymnasion* culture within Rome. However, Roman models for physical training often diverged from their Greek equivalents, which tended to be more firmly bound up with the training of young men in their duties as citizens.[42] Similarly, Greek athletic statues were often used to decorate private spaces within Roman houses, far removed from their original contexts of civic dedication.[43] In one of his letters (*Letters to Atticus* 1.10) Cicero asks his friend Atticus to send statues of Hermes, to be placed in the *palaistra* and *gymnasion* within Cicero's own house.[44] Much of Cicero's writing contains criticism of Greek

---

[40] See Caldelli (1993) 18, esp. n. 47.
[41] Thuillier (1996a) 140–1, (1988) and (1982) 115 argues for resistance to Greek-style nudity amongst Romans in their own practice of athletics, in contrast with the nudity of imported Greek athletes on display in Republican *ludi*; like Crowther (1980/1), however, he also suggests that there may have been some softening in that resistance over time, if we are to judge by the decreasing frequency of negative judgements of Greek nudity within Latin literature.
[42] The Roman institution of the *collegia iuvenum* did have some parallels with the Greek system of training (physical and otherwise) for ephebes and *neoi*, but it is hard to find any close resemblance or specific evidence for mutual influence between them, and *collegia iuvenum* were in some elements firmly marked as western institutions, for example by the occasional participation of aristocratic *pueri* in the *Lusus Troiae*: see Vanoyeke (1992) 69–70; Ginestet (1991); Kleijwegt (1991) 101–16.
[43] See Newby (forthcoming); Neudecker (1988) 60–4.
[44] =Miller 141; discussed by Marvin (1993) 161–7, along with other letters related to this one, with translation of all the relevant texts in an appendix (180–4).

athletics,[45] and this request to Atticus is at first sight surprising. However, Cicero seems to be more interested in exercising cultured connoisseurship, and in exploiting the philosophical associations of the *gymnasion*, than in taking seriously its role as a place of physical training and education. He also departs from the Greek model of the *gymnasion* and *palaistra* as civic institutions, or at least institutions which were open for public use, even when they were privately owned. In that sense this letter gives a far from unusual illustration of Roman selectiveness in the adaptation of Greek custom.

In some areas, however, traditional Greek practice was more closely (if not always scrupulously) followed, increasingly so from the first century AD. That was especially the case within the many *agones* of Rome which were founded to play a prominent role within the Greek agonistic calendar, and which gradually transformed the city into a major Greek athletic centre. Many viewers within Rome would surely have sensed differences of framing between the appearance of athletes within *ludi* (events which were traditionally associated with the oldest moments of Roman history, as Livy and others suggest),[46] or within gladiatorial *munera* (one of whose functions seems to have been the display of Roman virtues, albeit in highly ambiguous form, within gladiatorial combat),[47] and the ambitious recreations of Greek agonistic contexts which Nero and Domitian and others attempted.[48]

The sporadically held *agones* of Rome thus tended to have conspicuous Greek overtones, in contrast with the city's more usual entertainments. And yet it turns out to be hard to draw an absolute dividing line between the style of Roman *ludi* and Greek *agones* within Rome, since even these latter more 'authentically' Greek events seem often to have been accompanied by a sense that the Hellenic role-playing they involved should have conspicuous limits, as Tacitus' image of the abandonment of Greek dress at the end of the first Neronian festival suggests. Nero's reputation for failing to observe those limits may even have provoked a more urgent sense of their importance. Moreover, even in the *agones* of Rome we find some significant

---

[45] See Crowther (2001b); however, he challenges the assumption that Cicero was unreservedly hostile to Greek athletics; cf. Rawson (1992) 25, notes 11–13.

[46] E.g., see Livy 1.9.6–14 and 1.35.7–10, discussed well by Helen Lovatt (forthcoming) on Statius, *Thebaid* Book 6.

[47] On gladiators and Roman identity, see (amongst others) Plass (1995) esp. 1–54; Toner (1995) 34–52; Wiedemann (1992); Hopkins (1983) 1–30, esp. 29; Müller (1995) 224–95 draws on much of the same material to argue for a fairly clear-cut contrast between Roman experiences of athletic and gladiatorial spectatorship.

[48] Cf. Robert (1970) 7, who insists on the distinction between *ludi* and *agones*, with criticism of Arnold (1960) 246; Caldelli (1993) 9–15 makes the same distinction.

departures from the Greek models on which these festivals were based, as we shall see in a moment for the Capitolia. The blurring of those boundaries is perhaps most obvious of all in the case of the *ludi pro valetudine Caesaris*, games held every four years in honour of Caesar, from 30 BC. The scheduling of this event fails to fit neatly into either of the two categories I have been working with up till now, and its exact status is debated.[49] Most significantly, it seems to have included gladiatorial events, unlike the *agones* of the Greek east, but it may also have been counted as a legitimate component of the Greek agonistic calendar, if we are to judge by (admittedly inconclusive) evidence for its mention in at least one Greek victory inscription.[50]

The Capitolia exemplifies these patterns well.[51] It was founded in AD 86, to include musical and equestrian events as well as athletics. It formed the first permanent Roman contribution to the Greek festival programme, and as such represented a turning-point in Rome's agonistic history, preparing the way for Greek athletic activity to play a more familiar and prominent role within the city's public life,[52] and opening the floodgates to a number of other Greek foundations in Rome during the next two centuries.[53] It was widely represented as part of the agonistic circuit in Greek victory inscriptions. Domitian's construction of Rome's first Greek-style *stadion*-building for the occasion may also have contributed to that impression of the festival's Hellenic character.[54] And the Capitolia's Hellenic characteristics were accompanied by distinctively Roman innovations, including the participation of freedmen in the musical competitions, use of the Roman circus building for horse events rather than the Greek-style hippodrome, and the introduction of *factiones* (teams) into the chariot-racing.[55] Suetonius gives a very similar picture of the adaptation of Greek convention in his account of the festival's foundation (*Domitian* 4.4), which I will discuss further in the next section.

Greek festivals were also prominent elsewhere in the west of the Empire. Here too they seem to have been used as vehicles for the display of distinctively western identities, rather than being taken as signs of 'hellenization'. The Sebasta at Naples, for example, which we have come across before, was arguably the most important of Augustus' foundations (founded in 2 BC), and certainly the one mentioned most often in Imperial literature.[56] Naples

---

[49] Caldelli (1993) 21–4 takes it as the first of Rome's 'proper' Greek *agones*; Thuillier (1996b) 267 is suspicious of that conclusion.
[50] See Caldelli (1993) 22, n. 65 on *I.Pergamon* 535 (=Moretti (1953) no. 58 (pp. 149–51)).
[51] See Caldelli (1993), esp. 53–168.   [52] See Caldelli (1993) 165.
[53] See Caldelli (1993) 45–52; Robert (1970) and (1930) 36–8.   [54] See Darwall-Smith (1996) 221–2.
[55] See Caldelli (1993) 165–6 for summary of these points.   [56] On the Sebasta, see Geer (1935).

was itself a hybrid community with a mixture of Greek- and Latin-speaking population, and a mixture of Greek and Roman institutions and traditions. Many of the Greek cities of the surrounding area of southern Italy (known as Magna Graecia) and of Sicily similarly maintained long-standing Greek traditions.[57] The Sebasta therefore cannot be used as evidence for the spread of athletics beyond its traditional eastern constituency in the same way as the Capitolia can. It is interesting, however, to see the pattern of qualified Hellenism which we have seen in Rome repeating itself in this very different community. The festival culture of Naples seems to have been one of the areas in which the city displayed its Hellenic characteristics and traditions most prominently (for example, with inscriptions in Greek, and with Greek-style funding arrangements and officials), in contrast with other areas of the city's public life which conformed more closely to models which were common in the west of the Empire.[58] It also seems to be the case that it was partly the interest of philhellenic Romans which served to maintain Naples' Hellenic atmosphere so securely.[59] The games in Naples thus fit well with the idea that Hellenic behaviour among the Roman elite tended to be very selective, and that devotion to Greek-style agonistic activity in the west was often an expression of Roman elite status as much as an expression of 'hellenization'.

Greek-style *agones* spread even to much smaller cities within the Latin-speaking west, and were often founded on local initiative. Here too we see some of the same patterns. Maria Caldelli's work on the agonistic culture of the west has extended beyond the boundaries of Rome to a study of the agonistic festivals of Gallia Narbonensis, in the cities of Massilia (Marseille), Nemausus (Nîmes) and Vienna (whose agonistic calendar was the subject of a letter of Pliny (*Ep.* 4.22), which describes debates about whether the city's *agôn* should be abolished).[60] The games in Nemausus in particular

---

[57] On Naples, see Leiwo (1994), esp. 30–2; cf. Lomas (1993), esp. 99–114 and 125–44 on the identity of Magna Graecia more broadly. Another important festival was founded nearby a century and a half later, when Antoninus Pius created the Eusebeia at Puteoli in honour of the recently deceased emperor Hadrian (see *Historia Augusta* 5 (*Hadrian*) 27.3); Caldelli (1993) 44 suggests that Puteoli may have been chosen as the venue for the Eusebeia because of its location in an area already endowed with a strong agonistic culture. Arnold (1960) lists a number of other smaller *agones* from Sicily and Magna Graecia.

[58] For example, agonistic inscriptions in Naples seem to have been almost exclusively in Greek (see Leiwo (1994) 45–8), whereas Latin was regularly used with Greek for other types of inscription in the city; cf. Kaimio (1979) 73 for a similar pattern in the inscriptions of Nemausus (Nîmes).

[59] See Bowersock (1995); d'Arms (1970), esp. 142–52.

[60] Caldelli (1997); I have also learnt a great deal – both about Pliny and about some of the wider themes I am concerned with in this chapter – from Greg Woolf's unpublished work on this letter; he argues that Pliny, like the men whose actions he writes about, is not primarily interested in issues of Greek and Roman cultural exchange, but rather uses the debate about Greek athletics in Vienna as a convenient vehicle for commenting on the politics and society of Rome itself.

are well attested, in seventeen documents, which also include evidence for local branches of the agonistic guilds (both athletic and musical) centred in the city. Caldelli acknowledges that the presence of games in Massilia can be partly explained by that city's Greek origins, although whether they are direct continuations of Massilia's Republican *agones* is unclear. There also seems to have been a large Greek population in Vienna, which might go some way towards explaining the existence of that city's *agones*. However, Caldelli also argues plausibly that the province's games were in part a result of the association between imperial cult and agonistic festivals, and perhaps also a response to the popularity of the Capitolia. In other words these *agones* may in some cases have been founded because they were felt to be appropriate vehicles for imperial worship. If that is right it represents another example of the way in which Greek games in the west tended to be marked by imperial influence, which was not just a later addition to already existing institutions, as it was in the east, but was rather the single most important factor in their formation within an area where such events had not previously been widespread.

The westward spread of Greek games thus seems to have been subject to a process of selective adaptation, and valued for the light it could shed on western identities and western society. That said, we should not overestimate the degree to which the expanding network of agonistic foundations in the west was in reality under firm imperial control, or part of any firm imperial policy, or even broadly uniform in its contours. For one thing, the debate which many of these foundations generated is one sign that their 'Romanized' characteristics did not go far enough for many observers. Nor would it be right to suggest that all of the agonistic foundations of the west were mediated directly through Rome. Many imperial foundations (the Capitolia included) must have been improvised attempts at harnessing the unstable and variable dictates of local taste, even when they were presented as carefully orchestrated, top-down impositions. Moreover, a more detailed examination of the situation in other western cities would no doubt show that the debates and trends which were at work within Rome itself were far from typical.

Finally I want to discuss evidence for the presence within Rome of the headquarters of the Universal Guild (*synodos*) of athletes within the second century AD, which must have both reflected and enhanced Rome's status as a major athletic centre.[61] We have already seen glimpses of the Empire's agonistic guilds in chapter three,[62] where I discussed their role as

---

[61] For overviews see Roueché (1993) 53–5; Millar (1977) 456–63; Pleket (1973); Forbes (1955); see also Frisch (1986) for a collection of papyrus documents relating to the agonistic guilds.
[62] Pp. 130–1.

one possible focus for the affiliation of competitors, in order to qualify the claim that athletic victory was a source of glory primarily for the victor's home city. I have postponed detailed discussion of their significance until now because of their close association with imperial patronage throughout their history. Their Roman-centredness is reflected in the fact that much of our best evidence for their organization comes from Rome itself. Their activities within Rome confirm the move I have outlined towards a more and more unqualified acceptance of Greek athletics within Rome. They also illustrate, however, the way in which even later athletic texts from the west of the Empire, composed once this process of institutionalization was well under way, still tend to place a markedly Roman slant on their material, holding their subject matter under the spotlight of specifically western concerns. In the case of guild-related inscriptions that effect is achieved above all through conspicuous mention of imperial control. Even the most self-glorificatory of Greek athletes in Rome tend to collude with that trend in their inscriptions.

We hear regularly of scenic guilds for musicians and actors from the early third century BC onwards, but it is not until the first century BC that we start to see evidence for the emergence of the worldwide guilds of athletes. That coincidence may in itself be a sign that the athletic guilds were from the start dependent upon Roman patronage and on the new political structures of the post-Hellenistic world.[63] The overall picture of the institutional development of the guilds is hard to reconstruct confidently, but it seems to be the case that there were two separate guilds of athletes co-existing for some time: the Guild of Ecumenical Athletes, whose members presumably were not required to have won sacred victories, and the Guild of Crowned Victors.[64] These two guilds later seem to have merged, and the headquarters of the combined Guild seems to have been moved to Rome at some time in the middle of the second century AD, to judge by two inscriptions which record the grant of land for Guild headquarters in Rome by Hadrian and Antoninus Pius respectively.[65] This Guild seems to have been represented by local branches in many cities of the Empire, as the two separate guilds from which it was formed also were.[66] Within Rome itself, most of the evidence we have comes from inscriptions in honour of the major officials of the organization, who seem to have been responsible amongst other things, and in a variety of capacities, for day-to-day administration of the Baths of Trajan where the Guild was based.[67] The Guild in Rome also

---

[63] See Potter (1999) 271 for that suggestion.
[64] See Pleket (1973) 202–3, with reference to Robert (1949) 123, n. 1.
[65] *IG* XIV, 1054 (=*IGUR* 235); *IG* XIV, 1055 (=*IGUR* 236).   [66] See Roueché (1993) 54.
[67] On administration of the baths, see Caldelli (1992).

Athletic institutions in Rome

seems to have been closely associated with the Capitolia, judging by the frequency with which that festival is mentioned in its inscriptions.[68] It is worth noting, however, that that picture is hard to guarantee in all its details. Most importantly, the institution's history is made difficult to decipher by the overlaps in terminology with which these guilds and other less formal groupings of athletes are described.[69] For example, we have records of impromptu athletic associations being formed at festivals, including Olympia. We also see sacred victors mentioned as a group in civic contexts where they do not seem to be representing any Empire-wide organization. There is even evidence that the worldwide theatrical and athletic guilds acted together in some contexts, although some scholars have overstated the permanence of that co-operation.[70]

We see some signs of the Athletic Guild's institutional hierarchies, and of the way in which those hierarchies were linked with imperial patronage, in the inscription recording Antoninus Pius' grant of land in the 140s AD which I mentioned briefly above. The grant is represented as a response to a request by M. Oulpios Domestikos, President (*xystarches*) of the Guild and Director of the Imperial Baths:[71]

> With Good Fortune. The emperor Caesar, son of the deified Hadrian, grandson of the deified Trajan Parthikos, descendant of the deified Nerva, Titus Aelius Hadrian Antoninus Augustus, *pontifex maximus*, tribune for the sixth time, emperor for the second time, consul for the third time, father of the fatherland, sends greetings to the Guild of the Heraklean Sacred Crown Athletic Victors. I have given orders for land to be handed over to you in which you can store your sacred prizes and records, next to the Baths which were built by my deified grandfather, where you come together for the Capitolian Games. Farewell. Oulpios Domestikos the Director of my Baths (ὁ ἐπὶ βαλανείων μου) negotiated this gift. This was written on 16 May from Rome in the consulship of Torquatus and Herodes. (*IG* XIV, 1055b (= *IGUR* 236b))[72]

The tone of the letter is proprietorial. The emperor stresses his own connection with the baths by stating their links with his ancestor Hadrian, and

---

[68] On links with the Capitolia, see Caldelli (1997) 97–105.
[69] See Millar (1977) 456; Pleket (1973) 203–13.   [70] See Roueché (1993) 55.
[71] West (1990) discusses fragmentary inscriptional evidence from Ephesus which records Domestikos' role in these same negotiations with the emperor; he also argues that Ephesus was the main headquarters of the Guild of Sacred Victors for many years before the move to Rome.
[72] Ἀγαθῆι Τύχηι | Αὐτοκράτωρ Καῖσαρ θεοῦ Ἀδριανοῦ υἱός, | θεοῦ Τραιανοῦ Παρθικοῦ υἱωνός, θεοῦ Νέρουα | ἔγγονος, Τίτος Αἴλιος Ἀδριανὸς Ἀντωνεῖνος | Σεβαστός, ἀρχιερεὺς μέγιστος, δημαρχικῆς ἐξουσίας | τὸ ϛ, αὐτοκράτωρ τὸ β΄, ὕπατος τὸ γ΄, πατὴρ πατρίδος συνόδῳ | ξυστικῇ τῶν περὶ τὸν Ἡρακλέα ἀθλητῶν ἱερονεικῶν στεφα ̄ | νειτῶν χαίρειν· | ἐκέλευσα ὑμεῖν ἀποδειχθῆναι χωρίον, ἐν ᾧ καὶ τὰ ἱερὰ κατα ̄ | θήσεσθε καὶ τὰ γράμματα, πρὸς αὐταῖς ταῖς Θερμαῖς ταῖς ὑπὸ | τοῦ θεοῦ πάππου μου γεγενημέναις, ὅπου καὶ μάλιστα τοῖς | Καπιτωλείοις συνέρχεσθε. εὐτυχεῖτε. ἐπρέσβευεν | Οὔλπιος Δομεστικὸς ὁ ἐπὶ βαλανείων μου. | ἐγράφη πρὸ ιζ καλ(ανδῶν) Ἰουν(ίων) ἀπὸ Ῥώμης Τορκουάτῳ καὶ Ἡρώδῃ ὑπάτοις (=Miller 152).

by casting Domestikos' high office within the Guild as a kind of personal service to him. The connection of the Guild with the Capitolian games (paralleled within a number of other inscriptions) is also stressed here, perhaps with the implication that the grant is a reward for long-term commitment to the games in the past. The emperor's accumulation of titles at the start of the letter and his emphasis on the way in which his control over the baths has been inherited from Trajan draws on common epigraphical conventions which are shared by several of the surviving honorific inscriptions for Guild officials, who list their titles with reference to ancestors who have held similar positions. In this inscription, the glory of Antoninus Pius far outweighs the distinctions of Domestikos, who is presented to us in very modest terms, in contrast with the much more extravagant celebration of his achievements which we find in another nearly contemporary inscription set up in his honour (*IG* XIV, 1109 (= *IGUR* 237)). The inscription quoted above thus foregrounds imperial pre-eminence and control even as it confirms Greek privilege.

The honorific conventions just mentioned recall the inscription set up by Markos Aurelios Asklepiades (*IG* XIV, 1102 (= *IGUR* 240)) which we have come across several times already. That is no accident. Asklepiades was himself President of the worldwide Athletic Guild in Rome, and the long inscription from which the opening quotation of this book is taken was found in Rome, as were the several other (shorter) surviving inscriptions set up by him or in honour of him.[73] Most of the inscription, as we have seen, is taken up with extravagant self-glorification. Asklepiades' fame is due not only to his athletic career, from which he retired at the age of twenty-five after just six years of competition, but also to the later glories of his administrative work in the Guild and elsewhere, which are enumerated in detail. Even here, however, as in his other inscriptions, the influence of the emperor hovers in the background. Like Domestikos, Asklepiades is described as Director of the Baths of the emperor (ἐπὶ βαλανείων τοῦ Σεβαστοῦ (line 7)). More strikingly, perhaps, he goes out of his way to avoid the accusation that any of his victories were won by imperial favour (μήτε κατὰ χάριν βασιλικὴν ἀγῶνα ἔχων (lines 14–15)), implicitly acknowledging the depth of his dependence on imperial patronage in the present, even while he denies its influence on his competitive career.

These inscriptions thus illustrate, most importantly, the way in which late second-century Rome had developed into one of the Empire's most

---

[73] The other inscriptions, as noted in chapter one (p. 3, n. 3), are *IG* XIV, 1104 (=*IGUR* 239); *IG* XIV, 1103 (=*IGUR* 241); and probably also *IGUR* 250, which is half in Latin (discussed by Moretti (1953–5) 73–8).

important agonistic centres, drawing in illustrious athletes like Asklepiades from all over the Mediterranean. In that sense they represent the culmination of a long history of growing familiarity with Greek athletic competition within Rome. And yet they also illustrate how the strong hand of imperial control was never far away, even after the tendency to adapt and distort Greek imports in the west started to lose its intensity. Roman influence over Greek agonistic institutions and athletes is of course proclaimed and celebrated as a matter of course in the east, and it may be that we should not take it as being any more strongly marked in these Guild inscriptions than it is there. I suspect, however, that this kind of standard acknowledgement of the emperor may have taken on slightly different overtones at least for some of its readers in this western context, informed by long-standing – albeit by this date less vigorous – Roman habits of displaying and interrogating Romanness through adaptation of Greek custom. Even Markos Aurelios Asklepiades, the most fiercely independent and invincible of self-publicists, whose boasts borrow from the conventions of imperial self-promotion, with their implications of territorial conquest, cannot quite succeed in bypassing imperial control. Even he cannot quite conquer Rome in the unconditional manner which has characterized all of his other victories.

GREEK CONTESTS AND ROMAN EMPERORS

I have suggested, then, that athletics in Rome – funding athletics, participating in athletics, even writing about athletics – was often about displaying and exploring distinctively Roman elite anxieties and identities, not about celebrating any increasing 'hellenization'. I have also pointed to the importance of imperial involvement for our understanding of those developments. The degree of that involvement – and the degree to which it was emphasized within contemporary assessments – is remarkable. Not only were emperors able to found new events and to adjust festival programmes in west and east alike, either in response to specific petitions or by personal initiative; but they also influenced agonistic fashions by their reputations and innovations. The confusing variety of different ways in which they did so is one of the things which makes it so difficult to generalize about Roman treatments of these Greek practices.

Why, then, did imperial intervention in the Empire's agonistic culture take so many different forms? One answer is that emperors often used athletics, and spectacle benefaction more broadly, as a particularly promising means of advertising their own distinctive relations with their subjects, and their own distinctive visions of the proper composition of Roman culture. It has often been stated that a society's public entertainments can throw light on its political and cognitive structures. There were many factors which made the spectacle culture of Rome itself crucial to the formation and confirmation of public perceptions of imperial power and Roman superiority, and of the social and cultural hierarchies those things were founded on.[74] For example, it displayed publicly the extraordinary prominence of the emperors of Rome, in their role as almost inconceivably wealthy benefactors, and their transcendence of the processes of competition they sponsored, which were deeply ingrained within both Greek and Roman tradition as metaphors for the struggle of elite individuals within a competitive society, and yet no longer applicable to the emperor himself in his position of unrivalled power (at least according to the conventions of imperial self-projection, even if in reality the emperor's position must have been open to the constant threat of scrutiny and challenge). Rome's spectacle culture also put on show the city's cultural cosmopolitanism and military power. And it encouraged Roman audiences to see themselves and their relation with the emperor as part of the spectacle, through hierarchical seating arrangements, and through the audience's ability to make the emperor respond (at least sometimes) to public opinion, in relation to the contests of the day, or even in relation to civic policy.[75]

Rome's rulers often seem to have exploited these conventions calculatingly. The different methods they chose in approaching the common challenges and opportunities which traditions of spectacle benefaction offered reveal a great deal about their different positions within Roman debates about both Roman culture and provincial policy. Greg Woolf has made a similar argument in assessing Roman reactions to Greek culture more broadly:

> For Romans under the empire, reactions to Hellenism were most often discussed in relation to the attitudes and actions of individual emperors. Partly this was because it provided a means of subjecting emperors to moral scrutiny in relation to existing frameworks of ethical debate, but it was also the case that emperors were grappling in public with the same moral and cultural dilemmas that preoccupied the rest of the Roman elite: the answers they found (and public responses to them) helped regulate and model the attitudes of other aristocrats to Greek culture.[76]

Selective acceptance of hellenizing influences, he suggests, did not at any stage restrict the maintenance of a firmly Roman identity: '. . . their

---

[74] Cf. Beacham (1999); Toner (1995) 34–52; Edwards (1993) 110–19 on theatre.
[75] On exchange between emperor and audience in spectacle contexts, see Millar (1977) 368–75.
[76] Woolf (1994) 133.

divergent attitudes exemplify their different positions within *Roman* debates about the proper nature of high culture. In fact the diversity of Hellenism opened up space for emperors to choose which Greek culture to patronize.'[77]

On that model, the varieties of imperial agonistic policy should tell us a great deal about the wider projects of their individual sponsors.[78] But they should also be able to tell us a great deal about the way in which the Roman senatorial classes and their provincial counterparts may have reacted to those projects, if we pay close attention to the way in which imperial agonistic policy and idiosyncrasy were debated and represented by near contemporaries. In the rest of this section I want to leave aside for the most part the problem of *why* individual emperors acted as they did. Instead I wish to take further some of Woolf's hints about the significance of contemporary *responses* to imperial self-presentation, in order to illustrate in more detail the claim that an emperor's spectacle policy often provided a highly charged starting-point for assessment of his moral and political significance, and also a basis for analysis of the changing contours of Roman identity as something which was inextricably entangled with each emperor's image.

To illustrate that point I want to look briefly at Suetonius' portrayal of three of the most 'agonistic' of the emperors of the first century – Augustus, Nero and Domitian – reading their separate biographies as part of a more or less coherent project in order to see how Suetonius' representations of their reactions to Greek athletic culture contribute to his contrasting assessments of them.[79] I hope it will be clear in the rest of this section that my presentation of the actions of these emperors is intended to be taken with implied quotation marks, as paraphrases of Suetonius' representation of them, which is my main interest here, unless it is specified that I am referring to actions or motives beyond Suetonius' account.

Suetonius' juxtaposition of the lives of successive emperors allows him to trace a number of developments within the imperial court and the public life of Rome within the first century AD. One of those developments is the increasing absorption of Hellenic ideas and activities within both of those spheres up to the reign of Nero, followed by a partial reaction to Nero's excesses of hellenization on the part of the Flavian emperors Vespasian,

---

[77] Woolf (1994) 135 (with his italics).
[78] E.g., see André (1996), Alcock (1994) and Kennell (1988) for exploration of the motives behind Nero's agonistic obsessions.
[79] Some of the same passages and issues are dealt with by Bradley (1981).

Titus and Domitian.[80] One of the indexes Suetonius uses to chart those changes, I will argue, is the changing character of imperial involvement in the spectacles of the city of Rome, Greek athletic spectacle included. Suetonius repeatedly gives detailed attention to scenes from the spectacular spaces of Rome and catalogues the precise mixture of events which each emperor has introduced, treating imperial entertainment policy as one of many standard categories into which he organizes his subject matter within all of the *Lives* alike.[81] Suetonius also pursued that interest elsewhere in even more detail, in a work on Greek and Roman games which seems to have been well-known by his contemporaries.[82] In the *Lives*, I believe, his repetition of scenes of spectacle conveys an impression of the similarities between the challenges and institutional conventions and expectations with which successive emperors were confronted, while also leaving space to chart their different responses to those challenges.[83] In doing so it exploits a tension within first-century imperial self-representation, and contemporary reactions to it, between Republican circularity, where political action conforms to repeated cycles, and the rhetoric of imperial innovation, whereby each new emperor seeks to revolutionize what has gone before. Suetonius' representations of the repetitive nature of changing public spectacle never allow us to forget that each of these emperors is trapped within familiar (though certainly not *purely* Republican) models, however distinctive each individual's manipulation of them. That effect has a certain amount in common with the way in which inscriptions commemorating Greek festival foundation inscribe their subjects in age-old institutional trends, whatever the specific differences between them.

Suetonius begins to establish these patterns in his account of Julius Caesar. There the gladiatorial benefactions of Caesar's early career are implicitly contrasted with his later, more extravagant involvement in public spectacle. In *Divus Iulius* 10.2, for example, we hear that the gladiatorial contest he had planned while aedile turned out to be less impressive than he had intended, because of a law which was passed, in response to his over-extravagant preparations, to limit the number of gladiators to be kept in the city by any individual. His spectacular impulses are thus kept in check (though only just) by the mechanisms of Republican law. By contrast, in

---

[80] See Wallace-Hadrill (1983) 181–9.
[81] See Wallace-Hadrill (1988) 66–72 on these standard categories.
[82] See Wallace-Hadrill (1988) 41, 46–7, 126–8.
[83] Some modern scholars seem to me to have underestimated the artfulness and intricacy of Suetonius' composition: e.g., see Wallace-Hadrill (1988) 19–22; see Barton (1994b) for a more sympathetic and complimentary appreciation of Suetonius' creative use of rhetorical and biographical patterns.

section 39,[84] as almost the first act Suetonius mentions after recounting the end of the war with Pompey, we hear about much more ambitious and successful benefactions: 'He gave spectacles of various kinds: a gladiatorial show (*munus*), games in every district throughout the whole city put on with actors of all languages (*per omnium linguarum histriones*), and also horse races in the Circus and athletes and a mock sea battle' (39.1).[85] The arrangement of Suetonius' material seems to imply that Caesar is unable to give free reign to this kind of extravagance until he has been freed from Republican constraints, although of course these celebrations also have much in common with the triumphal games held by other Republican generals, as we saw in the previous section, and their celebration in 45 BC may have been designed to gloss over the fact that Caesar's conquest was a conquest of fellow Romans as well as foreign enemies. From there, Caesar turns immediately to the business of setting the state in order, as we hear in the opening sentence of 40, as if the reordering of the city's entertainments and the reordering of its government are parallel processes.

This scene of culturally mixed and extravagant spectacle as something implicitly linked with the order of the city more broadly is one which is replayed with telling variations in many of the lives which follow. It is also linked with the conventions of imperial self-presentation. For example, the catalogue of spectacles which occurs at an equivalent stage halfway through the *Divus Augustus* has close verbal links with this passage from the *Divus Iulius*, while also closely following Augustus' own account of his achievements in *Res Gestae* 22–3. We hear that:

He surpassed all his predecessors in the frequency and variety and magnificence of his spectacles. He said that he gave games four times in his own name, and twenty-three times on behalf of other magistrates who were either away or unable to afford the expense. In some cases he put on spectacles in all the different regions of the city and on lots of different stages with actors of all languages (*per omnium linguarum histriones*), and he gave shows (*munera*) not only in the Forum and amphitheatre, but also in the Circus and the Saepta, although sometimes he gave nothing but a wild beast show. (*Divus Augustus* 43.1)[86]

The repetitions from Suetonius' biography of Caesar mirror the sense of an endless and endlessly varied succession of spectacles within the traditions

---

[84] =Miller 142.
[85] *edidit spectacula varii generis: munus gladiatorium, ludos etiam regionatim urbe tota et quidem per omnium linguarum histriones, item circenses athletas naumachiam.*
[86] *spectaculorum et assiduitate et varietate et magnificentia omnes antecessit. fecisse se ludos ait suo nomine quater, pro aliis magistratibus, qui aut abessent aut non sufficerent, ter et vicies. fecitque nonnumquam etiam vicatim ac pluribus scaenis per omnium linguarum histriones, munera non in Foro modo, nec in amphitheatro, sed et in Circo et in Saeptis, et aliquando nihil praeter venationem edidit.*

of Roman public life, based on repetitive Republican convention, but now also developing momentum as a distinctively imperial festival system. In many ways Augustus seems to be following his predecessor closely, but he also departs from his example in significant ways. The most obvious adjustment lies simply in the frequency of these events, which surpasses anything which has come before, as the opening lines of the paragraph inform us, in contrast with the matter-of-fact description of a one-off event in the opening words of the passage from *Divus Iulius* 39.1 (*edidit spectacula varii generis*). Caesar's great triumphal games are replayed almost countlessly within the new Augustan city. Augustus' exploitation of the absences and financial weaknesses of his 'colleagues' echoes the actions of Julius Caesar (described in *Divus Iulius* 10.1) who is said to have taken credit for shows which he had put on jointly with his fellow aediles. Augustus has more than matched that achievement, repeatedly and systematically taking over the duties of his fellow magistrates, although in a way which still manages to look as though it is consistent with Republican convention. There is also a strong sense – even stronger than for Julius Caesar – of Augustus' concern with enforcing civic order through the games. He goes out of his way (e.g. in 44) to ensure orderly viewing amongst the Roman audience. Moreover, at the beginning of 46.1, immediately after the description of the games, we hear that Augustus turned his attention outside Rome, 'having thus (*ad hunc modum*) set in order the city and the affairs of the city'.[87] That transitional phrase implies that Augustus' spectacular innovations actually contributed to or even constituted the enforcement of order, rather than simply being parallel to it, as Caesar's innovations are, in the transitional sentence following Suetonius' description of them in *Divus Iulius* 40.1.

We also hear (in *Divus Augustus* 45.1) that Augustus was a better watcher of the games than Caesar had been, giving them his full attention more successfully. That picture may be meant to reinforce the sense that Augustus has given his attention to the challenges of orchestrating the city's entertainments in a more sustained and careful way than Caesar had. The theme of watching is also relevant to Augustus' broader cultural 'policy', at least as Suetonius presents it, and is in fact applied to him in a range of contexts throughout the work. He seems to have no difficulty in finding the right balance between enthusiasm and unseemly involvement, maintaining a dignified detachment from spectacle in a way which later emperors like Nero spectacularly fail to match, as we shall see in a moment. At several points, Suetonius underlines the cultural affiliations of the competitors Augustus

---

[87] *ad hunc modum urbe urbanisque rebus administratis.*

views. We are told, for example, that he loved to watch Latin boxers fighting with Greeks (45.2). Suetonius also gives a long description of his final days in the Bay of Naples, where he spent his time watching the contests of the ephebes in Capreae (98.3) and later a quinquennial athletic contest in Naples which had been established in his honour (98.5). At Capreae he also distributed gifts of clothing 'stipulating that the Romans should use Greek clothing and language and the Greeks Roman' (98.3).[88] That detail echoes the earlier picture of mixed boxing, and suggests a fascination with viewing the processes of exchange between Greek and Roman culture. It acts as a final image of Augustus' characteristically inconspicuous surveillance of the cultural and political fusions of the Empire which his rule had brought about, at least on Suetonius' account, and within which Naples itself and its Sebastan festival had played such an important role.

In Suetonius' biography of Augustus, then, the emperor's benefactions and enthusiasms provide a vehicle for characterizing his careful attention to wider cultural transformations within the Empire, and his calculating extension of the precedent Julius Caesar had bequeathed to him. Nero is similarly characterized through his entertainment policy. He too follows the models set up by his predecessors, but he does so with distortions which are far more drastic and obtrusive than any of the changes Augustus attempts, and with a narrow-mindedness which is dangerous for the Empire as a whole, and strikingly in contrast with Augustus' ability to juggle different political and cultural commitments while giving proper attention to each of them.[89] The main problem, so Suetonius suggests, is Nero's obsessive desire to participate in public competition in a way which tends to confuse conventional boundaries between spectacle and life, a trait which is paralleled in Suetonius' representation of Caligula's reactions to public spectacle.[90] That characterization is related to Suetonius' wider interest in the signs of personal involvement by emperors in the running of the Empire, for example in judicial and military activity, involvement which he represents as crucially important but also dangerous when carried to excess and with too restricted a focus on any single area.[91] Nero's commitment to personal involvement is characterized as dangerously uneven, leading him to neglect crucial areas of policy, and his agonistic obsession is one of the things which signals that unevenness most clearly.

---

[88] *lege proposita ut Romani Graeco, Graeci Romano habitu et sermone uterentur.*
[89] For other perspectives on ancient representations of Nero's agonistic enthusiasms, see Whitmarsh (1999); Elsner and Masters (1994), esp. the essays by Alcock (1994) and Edwards (1994) in that volume; Woodman (1993).
[90] See Wallace-Hadrill (1983) 125.   [91] See Wallace-Hadrill (1983) 122–5.

In describing Nero's policy towards the games of Rome, Suetonius emphasizes his imitation of Augustus, but also his failure to live up to Augustus' example. Nero's spectacle benefactions are introduced in what is by now standard fashion: 'The spectacles he put on were many and varied: the Iuvenal games, horse races, theatrical shows, and gladiatorial contests' (*Nero* 11.1).[92] In addition he extends the precedent of Augustus' agonistic foundations outside Rome by founding the Neronian *agôn* within the city itself (12.3–4). He proves unable to resist the temptation of appearing on stage himself to receive the prize for Latin oratory and verse, despite the fact that he does not seem to have competed. These early signs of unusual personal interest in public competition rapidly degenerate into obsession, culminating in his notorious agonistic tour of Greece,[93] which is in turn followed by vigorous advertisement within Rome itself of his commitments to a distinctively theatrical form of Hellenism. He ostentatiously rejects the stereotypical Roman strategy of holding back from adopting Greek agonistic interests too whole-heartedly in order to shield oneself from criticism. In that sense the Nero Suetonius presents us with is a metaphor for the consequences of taking cultural 'borrowing' too literally, without maintaining the necessary qualifications and restraints. Through these commitments, which prompt him to degrading appearances on stage, Nero threatens traditional Roman social hierarchies which debarred those of senatorial rank from participation in public entertainment. The image of Nero's public competition is used by Suetonius to underline the immensity of the challenge to Roman social, political and moral order which his reign represented in all areas; it serves to emphasize the monstrous extent of the emperor's power, which not only exhibits the destruction and appropriation of foreign enemies, but can also afford to parade its disregard for the underlying foundations of Roman self-perception and social structure.

The organization of the narrative articulates the process vividly. Instead of confining himself to one main section on the emperor's spectacle benefactions, as he does for Julius Caesar and Augustus and others, Suetonius here finds himself dragged back to that subject insistently, so that Nero's agonistic obsession threatens to take over the whole narrative, just as it threatens to destroy the proper government of the Empire. The account slides immediately from Nero's triumphal return to Greece as agonistic victor into an catalogue of his moral degeneration, as if the two are inevitably connected with one another. Even Suetonius' description of the final hours

---

[92] *spectaculorum plurima et varia genera edidit: iuvenales, circenses, scaenicos ludos, gladiatorium munus.*
[93] See esp. Suetonius, *Nero* 22–4 (=Miller 144).

of Nero's life is pervaded by a sense of theatricality, as if Nero is still playing to an audience, unable to separate dramatic performance from reality. Like Augustus, he is in Naples shortly before his death. Like Augustus, he takes the opportunity to enjoy the city's agonistic culture – but Nero goes to the *gymnasion* to watch athletes competing as soon as he hears news of the uprising in Gaul (*Nero* 40.4). In showing us Nero attending the *gymnasion* at an inappropriate time Suetonius is surely offering us a parody of Augustus' calmness in the face of illness, transforming this scene into a characteristic example of Nero's refusal to accept the conventional wisdom that there should ultimately be boundaries between Greek spectacle and Roman reality, and a limit to Roman imitation of such spectacle. That characterization, which resurfaces again and again throughout the work, seems to be a reaction on Suetonius' part not only to Nero's personal manias, but also to the narrow-mindedness of his provincial and domestic 'policy', as Suetonius represents it. Nero's refusal to maintain the selectiveness and restraint exemplified by Augustus, and to give his attention to all areas of the Empire and of imperial policy equally and in turn, ultimately makes him unable to fulfil his proper role as emperor, as we see from the final irruption into the narrative of the military sphere he has consistently neglected, and which he has attempted to replace with the triumphs and victories of his own agonistic 'campaign' in Achaia.[94]

Domitian, finally, is represented by Suetonius as very much less committed to an unqualified Hellenism than Nero is, and there are signs that we are meant to see some of his decisions – for example his forbidding of the appearance of actors on the public stage (7.1) – as reactions to the continuing memory of Nero's debauchery. Nevertheless, Domitian followed Nero's example of introducing a Greek *agôn* within Rome, as we have seen. That inconsistent reaction to Nero's Hellenism could be explained simply as an example of typically Roman selectiveness in the treatment of Hellenic culture, but in the context of Suetonius' representation it also contributes to the impression of capriciousness which is one of the dominating themes of the work. Domitian is distinguished above all by his inconsistency. That quality manifests itself in his military policy, which mixed necessary with unnecessary campaigns (*Domitianus* 6.1), and in his random acts of cruelty (11.1), which frequently followed displays of generosity or scrupulous fairness, and which were related to a wider picture of oscillation between virtue and vice in his administration of the Empire, which finally inclined towards the latter (3.2). Domitian's spectacles are closely associated with his

---

[94] Cf. Edwards (1993) 135–6 on Nero's neglect of the army in favour of the theatre.

capriciousness in part because they provide him with a conspicuous arena in which to display it, for example in his public execution of an audience member who has criticized him (10.1). They are even represented as a direct cause of it, because his overspending on public entertainments forces him to confiscate the property of men who have recently died (12.1–2). The biography's spectacular material is introduced in characteristic fashion: 'He repeatedly gave magnificent and luxurious spectacles, not only in the amphitheatre, but also in the Circus, where beyond the established races of two-horse and four-horse chariots he also staged two battles, one between cavalry soldiers and one between infantrymen; and he even gave a naval battle in the amphitheatre' (*Domitianus* 4.1).[95] At first sight that formulaic introductory sentence seems to be just another variation on the standard theme whereby emperors seek to outdo or adjust the innovations of their predecessors. Within this biography, however, Domitian's pointedly unusual innovations take on greater significance, consistent with his urge elsewhere always to do the unexpected, often for no specified reason. The description of Domitian's foundation of the Capitolia gives a similar impression of his gratuitous distortion of conventions (4.4).[96] Suetonius suggests that Domitian introduced a number of new events, including even races for women (which are uncommon elsewhere, although not unparalleled),[97] with the result that the first instalment of the festival had 'quite a few more prizes than it does in the present' (*aliquanto plurium quam nunc est coronatorum*). Suetonius thus contrasts the original foundation with its less outlandish contemporary manifestations, no longer influenced by Domitian's idiosyncrasies, as if to suggest that these have been ironed out into a more moderate, less ostentatious form of Hellenism within his own contemporary Hadrianic society. This is one of the few places where we can see clear signs of pointed comparison between Hadrian's festival policy and its first-century precursors, although that comparison would no doubt have been readily made in other places too by many of Suetonius' readers. Here again, then, as for Domitian's predecessors within Suetonius's *Lives*, Suetonius shows how each emperor's distinctive treatment of Greek and Roman spectacular traditions can be used as an index for broader evaluation of his political and moral qualities, and of their interrelation. In Domitian's case, however, the most distinctive feature of that policy and character is precisely its unpredictability.

---

[95] *spectacula assidue magnifica et sumptuosa edidit non in amphitheatro modo, verum etiam in Circo, ubi praeter sollemnes bigarum quadrigarumque cursus proelium etiam duplex, equestre ac pedestre, commisit; at in amphitheatro navale quoque.*

[96] =Miller 145.   [97] As discussed in chapter two (p. 66).

I have argued, then, that talking about an emperor's agonistic commitments was often a way of evaluating his qualities and achievements within an established conceptual template. Suetonius' recurrent discussion of agonistic and spectacular decision-making exemplifies that tendency well, articulating differences in character and policy, while never losing sight of the fact that all of the emperors he describes, like the city of Rome itself under its imperial masters, are ultimately trapped within repetitive conventions. Those insights should go some way towards confirming the conclusion I drew in analysing Tacitus, *Annals* 14 in the opening section of this chapter, that the practice and representation of Greek agonistic activity, and of its relation with Roman entertainment traditions, was often a highly charged and adaptable focus for the definition and evaluation of Roman and imperial identity.

SILIUS ITALICUS AND THE ATHLETICS OF ROMAN EPIC

In this final section I will turn to the funeral *agones* of Latin epic, in the poems of Virgil and Statius and (especially) Silius Italicus. Here too, as we shall see, representations of Greek athletic activity act as vehicles for articulating their authors' distinctive visions of Roman virtue, Roman history and contemporary Roman identity.

The most conspicuous archetype for the athletic scenes of Latin epic is the Homeric funeral *agôn* for Patroclus in *Iliad* 23.[98] That episode plays a prominent thematic role within the *Iliad*, as has often been noted.[99] It stages a scene of reconciliation between Achilles and Agamemnon, although not without continuing tension between them,[100] and so prepares for Achilles' uneasy resolution of his differences with Priam in Book 24. It dramatizes the problem of marking boundaries between peace and war, and thus extends questions – which are crucial to the poem as a whole – about the extent to which conflict may be made compatible with the maintenance of social order. In the process it also interrogates the differences between divine and human perspective, since the human spectators view athletic conflict in much the same way as the gods view contests of human battle. The distinction between these different objects of viewing – in other words the distinction between the violence of warfare and the non-violence of the athletic *agôn* – is constantly eroded, although never finally breached. The fight in arms (*hoplomachia*) between Aias and Diomedes (*Iliad* 23.798–825)

---

[98] =Miller 1. [99] E.g. see Visa-Ondarçuhu (1999) 17–72; Golden (1998) 93–5.
[100] Taplin (1992) 251–60 emphasizes the atmosphere of reconciliation, but surely underestimates (especially at 257, n. 12) the degree of tension which hides beneath the surface of this.

is the most powerful example of that effect. It seems for a moment that they will take their duelling to a fatal conclusion, but at the climax of the contest the crowd protests, fearing that one of them will die, and Achilles steps in to separate them, confirming the ultimate inviolability of the gulf between men and gods, and reasserting – at least temporarily – the possibility of containing conflict within the structures of human society. *Iliad* 23 also gestures towards the contemporary 'realities' of the society within which it arose, in recalling the traditions of Panhellenic competition which were coming to play a more and more prominent role in inter-state relations at the time of its composition,[101] and so inviting the poem's audience to reflect on the extent to which the traditional virtues on display are relevant within the poem's present-day society, much as the heroes of the poems compare themselves with their over-performing predecessors. The *Iliad* as a whole is focused around the peculiar problems faced by the Panhellenic community of the Greek army, with its need to reconcile the competing agendas and egos of different communities and leaders, in contrast with the relative unity of the Trojan *polis*, problems whose relevance for the poem's original audiences is clear, albeit hard to identify as highly marked within any specific passage. Many of the thematic functions of *Iliad* 23 I have outlined have resonances with these challenges of Archaic Panhellenism. For example, the impression of uneasy reconciliation between Achilles and Agamemnon and the communities they represent surely draws on the conventions of the Panhellenic truce.

Iliad 23 thus occupies a conspicuous position within the poem, while also glancing outside itself at the real world, weaving in fleeting impressions of contemporary social and political institutions within its complex texture. As we shall see, many of the same thematic issues are refashioned and recontextualized in provocative ways within the games of later epic, which also follow the Homeric precedent of making tantalizing reference beyond their own mythical or historical contexts. There are many surviving imitations of these funeral games within both Greek and Latin epic, and the convention continues within Greek epic long beyond the Flavian period which I will mainly deal with here.[102] Quintus Smyrnaeus, for example, writing in the third century AD, includes a long account of contests following the funeral of Achilles in Book 4 of his *Posthomerica*. These more or less harmonious games are then followed in Book 5 by the bitter quarrel

---

[101] On the mixture of contemporary and traditional practices which may lie behind *Iliad* 23, see Golden (1998) 90–3; on relations between the Homeric poems and their contemporary context, see Osborne (1996) 137–60; on Panhellenism in the *Iliad*, see, e.g., Nagy (1979) 7–9, 115–17.
[102] Willis (1941) surveys all the surviving examples of epic funeral games.

between Aias and Odysseus over the arms of Achilles, which makes explicit the overtones of future disharmony which we find within the end of the *Iliad*. Quintus modernizes the Homeric games by presenting many more events than we find in *Iliad* 23, including even a contest of rhetoric (of the kind we hear about in many Imperial-period inscriptions), as if to bring his games in line with contemporary agonistic programmes, in a way which contributes to the impression that his poem has taken us into a new world which the heavy sense of closure within the final books of the *Iliad* can only hint at.[103] Similarly, Nonnus, writing in the sixth century AD, dazzlingly restages *Iliad* 23 in the wild and intoxicating musical and pantomimic contests staged by the god Dionysus, in *Dionysiaka* Book 19. Nonnus exploits the implicit links between intertextuality and agonistic contest which run through Greek poetic tradition in order to glory in his own bewildering, Dionysiac outrunning of his Homeric rival.[104]

There are also other Homeric models for athletics in Imperial-period epic. Most importantly, the Phaiacian games of *Odyssey* 8,[105] where the returning hero Odysseus defeats his peace-loving hosts in athletic contest, offer an image of a less conflict-riven style of athletic competition, much further removed than the funeral games for Patroclus from the horrors of war, and less marked by divisions between the different participating communities (although that is not to suggest that overtones of conflict are entirely absent from this episode, which in some ways prefigures Odysseus' contest with the suitors). Virgil engages with this alternative Odyssean tradition in order to modify the Iliadic atmosphere of *Aeneid* Book 5 (as we shall see further in a moment), echoing the way in which the poem as a whole charts the earliest formation, from loosely connected strands, of a communal Roman identity which can ultimately sidestep the Iliadic dangers of conflict and division[106] (although the pacific Phaiacian overtones which these echoes bring to *Aeneid* 5 will of course be challenged in later books of the poem).

Apollonius of Rhodes was another influential model for Roman epic. In his third-century BC *Argonautika* he chooses not to imitate Homer's funeral games directly, although he does include a boxing-match in Book 2, between Polydeukes and the monstrous Bebrykian leader Amykos, whose defeat leads to war. This incident exemplifies well the poem's preoccupation with mortal dangers which arise from unconventional, unmilitary contexts. That preoccupation is further reinforced by Apollonius' echoes of *Iliad* 23 within

---

[103] See Vian (1963) 129–35 and Vian (1959) 35–9 for brief discussion.
[104] See Shorrock (2001) 156–61 and 178–84.   [105] =Miller 2.   [106] See Cairns (1989) 215–48.

Jason's contests in Book 3, where he has to struggle against the magical challenges set for him by King Aiakos. Within the *Iliad*, dangers are for the most part confined within the context of the battlefield, which is defined by its contrast with the agonistic arena. In the world of Apollonius, they are harder to recognize and anticipate. Agonistic competition becomes deadly. The recasting of Homeric athletics throughout the poem thus reinforces the sense that here the rules of war, with its (albeit precariously maintained) separation from everyday life in the *Iliad*, have changed.

Lucan, amongst others, follows the Apollonian model by choosing not to include funeral games in his poem, a decision which I suspect hints at the uncontainable nature of the civil conflict he describes: here conflict tends to spill out beyond the conventional institutions which on the Homeric model should be able to restrain it. That impression is reinforced by the obsessive recurrence of gladiatorial imagery within the poem,[107] which displaces Homeric agonistic activity as if to emphasize the difficulty – within a world where the possibility of normal functioning of peace-time society has been lost – of envisaging rivalry which is anything other than fatal. Lucan does, however, replay Apollonius' boxing match in a description of the mythical wrestling contest between Hercules and the gigantic Antaeus, son of Earth (*Bellum Civile* 4.592–660). That story is related as an event of cosmic significance, as a reminder of the ever-present potential for violence in the world. Hercules' triumph is represented as a victory for civilization over barbarism, and the listening general Curio takes it as a good omen for his own struggles on behalf of Caesar. In the context of the poem's condemnation of civil conflict elsewhere, however, we might doubt whether the destructive victories of Caesar are quite so one-sidedly civilized and benevolent as Curio seems to assume.

These features of the *Bellum Civile* exemplify well the way in which Greek poetic traditions of the athletic *agôn* develop new dynamics within Latin epic, through their participation in projects which interrogate the significance of the horrors of Roman war for Roman self-perception. In this respect the most important Latin precursor of Flavian epic is of course the *Aeneid*, which charts so influentially the costs and the glories associated with Rome's forging of a new identity through the processes of conquest and incorporation. The games of *Aeneid* 5, conspicuously placed at the point of transition between the Trojan and Italian halves of the poem, play a central role within that project. They showcase virtues which have a

---

[107] On gladiatorial imagery in Lucan, including brief discussion of this wrestling match, see Ahl (1976) 82–115; however, Hardie (1993) 29–30 also notes Lucan's dependence on Virgil in this respect.

distinctively Virgilian, rather than Iliadic, resonance, for example through the impression they give that praying to the gods leads directly to victory, which parallels the emphasis on the *pietas* of Aeneas throughout the poem. Aeneas is given a role very different from that of Achilles, more remote but also more imperious, as if to signal the poem's overlaps with contemporary representations of Augustus' imperial power. As has often been noted, the games also invite comparison with Augustus' own festival foundations, which played such a crucial role within the development of a new identity for the Empire.[108] And there are signs of fascination with the cultural mixing which was one of the most prominent effects of those events, at least in idealized representations of them, and which is reminiscent of Suetonius' account of Augustus' interest in culturally mixed boxing matches. Virgil's boxing match, for example, is between the terrifying Dares, who has fought against Paris and Amycus, and Entellus, a western Greek from Sicily whose eventual victory offers a picture of western confrontation with and ultimate dominance over the old world of the Greek epic.[109]

What, then, of the Flavian epic poetry which so many of these models inform?[110] Statius' *Thebaid* is an apocalyptic relocation of Roman epic tradition within the framework of ancient Greek civil strife, the story of the struggle between the brothers Polyneikes and Eteokles over the throne of Thebes, which culminates in their mutual killing in combat. Civil war was deeply ingrained within Imperial history, first within Augustus' conflict with Mark Antony, resolved by the battle of Actium and the post-Actian peace, events which hover in the background of the *Aeneid*; and more recently within the vicious fighting over the throne of Rome itself, which saw four emperors within the single year of AD 69.[111] One of the things which Statius' rewriting of Virgilian concerns achieves – his transformation of the Virgilian funeral *agôn* within *Thebaid* Book 6 included – is a questioning of the cultural implications of these more recent wars of imperial succession. What did it mean to be Roman, and to live under autocratic Roman

---

[108] E.g., see Feldherr (1995); Briggs (1975); Cairns (1989) 215–17, by contrast, tends to downplay the significance of this.

[109] As Lovatt (forthcoming) points out.

[110] On the boxing match between Pollux and Amycus in Valerius Flaccus, *Argonautica* 4.99–343, which I will not be discussing at length, see Zissos (2002) 89–92, who argues that Valerius distances himself from the models provided by Virgil and Apollonius through his engagement with Homeric epic in this passage; that conclusion supports the impression that athletic scenes in epic tend to invite comparison with similar scenes in earlier poetry.

[111] On the way in which the horrors of civil war impact on Imperial Latin literature, see, amongst many other things, the articles reprinted and revised in Henderson (1998), esp. 165–211 on Lucan and 212–54 on Statius.

government, after AD 69? And how had the answer to that question changed in the hundred years since Actium?

Helen Lovatt has discussed at length the political and poetic projects which underlie Statius' funeral games.[112] She emphasizes Statius' own association not only with Domitian, but also with the imperially sponsored agonistic culture of the late first-century AD, the Capitolia included, in which Statius tells us he competed.[113] It seems hard to suppress the possibility, with that statement in mind, that *Thebaid* 6 is meant in part as a meditation on the links between the horrors of Greek myth and the image of contemporary order in which Domitian, like his predecessors, invested so heavily, within his spectacle benefactions and elsewhere. Lovatt argues that the games are important in part because of their thematic foreshadowing of the military conflicts of the rest of the poem; but at the same time she emphasizes the fact that the clear separation between war and *agôn* which that model implies cannot ultimately be upheld, because of the way in which conflict repeatedly threatens – far more consistently than for Virgil or Homer, and paralleled more closely by Lucan – to burst out from the veneer of control which overlies it. She suggests that the book stages a crisis of masculinity, through the way in which signs of failure and effeminization are inscribed on the heroic bodies which are on show; and that it stages a confusion between the morally charged categories of Greekness and Romanness which form the basis of traditional Roman elite identity. She also pays close attention to Statius' representations of the audience and of the orchestrator of the games, to show how their struggle for the control of meaning is undermined within this mythical spectacle of public contest, as it is within so many contemporary representations of the Flavian political arena. Those confusions constantly threaten to fracture Statius' own poetic voice, pulled between different models and identities, in ways which are signalled through Statius' use of agonistic competition as a metaphor for intertextual contest and poetic display. Statius' funeral games thus exemplify well the characteristic pattern in Latin epic of presenting Greek athletics in a way which invites reflection on Roman society. In what follows I wish to extend that insight to the epic of Silius Italicus. In doing so I do not intend to restate or add to the details of Lovatt's reading of Statius in any sustained way. Neverthless my reading of Silius should extend our appreciation of the context in which Statius is working. Analysis of the close intertextual relation between Statius

---

[112] See Lovatt (forthcoming); see also Vessey (1970).
[113] See Statius, *Silvae* 3.5 and 5.3; cf. Hardie (1983), esp. 1–49 for the contexts of poetry and patronage lying behind Statius' career.

and Silius Italicus seems to me to be crucial for understanding of either of them.[114]

Silius Italicus' *Punica* charts the struggles of Hannibal and Scipio within the Second Punic War. The poem shares many of the preoccupations of Virgil's other epic successors – preoccupations with the processes of historical and poetic succession and repetition, which endlessly refashion their models but always fail to break free of the polluting paradigms which lie at the heart of Roman identity; and with the horrifying processes of sacrificial violence, which always in the end deny the possibility of resolution, and which ultimately lead to a dreadful symmetry between victim and victor[115] – but it often articulates these preoccupations in an understated form,[116] which for many readers has seemed to fall short of the extravagant (and now increasingly celebrated) horrors of Lucan and Statius. One of my aims here is to take a brief look, via the funeral games of *Punica* Book 16, at the poem's representations of heroic achievement, and at the ways in which that impacts on and is viewed by those who must bear the consequences of it, in order to give some impression of what is distinctive about Silius' own under-appreciated evocation of epic virtues and horrors, and about the resonances with Rome's recent history and contemporary politics which that evocation sets up.

The games of *Punica* Book 16 (the poem's penultimate book) come at a moment of triumph for Scipio, following his removal of the Carthaginians from Spain, and shortly preceding his final confrontation with Hannibal, which the poem has been building up to (and endlessly deferring) throughout. They represent a moment of calm before the final episodes of conflict, a chance to review the virtues which have contributed to victory, and which will further contribute to Scipio's success in the final act; and perhaps even to cast glances forward at what those virtues may become after the events the poem describes. In what follows I want to examine first the extent to which the *agôn* is marked as a display of Romanness, by comparison with the culturally ambiguous games of Virgil and Statius which represent such important intertexts. I will then turn to two specific aspects of the *agôn* – its representation of the boundaries between

---

[114] There are a number of very close linguistic and thematic parallels and contrasts between the epics of Statius and Silius, but I am not committed to a relative chronology in my analysis of intertexts between them; rather I aim to discuss the different effects of their very different manipulations of common resources and traditions.

[115] See Hardie (1993); for overviews of Silius' life and work, see Leigh (2000) 478–83; Wilson (1993); Ahl, Davis and Pomeroy (1986).

[116] See Ahl, Davis and Pomeroy (1986) (e.g. 2556) for detailed and (unusually) appreciative characterization of Silius' work in those terms.

war and peace, and its representation of the processes of viewing – in the hope of conjuring up a more precise characterization of the Roman identities Silius evokes. In respect of both aspects I will be interested especially in the extraordinary penultimate event of the *agôn*, the fight in armour between two Spanish brothers whose feud spills over into mutual slaughter, breaking the taboo on human bloodshed as spectacle which Homer and Virgil and even Statius enforce so carefully in their own funeral *agones*.

First though, some framing, through two other episodes which should help to nuance my account of the poem's play with long-standing paradigms of heroism. Hannibal is in many ways the poem's dominant hero, especially within the opening books, where he plays an Achillean role, sweeping all before him on the battlefield, from the very opening books of the poem in the siege of Saguntum, where we see him chasing the priest Theron – who can provide only the weakest version of Hectorian resistance to his monstrous opponent – around the walls of the city (*Punica* 2.233–64). Hannibal's advance towards Rome continues inexorably, while the Romans can only counter him, with mixed success, through debate and delay. The turning point comes only in Book 11 when Hannibal winters in the city of Capua, which has come over to his side like many of Italy's other cities. There, in a disaster orchestrated by Venus – whose actions are given no clearly stated motive apart from the desire to infect all those who drop their guard enough to make it possible – Hannibal and his troops are enfeebled by luxurious pleasures. That submission is implicitly contrasted with the firm adherence to virtue which we see in Scipio and his compatriots, just as it stands in contrast to Aeneas' destiny-conscious resistance to the blandishments of Dido at the end of *Aeneid* Book 4 (although that is not to suggest that Aeneas escapes from love's destabilizing influence entirely). Virgil's Dido, of course, is the original Carthaginian, and herself succumbs to the power of Venus, in a way which shows her kinship with Hannibal and his men. And yet at the same time there is enough here to make us hesitate before accepting an unequivocal vision of Punic weakness in contrast with Rome. For one thing, Venus's assault on Hannibal's men is represented in military terms as the action of a protecting goddess, and we might therefore suspect that desire to protect Rome is her real if unstated reason for the attack on Hannibal. She uses her native arts to ward off danger from Rome, much as she infects Dido with lust out of a desire to protect her son Aeneas. More importantly, perhaps, it is striking that Capua itself is characterized as an epicentre for all of the vices which spread to the Carthaginians. Hannibal himself 'gradually becomes degenerate (literally "loses his natural colour"), discarding the qualities of his race' (*Punica* 11.422–3)),[117] ancestral virtues which up to this point have seemed very much like the traits of an ideal Roman general, an impression enhanced by the often-noticed resemblance between Hannibal and Scipio.[118] By contrast with this implicit praise of natural Carthaginian manliness, we hear that 'for the men of Campania there is no limit to luxury or to lives overwhelmed by lust' (11.427–8)).[119] This characterization, with its lack of main verb, and consequent temporal vagueness, perhaps glances forward in time to the reputation of Campania (where Silius himself is said to have lived in retirement) as the centre of Greek influence on Italy, through Naples in particular. That reminder of the complex identity of later Rome, which will absorb Capua, like so many other cities, after this war and after others, adds an ominous note to the ostensibly straightforward distinction between Roman virtue and Punic weakness in the face of temptation. Perhaps we are to imagine that the Rome of Scipio risks the same fate as Hannibal in Capua, if its conquests continue.[120]

Soon afterwards, the Romans duly retake Capua, and the tide of campaigning begins to turn. In Book 14, the action moves to Sicily, where the Roman army under Marcellus campaigns against the Syracusans, who are allied with Carthage. The episode replays Thucydides' account of the disastrous Athenian campaign against Sicily in the Peloponnesian War, with the obvious difference that the Roman army in this case claims a resounding success. Here I want to revisit the athletic stereotypes which the poem applies to the Syracusans at several points during the book. I discussed briefly, in the first section of this chapter, the accusation of Greek effeminacy which Marcellus flings against the opposition in encouraging his own troops. As I suggested there, the surrounding action at first sight confirms the validity of his judgement, as the weakness of the Sicilians leads them to crumble before their more steadfast opponents, temporarily saved only by the Greek ingenuity of Archimedes, who devises complex war machines to keep the Romans at bay. On closer inspection, however, Marcellus' accusation turns out to carry disturbing implications.

One might argue that the stereotypical contrast between Greek and Roman is undermined by the presence of Greek allies in the army of Marcellus (listed in 14.248–57), and by the overtones of civil war which

---

[117] *et patrias paulatim decolor artes | exuit.*   [118] E.g., see Hardie (1993) 24–5.
[119] *nec luxus ullus mersaeque libidine vitae | Campanis modus.*
[120] Cf. Ahl, Davis and Pomeroy (1986) 2501–4 on the way in which Silius hints at the paradox that victory may be more damaging to Rome than defeat, through the future consequences of decadence it will bring with it.

the intertexts with Thucydides' account of intra-Hellenic conflict convey.[121] Here, however, I want to emphasize more – through the example of Silius' authorial comment on the death of the Syracusan youth Podaetus in 14.492-515 – the way in which these stereotypes of Greek luxury are made to contaminate Silius' representation of Rome not in any literal sense, but rather as a metaphor for the dangers inherent in Roman action in other spheres, spheres far removed from the *gymnasion*, or from the banquets which corrupt Hannibal in Capua. Podaetus' glory is only fleeting, but for the brief moments of his appearance the narrative slows its pace to linger over him. We hear that he is a youth unready for battle, who has 'not yet left the *ephebeia*' (*nondum excessisset ephebos* (14.493)). Silius stresses his boyish enthusiasm through the pleasure he takes in disturbing the surface of the sea with his ship, and in outstripping the Roman and Carthaginian boats, as if the battle is no more than a childish game, or else a re-run of the ship race which forms the first contest of Virgil's games in *Aeneid* 5.[122] At the moment of the fatal spear-wound inflicted on him by Marcellus, the text withdraws even further from the reality of the battle to mourn his lost potential, much like the honorific inscriptions for deceased athletes which I discussed in chapter three[123], which offer idealized and eroticized visions of youthful athletic prowess. However, the regret Silius expresses here is not just at the boy's loss, but also at the way in which his agonistic spirit has brought its own destruction: 'There was enough, quite enough of glory and praise to be gained in safe contests. Why, boy, why did you strive for deeds which were too great?' (*cur facta, puer, maiora petebas?*) (14.510–11).[124] That anguished question resonates with the theme of over-ambitious expansionism which runs throughout the poem, not only in the arrogance of Hannibal, but also in repeated hints that Scipio's desire for glory will commit Rome itself to an imperial destiny which carries the seeds of its own destruction. For the moment, the Romans have got away with the kind of over-reaching which destroys the Athenians of Thucydides – who overextend themselves by fighting on more than one front – but we might be less confident about whether they will be so fortunate in the future. Here, criticism of Greek weakness, articulated through athletic imagery, is not used to suggest that Rome is literally contaminated by the foreign

---

[121] Livy 29.19 also tells us that Scipio was himself accused in the Senate of allowing his army to be corrupted by the charms of Syracuse.

[122] Spaltenstein (1990) 324 (on *Punica* 14.498) suggests a parallel between one of the ships Podaetus has sunk, the 'Nessus' (named after the famous centaur), and the ship 'Centaurus' which participates in the ship-race in *Aeneid* 5.122.

[123] Pp. 127 and 130–1.

[124] *sat prorsus, sat erat decoris discrimine tuto, | sat laudis: cur facta, puer, maiora petebas?*

influences it defines itself against. Rather, Silius uses it as a metaphor, to hint at the way in which Rome faces its own, very different dangers, in the possibility that its characteristic impulses of aggression may be infected by a lack of restraint far more consequential than the Hellenic luxury of the *gymnasion*.

The games of *Punica* Book 16 follow a similar course, in the sense that Silius draws back from the temptation of contaminating Scipio's triumph by associating it directly with traditions of corrupting Republican philhellenism, despite the fact that there was material within historical tradition which would have made that option available. Plutarch, amongst others, tells us that Scipio's contemporaries – including Cato, the great scourge of Roman philhellenism – disapproved of Scipio's interest in Greek culture, exemplified by extravagant devotion to the *gymnasion* and to theatrical display.[125] Silius, however, goes out of his way to exclude those elements within the athletic traditions of epic which were most closely associated with eastern agonistic tradition. In that sense he avoids an abrupt departure from the picture presented by the other surviving historical sources for this event, which similarly emphasize its gladiatorial nature.[126] He includes only a horse race – whose catalogue of competing horses is emphatically western, echoing the catalogue of western troops fighting for Rome in Book 3 – a running race, a set of gladiatorial-style fights in armour (more obviously 'gladiatorial' than the *hoplomachia* accounts within Homer and others simply because at least one of the fights results in death) and a javelin contest. By contrast, Statius' games (which retell the foundation-myth of the Nemean festival) offer a vision of epic heroism and epic spectacle which mixes Greek and Roman influence in destabilizing and uncertainly delimited ways. Statius includes specialized Greek events like discus-throwing and boxing and wrestling, which were less obviously connected with the demands of Roman militarism; and his competitors exercise naked, whereas Silius has no explicit mention of nudity.

That difference is of course partly due to the fact that Statius is describing scenes from the Greek heroic past, whereas Silius' protagonists are Roman. But there is more to it than that. Silius' strategy of suppressing the hellenizing possibilities taken up by his contemporary seems to me to be part of his more understated approach to the questioning and undermining of Scipio's Roman heroism. Scipio here seems to have no trouble maintaining a Roman style even in moments of quasi-philhellenic role-playing, just as Silius' Romans elsewhere easily resist the charge of being subject to

---

[125] Plutarch, *Cato Maior* 3.5–7; cf. Livy 29.19.   [126] Livy 28.21 and Valerius Maximus 9.11, ext. 1.

corrupting foreign influence, with some exceptions like the scenes in Capua which point forward to the Republic's *future potential* for such subjection. However, even autonomous Roman identity turns out to have parallel, and perhaps more serious, problems implict within it; in much the same way as Roman culture is implicated in the failings of Podaetus not literally but metaphorically.

On the whole, Silius is also less explicit than Statius about problematizing the boundaries between games and war. Statius' *agôn* is described as similar to war in its intensity, and repeatedly threatens to spill over into conflict and slaughter between competitors and spectators alike. For example, the opening lines of *Thebaid* Book 6 announce that Adrastus and the other leaders of the Argive expedition against Thebes have ordered an *agôn* 'in which the valour of Mars (*Martia... virtus*) might prepare to rouse itself and sweat in advance of war' (*Thebaid* 6.3–4).[127] Similarly, when the chariots gather before the opening contest, we hear that 'never before had any more noble battle-line (*acies*) of wing-footed horses been brought together (*conlata*)' (6.297–8).[128] These reminders of warfare gain further momentum as the *agôn* proceeds. At the end of the running race, when Parthenopaeus is cheated of victory by Idas, the Arcadians prepare to fight to restore their runner's honour, until Adrastus calms them (6.618–30). And then at the beginning of the boxing match the Argive Capaneus announces his intention to kill whoever fights against him – as if he is taking on the role of the monstrous Bebrykian Amykos of Apollonius' *Argonautika*. However, he stops short of importing the fratricidal overtones of the conflict between Polyneikes and Eteokles by calling for a Theban opponent, so that he will not be guilty of slaughtering one of his own kinsmen (6.731–8). Finally, in the last event before the closing archery contest, two fighters step forward to fight in arms, and are held back only by Adrastus' exhortation that they should save themselves for the bloodshed of the battlefield which is to come (6.911–23).

Statius' games, then, return obsessively to the image of warfare threatening to burst in upon the funeral celebrations, although in the end it is held in check. Silius, by contrast, tends to avoid this recurring language and threat of battle, at least in the early events, and yet curiously his *agôn* in the end transgresses the boundary of human bloodshed which Statius always stops short of. Silius' games come at the end of his campaign in Spain – in contrast with Statius whose *agôn* is explicitly represented as preparation for

---

[127] *quo Martia bellis | praesudare paret seseque accendere virtus.*
[128] *neque enim generosior umquam | alipedum conlata acies.*

fighting in store – and are followed immediately, in fact abruptly, by Scipio's return to Rome (although there is of course still one last battle to come in Book 17). They also tend not to involve the poem's great fighters to the same degree. And the first two events, the chariot-race and the running, pass off without conflict. Immediately afterwards, however, things become more serious, and the language of warfare starts to intrude: 'Then came the more serious contests of men (*graviora virum certamina*). Swords are unsheathed at close quarters, and images of fierce warfare are stirred (*bellique feri simulacra cientur*)' (16.527–8).[129] That last phrase echoes and grimly rewrites Virgil's description of the way in which the celebratory drill exercise of the *Lusus Troiae*, performed by the youth of Troy once the athletic events of *Aeneid* 5 are over, mimics the movements of battle: 'they stir up images of battle under arms (*pugnaeque cient simulacra sub armis*)' (*Aeneid* 5.585). And the reference to 'more serious contests of men (*graviora virum certamina*)' in the opening line of this passage from the *Punica* presents this move from the child's play of racing to the manly activity of armed conflict as a more horrifying version of the switches between age categories which structured the programming of Greek *agones*. Silius thus signals with ironic humour the way in which his own third contest diverges in seriousness from the two which have come before, and also from the spectacles which have preceded it within epic tradition.

Silius tells us that many men fought in arms, but the only competitors identified are the Spanish princes who fight to the death over their father's throne:

Nor were the fighters guilty men, whose lives had been marked by crime; instead manly virtue (*virtus*) and fierce spirit drove them on to desire for glory. These were the men who sprang up to face each other with their swords. It was a spectacle worthy of this people born of Mars (*spectacula digna Martigena vulgo*), a mirror-image of their accustomed work. Amongst them twin brothers entered on an impious battle with armed right hands for the sake of the sceptre before this innumerable circus of spectators, though the auditorium condemned their madness (*cavea damnante furorem*). What deed, once this had been done (*iam*), has been left undared by kings? What crime remains uncommitted for the sake of kingship? That was the grim custom of their people (*is genti mos dirus erat*). They sought their father's throne in a contest to the death. (16.529–38)[130]

---

[129] *hinc graviora virum certamina, comminus ensis | destrictus bellique feri simulacra cientur.*

[130] *nec, quos culpa tulit, quos crimine noxia vita, | sed virtus animusque ferox ad laudis amorem, | hi crevere pares ferro; spectacula digna | Martigena vulgo suetique laboris imago. | hos inter gemini (quid iam non regibus ausum? | aut quod iam regni restat scelus?) impia circo | innumero fratres, cavea damnante furorem, | pro sceptro armatis inierunt proelia dextris. | is genti mos dirus erat; patriumque petebant | orbati solium lucis discrimine fratres.*

This passage, I believe, intersects in extraordinary ways with the themes of civil war and fratricide which are so prominent throughout Neronian and Flavian epic, and in the historical events which those works respond to. The civil wars of AD 69 – in which many of Silius' first readers must have been involved, as Silius himself was – had threatened to tear apart the surface harmonies of Roman elite society and politics. As has often been noted, this campaigning, like many of the other wars and political intrigues of the previous two centuries, had seen prominent examples of intrafamilial conflict.[131] Lucan had introduced his *Bellum Civile*, in the very opening words of his poem, not just as an account of civil war, but also as a tale of confrontation between relatives, Pompey and his son-in-law Caesar. Statius' tale of the mutual killing of Polyneikes and Eteokles entails a similarly conspicuous poetic engagement with those historical trends. This passage of Silius forms part of the same pattern.[132] More specifically, it has close intertexts with Statius' account of the duel between Polyneikes and Eteokles in *Thebaid* Book 12, since in both cases (*Punica* 16.546–8 and *Thebaid* 12.429–46) the brothers involved are cremated in joint funeral pyres, which burn with distinct and competing sets of flames, as if to enact their continuing hostility after death.[133]

It is striking, however, that the very crowning moment of the *Thebaid*'s horror is condensed by Silius into a brief event within a programme of spectacular entertainment,[134] albeit one which is initially condemned by the spectators. It is tempting to feel that this condensation and spectacularization of the scene of fratricide is meant as a comment on the routinization of violence within the Roman heritage, and on the way in which so many similar moments of barbarity have been met without effective resistance throughout the course of Roman history. Certainly there are pointed references in this passage to the way in which particular styles of fighting and watching can be associated with specific peoples, for example in Silius'

---

[131] E.g., see Hardie (1993) 93–5.

[132] See McGuire (1997) 88–146 on the theme of civil war in the Flavian epic. He makes the point, with reference to Silius in particular, that within these poems 'even wars that are not precisely civil take on the attributes of civil war . . .' (103).

[133] See McGuire (1997) 98–100 on the way in which this episode's miniaturization of the duel of Eteokles and Polyneikes (identified as such also by Ahl (1986) 2814–16 and Venini (1969) 778–83, as McGuire points out) enhances the *Punica*'s obsession with civil war. Livy 28.21 had recorded the event as a fight between two cousins, with a clear victory for one of them (unlike Valerius Maximus 9.11, ext. 1, who like Silius has two brothers); the existence of that passage may be a sign that Silius deliberately rejected the possibility of following a less fratricidal model.

[134] Cf. Hardie (1993) 22–3, n. 8, who points out that *Punica* 16.531 recalls the climactic killing of Turnus by Aeneas in *Aeneid* Book 12, perhaps another sign of Silius' technique of routinizing defining moments of violence within the epic tradition.

aside in line 537: 'that was the grim custom of their people (*is genti mos dirus erat*)'. The precise meaning of that phrase is made vague by the fact that the narrative does not tell us explicitly whether any of the other fighters who face each other are killed. It is not clear, in other words, whether the custom being criticized is the killing of noble men in public duelling, or just the duelling of brothers over their inheritances.[135] Either way, however, the phrase might prompt reflection on how the 'custom' of the Roman people compares. We may be reminded not only that gladiatorial spectacle is ingrained in Roman tradition (as Silius' point about the suitability of this spectacle for the 'people born from Mars' implies), but also that this kind of intra-familial rivalry here described *will* be common after the events of the poem within the Roman history of the late Republic and early principate.

Moreover, the incident's brevity seems to me to be strikingly consistent with Silius' perfunctory representation of the polluting and violent consequences of warfare elsewhere in the poem. It acts as a characteristically fleeting reminder – through the implication of metaphorical links between Spanish fratricide and Roman civil destruction – of the costs which pursuit of power brings with it, and of the terrible consequences which may eventually follow from Scipio's own ambitions, unsuspected by any of those involved in his campaigns at the time. It perhaps also suggests that blindness to horror, or at least resignation to horror stemming from the inability to prevent it – the kind of resignation this audience is forced into here in its failure to prevent the duel – has been deeply ingrained in Roman action not just within Silius' own Neronian and Flavian lifetime, but also from the very beginning of Roman expansionist history. Silius' desire to foreground impressions of this sort seems to me to be one important – and generally unacknowledged – explanation for his tendency throughout the *Punica* to push signs of anxiety and horrified reaction beneath the surface of his text, allowing them to reappear only sporadically. In other words, Silius' characteristic 'understatement', and the very unStatian suppression of conspicuous and apocalyptic tensions within his representations of heroic virtue, may itself, I suggest, be a provocative enactment of the way in which Roman culture has been driven to selective blindness and desensitization in its viewing of political violence, rather than a sign of the mechanical nature of his poetic style, for which he has so often been criticized.

---

[135] The text also gives no explicit mention of the princes' Spanish origin (that detail comes from other sources), and we could therefore easily be drawn into seeing them as Romans on a first reading, although the fact that they are fighting over inheritance of a 'kingship' gives the game away on reflection.

A closer look at the poem's representation of the viewing of conflict, both during the *agôn* and at other times, may help to clarify some of those issues. I have certainly not meant to suggest that the audience of this gladiatorial contest is entirely accepting of the mutual fratricide. As we have seen, there is a prominent expression of horror and condemnation of the fight interjected in line 535 in the phrase *cavea damnante furorem* ('though the auditorium condemned their madness'). Just as striking as this resistance, however, is the fact that it has no effect. All they can do is continue their watching, as the brief ablative absolute phrase which expresses their objection is swept away by the hesitant and convoluted but ultimately relentless sentence which surrounds it. Nor is there any sign that Scipio contemplates intervention. That lack of intervention is in line with the way in which the outcome of the other events of the *agôn* attracts almost no debate or uncertainty, despite the initial involvement and partisan excitement of their audience. That passiveness is strikingly in contrast with what we see in Homer and Virgil and Statius, where the generals responsible for the games repeatedly intervene in the events, or alter their plans for prize-giving in response to audience outrage. At the end of the *Punica*'s running race, for example, the final result goes unchallenged, despite the fact that Hesperus has pulled Theron's hair to hold him back, in a way which allows Eurytus to claim victory. It is the equivalent event in the *Thebaid*, where Idas pulls the hair of Parthenopaeus to deprive him of victory, which drives the Argives to take up arms in defence of their honour. Similarly, the final omen of Scipio's javelin throw, where his spear turns into a tree at the end of the *Punica*'s funeral games, is given an ostensibly straightforward interpretation, as a foreshadowing of his future victories; whereas the equivalent omen in the *Thebaid*, Adrastus' boomerang-like arrow shot, attracts a great range of interpretations, none of them correct, so the poet tells us. Silius' audience, the games' orchestrator, Scipio, included, accept almost without hesitation whatever fate presents them with. Anxiety about such acceptance is suppressed, although that should not exclude the possibility that this pose of (excessive?) passivity – which is so unusual by comparison with the traditions it draws on – may be ominous in itself.

The viewing of political and military events elsewhere in the poem follows similar patterns.[136] There are numerous scenes of debate within the Roman and Carthaginian senates, and yet Silius repeatedly shows us the

---

[136] Wilson (1993) describes similar effects – in particular the poem's tendency to take more interest in viewing than in explaining – in terms of a mythicization of history, which rejects historiographical convention.

will of individual commanders bypassing senatorial decisions. The poem itself ends with extraordinary abruptness, resolving all its complex agonistic movements of military advance and retreat into a final image of Scipio's triumphant entry into Rome, where he is compared with Bacchus triumphing over the Indians or Hercules celebrating victory over the giants, as if Scipio's achievements have at last been fixed irrevocably in artistic form. The poem has expressed uncertainty about the legacy of Scipio's campaigns often enough to make us wary of this static final image, which skates over, amongst many other things, the disgraceful exile which lies in store for Scipio at the end of his career. Nevertheless Silius goes out of his way to avoid such uncertainty within this passage itself, as if enacting the way in which the Roman elite has knowingly colluded with the myth of the glorious and inexorable progress of Roman imperial dominance, as the only option which remains open to it.[137] That gesture of abrupt and undisputed closure mirrors the undebated endings to each of the events of the *agôn* of Book 16, and the way in which in the end the spectators are powerless, or unwilling, to prevent the transgressive slaughter they are witnessing. Even Scipio – perhaps not unlike the emperors of Rome, in their confrontations with history – is ultimately unable to do anything but watch and accept the unfolding of the events of the *agôn*, as if they are being orchestrated by some higher force of destiny. Similarly, the most prominent sign of denigratory connotations underlying the glory of Scipio in the work's final tableau may be the fact that Scipio is no more in control of his own glorious image than those who are watching it, just as he is swept along by the course of events in his unquestioning distribution of prizes in Book 16. Silius himself is said to have retired from a senatorial career to a life of art-collecting and political detachment.[138] I suspect that this biographical story of retreat into aestheticization of the Roman past as a reaction to political experience is connected with the poetic experiment which the *Punica* represents, whether because Silius' reputation gained currency partly in reaction to the experience of reading his work, or whether because he modelled his own life and poetry together, on a principle of unavoidable, though certainly not unequivocal, resignation and passivity.

---

[137] Cf. Fowler (1996) for discussion of the many implied viewpoints in the ekphrasis of temple paintings of the First Punic War in Liternum in *Punica* 6.653–715, paintings which include several scenes of triumph; the multiplicity of these viewpoints, and Hannibal's ultimately unsuccessful attempt to impose his own view of history on the events they represent by burning them, might make us suspicious of the ostensible simplicity of the poem's final lines.

[138] E.g., see Pliny, *Ep.* 3.7; Leigh (2000) 478–83 analyses Silius' poem as the work of a collector, whose interest in accumulating artworks is paralleled by his appropriation of models within the work.

I have argued in this chapter that Greek athletics, in fact Greek agonistic activity more generally, was repeatedly used in the west of the Empire as a starting-point for performance and problematization of Roman identity. I suggested that the transfer of agonistic institutions to a western context was often marked by conspicuous changes which reflected – and sometimes deliberately advertised – the way in which these Greek activities had been made compatible with Roman social norms, and made subject to Roman, especially imperial, control. That tendency to adapt Hellenic imports was most conspicuous within the Republican period and in the first century or so of the principate, but I also argued that we see versions of it continuing well into the next century, well after Domitian's foundation of the Capitolia began to turn Rome into one of the Empire's greatest agonistic centres. I also argued that those processes in the west of the Empire are mirrored by, and contribute to, long-standing trends within Latin literature of using agonistic narrative as a starting-point for defining and also debating the distinctive qualities and problems of Roman identity. I looked in particular at some of the highly charged textual functions performed by recurrent Roman stereotyping of Greek athletic vices, by representations of Roman imperial interest in Greek agonistic activity within historical writing, and finally by rewritings of the agonistic scenes of Greek epic tradition.

In the context of these provocative literary developments, and in the context of the much-debated imperial support for Greek agonistic institutions which continued throughout the period when he was writing, the *agôn* of Silius Italicus' *Punica* comes to seem very far from the mechanical and dutiful rewriting of epic convention which modern scholarly consensus, at least until recently, has judged it to be. I have argued here that Silius resists the temptation of introducing hellenizing material into the games of Book 16, despite the fact that Scipio (like Nero and other first-century emperors) had been accused by his contemporaries of wasteful philhellenism. In that sense Silius stands out from his epic rivals. Virgil, for example, had mixed Homeric, Greek events with markedly Roman-style innovations, in order to reflect on the mixed cultural origins of the Roman people whose foundation his *Aeneid* charts; while Silius' near contemporary Statius reverted to a more extravagantly Hellenic model than Virgil in his morally ambiguous representation of heroic virtue. Silius, by contrast, marks the Romanness of his *agôn* – especially in his account of audience reactions to the mutual fratricide of brothers from Spain in gladiatorial contest – and uses his account to invite reflection, in a manner which is exemplary of many of the effects we find throughout the rest of his poem, on specifically Roman qualities, and on the ways in which the conflicts of Roman history have been viewed by their Roman audiences. In doing so, I believe, he hints at parallels between the passivity of the audience of Scipio's games, and the passivity which the Roman people have chosen, or been forced to choose, in their viewing of the horrors of contemporary warfare.

CHAPTER 6

Athletes and doctors: Galen's agonistic medicine

> These men won the *agôn* of the doctors. The contest of medical composition: P. Vedios Rufeinos; the surgery contest: P. Ailios Menandros the head doctor (ἀρχιατρός); the contest of problem-solving: P. Ailios Menandros the head doctor; the contest in use of instruments: P. Ailios Menandros the head doctor.
>
> (*I.Eph.* 1162, lines 4–8)[1]

DOCTORS IN COMPETITION

This inscription records the victories of doctors in a public medical *agôn*, held at the festival of the Asklepieia in Ephesus during the first half of the second century AD.[2] It illustrates vividly the way in which physicians could be involved in the agonistic life of the cities of the east, and the way in which they sometimes drew on agonistic convention in their professional self-advertisement, marked here by close imitation of the form of musical and athletic victory inscriptions. The exact wording of the inscription is uncertain (although the restorations made within the text quoted above seem fairly secure, since they are paralleled within the ten or so other inscriptions from Ephesus which celebrate victories in the same *agôn*), and it is not clear exactly what each of the contests listed may have involved. It does seem clear, however, that they required the display of serious medical skills. These were not dumbed-down and spectacularized versions of more serious medical practice (although it may be the case that not all onlookers would have agreed with that judgement, given that

---

[1] οἵδε ἐνεί̄|[κησαν τὸν ἀγῶνα τῶν ἰατρ]ῶν· συντάγματος· Πο. Οὐή. Ῥουφεῖνος ||χειρουργίας· Πο. Αἴλιο]ς Μένανδρος ἀρχιατρός, προ̄| [βλήματος· Πο. Αἴλ. Μένανδρο]ς ἀρχιατρός, ὀργάνων· Πο. ΑἴλΓ||ος Μένανδρος ἀρχ.] . . .
[2] For the full series of medical *agôn* inscriptions from Ephesus, see *I.Eph.* 1161–9 and 4101b; with Knibbe and Iplikçioglu (1981/2) no. 146 (p. 136) for dating. For discussion of these inscriptions and related practices, see Nutton (1995) 7–8; Barton (1994a) 148, with 223, n. 73; Keil (1905).

some Imperial-period writers criticize doctors who debase medical and philosophical principles by their public appearances).³ For one thing, the term 'head doctor' (ἀρχιατρός) which the inscription applies to Menandros refers to a physician with official civic recognition.⁴ Moreover, the words applied to the first contest (the contest of composition (σύνταγμα)) and the third contest (the contest of problem-solving (πρόβλημα)) have strong philosophical and rhetorical overtones. Both words are used by Galen, for example, in the late second century AD, to describe the activities of research and debate which he represents as central to the most elevated versions of both medical and philosophical activity. By that parallel it seems likely that the first contest involves the presentation of research, whether in written form or through oration on a previously prepared theme, while the third may have involved the solution of theoretical questions proposed by the judges.⁵

In this chapter I will be revealing some of the ways in which medicine in the Roman Empire was intertwined with athletics and with agonistic culture in general. The inscription quoted above is just one of many examples of that kind of interconnection. My argument will be that athletes and their trainers often acted as important defining images through and against which doctors could structure their own professional self-definition. Sometimes we see doctors acting in concert with athletic trainers and laying claim to a share in their expertise, or else using the image of the athletic victory metaphorically to advertise their own civic importance or pre-eminence over their rivals. At other times, by contrast – most conspicuously in some (though not all) of the writing of Galen⁶ – we see doctors rejecting any association with athletic training, contrasting their own knowledge and practice with that of the *palaistra*. I suggest that the association of athletics with medical self-definition centred around two main (interrelated) areas. First, the image of athletic competition allowed doctors to think through and advertise their own distinctive relations with the competitive processes which were central to the medical profession, both in their relations with individual rivals, and in the jostling for position between medicine and other disciplines. Secondly I will be arguing that athletic training offered distinctive but controversial models for the training and care of the human

---

³ E.g., see Dio Chrysostom 33.6.   ⁴ See Nutton (1977).
⁵ For discussion of the different possibilities, see Nutton (1995) 7–8; Barton (1994a) 223, n. 73; Keil (1905) 133–5.
⁶ See Müller (1995) 306–16 for a useful short analysis of Galen's athletic writing. Singer (1997) translates many of Galen's most important works on athletics, and his book is thus an important resource for the subjects discussed in this chapter.

body. For some, the fitness of athletes was attained only by carrying the techniques of bodily self-care to their highest peak of perfection, techniques which were in many ways close to the principles of preservative medicine with which the medicine of this period had come to be increasingly preoccupied, in moving beyond a more exclusive focus on the healing of disease. For others, Galen most conspicuously, athletic exercise – at least when it was wrongly practised – was distinguished above all by its lack of moderation, and represented a limit-case of misapplication of medical principle, and a perfect example of the dangers of pushing the body to extremes. Galen and others repeatedly defined their own approaches to bodily regimen by their reactions to practices of athletic training. Having discussed these two central areas of medical self-definition, I will then turn to Galen's *Protrepticus* – which is both his most passionate plea for the importance of medicine and also his most scathing tirade against the dangers of athletic training – in order to show how his strategy of distancing himself from the work of athletic trainers forms a central plank of his professional self-presentation. In the chapter following this one, finally, I will then extend that picture of interrelation between different disciplines and methods of bodily training in discussing the profession of athletic training, through Philostratus' defence of the art of the athletic trainer in his *Gymnasticus* (written in the early third century AD). Between them, the contradictory testimonies of Galen and Philostratus give a vivid illustration of the way in which athletic training acted as a battleground both for opposing disciplines, and also (in line with what we have seen already in earlier chapters) for opposing views of how contemporary life should be lived in relation to earlier Greek traditions.

To begin with, then, let us look at some of the reasons why the image of athletic competition might have been seen as an appropriate one for medical activity. For one thing, doctors seem to have had regular contact with athletes and their trainers in educational contexts. That contact may have contributed to a widespread perception that the medical *technê* ('art' or 'skill') could play a crucial role in training young men for physical fitness and competition. Such a perception would have been reinforced by the existence of gymnastic treatises which had serious medical and even philosophical pretensions, and by the claims made within at least some medical and philosophical writing that gymnastic exercise of the right sort could contribute usefully to bodily self-care.[7] We shall see more evidence

---

[7] See, e.g., Jüthner (1909) 3–74; he points out that there were famous examples of men who had combined gymnastic and medical expertise; Herodikos of Megara is said to have been the first to do

Doctors in competition 257

for those claims in the section following this one. There is, moreover, extensive evidence for doctors lecturing in *gymnasia*,[8] or else more permanently attached to *gymnasia* in an official capacity, which sometimes led to their being listed among instructors in inscriptions recording end-of-year ephebic competitions, in the Imperial period and before.[9] Others seem to have travelled with athletes to festivals as part of their retinues, along with trainers.[10] We have one second- or early third-century AD epitaph which honours a man as official doctor of the worldwide guild (ἀρχιατρός τοῦ σύμπαντος ξυστοῦ).[11] He was presumably required to treat wounded and injured athletes. Louis Robert gives an example of an inscription from Lydia, set up in honour of a young man who had recently died.[12] It contains a long list of the man's relatives and associates, including, towards the end, a doctor and a trainer: 'Antoneinos the trainer and Tatianos the doctor honour their pupil' (Ἀντωνεῖνος ὁ ἐπιστάτης, Τατιανὸς ὁ ἰητρὸς τὸν μαθητὴν [ἐτίμησαν]). It is not clear whether they had been preparing the boy for athletics, or rather instructing him separately in their own professions of medicine and *gymnastikê* ('athletic training'), but either way the inscription gives the impression of co-operation in the education and commemoration of a promising pupil. There are even signs of a midway category between doctors and trainers, in the widely attested term ἰατραλείπτης (*iatraleiptês* ('doctor-trainer')), which seems to have straddled both specialisms.[13]

Doctors were also often involved in the public life of Greek cities outside these educational contexts, festivals included. The most successful doctors were wealthy enough to act as public benefactors and were honoured publicly for their achievements throughout the Hellenistic and Imperial periods, in much the same way as agonistic stars and other members of

---

so (Jüthner (1909) 9–16), although his work would not necessarily have provided an attractive model since he is criticized by many writers for his innovations (e.g., by Plato, *Republic* 3, 406a–b [=Miller 158A]).

[8] See Kleijwegt (1991) 155–6; Nutton (1979) 187; Marrou (1965) 281; Robert (1946) 36, citing Wilhelm (1915) 53–60.

[9] E.g., see Forbes (1955) 249; Robert (1950) 26; Oliver (1942) no. 37 (pp. 71–4), line 48; Jüthner (1909) 4, who refers to *IG* III, 1199, line 38 and 1202, line 38.

[10] See Robert (1950) 26, citing the first-century BC inscription *I.Priene* 111, lines 175–6; cf. van Nijf (1997) 185 on the same text, who suggests (citing *I.Priene* 112 and 118 as parallels) that the listing of doctors and trainers together with athletes and ephebes in these inscriptions is a sign of the tendency to feast those who had been closely associated with a festival's success.

[11] See Robert (1950) 25–7, citing a fourth-century AD parallel in *Codex Theodosianus* 13.3.8; see also Forbes (1955) 249.

[12] Robert (1974b) 525–7, commenting on an inscription published by Tsakyroglous (1892) 198–200.

[13] See Robert (1965) 168–9, with further references; there is, however, very little evidence for the word's precise significance.

the elite. There are many examples of doctors being awarded the right of *proedria* (reserved seating) at a city's festivals and theatres, as part of a standard package of rewards for public service, in recognition of the public benefactions they have provided through their medical expertise.[14] Several Hellenistic inscriptions give vivid descriptions of honours to be presented regularly to doctors at public festivals, organization of which was the responsibility of those festivals' agonothetes.[15] Vivian Nutton has argued for continuity between the Hellenistic and Imperial periods in the practice of honouring official doctors (men like P. Ailios Menandros, the victor recorded in the inscription I quoted from Ephesus) for public service, although he also charts a move away from the positive honours associated with rights like *proedria*, towards the privilege of exemption from *munera* (the duty of providing funding for public benefactions, including funding for spectacular entertainment). Even after that development was well-established, however, it is clear that successful doctors continued to be involved in festival and *gymnasion* benefaction because of the financial need for wealthy men to contribute to civic life.[16] A number of surviving inscriptions from the Imperial period honour doctors for their generosity as agonothetes or gymnasiarchs.[17] A surviving edict of Hadrian grants doctors, along with rhetors and grammarians, immunity from gymnasiarchy and a number of other types of public service.[18] However, we also have a letter from his successor Antoninus Pius to the council of Asia which partially reverses that decision, apparently for reasons of financial prudence, by placing limits on the numbers of men from each of these categories who could be exempted from *munera* (duties of public benefaction) in any one place.[19] Doctors were also typical of other professions in their customs of communal self-representation, centred around civic medical associations which would often have been represented as a group at public festivals and festival banquets. These associations functioned in much the same way as the civic associations of many other professions,[20] and were also similar in

---

[14] For a doctor honoured with *proedria* in the Imperial period, see Flacelière (1949) no. 3 (pp. 467–8), lines 4–5; for good Hellenistic examples, see Robert (1954), line 16 and (1928a) 172–3, line 8.

[15] For Hellenistic examples from Cos, see Benedum (1977) no. 3 (pp. 272–4), lines 8–13; Laurenzi (1941) no. 4 (pp. 37–9), lines 4–5 and 14–16.

[16] See Nutton (1977) 199–201.

[17] For Imperial-period doctors as gymnasiarchs, see *IGR* IV, 182; Danoff (1937) no. 4 (pp. 84–6); for doctors as agonothetes, see the inscription discussed below in honour of Herakleitos of Rhodiapolis, who provides money for games despite having been granted immunity.

[18] *Dig.* 27.1.6.8.

[19] *Dig.* 27.1.6.2–4; both of these texts are discussed by Nutton (1977) 200–1 and (in more detail) (1971).

[20] See van Nijf (1997) 61, 149, 170–6 and 185 on groups of physicians listed with other professional associations.

form to the guilds of athletes and musicians and actors, whose Empire-wide organizations seem to have been structured around local branches, as we saw in chapter five,[21] and which would have been similarly visible as a group during many public events. Of course none of these honours would have been confined to doctors; all of them were similarly open to prominent men from other professions. However, there is also some evidence of more specific links between doctors and festivals. We know, for instance, that elected public physicians[22] – of whom there were many in the cities of the Greek east – would sometimes have been present at festivals in an official capacity not only to look after athletes, but also to care for the many visitors in attendance.[23] For example, we have one Hellenistic example of honours voted to a doctor who has cured some of the city's prominent guests attending a festival.[24]

That kind of familiarity with civic festival culture must have made the use of agonistic imagery a natural choice for doctors trying to advertise their own civic usefulness and professional pre-eminence. One final example should help to make those conventions of medical self-advertisement clearer. Herakleitos of Rhodiapolis in Asia Minor was a prolific medical writer and doctor. An inscription from a statue base set up in his home town at some time in the first or early second century AD praises him in language closely reminiscent of the inscribed boasts of athletes and musicians:

To Asklepios and *Hygeia*. The City Council and Demos and Gerousia of the Rhodiapolitans have voted continual yearly honours to Herakleitos, son of Herakleitos Oreios, their fellow citizen and citizen of Rhodes, a lover of his country and priest of Asklepios and Hygeia. They have honoured him with a gold portrait and with a statue commemorating his learning. He has been honoured in the same way by the Alexandrians, the Rhodians, the Athenians and the most sacred Council of the Areopagos and the Epicurean philosophers in Athens and the Sacred Thymelic Guild. He is the first man ever (πρῶτον ἀπ' αἰῶνος) to be a doctor and author and poet of works of medicine and philosophy; he has been called the Homer of medical poems; he has been honoured with exemption from liturgy; he has served for free as a physician; he has built a temple and dedicated images in honour of Asklepios and *Hygeia*, he has given his treatises and poems to his own city and to the Alexandrians, the Rhodians, the Athenians; and he has given to his own

---

[21] Pp. 221–5.
[22] See Cohn-Haft (1956) on public doctors in the Classical and Hellenistic periods; on the Roman period, see Nutton (1977).
[23] See Cohn-Haft (1956) 23, n. 71 (with the criticisms of BE 1958 no. 85 (pp. 201–2) and Robert (1966d) 24, n. 5).
[24] See Robert (1978b), with reference to an inscription published by Benedum (1977) no. 1 (pp. 265–70).

city a donation of 15,000 denarii to use for distributions and contests (χαρισάμενον τῇ πατρίδι εἰς διανομὰς καὶ ἀγῶνας Ἀησκληπίων καὶ ἀργυρίου μύρια καὶ πεντάκις χίλια). His city has honoured him with a permanent front seat (προεδρία). (*TAM* 11.910)[25]

This representation of Herakleitos conforms to the demand made by Galen and others that medicine should be an elevated, intellectual profession, able to hold its own against the high literary culture of the Empire. However, it also integrates that achievement with claims about Herakleitos' longstanding and generous involvement with the public life of his own city and others. In doing so it draws on epigraphic conventions which are common to decrees for agonistic performers and for a whole range of other prominent figures, for example in the mention of benefactions and multiple citizenships. Some of those achievements are tied to festival activity in familiar ways. For example, we hear of money given for contests, and the final word of the decree reminds us that the city's gratitude will be perpetually enshrined in Herakleitos' right to a front seat in the city's festivals. Moreover, in addition to these fairly standard honorific details there are features here which give Herakleitos' career unusually intense agonistic overtones. For example, the honours received from the Sacred Thymelic Guild of musicians imply public recognition of a connection between his literary skills and the competitive prowess of poets and musicians. The agonistic flavour of the inscription affects even its language. The phrase 'first of all time' (πρῶτον ἀπ' αἰῶνος) is one which is used regularly in agonistic inscriptions to signal unprecedented achievements, such as unparalleled combinations of victories.

I have suggested, then, that the frequent application of agonistic imagery to medical activity may be explicable partly by the fact that doctors often had close contact with the *gymnasia* and festivals of the cities of the east. This inscription for Herakleitos illustrates well both that kind of institutional contact and the way in which it filtered through into the honorific language used for prominent doctors (as for men from many other

---

[25] Ἀσκληπιῶι καὶ Ὑγίαι. | Ῥοδιαπολειτῶν ἡ βουλὴ καὶ ὁ δῆμος | καὶ ἡ γερουσία ἐτείμησαν ταῖς διηνε̄ | κέσιν κατ' ἔτος τειμαῖς Ἡράκλειτον | Ἡρακλείτου Ὀρείου, τὸν πολείτην καὶ | Ῥόδιον, φιλόπατριν, ἱερέα Ἀσκληπιοῦ | καὶ Ὑγίας, ἰκόνι ἐπιχρύσῳ καὶ τῷ τῆς | παιδείας ἀνδριάντι· ὃν ἐτείμησαν ὁμοί̄ | ως Ἀλεξανδρεῖς Ῥόδιοι Ἀθηναῖοι καὶ ἡ | ἱερωτάτη Ἀρεοπαγειτῶν βουλὴ καὶ οἱ | Ἀθήνησιν Ἐπικούρειοι φιλόσοφοι καὶ ἡ | ἱερὰ θυμελικὴ σύνοδος, πρῶτον ἀπ' αἰ̄]ῶνος ἰατρὸν καὶ συγγραφέα καὶ ποιη̄̄ | τὴν ἔργων ἰατρικῆς καὶ φιλοσοφίας, | ὃν ἀνέγραψαν ἰατρικῶν ποιημάτων | Ὅμηρον εἶναι, ἀλιτουργησία τιμηθέντα, | ἰατρεύσαντα προῖκα ναὸν κατασκεῡ | άσαντα καὶ ἀγάλματα ἀναθέντα Ἀσκλῃ̄ | πιοῦ καὶ Ὑγείας καὶ τὰ συγγράμματα αὐ̄ | τοῦ καὶ ποιήματα τῇ πατρίδι Ἀλεξαν | δρεῦσι Ῥοδίοις Ἀθηναίοις, χαρισά̄ | μενον τῇ πατρίδι εἰς διανομὰς καὶ | ἀγῶνας Ἀσκληπίων καὶ ἀργυρίου | * μύρια καὶ πεντάκις χίλια· ὃν ἐτεί̄ | μησεν ἡ πατρὶς καὶ προεδρία. See Oliver (1975) for brief commentary.

walks of life). It also gives one example of the way in which that agonistic imagery could be made compatible with conceptions of medicine as a philosophically elevated profession. We will see Galen enforcing a similar kind of compatibility between medicine and athletics in what follows, although he uses very different means to achieve that effect, acting on the conviction that 'athletics' can only be compatible with medicine if it is radically redefined.

An equally important factor in the relevance of agonistic imagery for doctors is the fact that medicine was itself a notoriously competitive profession, and not only in the sense that modern professions might be described as competitive when they have large numbers of people fighting for recognition. Greek science was competitive above all through being unregulated.[26] Doctors relied on rhetorical self-advertisement in their attempts to enhance their reputations and compete for custom, often in the context of public refutation of rivals. Tamsyn Barton has drawn on that insight in discussing Imperial-period medicine in the context of other scientific disciplines of the same period (especially astrology and physiognomics), in an attempt to relate the distinctive features of these different but related bodies of scientific knowledge to the social functions they performed.[27] She emphasizes in particular the way in which doctors tended to foreground their own moral propriety and literary sophistication by contrast with those of their rivals. She also draws attention to the habit, which ancient doctors shared with practitioners in other areas of scientific study, of outstripping one's rivals by presenting theories of greater and greater complexity.[28] Within that system the urge to denigrate rivals by recategorizing their activity as different from one's own was strong. Lloyd, for example (writing about Greek science and philosophy broadly speaking, rather than medicine specifically), describes 'the need some of the philosophers felt to distance themselves from those whom they generally considered to be no more than mere opportunistic conveyors of the plausible'.[29] In that sense the boundaries between different disciplines which medical writers sometimes assert so stridently were often extremely flexible, a function of self-serving and tendentious self-positioning as well as a reflection of widely acknowledged norms. The assertion of differences in the degree of technical worth of different disciplines often also extended to social differentiation. Doctors

---

[26] On the relation between competitive rhetoric and the development of philosophy and science in the Classical period, see Lloyd (1987) 83–102 and (1979) 86–98.
[27] Barton (1994a), esp. 133–68 on Galen and medical rhetoric.
[28] E.g., see Barton (1994a) 14 and 172–3 for summary of that technique within a number of different *technai*.
[29] Lloyd (1996) 73.

occupied a great range of social levels.³⁰ It may be that the great variety of social levels the ancient evidence attests to is not only a reflection of self-evident divisions, but also a function of the way in which the competitive processes of praise and blame granted doctors high or low social prestige.³¹

At the same time, however, it is important to be cautious about the characterization of Greek medicine as agonistic. The Ephesus inscriptions quoted above have often been used, along with evidence for contests in other activities which would seem out of place in a modern sporting context – ox-eating and wool-carding competitions, for example – to illustrate the claim that Greek society was structured around competition.³² One of my aims here, in exposing a deep-rooted ambivalence about competitiveness within at least some areas of the medical discourse which lies behind these inscriptions, is to draw attention to ways in which that unhelpfully broad characterization in some circumstances needs to be nuanced, in order to take into account the widely perceived negative connotations of agonistic prowess, as well as its attractions. The medical practice of the Empire, in other words, was not distinguished only by its competitiveness. It also had co-operative ideals and suspicion of competitive rhetoric deeply ingrained in it.³³ Geoffrey Lloyd has recently analysed the complex patterns underlying the competitive facade of Greek science through a comparison with Chinese practice.³⁴ One of the things he notes is a tendency within Greek science to seek logical certainty in order to avoid the impression of having used showy techniques of persuasion. He also notes the difficulty of maintaining that impression given that the claim to be speaking the truth was itself recognized as a rhetorical technique of persuasion.³⁵ Both of those points illustrate well the desire many scientists had to avoid overtly competitive behaviour in intellectual exchange, and also the difficulty of doing so. Moreover, Vivian Nutton has suggested that public physicians in small

---

³⁰ For a good overview of the varied social status of doctors, see Kleijwegt (1991) 135–63; cf. van Nijf (1997) 170–6; Nutton (1995) argues for a variety of different types of doctor, most of whom were not members of the elite; Pleket (1995) argues that medicine was most often a low-status *technê*; Nutton (1977) and Broughton (1938) 851–3 give examples of doctors occupying very high social status; for discussion of the varied social status of doctors in Rome, where Galen spent much of his career, see Nutton (1992), esp. 38–49, who suggests that the status of doctors tended to be lower in the west of the Empire than in the east; see also Singer (1997) xix–xxiii; Scarborough (1993) esp. 37–8; Kleijwegt (1991) 144–8; Kudlien (1986); Rawson (1985) 170–84; Edelstein (1966) 385–6.
³¹ Cf. Perkins (1995) 167–9.
³² For example, see Poliakoff (1987b) 104; Golden (1998) 29 discusses these examples in the course of challenging the idea that Greek society was uniquely agonistic.
³³ Cf. Brown (1978) 38–9 on the avoidance of overt competitiveness as a common pose in the Greek elite of the second century AD.
³⁴ Lloyd (1996).   ³⁵ Cf. Lloyd (1996) 74–92 (esp. 90–2).

cities in the east would often have been very secure in their professional standing, more so, presumably, than doctors in large cities like Rome, where Galen spent much of his life.[36] That reminder provides another valuable corrective to the dominant view – which Galen's work has tended to inspire – that medicine was uncontrollably agonistic. Co-operation between disciplines is implied by the evidence for close association between doctors and others in the civic contexts I have discussed. Men like Herakleitos of Rhodiapolis are praised for their intellectual pre-eminence, but in terms which tend to obscure the processes of contest which have produced it. Herakleitos stands above the petty struggles of everyday life, and so can afford to advertise his affinities with other intellectuals rather than debunking them.

In the context of the competitive practices of ancient medicine, the use of agonistic imagery within medical self-definition of the kind we see in the inscription quoted at the beginning of the chapter comes to look less surprising. The voluminous writings of Galen, the second-century physician who dominates our view of Imperial medicine, and whose influence overshadowed later European medical practice for many hundreds of years, provide a good (albeit extreme) example of those competitive practices.[37] His writing displays an extraordinary degree of technical and philosophical sophistication,[38] which carries to its limits the habit of asserting professional pre-eminence by means of the complexity and comprehensiveness of one's work.[39] He also often denigrates his rivals fiercely, in moral as well as technical terms, in distinguishing between his own elevated medical *technê* and the debased, superficial versions of it, unworthy of the name of true medicine, which those rivals espouse.[40] However, the categories Galen works with – in line with the tendency towards contentious and self-serving redefinition of boundaries which I have outlined above – are in many ways highly controversial products of his own rhetorical self-promotion. In fact, Galen himself seems to be partly responsible for establishing a conceptual split between high medicine and its debased rivals.[41] Such a split was out of step with the signs of close association between medicine and other professions which we see from the Empire's inscriptional record, as I suggested above.

---

[36] Nutton (1977) 200.   [37] See Barton (1994a) 133–68; cf. Singer (1997) xx–xxiii.
[38] On Galen as philosopher, see Hankinson (1992); Donini (1992); Moraux (1981); Frede (1981) on Galen's epistemology; Kieffer (1964) 1–30 on Galen's study of logic.
[39] E.g., see Barton (1994a) 152–63 on Galen's complex subdivisions in his work on the pulse.
[40] See Barton (1994a) 143–7; Lloyd (1973) 152–3.
[41] See Riddle (1993) 113–17; cf. Stok (1993) 418–21 on Galen's attempt to reclassify the arts in the *Protrepticus*, which I will discuss at the end of this chapter.

Galen's competitiveness does not confine itself to duelling with his rivals on paper. Over and over again he comes back to the scene of confrontation with other claimants to medical expertise in public; in fact his work provides some of the most vivid evidence we have for the prevalence of public medical debate.[42] We see him trumping his ignorant rivals with his own diagnoses and theories. The most spectacular examples are his interventions in displays of dissection, carried out on animals as exotic as the elephant described in *On Anatomical Procedures* 7.10 [K2.618–23], where Galen correctly predicts that the animal's heart will have a 'bone' in it (really a bone-like piece of cartilage), a fact denied by all of the other doctors present. Moreover, Galen's autobiographical works in some ways confirm the picture of doctors involved in the public agonistic culture of the cities of the east. For example, he describes his own early career as doctor to a school of gladiators in Pergamon.[43] His familiarity with the ubiquitous festival and spectacle culture of the Empire must surely be one of the factors which make the agonistic elements of his own professional self-representation so prevalent. Galen's competitiveness has often been treated as a close relative of the fierce rivalries of sophistic rhetoric which were so much a part of the intellectual scene of this period.[44] I want to suggest here, in addition, that a full understanding of Galen's attitudes to agonistic processes requires examination of his representations of athletics as much as his relations with sophistry. The tendency to emphasize Galen's links with rhetorical activity at the expense of examining his relations with athletic competition is, I believe, one consequence of the dominant, and too narrow modern scholarly emphasis on sophistry as the most important form of elite participation in public spectacle in this period.

Galen, then, is the most agonistic of medical writers; in fact his competitiveness is so obsessive that we should probably be wary of using his work straightforwardly as evidence for the agonistic nature of ancient medical practice.[45] It is striking, however, that there are also many ways in which he resists agonistic imagery, dissociating himself from the vulgar and strident squabbling and self-advertisement of his rivals. That is a point which

---

[42] Debru (1995) summarizes the evidence from Galen's own writing for his involvement in public debate; cf. Flemming (2000) 262–3; Nutton (1972) on Galen's *On Prognosis*.

[43] See Nutton (1973) 162–4.

[44] E.g., see von Staden (1997) (who focuses on Galen's anatomical displays in particular) and (1995); see also Pearcy (1993); Kollesch (1981); Reardon (1971) 45–63; Bowersock (1969) 59–75; by contrast, Brunt (1994) 43–4 importantly reminds us that many of the 'sophistic' characteristics of Galen and his contemporaries were in no way exclusive to this period.

[45] Equally, however, we should probably be cautious about doubting the picture he paints of his own pre-eminence, as Nutton (1984) argues.

modern discussion of his work has often ignored.⁴⁶ In much the same way he tends to represent himself as superior to the wranglings of rival medical sects, in avoiding narrow-minded allegiance to any one of them.⁴⁷ Even in the descriptions of public debate which I have just referred to, he often goes out of his way to avoid the impression that he has been interested in scoring cheap points off his competitors.⁴⁸ For example, he often plays down the possibility that the gatherings he describes might have been public ones, emphasizing the presence of experts – or at least pretended experts – rather than entirely unqualified bystanders.⁴⁹ He also frequently announces that he has agreed to write or speak only reluctantly, after a great deal of persuasion.⁵⁰ And on other occasions he chooses not to correct his rivals' faults face to face, preferring to wait instead for the opportunity to do so on paper.⁵¹ He thus transfigures sordid rivalries into the much more elevated arena of his own philosophical composition, advertising his indifference towards the spectacle of public dissection, as if he is saving his energy for the much more exalted task of looking beneath the surface of nature and dissecting the secret workings of the universe in all their most intricate detail.⁵² Even while he indulges in fierce denunciation of his competitors and in opportunistic self-promotion of unparalleled brilliance and complexity, he simultaneously denies any significant connection between his own activities and the ideals of public contest and spectacle which were so widespread within the Roman Empire's civic culture, lifting his own struggles on to an incomparably higher plane.

Elsewhere he goes out of his way above all to deprecate the kind of victory which is based on showy rhetoric, without any substance underlying it. The opening metaphor of his treatise *The Best Doctor is also a Philosopher*

---

⁴⁶ E.g., Barton (1994a) 147–9, like others, underemphasizes that pattern.
⁴⁷ See, e.g., Boudon (1994) 1436–41; Grmek and Gourevitch (1994) 1524–5.
⁴⁸ Cf. Pearcy (1993) and (1983) on Galen's (only partially successful) attempts to dissociate medicine from rhetoric; Galen's avoidance of excessive atticism may be related to this pose, as an attempt to escape from the charge of excessively showy erudition: e.g., see *The Order of My Own Books* 5 [K19.60–61]; Swain (1996) 56–63.
⁴⁹ E.g., see *On Anatomical Procedures* 7.10 [K2.619–20], describing the presence of 'many doctors' at the dissection of the elephant; cf. *On Examinations by which the Best Physicians are Recognized* 9.6–7 (only surviving in Arabic translation: see Iskandar (1988) 104–5).
⁵⁰ E.g., see *On My Own Books* [K19.21–2] for the claim that he had to be persuaded by his friends to give a public demonstration and to write up the results.
⁵¹ E.g., see *On Anatomical Procedures* 7.16 [K2.642–3], where he describes other people – rather than himself – humiliating an incompetent dissector; cf. *On Anatomical Procedures* 7.10 [K2.619–20], although here it is his companions who persuade him not to waste his energy on demonstrating the truth about the elephant's heart to the ignorant men who are present.
⁵² See Hankinson (1994) and (1988) on Galen's conception of anatomy as an important foundation for his teleological views on the workings of the universe.

makes that claim clearly. Here he criticizes doctors who claim to imitate Hippocrates without being willing to put in the hard work of reading his texts. He compares these people with lazy but self-glorifying athletes who are unwilling to undertake the training they would need to reach the top of their profession: 'Many athletes suffer from wanting to become Olympic victors, but without going to the trouble of doing anything to bring that about; much the same thing happens to the majority of doctors' (*The Best Doctor is also a Philosopher* 1 [K1.53]).[53] The implications for Galen's position are clear. His Olympian standing in the field of medicine is due to hard work, as he often tells us elsewhere in his more autobiographical moods.[54] Professional pre-eminence can only be acquired by hard work, and before that by a painstaking education in logical method and philosophical principle. The image of athletic training which Galen exploits here is in fact one which he uses again and again throughout his work, most often through the word γυμνάζειν ('to train'), which he applies to his own meticulous preparation and learning in order to reinforce this same point about the importance of solid medical education. That gymnastic metaphor supplements the equally athletic image of 'stripping bare' (γυμνοῦν) which he often applies to the activity of dissection discussed in the last paragraph, and to his own logical method of 'stripping bare' arguments and theories, examining them in a form unadorned by any rhetorical clothing.[55] He appropriates this athletic imagery for his own skills, transforming it to something far more elevated than the activities of the *gymnasion* to which it is usually applied.

Galen's work thus points, I believe, to the deeply ingrained nature of the medical mistrust of competitiveness which I drew attention to above. He participates energetically in agonistic rivalries, but he also at least pays lip-service to more anti-rhetorical co-operative ideals of medical practice, in shying away from personal confrontation even as he attempts to impose a view of intellectual hierarchies which bolsters his own pre-eminence. Galen, in other words, is one of the most agonistic writers of the ancient world, but he is also, paradoxically, one of the ancient writers who goes furthest in distancing himself from agonistic processes. In that sense he takes to its furthest extreme the ambivalence about competitiveness which

---

[53] Οἷόν τι πεπόνθασιν οἱ πολλοὶ τῶν ἀθλητῶν, ἐπιθυμοῦντες μὲν ὀλυμπιονῖκαι γενέσθαι, μηδὲν δὲ πράττειν, ὡς τούτου τυχεῖν, ἐπιτηδεύοντες, τοιοῦτόν τι καὶ τοῖς πολλοῖς τῶν ἰατρῶν συμβέβηκεν.

[54] Cf. Flemming (2000) 257.

[55] There are good examples of both words in the short description of the dissection of the elephant from *On Anatomical Procedures* 7.10 [K2.618–23] which I mentioned above (for training imagery, see 619, line 19; 620, line 14; 621, lines 2 and 5; and for the image of 'stripping bare' (γυμνώσας), see 622, lines 12–13).

I have suggested is a direct consequence of the rhetorical nature of ancient medical practice.

In the rest of this section I want to look a little more closely at Galen's representation of his own involvement in competitive processes by reading his *Thrasyboulos* [K5.806–98] (subtitled *Whether Healthiness is a Part of Medicine or Gymnastics*).[56] In this work, Galen refutes the opinions of athletic trainers, who according to his account categorize medicine as an exclusively 'restorative' *technê*, whose only function is to return the body to good health when ill. As such, they suggest, medicine is unconnected with the 'preservative' functions of day-to-day exercise and regimen, which they claim as the exclusive province of the *gymnasion*. Galen argues instead that all of the different skills concerned with the well-being of the body are part of a single overall art, which he associates with his own Hippocratic, medical expertise; and he suggests that the expertise of the trainer is only one tiny subdivision of this overall medical art, and is useless without the overall art to guide it. He thus leaves some room for athletics as a valuable if relatively insignificant contributor to medical care, although he also suggests that there are few who still practise it in an appropriately modest fashion. Training (*gymnastikê*) used to be valuable, he tells us, until trainers became preoccupied with how to defeat their opponents (36 [K5.874]). It was after this that everything began to go wrong.

The arguments he uses are often complex, although they are presented in a more user-friendly form than in some of his most technical works, partly, I think, to give the impression that the work is relevant for non-specialists and students as much as for established practitioners.[57] He begins by pointing to some of the problems which follow from suggesting that there is more than one art concerned with the body (*Thrasyboulos* 4–9). In doing so he exposes the faulty logic some of his opponents use in defending their cause. He then demonstrates instead that there can only be one single *technê* concerned with the body (10–29). That demonstration is based on the claim that 'good condition' (εὐεξία, the aim of preservative 'regimen') and 'health' (ὑγίεια, the aim of restorative 'therapy') are caused by the same good bodily state. Regimen and medical therapy must therefore be inextricably related to each other, since actions which aim for identical results are necessarily part of the same *technê*. Then, in 30–45, he shows us how this overarching art concerning the body should be divided. He suggests a basic distinction

---

[56] See Kollesch and Nickel (1994) 1420 for further bibliography on the *Thrasyboulos*; I have not had the opportunity to see the work of Englert (1929).
[57] On the variation in levels of audience sophistication which Galen envisages for his different works, see Barton (1994a) 146–7.

between the restorative part of it and the preservative part of it, each of which can be further subdivided. He then explains that the art of the *paidotribês* is a very tiny subsection of the latter (41–5). He concludes (46–7) with more general points about the uselessness of athletics, and contrasts the great doctors of the past, who have displayed a knowledge of the whole art of the body, with those who have set themselves up as experts in athletic training. In the process he describes a recent encounter with an ignorant athletic trainer, who has been impudent enough to attack his views in public.

The text is shaped by interdisciplinary rivalries of the kind I have been discussing. A number of features stand out. Galen's crushing of rival theories is represented as effortless and complete, but also methodical and unostentatious. He replaces the over-ambitious assertions of the athletic trainers' claims with his own more powerful vision of philosophical medicine as an overarching discipline which holds all other types of bodily knowledge in its power. The complex categorizations he uses to achieve that effect exemplify well the technique I discussed above of outstripping one's rivals by increasingly subtle and convoluted logical subdivisions.[58] Those subdivisions give an impression of depth to his own logical method, in contrast with the superficiality of athletes and athletic trainers, who are portrayed as both logically and morally bankrupt and whose concern with empty spectacle manifests itself not only in the superficial posturing of their public appearances, but also in the shallowness of their arguments. At the same time, despite the ferocity of his point-scoring, he devotes the vast bulk of the work to careful exposition of the arguments underlying his position, as if to stress his lack of interest in *ad hominem* criticism of the kind the trainers themselves indulge in.[59] The work also envisages a number of possible audiences, distinguishing between those who are able to follow the different stages of a complex argument through a willingness to submit to Galen's guidance, and others whose unthinking adherence to superficially attractive but illogical arguments makes them incurably ignorant and so unable to respond properly to what they read. Galen thus advertises his own superiority in the struggle between different disciplines for adherents. The implication is that any students whose receptiveness and intelligence make them worth having will side with Galen unhesitatingly.

---

[58] Cf. Barton (1994a) 152 and 224–5, n. 103 on the similar way in which Galen reacts to trainers in his *De sanitate tuenda* – which I will discuss further in the next section – responding to the complexity of their systems of classification by constructing alternative systems which are equally complex, if not more so.

[59] Cf. Smith (1979) 107 on the *Thrasyboulos*: 'In his usual fashion, Galen deprecates quarrels over words, while showing his own adeptness in such quarrels.'

The text's long central section of theoretical argument is framed by two scenes of public debate which enhance these contrasts between Galen's own position and the false logic of his competitors. These scenes also help to convey some of Galen's distinctive attitudes to his own professional competitiveness and display. The work opens with immediate reference to a previous discussion:

> It is not the case, Thrasyboulos, that my initial answer to the problem you set for me (περὶ τοῦ προβληθέντος ὑπὸ σοῦ ζητήματος) is different from what I will write in this treatise. For you know perfectly well, I think, that I always make the same argument about the same subject, and that I never attempt to speak on a subject without first learning the right method for discussing it, and without training myself in that method (ὧν οὔτε μέθοδον ἔμαθον οὔτ' ἐγυμνασάμην πω κατ' αὐτήν). (*Thrasyboulos* 1 [K5.806])[60]

This opening hints at a scene of public lecturing or public debate, but that hint is kept in check in order to stress the dominant impression of a very private gathering. Galen suggests that Thrasyboulos will be familiar with his methods, with the implication that this conversation is related to a long history of friendship and intellectual exchange between the two men, rather than any single encounter. In that context, the personal, one-to-one style of the opening paragraphs gives the impression of being an appropriate extension of intimate discussion. Galen is also careful to proclaim his consistency, as if to remove any doubt that he might have pandered to his listeners at the time of the original debate, or that his responses to the questions he is presented with are just opportunistic expressions of whatever ideas occur to him on each separate occasion. In fact he bases his responses on careful preparation in logical method. He draws attention to the way in which he never embarks on a subject unless he has 'trained himself' (ἐγυμνασάμην) in it. Here, as so often, he transfers the vocabulary of agonistic activity to a more elevated sphere. He implicitly contrasts his own preparations with the lack of self-attention exhibited by the athletic trainers who will be prominent in the closing paragraphs of the work, and whose self-care never moves beyond the most debased and superficial version of bodily training. The word 'problem' (πρόβλημα), which is used at the beginning of the next paragraph (2 [K5.807]) to describe the question under discussion, and which picks up on Galen's initial mention of the query Thrasyboulos has 'thrown forward' (προβληθέντος), is often

---

[60] Οὐκ ἄλλα μέν, ὦ Θρασύβουλε, παραχρῆμα περὶ τοῦ προβληθέντος ὑπὸ σοῦ ζητήματος εἶπον, ἄλλα δὲ συγγράψασθαι τοῖσδε τοῖς ὑπομνήμασιν ἔχω· πάντως γάρ που γιγνώσκεις, ὡς ἀεί τε τὰ αὐτὰ περὶ τῶν αὐτῶν διεξέρχομαι καὶ ὡς εἰς οὐδὲν ἐπιχειρῶ λέγειν, ὧν οὔτε μέθοδον ἔμαθον οὔτ' ἐγυμνασάμην πω κατ' αὐτήν.

applied to topics under consideration in philosophical dialogue and here perhaps contributes to a sense of detached, theoretical speculation. It is also worth remembering, however, that the same word πρόβλημα was used for one of the contests in the Ephesian medical *agôn*, and that it was used to describe the presentation of subjects to orators as starting-points for rhetorical improvisation. As those parallels remind us, the imagery of public rhetoric and competition constantly lies in the background to Galen's representation of this occasion, even if it is an image he goes out of his way to resist.

Many of the same themes are extended within the introductory paragraphs which come next. Galen mentions the fact that Thrasyboulos was interested in the topic because he had often heard it discussed in disputes between doctors and athletic trainers (2 [K5.807]). He thus emphasizes the way in which his contribution is related to a wider context of disciplinary dispute, but he also represents it as a contribution which sidesteps some of the more adversarial characteristics of that context, if nothing else because he makes no mention of any athletic trainer being present on the specific occasion he is describing. He is careful to avoid the impression of any crass over-certainty or any claim to complete knowledge on his own part or on the part of his interlocutors. He tells us that he was very tentative about beginning the exposition because he wanted to be sure that all were agreed on what exactly was under discussion, and what exactly the terms of the discussion meant, for fear of presenting an argument which was superficial, or which addressed the topic 'in name only' (πρὸς τοὔνομα μόνον) (2 [K5.807]). That concern is picked up in paragraph 5 [K5.810–11], where he points out the absurdity of using arguments which prejudge the answer to the question, as the athletic trainers do in simply stating their view of the categories of bodily care under discussion rather than arguing for them logically. Once again, Galen there constructs his own professional persona in contrast with athletic superficiality and stridency. He also mentions the tentativeness Thrasyboulos showed in acting as Galen's interlocutor, and tells us that Thrasyboulos' place was soon taken by a philosopher who happened to be present, who was 'one of those who are *well-trained* in logical argument' (τῶν τινα γεγυμνασμένων ἐν λογικῇ θεωρίᾳ) (2 [K5.809]). That detail bolsters the impression of a respectable, philosophical gathering, far removed from public, spectacular wrangling where men speak on subjects they know nothing about. It also contributes, once again, to Galen's familiar technique of transferring the language of athletic training to describe more elevated intellectual activities.

These effects are further enhanced in Galen's reminder of the need for all readers to bring their own responses to bear on the arguments they encounter. He tells us that he was very reluctant to write up the argument, reminding us of his own preference for avoiding the limelight. And he announces that the text is only a very incomplete study, designed above all to provide a model for logical analysis of other problems. Solutions to set problems are on their own useless, he suggests, unless a reader has the logical expertise to respond to them. The method Galen offers here is related to skills he has 'worked at on his own' (ὅπερ αὐτὸς ἐπ' ἐμαυτοῦ πράξας ἔτυχον) (3 [K5.809–10]). Logical method, he explains, will allow 'one who has trained himself in it sufficiently' (ὅστις ἂν ἱκανῶς ἀσκήσῃ) (4 [K5.810]) to undertake any enquiry with equal success. Yet again, the imagery of disciplined athletic training is applied to intellectual enquiry, instead of gymnastic contest. And through that reapplication of imagery Galen once again avoids the impression of superficial display and exaggerated self-advertisement for his own work. Good readership, it seems, is based on hard training. It stands in contrast with the unthinking absorption which is commonly shown in viewing both athletic spectacle and the self-promoting antics of athletic trainers on the debating floor.

The detailed argument which follows, and which I have outlined above, enhances the impression of depth and solidity within Galen's own argument. When it draws to a close at the end of paragraph 45, Galen steps back from the text's relentless logical progression, and turns for a moment to a second, very different scene of public debate. Here, he finally makes a more direct attack on the athletic trainers, whose presence in the dialogue as espousers of the arguments Galen rejects has so far been a shadowy one. Galen's final, vivid condemnation of their crowd-pulling vulgarity, conveyed through a fleeting glimpse of one of them in action in debate, gives the impression of being just a small footnote to the more important topic of their illogicality which has so far been Galen's main focus. The implication may be that for Galen debunking the personal characteristics of his rivals is relatively unimportant. At the same time, however, the position of this scene at the end of the work gives it a lingering intensity, as if it is only now, when the logical justification for his views has been presented, that Galen will allow himself an open expression of the opinion which he has been moving towards all along.

This short final section of the *Thrasyboulos* opens with denunciation of the uselessness of athletic activity. Galen here emphasizes the falsity of even those virtues which athletics purports to produce, suggesting, for example, that the strength of athletes has no useful function in any real-life context outside the *stadion*. This impression of underlying emptiness matches the sense of hollowness which Galen has repeatedly applied to the trainers' arguments. He also suggests here that the narrow selectiveness with which athletes train themselves makes them unsuited to any other kind of activity. Most importantly it makes them unsuited to the activities of writing and debate in which many of them attempt to participate, failing to recognize their own incompetence, when they become trainers on retirement:[61] 'Nevertheless the most unfortunate of them, all the ones who have never won anything, immediately start to call themselves trainers, and then they begin screeching, just like pigs, in a discordant and barbarous voice' (κεκράγασιν οὐδὲν ἧττον τῶν συῶν ἐκμελεῖ καὶ βαρβάρῳ φωνῇ) (46 [K5.894]).[62] The animal imagery suggests a loss of restraint and reason, which leads to a barbaric mistreatment of the Hellenic, Hippocratic heritage of which Galen represents himself as the guardian.[63] For a moment Galen almost takes on the strident, screeching voice of the trainers in his denunciation of them, abandoning temporarily the measured tone of all that has come before, as if to remind us of how his criticisms would sound if they were converted to the conventional idioms of vulgar professional rivalry, before returning to a more sober, step-by-step summary of some of the text's main conclusions in his closing pages.

We then hear about one particularly impudent athletic trainer who is said to have quarrelled recently with Galen in public (on an occasion separate from the one which the *Thrasyboulos* itself is dedicated to replaying). We hear that the man had been criticizing Hippocrates' views on massage in front of an audience partly composed of doctors and philosophers, who then asked Galen for his opinion when he arrived on the scene. Galen duly explains that Hippocrates was the very first person to write an important work on the subject. At that point he is interrupted:

That self-taught trainer came forward at once into the middle of the gathering (παρελθὼν εἰς τὸ μέσον), and stripped a boy, ordering us to massage him and train him, or else to be silent about massage and training. And after that he kept shouting, 'Where did Hippokrates ever go to do the long-jump? When did he ever go to the *palaistra*? He probably didn't even know how to rub oil on himself properly.' (46 [K5.895])[64]

[61] Galen makes a similar attack (at 22 [K5.842–3]) on public lecturers who have no knowledge of logic.
[62] ἀλλ' ὅμως οἱ τούτων ἀτυχέστατοι καὶ μηδεπώποτε νικήσαντες ἐξαίφνης ἑαυτοὺς ὀνομάζουσι γυμναστάς, εἶτ' οἶμαι καὶ κεκράγασιν οὐδὲν ἧττον τῶν συῶν ἐκμελεῖ καὶ βαρβάρῳ φωνῇ.
[63] Cf. *De sanitate tuenda* 1.10 [K6.51] for a similar link between animality and barbarism.
[64] παρελθὼν εἰς τὸ μέσον ἐξαίφνης ὁ αὐτοδίδακτος ἐκεῖνος γυμναστὴς ἐκδύσας παιδάριον ἐκέλευσεν ἡμᾶς τρίβειν τε τοῦτο καὶ γυμνάζειν ἢ σιωπᾶν περὶ τρίψεως καὶ γυμνασίων, εἶτ'

The trainer's stock reflex in any situation of public display is to strip his athletes, a response which might be suitable for the *stadion*, but which is clearly inappropriate here. He thrusts himself forward into the limelight (εἰς τὸ μέσον), in a way which contrasts with Galen's more self-effacing approach, which involves speaking only when he is asked to do so, just as he claims to have written the *Thrasyboulos* only after repeated requests. Galen goes on to refute the challenge, although the trainer himself continues to shout unrelentingly and is therefore unable to take in any of the argument. In that sense the trainer stands in contrast to Galen's ideal readers as the text envisages them. Galen explains the truth to those who will listen in a leisurely way (κατὰ σχολήν) (46 [K5.895]), just as the text itself has moved patiently from one point to the next, in a way which makes it accessible even for readers like Thrasyboulos who are not confident in their grasp of logical method, but which leaves no chance for ignorant readers who are not willing to make the effort of following.

I have argued, then, that the *Thrasyboulos* participates with extreme vehemence – as many of Galen's other works also do – in widespread processes of disciplinary rivalry. At the same time, however, it avoids aggressive overtones, rejecting overt competitiveness in favour of a more co-operative and non-aggressive image of professional endeavour. It is thus, I believe, typical of broad patterns of medical self-portrayal amongst Galen's contemporaries, in the sense that it reveals a fundamental tension between the need for competitive self-promotion on the one hand, and the need for avoidance of spectacular and unco-operative rivalry on the other. However, Galen is unusual in the extravagance with which he commits himself to both sides of this balance simultaneously, in the degree to which he is agonistic and anti-agonistic at the same time. That double motivation goes a long way towards explaining the text's ambivalent use of athletic imagery. His denigration of trainers is used to back up his claims to pre-eminence. The vocabulary of athletic training is used for Galen's own philosophical labours. We see standard techniques of rhetorical denigration turned against Galen's rivals in order to emphasize his victory over them. In the process, however, the same imagery is used to illustrate his suspicion of blatant self-advertisement, in a way which makes the image of the athletic trainer a negative point of reference for Galen's professional self-projection, helping him to articulate by contrast his own restrained attitudes to the very

---

ἐφεξῆς ἐβόα· ποῦ γὰρ Ἱπποκράτης εἰσῆλθεν εἰς σκάμμα; ποῦ δ' εἰς παλαίστραν; ἴσως οὐδ' ἀναχέασθαι καλῶς ἠπίστατο.

processes of professional display and competition in which the *Thrasyboulos* participates so forcefully. The trainers of this text are obsessively concerned with public appearance and *ad hominem* rivalry instead of philosophical substance. Their superficiality is apparent both in the failings of their logic and in their personal and professional conduct. In that sense they are far removed from Galen's own shining example of unostentatious logical solidity, which goes hand-in-hand with his modest and hard-working professional practices, but which nevertheless, on Galen's own account, wins an almost effortless victory within the struggles for medical renown.[65] The final image of the shrieking athletic trainer in *Thrasyboulos* 46 gives us a concrete image of everything Galen is not.

TRAINING IN MODERATION

How, then, did Galen believe the body should be treated? How did his accounts of gymnastic exercise help to articulate his responses to that question? And how widely paralleled were his views on these issues? Like many other medical writers, Galen combines an interest in the value of carefully regulated exercise with a mistrust of the dangerous excesses of top athletes, using athletic subject matter in both cases as a vehicle for presenting the fundamental principles of his own medical doctrine. Galen savages the athletic trainers, in other words, not only in order to define his own preferred mode of professional conduct, but also, perhaps more importantly, to hold them up as paradigmatic examples of the misapplication of medical principle, with which his own recommendations for bodily care are contrasted. At the same time, he embraces the project of constructing a positive version of *gymnasion* training, making the *gymnasion* compatible with his broader views on what properly philosophical medical knowledge should involve, especially in his *De sanitate tuenda*, which outlines exhaustively (and exhaustingly) his recommended scheme for gymnastic regimen, and which was one of the ancient works which had most influence on the growth in sixteenth- and seventeenth-century European interest in sporting activity.[66]

The idea of all-embracing philosophical discipline, which could exercise control over the body as well as the mind, was of course very far from being

---

[65] Cf. Flemming (2000) 256–83 for an overview of the way in which Galen combines autobiographical and professional self-presentation in a way which makes his personal and philosophical authority seem to spring from the same source.
[66] See Brailsford (1969) 15, 18, 165.

new.⁶⁷ Nor is it unrelated to what we find in medical writing contemporary with Galen. As we have already seen in chapter three,⁶⁸ Michel Foucault has argued that the Imperial period was marked by an intensification of Classical interest in bodily self-care as a project which requires and enhances care of the individual's soul.⁶⁹ In line with those tendencies, this period sees a huge increase in the production of treatises devoted to accounts of the relationship between daily regimen and preservation of health. Galen's interest in athletic training is clearly related to these trends. However, he also intensifies them and manipulates them in highly original and influential ways. In that sense his work provides a vivid illustration of how widely the changes which Foucault identifies were contested.⁷⁰ The most striking feature of his work on this subject is its uncompromising nature, the intensity of his insistence that all fields of action should come under the aegis of his own philosophical and medical guidance. That refusal to compromise may be one explanation for the intensity of his interest in athletic subject matter. The vehemence of his attempts to reform athletic training is a sign of his determination that no sphere of human activity can be allowed to escape from subjection to the principles of balance and self-knowledge which are the central features of his own philosophical medicine.

In making that argument I am moving from questions of form (as outlined in my discussion of Galen's attitudes to competitive self-presentation) to questions of content, moving from questions about how medical practice was presented to the world to questions about what principles and doctrines it was based on. Ultimately, however, I believe that that distinction is difficult to maintain, since Galen's demands for unathletic moderation and balanced treatment of the body spill over into his portrayal of his own didactic style. The principle of philosophical self-attention and moderation is an all-embracing concept for Galen, which must be applied to all

---

⁶⁷ Jouanna (1999) 258–85 discusses the idea of philosophical medicine in the Classical period; however, he also draws attention to the way in which much of the Hippocratic Corpus, which had such a strong influence on Galen, as we shall see in a moment, participated in a reaction against the philosophization of medical practice.

⁶⁸ Pp. 99–100.

⁶⁹ Foucault (1986), esp. 39–68; see also Flemming (2000) 63–6 for an overview of the applicability of Foucault's ideas to ancient medicine.

⁷⁰ For an analysis of Galen's unique but also influential contribution to these trends, see Perkins (1995) 142–72, esp. 145–50 on contest over care of the body in the Imperial period, focusing on rivalry between different medical sects. See also chapter one (pp. 14 and 29) and chapter three (pp. 99–101) above, where I discuss further the need to nuance Foucault's mappings of cultural change; cf. Miller (1998), Davidson (1997), esp. xxiv and Goldhill (1995), esp. xi–xii; that is not to suggest, however, that Foucault was consistently oblivious to these complexities – in fact the opening paragraph of his chapter on 'The Body' (Foucault (1986) 99) foregrounds precisely the phenomenon of debate about the relations between medicine and philosophy.

forms of physical activity; and the universal applicability of that principle does not stop at bodily exercise. It also takes over the whole of Galen's persona, in ways which are related to the professional virtues which we have seen him advertising in the *Thrasyboulos*. His style of teaching and his ostensibly non-aggressive professional self-advertisement are themselves embodiments of moderation and self-knowledge, in just the same way as the exercises he recommends.

I will be coming back to Galen's work in a moment, in order to look at the way in which he conveys his ideals of moderate and balanced bodily training as something compatible with philosophical self-knowledge, and the way in which he uses athletic imagery and subject matter to enforce that prescription. First, though, I want to look briefly at the way in which athletic subjects are addressed — similarly, but more sporadically — by other medical writers. I take two main examples, one Classical, from the works ascribed to Hippocrates, and the other roughly contemporary with Galen, from the works of Antyllos, recorded in the medical compendium of the fourth-century writer Oribasios.

Analysis of the Hippocratic Corpus is complicated by the fact that it is the product of work by a number of different writers, whose perspectives are not always easily compatible with each other, a fact which Galen's analysis of those texts does not acknowledge. Galen attempted, more systematically than anyone, to extract coherent views from the Corpus on a great range of subjects, athletic activity included.[71] He presents the Hippocratic Corpus as the work of a single writer (in line with what was generally believed at the time), and integrates it with his own medical views, although he does not shy away from correcting Hippocratean conclusions in places. He claims Hippocrates as the great father of Greek medicine, representing himself as Hippocrates' most faithful follower, as others had before him. At times his desire for coherence between these texts and his own means that his interpretations of Hippocrates are opportunistic, although that need not mean that they were not sincerely held.[72] The same is also true of his treatment of a number of other famous forerunners. After Hippocrates, Galen's most important role model was Plato.[73] In several places he quotes Plato's views from *Republic* Book 3 on the importance of education which balances physical elements with intellectual, spiritual components, but at times he exaggerates the consistency and urgency of Plato's interest in a rigid re-categorization of athletic training as a *technê* subordinate

---

[71] On Galen and Hippocrates, see Flemming (2000) 278–9; Lloyd (1991); Temkin (1991) 47–50; Smith (1979) 61–176.
[72] See esp. Lloyd (1991). [73] See Flemming (2000) 278; de Lacy (1972).

to medicine.[74] I will discuss Galen's Platonism in more detail in chapter seven, especially in looking at the way in which his interpretation of Plato's *Gorgias* differs from the response we find in Philostratus' *Gymnasticus*.[75] Galen's dependence on these models is partly a response to the need many scientific writers seem to have felt to avoid the impression of excessive innovation – represented as excessive competitiveness with the great men of the past – although that urge was also balanced by the desire to avoid any accusation of excessive dependence on authority.[76]

We should therefore be wary of accepting Galen's interpretation of Hippocrates wholesale. Often the views we find in the Hippocratic Corpus are not as coherent as Galen claims. Often, too, they do not fit with his own opinions quite so neatly as he suggests. Galen's treatment of Hippocrates' views on athletics is a good example of that phenomenon. The techniques of healing disease seem to have been the main priority for medical knowledge at the time these works were written, and Galen's own interest in daily regimen and preventative medicine is not one which the Hippocratic Corpus shares to anything like the same degree,[77] although there are conspicuous exceptions to that in the Hippocratic work *Regimen*, which catalogues the best types of exercise in several places, most extensively in 2.61–6.[78] The Hippocratic Corpus also contains several expressions of anxiety about the dangers of immoderate athletic training, and the imagery of violent and self-destructive over-exercise which these texts attach to athletes has something in common with the imagery Galen uses, but it occurs far less frequently than it does within Galen's work. Galen puts a great deal of weight on these statements, most prominently in *Good Condition* and in the *Protrepticus*, as we shall see in the final section of this chapter. In some ways, however, the Hippocratic writings do not support the extreme view Galen attempts to use them for. In the Hippocratic text *Nutriment* 34, for example, we are told that: 'The condition of the athlete is not in accordance with nature. The healthy condition is better in all things.'[79] It has been shown, however, that this treatise is a Hellenistic work much later than most of the other Hippocratic texts,[80] and we should therefore, I think, be cautious about taking this seemingly programmatic statement as an idea which informs the principles lying behind the whole of the Hippocratic Corpus, as Galen does.

---

[74] E.g., see *Good Condition* [K4.753].   [75] Pp. 321–4.
[76] See Barton (1994a) 149–52; Lloyd (1991).   [77] See Jouanna (1999) 324.
[78] For a brief account of this text see Jouanna (1999) 408–9.
[79] διάθεσις ἀθλητικὴ οὐ φύσει· ἕξις ὑγιεινὴ κρείσσων ἐν πᾶσιν.
[80] See Jouanna (1999) 401.

Elsewhere, we hear that athletic fitness can be risky because it is always in danger of breaking down abruptly when it is carried to its highest peak of perfection, but here too we should be cautious about Galen's claims that this principle was a central plank of Hippocratean medical doctrine. The idea occurs in *Nature of Man* 22 (=*Regimen in Health* 7),[81] and in *Aphorisms* 1.3, quoted here: 'In athletes perfect good condition is dangerous if it is at its highest peak. In that situation it cannot remain the same or be at rest, and, since improvement is impossible, the only possible change is for the worse.'[82] Galen quotes this passage several times in his attacks on athletic training, as we shall see further below. Clearly it does signal a degree of anxiety within the original Hippocratic text about dangers which are specific to athletic exercise. However, these passages do not back up Galen's claims about Hippocratean anti-athleticism so firmly as he wishes to suggest. For one thing, the *Aphorisms* seems to be a collection of extracts and sayings compiled well after many of the original sentences were composed, whereas Galen and his contemporaries viewed it as the Hippocratic work par excellence.[83] A single critical representation of athletics is therefore not necessarily a reliable indicator of the work's overall themes. There might also be reasons to doubt Galen's conclusions on thematic grounds, even if we adopt the ancient strategy of viewing the *Aphorisms* as a single work. One reason for the inclusion of this aphorism at this point, very close to the opening of the text, is the author's (or compiler's) interest in the question of how one should judge and respond to turning-points and extremes in a great range of different circumstances, both in disease and in the constitutions of individuals. In other words, this aphorism uses the example of gymnastic training to articulate challenges which athletics shares with many other areas of medical practice. Galen, by contrast, goes out of his way to demonstrate the *differences* between athletic and other bodies. He attempts to integrate these Hippocratean passages with his own perspective by denying that Hippocrates has ascribed any positive value to athletic health by the phrase 'athletic good condition', a denial which is far from conclusive. He claims that Hippocrates is portraying specifically 'athletic' good condition – which is not something to be valued in itself – as unhealthy, in contrast with 'proper' good condition,

---

[81] See Jouanna (1999) 399–400.
[82] Ἐν τοῖσι γυμναστικοῖσιν αἱ ἐπ' ἄκρον εὐεξίαι σφαλεραί, ἢν ἐν τῷ ἐσχάτῳ ἔωσιν· οὐ γὰρ δύνανται μένειν ἐν τῷ αὐτῷ οὐδὲ ἀτρεμεῖν· ἐπεὶ δὲ οὐκ ἀτρεμέουσιν, οὐκέτι δύνανται ἐπὶ τὸ βέλτιον ἐπιδιδόναι· λείπεται οὖν ἐπὶ τὸ χεῖρον.
[83] See Jouanna (1999) 376–7.

where the highest pitch of healthiness will always be worth aiming for.[84] Within the Hippocratic Corpus, then, we can see some signs of anxiety about the dangers of immoderate athletic exercise, and also some interest in the uses of athletic exercise within day-to-day preventative medicine. However, these passages do not guarantee any systematic distinction comparable to the one Galen makes between athletic excess and properly philosophical regimen.

How did medical writers contemporary with Galen view athletic exercises? Here again there are many important similarities, in fact the similarities tend to be closer and also more frequent than those we can find between Galen and Hippocrates. A number of other medical writers express concerns about athletic excess which are similar to Galen's, albeit in less vehement form. Celsus, for example, denounces the athletic physique in the opening paragraphs of Book 1 of his *De medicina*, in attempting to outline some of the characteristics associated with good health.[85] Galen's detailed interest in the positive uses of physical exercise is also widely paralleled within works dedicated to systematic accounts of the techniques of day-to-day regimen designed for the preservation of health, which sometimes included gymnastic-style exercise. Those works often emphasize the importance of scrupulous understanding of the usefulness of each different type of exercise, and catalogue extensively the effects of these different types of exercise on different parts of the body. Extensive cataloguing of that sort draws on the techniques of advertising professional sophistication by complex subdivision which I discussed in the previous section. It also implies a conception of regimen as a process which must be tailored to suit the needs of the individual through the exercise of sensitive and varied personal response.[86] The reader must choose and adapt whichever of the many options offered is most suited to his or her requirements. In some ways, then, Galen is a product of his time, although he twists the patterns he finds around him in some extraordinary ways, as we shall see in a moment.

Our view of these things is complicated by the fact that much of the non-Galenic medical writing of the second century survives only in much later anthologizations; these are themselves heavily influenced by Galenic ideas, and quote repeatedly from Galen's work. It is sometimes hard to draw firm

---

[84] See *Good Condition* K4.750–3 and *Thrasyboulos* 9 [K5.819–21]; the passage is also quoted without discussion of these terminological problems in *Protrepticus* 11 [K1.27].
[85] Celsus *De medicina* 1.1.3 and 1.1.7; cf. 1.2.7.
[86] On the requirement for active individual response in regimen, see Foucault (1986) 99–101.

conclusions about the agendas underlying these works when they survive only in excerpted form. Nevertheless there is enough here for us to get a good flavour of what other medical authors from the same period were attempting. Antyllos – whose work has had very little attention even within recent scholarship on ancient medicine – was more or less contemporary with Galen, and some of his work survives in the compilations of Oribasios, which were made in the fourth century AD.[87] Antyllos may or may not have been influenced himself by Galen's work, but either way his writing gives us a good reference-point, enabling us to illuminate by comparison the choices Galen made in his medical writing. The work of Antyllos among others has a great deal in common with Galen's own work on regimen, but there are a number of additional features which are, as far as we can tell, more or less unique to Galen, and which this comparison can throw into a clearer light.

Antyllos' writing on physical exercise, preserved in Oribasios' *Collectiones Medicae* 6.21–4 and 6.25–36 (=*CMG* 6.1.1.177–87), deals with a wide variety of different exercise types, including running, horse-riding, hoop-rolling, swimming, wrestling and shadow-boxing, all of them presented in ways which are reminiscent of Galen's systematic coverage of the many different topics he discusses. All of these events are carefully categorized by Antyllos into their different forms. In his section on wrestling, for example (6.28), he divides the exercise into two different varieties, vigorous wrestling and gentle wrestling. The first of those, he tells us, improves breathing, makes the body firm and muscular, strengthens the sinews, sharpens the senses and intensifies natural vigour, produces flesh which is dense but not bulky or uneven, reduces fatness and swellings and dropsy, but is not suitable for developing the trunk. The second of the two by contrast produces a different kind of flesh which is more suitable for beginners. He then introduces two further categories, explaining the different benefits of upright-wrestling and floor-wrestling for different parts of the body. The complex categorization of the information presented requires a certain amount of self-awareness from the patient (or from the patient's adviser), which will allow him or her to choose between the many different possibilities presented according to individual need. The mention of the difficulty beginners face acts as a reminder that care of the body, just like athletic technique, takes practice.

One of Antyllos' other sections here is on the many different varieties of ball-play. It provides a useful backdrop to Galen's more ambitious and

---

[87] On Oribasios, see de Lucia (1999), especially on his approval of Galen.

self-reflexive treatise *On Exercise with the Small Ball*, which I will be turning to in a moment. Ball play seems to have been popular in the Imperial period.[88] It is mentioned in a number of other medical treatises as a beneficial exercise.[89] It also seems to have been practised regularly in the *gymnasion*, as far as we can tell from evidence for ball-rooms (*sphairisteria*) in many *gymnasion* complexes.[90] It was not, however, an activity which featured in agonistic festival competition. By including it here, along with other exercises like hoop-rolling which similarly had no place in agonistic festivals, Antyllos, like Galen, rejects the idea that the exercises he describes may be useful primarily for training athletes to compete. The passage has a complexity in its many subdivisions which is similar to what we find in the wrestling section. Antyllos outlines a great variety of different types of ball-play, emphasizing that each one of them is a separate exercise, and outlining the particular techniques and bodily benefits associated with all of them. To begin with he lists five types: 'the small ball, the large ball, the medium ball, the good-sized ball, and the hollow ball' (6.32.2).[91] He then immediately subdivides the small ball again. The very small ball, he tells us, is useful for the legs and the back and the upper arms and for those whose ribs have gone soft, and also strengthens the flesh. The kind of small ball which is slightly larger is used differently, and he praises it as the best of all the ball exercises because it makes the whole body healthy and mobile and strong, while also benefiting the eyesight and the head. The third type of small ball, which is slightly larger again, can itself be used in two different ways, either for standing exercises or for running exercises, both of which benefit the arms and the eyesight, while the running version, perhaps not surprisingly, also benefits the legs and the flanks. The catalogue continues in similar vein, ending with a sharp dismissal of the hollow ball for its failure to provide exercise which is agile or graceful.

This extract from Antyllos is in many ways typical of the non-Galenic writing on regimen from this period. Many of its distinctive features are also prominent within Galen's own writing, as we shall see. Galen, however, refashions those techniques in distinctive ways. For example, Antyllos' work shares with Galen's writing a sense of comprehensiveness in its cataloguing of different types of exercise, and so demands active involvement and self-knowledge from anyone who wishes to use these instructions. However,

---

[88] On ball games in the ancient world see Harris (1972) 75–111, who takes much of his evidence from both Greek and Latin texts of the Imperial period.
[89] E.g., see Celsus, *De medicina* 1.2.6, 1.6.1, 1.8.1 and 3.27.3.   [90] See Roux (1980).
[91] ἡ μὲν γάρ ἐστι μικρά, ἡ δὲ μεγάλη, ἡ δὲ μέση, ἡ δὲ εὐμεγέθης, ἡ δὲ κενή.

Galen goes much further in theorizing the philosophical implications of his prescriptions (although there may conceivably have been some philosophical material surrounding the sections Oribasios has excerpted from Antyllos). Galen is also much more explicit about combining recommendation of his own system of physical exercise with the enumeration and rejection of misguided styles of athletic training. Removing authority of any sort from the gymnastic trainers has become a necessary prerequisite for his own writing on regimen. He thus emphasizes the way in which his all-embracing principles of philosophical medicine claim control over the whole of the human body, and cannot allow any unphilosophical system to coexist with them.

The nature of Galen's quarrel with the medical content of athletic instruction is set out clearly and briefly in his work *Good Condition* [K4.750–6], which draws on some of the Hippocratic and Platonic passages I mentioned earlier. As I have already noted, he here discusses Hippocrates' claim that athletes who reach a peak of good condition are likely to be in danger of descending rapidly into ill-health. According to Galen, Hippocrates did not believe that athletic good condition could ever be an admirable bodily state; he argues instead that the phrase 'athletic good condition' in the Hippocratic Corpus must always mean 'the kind of condition athletes aim for', a condition which is on Galen's account very far from being praiseworthy. Having dealt with that point he states the principle that understanding athletic misuse of the human body is an essential starting point for building up a positive picture of the proper alternatives:[92] 'Therefore, in order to reach a proper understanding of genuine good condition, we must compare with it similarly named athletic good condition asking what they have in common and what the differences are between them' [K4.753–4].[93] He concedes certain similarities between them, for example the fact that both of them entail a good balance between the different parts of the body and between the different humours. But he then launches into vivid criticism of what trainers do wrong in exercising their charges. His main objection seems to lie in the fact that athletic training aims for the acquisition of bodily mass, as well as bodily balance, which leads to an imbalance in the matter which fills the body's internal space:

---

[92] Cf. *Thrasyboulos* 8 [K5.817], where Galen states the principle (which many do not understand, he says), that understanding of a thing (in this case healthiness) also entails understanding of its opposite.

[93] ἵνα τοίνυν τῆς ὄντως εὐεξίας εἰς ἀκριβῆ γνῶσιν ἀφικώμεθα, παραλαβεῖν αὐτῇ χρὴ τὴν ὁμώνυμον εὐεξίαν τὴν ἀθλητικήν, καὶ σκέψασθαι, τί ταὐτὸν ἑκατέραις ὑπάρχει, τί τε ἐναντίον.

The differences between them are as follows: genuine good condition entails a proper balance in the blood and in the whole mass of solid bodies. Athletic varieties of good condition entail the opposite: disproportion in all of the same areas, especially for those athletes of the 'fleshy' type. Danger necessarily follows from that bodily state, whenever the athletic good condition reaches its peak. [K4.754][94]

One of the main causes of this problem, Galen tells us, is overeating, which leads to the overfilling of the veins with blood, since there is nowhere else for the matter which the body has absorbed to go. This in turn leads the body's innate heat to be dissipated. For proof of this inevitable chain of consequences he refers the reader to one of his own previous works. There is a conspicuous emphasis throughout — in line with so much of his other work — on the importance of balance, which guides both his brief initial approval of what athletic training does right and his much longer account of where it goes wrong. The second half of the work overflows with the language of immoderation, which gives a horrifying impression of the violence which is done to the workings of the human body as athletic mismanagement almost literally rips its internal organs apart. We will see similar language being used in more sustained form in the *Protrepticus*. Galen's clear gaze sees effortlessly through the surface of the human body to reveal processes which the athletic trainers are unable — or unwilling — to investigate. And his step-by-step account of these consequences reveals by contrast the more beneficial and ordered operations which the veins and the digestive system will carry out when they are subject to correct medical control, of the kind which he is uniquely qualified to impose, as his reference to his own previous works seems to claim.

Elsewhere Galen outlines more clearly the admirable physical exercises with which the recommendations of false athletic trainers should be replaced. The most important example of his project of refashioning the exercises of the *gymnasion* to fit them in with his own conceptions of medical regimen comes in his long work *De sanitate tuenda* [K6.1–452] (=*CMG* 5.4.2.1–198), where he claims to give a comprehensive account of the techniques for preservation of health. Within this work the topic of physical exercise, along with related topics like massage techniques and the treatment of different types of fatigue, dominates three books out of six

---

[94] τὰ δὲ ἐναντία συμμετρία μὲν αἵματός τε καὶ τοῦ τῶν στερεῶν σωμάτων ὄγκου παντὸς ἐν ταῖς ὄντως εὐεξίαις, ἀμετρία δὲ τῶν αὐτῶν τούτων καὶ μάλιστα τοῦ σαρκώδους γένους ἐν ταῖς ἀθλητικαῖς. αἷς ἐξ ἀνάγκης ἕπεται τὸ σφαλερόν, ἐπειδὰν εἰς ἄκρον ἀφίκηται.

(2, 3 and 4) and also spills over into the others.⁹⁵ Galen follows the model of comprehensive cataloguing which was so important to Antyllos – as it also was to many non-medical writers – although he steps back from that task more often than Antyllos to reflect explicitly on the importance of balance in the maintenance of health;⁹⁶ and on the importance of caring for the soul at the same time as the body, especially in the section dealing with the upbringing of children.⁹⁷ He also repeatedly returns to the challenge of defining his subject, emphasizing the fact that proper understanding of the scope of the topic under discussion is a necessary prerequisite for treating it adequately. He argues for a wide definition of physical exercise, which is not confined simply to the exercise of the *gymnasion*,⁹⁸ and he attempts to show us how important it is that all types of preservative exercise should be under the care of the overarching medical art, whatever name one gives to it, which he had defined in the *Thrasyboulos*. In fact he refers repeatedly to the principles of the *Thrasyboulos*, portraying it as a companion piece and forerunner of the present work, as if the humiliation of the art of training is a necessary corollary of his own reformation of it.⁹⁹ At several points he pauses from his positive recommendations to reinforce the contrast between normal regimen and the more extravagant features of athletic training which are so different from the exercises of everyday life, although he tends to do that with much less hostility than in the *Thrasyboulos* and elsewhere, in line with his slide towards a more positive version of what the trainer (γυμναστής) can achieve once he is under Galen's command.¹⁰⁰

In both of these works, then – *Good Condition* and *De sanitate tuenda* – Galen stresses the requirements for moderation and balance which are central to his own medical method. He also stresses the importance of rejecting the narrow and unintelligent techniques of athletic training, as if that rejection is a necessary part of the process of defining and constructing his own all-embracing principles of philosophically aware self-attention. At this stage I want to turn briefly to Galen's own work on the benefits of ball-play, *On Exercise with the Small Ball*.¹⁰¹ I will be arguing

---

⁹⁵ For brief analysis of *De sanitate tuenda* and its relations with older texts on regimen (especially its not entirely convincing attempts to align itself with Hippocratic precedent), see Smith (1979) 106–14.
⁹⁶ E.g., see 1.1.3–4 [K6.2]; 1.5.1–12 [K6.13–15].
⁹⁷ E.g., see 1.8.24 [K6.42]; 1.11.3 [K6.54–5]; 1.12.5 [K6.60].
⁹⁸ E.g., see 2.2.6–12 [K6.85–6]; 2.8.1–7 [K6.133–5].
⁹⁹ E.g., see 1.1.1 [K6.1] (the opening lines of the work); cf. 1.4.12 [K6.12]; 2.8.11 [K6.136].
¹⁰⁰ E.g., see 3.2.2–12 [K6.167–9].
¹⁰¹ See Kollesch and Nickel (1994) 1400–1 for the small bibliography on this work.

that this work is imbued with a sense of its own difference from athletic excess, even though it does not say anything until its very final paragraphs about the importance of competitive athletics as a defining point of contrast. I will also be arguing that Galen's recommendations for balance and moderation as all-embracing requirements within physical training are related to what we saw of his professional self-representation in the previous section, and overflow even into his style. Galen's works do not simply contain technical instructions on how to apply principles of philosophical moderation. They are also, inevitably, saturated with those principles, offering an embodied example of their universal relevance.

The work opens with humorously extravagant praise of the small ball, which has the effect of undermining the pretensions of the more prestigious forms of exercise with which it is contrasted:

> The men of the past – the best of doctors and philosophers – have given a full account, Epigenes, of the usefulness of physical exercise (γυμνάσια) for health, and of its precedence over food in that respect. But as for the pre-eminence of the exercises of the small ball (τὰ διὰ τῆς σμικρᾶς σφαίρας) over all other types of exercise, this has not ever been adequately explained by any of my predecessors. (*Small Ball* 1 [K5.899])[102]

The word γυμνάσια is used in its standard sense from *De sanitate tuenda*, signalling not those exercises which are the province of the fraudster athletic trainers, but rather the medically sanctioned techniques of bodily care with which Galen has replaced them. Of those, the best of all, he tells us, is the small ball. There is an arresting – and I think very funny – sense of paradox here in the idea that something so small and simple can be the source of the very greatest of benefits. That paradox is not intended to undermine Galen's claims for ball-play as a useful exercise. This is not, in other words, a straightforward example of the common rhetorical exercise of praising objects which would not usually attract praise. Nor is it the case that the small ball is being used only as a metaphor for broader principles, although that is one of its important functions in the text, as we shall see shortly. If nothing else, the serious attention given to ball-play in other medical works like that of Antyllos should make us wary of those conclusions. Instead, this paradox serves more than anything to mock the many other exercises

---

[102] Πηλίκον μὲν ἀγαθόν ἐστιν εἰς ὑγίειαν, ὦ 'Επίγενες, γυμνάσια, καὶ ὡς χρὴ τῶν σιτίων ἡγεῖσθαι αὐτά, παλαιοῖς ἀνδράσιν αὐτάρκως εἴρηται, φιλοσόφων τε καὶ ἰατρῶν τοῖς ἀρίστοις· ὅσον δ' ὑπὲρ τἄλλα τὰ διὰ τῆς σμικρᾶς σφαίρας ἐστί, τοῦτ' οὐδέπω τῶν πρόσθεν ἱκανῶς οὐδεὶς ἐξηγήσατο.

which are said to fall short of the small ball's usefulness. The humour lies in the fact that activities like athletics, despite the extravagant claims they make for their own benefits, are so easily defeated even by the most tiny and unpretentious of objects.

That humorous effect is echoed several times in what follows. For example, in *Small Ball* 3 [K5.905], Galen tells us that the exercise will be more useful than any other to men who wish to improve in the art of generalship, since the skills of protecting territory and anticipating the enemy's moves are all things which ball-play teaches: 'Is there any other exercise so capable of training one to guard what one has gained or to recapture what one has lost, or to anticipate the state of mind of one's enemies? I would be amazed if anyone could name one (θαυμάζοιμ' ἄν, εἴ τις εἰπεῖν ἔχοι)'.[103] That provocatively extravagant claim is meant as much as anything to mock the pretensions of other types of exercise for their failure to give useful preparation for political or military life, as the sentences which follow make clear: 'Most exercises have exactly the opposite effect on one's mind, making it lazy and sleepy and slow. Indeed all those who toil in the *palaistra* (ὅσοι κατὰ παλαίστραν πονοῦσιν) are led by their exercises towards excessive fleshiness rather than the exercise of virtue' (3 [K5.905]).[104] The small ball stands in a position of effortless pre-eminence, mocking the pretensions of Greek traditions of physical education which claim to be able to prepare young men for public life.

After the opening words of the text, Galen goes on to praise exercises which benefit the soul as well as the body. The small ball is one such exercise, which benefits the soul above all through its capacity to give pleasure. This praise of the ball's capacity to bring physical and spiritual benefits together, which recurs a number of times in what follows,[105] sets the argument within a Platonic frame of reference. The small ball, it seems, is not only the most useful of exercises for military and political life, but also one of the most Platonic. Once again that reflects badly on the dullness of those who follow more conventional agonistic training patterns. There may also be a dig at athletic regimen in Galen's mention of the pleasure the small ball brings, given that he criticizes athletics in the *Protrepticus*, as we shall see in a moment, not only for failing to produce the worldly benefits it promises, but also for failing even to be enjoyable in the process.

---

[103] ἆρ' οὖν ἄλλο τι γυμνάσιον οὕτω προεθίζειν ἱκανὸν ἢ φυλάττειν τὸ κτηθὲν ἢ ἀνασώζειν τὸ μεθεθὲν ἢ τῶν ἐναντίων τὴν γνώμην προαισθάνεσθαι; θαυμάζοιμ' ἄν, εἴ τις εἰπεῖν ἔχοι.
[104] τὰ πολλὰ γὰρ αὐτῶν αὐτὸ τοὐναντίον ἀργοὺς καὶ ὑπνηλοὺς καὶ βραδεῖς τὴν γνώμην ἐργάζεται· καὶ γὰρ καί, ὅσοι κατὰ παλαίστραν πονοῦσιν, εἰς πολυσαρκίαν μᾶλλον ἢ ἀρετῆς ἄσκησιν φέρει.
[105] E.g. in 3 [K5.904].

Galen then outlines a number of advantages which are more specific to the small ball, all of them focused around the idea that it has a universal applicability. First, he mentions its accessibility, available even to the poorest of people, and suitable even for those who are most busy with public affairs and so have little time to spare. Then he discusses its adaptability, explaining that it is good for all types of patient, and capable of benefiting all parts of the body evenly, or else of being used to exercise different parts of the body according to need, for those who have more specific requirements. It is thus better able to produce a balanced and rounded physical condition than any other type of exercise. These details have a certain amount in common with what we see in the work of Antyllos, where the effects of different types of ball-play on different parts of the body are enumerated separately. It is striking, however, that Galen is less concerned than Antyllos with establishing divisions between different types of ball. His small ball encompasses all the conceivable benefits of the *gymnasion* within its small volume, in a way which makes it entirely self-contained, removing any need for reference to other pieces of gymnastic equipment. In that sense it is a more extravagant – and humorously paradoxical – version of the middle of Antyllos' three small balls, which Antyllos praises as the best of them because of its capacity to benefit the whole of the body.

One of the other features which differentiates Galen's account from that of Antyllos is the way in which he repeatedly steps back from the enumeration of practicalities in order to reflect on the broader significance of the exercises he describes. In that sense the small ball becomes not only a useful exercise in its own right, but also an exemplar for all that is most to be desired from physical regimen and indeed philosophical self-care more generally. The most important of its qualities, Galen suggests, is its capacity to maintain moderation and balance. Those hints of universal significance might for some readers have been reinforced by the cosmic overtones of the word σφαίρα (meaning 'ball', but also in some contexts 'globe').[106] Obviously those overtones would not always have been prominent within day-to-day use of that word, but they may have some significance in the context of Galen's repeated insistence on the ball's perfectly complete universal powers. In 4 [K5.906–7], for example, he lists the most important criteria for an exercise to be useful, and then repeats his claim that the small ball fulfils all of them:

---

[106] For an example of a universally significant ball in the Greek poetic tradition, see Apollonius *Argonautika* 3.129–44, where the ball (σφαῖραν) which Aphrodite offers to Eros 'symbolises Eros' universal power' (Hunter (1989) 113).

The form of exercise which I praise most of all is therefore the one which is able to provide bodily health (σώματος ὑγίειαν), harmony between the parts of the body (μερῶν εὐαρμοστίαν), and virtue in the soul (ψυχῆς ἀρετήν); and all these things apply to exercise with the small ball. It has the capacity to benefit the soul in every way (ψυχὴν εἰς πάντα δυνατὸν ὠφελεῖν), and it exercises the different parts of the body evenly (τοῦ σώματος τὰ μέρη δι' ἴσου πάντα γυμνάζει). This is the thing most useful of all for health, and it produces balance in one's bodily state (συμμετρίαν ἕξεως) . . .[107]

The extraordinary clustering here, and in the lines following these, of phrases describing evenness and universality intensifies the text's earlier emphasis on those qualities. In the process, this passage is explicit about the fact that the small ball is a perfect match for these requirements, a paradigm of the capacity to improve health. Galen has earlier made even clearer the universal significance of the qualities he is praising in this work, in describing his opposition to running, which leads to lack of bodily proportion: 'For I object to lack of proportion (ἀμετρίαν) in all cases (πανταχοῦ), and I believe that every art must cultivate good proportion (πᾶσαν τέχνην ἀσκεῖν φημι χρῆναι τὸ σύμμετρον); any loss of proportion (εἴ τι μέτρου στερεῖται) is bad' (3 [K5.906]).[108] Once again the vocabulary of moderation and immoderation (ἀμετρίαν, τὸ σύμμετρον, μέτρου) is packed into this pronouncement, as if to emphasize the necessity of keeping it constantly in mind, like some endlessly repeated mantra. The passage also looks beyond the immediate context of the ball-play it describes by the word πανταχοῦ ('in all cases', 'everywhere'), and by the phrase πᾶσαν τέχνην ('every art'), as if to emphasize the applicability of these principles even well outside the arena of private regimen.

In the process, I suggest, this passage shows us how the virtues of balance which Galen describes as crucial to health may also be applicable to the kind of enterprise he is engaged in in writing this work. It does so especially through its use of the word *technê* (τέχνη, meaning 'art' or 'profession'), which Galen employs so often to describe his own activity in works like the *Thrasyboulos*, following a long philosophical tradition. It may not be too fanciful to imagine that the small ball's evenness is a metaphor for Galen's own didactic style. Certainly the rounded nature of the small ball's effects filters through into the evenness of Galen's text, which mirrors the

---

[107] Μάλιστ' οὖν ἐπαινῶ γυμνάσιον, ὃ καὶ σώματος ὑγίειαν ἱκανὸν ἐκπορίζειν καὶ μερῶν εὐαρμοστίαν καὶ ψυχῆς ἀρετήν, ἃ πάντα τῷ διὰ τῆς σμικρᾶς σφαίρας ὑπάρχει. καὶ γὰρ ψυχὴν εἰς πάντα δυνατὸν ὠφελεῖν καὶ τοῦ σώματος τὰ μέρη δι' ἴσου πάντα γυμνάζει, ὃ καὶ μάλιστ' εἰς ὑγίειαν συμφέρει καὶ συμμετρίαν ἕξεως ἐργάζεται . . .
[108] τὴν γὰρ ἀμετρίαν ἐγὼ πανταχοῦ ψέγω, καὶ πᾶσαν τέχνην ἀσκεῖν φημι χρῆναι τὸ σύμμετρον, καὶ εἴ τι μέτρου στερεῖται, τοῦτ' οὐκ εἶναι καλόν.

regular rhythms of those effects within its balanced description of them. He repeatedly uses pairs of words or phrases in juxtaposition, making his own description echo the repetitions and variations of the actions he is describing. He moves from one part of the body to the next, as if to emphasize the way in which his own medical writing and his own medical expertise share the small ball's comprehensiveness, in their ability to act on all parts of the human physique equally.[109] His claims about the small ball's accessibility in the early part of the work have resonances with his claim to be capable of writing in ways which all of his readers can follow, at least in works like the *Thrasyboulos*, where the difficulty of the subject matter is in part mitigated by the methodical and user-friendly nature of his exposition of it. And like the small ball his work may be used differently by different readers, in line with the requirement that properly philosophical reception – like properly philosophical regimen – must always entail personal response.[110] The opening paragraph of the text foregrounds the different uses to which the work may be put, in mentioning the possibility that the addressee, Epigenes, may pass it on to others once he has read it. And in the last sentence of his penultimate paragraph Galen tells us explicitly that the instruction he has offered in this work must be adapted to the situation of each individual reader before it is applied:

It is not possible to record in writing the degree to which one should increase or reduce the intensity of these exercises in different circumstances – for the requirement for each separate case is not quantifiable – but rather it can only be discovered and taught through experience of the exercises themselves. This point is very important. For the right quality of exercise is useless if it is damaged by the wrong quantity. It should be the job of the trainer (τῷ παιδοτρίβῃ) to explain these things to those who are about to take exercise. (4 [K5.909])[111]

Galen's text, like the small ball, will only be useful if we use it in the right way.

This mention of the role of the athletic trainer signals a turn towards more explicit rejection of athletic excess in the closing paragraph of the work. It confirms the belittlement of the art of the trainer which we have already seen Galen making in the *Thrasyboulos*, and so intensifies the demand for subordination of all types of physical training to the overarching art of

---

[109] See esp. 2 [K6.902] and 4 [K6.908–9].
[110] Cf. Plutarch, *On Studying Poetry* 38e for a similar example of ball-play as a metaphor for reading.
[111] ἐφ' ὅσον δὲ δεῖ καθ' ἑκάστην χρείαν ἐπιτείνειν τε καὶ ἀνιέναι, γράψαι μὲν οὐχ οἷόν τε – τὸ γὰρ ἐν ἑκάστῳ ποσὸν ἄρρητον – ἐπ' αὐτῶν δὲ τῶν ἔργων εὑρεῖν τε καὶ διδάξαι δυνατόν, ἐν ᾧ δὴ καὶ μάλιστα τὸ πᾶν κῦρος· οὐδὲ γὰρ ἡ ποιότης ἐστὶ χρήσιμος, εἰ τῷ ποσῷ διαφθείροιτο. τούτου μὲν δὴ τῷ παιδοτρίβῃ μετέστω τῷ μέλλοντι τῶν γυμνασίων ἀφηγεῖσθαι.

Galenic medicine, which has been implicit throughout the work, as if to emphasize the fact that physical exercise can only be valuable under those circumstances. His argument in this closing paragraph is centred on the final benefit of the small ball, the fact that it is free from risk, by contrast with the destructive violence of less moderate exercises like running, jumping, discus-throwing and wrestling. He applies Homer's description of the Prayers (Λιταί) – who follow behind destructive madness (Ἄτη), attempting to salvage what they can from disaster – to athletes who have been washed up by their violent exertions: 'Limping, shrivelled up, squinting' (5 [K5.910] (quoting Homer, *Iliad* 9.503).[112] These blind and lame and desperate athletes are as far removed as one can imagine from the fantasy image of youthful athletic perfection. However, Galen also hints at a positive function for them – parallel to their healing function in this passage from Homer. Perhaps we are to see the damaged athletes as figures who can point the way to salvation for young men who have been led astray, by revealing so clearly the horrors of the course they have themselves chosen.

The work thus ends with a ringing contrast between athletic mistreatment of the body and the wonderful benefactions of the small ball, as if those benefactions can best be described precisely by contrast with the dangers of conventional athletic activity. This final paragraph thus confirms the significance of athletic training as a defining negative image for Galen's representation of medical moderation, significance which has been hinted at repeatedly throughout the work. It also suggests, through its mention of the *paidotribês*, that the subordination of the athletic trainer to philosophical control is a prerequisite for any kind of beneficial regimen – that the *paidotribês* cannot play a valuable role without philosophical guidance. That demand is reminiscent of the strategy Galen uses in *De sanitate tuenda*, where the conclusions of the *Thrasyboulos* are mentioned as an essential starting-point for Galen's project of discussing regimen as it should be done. In the *Small Ball*, Galen similarly hints that all training must be philosophically self-aware if it is to be worth anything. In making that suggestion, he goes far beyond the much less philosophical and more evenly practical works of Antyllos. In fact the *Small Ball* is imbued with an atmosphere of philosophical balance, not only in the frequent theorization of the philosophical significance of the actions it describes, but also in the very rhythms of the text itself. Through those rhythms Galen enacts the way in which the principles of moderation and balance which are central

---

[112] χωλαί τε ῥυσαί τε παραβλῶπές τ' ὀφθαλμώ.

to his technical, medical recommendations also overflow into his professional practice, in line with his claims for their universal applicability and importance.

GALEN'S *PROTREPTICUS*

We have seen, then, that athletics and medicine were closely linked with each other, both institutionally and conceptually. We see doctors sharing the expertise of trainers in a spirit of co-operation, and applying agonistic imagery to their own endeavours. At the same time doctors sometimes reject what they see as the worst elements of athletic excess in order to define more clearly the technical and professional features which make medicine what it is. Galen exploits those trends in very distinctive ways — just like all of the authors I have examined in other chapters, who manipulate widespread patterns of athletic representation for their own particular ends — not least by combining these two different poses, of criticism and appropriation, so systematically. He uses athletic imagery to attack excessive and superficial competitiveness, but also at the same time to advertise his professional victories, which he suggests are made possible precisely by that avoidance of superficiality. He also makes rejection of the disciplinary authority of trainers a prerequisite for his own construction of a system of medical regimen which maintains the whole of the human body under philosophical control.

Here, finally, I want to return to Galen's *Protrepticus ad artes addiscendas* (*Exhortation to Study the Arts*) [K1.1–39], which provided one of the two quotations with which this book opened.[113] This is Galen's most extravagant and explicitly programmatic attack on athletes and their trainers. It is also, I think, the one which looks most surprising at first sight to a modern reader. I hope, however, that we will by now be in a better position to make sense of Galen's claims in this work, in the light of some of the distinctive preoccupations of his work which I have been discussing above.

The *Protrepticus* opens with the claim that the defining characteristic of man, which separates him from the animals and brings him close to the gods, is his rationality. Galen denounces the disorderly followers of Fortune who neglect reason (*Protrepticus* 2, 4), in contrast with the followers of Hermes (3, 5), who devote themselves to the cultivation of the genuine arts (*technai*). In the former group he categorizes especially those who give

---

[113] On the *Protrepticus*, see Boudon (2000) for commentary with long introduction, especially good on parallels from other literary and philosophical texts; Müller (1995) 306–16; Kollesch and Nickel (1994) 308–9 for further bibliography.

too much attention to wealth (6), noble birth (7) or beauty (8). None of these things, we are told, is a stable blessing, and none of them is on its own admirable, unless it can also be combined with virtues of the soul. In paragraph 9 there is then an extraordinary shift, as Galen moves into a denunciation of athletics, in the passage I quoted in my introduction. He tells us that athletics is the only one of the false *technai* which poses any real threat to society, through its horrifying capacity to seduce young men into following it. He focuses on its uselessness (10), the damage it does to physical health (11), and its failure to provide beauty (12), useful strength (13) or a secure income (14), despite its claims to do so. Finally he returns to his original categorization of the *technai*, exhorting his reader to choose one of the true arts. Of these, medicine, he suggests, is the most valuable of all.

It is hard not to come away with the impression of a very odd disjunction between the two halves of the text. One of the things I want to show here is that that disjunction is very carefully managed.[114] The abruptness of Galen's shift of focus is designed as a challenge to the reader. Have we understood the dangers athletics brings with it? Or have we, too, been seduced into a kind of blindness by its superficial attractions, which prevent us from realizing that athletes themselves possess all the archetypal faults of those who devote themselves to Fortune and to the false arts? At the same time, despite the abruptness of the shift, the two halves turn out on closer inspection to be more closely linked than one would initially imagine. The first half of the work has athletic overtones partly in the sense that the faults Galen criticizes there are reminiscent of the faults he denigrates in his attacks on athletics elsewhere. More importantly, there are a number of points in the first half which directly prepare for material Galen uses after paragraph 9. There are also several quotations or details of narrative before paragraph 9 which turn out to be closely related to athletic activity even though their connections with it are not made explicit.

For example, the opening emphasis on the rationality of man as the thing which distinguishes him from the animals looks forward to the imagery of animality which is repeatedly applied to athletes in the second half, and within Galen's other works. The extraordinary thing about man, Galen tells us, is the fact that he has the freedom to practise whichever *technai* he wishes. That involves choosing between the basic *technai* which animals

---

[114] See Müller (1995) 308–9 on the originality of Galen's linking of the themes in the two halves of the work, even though they both have many conventional elements taken individually.

also follow, and the rational *technai* which are the province of the gods. Making the right choice between those options is crucial, Galen suggests, hence the importance of his own exhortation in this work. To choose the *technai* of the animals when a more exalted option lies open is absurd. As we learn later, that is exactly the mistake athletes make. Galen in fact returns to this contrast between the irrational arts of the animals and the rational arts of the gods at the very beginning of his discussion of the faults of athletes, in a way which makes the second half structurally reminiscent of the first. He draws on traditional Cynic imagery in *Protrepticus* 9 to remind us of the absurdity of athletic claims to speed or strength, given that no athlete could ever defeat the animals if he had to compete with them. That point is repeated with more vivid and ridiculous examples in *Protrepticus* 13 [K1.35–7]. Athletics is thus shown to be the prime example of the neglect of divine activities which Galen has condemned at the very start of the work, and the prime example of the futility of espousing the *technai* of the animals.

Much of the first half of the work is taken up with enumeration of the illusory blessings which are associated with the false *technai*. That enumeration has many close overlaps with the similar list which is later applied to athletics, as I shall show in more detail in a moment. There are also, I suggest, several passages in the first half where Galen refers to athletic subject matter implicitly, but chooses not to make his criticism of it blatant. Perhaps the most ingenious example of that is his quotation from *Odyssey* 8.169–73 in *Protrepticus* 8, which he uses to demonstrate his point that the qualities of the soul are more important than physical beauty. The lines are taken from a speech of Odysseus in reply to the Phaiacian Euryalos.[115] Euryalos has criticized him for his unathletic appearance, in response to Odysseus' refusal to compete in the Phaiacians' contests. Odysseus replies angrily that physical beauty may not be the only indicator of a man's worth. He then goes on to take up the Phaiacians' challenge victoriously, despite being weighed down by sorrow. It is striking that Galen's use of these lines obscures their original athletic context. For those who do not recall the original context of the lines, the quotation simply acts as one of many examples of Galen's appeals to literary authority throughout the work. For those who do, it prepares for the shift of focus in the second half of the text. Odysseus' initial lack of interest in competing matches Galen's own deprecation of agonistic activity. It also reinforces the sense that those who value athletic beauty, and who practise athletics at the expense of more serious pursuits like warfare, as the

---

[115] =Miller 2.

Phaiacians do, may not even be good at the things they claim to be good at. That suggestion is in line with the idea we find repeatedly later in the work that athletic training does not even bring with it the benefits and skills it purports to bring.

It is also striking that specific mention of athletic activity is often absent in Galen's description of areas where we might expect it to play a conspicuous role, as if he has chosen to expunge it in a deliberately conspicuous way from his account of the virtues he recommends. Hermes, for example – along with Herakles, who is criticized for his athletic associations later in the work (in 13 [K1.33 and 1.36]) – was one of the patron gods of the *gymnasion*.[116] It seems extraordinary, no doubt designedly so, that this function is omitted in Galen's praise of the arts which are associated with him. Galen seems to be provocatively disallowing the possibility that athletic training should be seen as one of the god's legitimate domains. Galen uses similar effects in telling the story of the shipwreck of the philosopher Aristippos, in the course of his listing of the most famous of the followers of Hermes (5 [K1.8–9]). He does so in order to convince us that the truly wise man will not be encumbered by worldly possessions, and will be content whatever disasters Fortune imposes. He describes Aristippos' joy at finding himself washed up amongst Greeks on the coast of Syracuse. Aristippos realizes that he has arrived amongst civilized people when he sees a geometrical diagram traced in the sand on the beach. That point glances back to Galen's classification of *technai* not many lines before, which makes geometry one of the highest of human arts. We also hear that Aristippos chose to announce himself to the Syracusans in the *gymnasion*. Strikingly, however, there is no mention of any physical activity there. The juxtaposition of this mention of the *gymnasion* with the story of the diagram in the sand suggests that Aristippos' excitement about encountering a Greek education system in the city is mainly due to having found himself surrounded by properly Greek intellectual pursuits. This passage contributes to the high priority Galen gives throughout the work to the virtues of proper interpretation of Hellenic tradition, of which we shall see more in a moment. It hints at a role for the *gymnasion* in that project, but refuses to acknowledge that it is to be valued for the physical education it offers.

---

[116] See Scanlon (2002) 250–5, citing Siska (1933), which I have not been able to see; ephebic contests in honour of Hermes are discussed in chapter two (pp. 64–5) above. The mention of the stable, cubic base on which the god Hermes stands (*Protrepticus* 3 [K1.5]), in contrast with Fortune, who stands on an unstable sphere, might remind us of the way in which Hermes was often represented in statues placed (on stone blocks) in the *gymnasion*.

Galen's abrupt turn to the dangers of athletic seductiveness comes in a stirring address to an imagined collective readership composed of the young men of Greece (as quoted at the beginning of my introduction):

> Come on, boys (παῖδες), all of you who have listened to my words and are preparing to commit yourselves to an art (*technê*), make sure that no swindlers and conjurers can deceive you by teaching *technai* that are useless or bad. You must realize that any activity whose aim is not useful for life is not really a *technê* . . . The only thing I am afraid of is the activity of the athletes, in case it deceives any one of our young men (τινα τῶν νέων) into preferring it to a genuine *technê*, through offering, as it does, bodily strength and popular fame and daily public payments from the elders of our cities and honours equal to those given to outstanding citizens. (9 [K1.20–21])[117]

Are we surprised by this move?, Galen seems to be asking. And if so, does that tell us something about our own share in the collective blindness of contemporary society, which is detailed so scathingly in the mention of the popular admiration athletes receive?

The criticism of athletics which follows clusters around many of the themes which are also central to works like the *Thrasyboulos* and *Good Condition*. For example, we hear about the damage which athletics does to the balance of human health in 11, where Galen returns to the theme of overfilling of the athletic body which dominates *Good Condition*, portraying athletic regimen as the furthest imaginable opposite to his own properly rounded medical care. At one point Galen quotes Homer's description of the shrivelled bodies of the Prayers, just as he had done at the end of the *Small Ball*, to describe the decline of the athletic physique. That quotation enhances the sense that the *Protrepticus* is a contribution to a coherent project, a sustained battle against all that is worst in human medicine. The consequences of a prolonged athletic career are described with sickening vividness, reversing the idealization of scarred athletic bodies which we saw in looking at 'realistic' victory statues in chapter three.[118] The bodies of athletes are described as being like the walls of cities which have been weakened so much by siege engines that they afterwards collapse when even the smallest of pressures is applied to them:

---

[117] Ἄγετ' οὖν, ὦ παῖδες, ὁπόσοι τῶν ἐμῶν ἀκηκοότες λόγων ἐπὶ τέχνης μάθησιν ὡρμῆσθε, μή τις ὑμᾶς ἀπατεὼν καὶ γόης ἀνὴρ παρακρουσάμενός ποτε ματαιοτεχνίαν ἢ κακοτεχνίαν ἐ<κ>διδάξηται γιγνώσκοντας, ὡς, ὁπόσοις τῶν ἐπιτηδευμάτων οὐκ ἔστι τὸ τέλος βιωφελές, ταῦτ' οὐκ εἰσὶ τέχναι . . . τὸ δὲ τῶν ἀθλητῶν ἐπιτήδευμα μόνον ὑποπτεύω, μή ποτ' ἄρα τοῦτο, καὶ ῥώμην σώματος ἐπαγγελόμενον καὶ τὴν παρὰ τοῖς πολλοῖς δόξαν ἐπαγόμενον, δημοσίᾳ παρὰ τοῖς πατράσι ἡμερεσίαις ἀργυρίου δόσεσιν καὶ ὅλως ἴσα τοῖς ἀριστεῦσι τετι[μη]μένον, ἐξαπατήσῃ τινὰ τῶν νέων ὡς προκριθῆναί τινος τέχνης.

[118] Pp. 115–24.

In just the same way the bodies of athletes become rotten and weak through the blows they receive in training, and are therefore ready to succumb to the slightest misfortune. For their eyes often have spaces hollowed out around them, and when their bodies no longer have the strength to resist, these spaces become filled with fluid; their teeth, having been shaken by repeated blows, fall out readily after a while, once their strength begins to fail; their joints, through having been twisted, become too weak to stand up to any kind of outside pressure; and all kinds of break or tear are easily re-opened. As far as bodily health is concerned, then, it is clear that no other group of people is more miserable (ἀθλιώτερον) than athletes. (11 [K1.30–31])[119]

The pun between ἀθλιώτερον ('more miserable', 'more badly off') and the word ἀθλητής ('athlete'), which Galen expands on in the lines following these, gives overtones of inevitability to the link between athletic condition and miserable ill-health. This section also insists on similarly inevitable links between physical degeneration and neglect of the soul:

They do not even know that they have a soul in the first place, so far are they from comprehending its rational qualities. For they are so busy accumulating a mass of flesh and blood that their soul is extinguished as if beneath a heap of filth, and they are incapable of thinking about anything clearly; instead they become mindless like the irrational animals. (11 [K1.27])[120]

The image of animality here carries forward the themes of the work's opening sentences, which I discussed above. This passage suggests an almost physical connection between the process of building up bodily mass and the problem of losing sight of the soul, which is the defining feature of the animal condition. Galen not only suggests that concentrating on the body makes it difficult to find time for giving attention to the soul, but also implies that the two are inevitably connected with each other, through the horrifyingly concrete image of the soul being swallowed up within the slime of athletic flesh.

The text also replays Galen's preoccupation with the image of the athletic trainers' superficial rhetoric and strident self-promotion, with which he

[119] οὕτω καὶ τὰ τῶν ἀθλητῶν σώματα σαθρὰ καὶ ἀσθενῆ ταῖς κατὰ τὴν ἐπιτήδευσιν γεγονότα πληγαῖς ἕτοιμα πρὸς τὸ πάσχειν ἐστὶν ἐπὶ ταῖς τυχούσαις προφάσεσιν. οἱ μὲν γὰρ ὀφθαλμοὶ περι<ορ>ωρυγμένοι πολλάκις, ὅθ' ἡ δύναμις οὐκέτ' ἀντέχει, πληροῦνται ῥευμάτων, οἱ δ' ὀδόντες ἅτε διασεισμένοι πολλάκις ἐπιλειπούσης ἐν τῷ χρόνῳ τῆς δυνάμεως αὐτοὺς ἑτοίμως ἐκπίπτουσι, τὰ δὲ λυγισθέντα τῶν ἄρθρων ἀσθενῆ πρὸς πᾶσαν τὴν ἔξωθεν βίαν γίγνεται, καὶ πᾶν ῥῆγμα καὶ σπάσμα ῥᾳδίως κινεῖται. Σωματικῆς μὲν οὖν ὑγιείας ἕνεκα φανερόν, ὡς οὐδὲν ἄλλο γένος ἀθλιώτερόν ἐστι τῶν ἀθλητῶν.
[120] τὴν ἀρχὴν γὰρ οὐδ', εἰ ψυχὴν ἔχουσι, γιγνώσκουσι· τοσοῦτον ἀποδέουσι τοῦ λογικὴν αὐτὴν ἐπίστασθαι. σαρκῶν γὰρ ἀεὶ καὶ αἵματος ἀθροίζοντες πλῆθος ὡς ἐν βορβόρῳ πολλῷ τὴν ψυχὴν <τὴν> ἑαυτῶν ἔχουσι κατεσβεσμένην, οὐδὲν ἀκριβὲς νοῆσαι δυναμένην, ἀλλ' ἄνουν ὁμοίως τοῖς ἀλόγοις ζῴοις.

contrasts his own ostensibly unassertive logical method. He relies throughout the second half of the work on the authority of great doctors and writers of the past, quoting most heavily of all from the work of Hippocrates. At the same time, however, he tells us that he is reluctant to use that strategy of quotation, as if he wishes to avoid any impression of excessive reliance on authority:

> I would certainly not like to base my judgement on arguments from authority. That is the trick of a rhetorical man, not of someone who honours truth. Nevertheless, since there are some people who take refuge in the attitudes of the majority and in their empty opinions, declining to look at the practice in question on its own terms (γυμνὸν τῶν ἔξωθεν), I have been forced to bring witnesses, in order they should know that they have no advantage over me even in this respect. (10 [K1.25])[121]

Galen suggests that he is forced to advertise the rightness of his own position in more forthright ways than he would choose because of the empty and deceptive sophistical tricks of his opponents. Presumably he would prefer to leave the conformity of his views with previous tradition implicit, as he does in his quotation from *Odyssey* Book 8 in the first half, where readers are left to make the connections for themselves. Ironically, however, and not untypically, this show of reluctance is precisely the thing which allows him to present his argument in such forthright and unnuanced terms, since his deprecation of over-dependence on quotation is an excuse to break off without any further justification or contextualization of the passages he has quoted. Moreover, the passage characteristically uses the imagery of the *gymnasion* to throw light on the distinctive features of his opponents' superficiality. The phrase γυμνὸν τῶν ἔξωθεν ('on their own terms', or more literally, 'naked of external considerations') describes the trainers' examination of the principles under debate in terms which are reminiscent of their techniques of instruction. They refuse to examine the matter 'nakedly', without obscuring the real issues. Their standard ploy of stripping athletes for examination and for training is thus shown to be, paradoxically, a gesture of concealment, a corollary of their unwillingness to carry out the logical 'laying bare' which is the necessary basis for any technical knowledge. That hint is reminiscent of the actions of the athletic trainer described at the end of the *Thrasyboulos*, whose gesture of stripping an athlete in public is his only response to logical debates which

---

[121] Ὅλως μὲν οὖν ἐπὶ μάρτυρος οὐκ ἐβουλόμην κρίνεσθαι· ῥητορικοῦ γὰρ τὸ τοιοῦτον μᾶλλον ἢ τιμῶντος ἀλήθειαν ἀνδρός· ὅμως δ' ἐπειδή τινες ἐπὶ τὸν τῶν πολλῶν ἔπαινον καταφεύγουσι καὶ τὴν παρὰ τούτων κενὴν δόξαν, ἀφέντες αὐτὸ <τὸ> ἐπιτήδευμα γυμνὸν τῶν ἔξωθεν σκοπεῖν, ἠναγκάσθην κἀν τούτοις προχειρίσασθαι τοὺς μάρτυρας, ἵν', ὅτι μηδ' ἐνταῦθα πλέον ἔχουσί τι, γιγνώσκωσιν.

he is too ignorant to understand, and works as an attempt to obstruct and obscure clear logical argument rather than enabling it. As so often, the showy, over-rhetorical trainers are a crucial point of contrast for Galen's own self-presentation.

The second half of the work also refers back to Galen's account of the three illusory blessings of wealth, noble birth and beauty (in *Protrepticus* 6, 7 and 8 respectively), as I suggested earlier. Athletic expertise, Galen claims, cannot guarantee any of these, just as it fails to provide any of the other benefits which it claims for itself. The idea of athletes as beautiful was a conventional one, although athletic beauty was also often treated with ambivalence as a self-undermining quality, which had corruption somehow implicit within it, as we saw throughout chapter three. Galen intensifies that characteristic ambivalence, giving his scepticism a specifically medical twist in claiming that permanent athletic beauty is impossible, in the light of the athletic disfigurements discussed above. Those disfigurements similarly undermine the possibility of athletes having any real and long-lasting kind of physical strength. The idea that athletics brings wealth is also misleading, Galen claims: 'Perhaps you will say that they pride themselves on making money more than anyone; and yet you can see that they are all in debt, not only during their careers, but also after they have retired' (14 [K1.37]).[122] The reference to retired athletes might remind us of the passage at the end of the *Thrasyboulos*, where we hear that the least successful and most bankrupt of athletes are the ones who become trainers on their retirement, driven by their need for money to inculcate greed for athletic success in others, in a way which makes the whole system self-perpetuating. The only skills which can provide a reliable income, and an income to be proud of, are the true *technai*, especially those like medicine which are not dependent on physical agility, and so can be carried forward indefinitely into old age.

The third of these false blessings – the blessing of noble birth – is not dealt with so explicitly in the second half as the other two. Nevertheless it may be implicit in Galen's anxiety about the dangers which face the young men of Greece, since the educational institutions of the *gymnasion*, signalled by the words 'boys' (παῖδες) and 'young men' (νέοι) in the passage quoted above from *Protrepticus* 9, were associated with a certain degree of social distinction. It is also implicit in Galen's repeated hints that the excesses of athletic activity represent a perversion of the heritage of Hellenic

---

[122] Τάχ' οὖν ἐπὶ τῷ χρήματα πάντων ἀθροίζειν πλεῖστα σεμνύνονται· καὶ μὴν ἔστιν ὑμῖν θεάσασθαι πάντας αὐτοὺς ὀφείλοντας οὐ μόνον ἐκεῖνον τὸν χρόνον, καθ' ὃν ἀθλοῦσιν, ἀλλὰ καὶ καταλύσαντας τὴν ἄσκησιν...

culture.¹²³ The virtue of noble birth (εὐγένεια) in *Protrepticus* 7 seems to be used to describe not only social standing, but also cultural inheritance. Several of Galen's examples there point to the conclusion that one's origins do nothing to guarantee one's virtue. He quotes the example of the Scythian Anacharsis, amongst others, whose wisdom outclassed so many of his non-barbarian contemporaries. Galen's quotation of Hippocrates and others in the second half of the text reminds us that his own medical pre-eminence, in contrast with the ignorance of his opponents, is inextricably grounded in correct interpretation of his medical and philosophical heritage.

The text ends with a final restatement of the pre-eminence of the true *technai*. Of those, Galen claims, medicine is the most admirable: 'Young men – apart from those whose souls are entirely brutish – should therefore take up and practise one of these arts; especially the best of them, which in my opinion is medicine. This is the very point to be demonstrated in what follows (ἐφεξῆς)' (14 [K1.39]).¹²⁴ Philosophy is not mentioned in the list of *technai* given before this closing sentence. That omission perhaps implies that all of these true *technai*, medicine especially, are themselves representatives of philosophy. The final sentence seems to be referring ahead either to another closely connected work or to a second half which is now missing, it is not clear which.¹²⁵ Either way, as in the transition from the *Thrasyboulos* to *De sanitate tuenda*, dismissing any claim to authority on the part of athletic training – which is precisely the project which the paragraphs preceding this concluding sentence have been dedicated to – once again seems to be a prerequisite for Galen's own demonstration of what the art of medicine should really involve.

Why then does Galen issue this extraordinary attack on athletes in the *Protrepticus*? And does it really have any connection with the opinions of his contemporaries? On one level, of course, it must be meant to shock, as an attempt to jolt its readers out of complacency. It is a provocatively extravagant response, like his claims about the pre-eminence of the small ball, to the overblown self-glorification of men like Markos Aurelios Asklepiades.

---

¹²³ Cf. Flemming (2000) 288–9 and Swain (1996) 357–77 (esp. 377–9) on the strength of Galen's continued espousal of Hellenic affiliation, despite the many years he spent in Rome and his close links with the imperial family.

¹²⁴ Ἐκ τούτων οὖν τινα τῶν τεχνῶν ἀναλαμβάνειν τε καὶ ἀσκεῖν χρὴ τὸν νέον, ὅτῳ μὴ παντάπασιν ἡ ψυχὴ βοσκηματώδης ἐστί· καὶ μᾶλλόν γε τὴν ἀρίστην ἐν ταύταις, ἥτις, ὡς ἡμεῖς φαμεν, ἐστὶν ἰατρική. τοῦτο δ' αὐτὸ δεικτέον ἐφεξῆς.

¹²⁵ Boudon (2000) 67 presents strong evidence from the later manuscript tradition for assuming that the *Protrepticus* itself had a second half; Singer (1997) 407 suggests this may be a reference to the *Thrasyboulos*.

More importantly, however, it is also part of a coherent and carefully constructed project of defining and prescribing the best form of medicine. In the *Protrepticus*, as so often in his work, Galen takes athletics as the single most important mirror-image of his medical art. The art of the athletic trainer is opposed to medicine both because of the imbalanced nature of its treatment of the human body and (inevitably connected with that) because of the superficial and therefore dangerously seductive nature of the form in which it presents itself. Galen makes his dismissal of it emblematic of the need to debunk any care of the human body which claims autonomy from philosophical medicine.

The choice of athletics as a defining mirror-image for medicine is partly explained by the prevalence of similar patterns of self-representation throughout the medical writing and medical practice of this period. Doctors and trainers were closely linked with each other institutionally, in ways which led them to share many areas of professional expertise, but also at the same time to compete against each other. That may have been the case increasingly at the time when Galen was writing, given the gradual intensification of interest in medical and philosophical regimen in the Imperial period, and given the variety of different theories about regimen which seems to have surrounded that development. We will see further signs of the controversial nature of these subjects in the next chapter, in looking at Philostratus' ingenious response to Galen's denigration of the *technê* of athletic training. And yet Galen's treatment of athletes is very far from being a straightforward reflection of the preoccupations of his age, or a conventional intervention in those debates. He carries these trends to an extraordinary degree of intensity, manipulating them in unique ways in order to articulate an unprecedentedly uncompromising and detailed vision of the philosophical foundations required for medical activity.

CHAPTER 7

Philostratus' Gymnasticus *and the rhetoric of the athletic body*

> As far as athletic training (γυμναστική) is concerned, I consider it a form of wisdom (σοφία), and one which is inferior to none of the other arts (οὐδεμιᾶς ἐλάττω τέχνης) . . .
> (Philostratus, *Gymnasticus* 1 [261.13–14])[1]

RHETORIC AND THE BODY

From the Classical period onwards athletic training had been a publicly celebrated and often prestigious profession. Trainers are praised within the victory odes of Pindar for guiding their young charges to glory; they are pictured on Attic vases observing and correcting athletic technique in the *gymnasion*; and they are honoured in end-of-year ephebic inscriptions for their instruction, throughout the Hellenistic period and beyond. And yet in many ways these trainers remain shadowy figures, playing only a supporting role to the athletes they guided, who are nearly always the main subject of inscriptions and literary accounts alike. One of my aims in this chapter is to bring the athletic trainers of the ancient world a little more to life. I aim to do so first of all through mapping out some of the glimpses we gain of their activity and self-presentation within the inscriptional record of the east of the Empire. With that background in mind I then want to examine the *Gymnasticus* of Philostratus, an early third-century AD text[2] which purports to offer practical instruction in the art of athletic training (*gymnastikê*) – and as such is the nearest we get to a sustained view of athletic activity from a trainer's perspective – but which also goes far beyond conventional claims for the value of that art.

This material will extend the themes of the previous chapter in two main ways. First, it will illuminate further the processes of inter-disciplinary

---

[1] περὶ δὲ γυμναστικῆς, σοφίαν λέγομεν οὐδεμιᾶς ἐλάττω τέχνης . . .
[2] The precise date of the *Gymnasticus* is unclear, but it is likely to have been written in the 220s or 230s AD; for a summary of debate see de Lannoy (1997) 2405–7; Müller (1995) 317.

rivalry and self-promotion which underlay the projects of moulding and comprehending the athletic body in the Imperial period. I have already offered one view of the place trainers occupied on the status-map of technical disciplines in the Greek cities by discussing their close association with doctors. Here I will be fleshing out that picture by illustrating the way in which the Greek inscriptions of this period often show us trainers verging on high status, and doing their best to enhance the legitimacy and complexity of their own expertise, while also at the same time grappling with the possibility of a less complimentary public view of the sophistication of their professional knowledge. We have also seen something of the way in which the processes of day-to-day competition between different disciplines are transposed into writing with more elevated, philosophical pretensions, in the work of Galen. Galen offers as sustained a portrait of the athletic trainer as any writer does before Philostratus, albeit an unsympathetic and in many ways unrepresentative portrait. He admits the possibility of a valuable kind of *gymnastikê*, but also quashes its claims to be an autonomous art (*technê*), and purports to unmask the unscrupulousness and ignorance of the majority of its practitioners. Philostratus' *Gymnasticus* gives us a valuable point of comparison. His claims for the powers of *gymnastikê* as an independent *technê*, exemplified in the opening quotation of this chapter, are a provocative response to the currents of criticism Galen's work exemplifies, and perhaps even a direct response to Galen's text. By Philostratus' account, I will argue, the athletic trainer is a paradigmatic representative of Greek wisdom, whose art is powerful enough to encompass analytical techniques which give access to understanding of the whole of the Hellenic heritage, as well as offering practical control over the performance of individual athletes. Philostratus makes his refashioning of *gymnastikê* compatible with many of Galen's views, accepting the point that only the most elevated versions of the art will be of value. But he diverges from Galen in placing those more elevated versions under the aegis of rhetoric, not of philosophy.

My second aim in this chapter – which is offered in part as an explanation for the reasons *why* Philostratus is attracted to the subject of athletic training in the first place – is to analyse further the way in which the male, athletic body acted as a vehicle for ideas and ideals which had far-reaching significance for Greek and Roman society. As we have seen already, images of the human body are often used by individuals to think through and experience the values and ideals they must grapple with in their lives. The body as it is encountered, in both self and others, is a crucial focus for our perceptions both of self-identity and of the organizing structures of society; and textual bodies, for that reason, are often highly charged carriers of meaning. In both cases, however – on paper as in the flesh – the human body gains something of its fascination partly through its inscrutability, through its refusal to conform to whatever significance we attempt to impose upon it. I have discussed that tension between significance and inscrutability in chapter three, in illustrating the way in which the beautiful athletic body is inscribed with moral significance, but also constantly refuses to yield up the moral edification it seems to promise. Philostratus, I believe, works with a similar tension between significance and inscrutability in the athletic body, but he also manipulates that familiar tension for his own very different ends, as we shall see.

Within the Roman Empire the male body was a vehicle of elite identity, but the question of exactly how such an identity might best be inscribed on the body and inculcated in it – or indeed the question of what kind of viewing of the bodies of others might be most compatible with such an identity – was open to a great range of answers. The athletic trainer, as master of one of this period's most popular 'technologies' of the body, could lay claim to great authority as one who was capable of filling the male body not only with health, of the kind Galen demands, but also with the distinctive physicality which was capable – at least according to some accounts – of signalling and bestowing high social status, making men into good citizens and embodied inheritors of the Hellenic past. That is a claim Galen implicitly rejects in attacking the trainers for their barbarism.[3]

Philostratus, I will argue, extends to its limits this idea – the idea that training could mark and comprehend the human body in distinctively Greek ways – by suggesting a fundamental similarity between gymnastic knowledge of the body and cultural knowledge of the Hellenic heritage. He does so in part by juxtaposing a detailed account of how the athletic body should be analysed with a long section on athletic history, as it is reflected in contemporary institutions and rituals. The historical details he includes fit in well with the patterns we have seen in the work of Lucian and Pausanias, whereby athletic history often becomes a source of fascination as soon as one chooses to look beneath the surface of conventional practices at the extraordinary range of traditions which lie beneath them. That fascination is partly due to the alluring mixture of familiarity and alienness – rather like the mixture of familiarity and unfathomability within the athletic body itself – which the athletic past had the capacity to conjure up. Philostratus applies similar techniques of analysis in both sections of his work, both to the Greek

---

[3] E.g. at *Thrasyboulos* 46 [K5.894], discussed above (pp. 271–3).

past and to the bodies of the *gymnasion*, in a way which casts the trainer as a representative of Hellenism in its most elevated form, wielder of analytical powers which are very similar to Philostratus' own. Delving into the secrets of the human body, he suggests, is the same as delving into the human past. In both cases he demands a form of interpretation which is flexible and ingenious — and often humorous — in its responses to the obscurities of its subject, but which also never loses sight of its moral responsibilities. It is a form of interpretation which confers exclusive authority, not available to all, as we see not least by the fact that the Philostratean athlete himself is always a passive figure, never a figure to be empowered with a capacity for self-analysis. The inscrutability of the body, like the tantalizing unknowability of the past, is thus the very thing which makes Philostratean interpretation possible, by providing room for the interpreter to manoeuvre, and the very thing which gives it such an unshakeable authority and exclusiveness, by frustrating all but the most sophisticated of rival analysts. Marking and deciphering the human body in a properly Hellenic way, on this model, is possible only for those who have command of the most elevated of rhetorical accomplishments.

The variably imagined cultural and social significance of the human body, and the great variety of views about the way in which the human body should best be treated, have been important issues for many of the texts and practices discussed in previous chapters. Their prominence in the *Gymnasticus* will make it an appropriate point of conclusion for this book. It is also an appropriate text with which to end simply because it is, as has often been acknowledged by scholars of ancient athletics, one of our most detailed 'sources' for athletic practice and ideology in the ancient world, but also, at the same, time, the athletic text which has proved most inscrutable of all. The questions most often asked of it are about its usefulness, as we shall see. Was this really a text which any real trainer could have used? Enquiries of that sort have often proved to be frustrating. Some writers have expressed their irritation at Philostratus' failure to provide a clear account of how the various techniques he discusses should be performed. Others have settled for bewilderment about why the work could possibly have been written. I do not claim to be able to unlock all of the text's secrets. Probably any claim to do so — like any claim to have full and unequivocal interpretative control over the workings of the Philostratean athletic body — would be misguided. I do intend, however, to map out one approach towards understanding the effects this extraordinary work achieves within its cultural and literary contexts. In the process I also wish to give some impression of the way in which it functions in relation to the rest of Philostratus' work, with which it shares so many central themes.[4] Questions about how 'useful' the text is are of limited value, I suggest, unless we acknowledge the fact that it aims at a much wider conception of athletic training than modern sports historians have tended to assume. It is anchored in the realities of contemporary *gymnasion* practice, but it also deliberately goes beyond those realities (just as all of the other texts we have looked at in previous chapters – the works of Galen, Silius Italicus, Pausanias, Dio Chrysostom, Lucian – take on common patterns of evaluating and representing athletics and transform them in extraordinary ways). Philostratus' innovation comes from linking the practical skill of athletic training with interpretative techniques of much broader value. That linking may have been not irrelevant to the self-perception of any athletic trainer who happened to read it, but it also has much broader implications for understanding of traditional culture even for readers who had no personal involvement in *gymnasion* activity. We have seen repeatedly in preceding chapters how the proper use of athletics tends to be taken as an emblem of other qualities and accomplishments: proper education, proper morality, proper use of tradition. The *Gymnasticus* exemplifies that tendency as well as any of the other texts I have discussed. Philostratus' athletic trainer, like Philostratus himself, by his own account, is a representative of Hellenic tradition in the broadest sense, constantly concerned with explicating and refashioning the embodied and institutionalized heritage of the Greek past.

ATHLETIC TRAINERS IN ACTION

Greek has a number of different words for athletic trainers. The word I have used most often up to now, following Galen and Philostratus, has been γυμναστής (*gymnastês*), but in many contexts other terms were more common, the most frequent of those being παιδοτρίβης (*paidotribês*), ἀλείπτης (*aleiptês*) and ἐπιστάτης (*epistatês*).[5] The differences between

---

[4] I assume, following de Lannoy (1997), esp. 2404–10 (and also Flinterman (1995) 5–14 and others), that the author of the *Gymnasticus* is the same as the author of the *Lives of the Sophists* (*VS*), *Life of Apollonius* (*VA*), and *Nero*, and probably also of the *Heroicus* and the first *Imagines*. The repeated interest in athletic subject matter which all of these works share (see de Lannoy (1997) 2407–8), is one convincing argument for common authorship (or at the very least for deliberate correspondence between the work of different authors, especially between the *Gymnasticus* and the *Heroicus*, whose subject matter is often strikingly close). Certainty about that is impossible, however, and I have therefore aimed for a reading of the *Gymnasticus* which is valid independently of any precise connections with other Philostratean texts, which I will discuss in the final section of the chapter.

[5] Louis Robert insisted repeatedly on the athletic meaning of the word *epistatês*, as well as discussing these other terms: e.g., Robert (1974b) 519–29; (1967) 30–1; (1937) 139, n. 1; cf. Robert (1965) 167–70 on the related term *keromatitês*, which becomes common in later centuries.

these terms may imply distinctions between different types of trainer. And they are sometimes due to regional and chronological variations in terminology (which also produced many other names for *gymnasion* personnel in addition to these). But they may also be a sign that the same activities were valued very differently in different contexts and by different people, and dignified with more or less prestigious labels accordingly. In that respect, one of the most marked distinctions seems to have been between the word *gymnastês* and the other three. That term seems to have been used relatively rarely within inscriptions and other 'non-literary' contexts,[6] although there are exceptions.[7] It occurs most frequently when training is discussed in generalizing or theoretical terms, outside specific institutional frameworks, for example within philosophical texts.[8] The elevated overtones Philostratus gives to the word *gymnastês* throughout his text may thus be in part a reflection of a widespread perception that training had a number of different levels of sophistication. His choice of vocabulary signals his desire to construct an idealized version of the category of athletic training which is on a higher level than the practicalities of the *paidotribês*. In much the same way Galen, in his less antagonistic moments, contrasts the detailed care of the *paidotribês* with the more supervisory role the *gymnastês* can play, so long as he remains under the proper guidance of philosophy.[9]

That is not to suggest that the only trainers held in high esteem were those referred to as *gymnastai*. In fact, trainers in all their manifestations were often publicly honoured, although that impression is sometimes undermined by the sense that they are subordinate figures, either public servants under the city's control and under the control of their gymnasiarchs, or else secondary in importance to the athletes they serve. Training of promising athletes, for example (beyond the institutions of ephebic education, which I will come back to in a moment) seems sometimes to have been funded and honoured by the local community, at least within the Hellenistic period, with the implication that the trainers involved were carrying out a publicly

---

[6] I am grateful to Onno van Nijf for pointing this out to me on a number of occasions; cf. Jüthner (1909) 3–8.
[7] E.g., *P. Lond.* 1178, line 63; *F. Delphes* 3.1.220.
[8] E.g., Aristotle, *Politics* 1338b (=Miller 130) offers explicit, though cautious, approval of the *gymnastês* and the *paidotribês* as important contributors to the education of the young, the former as overall supervisors of the condition of the body, the latter as supervisors of its actions; Kyle (1987) 141–2 seems to me to be incautious in relying only on the testimony of Galen and Philostratus, in addition to this passage from Aristotle, to back up his claims for a clear, 'real-life' separation between the *gymnastês* and the *paidotribês*.
[9] E.g., see *De sanitate tuenda* 2.9.25, 2.11.42–4.

useful duty, albeit for financial reward.[10] Louis Robert, for example, has analysed a Hellenistic decree from the region of Epiros, in what is now Southern Albania, put up by the confederation of the Prasaiboi (which was composed of a number of local cities) in honour of an athletic trainer brought from Ionia to train a young man from the area.[11] Some trainers seem to have been of fairly high social status, and to have held political office within their own cities or even in others. One Imperial-period inscription from Smyrna (*I.Smyrna* 246), from the tomb of a βουλευτής (*bouleutês*, 'councillor'), explains that the man was also a *paidotribês*.[12] We also have two Imperial-period inscriptions from Delphi rewarding trainers from other cities with Delphic citizenship and honorary membership of the Delphic *boulê*.[13] These texts form part of a long series of inscriptions granting honours to distinguished outsiders. It may be the case that these men had served the city in some way through their *technê*, whether by training local athletes or by giving public displays and lectures of the kind which are widely attested within Delphi and elsewhere, especially within the *gymnasion*, although the inscriptions are not explicit on that point.[14] Trainers are also honoured regularly for holding office within the athletic guilds.[15] At least one of the trainers mentioned in guild documents seems to have had a glorious athletic career himself, presumably with all the wealth and fame which usually accompanied such a career.[16] That testimony accords in everything but its honorific tone with Galen's criticism of trainers who are retired athletes. Trainers often shared in the glory of those they had

---

[10] See Robert (1967) 27–32 on two Hellenistic inscriptions from Ephesus (*I. Eph.* 1416 and 2005) both of which record the decision to fund the training of athletes, in anticipation of the glory their victories will bring to the city; in the second of these inscriptions, the training is to be paid for by the sale of citizenships. On the expense of training, see also *P. Zenon* 59060 (=Miller 147) for a third-century BC papyrus letter addressed to Zenon, business manager of the politician Apollonios; Zenon has sent a boy to Alexandria to be trained, apparently at considerable expense, to judge by lines 1–3 where the writer reminds Zenon that he had asked for the money not to be wasted on training the boy unless he turned out to be exceptionally promising.
[11] Robert (1974b) on Cabanes (1974) no. 32 (pp. 164–7).
[12] Discussed by van Nijf (1997) 42, n. 54 and 59, n. 144, although we should probably not assume that the man's social or political status was exceptional, as van Nijf stresses.
[13] *F. Delphes* 3.1.200 and 3.1.220. [14] For honours of this sort in Delphi and elsewhere see pp. 49–51.
[15] E.g., see the two trainers listed in *P. Lond.* 1178 (the first in lines 63 and 73, the second in line 94), included by Perpillou-Thomas (1995) numbers 250 and 309 in her catalogue of Egyptian artists and athletes; for an *aleiptês* representing one of the guilds in negotiations with Mark Antony, see Robert (1949) 122 on *P. Lond.* 137 (=Miller 149) (text in Kenyon (1893); also translated by Sherk (1984) no. 85 (pp. 105–6)); on trainers honouring deceased guild members together with the athletes of their guild, see Robert (1968) 406–7 and BE 1968 no. 442 (p. 504) on *GIBM* 794, and on lines 1–3 of the inscription for Markos Alfidios (Bean (1965) no. 2) which I discussed above (pp. 130–1).
[16] See *P. Lond.* 1178, lines 73–4; however, Perpillou-Thomas (1995) is wrong to list as a trainer the athlete honoured in *IG* v, 1, 666 (in no. 316 of her catalogue), basing her categorization on the mistaken reading corrected by Robert (1929b) 35, n. 1.

trained. In many cases they seem to have accompanied athletes when they travelled to festivals. We see a vivid example of that in the first-century BC inscriptions from Priene, where both foreign trainers and doctors are recorded as attendants at a festival banquet together with their athletes.[17] Trainers are also frequently honoured in inscriptions put up by athletes to celebrate their victories.[18]

All of these indications of the prestige of training in the Imperial and Hellenistic periods must have been reinforced by Classical images of trainers as influential (and highly paid) figures, most extravagantly within the poetry of Pindar,[19] although the day-to-day reality of *gymnasion* training would often have fallen short of these glamorous visions of the trainer as recipient of royal patronage. That said, there are inscriptions which honour men with the title 'trainer of the emperor' or 'trainer of the imperial children'.[20] The emperor Marcus Aurelius also seems to have had an interest in athletic training, and mentions his trainer in one of his letters to Fronto.[21] The imperial patronage those details imply can perhaps not tell us much about the status of trainers in the cities of the east, but it does seem to be a relevant background detail for the account given by Galen, given that he spent much of his career working for the imperial family, Marcus Aurelius included.[22] These indications of the interest some emperors had in physical training, as well as in Galen's medicine, are another sign that Galen's claim about his superiority over the Empire's athletic trainers may not have been quite so self-evident as he claimed.

We also have a great deal of evidence, from both the Hellenistic and Imperial periods, for trainers attached to *gymnasia* and *palaistrai* in permanent positions, most often with the label *paidotribês*. Most of this evidence comes from ephebic inscriptions, and so relates to men who were elected to instruct the young men of the city in an official capacity, although it is worth remembering that there were also many trainers who provided similar services in private *palaistrai*, but who are less visible in the inscriptional

---

[17] *I. Priene* 111 (lines 175–6); on the practice of trainers accompanying athletes, and on that inscription specifically, see Robert (1967) 31, esp. n. 3.
[18] For many examples, see Robert (1974b) 520–3 and (1937) 139, n. 1.
[19] See Golden (1998) 83–4 on the Pindaric tradition of praising athletic trainers; 160 on high rewards for some Classical trainers; for varied opinions on trainers in fifth-century BC Athens, see Kyle (1987) 141–5.
[20] See Robert (1959) 662–3 on *I. Didyma* 108, citing several parallels.
[21] Fronto, *Ad M. Caesarem* 2.16 (Teubner p. 34): . . . *et meus me alipta faucibus urgebat*; it seems wrong to put too much weight on this reference, however, since the first half of the sentence is missing and since the rest of the letter seems to be unconnected with it; cf. *Historia Augusta, Marcus Antoninus* 4 for further testimony to his interest in athletics.
[22] See Swain (1996) 375–6.

record.²³ The overriding impression most of this evidence gives is of trainers receiving considerable respect for their work. At the same time, however, it is sometimes stressed that the trainer's services to the city in question are on a much more restricted and less elevated level (perhaps not surprisingly) than that of the gymnasiarch. For example, many of the ephebic inscriptions put up to record membership of the year's *ephebeia* mention trainers along with other *gymnasion* and city officials, presumably with the intention of acknowledging their instruction as well as identifying more clearly the year and the ephebic intake in question. Other ephebic inscriptions honour trainers more directly for their services, often along with other instructors. The long series of honorific *gymnasion* inscriptions and ephebic catalogues from Imperial-period Athens (recorded in *IG* III, 735–68 and 1076–1275), where the *ephebeia* seems to have flourished increasingly from the reign of Tiberius onwards, gives many examples of both of these practices.²⁴ The *paidotribai* of Athens in fact seem to have occupied a fairly high position in relation to their colleagues, if we are to judge by the fact that they tend to come first in the list when they are honoured together with other instructors.²⁵ Moreover, from the second century AD onwards the Athenian office of *paidotribês* became a lifetime appointment, a move which must surely have reflected and contributed to an increase in its prestige (although we do see signs that a number of other *gymnasion* officials had the same tenure).²⁶

In some cases, however, especially outside Athens, the *paidotribês* is clearly separated from gymnasiarchs and other benefactors and public officials mentioned in the same inscriptions, perhaps because his services cannot quite make the jump to being on an equal level with theirs. In some inscriptions, for example, the ephebic year is labelled by reference to the gymnasiarch at the very beginning (sometimes supplemented or supplanted by other major officials and benefactors), followed by the ephebic catalogue, while mention of the *paidotribês* is held back to the end of the inscription, as if to enforce a separation between the trainer and his more important counterparts. This idiom is conspicuous in the series of ephebic inscriptions which survive from second- and first-century BC Delos (recorded in *I.Délos*

---

²³ See Pélékidis (1962) 235 for that point in relation to *paidotribai* in Hellenistic Athens.
²⁴ On the Athenian *ephebeia* in the first and second centuries AD, see Graindor (1931) 85–97, esp. 94–6 on *gymnasion* staff, and (1934) 98–102; cf. Pélékidis (1962) 108–9 for an overview of the role of the *paidotribês*, along with many other teachers, most of them military instructors, in the Hellenistic *ephebeia* of Athens.
²⁵ Cf. Pélékidis (1962) 109, 169, 179–80 and 206–7 on Hellenistic Athens; he makes the point that from the reforms of the third century BC onwards the *paidotribês*, of whom there is usually only one per year from this date (rather than two, as described by Ps.-Aristotle, *Constitution of the Athenians* 42.3 [=Miller 127]) is generally listed in the place of honour at the head of the other instructors.
²⁶ See Follet (1976) 201–46; Graindor (1934) 99.

1922–40). Many of these texts omit any mention of the *paidotribês*, labelling the year in question by reference to the gymnasiarch, sometimes combined with the city's *archôn* and others. Of the seven inscriptions in this series which do mark the year by mention of the *paidotribês* (or *paidotribaî*), four (*I.Délos* 1922, 1924, 1925 and 1926) hold back any mention of him until the end, having labelled the year by reference to the gymnasiarch and *archôn* in standard terms in the opening lines. Even in inscriptions where there is not such a clear separation between *paidotribês* and others, the *paidotribês* still tends to keep his characteristic final place. It is hard to be certain about the implications of those patterns – in fact the exercise of drawing conclusions about an individual's status from his or her position in an inscription is clearly a precarious one – but it may be the case that these texts are drawing on and confirming the impression of a fundamental difference in function and status, at least within this community, between the *paidotribai* and the men who funded and organized the activity they were engaged in.

We see a similar effect in a late first-century AD Macedonian inscription put up by ephebes in honour of their gymnasiarch.[27] The gymnasiarch, who is still a young boy, is named in the opening lines, with a number of other *gymnasion* office holders for the year, including the deputies who were responsible for the practical details of his benefaction, if that is the correct meaning of the word *epimeletês* here:[28] 'Neikokleos, son of Philotos, son of Neikokleos is here honoured as boy-gymnasiarch by the ephebes, in the year when Tryphon son of Attalos is ephebarch, with the *epimeletai* Chairophanos son of Kriton, Neikon son of Daseilos, Menandros son of Eros, Teimokrates son of Teimokrates, with Krinios son of Philotos as *protostatês* . . .' (lines 1–9).[29] That opening is followed by a long list of eighty-eight ephebes, and then finally the name of the *paidotribês*: 'in the trainership of Titos Klaudios Zosimos' (παιδοτριβοῦντος Τ. Κλαυδίου Ζώσιμου) (lines 98–100). Here, the *paidotribês* has a very prominent role, helping to fix the identity of the year, and mirroring the opening position of the young gymnasiarch, in a way which makes the two officials seem to encompass the intervening list of ephebes in their joint care, as they have done throughout the year. The trainer's contribution may be particularly important given the young age of his gymnasiarch. It is also clear,

---

[27] Hatzopoulos and Loukopoulou (1992) K9 (pp. 87–90).   [28] As discussed above, p. 70.
[29] Νεικοκλέα Φιλώτου τοῦ Νει‾ | κοκλέους γυμνασιαρχή‾ | σαντα ἐν παιδί, οἱ ἔφηβοι, | ἐφηβαρ-χοῦντος Τρυφωνᾶ τοῦ Ἀττάλου, | δι' ἐπιμελητῶν Χαιροφάνου τοῦ Κρίτω‾ | νος, Νείκωνος τοῦ Δασείλου, Με‾ | νάνδρου τοῦ Ἔρωτος, Τειμοκράτου | του Τειμοκράτου, πρωτοστατοῦντος | Κρινίου τοῦ Φιλώτου . . .

however, that the trainer is not the main subject of the decree, or even its main initiator. The final position of his name, separated from the list of ephebes by a physical gap in the inscription, gives the impression of a degree of detachment, as if he is standing to one side in a supervisory role to those whose youthful achievements are the most important object of celebration.

Surviving Hellenistic *gymnasion* laws, most notably the decree from Beroia which I discussed in chapter two,[30] also give a vivid picture of the crucial role played by *paidotribai* in the city's day-to-day education. Here too, however, there is also a consistent emphasis on the trainer's subordinate status. He is subordinate both to the city, in general terms, as a public servant, and also to the gymnasiarch, to whom he is answerable. One third-century BC *gymnasion* decree from Miletos (*SIG*³ 577) gives a detailed description of the yearly election process for *paidotribai*, along with other teachers, which implies that great care was taken over their appointment. But in this case, and perhaps in contrast with Athens, where *paidotribai* are often honoured first among their fellow-instructors, the trainers may not have been valued quite so highly as some of their colleagues, if we are to judge by the fact that their salaries often do not reach the top level. The salary of elected *gymnasion* officials is specified immediately after the instructions for election procedure, with *paidotribai* listed at three-quarters of the salary given to grammar teachers.[31] There are signs of a similar inequality of pay elsewhere.[32] The Beroia decree lays down some of the trainers' most important duties, among them the requirement that they organize the *paides* for special occasions like sacrifices and regular examinations.[33] Those details emphasize the crucial nature of their contribution to the smooth running of the *gymnasion*. However, the inscription also threatens trainers with a disciplinary appearance before the gymnasiarch and a specified fine if they fail to attend twice daily at the times decided on by the gymnasiarch, a punishment which echoes on a much smaller scale the

---

[30] Pp. 51–5. See Gauthier and Hatzopoulos (1993) (= *SEG* 27.261) (=Miller 126).

[31] *SIG*³ 577, lines 51–3; translated by Austin (1981) no. 119 (pp. 207–10).

[32] See *SIG*³ 578, lines 7–28 (translated in part by Miller 125), a third-century BC inscription from a *palaistra* in Teos, where the *paidotribês* earns less than all but one of the grammar teachers and musicians, but more than the javelin teacher and the teacher of fighting in armour. However, the fact that the decree specifies a minimum of two months per year teaching time for the last of those instructors should make us cautious about assuming a direct correlation between the sum granted and the value implied in all cases; it may even be the case that the *paidotribês* earned more than these less well-paid instructors simply because he worked there full-time in contrast with them, rather than through being more highly appreciated.

[33] The *paidotribai* in Beroia were apparently responsible for the *paides* only, whereas in Athens they also trained the ephebes: see Gauthier and Hatzopoulos (1993) 73.

huge financial punishments which are to be imposed on the gymnasiarch by the city in the case of wrong-doing:

> The *paidotribai* are to attend the *gymnasion* twice a day at the times specified by the gymnasiarch, except in the case of illness or other unavoidable reasons for absence. If any one of them does not, he must explain himself before the gymnasiarch; and if any of the *paidotribai* seems to be neglecting his duty and not appearing at the designated times, the gymnasiarch is to fine him at a rate of five drachmas per day. The gymnasiarch is also to be in charge of whipping *paides* who are disorderly, and *paidagogoi*, those who are not free; those who are free he must fine. He must also arrange for the *paidotribai* to make an examination of the *paides* three times each year, every four months; and he must choose judges for that examination and crown the winners with olive branches. (B15–26)[34]

The *paidotribês* is here subordinate to the gymnasiarch in much the same way as the gymnasiarch is subordinate (though with very much more at stake) to the city. At the same time he seems to outrank the other groups mentioned here. He is portrayed as occupying a midway position between the gymnasiarch and other less high-ranking individuals who are punished in more humiliating and less consequential ways for misbehaviour: the *paides* themselves, who are to be punished by flogging; and the *paidagogoi* (men responsible for supervising and accompanying the *paides*) who are to be flogged, if they are slaves, and fined if they are free. Even the fines to be levied on free *paidagogoi* are cast as less significant than those applied to the *paidotribês* (and of course less so than the much greater fines applied to the gymnasiarch) by the fact that the decree declines to specify their magnitude. The relative frequency with which trainers and gymnasiarchs are honoured points to similar (and no doubt similarly unsurprising) conclusions about their relative importance. The trainer's services may be crucial, and comparable to those of the gymnasiarch, but he never receives anything like the same level of public recognition.

We should of course be wary of assuming that these decrees can give us an accurate general picture of the situation some three or four centuries later, at the time when Philostratus and Galen were writing. There are no Imperial *gymnasion* decrees to compare them with. However, there are

---

[34] ἅπαν⁻ | τάτωσαν δὲ καὶ οἱ παιδοτρίβαι ἑκάστης ἡμέρας δὶς εἰς τὸ γυμνάσιον | τὴν ὥραν ἣν ἂν ὁ γυμνασίαρχος ἀποδείξῃ, ἐὰν μή τις ἀρρωστήσῃ | ἢ ἄλλη τις ἀναγκαία ἀσχολία γένηται· εἰ δὲ μή, ἐμφανισάτω τῶι γυ⁻ | μνασιάρχηι· ἐὰν δέ τις δοκῆι ὀλιγωρεῖν τῶν παιδοτριβῶν καὶ μὴ παραγίνε⁻ | σθαι τὴν τεταγμένην ὥραν ἐπὶ τοὺς παῖδας, ζημιούτω αὐτὸν καθ' ἡμέ⁻ | [ρ]αν δραχμαῖς πέντε· κύριος δὲ ἔστω ὁ γυμνασίαρχος καὶ τῶν | παίδων τοὺς ἀτακτοῦντας μαστιγῶν καὶ τῶν παιδαγωγῶν, | ὅσοι ἂν μὴ ἐλεύθεροι ὦσιν, τοὺς δὲ ἐλευθέρους ζημιῶν· ἐπαναγ⁻ | καζέτω <ι> δὲ καὶ τοὺς παιδοτρίβας ποιεῖσθαι ἀπόδειξιν τῶν παίδων | [τ]ρὶς ἐν τῶι ἐνιαυτῶι κατὰ τετράμηνον καὶ καθιστάτω αὐτοῖς κριτάς, | [τ]ὸν δὲ νικῶντα στεφανούτω θαλλοῦ στεφάνωι.

enough similarities between the Imperial and Hellenistic ephebic catalogues which I analysed in the previous paragraphs to suggest that the organization of these institutions would have remained fairly static within many cities, at least in their staffing structures, and that stability may imply that the prestige levels of *paidotribai* within these systems did not change drastically, despite some local variation. Stability of that sort would have been due in part to a widespread perception of the *ephebeia* as an education system fixed and sanctioned by long tradition.

Some *paidotribai* may have had pretensions to a high level of general education, and may even have found themselves in situations where the skills such an education provided were necessary. Certainly trainers do not hesitate to use the word *technê*, which we have seen already in Galen, for their own activity.[35] However, that fact may not on its own be very significant, since this seems to have been a standard term for many different types of professional activity in the Imperial period, and need not imply any very elevated claims to philosophical or logical sophistication.[36] In fact, the overlap between Galen's use of the word and its use by trainers may be better explained in other ways, in the sense that it may have been more a sign of Galen's tendency to insist on the elevated, Platonic connotations of words and practices which were used less ostentatiously elsewhere, than a sign of any desire on the part of trainers to appropriate philosophical language for their own expertise. More significant, perhaps, is the possibility that trainers may have required rhetorical expertise in some circumstances.[37] The public election procedures from Miletos, for example, may have left room for candidates to argue their cases themselves, although that is not specified. One of the examples of public funding for a promising athlete which I discussed above sees the trainer of the athlete in question putting his case to the city's assembly.[38] And it may be that high office in the Empire-wide guilds would have required regular advocacy on behalf of guild members, as in the example of the *aleiptês* who negotiates with Mark Antony on behalf of the Guild of Sacred Victors in *P.Lond.* 137.[39] The rhetorical treatises of Pseudo-Dionysius contain instructions, amongst many other categories, for the type of speeches which are delivered to athletes.[40] The sample speech provided is described as an 'exhortation to competing athletes', and seems to envisage a fairly large group of assembled contestants before the

---

[35] E.g., see Robert (1974b) 519–20 and 528.   [36] See Robert (1974b), esp. 519, n. 29 and (1960a) 26–7.
[37] I am once again grateful to Onno van Nijf for reminding me of that.
[38] See Robert (1967) 28–32.   [39] =Miller 149.
[40] Ps.-Dionysius, *Ars rhetorica*, speech 7; the treatise was probably written in the fourth or fifth century AD; speech 7 is translated with notes by Russell and Wilson (1981) 377–81; it is similar in some of its details to speech 1 (pp. 362–5), which gives instructions for speeches at festivals.

beginning of an *agôn*. It is possible that the text reflects a regular practice of exhortatory speech-making to athletes before festivals. The instructions state at the very beginning that speeches of this sort can be delivered by officials and participants of many different sorts. While there is no particular sign that trainers form one of the groups the author has in mind, it may be that speeches of this sort were regularly delivered as a feature of guild activities, and if so they might sometimes have been the responsibility of trainers who held senior guild offices.

Much of this evidence is highly speculative, of course, and none of it can bear much weight, but collectively it does at least hint at a range of contexts in which we can plausibly imagine trainers – at least the most senior of them – exercising a degree of rhetorical skill. And yet, despite all of these factors, there are signs even beyond the work of Galen that the idea of the trainer as *pepaideumenos* would sometimes have been suspect. For example, Dio Chrysostom's portrait of the athletic trainer in his second Melankomas text, *Oratio* 28, seems to draw on a widespread perception that trainers in practice fell short of these requirements. The athletic trainer there, as I argued in chapter three,[41] seems rather lacking in intellectual sophistication, at least until Dio (or whoever the first-person speaker is supposed to be) interprets the situation for him in more philosophical terms.

There are, finally, signs of a body of theoretical writing associated specifically with the trainer's art. Manuals of training seem to have been written long before the *Gymnasticus*, as far back as the fifth century BC.[42] Many of these texts seem to have been relatively complex and erudite, and some of them may have been similar at least in form to the kind of medical treatises on regimen which I discussed in the last chapter, although it is of course very hard to know how widely they were used or read by *gymnasion* instructors. We also have one brief surviving extract from what seems to be a book of instruction in wrestling technique, surviving in a second-century AD papyrus fragment from Egypt (*P.Oxy.* 3.466). This text contains a series of wrestling moves described in extensive technical detail,[43] and seems to testify to an industry of theorization of athletic method within the Imperial period, although it is again difficult without parallels to know how widely used instructions of this sort may have been. The text may fall short of

---

[41] See pp. 152–6.
[42] See Jüthner (1909) 8–26 on Ikkos, Herodikos, Theon and others; Galen discusses, and refutes, the work of Theon at length in his *De sanitate tuenda*, citing two of his works on gymnastic subjects by name.
[43] Poliakoff (1986) 161–72 argues that the format of the work makes it likely that it was written to be sold; he also compares the fragment with a passage from Galen (from *De sanitate tuenda* Book 2 [K6.141–3]) with which it has many similarities; cf. Poliakoff (1987b) 51–3; Jüthner (1909) 26–30.

Galen's demands for a medical and philosophical form of athletics, but it seems at least to have had pretensions to match the intricacy of elaboration which was such an important requirement for any kind of professional standing,[44] and to have had some claims to be a sophisticated body of expertise.

I have argued, then – albeit with repeated qualifications due to the provisional nature of the evidence we have – that training was often a relatively prestigious career, even if it was sometimes represented in terms which imposed limits on that prestige. There may be signs, in other words, that Galen's vision of ignorant and despised athletic trainers is highly suspect as a generalization about the importance of their profession. At the same time, however, the tension between authority and subordinate status which some of these inscriptions reveal should make us equally cautious about taking at face value Philostratus' version of an elevated and autonomous *gymnastikê*. Just like Galen's idealized view of philosophical medicine, Philostratean *gymnastikê* is related to routine practice, but also very deliberately elevated above it.

MEDICINE AND TRAINING IN THE *GYMNASTICUS*

My aim in this section, reversing the perspective of chapter six, is to discuss the way in which Philostratus' representation of *gymnastikê* relates to his portrayal of medicine. I will argue that *gymnastikê* is here defined, like Galenic medicine, by its relations with alternative and rival *technai*. I will be using the work of Galen as a recurrent point of reference, in order to highlight some of the most distinctive features of the choices these two writers have made in navigating through a shared literary and philosophical tradition, and against a shared background of cultural activity (despite the fact that some of Galen's athletic works may have been written as much as thirty or forty years before the *Gymnasticus*). Probably Philostratus knew Galen's work well, and he may well have intended the *Gymnasticus* as a specific response to it. The repeated similarities between their works make that highly likely.[45] It is, however, a difficult claim to prove, and my

---

[44] Pp. 261, 263, 268.
[45] Jüthner (1909) 118–20 claims that Philostratus' knowledge of medical texts is probably not direct, but rather mediated through the treatises of trainers; while that conclusion may well be right, and while it is not in conflict with the interpretations I propose, it nevertheless seems to me far less self-evident than he claims (see p. 329, n. 70 below); Brophy and Brophy (1989) 161–4, by contrast, are surely too confident in claiming to have detected precise echoes of Galen's own work in the parodies of medical writing on diet discussed further pp. 323, 335–6 below, and they certainly go too far in assuming that Galen and Philostratus were 'friendly rivals at court' (157).

argument here will not depend on it. The more important point is that their shared intertextual engagement with similar philosophical models, and with similar patterns of professional self-presentation, of the kind I outlined in the previous chapter, means that they are significantly in dialogue with each other in ways which any contemporary reader who knew the work of both authors is likely to have sensed.

These intertextual relations between them are prominent at a number of different stages within the *Gymnasticus*. In some ways Philostratus' project is actually very close to Galen's, not least because both of them set out to construct a variety of *gymnastikê* which is avowedly elevated above the level of actual contemporary practice. Philostratus represents his work as an attempt to rescue *gymnastikê* from the degeneration into which it has fallen, much as Galen represents his work as an attempt to reclaim a degenerate art for the forces of rational medicine. In the process, however, Philostratus goes out of his way to neutralize the predominantly negative tone which pervades much of Galen's work on athletics. He emphasizes more consistently than Galen the positive aspects of Plato's account of *gymnastikê*.[46] He suggests, through his acknowledgement of a recent decline in athletic training, that Galen's criticisms of the malpractice of unscrupulous trainers who have abandoned the true path of their art are not relevant to any discussion of how the real *gymnastikê* should be valued. He plays up medicine's most absurd and disreputable elements in a way which purports to undermine the *technê* as a whole, in order to show that the same trick of Galenic denigration could very easily be directed at medicine itself. And he insists throughout that *gymnastikê* is at least as autonomous a *technê* as medicine. In making that point he opts for a relatively simple statement of the features which make it distinct from medicine, and so refuses to enter into competition with Galen's technique of complex subdivision and categorization, which had been used to cast *gymnastikê* as a tiny portion of medical knowledge (although, as we shall see, Philostratus is not shy of presenting us with his own kind of complex categorization at a later stage, in the physiological details of the second half of the work).

Philostratus thus introduces subtle and original variations into the patterns of technical categories and hierarchies which Galen, like others, had manipulated before him. There are also both similarities and differences between the techniques of analysis they recommend. Both of them are similarly interested in the project of looking beneath the surface of their subjects, laying bare the workings of the world, a project which also played a large role in many other areas of expertise, not least in the techniques of

---

[46] Cf. Müller (1995) 324–6 on Platonic allusions in the *Gymnasticus*.

physiognomical interpretation which both of these writers show an interest in. But the subject matter Philostratus chooses for that project is in many ways different from what we find in the writing of Galen. The often bizarre texture of the historical subject matter in the first half of the *Gymnasticus* signals that difference strongly, setting the reader adrift in a text which at first sight seems far removed from the physiological focus of Galen's writing, although the work also increasingly builds up an impression of alluring but only barely graspable links between bodily and historical analysis, as we shall see further in the next section. Philostratus seems to be accepting the need for some wider guiding force to stand over his *technê* of *gymnastikê*. But he rejects the Galenic idea that philosophical medicine can do that job of guardianship in adequate ways, not least because it is just as much at risk of degenerating into morally corrupt and irrational action as *gymnastikê* is. He chooses rather to put all of these individual *technai* under the overarching control of a much broader form of morally aware and rhetorically flexible interpretative skill, which can be applied to contemporary culture in all its forms.[47]

Before turning to more sustained comparison I want first to run through a brief outline of the structure of the *Gymnasticus*, and of some of the most conspicuous trends in modern responses to it.[48] The opening of the work (paragraphs 1–2) asserts the prestigious position held by *gymnastikê* within the hierarchy of professional skills. Following this we might expect, on the model of Galen's *Thrasyboulos*, an involved analysis of those categories, and a robust presentation of the technical complexities on which *gymnastikê* relies. Philostratus, however, launches at once (paragraphs 3–19) into a long account of the origins of the various athletic events, which for the most part has no immediately obvious connection with techniques of training. Only then does the figure of the trainer return to the limelight. The rest of the work (paragraphs 20–58) focuses on the skills required by the *gymnastês*, presenting famous examples of encouragement given by trainers to their athletes, and illustrating – often very entertainingly – some of the techniques of physiognomical analysis required for evaluating the strengths and weaknesses of aspiring competitors.

The initial foray into athletic history looks at first sight like an own goal for Philostratus, a move which is only likely to increase the suspicion that we are dealing with a discipline which cannot hold its own against Galen's heavyweight philosophical medicine, but it is, I believe, an essential part of Philostratus' argument. Many modern commentators on the *Gymnasticus*

---

[47] Van Nijf (2003) 283 briefly discusses Philostratus' combination of rhetoric and training.
[48] For commentary see Jüthner (1909) and (less detailed) Coretta (1995).

have been unimpressed by the historical details of the first half, no doubt influenced by a tendency to undervalue athletic 'antiquarianism', without acknowledging the prestige and fascination associated with the project of anchoring contemporary festival life within a long historical framework. I will argue in what follows, by contrast, that Philostratus' juxtaposition of the physical and the historical is a deliberate and bold attempt to give *gymnastikē* a central space within the contours of contemporary *paideia*, as something which draws on and exemplifies processes on which all educated men must rely. It also suggests that Philostratus' own transformative skills of cultural analysis have a kind of universal power and relevance. That universal power is also signalled by their capacity to reconfigure even a discipline whose value is far from self-evident, a discipline which in the world of the second and third centuries AD attracted widespread devotion, but nevertheless still hovered on the edges of social and intellectual prestige.

My aim is thus partly to suggest that the *Gymnasticus* is a work of greater sophistication than has usually been acknowledged. It has often been criticized as a 'sophistic' text, a playful reworking of a traditional 'textbook' topic, linked with rhetorical traditions of adoxography, the exercise of defending activities which cannot easily be defended.[49] The *Gymnasticus* has also been denigrated as an incoherent, 'encyclopedic' piece of writing.[50] Even Alain Billault, who usefully attempts a rehabilitation of the *Gymnasticus*, seems unable to escape from a terminology of 'encyclopedism'.[51] Such assessments suffer from underestimating the central importance to contemporary culture of the institution Philostratus describes. They also suffer, I suggest, from a misunderstanding of the fundamentally rhetorical character of much ancient scientific writing, and of the prestigious role played by creative compilation within Imperial-period literature, of the kind we saw in looking at Pausanias in chapter four. More specifically, all of them fail to show that there are very strong thematic links between the many different sections of the work. The elements of ingenuity which resurface throughout the *Gymnasticus*, and which others have seen as signs of the author's lack of serious investment in the things he defends, are in fact an important part of his justification of it, and the humour of the work plays a deliberate role, as a central element in the sophisticated styles of analysis and display which Philostratus illustrates for us.

Where the *Gymnasticus* has received more attention, as I suggested in the introductory section of this chapter, is from scholars interested in

---

[49] See, e.g., Müller (1995) 328; Anderson (1986) 269; Jüthner (1909) 97–107.
[50] See, e.g., Reardon (1971) 195–8.   [51] Esp. Billault (1993) 161–2.

reconstructing the realities of ancient athletic practice. Many of these studies have been reluctant, however, to situate the *Gymnasticus* within its wider context of cultural and disciplinary polemics, and have failed to take account of the rhetorical strategies which are distinctive to it.[52] This is not to say that the *Gymnasticus* has no value for reconstructions of athletic practice; rather that its value will be limited if one does not take into account the way in which Philostratus' work, along with other literary representations of athletic activity in this period, carries with it a much wider agenda than the 'faithful' reflection of what actually happened in the *gymnasion* and the *stadion*. It is clear that the *Gymnasticus* is not meant simply as a systematic manual of instruction, to be mechanically applied (as is more likely to be the case with the wrestling manual of *P.Oxy.* 3.466), but in a sense that is precisely the point, since for Philostratus, as for Galen in a different way, the idealized *gymnastês* must be able to see very far beyond the technical details of the more lowly *paidotribês*.

The *Gymnasticus* opens with the claim that *gymnastikê* is a form of *sophia* (wisdom) equal to any. The passage has fascinating overlaps with a number of passages in Galen's *Protrepticus*, especially with the categorization of good and bad *technai* in *Protrepticus* 5 and 14. These overlaps are partly due, no doubt, to the fact that Galen and Philostratus are both similarly drawing on long traditions of categorization of the *technai* in protreptic writing.[53] I quote here, for reference, an extract from the final paragraph of Galen's text:

Given that there is a distinction between two different types of art (*technê*) – some of them are rational and highly respected, whereas others are contemptible, and centred around bodily labour, in other words the ones we refer to as banausic or manual – it is better to take up one of the first category ... In the first category are medicine, rhetoric, music, geometry, arithmetic, logic, astronomy, grammar and law; and you can also add sculpting and drawing if you wish. (*Protrepticus* 14 [K1.38–9])[54]

---

[52] So much so that the only translations of this text into English (in athletic sourcebooks by Robinson (1955) 212–32 and Sweet (1987) 212–30 are incomplete; Robinson even omits the opening paragraph of the work. Golden (1998) 48–50 recognizes the text's limitations as a reliable source, but he does not attempt a coherent exposition of it. Harris (1972) gives up in exasperation, and accuses Philostratus of including material which is 'silly' (24) and 'feeble' (33); cf. Harris (1964) 26.
[53] See Boudon (2000) 16–35 on Galen's treatment of these traditions in his *Protrepticus*.
[54] Ἀλλὰ διττῆς οὔσης διαφορᾶς τῆς πρώτης ἐν ταῖς τέχναις – ἔνιαι μὲν γὰρ αὐτῶν λογικαί τ' εἰσὶ καὶ σεμναί, τινὲς δ' εὐκαταφρόνητοι καὶ διὰ τῶν τοῦ σώματος πόνων, ἃς δὴ βαναύσους τε καὶ χειρωνακτικὰς ὀνομάζουσιν – ἄμεινον ἂν εἴη τοῦ προτέρου γένους τῶν τεχνῶν μετέρχεσθαί τινα· ... εἰσὶ δ' ἐκ τοῦ προτέρου γένους ἰατρική τε καὶ ῥητορικὴ καὶ μουσικὴ γεωμετρία τε καὶ ἀριθμητικὴ καὶ λογιστικὴ καὶ ἀστρονομία καὶ γραμματικὴ καὶ νομική. πρόσθες δ', εἰ βούλει, ταύταις πλαστικήν τε καὶ γραφικήν.

The best of all, Galen tells us finally, is medicine. Athletic training, meanwhile, has already been ejected from the categorization altogether, as we saw in chapter six[55] and at the beginning of my introduction, counted along with acrobatics and tight-rope walking as a 'bad art' (κακοτεχνία) (9).

Philostratus begins his work in similar vein, identifying a number of types of wisdom (*sophiai*), in ways which implicitly challenge Galen's account:

> Let us consider the following things as examples of wisdom – things like poetry and speaking artfully and undertaking poetry and music and geometry (ποιητκῆς τε ἅψασθαι καὶ μουσικῆς καὶ γεωμετρίας), and even astronomy, as long as you don't overdo it (ὁπόση μὴ περιττή), and also the art of organizing armies, and even things like the following (καὶ ἔτι τὰ τοιαῦτα): the whole of medicine and painting and modelling, and all types of sculpting and gem-cutting and metal-engraving. The banausic activities can be granted the status of *technai*, since they are capable of producing their own tools, but let the label of *sophia* be reserved for those I have mentioned . . . And I consider *gymnastikê* a form of *sophia*, and one which is inferior to none of the other arts (*technai*), so much so that treatises (ὑπομνήματα) have been composed on the subject for the benefit of those who may wish to take up training. (*Gymnasticus* 1 [261.1–15])[56]

Galen had chosen the word *technê* to describe his idealized forms of professional expertise. It is immediately striking that Philostratus here moves beyond that usage, insisting that qualifying as a *technê* is not enough to guarantee the highest level of prestige. His ideal forms of expertise will instead be types of 'wisdom'. It is almost as though he is signalling here the differences between Galen's project and his own, lifting the latter on to a higher level of ambition. He includes the arts of painting and sculpting in his list in a more comprehensive form than Galen does, and thus signals a readiness to expand the canon of respectable expertise beyond Galen's narrow conception of it. At the same time, however, he emphasizes throughout this opening the discriminating nature of his own categorization. For example the exclusion of astronomy in its more extreme forms advertises the fact that activities which have the potential to make the grade will be automatically excluded as soon as they overstep the bounds of propriety, just as medicine and training will be criticized in later parts of the

---

[55] P. 295.
[56] Σοφίαν ἡγώμεθα καὶ τὰ τοιαῦτα μὲν οἷον φιλοσοφῆσαι καὶ εἰπεῖν ξὺν τέχνῃ ποιητικῆς τε ἅψασθαι καὶ μουσικῆς καὶ γεωμετρίας καὶ νὴ Δί' ἀστρονομίας, ὁπόση μὴ περιττή, σοφία δὲ καὶ τὸ κοσμῆσαι στρατιὰν καὶ ἔτι τὰ τοιαῦτα· ἰατρικὴ πᾶσα καὶ ζωγραφία καὶ πλάσται καὶ ἀγαλμάτων εἴδη καὶ κοῖλοι λίθοι καὶ κοῖλος σίδηρος. βάναυσοι δὲ ὁπόσαι, δεδόσθω μὲν αὐταῖς τέχνη, καθ' ἣν ὄργανόν τι καὶ σκεῦος ὀρθῶς ἀποτελεσθήσεται, σοφία δὲ ἐς ἐκείνας ἀποκείσθω μόνας ἃς εἶπον . . . περὶ δὲ γυμναστικῆς, σοφίαν λέγομεν οὐδεμιᾶς ἐλάττω τέχνης, ὥστε εἰς ὑπομνήματα ξυνθεῖναι τοῖς βουλομένοις γυμνάζειν.

text for any failure to live up to the standards required of them. He generously includes medicine (*iatrikê*), as if he is trying to avoid the impression of disagreeing with Galen outright, but the phrase ἔτι τὰ τοιαῦτα ('*even things like the following* [will be included]'), perhaps suggests that it is only there on sufferance, like astronomy, on the condition that it does not succumb to the luxurious influences which Philostratus condemns later in the work. He then states the pre-eminence of *gymnastikê* in pride of place at the end of the list, echoing Galen's final mention of medicine, in a way which sets up a blunt challenge to the assumptions of superiority which underlie Galenic medicine, although his claim is a more modest one than Galen's, and so by implication less controversial, since he insists only on making athletic training *no less valuable* than its counterparts. He also reminds us that he is very far from being the first to undertake this kind of project. The word 'treatises' (ὑπομνήματα) signals the many athletic works which seem to have preceded Philostratus' own, and thus sets the *Gymnasticus* within a long tradition of intellectually distinguished composition,[57] while also perhaps reminding us (if we translate ὑπομνήματα as 'monuments' or 'memorials') of the role his own work plays in commemorating and preserving the traditions of the past.

Philostratus also anchors his treatise in philosophical precedent in this opening passage, not least by his use of the phrase 'undertaking poetry and music and geometry' (ποιητικῆς τε ἅψασθαι καὶ μουσικῆς καὶ γεωμετρίας), which recalls the language of Plato, *Republic* Book 3. There Socrates advocates a balanced education, saying that a man who toils hard at athletics and eats luxuriously and takes no notice of music and philosophy (μουσικῆς δὲ καὶ φιλοσοφίας μὴ ἅπτηται) (411c) at first becomes very fit and proud, but later loses all his love of knowledge. The reference signals Philostratus' knowledge of Plato, and hints at an alignment of Philostratus' own opinions with Plato's. More specifically, it reinforces Philostratus' insistence that he is not condoning the practice of athletics to excess, and that he is not under any obligation to defend those who practise athletics wrongly – immoderately and unphilosophically. As we saw in chapter six,[58] this book of the *Republic*, along with other Platonic passages, had been used by Galen as a central plank of his own criticism of athletic training.[59] Galen does not always give as much weight to the positive side of Plato's representations of athletic activity as he might do, at least in those

---

[57] See Jüthner (1909) 116–18 on the significance of this phrase.   [58] Pp. 276–7.
[59] For example at *Thrasyboulos* 36 [K5.874–6], where Galen quotes Plato, *Republic* 407b–c and 410b, obscuring their full contexts, as examples of philosophical condemnation of training; cf. *Thrasyboulos* 47 [K5.898]; *Good Condition* K4.753.

passages where he attacks trainers most uncompromisingly. Philostratus here seems to be correcting Galen's unbalanced representation of Platonic opinion, reminding us that Plato does not even come close to condemning athletics outright. He thus side-steps many of the criticisms of Galen and others, through the implication that any problems associated with *gymnastikê* are due simply to (unPlatonic) misuse of it by modern practitioners; and through the implication that his own version of *gymnastikê* can have a fruitful co-operation, like Platonic *gymnastikê*, with a whole range of other cultured and intellectual arts.

He then states his intention to 'defend nature' by demonstrating that the present-day shortage of excellent athletes is due to mistraining rather than inborn deficiencies; that claim is followed immediately by his account of athletic history; and then in 14–15, before finally focusing on the figure of the trainer in more detail, Philostratus returns again to the problem of how the expertise of the trainer should be categorized. This section responds to Galen's argument that the art of the trainer is only one tiny subdivision of the overarching *technê* of the doctor. Philostratus tells us, for example: 'How then should one understand *gymnastikê*? How else should one think of it than as a form of wisdom composed of medicine and of the art of the *paidotribês*, being more perfect than the latter, and a part of the former?' (*Gymnasticus* 14) [268.30–269.1].[60] Philostratus here sidesteps Galen's logical complexities and argues for a view of training as a *technê* which takes elements both from the art of the *paidotribês* and the art of the doctor. The admission that it is a part of medicine might seem like too submissive an attitude to Galen's claims about the subordinate status of *gymnastikê*. But the qualifications which follow in the rest of the paragraph largely undermine that impression, as Philostratus goes on to outline the mainly separate bodies of expertise associated with doctor and trainer respectively. It is tempting, in fact, to feel that the passage quoted above is using 'medicine' in the overarching Platonic sense which Galen himself argues for so often, following the *Gorgias* – which I will examine further in a moment – to mean 'care of the body as a whole'. This overarching care of the body can then be divided into the two equal spheres of restorative medicine (dedicated to making the body better in times of illness and injury) and preventative athletic training (dedicated to strengthening the body and so preventing illness and injury). Certainly that impression of equal division is supported by the lines which follow, where

[60] Τί οὖν χρὴ περὶ γυμναστικῆς γινώσκειν; τί δ' ἄλλο ἢ σοφίαν αὐτὴν ἡγεῖσθαι ξυγκειμένην μὲν ἐξ ἰατρικῆς τε καὶ παιδοτριβικῆς, οὖσαν δὲ τῆς μὲν τελεωτέραν, τῆς δὲ μόριον.

we hear that the doctor and the trainer are to be distinguished from each other by the different techniques they use for the same end of healing the body. The doctor uses drugs and plasters, whereas the trainer uses massage and regimen. And there will often be cases where only one of the two is qualified to intervene. The passage as a whole thus offers a refutation, based on both common sense and Platonic precedent, of Galen's insistence that the art of *gymnastikê* cannot be admitted to have any areas of expertise independent of the art of the doctor.

There are also points where Philostratus criticizes and parodies medical writing explicitly, most conspicuously in *Gymnasticus* 44. There he suggests that medicine (*iatrikê*) – in harness with *opsophagia* ('the love of luxurious food') – has been one of the main vehicles for the luxury which has ruined the true art of *gymnastikê*. He ridicules the way in which doctors classify different types of fish according to their origins, with the implication that such classifications have been used mainly to achieve greater gastronomic satisfaction – to get hold of the best tasting fish – rather than for the purpose of guaranteeing good health (although in many ways the technique of classification Philostratus mocks at this point seems worryingly close to the techniques he recommends himself in the second half of the work, as we shall see later). Philostratus' parodic account is reminiscent of the style of Galen's dietary texts, for example his discussion of the effects of different types of fish on human health in *On the Faculties of Foodstuffs* Book 3 [K6.554–659].[61] Philostratus surely has established techniques of medical dietetic writing in mind here, even if he is not referring to Galen specifically. Medicine is claimed to be responsible for exactly the kind of vices which Galen and others have blamed *gymnastikê* for introducing.

He even suggests that medicine has 'flattered' (ἐκολάκευσε) athletics. That odd expression alludes to Plato's *Gorgias*. In that text, Socrates – in conversation with the famous teacher of rhetoric, Gorgias, and some of his supporters – denigrates rhetoric for its damaging influence on civic life. He subdivides the human sphere of action into two main areas, care for the soul, which he calls 'politics', and care of the body. He then further divides politics into the spheres of legislation and of justice; and he divides the care of the body into *iatrikê* and *gymnastikê*. He suggests that sophistry is a degenerate and seductive version of legislation. It 'flatters' legislation, purporting to provide gratification, but in fact leading it astray. Similarly, oratory 'flatters' justice. Finally, he illustrates his concept of 'flattery' more

---

[61] See Powell (2003) for translation and commentary.

clearly by reference to the other half of human activity. *Gymnastikê*, he suggests, is 'flattered' by the art of cosmetics, which purports to achieve the same ends as conventional *gymnastikê*, but actually replaces it, with disastrous consequences. Similarly *opsopoiikê* – the art of cookery – flatters medicine, leading it astray.

Galen makes the overall art of bodily care equivalent to his own medical expertise, as we have already seen several times. At the same time he downgrades *gymnastikê* as it is actually practised, in order to make it a very tiny part of the much more significant sphere Plato himself refers to as *gymnastikê*. He thus brings Plato in line with his own view of disciplinary hierarchies by suggesting that common usage of the terms for medicine (*iatrikê*) and training (*gymnastikê*) does not correspond to what Plato really intended. Plato, he suggests, was certainly not thinking of the routine work of the athletic trainer when he wrote about *gymnastikê*. Galen also picks up the Platonic hint about cosmetics as the art which flatters *gymnastikê*, by emphasizing the way in which athletes and their trainers have succumbed to the obsession with surface appearance.

Philostratus resists those conclusions. Not only does he give back to *gymnastikê* its full meaning, making it equivalent to the Platonic category which is responsible for half of the care of the body, as one quarter of the whole sphere of human activity, but he also downgrades medicine, audaciously reversing Galen's strategy of demoting athletic training. He suggests not only that medicine has succumbed to the flattering wiles of cookery; but also that it has itself become, as a consequence, one of the *technai* which 'flatters' and endangers *gymnastikê*. In doing so he invokes Plato's authority (albeit with a humorous, almost 'sophistical' display of logical dexterity) for his portrayal of athletics as a respectable *technê*, and at the same time signals his own knowledge of the *Gorgias*, and thus also his awareness of the dangers of misusing rhetoric which are a central concern of that work. This effect is in line with his insistence throughout the *Gymnasticus* that the trainer must use words rationally and responsibly. One of his main aims in this passage, then, is to emphasize the fact that medicine itself does not have an undisputed claim to authority. It too is subject to absurd weaknesses, which threaten to drag it below the standards required to qualify as a kind of wisdom.

I have argued, then, that Philostratus' work responds, whether 'intentionally' or not, to Galen's denigration of athletic training. Like Galen, he defines the subject of his work by its relation with other forms of professional activity. Like Galen he participates in the process of debate between different forms of expertise which was so widespread in Imperial-period culture, where individuals and the bodies of knowledge they claim for themselves are constantly jostling for position, in a way which often produces surprising alliances and antipathies. Philostratus carves out a space for *gymnastikê* against that background. In the process, through the alliance he presents between athletic training and cultural analysis (more on that in a moment), he also carves out a pre-eminent space for the interpretative skills on which so much of his own writing relies. Philostratus aligns himself with a Galenic view of the decline of gymnastic practice, but he also emphasizes more insistently, and in different ways, the continuing validity of *gymnastikê* in its ideal form. He demonstrates that medicine itself is just as much at risk from the kind of degeneration Galen imputes to *gymnastikê*. And in the process he demonstrates the importance of offering the true *gymnastikê* a very different space from the one Galen offers it. He places it not, as Galen does, under the care of medical expertise, but rather under the aegis of a very different and even more ambitious form of knowledge, one which encompasses Philostratus' own powerful and flexible skills of cultural interpretation, as we shall see.

INTERPRETING THE BODY AND ANALYSING THE PAST

What kind of positive picture does Philostratus offer to replace Galen's portrayal of philosophical medicine as the only valid guiding principle for bodily training? Clearly the rooting of contemporary athletic custom in long tradition is important for Philostratus, and one implication of the text's long sections on athletic history may be that he expects the ideal trainer to have some historical knowledge of the development of the discipline, although that is not stated explicitly at any stage. His statements about recent athletic decline also suggest a certain amount of admiration for the athletes and trainers of the past. None of that means, however, that his interest in training is a nostalgically antiquarian one. Rather, I will argue, he sets out a vision of idealized present-day *gymnastikê* as something which is capable of continually reshaping the traditions of the past in a dynamic and inventive way. That kind of reshaping is of course in line with many contemporary institutional reshapings and adaptations of received athletic tradition, as we have seen throughout this book. The past, by Philostratus' account, is a resource to be interpreted and refashioned as much as imitated.

In making that point, Philostratus is very much aware of the difficulty of the task he sets himself. Acting as mediator between the past and the present, he suggests, is not an easily acquired skill. He declares his intention to use the most reliable sources available, the official Olympic records of Elis (*Gymnasticus* 2 [136.5–8]), but even then he repeatedly comes up against disputed points of tradition. His explanations take him back into the heroic past, requiring him to delve into moments in Greek historical and mythical tradition which have long been obscured by time. For example, he explains the origin of the long-distance *dolichos* race by the old custom of training Arkadian heralds for the job of running with messages during times of warfare, when they were forbidden to ride on horseback (4). And he explains the origin of the *stadion* race as an ancient sprinting competition, whose reward was to light the fire on the altar at the end of the course (5). Some modern scholarship has taken these explanations as evidence for widespread ancient perceptions of the origins of athletics, or even as evidence for the origins of ancient sport in religious and military ritual.[62] While that may be right, we should not underestimate the sense of alienness these visions might have had even for Philostratus' contemporary readers. Nor should we underestimate the sense of wonderment which Philostratus' text might have had the capacity to inspire, through its ability to unlock the secrets of customs which were often taken for granted in their contemporary manifestations, although that kind of wonderment might often also have been combined with sceptical enjoyment of the techniques of entertaining speculation by which much of this 'unlocking' takes place.

As a consequence of their difficulty, Philostratus' historical explanations give him an aura of authority,[63] partly because the erudition and judgement which they require are hard to match. In much the same way, the techniques of bodily analysis which are prescribed for the trainer in the second half are not only entertaining and perceptive, but also at the same time frustrating and bewildering and almost impossible to reproduce from the information we are given. That effect is not untypical of the many 'technical' didactic texts of the Roman Empire, which often resist the temptation of spoon-feeding their readers, and so implicitly challenge them to grapple for themselves with the process of applying in practice the information and techniques which are presented. We saw a good example of that avoidance of spoon-feeding in Galen's *Thrasyboulos*, in chapter six.[64] But Philostratus I think carries further than most the strategy of making his own recommendations difficult to apply in practice. Moreover, that difficulty seems to apply not only to the reader, but also to the aspiring

---

[62] See Sansone (1988), e.g. 82–3, with the criticisms of Golden (1998) 17–19.
[63] Cf. Billault (1993) 156–7 and 161 on the conspicuous and authoritative position of the author within the text.
[64] P. 271.

athlete, who is always represented in the *Gymnasticus* as a passive figure, subjected to and dependent on the trainer's interpreting gaze, rather than a figure who can be given the material needed for autonomous self-analysis. The authority of the trainer, it seems, cannot easily be disseminated and reproduced. The trainer's authority, like that of Philostratus himself, is also a moral authority. As we shall see in a moment, Philostratus emphasizes at several points the importance of giving historical interpretations which are morally admirable and efficacious. Similarly he stresses the responsibility of the trainer to choose morally suitable charges and to educate them in morally suitable ways. Training is not a job which just anyone will be qualified for.

I have argued that Philostratus represents the athletic trainer, like himself, as a prodigiously perceptive and morally authoritative interpreter. How, then, does the work articulate these impressions through its detailed texture? The relation between modern *gymnastikê* and its ancient counterparts is prominent from the earliest chapters. There is an insistence right from the start that the present should be related to the past, but also an awareness that for most areas of *gymnastikê* that is no longer the case. That fissure between the past and the present, the fact that present-day *gymnastikê* has been cut free from its ancient roots, is presumably one of the things which makes it all the more important to have someone to bridge the gap, someone to mediate between the past and the present, and to interpret athletic tradition properly.

In the opening paragraphs of the *Gymnasticus*, for example, immediately after his categorization of *gymnastikê* as a *sophia*, Philostratus proclaims the ancient glory of the art of training, listing heroic and Classical examples of great athletes. He then explains that the art has degenerated:

Present-day *gymnastikê* has so much changed the condition of athletes that even the majority (τοὺς πολλούς) are irritated by lovers of athletics. But my aim is to teach the causes of this degeneration, and to contribute (ξυμβάλεσθαι) for trainers and their subjects alike everything I know, and to defend nature, which has gained a bad reputation . . . (*Gymnasticus* 1–2 [261.21–262.6])[65]

That proclamation of decline has sometimes been taken as a sign of Philostratus' nostalgia for the athletic past,[66] but it is in fact very far from being a backward-looking and pessimistic claim, and it certainly does not

---

[65] ἡ δὲ νῦν καθεστηκυῖα μεταβέβληκεν οὕτω τὰ τῶν ἀθλητῶν, ὡς καὶ τοῖς φιλογυμναστοῦσι τοὺς πολλοὺς ἄχθεσθαι. δοκεῖ δέ μοι διδάξαι μὲν τὰς αἰτίας, δι' ἃς ὑποδέδωκε ταῦτα, ξυμβαλέσθαι δὲ γυμνάζουσί τε καὶ γυμναζομένοις, ὁπόσα οἶδα, ἀπολογήσασθαί τε ὑπὲρ τῆς φύσεως ἀκουούσης κακῶς . . .
[66] E.g. by Gardiner (1930) 115–16.

imply that Philostratus takes a despairing view of the gymnastic profession.⁶⁷ He does emphasize the difficulty of recreating the glorious athletic past. At the same time, however, he also states clearly his intention to take up the challenge of doing so. In the process he casts that determination as a sign of intellectual distinction, which is not widely paralleled. The phrase τοὺς πολλούς ('the majority') conspicuously ignores the huge popular admiration for athletic spectacle in this period, and in doing so ingeniously hints at an equation between intellectual opponents of athletics like Galen, whose opinions carry great weight within literary tradition, and the ignorant masses, setting up Philostratus' own version of learned *gymnastikê* as a product of his refined, sophisticated sensibilities. The forward-looking nature of this passage is later paralleled by Philostratus' final statement of intent at the end of 54, in the closing pages of the work: '. . . following these principles we will show that *gymnastikê* is a form of *sophia*, and we will strengthen the athletes, and the *stadia* will regain their youth (ἀνηβήσει) through good training practices' (54 [291.17–19]).⁶⁸ That claim implies a link between Philostratus' aims and the aims of the trainer, both of whom set out to bring strength to athletes and to the discipline as a whole.

Philostratus is thus very far from suggesting that ancient athletic virtues have been irreparably diluted. On closer inspection, moreover, it becomes clear that Philostratus' attitude to the heroic past is highly ambivalent. In 43–4, for example, in the middle of his discussion of physiognomical principles, he gives a long account of the athletic and military prowess of the ancient heroes, before returning to the topic of decline. At first sight his admiration of these warrior-heroes seems to be at its most explicit here. The opening sentence of 43, however, throws doubt on that assumption by foregrounding the lack of any scientific basis for heroic training:

That is all I wish to say about the mixture of humours as modern *gymnastikê* describes them. The old *gymnastikê* did not even recognize these mixtures, but trained only strength. By *gymnastikê* the men of the past meant any exercise whatsoever. Some trained themselves by carrying weights which were hard to lift, some

---

⁶⁷ Philostratus' model of the mechanisms of athletic decline is an unconventional one, as Weiler (1981) recognizes in commenting on the passage following this one, where Philostratus insists that the physical specimens nature produces, among men as among animals and plants and minerals, are in no way inferior to those of the past, only less well trained; Philostratus' resistance to standard models of golden-age supremacy, I suggest, helps to bolster the impression that he is writing with the possibility of reinvigoration always in view.

⁶⁸ οἷς ἑπόμενοι σοφίαν τε γυμναστικὴν ἐνδειξόμεθα καὶ τοὺς ἀθλητὰς ἐπιρρώσομεν καὶ ἀνηβήσει τὰ στάδια ὑπὸ τοῦ εὖ γυμνάζειν.

by competing for speed with horses and hares, others by straightening or bending pieces of wrought iron, while some yoked themselves with powerful, waggon-drawing oxen, and others wrestled bulls and even lions by the throat. (43 [284.19–27])[69]

This follows immediately after a long discussion of the benefits for the trainer of understanding the theory of humours, which is represented as so basic as to be entirely uncontroversial:

As far as the topic of bodily proportions is concerned, and the question of whether one kind is best, or another kind, there are some slight disagreements amongst those who have not examined the matter rationally (ξὺν λόγῳ). But as far as the mixture of the humours is concerned, it has never been disputed, nor would it ever be disputed, that the best type of mixture is the warm and moist one. (42 [283.29–284.2])[70]

His emphasis on the fact that the heroes trained only for strength, rather than for competition (echoed in his dismissive reference to the strength-based exercises of the Spartans at the very end of the work),[71] and without the benefit of even the most basic scientific principles, problematizes the status of the heroic way of life as a direct model for the Greek athletic culture of the present.

The past cannot be imitated incautiously, then. Instead, Philostratus emphasizes the need to interpret it flexibly, with the needs of the present in mind. For one thing, *gymnastikê* is represented as a *technê* which has always been keen to look to the future, as a catalyst for progress beyond heroic practices. At the end of his account of the different Olympic events, for example, he tells us that it is the art of the athletic trainer which has been responsible for the development of modern festival culture: 'These things were not introduced into the festivals all at once, but rather were discovered (εὑρισκόμενον) and refined (ἀποτελούμενον) one at a time by

---

[69] Ταῦτα εἰρήσθω μοι περὶ κράσεως ἐκ τῆς νῦν γυμναστικῆς, ὡς ἡ ἀρχαία γε οὐδὲ ἐγίνωσκε κρᾶσιν, ἀλλὰ μόνην τὴν ἰσχὺν ἐγύμναζεν. γυμναστικὴν δὲ οἱ παλαιοὶ καὶ αὐτὸ τὸ ὁτιοῦν γυμνάζεσθαι· ἐγυμνάζοντο δὲ οἱ μὲν ἄχθη φέροντες οὐκ εὔφορα, οἱ δ᾿ ὑπὲρ τάχους ἁμιλλώμενοι πρὸς ἵππους καὶ πτῶκας, οἱ δ᾿ ὀρθοῦντές τε καὶ κάμπτοντες σίδηρον ἐλληλαμένον εἰς παχύ, οἱ δὲ βουσὶ συνεζευγμένοι καρτεροῖς τε καὶ ἁμαξεύουσιν, οἱ δὲ ταύρους ἀπαυχενίζοντες οἱ δ᾿ αὐτοὺς λέοντας.

[70] Περὶ μὲν δὴ σώματος ἀναλογίας καὶ εἴτε ὁ τοιόσδε βελτίων, εἴτε ὁ τοιόσδε, εἰσί που καὶ λεπταὶ ἀντιλογίαι παρὰ τοῖς μὴ ξὺν λόγῳ διεσκεμμένοις ταῦτα, περὶ δὲ κράσεων, ὁπόσαι εἰσίν, οὔτε ἀντείρηταί πω οὔτε ἀντιλεχθείη ἂν τὸ μὴ οὐκ ἀρίστην κράσεων τὴν θερμήν τε καὶ ὑγρὰν εἶναι. Jüthner (1909) 118–20 takes this as evidence for Philostratus' ignorance of Galen, whose own work prominently contradicts Philostratus' claim, but his argument seems to me highly inconclusive; it is just as likely, given the close correspondence with Galen's interests elsewhere in the *Gymnasticus*, that Philostratus is here deliberately disregarding, perhaps even mocking, Galen's conclusions.

[71] *Gymnasticus* 58, discussed further below.

gymnastikê' (12 [267.6–8]).⁷² The words 'discovered' and 'refined' equate *gymnastikê*'s moulding of the Greek festival with the skill of training athletes, which involves both 'discovering' the best pupils, and 'refining' their bodies and their technique, as the second half of the work is largely dedicated to demonstrating. That equation casts *gymnastikê* as a *technê* which is able to act in a number of different spheres, using similar skills for each.

The text also shows a repeated interest in speculating about the precise origin of these events and customs, often suggesting a variety of possible explanations, in a way which foregrounds the value of flexible and even ingenious skills of interpretation. Between 3 and 13, Philostratus discusses the origins of the pentathlon, the *dolichos*, the *stadion*, the *diaulos*, the hoplite race, and all three combat events, focusing especially on religious and military explanations. In doing so he seems to be constantly aware of the possibility of multiple explanations for these phenomena, and also of the possibility that this variety of explanations may be partly the consequence of the self-representation of the various cities which make them. In 7 [263.32–264.11], for example, he tells us that the Eleans include the hoplite race in the Olympic programme in order to commemorate the arrival of an armed hoplite from the field of battle during the festival, with news of victory in the war with Dyme. He also tells us, however, that he has heard the same story told by the inhabitants of a number of different cities with reference to their own wars. Finally he gives his own explanation, suggesting that the hoplite race is included, at the end of festivals, to signal a return to war after truce. One of the effects of offering more than one explanation is presumably to invite readers to judge the matter for themselves. The techniques of ingenious, often multiple, explanation held an important place in scientific and religious analysis, and also in literary records of learned and entertaining conversation, within the Greek culture of the Roman Empire and before.⁷³ Philostratus seems to value such techniques

---

⁷² Παρελθεῖν δὲ ταῦτα οὐχ ὁμοῦ πάντα ἐς τοὺς ἀγῶνας, ἐπ' ἄλλῳ δὲ ἄλλο εὑρισκόμενόν τε ὑπὸ τῆς γυμναστικῆς καὶ ἀποτελούμενον. Cf. *Gymnasticus* 13 [268.24–27]: '. . . these things, in my opinion, would not have been introduced and become popular amongst the Eleans and the rest of the Greeks if *gymnastikê* had not improved them and refined them' (ταῦτα οὐκ ἄν μοι δοκεῖ καθ' ἓν οὑτωσὶ παρελθεῖν εἰς ἀγῶνας οὐδ' ἂν σπουδασθῆναί ποτε Ἡλείοις καὶ Ἕλλησι πᾶσιν, εἰ μὴ γυμναστικὴ ἐπεδίδου καὶ ἤσκει αὐτά). The gymnastic imagery of ἤσκει ('refined', 'trained') characteristically equates the day-to-day skills of training with the more theoretical skills required to develop the discipline as a whole.

⁷³ See Barton (1994a) on scientific explanation; e.g. 14 on the agonistic context of scientific analysis in the Roman Empire: 'it seems that (in my period at least) the ἀγών, far from narrowing down the options in any direction, encourages the proliferation of answers to questions'; and 172 on 'the way the principle of noncontradiction loses its privilege to the ideal of completeness' in ancient scientific writing; cf. Feeney (1998) 115–36, esp. 127–31, on multiple explanations of Roman religious

highly in this work; in fact he draws attention quite self-consciously to their usefulness.

His analysis of customs connected specifically with athletic trainers has a similar focus, paragraph 18 most strikingly so. There Philostratus sets out to explain why the coach at Olympia must carry a strigil. He offers two explanations and seems, as often, to be equally satisfied with both. The first is that it reminds the athlete to care for his body properly by using oil. As an alternative, however, he tells the story of a trainer who killed an under-performing athlete with a sharpened strigil, and explains that the strigil is therefore a symbol of the trainer's power, and a reminder to the athlete always to exert himself. He says, remarkably, of the second explanation: 'And I agree with the story; for it is better for it to be believed than not. Indeed let the strigil be a sword against bad athletes, and may the trainer have some authority above that of the *hellanodikês* in Olympia' (18 [271.19–22]).[74] This is Philostratus' clearest statement of the principle that the criterion for judging whether or not a story is to be accepted may not be its accuracy, but rather its usefulness. He also hints at the idea that any retelling of the past will necessarily involve recreation of it, shaped by the needs of the present. At the same time, his reference here to the *hellanodikai*, the Olympic judges, who were responsible amongst other things (at least in earlier periods of Olympic history) for ensuring that competitors were of Greek descent, reinforces the impression that the trainer will play an archetypal role as an arbiter of Hellenism. It may even be a more important role, with its duty of moral guardianship, than the superficial judgements about ancestry for which the Olympic officials are responsible. This point is later made much more forcefully at *Gymnasticus* 25, where we hear that the *hellanodikês* judges ancestry, whereas the *gymnastês*, fulfilling an equivalent, but more difficult function, must judge moral character in choosing which of his potential students to accept. Moreover, the trainer's status as moral guardian of Hellenism seems in some ways equivalent to Philostratus' own, given his preference for morally valuable aetiologies. In fact, that equation

---

ritual, although he is surely wrong to confine the importance of that phenomenon to Roman culture (129); for example, his distinction between the multiple style of explanation of Plutarch's *Roman Questions* and the more unitary explanations of his *Greek Questions* ignores the fact that Plutarch often treats Greek tradition with varied explanation elsewhere; Plutarch's *Quaestiones Convivales*, for instance, illustrates the important role of multiple explanation within Greek culture, used for both scientific and religious analysis, at least as they are to be performed in the context of playful sympotic conversation: see, e.g., Hardie (1992), esp. 4751–61 on 'interpretative pluralism' in the *Quaestiones Convivales* in the context of Plutarch's treatment of myth.

[74] καὶ ξυγχωρῶ τῷ λόγῳ· βέλτιον γὰρ πιστεύεσθαι ἢ ἀπιστεῖσθαι. ξίφος μὲν δὴ ἐπὶ τοὺς πονηροὺς τῶν ἀθλητῶν στλεγγὶς ἔστω καὶ ἐχέτω δή τι ὑπὲρ τὸν ἑλληνοδίκην ὁ γυμναστὴς ἐν Ὀλυμπίᾳ.

between the trainer's moral discrimination and Philostratus' own is implied within the passage quoted, which juxtaposes in one sentence the idea that both Philostratus and the *gymnastês* are obliged to make consequential choices about what is acceptable.

Some of these themes are continued, finally, in the stories of paragraphs 20–4, where we are presented with famous examples of advice and encouragement given to athletes by their trainers, all of which foreground the way in which the telling of stories and the right use of words can provide inspiration. For example, we hear that the boxer Glaukos was inspired (20) when his coach reminded him of the way in which he had straightened a ploughshare in his youth with his bare hands. Similarly Promachos was spurred on to victory when his trainer discovered that he was in love, and invented a note of encouragement from his beloved: 'a note (λόγον) that was not true, but very valuable to one in love' (22 [272.21–2]).[75] These stories between them again seem to recommend a flexible, improvisatory attitude to retellings of the past.

What relevance does all of this have, however, to the apparently more technical details of the second half of the *Gymnasticus*? For one thing, Philostratus' historical style of analysis is shown to be in many ways close to that of his ideal trainer; in fact the stories in 20–4 in themselves point towards that conclusion, since here we begin to get a more specific illustration of how an athletic trainer, much like Philostratus himself, may benefit from using words effectively and ingeniously. Often, moreover, we find gymnastic language used of Philostratus' own strategies in the *Gymnasticus*, or rhetorical language used for the skills of the *gymnastês*, in ways which strengthen the connection between them. Some of the most prominent examples of this effect come within the transitional passages between the historical half of the *Gymnasticus* and its more technical material. In 25–6, for example, Philostratus introduces the turn to physiognomics, which will dominate the rest of the work, as follows:

> Since a crowd of such examples comes pouring out, and since I am mixing ancient and modern stories together, let us have a look at the trainer himself (σκεψώμεθα τὸν γυμναστὴν αὐτόν), to see what sort of man will supervise the athlete, and what sort of knowledge he must have. Let the trainer be neither garrulous, nor untrained in speech (ἀγύμναστος τὴν γλῶτταν), so that the effectiveness of his speech may not be reduced because of his talkativeness, nor his actions appear unsophisticated through being performed irrationally (μὴ ξὺν λόγῳ δρώμενον)... (25 [273.15–21])[76]

---

[75] λόγον οὐκ ἀληθῆ, πλείστου δὲ ἄξιον τῷ ἐρῶντι.
[76] Ἐπεὶ δὲ ἐπιρρεῖ τῶν τοιούτων ὄχλος ἐγκαταμιγνύντων ἡμῶν παλαιοῖς νέα, σκεψώμεθα τὸν γυμναστὴν αὐτόν, ὁποῖός τις ὢν καὶ ὁπόσα εἰδὼς τῷ ἀθλητῇ ἐφεστήξει. ἔστω δὴ ὁ γυμναστὴς

Training requires action which is governed by rational principles (ξὺν λόγῳ δρώμενον), and perhaps even by words (ξὺν λόγῳ) – the ability to talk well – in a more concrete sense. The development of the powers of reasoning and persuasive speech is itself equated with athletic training by the word ἀγύμναστος, as if the two are inextricably connected with one another. Philostratus' desire to look at the trainer recalls the processes of inspecting potential athletes, and he thus sets himself up as a trainer to the *gymnastês*, with the authority to supervise and judge, just as the *gymnastês* is able to supervise and judge between potential athletes. The process of rational consideration (σκεψώμεθα) is equated with the processes of looking and analysing (for which the word σκεψώμεθα could equally be used) which are essential preliminaries to physical education. Both Philostratus and the ideal trainer, it seems, share the capacity of being able to see beneath the surface of things, to extract the truth from surface appearance, a requirement which often similarly preoccupies Galen in his medical writing, as I have suggested.

This strategy of equating Philostratus himself with the hypothetical trainer of the treatise is carried further by what we find in the following paragraph, where Philostratus similarly announces his intention to inspect (metaphorically) the many different types of athlete: 'At the close of these remarks, we should not get the impression that the topic of exercises is coming next, but the person to take the exercises is to strip now and submit to an examination of his natural qualifications, that is, what they are, and of what use' (26 [274.15–18]).[77] Philostratus himself strips his imaginary athletes. The order the trainer must impose on his work, beginning from analysis of his subject, coincides, by this metaphor, with Philostratus' own ordering of his text, reinforcing the impression of a fundamental similarity between their tasks.

In what follows we hear first of all (27–30) about the way in which the state of the athlete's parents at conception affects his appearance and his performance; and then (31–41) about the differences of physical appearance between different types of athletes. Finally, after discussion of the best combination of humours (42), and the analysis of decline from heroic athletics which I have mentioned already, and which I will return to shortly (43–7), there is a series of paragraphs focused on specific techniques and problems: the dangers and cures of over-indulgence and anxiety (48–54); the use of jumping weights (55); dust (56); punch bags (57); and sun-bathing

μήτε ἀδολέσχης, μήτε ἀγύμναστος τὴν γλῶτταν, ὡς μήτε τὸ ἐνεργὸν τῆς τέχνης ἐκλύοιτο ὑπὸ τῆς ἀδολεσχίας, μήτε ἀγροικότερον φαίνοιτο μὴ ξὺν λόγῳ δρώμενον.

[77] Τούτων ὧδέ μοι εἰρημένων μὴ τὸ γυμνάζειν ἡγώμεθα ἔπεσθαι τούτοις ἀλλὰ τὸ ἀποδῦσαι τὸν γυμναζόμενον καὶ ἐς δοκιμασίαν καταστῆσαι τῆς φύσεως, ὅπη τε σύγκειται καὶ πρὸς ὅ.

(58).⁷⁸ All of this material broadly speaking shares the concern with origins, and with getting to the truth behind surface appearance, which I have pointed to elsewhere in the text. In particular it seems significant that establishing the 'origin' of each athlete is presented as the first task for the trainer (28), just as Philostratus himself began his treatise on athletic training by reference to its origins and developments.

This section as a whole relies on rhetorical techniques of argument, which are used for detailed categorization of athletes by physical appearance, but must also, as Philostratus sometimes emphasizes, be applied flexibly, according to the individual circumstances of each case. Often his examples threaten to spill over into humour and absurdity. For Philostratus, it seems, the art of the trainer must always make room for inventive and entertaining speech. The problem that presents us with is that it is sometimes hard to see where to draw the line between plausible, morally useful improvisation and frivolous invention. Partly, no doubt, that problem comes for modern readers from lack of familiarity with the idiom of ancient science. I will also argue, however, that it is a problem which this text poses for us conspicuously and deliberately, although without ever offering an unequivocal solution. Philostratus slyly and repeatedly draws attention to the possibility that his own explanations should be seen as humorous or sophistical in character. He offers us authoritative interpretation, in other words, but without ever allowing us to drop our guard, without ever quite allowing us to be confident that any of the individual explanations he makes is reliable or straightforwardly admirable or imitable.

In order to illustrate some of these general points I take just one example of Philostratus' instructions, that is the claim that athletes born to old parents will resemble old people:

> I have shown what kind of children good stock and youthful parentage will produce; what is produced by parents more advanced in years can be detected in the following way: the skin of such persons is soft, the collar bones shaped like ladles, and the veins are prominent as in people who have worked hard, their hips are poorly built, and the muscular system is weak ... nor are they able to do any lifting but require pauses for rest, and they are exhausted by their efforts out of proportion to their achievements. (29 [276.4–16])⁷⁹

---

⁷⁸ It has often been assumed, e.g. by Harris (1964) 26 and Golden (1998) 49, that the dialogue is unfinished, but Philostratus' closing mention of the Spartan whipping ceremony (*Gymnasticus* 58), after his discussion of sunbathing, perhaps points in the other direction, given that it echoes Lucian's *Anacharsis* (38–40) which similarly closes with a reference to this Spartan custom, as we saw in chapter two (pp. 92–3); it may even be that Philostratus is aligning himself here with Lucian's challenge to unthinking acceptance of received tradition.

⁷⁹ Ἡ μὲν οὖν γενναία σπορὰ καὶ νεᾶνις ὁποίους ἀνήσει δεδήλωκα, ἡ δὲ ἐκ προηκόντων ὧδε ἐλεγκτέα· λεπτὸν μὲν τούτοις τὸ δέρμα, κυαθώδεις δὲ αἱ κλεῖδες, ὑπανεστηκυῖαι δὲ αἱ φλέβες

The reasoning here is typical of the passages surrounding it, and of other medical and physiognomical writing, both from the Roman Empire and before, in the sense that it uses surface similarities to interpret physical signs as indicators of inner reality,[80] arguing from what is superficially likely, much as Philostratus does in his discussion of athletic custom. It is also, however, very hard to know whether this idea – that children of old parents will look like old people – is to be taken seriously. The impression of absurd humour is hard to suppress.

Presumably this is the kind of argument which has worried so many of the modern scholars who have written about the *Gymnasticus*, and has led to the assumption that the work is somehow 'frivolous'. One answer to the problem is that 'entertainment' was in many ways compatible with the techniques of ancient science, which grew out of the need for speaking persuasively and engagingly in specific contexts. However, the text itself also seems interested in exploring the boundaries of acceptable ingenuity. Through explicitly characterizing certain forms of analysis as unsuitable, Philostratus suggests that there are ways of drawing a line between acceptable humour, which adds rhetorical force through entertainment, and unacceptable absurdities, which deserve only the laughter of mockery. The *Gymnasticus* tends to represent rhetorical manipulation which is applied for immoral ends, or else too rigidly, without adaptation to individual circumstances, as the main problem. At the same time it enacts the difficulty of making this kind of distinction in practice, between good and bad forms of analysis. If the seriousness or otherwise of the example quoted above is – like some others in the text – hard to judge, that may in part be a deliberately destabilizing effect.

To illustrate Philostratus' rejection of unacceptable uses of reason, I return to his criticism of medicine (43–4) for its contribution to the degeneration of modern training. One particular sign of medically inspired degeneracy is said to be the habit of distinguishing between different types of fish, and also different types of pig flesh, as harmful or beneficial according to where they have come from: 'unlawfully, they stuffed themselves with fish, deciding on the nature of the fish from their habitat in the sea: saying that those from swampy places are fat; the soft ones come from near cliffs, fleshy ones from the deep sea; that seaweed produces thin ones and other kinds of sea-moss produce a tasteless kind'

καθάπερ τοῖς πεπονηκόσι, καὶ ἰσχίον τούτοις ἄναρμον καὶ τὰ μυώδη ἀσθενῆ . . . οὐδὲ ἐπιτήδειοι ἆραι οὐδέν, ἀλλὰ ἀνοχῶν δέονται· ἀναλίσκονται δὲ καὶ πόνοις ὑπὲρ τὰ πονηθέντα.

[80] See Barton (1994a) 95–131 on the rhetorical language on which physiognomical study is based; cf. examples in Gleason (1995), esp. 21–54.

(44 [285.25–30]).⁸¹ Clearly one of the problems with this process is the way in which it introduces luxurious fussiness into athletic diets, not to mention unheroic fish-eating habits. However, Philostratus' mockery also seems to be directed specifically at the kinds of arguments these people use, as well as mocking the aims they are used to achieve, and it is striking, and at first sight perhaps worrying, that the forms of analysis he mocks are in many ways close to those he has been recommending in previous paragraphs, in particular the technique of linking outward appearance and inner nature with origins. But perhaps the thing which worries him here is the application of categories which are excessively rigid. If that is the case it would imply that one of the things the *gymnastês* must always avoid is over-schematization. That may be why Philostratus' parodic version of medical categorizations of fish is strikingly brief – as if to illustrate its inadequate, oversimplifying nature – in contrast with his own exhaustive account of physiognomical signs, which resists the temptation of making easy generalizations about the ways in which different types of athlete can be identified.

That reading is reinforced by his denigration of the tetrad system of training, which comes soon afterwards, whereby athletes are exercised on a dangerously inflexible four-day cycle: 'in this way they do all their training harmoniously, and thus, rotating these tetrads, they deprive *gymnastikê* of the ability to understand the bare athlete (τὸ ξυνιέναι τοῦ ἀθλητοῦ τοῦ γυμνοῦ)' (47 [288.3–6]).⁸² This final phrase ingeniously equates understanding of the naked athlete with sensitivity to the specificity of each individual case, in other words the ability, again, to look beneath the surface, to see the naked truth of each 'subject'. Later, in 54, he mocks the absurdity of the tetrad system via the story of the wrestler Gerenos, whose trainer, following this scheme, forced him to undertake heavy exercise despite the fact that he was hung over from celebration of his Olympic victory, and so drove him to his death. Modern trainers, we hear, make similar mistakes in training young boys as if they were men (46).⁸³ Once again, it seems, the worst misuses of classification are those which follow set patterns inflexibly.

I have argued, then, that it is often made difficult, designedly so, to judge the degree of humour or seriousness in Philostratus' specific

---

⁸¹ ἰχθύων παρανομωτάτης βρώσεως ἐμφοροῦσα καὶ φυσιολογοῦσα τοὺς ἰχθῦς ἀπὸ τῶν τῆς θαλάσσης δήμων – ὡς παχεῖς μὲν οἱ ἐξ ἰλύων, ἁπαλοὶ δὲ οἱ ἐκ πετρῶν, κρεώδεις δὲ οἱ πελάγιοι, λεπτούς τε βόσκουσι θαλίαι, τὰ φυκία δὲ ἐξιτήλους.
⁸² καὶ τὴν τοιάνδε ἰδέαν πᾶσαν ἁρμονικῶς γυμνάζοντες καὶ τὰς τετράδας ταύτας ὧδε ἀνακυκλοῦντες ἀφαιροῦνται τὴν ἐπιστήμην τὸ ξυνιέναι τοῦ ἀθλητοῦ τοῦ γυμνοῦ.
⁸³ Cf. Aristotle, *Politics* 1338b–39a (=Miller 130).

examples. That difficulty dramatizes the constant challenge the trainer faces to maintain the integrity of his art, to avoid slipping into degenerate forms of analysis. Philostratus does, however, hint at a number of principles which might allow us to decide when inventive interpretations will be unacceptable. In particular, he foregrounds the absurdities which arise from applying interpretative schemes which are driven by immoral or luxurious motives; or else schemes which are excessively rigid (much as the physiognomist Polemo had stressed the importance of examining each of his subjects as a whole, rather than fixing on just one symptom).[84]

Philostratus thus represents athletic analysis not as a fixed repertoire of procedures, but rather as a flexible process which can reshape the material it inherits with the future as well as the past always in mind. The alluring inscrutability of the athletic body, like the athletic past, will not yield up its secrets to those who approach it ignorantly; nor will it respond to the rigid application of mechanically learned knowledge. Properly flexible and ingenious but also morally responsible forms of interpretation are not ones which all people have the capacity to wield. That is one reason, no doubt, why the technique of seeing through the complexities of athletic history and athletic physiology which Philostratus displays here is one which he represents as both awe-inspiring and bewildering at the same time, as well as being worryingly close to sophistical implausibility. Philostratus deliberately frustrates any desire we might have for an unequivocal vision of how authoritative *gymnastikē* can be imitated and learned and applied. But he does leaves challenging hints about the kinds of intellectual accomplishment – based not only on painstaking erudition but also on the development of humorous ingenuity and moral integrity – which will be necessary for anyone who wants to reproduce the techniques of Philostratean *gymnastikē* for him- or herself.

PHILOSTRATEAN ATHLETICS AND THE USES OF HELLENISM

My final point is that this vision of athletics as something which requires and invites interpretation, but which also needs moral guidance, like the heritage of the Greek past more generally, is backed up by the picture we find in the other works usually ascribed to Philostratus. These close similarities I believe reinforce the assumption of common authorship. They also suggest, in turn, strong reasons for seeing the *Gymnasticus* as part of a wider project

[84] See Gleason (1995) 33–6.

of questioning exactly how Hellenic tradition as a whole should be treated and defined in the present day.[85]

My starting-point for comparison here is the *Heroicus*. This text is an account of a conversation between a Phoinician sailor, who has briefly put into shore on the Thracian Chersonese to wait for favourable winds, and a local vine-dresser. The vine-dresser claims to have regular contact with the semi-divine Homeric hero Protesileos, and gives a long account of their many conversations. According to the vine-dresser's claims, Protesileos is an expert athlete. He trains regularly in the nearby fields, and he has given aid to contemporary athletes who have prayed for his help.[86] He also often describes the many heroes he fought with at Troy, taking a particular interest in their athletic prowess. The *Heroicus* thus resembles the *Gymnasticus* in its presentation of a selection of prodigiously strong and warlike heroic athletes; in fact in a number of places the two texts share strikingly similar passages.[87] Instead of distancing these ancient heroes from the techniques of modern training, however, as he does in the *Gymnasticus*, Philostratus here chooses to portray them in great detail, almost as though they are modern athletes under the scrutiny of a trainer. At one point, to take just one example, we hear a long description of Palamedes, which includes the observation that he was halfway between a heavy athlete and a light athlete in physique, when seen naked.[88] This is reminiscent of the tendency to categorize athletes into light or heavy, to different degrees, throughout the *Gymnasticus*. More specifically, it is reminiscent of the characterization of the ideal pentathlete in *Gymnasticus* 31 as halfway between the two. Protesileos' repeated comparison of different heroes in terms of their athletic as well as military prowess also brings them close to resembling contemporary members of the Imperial-period elite, whose social standing was likely

---

[85] On Philostratus' interest in Hellenism and its boundaries, see Whitmarsh (2001) 225–44 and (1999); Swain (1996) 380–400. See also Swain (1999), esp. 181–2, who argues that early third-century threats to Hellenic culture go some way towards explaining the passionate defence of Hellenism which we find within Philostratus' *Life of Apollonius* (*VA*). He cites factors like the Syrian identity of some members of the imperial family, and the imperial-sponsored encroachment of eastern religious ritual on to Hellenic religious territory. If that is right, it may be the case that the *Gymnasticus* is responding to some of the same developments – certainly its pose of preserving and reviving traditional Greek culture is similar to Philostratus' pose in the *VA* – although that possibility should not be allowed to disguise the fact that the popularity of Greek athletics under the Severans continued unabated.

[86] On help given to modern athletes, see *Heroicus* pp. 146–7.

[87] See de Lannoy (1997) 2407–9, who deals with a number of parallels in addition to those discussed below.

[88] *Heroicus* p. 183. For other athletic material, see, e.g., *Heroicus* pp. 141–2, for a description of Protesileos, admirable for his physical beauty and athletic prowess; p. 167 on Nestor's ears disfigured by wrestling, and on Antilochos' superiority to Nestor in running; and p. 204 on Patroclus' athletic neck.

to be just as much dependent on agonistic prowess as it was on military accomplishment. Philostratus thus brings Homer humorously up to date, although it is never quite clear who is responsible for this modernization. Were all the Greek heroes sophisticated followers of the art of *gymnastikē*?[89] Or is it only Protesileos, looking back with the benefit of what he has learnt from modern science, and from his interactions with modern athletes? Or is the vine-dresser himself – the character who tells the story within the dialogue – wholly responsible for refashioning the words of Protesileos and/or of Homer? The sailor's reaction, veering between gullibility and scepticism, draws attention to the difficulty of answering those questions. One way of dealing with the strangeness of the past, in other words, is to reshape it ingeniously, to make it fit in with the modern world, as Philostratus has done here, but the degree of authenticity of that reshaping will always be hard to identify. That effect has a great deal in common with the way in which the *Gymnasticus* sets out to modernize the art of athletic training while simultaneously admitting the possibility that the process of modernization necessarily involves distortion and refashioning of the past as much as preservation of it.

There are similar effects in the *Imagines*, which is a collection of descriptions of paintings in an art gallery. The text is full of detailed descriptions of beautiful, male athletic bodies, which Philostratus takes as promising starting points for rhetorical display. Often the ekphrases which such bodies prompt echo the physiognomical language of the *Gymnasticus* and the *Heroicus*.[90] In *Imagines* 2.2, for example, we are given a glimpse of Achilles as a child undergoing his education at the hands of Cheiron. His athletic potential is as yet unfulfilled, but unmistakeable to the practised eye: 'For the boy's leg is straight and his arms come down to his knees; for such arms are excellent assistants in running . . .' (*Imagines* 2.2.2).[91] In 2.7.5 the dead Antilochos, whose potential will now never be realized, but acts instead as a spur to the grief of the Achaians, is described in similar terms: 'His leg is slender and his body proportioned for running with ease.'[92] One of the things the *Imagines* sets out to show, as much recent scholarship has suggested, is the way in which all viewing requires and prompts

---

[89] See Anderson (1986) 244, 246; cf. Schmitz (1997) 143–6 on Homeric heroes portrayed as sophists in sophistic texts.

[90] For examples other than those mentioned below, see 1.24.3 (=Miller 40), 1.28.8, 2.6 (=Miller 31), 2.19, 2.21 and 2.32. The second *Imagines*, usually not ascribed to the same author as the first *Imagines* and the *Gymnasticus*, contains very little athletic description.

[91] εὐθεῖα μὲν γὰρ ἡ κνήμη τῷ παιδί, ἐς γόνυ δὲ αἱ χεῖρες – ἀγαθαὶ γὰρ δὴ αὗται πομποὶ τοῦ δρόμου.

[92] κοῦφος ἡ κνήμη καὶ τὸ σῶμα σύμμετρον ἐς ῥᾳστώνην τοῦ δρόμου . . .

interpretation.⁹³ In other words, viewing of art, and of the athletic body as portrayed in art, relies in the *Imagines* on flexible response. The techniques of artistic interpretation which this text embodies thus have a great deal in common with the techniques which Philostratus recommends for the trainer in the *Gymnasticus*.

These two works, then, reinterpret the athletic past for a modern world, much as the first half of the *Gymnasticus* does. In the *Lives of the Sophists* (*VS*), by contrast, Philostratus takes a different tack, at least in his description of the companion of Herodes Atticus, Agathion (*VS* 552–4), where he emphasizes instead the difficulty of harmonizing the heroic past and the Imperial present. Agathion, also known as Herakles, was renowned, Philostratus tells us, for his great size and strength, for his perfect Attic speech, and for his imitation of the lifestyle of the ancient heroes of Greece, which involved, amongst other things, wrestling with animals, like the heroes of *Gymnasticus* 43. The interest in Agathion's physical appearance – his solidly built neck, his chest, which is well formed and slim, his legs, which are bowed slightly outwards, making it easier for him to stand firm – has a great deal in common with the detailed attention to such things in the categorization of athletes best suited to the different events in *Gymnasticus* 31–42, where the shape of the legs and chest and neck, amongst other things, occupies a great deal of attention. Despite his heroic athleticism, however, Agathion seems to have a highly ambivalent relationship with other elements of traditional culture. In particular he shows a Cynic suspicion of the athletic competition to which he should be perfectly suited:

Even more do I laugh at them when I see men struggling with one another in the *pankration*, and boxing, running, wrestling, and winning crowns for all this. Let the athlete who is a runner receive a crown for running faster than a deer or a horse, and let him who trains for a weightier contest be crowned for wrestling with a bull or a bear, a thing which I do every day. (*VS* 554)⁹⁴

Agathion is included here partly to draw attention to the fact that the Greek past, and more specifically the Greek heroic past, needs a degree of reshaping and reinterpretation if it is to be made compatible with present-day cultural norms, a conclusion which brings with it difficult problems about how far those reinterpretations should go, very much in line with

---

⁹³ See, e.g., Elsner (1995) 21–48; Blanchard (1986).
⁹⁴ ἐκείνων, ἔφη, καταγελῶ μᾶλλον ὁρῶν τοὺς ἀνθρώπους διαγωνιζομένους ἀλλήλοις παγκράτιον καὶ πυγμὴν καὶ δρόμον καὶ πάλην καὶ στεφανουμένους ὑπὲρ τούτου· στεφανούσθω δὲ ὁ μὲν δρομικὸς ἀθλητὴς ἔλαφον παρελθὼν ἢ ἵππον, ὁ δὲ τὰ βαρύτερα ἀσκῶν ταύρῳ συμπλακεὶς ἢ ἄρκτῳ, ὃ ἐγὼ ὁσημέραι πράττω.

the concerns of the *Gymnasticus* outlined above.⁹⁵ Broadly speaking this is a difficulty which the sophists of the *VS* must grapple with constantly, as living and highly public embodiments of the links between present and past. More specifically, it is a particularly pointed problem in the context of so controversial a character as Herodes Atticus, whose Roman Hellenism attracted a great deal of suspicion, and who is represented as an ambiguous figure within Philostratus' version of second-century Greek culture.⁹⁶

My final example comes from the *Life of Apollonius* (*VA*), which similarly explores the processes by which the Greek heritage is to be reinterpreted for the present. In Book 4, Philostratus describes a visit made by Apollonius to the Olympic festival. On the way there, we are told, he is met by a group of Spartan envoys who ask him to visit their city (4.27). Apollonius is so shocked by their effeminate appearance that he sends a letter of complaint to the ephors, and in response the Spartans decide to go back to the old way of doing things (ἐς τὸ ἀρχαῖόν τε καθισταμένους πάντα), with successful results: 'The consequence was that the wrestling grounds regained their youth (ἀνήβησαν), and the contests and the common meals were restored, and Lakedaimon became once more like itself (ἑαυτῇ ὁμοία).'⁹⁷ This anecdote displays sentiments which are strikingly similar to many of those we find in the *Gymnasticus*,⁹⁸ in particular in Apollonius' concern to arrest degeneration of educational traditions, which is consistent with his interest in correcting religious ritual throughout the *VA*.⁹⁹ The unusual word ἀνήβησαν echoes *Gymnasticus* 54, quoted earlier.¹⁰⁰ Simone Follet discusses Philostratus' conception of Hellenism as the ability to manipulate a set of common themes and images, and traditional language; she also points out, however, his insistence on going beyond such things in order to achieve a morally good way of life.¹⁰¹ The demands of Apollonius here fit in with her scheme well, with their insistence on learned and precise knowledge of the past, which must sometimes be manipulated in an ingenious way, as we shall see more clearly in a moment, but which must nevertheless always keep in sight moral considerations. That emphasis is clear particularly if we compare this passage with the letters preserved under the name

---

⁹⁵ Cf. Swain (1996) 79–83 on the ambiguities of Agathion's hyper-atticism.
⁹⁶ Whitmarsh (2001) 105–8 discusses the way in which Agathion's model of Hellenism is opposed to the more cosmopolitan one embodied by Herodes himself, while neither of them is clearly validated.
⁹⁷ ὅθεν παλαῖστραί τε ἀνήβησαν καὶ σπουδαί, καὶ τὰ φιλίτια ἐπανῆλθε, καὶ ἐγένετο ἡ Λακεδαίμων ἑαυτῇ ὁμοία.
⁹⁸ As Bowie (1978) 1680 points out.   ⁹⁹ See Elsner (1997), esp. 26–7.
¹⁰⁰ P. 328.   ¹⁰¹ Follet (1991) esp. 212.

of Apollonius, on which Philostratus draws.[102] They emphasize moral condemnation of luxury, whereas the *VA* tends to *combine* moral concerns with an interest in the ingenious display of *paideia*, and in *outward* adherence to Greek tradition. Here the speed of the Spartan recovery suggests an optimistic attitude to the possibility of rescuing degenerate Hellenic culture (much more so than the letters),[103] although the phrase ἑαυτῇ ὁμοία ('like itself' rather than 'exactly as it was before') characteristically leaves some doubt about the depth and moral effectiveness of the cure, as if to warn us against assuming that outward adherence to Hellenic values is in itself sufficient. Once again, these assumptions fit closely with the preoccupations of the *Gymnasticus*, especially with Philostratus' interest in the challenge of getting the right balance between ingenuity and morality in interpreting the past.

The recommendation of flexible reinterpretations of the past continues in the rest of the anecdote, sometimes, though not always, mixed with prioritization of moral considerations. In 4.28 we hear about Apollonius' comments in Olympia, in particular about his ingenious reinterpretation of a statue of the athlete Milo, which supplements received wisdom with an explanation based on Apollonius' own knowledge of traditional ritual and art history, in a way which is highly reminiscent of the aetiologizing of the *Gymnasticus*.[104] And finally he compliments the Eleans intriguingly on their running of the festival, praising them for the care and accuracy of their organization: '"Whether they are wise (σοφούς)," he said, "I do not know, but I am sure that they are sophists (σοφιστάς)"' (4.29).[105] The word σοφιστάς not only connotes 'skill', but also equates the Eleans with the representatives of rhetorical culture to whom Philostratus devotes so much attention in the *VS*, and thus once again suggests a link between athletics and learned interpretation and performance of tradition. It also sounds, however, as though Philostratus is holding back from full approval,

---

[102] This incident draws closely on Letters 42a and 63 (see Penella (1979) 52–3 and 111 on *Ep.* 42a; 72–3 and 122–3 on *Ep.* 63). Flinterman (1995) 89–100 illustrates the way in which the *VA* concentrates on moral stricture less firmly than the letters; Bowie (1991) 203–4 argues that the letters are an early second-century parody of 'lunatic' philosophical moralizing; cf. Swain (1996) 395–6.

[103] Sparta is of course far from typical of Hellenic culture at large, but this anecdote is consistent with Philostratus' interest in the diversity of Hellenism, sometimes illustrated precisely through discussion of Sparta: e.g. see *VA* 6.20, where Apollonius defends the Spartan whipping contest as part of a broader defence of Hellenic religion.

[104] Apollonius (or Philostratus) here puts greater emphasis on knowledge and interpretation of religious and sculptural tradition than on moralizing and philosophical speechmaking, in contrast, for example, with Dio Chrysostom's Olympic oration (*Or.* 12); cf. Fowler (1996) 58–61 on creative interpretation as an integral part of viewing in the *VA*.

[105] εἰ μὲν σοφούς, ἔφη, οὐκ οἶδα, σοφιστὰς μέντοι.

in expressing his uncertainty about their *sophia*, as if being sophists is not the most important thing of all.[106] Preoccupation with tradition, it seems, must never be divorced from philosophy. In this sense the story has a great deal in common with the positive valuation of rhetorical skills in the *Gymnasticus* and of their use in reinterpreting the past, but also with the warnings which that text presents us with about the dangers of using rhetoric irresponsibly and immorally.

In all of these Philostratean texts, to summarize, there are close similarities with the athletic material which we find in the *Gymnasticus*. These are partly similarities of subject matter, which sometimes even involve close verbal parallels with the *Gymnasticus*. But they are also similarities of treatment. Most importantly, all of these texts parallel the *Gymnasticus* by the manner in which they insert their discussions of athletic activity within a much wider framework, linking it with their wider projects of debating the values of contemporary culture and of interpreting the Hellenic past for the present, in ways which repeatedly strive for a (precarious) balance between rhetorical ingenuity and moral integrity.

Training, then, was often a relatively prestigious profession within Roman Imperial culture, partly because of its capacity to mark male, elite bodies with the signs of cultural and social standing, although its authority was sometimes undermined by the sense that its autonomy and applicability were limited to a fairly narrow sphere of activity. Galen's overwhelmingly negative picture of morally and logically degenerate trainers is therefore unlikely to be broadly representative. Philostratus – much like Galen in the works where he chooses to foreground the more positive possibilities for *gymnastikê* – refashions the view that training was an important activity, carrying it to a much higher level than the majority of trainers must ever have claimed for themselves. The *Gymnasticus* reflects processes of disciplinary rivalry which are similarly important for Galen, defining *gymnastikê* in part by its relation with a range of other professions and bodies of knowledge. However, Philostratus takes those processes to their extremes, making knowledge of the body into a broader kind of expertise or wisdom (*sophia*) than even Galen had done, by linking it with techniques of analysis which are crucial to the project of interpreting the Classical past for the early third-century present. Proper interpretation of the human body, he

---

[106] See Swain (1996) 97–100 on the variety of meanings, many of them uncomplimentary, attached to the word 'sophist' in Roman Empire writing. There is some disagreement about the degree to which Philostratus approves of sophistic activity: see Flinterman (1995) 29 for the claim that Philostratus values sophistic rhetoric highly in the *VS*; Brancacci (1986) for the claim that Philostratus dissociates himself from popular, sophistic rhetoric.

suggests, as of the ancient past, is difficult to achieve. It must be flexible and creative and entertaining, but also morally responsible. As such it confers great authority on the ideal trainer, as also on Philostratus himself. In making these claims Philostratus represents appropriate use of athletics, and appropriate analysis of the human body, as emblematic of the proper use of inherited Hellenic tradition. In that sense his work exemplifies many of the trends I have attempted to illuminate throughout this book, in showing how representations of athletics and of the athletic body were so often vehicles for perceptions and representations of the actual or ideal treatment of the past within the contemporary world.

Conclusion

The athletic culture of the Roman Empire, as we have seen, was subject to a wide range of different assessments and different representations. Athletics was popular throughout the Greek east, and was well established also in the west of the Empire. It was a central part of the common forms of education and public spectacle which occupied so much of public and private life. For those who competed, athletic prowess was an alluring goal, charged with risks and expense and rewards, which held in its extreme forms the promise of almost unimaginable fame. For others, whose ambitions did not stretch so far, it was nevertheless close to being a necessary accomplishment, a standard element in the progress of young men towards high social status and manly citizen identity. And for many it was one of the most widely valued and applauded forms of public entertainment. And yet at the same time there were many who resisted its allure, criticizing athletics or ignoring it. Some of these are writers whose voices have been influential in forming modern views of elite culture in this period. Others sought to refashion that allure, to make it safe by modifying its excesses and fitting it into Platonic ideals of balanced education; or else to make it compatible – often in audacious and original ways – with their own more idiosyncratic views of how contemporary culture should be ordered.

We see signs of that variety of assessments in the deeply ingrained tensions and ambiguities which lie beneath the surface of so many ancient representations of athletics. Those tensions and ambiguities are often present within both literary and epigraphical texts of many different types. The texts I have discussed have too often been mined individually for evidence in the service of a narrow conception of athletic history. Failure to address their broader relation with the great variety of opinions and representations that lie behind them has led to a tendency to underestimate their literary and rhetorical sophistication, and the complexity of the tensions and debates which they articulate. That habit of narrowly focused, unnuanced reading of representations of ancient athletics is one of things this book has tried to correct. Even the most confident of ancient evaluations of athletics, even the most confident of statements about the significance of athletics for individual and communal identity, as I argued in my introduction, has signs of controversy and anxiety ingrained in it. It is only through close reading of these texts – through close reading of their mutual interaction and of their internal ambiguities – that we can even approach an adequate understanding of the significances of athletic activity for ancient society.

Tension between alternative viewpoints thus lies at the heart of athletic representation. One reason for that is the fact that athletics is often caught up in other areas of cultural controversy, and thought to have significance for other areas of cultural activity. Textual portayal of athletics tends to act as a vehicle for navigating through a whole range of wider debates about contemporary culture. There is often very much more at stake in debating the value of athletic activities than simply the proper conduct of the activities themselves. We should now be in a position to sketch a more comprehensive picture of the forms these debates most commonly take, and of the areas around which the ambiguities of athletic representation most often cluster.

In Lucian's case satirical juxtaposition of the conflicting conventions of praise and denigration of Greek athletics allows him to explore humorously the value of Hellenic tradition and especially Hellenic education as they are enshrined within specific institutions. He self-consciously and artfully sets together two contradictory strands within contemporary and traditional thought, one of which mocks the *gymnasion* for its irrelevance to the practical demands of warfare and political activity and underlines the absurdity of attempts to recreate the Classical past within the present; and the other of which suggests that the *gymnasion* is to be valued precisely for its insulation from the realities of everyday life, for its preservation of authentic Hellenic tradition. Those contradictory viewpoints find echoes in the inscriptional record of the *gymnasion*, which often flaunts its connections with festival competition, but at other times sets itself apart from the apparently more frivolous activities of the public *agôn*, as if to demonstrate its own practical educational usefulness; or else it advertises its own insulation from other types of cultural activity as something which enhances its capacity to provide military skills and social distinction. Lucian juxtaposes and comically undermines those conflicting patterns of representation, exposing with characteristic flair the absurdities and contradictions which are inherent within Hellenic tradition in all its forms.

For Dio, in his Melankomas orations and elsewhere, discussion of athletic ideals is an opportunity to explore the practical difficulties of harmonizing philosophical lifestyle with participation in civic and political life. Dio repeatedly presents us with an idealized picture of athletic beauty and athletic virtue, which has the power to lead those who view it towards moral self-improvement, but he is also acutely aware of the difficulties of living up to those ideals in practice, without falling short of the requirements of philosophical virtue. In that sense the oscillation between praise and denigration of athletics in his work is not a sign of his inconsistency, nor of the fact that his opinions changed in the course of his career, but rather an indication of an unresolved tension which runs right through his thinking. It is a tension which he presents in its most challenging, extended and humorous form in the Melankomas texts, which show us a figure who seems at first sight to embody a paradoxical mixture of philosophical virtue and athletic prowess, and yet is never able to escape from the negative overtones of athletic denigration entirely. There are similar tensions ingrained in less intensive form within epigraphical representations, which frequently proclaim the beauty and virtue of athletic victors, setting them up as role models, but at the same time tend to emphasize the almost fantastical unattainability of precisely the qualities they praise. Dio manipulates those patterns in his praise of Melankomas, and in the process hints at broader problems which he struggled with throughout his career, about how to combine philosophical commitment with traditions of elite virtue and elite activity which were based on participation in the public world of civic politics.

Pausanias' examination of the athletic past as it is enshrined within Olympia, the greatest of all Panhellenic sanctuaries, is a central element in his exploration of the relations between past and present in the Greek world. He reads the traces of the Classical past as they are enshrined in the inscriptions and statues of the Olympian Altis, characteristically using them as points of access to a virtual world of Panhellenic history, where each statue base has the potential to point to a dazzlingly varied range of geographical and historical detail lying behind it. At the same time, however, he also emphasizes the absence of that Olympic past, and the incompleteness and precariousness of the traces it has left behind it. The practices of athletic, especially Panhellenic, commemoration and of Olympic chronography, I suggested, are imbued with similar tensions between the aims of recapturing and of distancing the past. And the experience of visiting Olympia would often have prompted visitors to awareness of those tensions in the physical space of the sanctuary itself. Pausanias latches on to these common features of athletic commemoration and sets them in an intensified form at the very heart of his vision of the interplay between past and present in the Hellenic landscape.

For Silius Italicus, manipulation of the Homeric tradition of epic funeral games is a vehicle for expression of anxieties about the effects of military conquest on Roman society. Greek athletic customs rarely seem to have been imitated wholesale in the west, but tended instead to be heavily adapted for their new Roman contexts and treated above all as vehicles for displaying and questioning Roman identity. Sometimes those Roman adaptations of athletic custom are represented as improving and sanitizing their Greek models; whereas sometimes they are represented as introducing new and distinctively Roman dangers in their wake. Silius manipulates those common patterns so that they come to serve the distinctive thematic preoccupations of his poem. He presents us with a markedly Roman version of epic funeral games, complete with gladiatorial combat. In doing so he resists the temptation to show us Scipio's soldiers corrupted by the effeminizing influence of Greek athletics. And yet he also suggests that the Roman alternative which Scipio orchestrates presents a much greater and distinctively Roman danger, foregrounding as it does their prolonged exposure to the brutalizing effects of war. The audience's passive spectatorship in the face of fatal mortal combat between two brothers at the climax of the games is implicitly equated with the enforced passivity of the Roman people through decades of civil warfare.

For Galen, discussion of athletics offers the opportunity to address two problems which are central to his conceptions of the medical profession and thus to his own professional self-representation: first, the problem of how far the doctor should involve himself in processes of disciplinary rivalry; and second, the question of how the obsession with bodily care which is necessary for physical and spiritual well-being can be harmonized with the requirement of maintaining moderation in treatment of the human body. Galen distances himself from the techniques of athletic trainers, making them into defining figures of the wrong way to do medicine, because of their shameless, self-advertising devotion to professional competitiveness, and because of their insistence on driving the bodies of their athletes to the limits of endurance. And yet Galen also paradoxically appropriates many of their characteristics and methods, representing his own medical-philosophical skills as elevated versions of the techniques of athletic training. Those skills allow him to defeat his own opponents effortlessly, and prompt him to find varieties of gymnastic exercise which benefit the body and soul, rather than damaging it. There is evidence from elsewhere of mutual suspicion between doctors and trainers, but also of close co-operation between them in other circumstances, and of widespread involvement of doctors in agonistic culture. Galen draws on that contradictory relationship between the two professions, intensifying it in original and provocative ways for his own aims of professional self-definition.

For Philostratus, lastly, examination of the profession of the athletic trainer provides an opportunity to explore the role of rhetoric in cultural analysis, and to emphasize the need for creative and inventive interpretation of the Hellenic tradition as it manifests itself in contemporary institutions. The profession of athletic training was generally a respected one, so far as we can judge from the inscriptional record, with some pretensions to intellectual complexity. Philostratus draws on that respected status, but he also transforms it, raising it to an altogether higher level and so making the ideal trainer into a representative of Hellenism who shares Philostratus' own skills of powerful but also flexible and entertaining analysis, able to interpret with equal perceptiveness the human body and the historical past.

There are many striking overlaps between the thematic preoccupations of these very different texts. For one thing, athletic activity and athletic commemoration offered a provocative space for thinking through the relations between present and past. Lucian, Pausanias and Philostratus all explore that space in different ways, although with a common interest in the capacity of athletics to make the past both closer and more distant or more alien at the same time. Relatedly, the athletic culture of the Roman Empire is repeatedly viewed, for example by Lucian and Philostratus, as a space for thinking through the value of traditions which are closely associated with Greek culture and identity (or Roman culture and identity, in the case of some of the Latin writers I examined in chapter five, who use Greek athletics as a peg on which to hang their own assessments of Roman qualities and ideals). Moreover, assessment of the value of longstanding tradition often involves these writers in debating the requirements of elite virtue as it was formed through elite education, in which athletics traditionally played such a central though controversial role. This is observed most notably in the case of Lucian, Dio and Galen. And that obsession with the place of physical training in education is in turn connected with the interest shown by several of these authors, especially Galen and Philostratus, in using athletics to define their own disciplines and to explore the relative value of different disciplines. Finally, both of these last projects — of debating educational practice and disciplinary hierarchies — tend to be informed by anxieties about the proper role of philosophy within contemporary life, especially for Dio and for Galen, perhaps not surprisingly given that the obsession with physical training and physical competition was so firmly entrenched in Greek and Roman culture, and yet was often thought to pose the greatest possible challenge to philosophical devotion.

Clearly it would be wrong to claim that athletics was never an important vehicle for cultural debate in the pre-Roman world. And yet the obsession with literary representations of athletics does seem to have reached new levels in the Roman era.[1] In many ways the preoccupations I have outlined here — and also the intensity with which they were treated — were unique to the Roman Empire, and especially to the second and third centuries AD when the athletic obsession was at its height, despite the fact that many of the authors I have examined draw heavily on earlier texts as starting points for expression of their opinions.

On one level the prominence of interest in athletics in the literary writing of this period is simply a consequence of the 'explosion'[2] of agonistic activity which took place in the eastern Mediterranean from the rule of Augustus onwards, and which would have been so hard for anyone to ignore. For example, the power of athletic paradigms of elite virtue — in a world where festival competition and *gymnasion* education were so widespread — must have made it almost impossible for anyone interested in assessing common patterns of elite self-representation, as for instance Dio and Lucian are, to ignore athletics entirely. And the sheer prevalence of athletic ideals, deeply ingrained within so many different areas of Roman Empire society, must have been one of the things which pushed writers like Dio and Galen to be influenced by those ideals in recommending philosophical education, even as they rejected them. In addition, widespread familiarity with the language of agonistic inscriptions, which were displayed even more densely than they had been in earlier centuries in the public places of all of the cities of the eastern Mediterranean, must be one explanation for the high degree of cross-fertilization between literary and epigraphical idioms and ideals. More than ever before, the language of public inscriptions seeped into other areas of textual production.

---

[1] See Kyle (1987) 6–7 for the point that fifth-century BC Athens produced a surprisingly small volume of literary writing on athletics, despite the prominence of athletic activity within Athenian society.

[2] Robert (1984) 38.

However, it is also clear, not surprisingly, that the agonistic 'explosion' and some of the most distinctive features of the Greek literature of the Roman Empire were themselves common symptoms of wider preoccupations within contemporary culture. For example, among the motives which drove agonistic expansion and increasing devotion to *gymnasion* education was an interest in replaying and reshaping Greek tradition and Greek elite identity, under conditions of Roman rule which threatened the ideals of unified and autonomous Greek tradition but also paradoxically made them possible. Those motives were also driving forces for much of the Greek literature of the Roman Empire, which was so interested in re-performing and recreating the literature and history of the past while also making it into something new. That may be one reason why athletics was seen as such a promising subject by so many of the authors of this period, Greek authors especially. The preoccupations which drove elite interest in athletics, I suggest, already overlapped significantly with the preoccupations which determined the shape of Imperial-period Greek writing, despite the many differences and antagonisms we often find between these two spheres of action.

Setting these different texts together, then, allows us to map out – at least in outline terms – the areas of cultural controversy with which athletic activity was most often associated during the first to third centuries AD. It also exposes very vividly the depth and intricacy of the many overlaps which we find between different types of text, which repeatedly borrow familiar patterns of athletic representation from each other and reconfigure them in distinctive ways. That said, it should also be clear by now that no simple, summary version of Imperial-period attitudes and opinions can be adequate. Ultimately, moreover, it is not these broad issues of periodicity and causation which men like Galen and Markos Aurelios Asklepiades would most have cared about (although both of them might in different ways have had a sense of themselves as central icons of an Empire-wide Hellenic culture). What mattered to them most of all was the immediate experience of engagement with the athletic culture of their contemporary world, and the urgent imperatives of self-presentation which were entangled with it. And it is the urgency and specificity of those experiences – the experiences of practising athletics, of talking about athletics and reading about it – which I want to re-emphasize above all in conclusion. All of the texts I have examined reconfigure the cultural significances of athletic practice and athletic history in passionate and unique ways. In doing so they reflect their cultural contexts, but also at the same time reshape and intervene in those contexts, manipulating common patterns of representation for their own particular ends. The warnings of Galen and the boasts of Markos Aurelios Asklepiades are windows on to a fascinatingly complex network of ideas and activities. And that network is important not only for our understanding of the education and entertainment of the Roman Empire, as they were practised and evaluated, and not only for our appreciation of that period's literary productions; they also help us to move towards a broader understanding of the ways in which cultural debate and elite self-presentation were intertwined with the athletic culture of the first to third centuries AD, and with the processes of textual production and reception in the same period.

Bibliography

Ahl, F. M. (1976) *Lucan. An Introduction*, Ithaca.
   (1986) 'Statius' *Thebaid*. A reconsideration', *ANRW* 2.32.5: 2803–912.
Ahl, F. M., Davis, M. A. and Pomeroy, A. (1986) 'Silius Italicus', *ANRW* 2.32.4: 2492–561.
Alcock, S. E. (1993) *Graecia Capta. The Landscapes of Roman Greece*, Cambridge.
   (1994) 'Nero at play? The emperor's Grecian odyssey', in Elsner and Masters (eds.): 98–111.
   (1996) 'Landscapes of memory and the authority of Pausanias', in Bingen (ed.): 241–67.
Alcock, S. E., Cherry, J. and Elsner, J. (eds.) (2001) *Pausanias. Travel and Memory in Roman Greece*, Oxford.
Alston, R. (1998) 'Arms and the man. Soldiers, masculinity and power in Republican and Imperial Rome', in Foxhall and Salmon (eds.) (1998b): 205–23.
Anderson, G. (1976) *Lucian. Theme and Variation in the Second Sophistic*, Leiden.
   (1986) *Philostratus. Biography and Belles Lettres in the Third Century AD*, London.
   (1989) 'The *pepaideumenos* in action: sophists and their outlook in the early Empire', *ANRW* 2.33.1: 79–208.
   (1990) 'The Second Sophistic: some problems of perspective', in Russell (ed.): 91–110.
   (1993) *The Second Sophistic. A Cultural Phenomenon in the Roman Empire*, London.
André, J.-M. (1996) 'Le *peregrinatio achaica* et le philhellénisme de Néron', *REL* 73: 168–82.
André, J.-M. and Fick, N. (eds.) (1990) *Theater und Gesellschaft im Imperium Romanum. Théâtre et société dans l'empire romain*, Tübingen.
Angeli Bernadini, P. (ed.) (1995) *Luciano. Anacarsi o Sull'atletica*, Pordenone.
Arafat, K. W. (1996) *Pausanias' Greece. Ancient Artists and Roman Rulers*, Cambridge.
Arnold, I. R. (1960) 'Agonistic festivals in Italy and Sicily', *AJA* 64: 245–51.
Arrigoni, G. (1985) 'Donne e sport nel mondo greco: religione e società', in Arrigoni, G. (ed.) *Le donne in Grecia*, Rome: 55–201.
Aubrian, E. (1990) 'L'historien Tacite face à l'évolution des jeux et des autres spectacles', in André and Fick (eds.): 197–211.

Austin, M. M. (ed.) (1981) *The Hellenistic World from Alexander to the Roman Conquest. A Selection of Sources in Translation*, Cambridge.
Badian, E. (1994) 'Herodotus on Alexander I of Macedon: a study in some subtle silences', in Hornblower, S. (ed.) *Greek Historiography*, Oxford: 107–30.
Baldwin, B. (1973) *Studies in Lucian*, Toronto.
Barton, T. S. (1994a) *Power and Knowledge. Astrology, Physiognomics, and Medicine under the Roman Empire*, Ann Arbor.
  (1994b) 'The *inventio* of Nero: Suetonius', in Elsner and Masters (eds.): 48–63.
Baslez, M.-F., Hoffmann, P. and Pernot, L. (1993) (eds.) *L'invention de l'autobiographie d'Hésiode à Saint Augustin*, Paris.
Bassnett, S. (1993) *Comparative Literature. A Critical Introduction*, Oxford.
Beacham, R. C. (1999) *Spectacle Entertainments of Early Imperial Rome*, New Haven.
Bean, G. E. (1956) Review of Moretti (ed.) (1953), *AJA* 60: 197–9.
  (1965) 'Inscriptions of Elaea and Lebedus', *Belleten* 29: 585–97.
Beard, M. (2001) '"Pausanias in petticoats," or *The Blue Jane*', in Alcock, Cherry and Elsner (eds.) (2001): 224–39.
Beard, M. and Henderson, J. (1995) *Classics. A Very Short Introduction*, Oxford.
Beardsley, M. C. (1966) *Aesthetics from Classical Greece to the Present. A Short History*, New York.
Beck, H., Bol, P. C. and Bückling, M. (1990) (eds.) *Polyklet. Der Bildhauer der griechischen Klassik*, Mainz am Rhein.
Bendlin, A. (1997) 'Peripheral centres – central peripheries. Religious communication in the Roman Empire', in Cancik and Rüpke (eds.): 35–68.
Benedum, J. (1977) 'Griechische Artzinschriften aus Kos', *ZPE* 25: 265–76.
Bergmann, B. and Kondoleon, C. (eds.) (1999) *The Art of Ancient Spectacle*, New Haven.
Berry, E. G. (1958) 'The *De liberis educandis* of Pseudo-Plutarch', *HSCP* 63: 387–99.
Bickerman, E. J. (1980) *Chronology of the Ancient World*, London (rev. edn.; first pub. 1968).
Biddiss, M. (1999) 'The invention of the modern Olympic tradition', in Biddiss, M. and Wyke, M. (eds.) *The Uses and Abuses of Antiquity*, Bern: 125–43.
Biliński, B. (1960) *L'agonistica sportiva nella Grecia antica. Aspetti sociali e ispirazioni letterarie*, Rome.
Billault, A. (1993) 'Le Γυμναστικός de Philostrate: a-t-il une signification littéraire?', *REG* 106: 142–62.
  (ed.) (1994) *Lucien de Samosate*, Lyon.
Bingen, J. (ed.) (1996) *Pausanias historien* (*Entretiens sur l'antiquité classique* 46), Geneva.
Blanchard, M. E. (1986) 'Problèmes du texte et du tableau: les limites de l'imitation à l'époque hellénistique et sous l'empire', in Cassin (ed.): 131–54.
Boatwright, M. T. (2000) *Hadrian and the Cities of the Roman Empire*, Princeton.
Bol, P. C. (1990) 'Diadumenos', in Beck, Bol and Bückling (eds.): 206–12.
Bol, R. (1984) *Das Statuenprogramm des Herodes-Atticus-Nymphäums*, Berlin.
Bompaire, J. (1958) *Lucien écrivain. Imitation et création*, Paris.

(1993) 'Quatre styles d'autobiographie au IIe siècle après J.-C.: Aelius-Aristide, Lucien, Marc-Aurèle, Galien', in Baslez, Hoffmann and Pernot (eds.): 199–209.
Bonfante, L. (1989) 'Nudity as costume in classical art', *AJA* 93: 543–70.
Boudon, V. (1994) 'Les oeuvres de Galien pour les débutants ('De sectis', 'De pulsibus ad tirones', 'De ossibus ad tirones', 'Ad Glauconem de methodo medendi' et 'Ars medica'): médecine et pédagogie au IIe s. ap. J.-C.', *ANRW* 2.37.2: 1421–67.
(ed.) (2000) *Galien. Tome II. Exhortation à l'étude de la médecine. Art médical*, Paris (Budé).
Boulogne, J. (1987) 'Le sens des "Questions romaines" de Plutarque', *REG* 100: 471–6.
(1992) 'Les "Questions romaines" de Plutarque', *ANRW* 2.33.6: 4682–708.
Bowersock, G. W. (1965) *Augustus and the Greek World*, Oxford.
(1969) *Greek Sophists in the Roman Empire*, Oxford.
(1995) 'The barbarism of the Greeks', *HSCP* 97: 3–14.
Bowie, A. M. (1998) '*Exuvias effigiemque*. Dido, Aeneas and the body as sign', in Montserrat (ed.): 57–79.
Bowie, E. L. (1974) 'Greeks and their past in the Second Sophistic', in Finley, M. I. (ed.) *Studies in Ancient Society*, London: 166–209 (rev. version; first pub. 1970).
(1978) 'Apollonius of Tyana: tradition and reality', *ANRW* 2.16.2: 1652–99.
(1982) 'The importance of sophists', *YCS* 27: 29–60.
(1991) 'Hellenes and Hellenism in writers of the early Second Sophistic', in Saïd (ed.): 183–204.
(1996) 'Past and present in Pausanias', in Bingen (ed.): 207–30.
(2001) 'Inspiration and aspiration. Date, genre and readership', in Alcock, Cherry and Elsner (eds.): 21–32.
Bowman, A. K. (1986) *Egypt after the Pharaohs. 332 BC–AD 642. From Alexander to the Arab Conquest*, Oxford.
Bowra, C. M. (1938) 'Xenophanes and the Olympic games', *AJP* 59: 257–79.
Bradley, K. R. (1981) 'The significance of the *spectacula* in Suetonius' *Caesares*', *RSA* 11: 129–37.
Brailsford, D. (1969) *Sport and Society. Elizabeth to Anne*, London.
Brancacci, A. (1977) 'Le orazioni diogeniane di Dione Crisostomo', in Giannantoni, G. (ed.) *Scuole socratiche minori e filosofia ellenistica*, Bologna: 141–71.
(1980) 'Tradizione cinica e problemi di datazione nelle orazioni diogeniane di Dione di Prusa', *Elenchos* 1: 92–122.
(1986) 'Seconde sophistique, historiographie et philosophie (Philostrate, Eunape, Synésios)', in Cassin (ed.): 87–110.
(2000) 'Dio, Socrates, and Cynicism', in Swain (ed.): 240–60.
Branham, R. B. (1985) 'Introducing a sophist: Lucian's prologues', *TAPA* 115: 237–43.
(1989) *Unruly Eloquence. Lucian and the Comedy of Traditions*. Cambridge, MA.
Brannigan, J. (1998) *New Historicism and Cultural Materialism*, London.

van Bremen, R. (1996) *The Limits of Participation. Women and Civic Life in the Greek East in the Hellenistic and Roman Periods*, Amsterdam.
Briggs, W. W. (1975) 'Augustan athletics and the games of *Aeneid* 5', *Stadion* 1: 277–83.
Broneer, O. (1962) 'The Isthmian victory crown', *AJA* 66: 259–63.
Brooks, P. (1993) *Body Work. Objects of Desire in Modern Narrative*, Cambridge, MA.
Brophy, R. and Brophy, M. O. (1989) 'Medical sports fitness: an ancient parody of Greek medicine', *Literature and Medicine* 8: 156–65.
Broughton, T. R. S. (1938) 'Roman Asia Minor', in Frank, T. (ed.) *An Economic Survey of Ancient Rome* (vol. IV), Baltimore: 499–916.
Brown, P. (1978) *The Making of Late Antiquity*, Cambridge, MA.
Brunt, P. A. (1973) 'Aspects of the social thought of Dio Chrysostom and the Stoics' *PCPS* 19: 9–34 (reprinted in Brunt, P. A. (1993) *Studies in Greek History and Thought*, Oxford: 210–44).
  (1994) 'The bubble of the Second Sophistic', *BICS* 39: 25–52.
Büchner, G. (1952) 'Epigraphe da Ischia. 154 d.C.', *PP* 7: 504.
Burckhardt, J. (1998) *The Greeks and Greek Civilization* (trans. S. Stern; ed. with introd. O. Murray), London.
Burke, P. (2000) *A Social History of Knowledge. From Gutenberg to Diderot*, Cambridge.
Butler, J. (1993) *Bodies That Matter. On the Discursive Limits of Sex*, London.
Cabanes, P. (1974) 'Les inscriptions du théâtre de Bouthrotos', in *Actes du Colloque sur l'esclavage 1972, Annales littéraires de l'Université de Besançon*: 105–209.
Cairns, F. (1989) *Virgil's Augustan Epic*, Cambridge.
Caldelli, M. L. (1992) 'Curia athletarum, iera xystike synodos e organizzazione a Roma', *ZPE* 93: 75–87.
  (1993) *L'Agon Capitolinus. Storia e protagonisti dall' istituzione domizianea al IV secolo*, Rome.
  (1997) 'Gli agoni alla greca nelle regioni occidentali dell' impero. La Gallia Narbonensis', *Atti della academia nazionale dei Lincei* 9.4: 389–481.
Cameron, A. (1993) *The Later Roman Empire, AD 284–430*, London.
Cancik, H. and Rüpke, J. (eds.) (1997) *Römische Reichsreligion und Provinzialreligion*, Tübingen.
Cartledge, P. (1994) Response to Usher (1994), in Khan (ed.): 146–55.
  (1997) 'Historiography of Greek self-definition', in Bentley, M. (ed.) *Companion to Historiography*, London: 23–42.
Cartledge, P. and Spawforth, A. (1989) *Hellenistic and Roman Sparta. A Tale of Two Cities*, London.
Casarico, L. (1982) 'Donne ginnasiarco', *ZPE* 48: 117–23.
Cassin, B. (ed.) (1986) *Le plaisir du parler. Études de sophistique comparée*, Paris.
Christou, C. A. (1959) 'Περὶ τὰ Σαραπεῖα τῆς Τανάγρας', *AEph*. 1956: 34–72.
Chuvin, P. (1990) *A Chronicle of the Last Pagans*, Cambridge, MA (trans. B. A. Archer; first pub. in French, 1990).

Clarke, K. (1999) *Between Geography and History. Hellenistic Constructions of the Roman World*, Oxford.
Clerc, M. (1885) 'Inscription de Nysa', *BCH* 9: 124–31.
Cohen, A. (2000) 'Introduction. Discriminating relations – identity, boundary and authenticity', in Cohen, A. (ed.) *Signifying Identities. Anthropological Perspectives on Boundaries and Contested Values*, London: 1–13.
Cohn-Haft, L. (1956) *The Public Physicians of Ancient Greece*, Northampton, MA.
Cohoon, J. W. (ed.) (1939) *Dio Chrysostom* (vol. II), Cambridge, MA (Loeb).
Coretta, A. (ed.) (1995) *Il manuale dell' alenatore. Filostrato di Lemno*, Novarra.
Cribiore, R. (2001) *Gymnastics of the Mind*, Princeton.
Criscuolo, L. (1995) 'Alessandria e l'agonistica greca', in Bonacasa, N., Naro, C., Portale, E. C. and Tullio, A. (eds.) *Alessandria e il mondo ellenistico-romano*, Rome: 43–8.
Crowther, N. B. (1980–81) 'Nudity and morality. Athletics in Italy', *CJ* 76: 119–23.
  (1983) 'Greek games in Republican Rome', *ClAnt* 52: 268–73.
  (1984–5) 'Studies in Greek athletics. Part 1', *CW* 78: 497–558.
  (1985) 'Male beauty contests in Greece: the euandria and the euexia', *AC* 54: 285–91.
  (1985–6) 'Studies in Greek athletics. Part 2', *CW* 79: 73–135.
  (1987) 'The *euandria* competition at the Panathenaia reconsidered', in *AncW* 15: 59–64.
  (1989) 'The Sebastan games in Naples (IvOl. 56)', *ZPE* 79: 100–2.
  (1991a) 'Euexia, eutaxia, philoponia: three contests of the Greek gymnasium', *ZPE* 85: 301–4.
  (1991b) 'The Olympic training period', *Nikephoros* 4: 161–6.
  (1992) 'Second-place finishes and lower in Greek athletics', *ZPE* 90: 97–102.
  (1993) 'Numbers of contestants in Greek athletic contests', *Nikephoros* 6: 39–52.
  (1995) 'Greek equestrian events in the late Republic and early Empire. Africanus and the Olympic victory lists', *Nikephoros* 8: 111–23.
  (2001a) 'Victories without competition in the Greek games', *Nikephoros* 14: 29–44.
  (2001b) 'Cicero's attitudes to Greek athletics', *Nikephoros* 14: 63–81.
Daniel, E. V. and Peck, J. M. (1996) 'Culture/contexture. An introduction', in Daniel, E. V. and Peck, J. M. (eds.) *Culture/Contexture. Explorations in Anthropology and Literary Studies*, Berkeley: 1–33.
Danoff, C. M. (1937) 'Neue Inschriften aus Bulgarien', *JÖAI* 30: Beiblatt 77–86.
d'Arms, J. H. (1970) *Romans on the Bay of Naples. A Study of Villas and their Owners from 150 BC to AD 400*, Cambridge, MA.
Darwall-Smith, R. H. (1996) *Emperors and Architecture. A Study of Flavian Rome*, Brussels.
Davidson, J. (1997) *Courtesans and Fishcakes. The Consuming Passions of Classical Athens*, London.
Davies, J. E. (2000) 'Introduction. Social change and the problem of identity', in Davies, J. E. (ed.) *Identity and Social Change*, New Brunswick: 1–10.
de Blois, L. (1984) 'The third century crisis and the Greek elite in the Roman Empire', *Historia* 33: 358–77.

de Lacy, P. (1972) 'Galen's Platonism', *AJP* 93: 27–39.
de Lannoy, L. (1997) 'Le problème des Philostrate (Etat de la question)', *ANRW* 2.34.3: 2362–449.
de Lucia, R. (1999) 'Doxographical hints in Oribasius' *Collectiones Medicae*', in van der Eijk, P. J. (ed.) *Ancient Histories of Medicine. Essays in Medical Doxography and Historiography in Classical Antiquity*, Leiden: 473–89.
Debru, A. (1995) 'Les démonstrations médicales à Rome au temps de Galien', in van der Eijk, Horstmanshoff and Schrijvers (eds.): 69–81.
Decker, W. (1995) *Sport in der griechischen Antike*, Munich.
DeLaine, J. (1997) *The Baths of Caracalla. A Study in the Design, Construction, and Economics of Large-Scale Building Projects in Imperial Rome*, Portsmouth, RI.
Delorme, J. (1960) *Gymnasion. Etude sur les monuments consacrés à l'éducation en Grèce*, Paris.
Delz, J. (1950) *Lukians Kenntnis der athenischen Antiquitaten*, Freiburg.
Derow, P. S. (1990) Review of Ferrary (1988), *JRS* 80: 197–200.
Desideri, P. (1978) *Dione di Prusa. Un intellettuale greco nell'impero romano*, Messina.
  (2000) 'City and country in Dio', in Swain (ed.): 93–107.
Dickie, M. (1993) 'Παλαιστρίτης/'palaestrita'. Callisthenics in the Greek and Roman gymnasion', *Nikephoros* 6: 105–51.
Dillon, M. (1997) *Pilgrims and pilgrimage in ancient Greece*, London.
  (2000) 'Did parthenoi attend the Olympic games? Girls and women competing, spectating, and carrying out cult roles at Greek religious festivals', *Hermes* 128: 457–80.
Dirks, N., Eley, G. and Ortner, S. (1994) 'Introduction', in Dirks, N., Eley, G. and Ortner, S. (eds.) (1994) *Culture/Power/History. A Reader in Contemporary Social Theory*, Princeton: 3–45.
Donini, P. L. (1992) 'Galeno e la filosofia', *ANRW* 2.36.5: 3484–504.
Downey, G. (1961) *A History of Antioch in Syria*, Princeton.
Drees, L. (1968) *Olympia. Gods, Artists and Athletes*, London (trans. G. Onn; first pub. in German, 1967).
Dubel, S. (1994) 'Dialogue et autoportrait: les masques de Lucien', in Billault (ed.): 19–26.
Dubuisson, M. (1984–6) 'Lucien et Rome', *AncSoc* 15–17: 185–207.
Dueck, D. (2000) *Strabo of Amasia. A Greek Man of Letters*, London.
Duff, T. (1999) *Plutarch's Lives. Exploring Virtue and Vice*, Oxford.
Duhamel, A. (1985) *Le complexe d'Astérix. Essai sur le caractère politique des Français*, Paris.
Dunbabin, K. M. D. (1999) *Mosaics of the Greek and Roman World*, Cambridge.
Eagleton, T. (1996) *Literary Theory. An Introduction*, Oxford (2nd edn.; first pub. 1984).
Ebert, J. (1981) 'Zum Epigramme auf den Schwerathleten Aurelius Achilleus aus Aphrodisias', *Stadion* 7: 203–10.
  (1982) 'Zur "Olympischen Chronik" *IG* II/III^2, 2326', *APF* 28: 5–14.

Edelstein, L. (1966) 'The distinctive Hellenism of Greek medicine', *BHM* 40: 197–255 (reprinted in Temkin, O. and Temkin, C. L. (eds.) (1967) *Ancient Medicine. Selected Papers of Ludwig Edelstein*, Baltimore: 367–97).
Edmondson, J. C. (1999) 'The cultural politics of public spectacle in Rome and the Greek East, 167–166 BCE', in Bergmann and Kondoleon (eds.): 77–95.
Edwards, C. (1993) *The Politics of Immorality in Ancient Rome*, Cambridge.
  (1994) 'Beware of imitations: theatre and the subversion of imperial identity', in Elsner and Masters (eds.): 83–97.
  (1999) 'The suffering body: philosophy and pain in Seneca's *Letters*', in Porter (ed.): 252–68.
van der Eijk, P. J., Horstmanshoff, H. F. J. and Schrijvers, P. H. (eds.) (1995) *Ancient Medicine in its Socio-Cultural Context* (2 vols.), Amsterdam.
Elsner, J. (1992) 'Pausanias: a Greek pilgrim in the Roman world', *P&P* 135: 3–29.
  (1994) 'From the pyramids to Pausanias and Piglet: monuments, travel and writing', in Goldhill, S. and Osborne, R. (eds.) *Art and Text in Ancient Greek Culture*, Cambridge: 224–54.
  (1995) *Art and the Roman Viewer. The Transformation of Art from the Pagan World to Christianity*, Cambridge.
  (1997) 'Hagiographic geography: travel and allegory in the *Life of Apollonius of Tyana*', *JHS* 117: 22–37.
  (2001a) 'Describing self in the language of the Other: Pseudo (?) Lucian at the temple of Hierapolis', in Goldhill (ed.): 123–53.
  (2001b) 'Structuring "Greece". Pausanias' *Periegesis* as a literary construct', in Alcock, Cherry and Elsner (eds.): 3–20.
Elsner, J. and Masters, J. (eds.) (1994) *Reflections of Nero. Culture, History and Representation*, London.
Engels, D. (1990) *Roman Corinth. An Alternative Model for the Classical City*, Chicago.
Englert, L. (1929) *Untersuchungen zu Galens Schrift* Thrasybulus, Leipzig.
Farrington, A. (1987) 'Imperial bath buildings in south-west Asia Minor', in Macready and Thompson (eds.): 50–9.
  (1995) *The Roman Baths of Lycia. An Architectural Study*, London.
  (1997) 'Olympic victors and the popularity of the Olympic games in the Imperial period', *Tyche* 12: 15–46.
  (1999) 'The introduction and spread of Roman bathing in Greece', in Delaine, J. and Johnston, D. E. (eds.) *Roman Baths and Bathing*, Portsmouth, RI: 58–65.
Feeney, D. (1998) *Literature and Religion at Rome. Cultures, Contexts and Beliefs*, Cambridge.
Feldherr, A. (1995) '*Aeneid* 5 and Augustan circus spectacle', *ClAnt* 14: 245–65.
Ferrary, J.-L. (1988) *Philhellénisme et impérialisme. Aspects idéologiques de la conquête romaine du monde hellénistique*, Rome.
Finley, M. I. and Pleket, H. W. (1976) *The Olympic Games. The First Thousand Years*, London.
Flacelière, R. (1949) 'Inscriptions de Delphes de l'époque impériale', *BCH* 73: 464–75.

Flemming, R. (2000) *Medicine and the Making of Roman Women. Gender, Nature, and Authority from Celsus to Galen*, Oxford.

Flinterman, J.-J. (1995) *Power, Paideia and Pythagoreanism. Greek Identity, Conceptions of the Relationship between Philosophers and Monarchs and Political Ideas in Philostratus' Life of Apollonius*, Amsterdam.

Follet, S. (1976) *Athènes au IIe et au IIIe siècle. Etudes chronologiques et prosopographiques*, Paris.

(1988) 'Ephèbes étrangers à Athènes: Romains, Milésiens, Chypriotes, etc.', *Centre d'Etudes Chypriotes* 9: 19–32.

(1991) 'Divers aspects de l'hellénisme chez Philostrate', in Saïd (ed.): 205–15.

(1994) 'Lucien et l'Athènes des Antonins', in Billault (ed.): 131–9.

Forbes, C. A. (1933) *Neoi. A Contribution to the Study of Greek Associations*, Middletown, CT.

(1945) 'Expanded uses of the Greek gymnasium', *CPh* 40: 32–42.

(1955) 'Ancient athletic guilds', *CPh* 50: 238–52.

Forni, G. (1953) *Il reclutamento delle legioni da Augusto a Diocleziano*, Milan.

Foucault, M. (1986) *The Care of the Self* (*The History of Sexuality*, vol. 3), London (trans. R. Hurley; first pub. in French, 1984).

Fowler, D. (1996) 'Even better than the real thing. A tale of two cities', in Elsner, J. (ed.) *Art and Text in Roman Culture*, Cambridge: 57–74.

Foxhall, L. and Salmon, J. (eds.) (1998a) *Thinking Men. Masculinity and its Self-Representation in the Classical Tradition*, New York.

(eds.) (1998b) *When Men were Men. Masculinity, Power and Identity in Classical Antiquity*, London.

Franke, A. (1999) *Keys to Controversies. Stereotypes in Modern American Novels*, New York.

Frede, M. (1981) 'On Galen's epistemology', in Nutton (ed.): 65–86.

Frei-Stolba, R. (1998) 'Frauen als Stifterinnen von Spielen', *Stadion* 24: 115–28.

Frisch, P. (1986) *Zehn agonistische Papyri*, Opladen.

(1988) 'Die Klassifikation der ΠΑΙΔΕΣ bei den Griechischen Agonen', *ZPE* 75: 179–85.

Gardiner, E. N. (1925) *Olympia. Its History and Remains*, Oxford.

(1930) *Athletics of the Ancient World*, Oxford.

Gauthier, P. (1985) *Les cités grecques et leurs bienfaiteurs*, Paris.

(1995) 'Notes sur le rôle du gymnase dans les cités hellénistiques', in Wörrle, M. and Zanker, P. (eds.) *Stadtbild und Bürgerbild im Hellenismus*, Munich: 1–11.

(1996) 'Bienfaiteurs du gymnase au Létôon de Xanthos', *REG* 109: 1–34.

Gauthier, P. and Hatzopoulos, M. B. (1993), *La loi gymnasiarque de Beroia*, Athens.

Geagan, D. J. (1979) 'Roman Athens: some aspects of life and culture 1. 86 BC–AD 267', *ANRW* 2.7.1, 371–437.

Gebhard, E. R. (1973) *The Theater at Isthmia*, Chicago.

(1993) 'The Isthmian games and the sanctuary of Poseidon in the early Empire', in Gregory, T. E. (ed.) *The Corinthia in the Roman Period*, Ann Arbor: 78–94.

Gebhard, E. R., Hemans, F. P. and Hayes, J. W. (1998) 'University of Chicago excavations at Isthmia, 1989: III', *Hesperia* 67: 405–56.

Geer, R. M. (1935) 'The Greek Games at Naples', *TAPA* 66: 208–21.
Georgiadou, A. and Larmour, D. H. J. (1998) *Lucian's Science Fiction Novel*, True Histories. *Interpretation and Commentary*, Leiden.
Gera, D. L. (1995) 'Lucian's choice: *Somnium* 6–16', in Innes, Hine and Pelling (eds.): 237–50.
Ginestet, P. (1991) *Les organisations de la jeunesse dans l'Occident romain*, Brussels.
Ginsburg, J. (1993) '*In maiores certamina*: past and present in the *Annals*', in Luce and Woodman (eds.): 86–103.
Giovannini, A. (1993) 'Greek cities and Greek commonwealth', in Bulloch, A., Gruen, E. S., Long, A. A. and Stewart, A. (eds.) *Images and Ideologies. Self-Definition in the Hellenistic World*, Berkeley: 265–86.
Glass, S. L. (1988) 'The Greek gymnasium. Some problems', in Raschke (ed.): 155–73.
Gleason, M. W. (1995) *Making Men. Sophists and Self-Presentation in Ancient Rome*, Princeton.
   (1999a) 'Elite male identity in the Roman Empire', in Potter and Mattingly (eds.): 67–84.
   (1999b) 'Truth contests and talking corpses', in Porter (ed.): 287–313.
   (2001) 'Mutilated messengers. Body language in Josephus', in Goldhill (ed.): 50–85.
Goffman, E. (1969) *The Presentation of Self in Everyday Life*, London.
Golden, M. (1998) *Sport and Society in Ancient Greece*, Cambridge.
Goldhill, S. (1995) *Foucault's Virginity. Ancient Erotic Fiction and the History of Sexuality*, Cambridge.
   (1999) 'Programme notes', in Goldhill and Osborne (eds.): 1–29.
   (2001a) 'Introduction. Setting an agenda: "Everything is Greece to the wise"', in Goldhill (ed.): 1–25.
   (2001b) 'The erotic eye. Visual stimulation and cultural conflict', in Goldhill (ed.): 154–94.
   (ed.) (2001c) *Being Greek under Rome. Cultural Identity, the Second Sophistic and Development of Empire*, Cambridge.
   (2002) *Who Needs Greek? Contests in the Cultural History of Hellenism*, Cambridge.
Goldhill, S. and Osborne, R. (eds.) (1999) *Performance Culture and Athenian Democracy*, Cambridge.
Goldhill, S. and von Reden, S. (1999) 'Plato and the performance of dialogue', in Goldhill and Osborne (eds.): 257–89.
Goldsworthy, A. K. (1996) *The Roman Army at War. 100 BC–AD 200*, Oxford.
Graindor, P. (1931) *Athènes de Tibère à Trajan*, Cairo.
   (1934) *Athènes sous Hadrien*, Cairo.
Grenfell, B. P. and Hunt, A. S. (eds.) (1899) *The Oxyrhynchus Papyri* (vol. II), London.
Grmek, M. D. and Gourevitch, D. (1994) 'Aux sources de la doctrine médicale de Galien: l'enseignement de Marinus, Quintus et Numisianus', *ANRW* 2.37.2: 1491–528.

Grodde, O. (1997) *Sport bei Quintilian*, Hildesheim.
Gruen, E. S. (1984) *The Hellenistic World and the Coming of Rome*, Berkeley.
  (1993) *Culture and National Identity in Republican Rome*, London.
Guttmann, A. (1978) *From Ritual to Record. The Nature of Modern Sports*, New York.
  (1994) *Games and Empires. Modern Sports and Cultural Imperialism*, New York.
Habicht, C. (1985) *Pausanias' Guide to Ancient Greece*, Berkeley.
Habinek, T. (1998) *The Politics of Latin Literature. Writing, Identity, and Empire in Ancient Rome*, Princeton.
Hadot, P. (1998) *The Inner Citadel. The* Meditations *of Marcus Aurelius*, Cambridge, MA (trans. M. Chase; first pub. in French, 1992).
Hall, A. and Milner, N. (1994) 'Education and athletics. Documents illustrating the festivals of Oenoanda', in French, D. (ed.) *Studies in the History and Topography of Lycia and Pisidia (In Memoriam A. S. Hall)*, London: 7–47.
Hall, E. (1995) 'Lawcourt dramas: the power of performance in Greek forensic oratory', *BICS* 40: 39–58.
Hall, J. M. (1995) 'The role of language in Greek ethnicities', *PCPS* 41: 83–100.
  (1997) *Ethnic Identity in Greek Antiquity*, Cambridge.
  (2002) *Hellenicity. Between Ethnicity and Culture*, Chicago.
Hall, S. (1996) 'Introduction. Who needs identity?', in Hall, S. and du Gay, P. (eds.) *Questions of Cultural Identity*, London: 1–17.
Hankinson, R. J. G. (1988) 'Galen explains the elephant', in Matthen, M. and Linsky, B. (eds.) *Philosophy and Biology*, Calgary.
  (1992) 'Galen's philosophical eclecticism', *ANRW* 2.36.5: 3505–22.
  (1994) 'Galen's anatomical procedures. A second-century debate in medical epistemology', in *ANRW* 2.37.2: 1834–55.
Hansen, W. (ed.) (1996) *Phlegon of Tralles. Book of Marvels* (trans. with introd. and commentary), Exeter.
Hardie, A. (1983) Statius *and the* Silvae. *Poets, Patrons and Epideixis in the Graeco-Roman World*, Liverpool.
Hardie, P. R. (1992) 'Plutarch and the interpretation of myth', *ANRW* 2.33.6: 4743–87.
  (1993) *The Epic Successors of Virgil. A Study in the Dynamics of a Tradition*, Cambridge.
  (2002) *Ovid's Poetics of Illusion*, Cambridge.
Harries, J. (1998) 'The cube and the square. Masculinity and male social roles in Roman Boiotia', in Foxhall and Salmon (eds.): 184–94.
Harris, H. A. (1962) 'Notes on three athletic inscriptions', *JHS* 82: 19–24.
  (1964) *Greek Athletes and Athletics*, London.
  (1972) *Sport in Greece and Rome*, London.
  (1976) *Greek Athletics and the Jews*, Cardiff.
Hatzopoulos, M. B. and Loukopoulou, L. D. (1992) *Recherches sur les marches orientales des Téménides*, Athens.
Hawley, R. (2000) 'Marriage, gender, and the family in Dio', in Swain (ed.): 125–39.

Heath, M. (1998) 'Was Homer a Roman?', *Papers of the Leeds International Latin Seminar* 10: 23–56.
Henderson, Jeffrey (1990) 'The *demos* and the comic competition', in Winkler, J. J. and Zeitlin, F. I. (eds.) *Nothing to Do with Dionysos? Athenian Drama in its Social Context*, Princeton: 271–313.
Henderson, John (1998) *Fighting for Rome. Poets and Caesars, History and Civil War*, Cambridge.
Herrmann, H.-V. (1972) *Olympia. Heiligtum und Wettkampfstätte*, Munich.
  (1988) 'Die Siegerstatuen von Olympia', *Nikephoros* 1: 119–83.
Herz, P. (1990) 'Die musische Agonistik und der Kunstbetrieb der Kaiserzeit', in André and Fick (eds.): 175–95.
Hill, C. R. (1992) *Olympic Politics*, Manchester.
Himmelmann, N. (1990) *Ideale Nacktheit in der griechischen Kunst*, Berlin.
Hitzl, K. (1991) *Die Kaiserzeitliche Statuenausstattung des Metroon*, Berlin.
Hobsbawm, E. J. (1983) 'Mass-producing traditions: Europe, 1870–1914', in Hobsbawm, E. J. and Ranger, T. (eds.) *The Invention of Tradition*, Cambridge: 263–307.
Holder, P. A. (1980) *Studies in the Auxilia of the Roman Army from Augustus to Trajan*, Oxford.
Hopkins, K. (1983) *Death and Renewal (Sociological Studies in Roman History* 2), Cambridge.
Humbert, S. (1991) 'Plutarque, Alexandre et l'hellénisme', in Saïd (ed.): 169–82.
Hunter, R. L. (ed.) (1989) *Apollonius of Rhodes. Argonautica Book 3*, Cambridge.
  (1994) 'History and historicity in the romance of Chariton', *ANRW* 2.34.2: 1055–86.
Hyde, W. W. (1921) *Olympic Victor Monuments and Greek Athletic Art*, Washington DC.
Innes, D., Hine, H. and Pelling, C. (eds.) (1995) *Ethics and Rhetoric. Classical Essays for Donald Russell on his Seventy-Fifth Birthday*, Oxford.
Iskandar, A. Z. (ed.) (1988) *Galen. On Examinations by which the Best Physicians are Recognised*, Berlin.
Jacob, C. (1991) *Géographie et ethnographie en Grèce ancienne*, Paris.
Jeu, B. (1986) 'Platon, Xenophon et l'idéologie du sport d'état', in Dumont, J.-P. and Bescond, L. (eds.) *Politique dans l'antiquité. Images, mythes et fantasmes*, Lille: 9–33.
Johnson, S. E. (1960) 'Preliminary epigraphic report on the inscriptions found at Sardis in 1958', *BASO* 158: 6–11.
Jones C. P. (1971) *Plutarch and Rome*, Oxford.
  (1973) 'The Date of Dio of Prusa's Alexandrian oration', *Historia* 22: 302–9.
  (1978) *The Roman World of Dio Chrysostom*, Cambridge, MA.
  (1981) 'Two inscriptions from Aphrodisias', *HSCP* 85: 107–29.
  (1986) *Culture and Society in Lucian*, Cambridge, MA.
  (1990) 'A new Lycian dossier establishing an artistic contest and festival in the reign of Hadrian', *JRA* 3: 484–8.
  (1996) 'The Panhellenion', *Chiron* 26: 29–56.

(1998) 'The pancratiasts Helix and Alexander on an Ostian mosaic', *JRA* 11: 293–8.
(1999) 'A Decree of Thyatira in Lydia', *Chiron* 29: 1–21.
(2001) 'Pausanias and his guides', in Alcock, Cherry and Elsner (eds.): 33–9.
Jones, S. (1997) *The Archaeology of Ethnicity. Constructing Identities in the Past and Present*, New York.
Jouan, F. (1993) 'Le Diogène de Dion Chrysostome', in Goulet-Cazé, M.-O. and Goulet, R. (eds.) *Le cynisme ancien et ses prolongements*, Paris: 381–97.
Jouanna, J. (1999) *Hippocrates*, Baltimore (trans. M. B. DeBevoise; first pub. in French, 1992).
Jüthner, J. (1904) 'Zu Dio Chrysostomus XXVIII', *WS* 26: 151–5.
(ed.) (1909) *Philostratos über Gymnastik*, Leipzig.
Kaimio, J. (1979) *The Romans and the Greek Language*, Helsinki.
Kajava, M. (2002) 'When did the Isthmian games return to the Isthmus? (Rereading Corinth 8.3.153)', *CPh* 97: 168–78.
Kayser, C. L. (ed.) (1870–71) *Flavii Philostrati opera* (2 vols., Teubner), Leipzig.
Keil, J. (1905) 'Artzeinschriften aus Ephesos', *JÖAI* 8: 128–38.
Kennell, N. M. (1988) 'ΝΕΡωΝ ΠΕΡΙΟΔΟΝΙΚΗΣ', *AJP* 109: 239–51.
(1995) *The Gymnasium of Virtue. Education and Culture in Ancient Sparta*, Chapel Hill.
Kent, J. H. (1966) *The Inscriptions 1926–1950 (Corinth. Results of Excavations*, vol. VIII, 3), Princeton.
Kenyon, F. G. (1893) 'A rescript of Marcus Antonius', *CR* 7: 476–8.
Keul-Deutscher, M. (1996) 'Heliodorstudien I. Die Schönheit in den "Aithiopika"', *RhM* 139: 319–33.
Khan, H. A. (ed.) (1994) *The Birth of the European Identity. The Europe-Asia Contrast in Greek Thought, 490–322 BC*, Nottingham.
Kieffer, J. S. (ed.) (1964) *Galen's Institutio Logica*, Baltimore.
Kindstrand, J. F. (ed.) (1981) *Anacharsis. The Legend and the Apophthegmata*, Uppsala.
Kleijwegt, M. (1991) *Ancient Youth. The Ambiguity of Youth and the Absence of Adolescence in Greco-Roman Society*, Amsterdam.
Knibbe, D. and Iplikçioglu, B. (1981–82) 'Neue Inschriften aus Ephesos VIII', *JÖAI* 53: 87–150.
Knoepfler, D. (1979) 'Contributions à l'épigraphie de Chalcis, II. Les couronnes de Théokles, fils de Pausanias', *BCH* 103: 165–88.
Knoepfler, D. and Piérart, M. (eds.) (2001) *Editer, traduire, commenter Pausanias en l'an 2000*, Geneva.
Kokolakis, M. (1958) 'Gladiatorial games and animal baiting in Lucian', *Platon* 10: 328–51.
Kollesch, J. (1981) 'Galen und die Zweite Sophistik' in Nutton (ed.): 1–11.
Kollesch, J. and Nickel, D. (1994) 'Bibliographia Galeniana. Die Beiträge des 20. Jahrhunderts zur Galenforschung', *ANRW* 2.37.2: 1351–420.
König, J. P. (2001) 'Favorinus' *Corinthian Oration* in its Corinthian context', *PCPS* 47: 141–71.

Konstan, D. (2001) 'The joys of Pausanias', in Alcock, Cherry and Elsner (eds.): 57–60.
Korenjak, M. (1999) *Publikum und Redner. Ihre Interaktion in der sophistischen Rhetorik der Kaiserzeit*, Munich.
Kudlien, F. (1986) *Die Stellung des Arztes in der römischen Gesellschaft*, Stuttgart.
Kuefler, M. (2001) *The Manly Eunuch. Masculinity, Gender Ambiguity, and Christian Ideology in Late Antiquity*, Chicago.
Kunze, E. (1956) *Bericht über die Ausgrabungen in Olympia*, vol. 5, Berlin.
  (1958) *Bericht über die Ausgrabungen in Olympia*, vol. 6, Berlin.
  (1961) *Bericht über die Ausgrabungen in Olympia*, vol. 7, Berlin.
Kurke, L. (1999) *Coins, Bodies, Games and Gold. The Politics of Meaning in Archaic Greece*, Princeton.
Kyle, D. G. (1984) 'Solon and Athletics', *AncW* 9: 91–105.
  (1987) *Athletics in Ancient Athens*, Leiden.
  (1990) 'E. Norman Gardiner and the decline of Greek sport', in Kyle, D. G. and Stark, G. D. (eds.) *Essays on Sport History and Sport Mythology*, College Station, TX: 7–44.
Lada-Richards, I. (2003) '"A worthless feminine thing"? Lucian and the "optic intoxication" of pantomime dancing', *Helios* 30: 21–75.
Lafond, Y. (1996) 'Pausanias et l'histoire du Péloponnèse depuis la conquête romaine', in Bingen (ed.): 167–98.
  (2001) 'Lire Pausanias à l'époque des Antonins. Réflexions sur la place de la *Périégèse* dans l'histoire culturelle, religieuse et sociale de la Grèce romaine', in Knoepfler and Piérart (eds.): 387–406.
Lahusen, G. (1990) 'Polyklet und Augustus', in Beck, Bol and Bückling (eds.): 393–6.
Larmour, D. H. (1999) *Stage and Stadium*, Hildesheim.
Laurence, R. and Berry, J. (eds.) (1998) *Cultural Identity in the Roman Empire*, London.
Laurenzi, L. (1941) 'Iscrizioni dell' Asclepieo di Coo', in *Clara Rhodos*, vol. x: 25–39.
Lee, H. M. (1983) 'Athletic arete in Pindar', in *AncW* 7: 31–7.
  (1988) 'Did women compete against men in Greek athletic festivals?', *Nikephoros* 1: 103–17.
  (2001) *The Programme and Schedule of the Ancient Olympic Games*, Hildesheim.
Lefkowitz, M. R. (1991) *First-Person Fictions. Pindar's Poetic 'I'*, Oxford.
Leftwich, G. V. (1995) 'Polykleitos and Hippokratic medicine', in Moon (ed.): 38–51.
Leibundgut, A. (1990) 'Polykleitische Elemente bei späthellenistischen und römischen Kleinbronzen'.
Leigh, M. (2000) 'Oblique politics. Epic of the imperial period', in Taplin, O. (ed.) *Literature in the Greek and Roman Worlds*, Oxford: 468–91.
Leiwo, M. (1994) *Neapolitana. A Study of Population and Language in Greco-Roman Naples*, Helsinki.
Lemarchand, L. (1926) *Dion de Pruse. Les oeuvres d'avant l'exil*, Paris.

Lendon, J. (1997) *Empire of Honour. The Art of Government in the Roman World*, Oxford.
Lesher, J. H. (ed.) (1992) *Xenophanes of Colophon. Fragments*, Toronto.
Levick, B. (2000) 'Greece and Asia Minor', in Bowman, A. K., Garnsey, P. and Rathbone, D. (eds.) *Cambridge Ancient History. The High Empire, AD 70–192* (vol. IX, 2nd edn.): 604–34.
Lloyd, G. E. R. (1973) *Greek Science after Aristotle*, London.
  (1979) *Magic, Reason and Experience. Studies in the Origins and Development of Greek Science*, Cambridge.
  (1987) *The Revolutions of Wisdom. Studies in the Claims and Practice of Greek Science*, Berkeley.
  (1991) 'Galen on Hellenistics and Hippocrateans: contemporary battles and past authorities', in *Methods and Problems in Greek Science*, Cambridge: 398–416.
  (1996) *Adversaries and Authorities. Investigations into Ancient Greek and Chinese Science*, Cambridge.
Lomas, K. (1993) *Rome and the Western Greeks, 350 BC–AD 200. Conquest and Acculturation in Southern Italy*, London.
Long, A. A. (2002) *Epictetus. A Stoic and Socratic Guide to Life*, Oxford.
Lovatt, H. (forthcoming) *Statius and Epic Games: Sport, Politics and Poetics in the Thebaid*, Cambridge.
Luce, T. J. and Woodman, A. J. (eds.) (1993) *Tacitus and the Tacitean Tradition*, Princeton
MacAloon, J. J. (1981) *This Great Symbol. Pierre de Coubertin and the Origins of the Modern Olympic Games*, Chicago.
MacClancy, J. (1996a) 'Sport, identity and ethnicity', in MacClancy (ed.): 1–20.
  (ed.) (1996b) *Sport, Identity and Ethnicity*, Oxford.
Macready, S. and Thompson, F. H. (eds.) (1987) *Roman Architecture in the Greek World*, London.
Maderna-Lauter, C. (1990) 'Polyklet in Rom', in Beck, Bol and Bückling (eds.): 328–92.
Mähl, E. (1974) *Gymnastik und Athletik im Denken der Römer*, Amsterdam.
Malkin, I. (ed.) (2001) *Ancient Perceptions of Greek Ethnicity*, Washington DC.
Manganaro, G. (1974) 'Una biblioteca storica nel ginnasio di Tauromenion e il P.Oxy. 1241', *PP* 29: 389–409.
Mantas, K. (1995) 'Women and athletics in the Roman East', *Nikephoros* 8: 125–44.
Markovich, M. (1978) 'Xenophanes on drinking parties and the Olympic games', *ICS* 3: 1–26.
Marrou, H. (1965) *Histoire de l'éducation dans l'antiquité*, Paris (rev. edn.; first pub. in French, 1948).
Marvin, M. (1983) 'Free-standing sculptures from the Baths of Caracalla', *AJA* 87: 347–84.
  (1993) 'Copying in Roman sculpture. The replica series', in d'Ambra, E. (ed.) *Roman Art in Context*, Englewood Cliffs, NJ: 161–88.
  (1997) 'Roman sculptural reproductions or Polykleitos: the sequel', in Hughes, A. and Ranfft, E. (eds.) *Sculpture and its Reproductions*, London.

McGuire, D. T. (1997) *Acts of Silence. Civil War, Tyranny, and Suicide in the Flavian Epics*, Hildesheim.
McNay, L. (1994) *Foucault. A Critical Introduction*, Cambridge.
Mehl, A. (1992) 'Erziehung zum Hellenen – Erziehung zum Weltbürger. Bemerkungen zum Gymnasion im hellenistischen Osten', *Nikephoros* 5: 43–74.
Meinburg, E. (1975) 'Gymnastische Erziehung in der platonischen Paideia', *Stadion* 1: 228–66.
Mellor, R. (1975) ΘΕΑ ΡШΜΗ. *The Worship of the Goddess Roma in the Greek World*, Göttingen.
  (1993) *Tacitus*, New York.
Merkelbach, R. (1970) 'Herakles und der Pankratiast', *ZPE* 6: 47–9.
  (1974a) 'Der unentschiedene Kampf des Pankratiasten Ti. Claudius Rufus in Olympia', *ZPE* 15: 99–104.
  (1974b) 'Zu der Festordnung für die Sebasta in Neapel', *ZPE* 15: 192–3.
  (1975) 'Der griechische Wortschatz und die Christen', *ZPE* 18: 101–48.
  (1982) 'Agonistisches Epigramm aus Aphrodisias', *ZPE* 49: 282–3.
Messner, M. A. and Sabo, D. F. (eds.) (1990) *Sport, Men and the Gender Order. Critical Feminist Perspectives*, Champaign, IL.
Métraux, G. P. R. (1995) *Sculptors and Physicians in Fifth-Century Greece. A Preliminary Study*, Montreal.
Millar, F. (1969) 'P. Herennius Dexippus: the Greek world and the third-century invasions', *JRS* 59: 12–29.
  (1977) *The Emperor in the Roman World*, London.
Miller, P. A. (1998) 'Catullan consciousness, the "care of the self", and the force of the negative in history', in Larmour, D. H. J., Miller, P. A. and Platter, C. (eds.) *Rethinking Sexuality. Foucault and Classical Antiquity*, Princeton: 171–203.
Miller, S. G. (ed.) (1991) *Arete. Greek Sports from Ancient Sources*, Berkeley (rev. edn.; first pub. 1979).
Millon, C. and Schouler, B. (1988) 'Les jeux olympiques d'Antioche', in *Les sports antiques. Toulouse et Domitien* (*Pallas* 34): 61–76.
Milner, N. P. (1991) 'Victors in the Meleagria and the Balbouran elite', *AS* 41: 23–62.
Milner, N. P. and Mitchell, S. (1995) 'An exedra for Demosthenes of Oenoanda and his relatives', *AS* 45: 91–104.
van Minnen, P. (2000) 'Euergetism in Greco-Roman Egypt', in Mooren, L. (ed.) *Politics and Administration in the Hellenistic and Roman World*, Leuven: 437–69.
Mitchell, S. (1977) 'R.E.C.A.M. notes and studies 1. Inscriptions of Ancyra', *AS* 27: 63–103.
  (1990) 'Festivals, games and civic life in Roman Asia Minor' (review of Wörrle (1988) and Ziegler (1985)), *JRS* 80: 183–93.
  (1993) *The Celts in Anatolia and the Impact of Roman Rule* (*Anatolia. Land, Men and Gods in Asia Minor*, vol. 1), Oxford.

(2002) 'In search of the Pontic community in antiquity', in Bowman, A. K., Cotton, H. M., Goodman, M. and Price, S. (eds.) *Representations of Empire. Rome and the Mediterranean World*, Oxford: 35–64.

Moles, J. L. (1978) 'The career and conversion of Dio Chrysostom', *JHS* 98, 79–100.

(1983) 'The date and purpose of the fourth *Kingship Oration* of Dio Chrysostom', *ClAnt* 2: 251–78.

(1990) 'The *Kingship Orations* of Dio Chrysostom', *Papers of the Leeds International Latin Seminar* 6: 297–375.

(1995) 'Dio Chrysostom, Greece and Rome', in Innes, Hine and Pelling (eds.): 177–92.

Montserrat, D. (ed.) (1998) *Changing Bodies, Changing Meanings. Studies on the Human Body in Antiquity*, London.

Moon, W. (ed.) (1995) *Polykleitos, the Doryphoros, and Tradition*, Madison, WI.

Morales, H. (1995) 'The taming of the view: natural curiosities in *Leukippe and Kleitophon*', in *Groningen Colloquia on the Novel* 6: 39–50.

Moraux, P. (1981) 'Galien comme philosophe: la philosophie de la nature', in Nutton (ed.): 87–116.

Moretti, L. (ed.) (1953) *Iscrizioni agonistiche greche*, Rome.

(1953–5) 'Iscrizioni greche inedite di Roma', *BCAR* 75: 73–89.

(1954) 'Note sugli antiche periodonikai', *Athenaeum* 32: 115–20.

(1957) 'Olympionikai, i vincitori negli antichi agoni olimpici', *MAL* 8.2: 55–198.

Morgan, C. (1990) *Athletes and Oracles. The Transformation of Olympia and Delphi in the Eighth Century BC*, Cambridge.

(1993) 'The origins of pan-Hellenism', in Marinatos, N. and Hägg, R. (eds.) *Greek Sanctuaries. New Approaches*, London: 18–44.

Morgan, J. R. (1985) 'Lucian's *True Histories* and the *Wonders beyond Thule* of Antonius Diogenes', *CQ* 35: 475–90.

(1998) 'Narrative doublets in Heliodorus' *Aethiopika*', in Hunter, R. L. (ed.) *Studies in Heliodorus*, Cambridge: 60–78.

Morgan, T. (1998) *Literate Education in the Hellenistic and Roman Worlds*, Cambridge.

Morris, I. (2000) *Archaeology as Cultural History. Words and Things in Iron Age Greece*, Oxford.

Mosshammer, A. A. (1979) *The Chronicle of Eusebius and Greek Chronographic Traditions*, London.

Müller, N. (1997) 'Coubertin und die Antike', *Nikephoros* 10: 289–302.

Müller, S. (1995) *Das Volk der Athleten. Untersuchungen zur Ideologie und Kritik des Sports in der griechisch-römischen Antike*, Trier.

Nagy, G. (1979) *The Best of the Achaeans. Concepts of the Hero in Archaic Greek Poetry*, Baltimore.

Nesselrath, H. G. (1990) 'Lucian's introductions', in Russell (ed.): 111–40.

Neudecker, R. (1988) *Die Skulpturenausstattung römischer Villen in Italien*, Mainz am Rhein.

Newby, Z. (2002) 'Greek athletics as Roman spectacle. The mosaics from Ostia and Rome', *PBSR* 57: 177–203.
　(forthcoming) *Victory and Virtue. Greek Athletics in the Roman World*, Oxford.
Nicolet, C. (1991) *Space, Geography, and Politics in the Early Roman Empire*, Ann Arbor (trans. H. Leclerc; first pub. in French, 1988).
van Nijf, O. M. (1997) *The Civic World of Professional Associations in the Roman East*, Amsterdam.
　(1999) 'Athletics, festivals and Greek identity in the Roman east', *PCPS* 45: 176–200.
　(2001) 'Local heroes: athletics, festivals, and elite self-fashioning in the Roman East', in Goldhill (ed.): 306–34.
　(2003) 'Athletics, *andreia* and the *askesis*-culture in the Roman East', in Rosen, M. and Sluiter, I. (eds.) *Andreia. Studies in Manliness and Courage in Classical Antiquity*, Leiden: 263–86.
Nollé, J. (1987) 'Pamphylische Studien 6–10', *Chiron* 17: 235–76.
Nutton, V. (1971) 'Two notes on immunities: Digest 27, 1, 6, 10 and 11', *JRS* 61: 52–63 (reprinted in Nutton (1988)).
　(1972) 'Galen and medical autobiography', *PCPS* 198: 50–62 (reprinted in Nutton (1988)).
　(1973) 'The chronology of Galen's early career', *CQ* 23: 158–71 (reprinted in Nutton (1988)).
　(1977) '*Archiatri* and the medical profession in Antiquity', *PBSR* 45: 191–226 (reprinted in Nutton (1988)).
　(ed.) (1979) *Galen. On Prognosis* (*CMG* v, 8.1), Berlin.
　(ed.) (1981) *Galen. Problems and Prospects*, London.
　(1984) 'Galen in the eyes of his contemporaries', *BHM* 58: 315–24 (reprinted in Nutton (1988)).
　(1988) *From Democedes to Harvey. Studies in the History of Medicine*, London.
　(1992) 'Healers in the medical market place; towards a sociology of Graeco-Roman medicine', in Wear, A. (ed.) *Medicine in Society. Historical Essays*, Cambridge: 15–58.
　(1995) 'The medical meeting place', in van der Eijk, Horstmanshoff and Schrijvers (eds.): 3–25.
Nye, R. B. (1980) 'Death of a Gaulois. René Goscinny and Astérix', *Journal of Popular Culture* 14: 181–95.
Ogilvie, R. M. and Richmond, I. (eds.) (1967) *Cornelii Taciti De Vita Agricolae*, Oxford.
Oliver, J. H. (1942) 'Greek inscriptions', *Hesperia* 11: 29–90.
　(1953) *The Ruling Power. A Study of the Roman Empire in the Second Century after Christ through the Roman Oration of Aelius Aristides*, Philadelphia.
　(1970) *Marcus Aurelius. Aspects of Civic and Cultural Policy in the East*, Princeton.
　(1975) 'The empress Plotina and the sacred thymelic synod', *Historia* 24: 125–8.

Osborne, R. (1993) 'Competitive festivals and the polis: a context for dramatic festivals at Athens', in Sommerstein, A. H., Halliwell, S., Henderson, J. and Zimmermann, B. (eds.) *Tragedy, Comedy and the Polis*, Bari: 21–37.
  (1996) *Greece in the Making, 1200–479 BC*, London.
  (1998a) 'Men without clothes. Heroic nakedness and Greek art', in Wyke (ed.) (1998a): 80–104.
  (1998b) *Archaic and Classical Greek Art*, Oxford.
  (1998c) 'Sculpted men of Athens. Masculinity and power in the field of vision', in Foxhall and Salmon (eds.) (1998a): 23–42.
Ostenfeld, E. N. (ed.) (2002) *Greek Romans and Roman Greeks. Studies in Cultural Interaction*, Aarhus.
Pearcy, L. T. (1983) 'Galen and Stoic Rhetoric', *GRBS* 24: 259–72.
  (1993) 'Medicine and rhetoric in the period of the Second Sophistic', *ANRW* 2.37.1: 445–56.
Peek, W. (1934) 'Griechische Inschriften', *MDAI(A)* 59: 35–80.
Pélékidis, C. (1962) *Histoire de l'éphébie attique*, Paris.
Pelling, C. B. R. (1989) 'Plutarch: Roman heroes and Greek culture', in Barnes, J. and Griffin, M. (eds.) *Philosophia Togata. Essays on Philosophy and Roman Society*, Oxford: 199–232.
Penella, R. J. (ed.) (1979) *The Letters of Apollonius of Tyana*, Leiden.
Perkins, J. (1995) *The Suffering Self. Pain and Narrative Representation in Early Christianity*, London.
Perlman, S. (1976) 'Panhellenism, the polis and imperialism', *Historia* 25: 1–30.
Pernot, L. (1993) *La rhétorique de l'éloge dans le monde gréco-romain* (2 vols.), Paris.
Perpillou-Thomas, F. (1995) 'Artistes et athlètes dans les papyrus grecs d'Egypte', *ZPE* 108: 225–51.
Perysinakis, I. N. (1990) 'The athlete as warrior: Pindar's *P.* 9.97–103 and *P.* 10.55–59,' *BICS* 37: 43–9.
Pfitzner, V. C. (1967) *Paul and the Agon Motif. Traditional Athletic Imagery in the Pauline Literature*, Leiden.
Philipp, H. and Koenigs, W. (1979) 'Zu den Basen des L. Mummius in Olympia', *MDAI(A)* 94: 193–216.
Piérart, M. (1998) 'Panthéon et hellénisation dans la colonie romaine de Corinthe: la "redécouverte" du culte de Palaimon à l'Isthme', *Kernos* 11: 85–109.
Pinet, C. (1977) 'Myth and stereotype in Astérix le Gaulois', *Contemporary French Civilization* 1: 317–36.
Plass, P. (1995) *The Game of Death in Ancient Rome. Arena Sport and Political Suicide*, Madison, WI.
Pleket, H. W. (1973) 'Some aspects of the history of athletic guilds', *ZPE* 10: 197–227.
  (1974) 'Zur Soziologie des antiken Sports', *MNIR* 36: 57–87.
  (1975) 'Games, prizes, athletes and ideology', *Stadion* 1: 49–89.
  (1976) 'Olympic benefactors', *ZPE* 20: 1–18.
  (1995) 'The social status of physicians in the Graeco-Roman world', in van der Eijk, Horstmanshoff and Schrijvers (eds.): 27–34.

(1998) 'Mass sport and local infrastructure in the Greek cities of Roman Asia Minor', *Stadion* 24: 151–72.
(1999a) Review of Gauthier and Hatzopoulos (eds.) (1993), *Gnomon* 71: 231–6.
(1999b) Review of Decker (1995), *Gnomon* 71: 512–15.
Poliakoff, M. (1981) 'ΑΣΥΝΕΞΩΣΤΟΣ', *ZPE* 44: 78–80.
(1986) *Studies in the Terminology of Greek Combat Sports*, Königstein/Ts.
(1987a) 'Melankomas, ἐκ κλίμακος, and Greek Boxing', *AJP* 108: 511–18.
(1987b) *Combat Sports in the Ancient World*, Yale.
Polley, M. (1998) *Moving the Goalposts. A History of Sport and Society since 1945*, London.
Pollini, J. (1995) 'The Augustus of the Prima Porta and the transformation of the Polykleitan heroic ideal. The rhetoric of art', in Moon (ed.): 262–82.
Porter, J. I. (ed.) (1999) *Constructions of the Classical Body*, Ann Arbor.
(2001) 'Ideals and ruins. Pausanias, Longinus, and the Second Sophistic', in Alcock, Cherry and Elsner (eds.): 63–92.
Potter, D. S. (1999) 'Entertainers in the Roman Empire', in Potter, D. S. and Mattingly, D. J. (eds.) *Life, Death and Entertainment in the Roman Empire*, Ann Arbor: 256–83.
Powell, O. (ed.) (2003) *Galen. On the Properties of Foodstuffs*, Cambridge.
Preston, R. (2001) 'Roman questions, Greek answers. Plutarch and the construction of identity', in Goldhill (ed.): 86–119.
Price, S. R. F. (1984) *Rituals and Power. The Roman Imperial Cult in Asia Minor*, Cambridge.
(1999) *Religions of the Ancient Greeks*, Cambridge.
Rader, B. G. (1979) 'Modern sports. In search of interpretations', *Journal of Social History* 13: 307–21.
Ramage, N. H. and Ramage, A. (1991) *The Cambridge Illustrated History of Roman Art*, Cambridge.
Raschke, W. J. (ed.) (1988) *The Archaeology of the Olympics. The Olympics and Other Festivals in Antiquity*, Madison, WI.
Rausa, F. (1994) *L'immagine del vincitore. L'atleta nella statuaria greca dell'età arcaica all'ellenismo*, Treviso.
Rawson, E. (1985) *Intellectual Life in the Late Roman Republic*, London.
(1992) 'The Romans', in Dover, K. J. (ed.) *Perceptions of the Ancient Greeks*, Oxford: 1–28.
Reardon, B. P. (1971) *Courants littéraires grecs des IIe et IIIe siècles après J-C*, Paris.
Reinach, T. (1908) 'ΠΑΡΘΕΝΩΝ', *BCH* 32: 499–513.
(1909) 'Note additionnelle à l'article ΠΑΡΘΕΝΩΝ', *BCH* 33: 547.
(1916) 'Inscriptions de Sinope', *RA* 3 (5e série): 329–58.
Reinmuth, O. W. (1948) 'The ephebate and citizenship in Athens', *TAPA* 79: 211–31.
(1961) 'Ephebic texts from Athens', *Hesperia* 30: 8–22.
(1974) 'A new ephebic inscription from the Athenian agora', *Hesperia* 43: 246–59.
Riddle, J. M. (1993) 'High medicine and low medicine in the Roman Empire', *ANRW* 2.37.1: 102–20.

Rigsby, K. J. (1979) 'An imperial letter from Balbura', *AJP* 100: 401–7.
Robert, J. and Robert, L. (1954) *La Carie. Histoire et géographie historique avec le recueil des inscriptions antiques, II. Le plateau de Tabai et ses environs*, Paris.
  (1989) *Claros 1. Décrets hellénistiques*, Paris.
Robert, L. (1925) 'Lesbiaca', *REG* 38: 423–6 (=*OMS* 2: 736–9).
  (1928a) 'Notes d'épigraphie hellénistique', *BCH* 52: 158–78 (=*OMS* 1: 87–107).
  (1928b) 'Etudes épigraphiques. Première série', *BCH* 52: 407–25 (=*OMS* 2: 878–96).
  (1929a) 'Epigraphica', *REG* 42: 426–38 (=*OMS* 1: 214–26).
  (1929b) 'ΠΥΚΤΕΥΕΙΝ', *RA* 2: 24–42 (=*OMS* 1: 691–708).
  (1929c) 'Etudes d'épigraphie grecque', *RPh* 3: 122–58 (=*OMS* 2: 1088–124).
  (1930) 'Etudes d'épigraphie grecque', *RPh* 4: 25–60 (=*OMS* 2: 1125–60).
  (1934a) 'Etudes d'épigraphie grecque', *RPh* 8: 267–92 (=*OMS* 2: 1166–91).
  (1934b) 'Notes de numismatique et d'épigraphie grecques', *RA* 3 (6e série): 48–61 (=*OMS* 2: 1012–25).
  (1935) 'Etudes sur les inscriptions et la topographie de la Grèce Centrale. VI –Décrets d'Akraiphia', *BCH* 59: 438–52 (=*OMS* 1.279–93).
  (1937) *Etudes anatoliennes. Recherches sur les inscriptions grecques de l'Asie mineure*, Paris.
  (1938) *Etudes épigraphiques et philologiques*, Paris.
  (1939a) 'Inscriptions grecques de Phénicie et d'Arabie', in *Mélanges Syriens offerts à René Dussaud*: 729–38 (=*OMS* 1: 601–10).
  (1939b) 'Inscriptions grecques d'Asie Mineure', in Calder, W. H. and Keil, J. (eds.) *Anatolian Studies presented to William Buckler*, Manchester: 227–48 (=*OMS* 1: 611–32).
  (1939c) 'Hellenica', *RPh* 13: 97–217 (=*OMS* 2: 1250–1370).
  (1940) *Les gladiateurs dans l'Orient grec*, Paris.
  (1944) 'Hellenica', *RPh* 18: 5–56 (=*OMS* 3: 1371–422).
  (1946) *Hellenica* II, Paris.
  (1948a) *Hellenica* V, Paris.
  (1948b) *Hellenica* VI, Paris.
  (1949) *Hellenica* VII, Paris.
  (1950) *Hellenica* IX, Paris.
  (1954) 'Décret de Delphes pour un médecin de Coronée', *BCH* 78: 68–73 (=*OMS* 1: 255–60).
  (1959) Review of Rehm, A. (ed.) (1958) *Die Inschriften von Didyma*, Berlin, in *Gnomon* 31: 657–74.
  (1960a) *Hellenica* XI–XII, Paris.
  (1960b) 'Recherches épigraphiques', *REA* 62: 276–361 (=*OMS* 2: 792–877).
  (1963) Review of Fraser, P. (1960) *The Inscriptions on Stone. Samothrace* (Volume II, 1), New York: *Gnomon* 35: 50–79.
  (1965) *D'Aphrodisias à la Lycaonie (Hellenica* XIII), Paris.
  (1966a) 'Inscriptions de l'antiquité et du bas-empire à Corinthe' (review of Kent (1966)), *REG* 79: 733–70
  (1966b) *Documents de l'Asie Mineure méridionale*, Paris.

(1966c) 'Inscriptions d'Aphrodisias', *AC* 35: 377–432 (=*OMS* 6: 1–56).
(1966d) *Monnaies antiques en Troade*, Paris.
(1967) 'Sur des inscriptions d'Ephèse. Fêtes, athlètes, empereurs, épigrammes', *RPh* 41: 7–84 (=*OMS* 5: 347–424).
(1968) 'Enterrements et épitaphes', *AC* 37: 406–48 (=*OMS* 6: 81–124).
(1969a) 'Les épigrammes satiriques de Lucilius sur les athlètes. Parodie et réalités,' in *L'épigramme grecque* (*Entretiens sur l'antiquité classique* 14), Geneva: 181–295 (=*OMS* 6: 317–431).
(1969b) 'Inscriptions d'Athènes et de Grèce centrale', *AEph* 1969: 1–58 (=*OMS* 7.707–64).
(1970) 'Deux concours grecques à Rome', *CRAI* 1970: 6–27 (=*OMS* 5: 647–68).
(1973) 'ΑΜΦΙΘΑΛΗΣ', in *Athenian Studies Presented to William Scott Ferguson*, Cambridge, MA: 509–19 (=*OMS* 1: 633–43).
(1974a) 'Les femmes théores à Ephèse', *CRAI* 1974: 176–81 (=*OMS* 5: 669–74).
(1974b) 'Un citoyen de Téos à Bouthrôtos d'Épire', *CRAI* 1974: 508–29 (=*OMS* 5: 675–96).
(1977) 'La titulature de Nicée et de Nicomédie. La gloire et la haine', *HSCP* 81: 1–39 (=*OMS* 6.211–49).
(1978a) 'Catalogue agonistique des Romaia de Xanthos', *RA* 1978: 277–90 (=*OMS* 7: 681–95).
(1978b) 'Decret pour un médecin de Cos', *RPh* 52: 242–51 (=*OMS* 5: 438–47).
(1980) *A travers l'Asie Mineure. Poètes et prosateurs, monnaies grecques, voyageurs et géographie*, Paris.
(1982) 'Une vision de Perpétue martyre à Carthage en 203', *CRAI* 1982: 228–76 (=*OMS* 5.791–839).
(1984) 'Discours d'ouverture', *Actes du VIIIe congrès international d'épigraphie grecque et latine à Athènes, 1982*, Athens: 35–45 (=*OMS* 6: 709–19).
Robinson, R. S. (ed.) (1955) *Sources for the History of Greek Athletics in English Translation*, Cincinnati.
Rogers, G. M. (1991a) *The Sacred Identity of Ephesos. Foundation Myths of a Roman City*, London.
(1991b) 'Demosthenes of Oenoanda and models of euergetism', *JRS* 81: 91–100.
Rojek, C. (1992) 'The field of play in sport and leisure studies', in Dunning, E. and Rojek, C. (eds.) *Sport and Leisure in the Civilizing Process. Critique and Counter-Critique*, Toronto: 1–35.
Roueché, C. (1993) *Performers and Partisans at Aphrodisias in the Roman and Late Roman Periods*, London.
Roux, G. (1980) 'A propos des gymnases de Delphes et de Délos. Le site du Damatrion de Delphes et le sens du mot sphairistérion', *BCH* 104: 127–49.
Russell, D. (ed.) (1990) *Antonine Literature*, Oxford.
Russell, D. A. and Wilson, N. G. (eds.) (1981) *Menander Rhetor*, Oxford.
Rutherford, I. (2000) '*Theoria* and *darshan*. Pilgrimage as gaze in Greece and India', *CQ* 50: 133–46.
(2001) 'Tourism and the sacred. Pausanias and the traditions of Greek pilgrimage', in Alcock, Cherry and Elsner (eds.): 40–52.

Rütten, U. (1997) *Phantasie und Lachkultur. Lukians "Wahre Geschichten"*, Tübingen.
Saïd, S. (ed.) (1991) ΕΛΛΗΝΙΣΜΟΣ *Quelques jalons pour une histoire de l'identité grecque*, Leiden.
  (1993) 'Le "je" de Lucien', in Baslez, Hoffmann and Pernot (eds.): 253–70.
  (1994a) 'Lucien ethnographe', in Billault (ed.): 149–70.
  (1994b) 'The city in the Greek novel', in Tatum, J. (ed.) *The Search for the Ancient Novel*, Baltimore: 216–36.
  (2001) 'The discourse of identity in Greek rhetoric from Isocrates to Aristides', in Malkin (ed.): 275–99.
Salmeri, G. (2000) 'Dio, Rome, and the civic life of Asia Minor', in Swain (ed.): 54–92.
Salomies, O. (ed.) (2001) *The Greek East in the Roman Context*, Helsinki.
Sansone, D. (1988) *Greek Athletics and the Genesis of Sport*, Berkeley.
Scaife, R. (1989) 'Alexander I in the *Histories* of Herodotus', *Hermes* 117: 129–37.
Scanlon, T. F. (1983) 'The vocabulary of competition: *agon* and *aethlos*, Greek terms for contest', *Arete. The Journal of Sports Literature* 1: 147–62.
  (1984a) *Greek and Roman Athletics. A Bibliography*, Chicago.
  (1984b) 'The footrace of the Heraia at Olympia', *AncW* 9: 77–90.
  (1988a) 'The ecumenical Olympics: the games in the Roman era', in Segrave, J. O. and Chu, D. (eds.) *The Olympic Games in Transition*, Champaign, IL: 37–64.
  (1988b) 'Virgineum gymnasium. Spartan females and early Greek athletics', in Raschke (ed.): 185–216.
  (2002) *Eros and Greek Athletics*, Oxford.
Scarborough, J. (1993) 'Roman medicine to Galen', *ANRW* 2.37.1: 3–48.
Schmitt-Pantel, P. (1992) *La cité au banquet. Histoire des repas publics dans les cités grecques*, Rome.
Schmitz, T. (1997) *Bildung und Macht. Zur sozialen und politischen Funktion der zweiten Sophistik in der griechischen Welt der Kaiserzeit*, Munich.
Shapiro, H. A. (1996) 'Democracy and imperialism. The Panathenaia in the age of Perikles', in Neils, J. (ed.) (1996) *Worshipping Athena. Panathenaia and Parthenon*, Madison, WI: 215–25.
Sherk, R. (ed.) (1984) *Rome and the Greek East to the Death of Augustus*, Cambridge.
Shilling, C. (1993) *The Body and Social Theory*, London.
Shorrock, R. (2001) *The Challenge of Epic. Allusive Engagement in the* Dionysiaca *of Nonnus*, Leiden.
Sidebottom, H. (1996) 'Dio of Prusa and the Flavian dynasty', *CQ* 46: 447–56.
Singer P. N. (ed.) (1997) *Galen. Selected Works*, Oxford.
Sinn, U. (1992) 'Bericht über das Forschungsprojekt "Olympia während der römischen Kaiserzeit". 1. Die Arbeiten von 1987–1992', *Nikephoros* 5: 75–84.
  (2000) *Olympia. Cult, Sport, and Ancient Festival*, Princeton (trans. T. Thornton; first pub. in German, 1996).
Siska, H. (1933) 'De Mercurio ceterisque deis ad artem gymnicam pertinentibus', PhD dissertation, University of Halle.

Smith, R. R. R. (1996) 'Typology and diversity in the portraits of Augustus', *JRA* 9: 31–47.
Smith, R. R. R. and Erim, K. T. (1991) 'Sculpture from the theatre. A preliminary report', in Smith, R. R. R. and Erim, K. T. (eds.) *Aphrodisias Papers* II, Ann Arbor: 67–97.
Smith, W. D. (1979) *The Hippocratic Tradition*, Ithaca.
Snodgrass, A. M. (2001) 'Pausanias and the chest of Kypselos', in Alcock, Cherry and Elsner (eds.): 127–41.
Spaltenstein, F. (ed.) (1990) *Commentaire des 'Punica' de Silius Italicus (livres 9 à 17)*, Geneva.
Spawforth, A. J. S. (1986) 'A Severan statue-group and an Olympic festival at Sparta', *ABSA* 81: 313–32.
 (1989) 'Agonistic festivals in Roman Greece', in Cameron, A. and Walker, S. (eds.) (1989) *The Greek Renaissance in the Roman Empire*, London: 193–7.
 (1994) 'Corinth, Argos and the imperial cult. Pseudo-Julian, *Letters* 198', *Hesperia* 63: 211–32.
 (1999) 'The Panhellenion again', *Chiron* 29: 339–52.
 (2001) 'Shades of Greekness. A Lydian case study', in Malkin, I. (ed.): 375–400.
Spawforth, A. J. S. and Walker, S. (1985) 'The world of the Panhellenion, I. Athens and Eleusis', *JRS* 75: 78–104.
 (1986) 'The world of the Panhellenion, II. Three Dorian cities', *JRS* 76: 88–105.
Speidel, M. P. (1980) 'Legionaries from Asia Minor', *ANRW* 2.7.2: 730–46.
Spivey, N. (1996) *Understanding Greek Sculpture. Ancient Meanings, Modern Readings*, London.
 (1997) 'Meditations on a Greek torso' (Review of Stewart (1997)), *CAJ* 7: 309–14.
von Staden, H. (1995) 'Anatomy as rhetoric. Galen on dissection and persuasion', *JHM* 50: 47–66.
 (1997) 'Galen and the "Second Sophistic"', in Sorabji, R. (ed.) *Aristotle and After*, London: 33–54.
Steiner, D. (1998) 'Moving images. Fifth-century victory monuments and the athlete's allure', *ClAnt* 17: 123–49.
 (2001) *Images in Mind. Statues in Archaic and Classical Greek Literature and Thought*, Princeton.
von Steuben, H. (1990) 'Der Doryphoros', in Beck, Bol and Bückling (eds.): 185–98.
Stewart, A. (1990) *Greek Sculpture. An Exploration*, New Haven.
 (1997) *Art, Desire and the Body in Ancient Greece*, Cambridge.
Stok, F. (1993) 'La medicina nell'enciclopedia latina e nei sistemi di classificazione delle *artes* nell' età romana', *ANRW* 2.37.1: 393–444.
Sutton, D. F. (1980) *The Greek Satyr Play*, Meisenheim am Glan.
Swaddling, J. (1980) *The Ancient Olympic Games*, London.
Swain, S. (1990) 'Hellenic culture and the Roman heroes of Plutarch', *JHS* 110: 126–45.
 (1996) *Hellenism and Empire. Language, Classicism, and Power in the Greek World AD 50–250*, Oxford.

(1999) 'Defending Hellenism: Philostratus, *In Honour of Apollonius*', in Edwards, M., Goodman, M. and Price, S. (eds.) *Apologetics in the Roman Empire. Pagans, Jews and Christians*, Oxford: 157–96.

(ed.) (2000) *Dio Chrysostom. Politics, Letters and Philosophy*, Oxford.

Sweet, W. E. (1987) (ed.) *Sport and Recreation in Ancient Greece. A Sourcebook with Translations*, New York.

Syme, R. (1958) *Tacitus* (2 vols.), Oxford.

Taplin, O. (1992) *Homeric Soundings. The Shaping of the* Iliad, Oxford.

Temkin, O. (1991) *Hippocrates in a World of Pagans and Christians*, Baltimore.

Themelis, P. (2001) 'Roman Messene. The gymnasium', in Salomies, O. (ed.): 119–26.

Thuillier, J.-P. (1982) 'Le programme "athlétique" des *Ludi Circenses* dans la Rome Républicaine', *REL* 60: 105–22.

(1988) 'La nudité athlétique (Grèce, Etrurie, Rome)', *Nikephoros* 1: 29–48.

(1993) *Spectacles sportifs et scéniques dans le monde étrusco-italique*, Rome.

(1996a) *Le sport dans la Rome antique*, Paris.

(1996b) Review of Caldelli (1993), *Nikephoros* 9: 266–9.

Tod, M. N. (1951) 'An ephebic inscription from Memphis', *JEA* 37: 86–99.

Toner, J. P. (1995) *Leisure and Ancient Rome*, Cambridge.

Trapp, M. (2000) 'Plato in Dio', in Swain (ed.): 213–39.

Tréheux, J. (1988) 'Une nouvelle lecture de l'inventaire du gymnase à Délos', *BCH* 112: 583–9.

Tsakyroglous, M. (1892) 'Μαιονικαὶ ἐπιγραφαὶ ἀνέκδοτοι', *MDAI(A)* 17: 198–201.

Turner, B. S. (1996) *The Body and Society. Explorations in Social Theory*, London (2nd edn.; first pub. 1984).

Tzifopoulos, Y. (1993) 'Mummius' dedications at Olympia', *GRBS* 34: 93–100.

Usher, S. (1994) 'Isocrates: paideia, kingship and the barbarians', in Khan (ed.): 131–45.

Vanoyeke, V. (1992) *La naissance des jeux olympiques et le sport dans l'antiquité*, Paris.

Venini, P. (1969) 'Silio Italico e il mito tebano', *RIL* 103: 778–83

Vessey, D. W. T. C. (1970) 'The games in *Thebaid 6*', *Latomus* 29: 426–41.

Veyne, P. (1990) *Bread and Circuses. Historical Sociology and Political Pluralism*, London (abridged with introd. O. Murray; trans. B. Pearce; first pub. in French 1976).

Vian, F. (1959) *Recherches sur les* Posthomerica *de Quintus de Smyrne*, Paris.

(ed.) (1963) *Quintus de Smyrne. La Suite d'Homère*, Paris.

Visa-Ondarçuhu, V. (1999) *L'image de l'athlète d'Homère à la fin du Ve siècle avant J.-C.*, Paris.

Walker, S. (1987) 'Roman nymphaea in the Greek world', in Macready and Thompson (eds.): 60–71.

Wallace-Hadrill, A. (1983) *Suetonius. The Scholar and his Caesars*, London.

(1998) 'To be Roman, go Greek. Thoughts on hellenization at Rome', in Austin, M., Harries, J. and Smith, C. (1998) *Modus Operandi. Essays in Honour of Geoffrey Rickman*, London: 79–91.

Weiler, I. (1981) 'Philostrats Gedanken über den Verfall des Sports', in Bachleitner, R. and Redl, S. (eds.) *Sportwirklichkeit. Beiträge zur Didaktik Geschichte und Soziologie des Sports*, Wien: 97–105.
Weiss, P. (1981) 'Ein agonistisches Bema und die isopythischen Spiele von Side', *Chiron* 11: 315–46.
Welch, K. (1998) 'Greek stadia and Roman spectacles. Asia, Athens, and the tomb of Herodes Atticus', *JRA* 11: 117–45.
  (1999) 'Negotiating Roman spectacle architecture in the Greek world: Athens and Corinth', in Bergmann and Kondoleon (eds.): 125–45.
West, M. L. (1967) 'The contest of Homer and Hesiod', *CQ* 17: 433–50.
West, W. C. (1990) 'M. Oulpios Domestikos and the athletic synod at Ephesus', *AHB* 4: 84–9.
Whitby, M. and Whitby, M. (eds.) (1989) *Chronicon Paschale. 284–286 AD* (trans. with notes and introd.), Liverpool.
Whitmarsh, T. (1998) 'Reading power in Roman Greece: the *paideia* of Dio Chrysostom', in Too, Y. L. and Livingstone, N. (eds.) (1998) *Pedagogy and Power. Rhetorics of Classical Learning*, Cambridge: 192–213.
  (1999) 'Greek and Roman in dialogue: the pseudo-Lucianic *Nero*', *JHS* 119: 142–60.
  (2001) *Greek Literature and the Roman Empire. The Politics of Imitation*, Oxford.
  (2002) 'Alexander's Hellenism and Plutarch's textualism', *CQ* 52: 174–92.
Whittaker, H. (1991) 'Pausanias and his use of inscriptions', *SO* 66: 171–86.
Wiedemann, T. (1992) *Emperors and Gladiators*, London.
Wilhelm, A. (1915) *Neue Beiträge zur griechischen Inschriftenkunde* (vol. IV), Wien.
Williams, C. A. (1999) *Roman Homosexuality. Ideologies of Masculinity in Classical Antiquity*, New York.
Willis, W. H. (1941) 'Athletic contests in the epic', *TAPA* 72: 392–417.
Wilson, M. (1993) 'Flavian variant: history. Silius' *Punica*', in Boyle, A. J. (ed.) *Roman Epic*, London: 218–36.
Wilson, P. (2000) *The Athenian Institution of the Khoregia. The Chorus, the City and the Stage*, Cambridge.
Woodman, A. J. (1993) 'Amateur dramatics at the court of Nero: *Annals* 15.48–74', in Luce and Woodman (eds.): 104–28.
Woolf, G. (1993) 'Roman peace', in Rich, J. and Shipley, G. (eds.) *War and Society in the Roman World*, London: 171–94.
  (1994) 'Becoming Roman, staying Greek: culture, identity and the civilizing process in the Roman East', *PCPS* 40: 116–43.
  (1997) 'Polis-religion and its alternatives in the Roman provinces', in Cancik and Rüpke (eds.): 71–84.
  (1998) *Becoming Roman. The Origins of Provincial Civilization in Gaul*, Cambridge.
Wörrle, M. (1988) *Stadt und Fest in kaiserzeitlichen Kleinasien. Studien zu einer agonistischen Stiftung aus Oinoanda*, Munich.
Wyke, M. (ed.) (1998a) *Gender and the Body in the Ancient Mediterranean*, Oxford.
  (ed.) (1998b) *Parchments of Gender. Deciphering the Bodies of Antiquity*, Oxford.

Yegül, F. (1992) *Baths and Bathing in Classical Antiquity*, Cambridge, MA.
Young, D. C. (1985) *The Olympic Myth of Greek Amateur Athletics*, Chicago.
  (1996) *The Modern Olympics. A Struggle for Revival*, Baltimore.
Zanker, P. (1988) *The Power of Images in the Age of Augustus*, Ann Arbor (trans. A. Shapiro; first pub. in German, 1987).
Ziegler, R. (1985) *Städtisches Prestige und kaiserliche Politik. Studien zum Festwesen in Ostkilikien im 2. und 3. Jahrhundert n. Chr.*, Düsseldorf.
Zissos, A. (2002) 'Reading models and the Homeric program in Valerius Flaccus's *Argonautica*', *Helios* 29: 69–96.

General index

Abraham 172
Achaia, Achaians (*see also names of individual cities*) 186–7, 202, 339
Achilles 76–7, 235–7, 339
acrobats, acrobatics 1–2, 4–5, 320
Actium, battle of 28, 239
Aelian 160
Aelius Alkibiades, P. 179
Aelius Alkibiades, T. 179–80
Aelius Aristides 40, 180, 191
Aemilius Paullus, L. 214, 216
Aemilius Scaurus, M. 216
Aeneas 239, 242
Agamemnon 77, 235, 236
Agathion 340–1
age categories (*see also paides*, ephebes, *neoi*) 53, 64, 129, 166, 198, 200, 202–3, 247
agôn (ἀγών), range of meanings 35
agones (agonistic festivals) (*see also gymnasion*, links with festival culture; *ludi*, distinction from *agones*; *and entries under the names of individual festivals*)
  and civic identity 4, 13, 27, 67–8, 165
  'crown', 'sacred' festivals 27, 29, 71, 164, 165, 185, 214
  held by Republican Roman generals 214
  in honour of Rome 213–14
  in the west (*see also* Capitolia; Neronia; Sebasta; Eusebeia) 218–21
  processes of foundation 7, 27, 29, 71, 164, 214
  themides (local, 'prize festivals') 27, 164
agonothete, *agonothesia* (*see also* euergetism; doctors, as agonistic benefactors) 27–8, 68, 76–7, 127, 166, 185
Aias 77, 235–6, 237
Aigina 201
Aktia (*agôn* in Nikopolis) 28, 51, 125, 169, 191
Alexander I of Macedon 26
Alexander the Great 200–1

Alexandria, Alexandrians (*see also under* Olympic festivals (in other cities)) 1, 3, 5, 6, 143, 167, 171, 259–60, 307
Alfidios, M. (athlete) 130–1, 138, 146, 307
Altis (*see* Olympia)
Alypos of Sikyon (sculptor) 197
alytarchai 166
amateurism 30, 37
Amphipolis 214
amphithalês 67
Amykos 237, 239, 246
Anacharsis (*see also* Lucian, *Anacharsis*) 299
  conversion to Hellenism 81, 83
  as a persona for Roman Empire writers 93–4
anagnosis ('reading' – title of a *gymnasion* festival contest) 65
Anaximenes (historian) 200–1
animals 142, 272, 291, 292–3, 296, 328, 340
Ankyra 169–70
Antaeus 238
anthologies 160
Antilochos 338, 339
Antisthenes 141–2
Antoninus Pius 220, 222, 223–4, 258
Antyllos 276, 280–2, 284, 285, 287
Aphrodisias 67, 119–24, 127–30, 131
Apollonia 56
Apollonius of Rhodes, *Argonautika* 237–8, 287
Apollonius of Tyana (*see also* Philostratus, *Life of Apollonius*)
  letters ascribed to 341–2
Appian 160
archery 246
Archimedes 243
archonship (Athenian) as means of dating 171, 174
Areios (athlete) 77
Aretê ('Virtue', deity of the *gymnasion*) 126
Argos (*see also* Shield Games of Hera at Argos) 167, 191, 194, 197
Aristippos 294

379

Aristotle 160, 172, 200, 306, 336
Arkadians 186–7, 326
army, Roman (*see also* Rome, military intervention in the Greek east) 56
Artemidorus 133
Artemis Orthia (*see* Sparta)
Artists of Dionysus (*see* guilds, musical)
Asia Minor (*see also names of individual cities*) 28, 70, 125, 168, 169
askeô (ἀσκέω), askesis (ἄσκησις), range of meanings 35
Asklepieia (*agôn* in Ephesus) 254–5
Asklepieia Sotereia Pythia (*agôn* in Ankyra) 169–70
Asklepios 259–60
Asterix comic series (Goscinny and Uderzo) 40–4
astrology (*see* astronomy)
astronomy 50–1, 261, 319, 320–21
Astyanax 91
Athenaeus 160
Athenodoros 178
Athens, Athenians (*see also under* Olympic festivals (in other cities)) 1, 3, 7, 26–7, 80–94, 141, 143, 169, 171, 177, 178, 183, 243, 244, 259, 309
    as host of modern Olympics 37, 38, 39
    as recipient of Hadrian's benefaction 28, 85, 163
    ephebeia 26, 27, 48, 55, 60, 64, 85, 309, 311
athletês (ἀθλητής), range of meanings 35
athletes
    as role models 97, 107–10, 126–39, 146–57
    dying young 127, 130–1, 146–57, 244
    family dynasties of 130, 147
    performing in Rome 216–17
athletics
    and civic identity 3, 4, 13, 19–20, 26
    and Greek identity (*see also* Panhellenism; *gymnasion* as marker of Hellenic culture; trainers, as representatives of Hellenic tradition) 13, 18, 25–6, 27
    as elite activity 6, 12–19, 23–5, 31, 58–63, 183, 303
    as metaphor 98, 129–30, 132–9, 183, 245, 266, 269, 270, 271, 288–9, 332
    as object of controversy 2–7, 8, 13–21, 95, 303, 345–6
    as preparation for political participation 59, 67, 87, 286
    Christian attitudes to 7, 133–4
    continuation beyond AD 400 29–30
    criticisms of military uselessness 47, 56–8, 90–1
    definition of 32–5
    in the Archaic/Classical period 23–7
    in the Hellenistic period 7, 27–8, 46–7, 51–2
    in the Imperial period 7, 28–30, 31, 46–7, 51–2, 350–2
    interaction between 'literary' and epigraphical representation 8, 21–2, 106–7, 350
    modern 23, 35–44
    origins of 23–5, 317, 326, 330–1
    Roman attitudes to (*see also* philhellenism) 7, 25–6, 28, 57–8, 90–1, 138, 205–53
athleuô (ἀθλεύω), range of meanings 35
Atlanta Olympics (1996) 38
Atticism 265, 341
Augustus 28, 46, 50, 51, 113–15, 213, 219, 227, 229–32, 233, 239
    Res Gestae 229
aulos 167
Aurelios Achilles (pankratiast) 127–30, 131, 132, 166
Aurelios Alexander (pankratiast) 3–4
Aurelios Artemon, M. (benefactor from Oinoanda) 71
Aurelios Asklepiades, M. 1–6, 29, 60, 124–6, 129, 130, 148, 168–9, 171, 211–12, 224–5, 299, 351–2
Aurelios Helix (pankratiast) 3–4

Bacchus (*see* Dionysus)
ball games 33–4, 49, 280–1, 284–91
baths 49, 214
    athletic statues in 107–10
Baths of Caracalla 107–10
Baths of Trajan (headquarters of the Athletic Guild) 1, 4, 110, 222, 223–4
beauty 22, 25–6, 97–9, 102, 134–5, 141, 144–5, 147–57, 298
benefaction (*see* euergetism)
Berlin Olympics (1936) 38
Beroia
    as centre for military training and administration 55
    gymnasion law 48, 51–5, 60, 63, 65, 311–12
Billault, A. 318
bodies 12, 14, 16–17, 97–157, 274–91, 295–6, 301–44
Borysthenes 84–5
Bourdieu, P. 100
boxers, boxing 77, 102, 115–24, 135, 146–57, 167, 176, 201, 216, 237, 238, 245, 246, 332, 340
    shadow-boxing 280
    techniques of 149
Branham, B. 73–4, 88

Caesarea (Palestine) 172
Caldelli, M. 220–1

General index

Caligula 231
Cape Araxos 202
Capitolia (*agôn* founded by Domitian in Rome) 28, 66, 125, 168, 169, 191, 211, 219, 220, 221, 222–3, 224, 234, 240, 252
Capreae 231
Capua 242–3, 244, 246
Caracalla 56
Castricius Regulus, L. 66
Cato the Elder 208–9, 245
Celsus, *De medicina* 279, 281
Certamen Homeri et Hesiodi 77
chariot racing (*see* horse racing)
Chariton 134
Cheiron 339
Chersonese, Thracian 338
Chinese science 262
Chronicon Paschale 172–3
chronography
  Christian 172–3
  general 160–1, 171
  Olympic (*see also* Phlegon, *Olympiads*) 159, 162, 171–80, 188, 196, 203
Cicero 217–18
citizenship, as a reward for agonistic victory 3, 13, 130, 260
civil war, as a theme in Roman epic 239–40, 248
coins 20, 59, 165
collegia iuvenum 217
Commodeia (*agôn* in Nikaia) 165
Commodus 165, 214
competition, competitiveness 5, 18, 24–5, 99–100, 127, 129–30, 262
  within and between scientific disciplines 261–74, 301–2, 315–25
'compilatory' texts 160–3, 173–4, 189, 318
complex categorization, as a rhetorical strategy in scientific writing 261, 263, 268, 279, 284, 316, 322, 336
consulship (Roman) as means of dating 171, 174
Corinth, Corinthians 66, 142, 184, 186–7, 189–93, 194, 213, 215–16
Cos 258
Cotswold Olympicks 39
Coubertin, Pierre de 36–7
Crete 177–8
'culture' (*see* identity, theories of)
Cynicism 133, 135, 140, 141–3, 150, 156, 293, 340

Dares 239
Delos 178, 180, 309–10
Delphi (*see also* Pythian festival) 50–1, 66, 134–5, 183, 186, 194, 216, 307
Demeter 166
democratic ideology 24
Demostheneia (festival at Oinoanda) 29, 67, 69, 71, 164
diaulos (*see* running)
Dido 242
Dio Chrysostom 21, 22, 91, 131, 133, 139–57, 305, 347, 349, 350
  career 140
  Orations 8 and 9 (Diogenes Orations) 141–3
  Oration 12 79, 143–4, 181, 342
  Oration 21 (*On Beauty*) 144–5, 150–1
  Oration 27 142
  Oration 28 (*Melankomas 2*) 97, 146–7, 152–6, 314
  Oration 29 (*Melankomas 1*) 146–52
  Oration 31 143, 215
  Oration 32 143
  Oration 33 255
  Oration 34 143
  Oration 36 84–5
  Oration 66 143
  Oration 80 143
Diodorus Siculus 84, 133, 160
Diogenes 136, 140, 141–3, 150, 156
Diogenes Laertius 84
Diomedes 235–6
Dionysius of Halicarnassus 160
Dionysopolis 54
Dionysus 237, 251
discus-throwing 245, 290
disfigurement 107, 115–19, 123, 135, 283, 298
dissection (*see* Galen, *On Anatomical Procedures*)
doctors (*see also under* trainers) 5, 22, 49, 104, 132–3, 254–300
  as agonistic benefactors 258, 259–60
  associations of 258–9
  honoured in festivals for public service 257–60
  in public medical competitions 254–5, 264–5, 270
  involved with athletic guilds 257
  official, public doctors 254, 255, 258, 259, 262–3
  on duty at festivals 259
  sects 265, 275
  social status of 261–2
  teaching in gymnasia 257
  techniques of self-promotion 261–3
dolichos (*see* running)
Domitian 28, 66, 140, 211, 218, 219, 227–8, 233–4, 240
Dorians 186–7

drawn contests 59, 77, 127
Dyme 330

Egypt (*see also names of individual cities*) 27, 59, 64, 169, 314–15
eiselastikos 165
ekphrasis 251, 339–40
Eleusis 158
Elis, Eleans 1, 3, 172, 176, 183, 185, 186–7, 193, 194, 197, 198, 199, 200, 202, 330, 342
    as keepers of Olympic records 184, 325–6
Elsner, J. 187, 188–9, 194–5
emperors, involvement in athletics (*see also* imperial cult; Rome, influence on Greek athletics; *and entries under names of individual emperors*) 211, 225–35
    granting permission for 'crown' festivals 71, 165, 214
    influence on athletic guilds 223–5
encomium, techniques of 149, 151
Entellus 239
Epeios (competitor in the boxing match in *Iliad* 23) 77
ephebeia, ephebes 27, 34, 46, 47–68, 126–7, 244, 301, 308–13
    as spectators 66–7
    competing in agonistic festivals 64
    membership outside one's native city 60
    taking part in festival ritual 67–8
Ephesus (*see also* Vibius Salutaris; Olympic festivals (in other cities)) 68, 127–30, 167, 223, 254–5, 262, 270, 307
epic poetry 235–53
Epictetus 133, 136–7, 139, 142
epimeletēs (deputy gymnasiarch) 70, 310
Epiros 307
epitomes 160
Eratosthenes 172
Eteokles 239, 246, 248
Etruscan influences on Roman sport 216
euandria ('good manliness' – title of a *gymnasion* festival contest) 126–7
Euarestos (Iulius Euarestos) (benefactor from Oinoanda) 50
euergetism (*see also* gymnasiarch, gymnasiarchy; agonothete, *agonothesia*; doctors, as agonistic benefactors) 2, 27–8, 68–70, 84, 132, 215, 220
euexia ('good condition' – title of a *gymnasion* festival contest) 65, 126–7
Euripides 84–5
    Autolykos fragment 57, 58, 90
Eusebeia (*agōn* at Puteoli) 125, 168, 220
Eusebius 172, 173, 174, 180

eutaxia ('discipline' – title of a *gymnasion* festival contest) 65, 72

Favorinus 16–17, 160
    Corinthian Oration 19, 190, 191–2
fees for *gymnasion* training 61
festivals (*see agones*)
fines 53–4, 311–12
finger-breaking 200
Flamininus (T. Quinctius Flamininus) 191, 214
Follet, S. 341
Foucault, M. 14, 29, 275
Franke, A. 207
fratricide, as a theme in Roman epic 239, 242, 247–50
Frontinus 160
Fronto 93–4, 308
Fulvius Nobilior, M. 216

Galba 184
Galen 22, 58, 160, 254–300, 305, 306, 312, 315–25, 329, 348–50, 351–2
    as philosopher (*see also below* use of Plato as model) 263, 268, 274–6, 281–2, 284, 299, 300, 302, 315, 317
    attitude to athletic trainers (*see also* Philostratus, engagement with Galen's criticisms of athletic training) 2, 4–5, 256, 267–74, 282–3, 289, 291–300, 314
    attitude to competition 263–74
    career 264, 299, 308
    encouragement of active reading 266, 268, 270–1, 279, 280–1, 289, 297, 326
    influence on sixteenth- and seventeenth-century sport 274
    recommendation of moderation in physical training 274–91, 300
    use of Plato as model 276–7, 282, 286, 316, 321–4
    De sanitate tuenda 268, 272, 274, 283–4, 285, 290, 299, 314
    Good Condition 277, 279, 282–3, 284, 295
    On Anatomical Procedures 264, 265, 266
    On Examinations by which the Best Physicians are Recognized 265
    On Exercise with the Small Ball 280–1, 284–91, 295, 299
    On the Faculties of Foodstuffs 323
    On My Own Books 265
    On Prognosis 264
    Protrepticus 1–6, 57, 62, 256, 263, 277, 279, 283, 286, 291–300, 319–20
    The Best Doctor is also a Philosopher 265–6
    The Order of My Own Books 265

Thrasyboulos 267–74, 279, 282, 284, 288, 289, 290, 295, 297–8, 299
Gardiner, E. N. 30
garlands (*see* prizes)
Gaul 206, 220–1
Gauthier, P. 55
Gellius, Aulus 160
geography 160
Gerenos (wrestler) 336
gladiators, gladiatorial games 15–16, 28–9, 74, 91, 132–3, 143, 214–17, 218, 228–9, 232
  Greek criticisms of 215–16
  imagery of, in epic (*see also hoplomachia*) 238, 249
Glaukos (boxer) 332
Gleason, M. 16–17, 18
'gloves', boxing (made of leather straps) 123–4
gluttony 97, 137, 154, 283, 323, 335–6
gods in epic 235–6
Golden, M. 24, 31
Gorgias 200
Gorgippia 64
Goscinny, R. 42
grammar teachers, grammarians 50, 66, 311
guides, at Olympia 195
guilds, athletic 29, 33, 221–5, 307, 313
  Athletic Guild of Sacred Victors 130–1, 222, 223, 313
  Guild of Ecumenical Athletes 222
  merging of the two original guilds to form the Universal Athletic Guild 222
  Universal Athletic Guild 1, 3, 5, 110, 221, 223–5
guilds, musical 33, 179–80, 220–1, 222, 259–60
Gulliver's Travels (Swift) 76
Guttmann, A. 32
gymnasiarch, gymnasiarchy (*see also* euergetism; doctors, as agonistic benefactors) 27–8, 48, 49, 52–4, 56, 68–9, 306, 309, 310–12
  boys acting as 70, 310–11
  difficulties of filling the office 69
  female 70
  for life 70
  posthumous cult worship of 69
gymnasion (*see also ephebeia*; *palaistra*) 28, 34, 45–96, 97, 153, 211, 217–18, 245, 284, 287, 308
  and education 4, 13, 27, 46, 47–63
  as a place of burial for benefactors 69
  as a venue for courtship and seduction 25, 104, 134, 207–8, 209
  as a venue for literate education 49–51, 88
  as a venue for military training 23–4, 47, 48–9, 51–9, 88–92

as marker of Hellenic culture 27, 54, 144–5, 294, 298–9
  at Olympia 181
  athletic statues in 107
  examinations for pupils 311, 312
  insulation from the outside world 47, 51, 52–4, 59, 63
  internal agonistic festivals (usually 'Hermaia', in honour of Hermes) 53, 64–5, 257
  layout 48
  lectures in 49–51, 257
  links with festival culture 46, 60, 63–72, 86, 126–7
  origins of 23–5
gymnastai (*see* trainers)
gymnastikê (*see* training)
gymnazô (γυμνάζω), range of meanings 35, 266, 269, 270

Hadrian 28, 68, 76–7, 163, 165, 210, 220, 222, 223, 234, 258
Hadrianus (M. Fabius Hadrianus) (Roman general) 177
Hall, S. 11
Hannibal (in Silius Italicus, *Punica*) 211, 241, 242–3, 244, 251
Harris, H. A. 30
Hatzopoulos, M. 55
Hector 91
Heliodorus 134, 135
hellanodikai (Olympic judges) 166, 170, 181, 182–3, 197, 198, 331
Heraia (*agôn* at Argos) (*see* Shield Games of Hera)
Herakleitos of Rhodiapolis 133, 258, 259–60, 263
Herakles 64, 175, 238, 251, 294
'Heraklid' (title given to an athlete who wins Olympic *pankration* and wrestling on the same day) 77
Hercules (*see* Herakles)
Hermaia (*see gymnasion*, internal agonistic festivals)
Hermes 64, 119, 291, 294
Hermesianax of Tralles 66
Hermopolis 1, 3
Herodes Atticus 184, 192–3, 340–1
Herodikos of Megara 256–7, 314
Herodotus 26, 76, 78, 79–80, 83, 188
heroes 76–9, 151, 327, 328–9, 335–6, 338–9, 340
Hesiod 16, 77
hieronikai ('sacred victors') 163–4, 169
Hippias 172

Hippocrates, Hippocratic Corpus 266, 272, 276, 282, 297, 299
  Aphorisms 278–9
  Nature of Man 278
  Nutriment 277
  Regimen 277
historiography, ancient 160
Homer 76, 77, 79–80, 82, 259, 290, 295
  Iliad 23 24, 76, 77–8, 211, 235–9, 240, 242, 250
  Odyssey 8 237, 293–4, 297
hoop-rolling 280, 281
hoplitodromos (race in armour) 33, 65, 66, 90, 176, 330
hoplomachia (contest of fighting with weapons), in epic 235–6, 245, 246, 247–50
horse racing 26, 33, 176, 181, 198–9, 219, 229, 232, 245
  chariot racing 184, 234, 246
horse riding (as daily exercise) 280
humours 329, 333
Hygeia ('Health', worshipped as divinity) 259–60

identity (*see also* athletics and civic identity; athletics as elite activity; athletics and Greek identity; Panhellenism)
  Greek 18–20
  interaction between Greek and Roman (*see also* philhellenism) 18, 190, 205–53
  local 19–20
  Roman 22, 205–53
  theories of 8–21, 205–6
Ikkos 314
imperial cult (*see also* neocorate) 29, 40, 71, 164–5, 185, 213, 214, 221
'interpretative pluralism', as a common feature in Roman Empire texts (*see also* Philostratus, use of speculative styles of explanation) 330–1
Ionia 307
Iphitos 175, 194
Isocrates, *Panegyricus* 26–7, 40, 57
'isolympian' *agones* 165–6, 185–6
'isopythian' *agones* 165–6
Isthmia (*see also* Isthmian festival) 186, 190–3
Isthmian festival (*see also* Isthmia; *periodos*) 3, 25, 66, 78, 125, 141–3, 168, 185, 190–1, 192, 213
Italy 125, 168
  south (*see also* names of individual cities) 206, 220
Iulius Africanus, S. (chronographer) 148, 172
Iuvenal games (Rome) 232

Jason 237–8
javelin contests 245, 250
Jones, C. 146
judges, Olympic (*see hellanodikai*)
Julian, *Caesares* 146
Julius Caesar 216–17, 219, 228–30, 231, 232, 238, 248
jumping weights 42–3, 333

kalligraphia ('writing' – title of a *gymnasion* festival contest) 65
Kapros (wrestler) 77
kithara 167
Kleon of Sikyon (sculptor) 198
Kleosthenes 175
knowledge, sociology of (*see also* 'compilatory' texts) 161–2
Konstan, D. 197

Lacan, J. 105–6
lampadedromia (torch race) 65
Larisos, River 202
Lasthenes 177, 178
lexicography 160
Livy 214, 216, 218, 244, 245
Lloyd, G. 262
long jump 272, 290
Lovatt, H. 240–1
Lucan, *Bellum Civile* 238, 240, 241, 248
Lucian 9, 18, 22, 40, 44, 46, 55, 60, 72–96, 305, 346–7, 349, 350
  Anacharsis 45, 47, 49, 57, 58, 63, 72–5, 78, 80–96, 106–7, 157, 215, 334
  Contemplantes 80
  De dea Syria 75
  De saltatione 81, 91
  Demonax 215
  Navigium 79
  Nigrinus 79, 94
  outsider's perspective 74–5, 78, 79–80, 94
  Peregrinus 181
  questioning of Hellenic tradition 75, 78–81, 86, 95
  relation with second-century society 73–5
  role-playing 74–5, 94
  Scytha 94
  Somnium 75
  True History (*VH*) 75–80, 94
Lucillius 1, 135
Lucius Verus 68
Lucullus (L. Licinius Lucullus) 177
ludi, distinction from *agones* 218–19
ludi pro valetudine Caesaris 219
Lusus Troiae 217, 247
Lycia (see also names of individual cities) 60

General index

Lykeion 49, 85–6
Lykourgos 92, 175
Lysippos (sculptor) 198

Macedonia (*see also* Beroia, *gymnasion* law) 51, 54–5, 67, 310–11
Magna Graecia (*see* Italy, south)
Magnesia (on the Maiandros) 164, 167
Marcellus (M. Claudius Marcellus) (in Silius Italicus, *Punica*) 205, 211–12, 243–4
Marcus Aurelius 56, 85, 308
Mark Antony 28, 239, 307, 313
Mars 247
masculinity 66, 99–100, 101, 105, 144–5, 240
Massilia (Marseilles) 220, 221
medicine (*see also* doctors; Galen; philosophy and medicine) 254–300
    categorization of, in relation to other arts 256, 259–61, 263, 267–74, 319–25
Melankomas (*see also* Dio Chrysostom, *Orationes* 28 and 29)
    as a real athlete? 146
Meleagria (festival at Balboura) 59
Mercury 115
Messene 59, 107, 192, 200
Metellus (Q. Caecilius Metellus Creticus) 177, 178
Miletos 176, 311, 313
military training (*see gymnasion* as a venue for military training)
Milo (athlete) 342
Miltiades (Athenian general) 183
Mithridates 177, 216
mosaics 3–4, 107–10
Mouseion of Alexandria 6
Mummius (L. Mummius Achaicus) 184–5, 190
'musical' contests 18, 26, 33, 181, 184, 186, 219
Myra 167
Myron, 'Diskobolos' 43

Naples (*see also* Sebasta) 1, 3, 138, 231, 233, 243
    cultural identity 219–20
Naukydes of Argos (sculptor) 197
neaniskoi (combined age category of ephebes and *neoi*) 53, 56
Nemausus (Nîmes) 220–1
Nemean festival (*see also periodos*) 3, 25, 125, 168, 214, 245
neocorate 165
neoi (*gymnasion* age category) 48, 53, 69, 81, 298–9
Nero 191, 192, 218, 227–8, 230, 231–3
    agonistic tour of Greece 28, 184, 191, 232
    Neronia, foundation of 209–11, 218, 232
Neronia (*see under* Nero)

Nerva 223
Nestor 338
New Historicism 10
Nikaia 165
Nikê (Goddess of Victory) 119
Nikomedia 165
Nonnus, *Dionysiaka* 237
novels, Greek 134–5
nudity 25–6, 136, 208–9, 217, 245, 272–3, 297
Nutton, V. 262–3
Nysa 179

Odessos 54
Odysseus (*see also* Homer, *Odyssey*) 77, 79–80, 140, 236–7
oil (applied prior to exercise in the *gymnasion*) 45, 52, 53–4, 66, 68, 82, 89, 272, 331
Oinoanda (*see also* Demostheneia) 50, 64, 71
Oinomaos 201
Olympia (*see also* Olympic festival (at Pisa)) 158–60, 180–6, 188, 192–204, 213, 342
    dedications of armour at 183
    hippodrome 181, 202
    Leonidaion 196, 201
    Metroön 184
    Nymphaion of Herodes Atticus 184, 192–3
    Pillar of Oinomaos 201
    stadion 181, 202
    Temple of Hera 193, 197
    Temple of Zeus (*see also* Pheidias) 181
    tension between past and present within 183–7
Olympic festival (at Pisa) (*see also* Olympia; *periodos*) 3, 6–7, 78, 125, 143–4, 168, 175–6, 216, 223, 266, 336
    demise 29–30
    foundation 23, 25, 175, 193–4
    programme 181, 184, 185–6
    traditions of speech-making 143–4, 181
    truce 25
Olympic festivals (in other cities) 166, 171
    Alexandria 1, 3, 171
    Antioch 30
    Athens 169, 170
    Ephesus 128, 166, 170
    Kyzikos 171
    Side 166
    Smyrna 16, 170, 171
    Sparta 166
    Tralles 166, 171
Olympic victory lists (*see* chronography, Olympic)
Olympics, modern 36–9
Opous 201

Oribasios 276, 280
Ostia 3–4, 107
Oulpios Domestikos, M. 223–4
Oxyrhynchos 173

paidagogoi (officials responsible for supervising *paides*) 312
paides (gymnasion age category) 48, 53, 66, 311, 312
paidotribai (see trainers)
palaistra 48, 49, 53, 218, 272, 286, 308–9, 311
  at Olympia 181
Palamedes 338
Panamara 56
Panhellenia (*agôn* in Athens) 85
Panhellenic festivals (see *agones*, 'crown' festivals)
Panhellenion 163
Panhellenism 22, 25, 26–7, 29, 38–40, 158–204, 236
  influence on local festival procedures 163–70, 203
pankratiasts, *pankration* 1, 3–4, 77–9, 124–6, 132, 168–9, 176, 200, 201, 340
pantomime dancing 5, 14, 81, 91, 98
paradoxography 160
Paris 239
Paros 59
Patara 167
Patroclus (see also Homer, *Iliad* Book 23) 338
Patron (Epicurean philosopher) 177
Paul, *Epistles* 133
Pausanias 22, 40, 56, 78, 158–204, 305, 347–8, 349
  Lydian identity 188
Pax Romana 55–6
peacock feathers 78–9
Peisos 175
Peloponnese 175, 186–7, 191
Pelops 175
pentathlon 330
Peregrinus 181
periodos 3, 25, 28, 159, 165, 168–70, 181
periodos-victors 1, 119–23, 124–6, 169
Perpetua, martyr 133–4
Persians 144, 183
Pescennius Niger 165–6
Pheidias 143–4, 181
Pheneos 197
Philadelphia 167
philhellenism 206–7, 210–11, 216, 219–21, 245
Philip II of Macedon 200–1
Philo 133

philoponia ('hard work')
  as a virtue praised in agonistic inscriptions 126
  title of a *gymnasion* festival contest 65, 72, 126
philosophy 160
  and athletics 2, 6, 29, 61–3, 85–6, 87–8, 102, 132–57, 183, 350
  and medicine (see also Galen, as philosopher; Galen, use of Plato as model) 255, 259
Philostratus 4, 9, 18, 22, 40, 58, 78, 301–44, 349–50
  analysis of athletic history 172, 325–32, 337, 342
  engagement with Galen's criticisms of athletic training 315–25, 335–6, 343
  engagement with Plato 316–24
  equation of athletic training with his own expertise 325, 332–3, 343–4
  Gymnasticus 172, 256, 277, 301–44
  Heroicus 4, 305, 338–9
  Imagines 305, 339–40
  Life of Apollonius (*VA*) 215, 305, 338, 341–2
  Lives of the Sophists (*VS*) 15–16, 305, 340–1, 343
  modern responses to the *Gymnasticus* 304, 317–19
  Nero 305
  use of speculative styles of explanation 326, 330–2, 334–7, 341, 342–3
Phlegon 160, 171
  as freedman of Hadrian 174–5, 179
  Book of Marvels 174, 179
  Long-Lived Persons 179
  Olympiads 160, 162, 167, 171, 172, 173–80, 193, 195, 199, 203
Photius 175, 178
physiognomics 261, 317, 328, 332, 333, 334–5, 337, 339, 340
Pindar 58, 301, 308
Plato (see also Galen, use of Plato as model; Philostratus, engagement with Plato) 7, 33, 58, 60, 61, 62, 85–6, 87–8, 149–50, 153
  Charmides 153
  Euthydemus 153
  Gorgias 277, 322, 323–4
  Laches 89, 153
  Laws 58, 61, 62, 87
  Lysis 27, 153
  Phaedo 150
  Phaedrus 88, 150
  Republic 58, 87, 149–50, 153, 256–7, 276–7, 321
  Symposium 150
Pliny the Elder 160

Pliny the Younger 220, 251
Plutarch 160, 289
   Cato Maior 208–9, 245
   Greek Questions 331
   On Studying Poetry 289
   Quaestiones Convivales 331
   Roman Questions 208, 331
   Solon 84
   Sulla 216
Polemo 16–17, 337
Polybius 213
Polydeukes 237
Polykleitos 103, 113–15
   'Diadoumenos' 110–13
   'Diskophoros' 119
   'Doryphoros' 107, 110, 113–15, 128
Polyneikes 239, 246, 248
Pompey 216, 228–9, 248
Pomponius Mela 160
Porter, J. 187–9
Poseidon 192–3
Priam 235
Priene 26, 257, 308
Prima Porta statue of Augustus 113–15
prize festivals (*see* under *agones*)
prizes
   garlands 27, 78–9, 86, 164
   money prizes 27, 164
proedria (reserved seating, as an honour given for public service) 258, 260
Promachos (athlete) 332
Protesileos 338–9
Prusa 140
(Pseudo)-Dionysius 126, 146, 313–14
(Pseudo)-Julian 191, 215
(Pseudo)-Plutarch, *Education of Children* 60–2, 63, 88
Puteoli 1, 3, 220
Pythian festival (at Delphi) (*see also periodos*) 3, 25, 50, 125, 168, 170, 182, 185
Pythian festivals in other cities 166, 170

Quintilian 133
Quintus Smyrnaeus, *Posthomerica* 236–7

race in armour (*see hoplitodromos*)
regimen 29, 267, 274–91, 322–4
rhetoric (*see also* sophistry, sophists)
   contests in 237
Rhodes, Rhodians 143, 259
Rhodiapolis (*see* Herakleitos of Rhodiapolis)
Riefenstahl, L. 38
Robert, L. 21–2, 76–7, 127, 133, 146, 148, 165, 179–80
Rogers, G. 67

Romaia (*agôn* in Xanthos) 166–8, 176, 213, 214
Roman involvement in the east 174–80
   influence on Greek architecture 214–15
   influence on Greek athletics 28–9, 71, 143, 159, 164–5, 167–8, 176–7, 191, 213–16
   influence on the Olympics 143, 184–5, 213
Rome 5, 22, 50–1, 177, 179–80, 242, 251, 263
   athletics in (*see also* athletes, performing in Rome; athletic guilds; Neronia; Capitolia) 212–13, 216–24, 225–35, 252
   circus buildings 219, 229, 234
   stadion buildings 219
running 198, 245, 246, 250, 280, 288, 290, 340
   diaulos 176, 330
   dolichos 167, 176–7, 180, 326, 330
   stadion 66, 142, 167, 171, 176, 202–3, 326, 330
Rutherford, I. 182

'sacred' *agones* (*see agones*, 'crown' festivals)
'sacred' victors (*see hieronikai*)
sacrifice, at Olympia 181, 195
Saguntum 242
Sardis 167
satyr plays 58
Satyros, statue of 115–19
Schmitz, T. 16, 17–18, 63
Scipio Africanus (P. Cornelius Scipio Aemilius Africanus) 214
   (in Silius Italicus, *Punica*) 212, 241, 242, 243, 244, 245–53
Scopelian 16
Scribonius Curio, C. 216, 238
Scythia 84–5
Sebasta (*agôn* at Naples) 66, 125, 130–1, 146, 169, 185–6, 219–20, 231
Sebasteia, as common title of imperial festivals 71
second prize 24, 127
'Second Sophistic' 15–16, 161, 187–8
self-care (*see also regimen*) 14, 29, 99–100, 275
Seneca the Younger 133, 135, 136–9, 142
   Letter 15 137–8
   Letter 80 138–9
Septimius Severus 165
Seria 202
Severans 165
Severeia (*agôn* in Nikomedia) 165
Shield Games of Hera (at Argos) 125, 159, 168
Shropshire Olympian games 39
Sicily (*see also names of individual cities*) 214, 220, 239, 243
Side 166
Sikyon 176, 191, 197, 199, 200

Silius Italicus 22, 205, 211–12, 235, 240–53, 305, 348
  intertextual relation with Statius 240–1, 245, 246
  retirement in Campania 243, 251
  'understated' style 241, 249–51
Smyrna 307
Socrates 7, 88, 140, 153, 323–4
soldiers (*see also* army, Roman) 99, 132–3
Solon, views on athletics (*see also* Lucian, *Anacharsis*) 84
sophistry, sophists 14–18, 63, 142, 264, 341, 342–3
sophrosynê (temperance) (as a virtue praised in agonistic inscriptions) 126, 131
Sophrosynê (Temperance, deity of the gymnasion) 126
Sparta, Spartans (*see also under* Olympic festivals (in other cities)) 26, 56, 82, 169, 329, 341–2
  whipping ceremony of Artemis Orthia 92–3, 334, 342
spectatorship 66–7, 97–9, 104–5, 143, 145, 150, 155, 156, 182–3, 225–6, 230–1, 303
  in epic 235–6, 249–51
sphairisteria (ball games attached to gymnasia) 33–4, 48, 49, 281
Sports Studies 31–2
stadion (*see under* running)
Stageira 200
Statius, *Thebaid* 30, 211, 218, 235, 239–42, 245, 246, 248, 250, 252
statues (non-athletic) 192–3, 259–60, 294
  at Olympia 181, 184–5, 194–5
statues of athletes 7, 102–24, 127–32, 144, 158–9, 162–3, 203, 295
  at Olympia 181, 183, 188, 189, 193, 195–202, 203–4
  copies 107, 110–13
  in the west 107–10, 217–18
  tension between idealism and realism 103–4, 107–24
stereotypes 207–12
Stoicism 133, 135–9, 149
Strabo 160
strigil 331
Suetonius
  Lives of the Emperors 66, 146, 184, 209, 211, 219, 227–35, 239
  use of repeated templates in the *Lives of the Emperors* 227–8
  work on Greek and Roman games 228
Sulla 184, 216
Swain, S. 18
swimming 280

Syracuse 205, 211–12, 243–5, 294
Syria 75, 169

Tacitus 91, 209–12, 218, 235
Tanagra 64
  Sarapeia (*agôn*) 68
Tarsos 143
team sports 34
Telmessos 168
Teos 50, 66, 311
Terme boxer, statue 115–19
Tertullian, *De Spectaculis* 134
'tetrad' training system 336
themides (*see agones*)
Themistius 146
Theodosius 29–30
Theon 314
theoria 182–3
Theseus 76–7
Thrace 54
Thucydides 82, 243–4
Tiberius 309
Tigranes 177
Titus (emperor) 146, 227–8
torch race (*see lampadedromia*)
Toxaris 94
trainers 22, 137, 146, 152–6, 301–44
  aleiptês 305–6, 307, 313
  epistatês 305–6
  gymnastês 284, 305–6, 317, 319, 325–37
  iatraleiptês 257
  keromatitês 305
  paidotribês 48, 54, 61, 268, 290, 305–6, 307, 308–13, 319, 322
  accompanying athletes to festivals 307–8
  as representatives of Hellenic tradition 302, 303–4, 305, 331–2, 343–4
  attached to private *palaistrai* 308–9
  in athletic guilds 307, 313–14
  involved in ephebic education 50, 53, 301, 308–13
  links with the imperial family 308
  need for rhetorical skills 313–14
  relations with doctors (*see also* Galen, attitudes to athletic trainers; Philostratus, engagement with Galen's criticisms of athletic training) 255–6, 257, 291, 300, 307–8
  salaries 54, 311
  social status of 302, 306–15
training (*gymnastikê*) (as an art) 301–2, 315–37, 339, 343–4
  treatises on 256–7, 314–15, 320, 321
Trajan (*see also* Baths of Trajan) 223, 224
Triarius, C. 178

truces 25, 38, 164, 236, 330
Tyrtaios 57

Valerius Flaccus, *Argonautica* 239
Valerius Maximus 245, 248
vase paintings 7, 301
Vedius Antoninus, P. (benefactor from Ephesus) 68
venationes (wild beast shows) 191, 214–15, 216, 229
Venus 242–3
Vespasian 227–8
Vibius Salutaris, foundation of (at Ephesus) 67–8
victory (*see also* prizes; statues of athletes)
  financial rewards for 27
  inscriptions commemorating 1–7, 119–23, 124–30, 166–70, 183, 254–5, 260
Vienna 220, 221
viewing (*see* spectatorship)
Virgil, *Aeneid* 235, 237, 238–9, 240, 241–2, 244, 247, 248, 250

virtue (*see* athletes as role models; *Aretê*, deity of the *gymnasion*)
Vitruvius 160

Whitmarsh, T. 19
wild beast shows (*see venationes*)
women
  in athletic training and competition 66, 234
  as gymnasiarchs 70
Woolf, G. 215, 226–7
wrestlers, wrestling 77, 167, 197, 200, 238, 245, 280, 290, 314, 319, 340, 341
Wyke, M. 101

Xanthos (*see also* Romaia) 69
Xenophanes 57, 84
Xenophon 60
  Symposium 145
Xenophon of Ephesus 134

Zappas, Evangelios 39

Index locorum

NB This index refers only to discussion of specified subsections of texts and of collections of texts; the general index lists all references to authors.

AELIUS ARISTIDES

On Rome (*Oration* 26) 97–9: 40, 180
Oratio 46, 20–24: 191

ANTYLLOS

Oribasios, *Collectiones Medicae* 6.21–4, 6.25–36: 280–1

APOLLONIUS OF RHODES

Argonautika 3.129–44: 287

APOLLONIUS OF TYANA

Letter 42a: 342
Letter 63: 342

ARISTOTLE

Politics 1338b: 306
1338b–39a: 336

AUGUSTUS

Res Gestae 22–3: 229

CASSIUS DIO

Roman History 62.14: 184

77.9–10: 56
77.16.7: 56
80.10.12: 4

CELSUS

De medicina 1.1.3: 279
1.1.7: 279
1.2.6: 281
1.2.7: 279
1.6.1: 281
1.8.1: 281
3.27.3: 281

CHARITON

Chaireas and Kallirhoe
1.1.4–6: 134
1.1.5: 134
1.1.10: 134
1.2.6: 134
2.3: 134

CICERO

Letters to Atticus 1.10: 217

CODEX THEODOSIANUS

13.3.8: 257

DIGESTA

27.1.6.2–4: 258
27.1.6.8: 258

DIO CHRYSOSTOM

Orations
8.3: 141–2
8.9: 142
8.36: 142
9.5–7: 142
9.10–13: 142
9.14–20: 142
9.22: 142
12.2–5: 79
21.1: 144
21.2: 145
21.13–14: 145
28.1–2: 153
28.2–3: 97, 102, 153–4
28.5: 154
28.6: 154–5
28.7: 149, 154
28.7–8: 154
28.8: 154
28.9: 154
28.10: 154
28.12: 150, 155
28.13: 155
29.1–2: 147
29.2–3: 147
29.3–5: 147
29.6: 147, 151–2
29.7: 147–8, 150, 151
29.8: 152
29.9: 148
29.9–10: 148
29.11: 147, 148
29.11–12: 148–9
29.13: 154
29.16–17: 150–1
29.17–20: 147
29.21–2: 150, 155
31.21: 143
31.110–11: 143
31.116: 143
31.121: 143, 215
31.163: 143
33.6: 255
34.31: 143
66.2: 78
66.5: 78, 143
80.2: 143

DIODORUS SICULUS

9.2.5: 84

DIOGENES LAERTIUS

1.55–6: 84

EPICTETUS

Discourses
1.24.7: 136
1.24.12: 136
2.17.29–31: 136
2.18.22–7: 136
3.20.9–10: 136
4.4.11–12: 136

EURIPIDES

fr. 282, lines 16–19, 21–4: 57

FAVORINUS

Corinthian Oration 26: 190

FRONTO

Ad M. Caesarem 2.3: 93–4
2.16: 308

GALEN

De sanitate tuenda 1.1.1 [K6.1]: 284
1.1.3–4 [K6.2]: 284
1.4.12 [K6.12]: 284
1.5.1–12 [K6.13–15]: 284
1.8.24 [K6.42]: 284
1.10 [K6.51]: 272
1.11.3 [K6.54–5]: 284
1.12.5 [K6.60]: 284
2.2.6–12 [K6.85–6]: 284
2.8.1–7 [K6.133–5]: 284
2.8.11 [K6.136]: 284
2 [K6. 141–3]: 314
2.9.25: 306
2.11.42–4: 306
3.2.2–12 [K6.167–9]: 284
Good Condition [K4.750–56]: 282–3
[K4.750–53]: 278–9
[K4.753]: 277, 321

On Anatomical Procedures 7.10
  [K2.619–20]: 265
7.10 [K2.618–23]: 264, 266
7.16 [K2.642–3]: 265
On Examinations by which the Best
  Physicians are Recognized 9.6–7: 265
On Exercise with the Small Ball 1
  [K5.899]: 285–6
3 [K5.904]: 286
3 [K5.905]: 286
3 [K5.906]: 288
4 [K5.906–7]: 287–8
4 [K5.909]: 289
5 [K5.910]: 290
On My Own Books [K19.21–2]: 265
Protrepticus 1: 291, 292–3
2: 291
3: 291
3 [K1.5]: 294
4: 291
5: 291, 319
5 [K1.8–9]: 294
6: 291–2
7: 291–2, 299
8: 291–2, 293–4
9: 292, 293, 298, 320
9 [K1.20–21]: 1–7, 295
10: 292
10 [K1.25]: 297–8
11: 292, 295–6
11 [K1.27]: 279, 296
11 [K1.30–31]: 295–6
12: 292
13: 292, 293
13 [K1.33]: 294
13 [K1.36]: 294
14: 292, 319–20
14 [K1.37]: 298
14 [K1.39]: 299
The Best Doctor is also a Philosopher 1 [K1.53]:
  265–6
The Order of My Own Books 5 [K19.60–61]: 265
Thrasyboulos 1 [K5.806]: 269
2 [K5.807]: 269–70
2 [K5.809]: 270
3 [K5.809–10]: 271
4 [K5.810]: 271
4–9: 267
5 [K5.810–11]: 270
8 [K5.817]: 282
9 [K5.819–21]: 278–9
10–29: 267
22 [K5.842–3]: 272
30–45: 267–8
36 [K5.874]: 267

36 [K5.874–6]: 321
41–5: 268
46 [K5.894]: 272, 303
46 [K5.895]: 272–3
46–7: 268
47 [K5.898]: 321

HELIODORUS

Aithiopika
1.4: 134
1.7: 134
1.19–21: 134
2.35–3.6: 134
4.1–4: 134
10.28–32: 134

HERODIAN

4.8.3: 56

HERODOTUS

4.76–7: 83
5.22: 26
8.144: 26

HIPPOCRATES

Aphorisms 1.3: 278–9
Nature of Man 22 (= *Regimen in Health* 7): 278
Nutriment 34: 277
Regimen 2.61–6: 277

HISTORIA AUGUSTA

Hadrian 27.3: 220
Antoninus Pius 5: 56
Marcus Antoninus 4: 308

HOMER

Iliad 3.350: 82
6.466–73: 91
10.577: 82
14.171: 82
23.735–7: 77
23.798–825: 235–6
Odyssey 3.466: 82
6.96: 82
10.364: 82

10.450: 82
19.505: 82

ISOCRATES

Panegyricus 1–2: 57

JULIAN

Caesares 7 (311a): 146

LIVY

1.9.6–14: 218
1.35.7–10: 218
28.21: 245, 248
29.19: 244, 245
39.22.1–2: 216
45.32.8–11: 214

LUCAN

Bellum Civile 4.592–660: 238

LUCIAN

Anacharsis 1: 45, 81–2
1–5: 83
6: 83
12: 87
12–13: 86
14–22: 86–7
16: 88
17: 83–4
18: 89–90
21: 87, 88
24: 87
24–30: 88–9
31–3: 90–1
33–5: 82
37: 91
38–40: 92–3, 334
40: 90
Contemplantes 8: 80
17: 80
Demonax 57: 215
Navigium 23: 79
Nigrinus 13: 79, 94
17: 94
Scytha 3: 94
True History (VH)
1.3: 79–80
2.17: 94
2.20: 79–80
2.22: 75–9

LUCILLIUS

Greek Anthology 11.78: 135
11.80: 135
11.85: 135

PAUSANIAS

1.26.4: 201
2.1.2: 191–2
2.1.5: 192
2.1.7–8: 192–3
2.3.7: 191
5.1.1–2: 186–7
5.1.1–5.5.1: 193–4
5.1.4: 193
5.1.5: 193
5.1.6: 193
5.2: 193
5.4.7: 194
5.5.2: 202
5.5.5–6: 193
5.5.2–5.7.5: 194
5.6.2: 193
5.7.6–5.9.6: 194
5.8.5: 194, 201
5.10.1: 158, 159
5.17.5–5.19.10: 193
6.1.2: 196–7
6.1.3: 197–8
6.1.4–5: 198–9
6.2.2–3: 199
6.2.3: 196
6.2.6: 199
6.2.10–11: 192
6.3.1: 193
6.4.1–2: 200
6.4.3–4: 200
6.4.7: 193
6.4.8: 200
6.5.3: 196
6.6.3: 198
6.6.4–11: 199
6.8.2: 199
6.9.1: 193
6.9.3: 199
6.9.4–5: 193
6.9.6–8: 199

6.10.5: 193
6.11.2–9: 199
6.13.1: 199
6.13.2: 193
6.13.8: 196
6.14.2–3: 198
6.17.1: 196, 201
6.18.2–6: 200–1
6.18.6: 199
6.18.7: 201–2
6.22.2–3: 194
6.25.1: 193
6.26.6: 202
6.26.10: 202–3
10.34.5: 56
10.36.9: 184

PHILOSTRATUS

Gymnasticus 1: 301, 320–2
1–2: 317, 327–8
2: 325–6
3–19: 317
4: 326
5: 326
7: 330
12: 329–30
13: 330
14–15: 322–3
18: 331
20: 332
20–4: 332
20–58: 317
22: 332
25: 331–2
25–6: 332–3
27–30: 333
28: 334
29: 334–5
31: 338
31–41: 333
31–42: 340
42: 329, 333
43: 340
43–4: 328–9, 335–6
43–7: 333
44: 323–4
46: 4, 336
47: 336
48–54: 333
54: 328, 336
55: 333
56: 333
57: 333
58: 329, 333–4
Heroicus pp. 141–2: 338
pp. 146–7: 338
p. 147, line 15: 4
p. 167: 338
p. 183: 338
p. 204: 338
Imagines 1.24.3: 339
1.28.8: 339
2.2: 339
2.6: 339
2.7.5: 339
2.19: 339
2.21: 339
2.32: 339
Life of Apollonius (*VA*) 4.22: 215
4.27: 341–2
4.28: 342
4.29: 342–3
6.20: 342
Lives of the Sophists (*VS*) 481: 15
490–91: 16
507: 15
514: 16
541: 15–16
541–2: 16
542: 16
552–4: 340–1

PHLEGON

Book of Marvels 35: 179
Long-Lived Persons (*FGH* 257, F37), 97: 179
Olympiads, *FGH* 257, F1: 175
F12: 175–8
T1: 180
T3: 179

PLATO

Euthydemus 271a: 153
Laches 181e–182d: 89
Laws 794d–796d: 58, 61
794c–796e: 58
829e–834d: 58
832d–834d: 62
Phaedo 78d–e: 150
Phaedrus 250b–e: 150
Republic 327a: 153
402d: 149–50
403c–412b: 58
406a–b: 257
407b–c: 321

410b: 321
411c: 321
Symposium 211a: 150

PLINY THE YOUNGER

Letter 3.7: 251
Letter 4.22: 220

PLUTARCH

Lives:
    Cato Maior 3.5–7: 245
        20.8: 208–9
    Solon 23.3: 84
Moralia:
    On Studying Poetry 38e: 289
    Roman Questions 40: 208

POLYBIUS

2.12.8: 213

(PSEUDO)-ARISTOTLE

Constitution of the Athenians 42.3: 309

(PSEUDO)-DIONYSIUS

Ars Rhetorica
1: 313
7: 146, 313–14
7.292: 126

(PSEUDO)-JULIAN

Letter 198: 191, 215

(PSEUDO)-PLUTARCH

Education of Children
7: 61
8 (5d–e): 62
9 (7a): 62
11 (8b–e): 61–2

SENECA THE YOUNGER

Letters

15: 137–8
15.2: 137
80: 138–9
80.1: 138
80.2: 138–9

SILIUS ITALICUS

Punica
2.233–64: 242
6.653–715: 251
11.422–3: 242–3
11.427–8: 243
14.134–9: 205, 211–12, 243
14.248–57: 243–4
14.492–515: 244–5
16.527–8: 247
16.529–38: 247–9
16.531: 248
16.535: 250
16.546–8: 248

STATIUS

Silvae
3.5: 240
5.3: 240
Thebaid
6.3–4: 246
6.297–8: 246
6.618–30: 246
6.731–8: 246
6.911–23: 246
12.429–46: 248

SUETONIUS

Divus Iulius 10.1: 230
10.2: 228
39: 216–17, 228–9
39.1: 230
40: 229
40.1: 230
Divus Augustus 43.1: 229–30
44: 230
45.1: 230
45.2: 231
46.1: 230
98.3: 231
98.5: 231
Nero 11.1: 232
12.3–4: 232

22–4: 232
23–4: 184
40.4: 233
Titus 7: 146
Domitianus 3.2: 233
4.1: 234
4.4: 219, 234
4.9: 66
6.1: 233
7.1: 233
10.1: 234
11.1: 233
12.1–2: 234

TACITUS

Agricola 11.4: 91
Annals 14.20–21: 209–11

THUCYDIDES

1.6.5: 82

TYRTAIOS

fr. 12 (*IE* 2.177–9): 57

VALERIUS FLACCUS

Argonautica 4.99–343: 239

VALERIUS MAXIMUS

9.11, ext. 1: 245, 248

VIRGIL

Aeneid 5.585: 247
5.122: 244

XENOPHANES

IE 2.186–7: 57

XENOPHON

Symposium 9–10: 145

XENOPHON OF EPHESUS

Ephesiaka 1.2–3: 134

Index of inscriptions and papyri

INSCRIPTIONS

Augustus, *Res Gestae*: 229

Bean (1965) no. 2 (pp. 588–93): 130–1, 307
Benedum (1977) no. 1: 259

Cabanes (1974) no. 32: 307
CID 2.139: 182
CIG 3088: 65
Clerc (1885) Face A (pp. 124–7): 179–80

Danoff (1937) no. 4: 258

EAH 1963, pp. 139–41: 59
1984, pp. 22–4: 51, 67

Flacelière (1949) no. 3: 258
F.Delphes 3.1.200: 307
3.1.220: 306, 307

GIBM 794: 307

Hatzopoulos and Loukopoulou (1992)
  K9: 310–11

I.Délos 1922–40: 309–10, 343
1922: 310
1924: 310
1925: 310
1926: 310
I.Didyma 108: 308
*I.Eph.*27: 67–8
621: 68
728: 68
1127: 170
1145: 68
1162: 254–5
1161–9, 4101b: 254
1416: 307
2005: 307

I.Erythrai 81: 65
IG II/III², 2326: 173
III, 735–68, 1076–1275: 309
III, 1199: 257
V, I, 666: 307
VII, 540: 68
VII, 2450: 64
XIV, 1054 (= *IGUR* 235): 222
XIV, 1055 (= *IGUR* 236): 222, 223–4
XIV, 1102 (= *IGUR* 240): 1–7, 124–6, 168–9, 171, 224–5
XIV, 1103 (= *IGUR* 241): 3, 6, 224
XIV, 1104 (= *IGUR* 239): 3, 24, 224
IG XIV, 1109 (= *IGUR* 237): 224
IGR IV, 182: 258
IV, 1252: 132
IGUR 250: 3, 224
I.Magnesia 17–87: 164
116: 68
180: 127
I.Milet. II, 500: 170
IOSPE IV, 432: 64
I.Pergamon 535: 219
I.Priene 111: 257, 308
112: 257
112–14: 68
118: 257
I.Smyrna 246: 307
IvO 56: 185–6
287: 184
319: 185

Kent (1966) no. 153: 66

Le Bas-Waddington 1620b: 169

Reinach (1916) no. 9: 169
Robert (1939b) 230–44: 127–30
  (1978a) 166–8
Roueché (1993) 66–87: 119

74–5: 123
89–92: 131

SEG 7.825: 127
14.602: 66
27.261: 51–5, 311–12
SIG³ 577: 311
578: 66, 311
771: 50–1
802: 66
959: 65

TAM II, 910: 133, 259–60
III.1, 199–213: 64

Tod (1951): 59, 64
Tsakyroglous (1892) 198–200: 257

Wörrle (1988): 29, 67, 71, 164

PAPYRI

CPHerm. 5.7: 3
P.Lond. 137: 307, 313
1178: 306, 307
P.Oxy. 2.222: 173–4, 175–6
3.466: 314–15, 319
9.1202: 59
P. Zenon 59060: 307